Alexander Shlyapnikov,
1885–1937

Historical Materialism Book Series

The Historical Materialism Book Series is a major publishing initiative of the radical left. The capitalist crisis of the twenty-first century has been met by a resurgence of interest in critical Marxist theory. At the same time, the publishing institutions committed to Marxism have contracted markedly since the high point of the 1970s. The Historical Materialism Book Series is dedicated to addressing this situation by making available important works of Marxist theory. The aim of the series is to publish important theoretical contributions as the basis for vigorous intellectual debate and exchange on the left.

The peer-reviewed series publishes original monographs, translated texts, and reprints of classics across the bounds of academic disciplinary agendas and across the divisions of the left. The series is particularly concerned to encourage the internationalization of Marxist debate and aims to translate significant studies from beyond the English-speaking world.

For a full list of titles in the Historical Materialism Book Series available in paperback from Haymarket Books, visit:
www.haymarketbooks.org/category/hm-series

Alexander Shlyapnikov, 1885–1937

Life of an Old Bolshevik

by
Barbara C. Allen

Haymarket Books
Chicago, IL

First published in 2015 by Brill Academic Publishers, The Netherlands
© 2015 Koninklijke Brill NV, Leiden, The Netherlands

Published in paperback in 2016 by
Haymarket Books
P.O. Box 180165
Chicago, IL 60618
773-583-7884
www.haymarketbooks.org

ISBN: 978-1-60846-558-3

Trade distribution:
In the US, Consortium Book Sales, www.cbsd.com
In Canada, Publishers Group Canada, www.pgcbooks.ca
In the UK, Turnaround Publisher Services, www.turnaround-uk.com
In all other countries, Publishers Group Worldwide, www.pgw.com

Cover design by Jamie Kerry of Belle Étoile Studios and Ragina Johnson.

This book was published with the generous support of
Lannan Foundation and the Wallace Global Fund.

Library of Congress Cataloging-in-Publication data is available.

Entered into digital printing, December 2017.

*To my son, Nicholas Syrgabaev, and to my parents,
Leonard R. and Ethelene M. Allen*

Contents

Acknowledgements ix
List of Illustrations xi
List of Abbreviations and Acronyms xiii

Introduction 1

1 From the Old Belief to Socialism 7

2 Emigration and the Revolutionary Underground 36

3 Organising Workers in the Revolutionary Year 1917 76

4 Labour Commissar 103

5 Defending Soviet Power and Unions in the Civil War 122

6 The Workers' Opposition and the Trade-Union Debate 157

7 Early NEP and the Trade Unions 191

8 Appeal of the 22 to the Communist International 227

9 Factional Politics in the NEP Era 253

10 Late NEP, Industrialisation and Renewed Repression 283

11 Purged from the Party 309

12 Exile, Arrest and Prison 331

Epilogue: Retribution Upon the Family and Rehabilitation 366
Conclusion 369

Bibliography 379
Index 403

Acknowledgements

Many people in Russia, the United States and other countries have encouraged and helped me to complete this biography. At the University of North Carolina at Chapel Hill, Donald J. Raleigh guided me in a readings course about early Soviet political history, near the end of my undergraduate studies in Russian language, literature and history. As portrayed in books by Robert V. Daniels and Jay B. Sorenson, Alexander Shlyapnikov's dry wit and the challenge he posed to Bolshevik Party leaders made me curious to learn more about him. Don Raleigh encouraged me to pursue a Ph.D. in Russian and Soviet history and to propose a biography of Shlyapnikov as a dissertation topic. At Indiana University Bloomington, my dissertation supervisor, Alexander Rabinowitch, as well as dissertation committee members David Ransel, Hiroaki Kuromiya and Michael Alexeev strongly supported this project and gave valuable advice.

While working as a research assistant for Indiana University Ph.D. candidate Suzanne Ament in Russia in 1990–1, I met Shlyapnikov's daughter Irina and conducted preliminary research in party and state archives. In 1995, I returned to Moscow for a full year of dissertation research, sponsored by the International Research and Exchanges Board (IREX) and the Fulbright-Hays Doctoral Dissertation Research Abroad programme. My thanks are due to the staff of Russian archives and libraries used in my research: the Russian State Archive of Socio-Political History, the Central Archive of the Federal Security Service, the State Archive of the Russian Federation, the Russian State Archive of the Economy, the Central Archive of Social Movements of Moscow and the Russian State Library. La Salle University, the Indiana University Russian and East European Institute and the International Institute of Social History in Amsterdam subsidised presentation of my work at conferences. La Salle awarded me summer grants that allowed me to conduct research in New York in 2009 and Moscow in 2012. The Slavic Reference Service at the University of Illinois at Urbana-Champaign libraries offered quick and informative answers to questions. Shlyapnikov's children Yuri, Irina and Alexander generously allowed me access to restricted archival files on their father and shared their memories, photographs and documents. Irina Medvedeva permitted me to see restricted materials on her father, Sergei Medvedev. Vladimir and Ritta Kollontai shared family stories and a photograph of Shlyapnikov with French workers.

Sebastian Budgen first contacted me about Shlyapnikov just months before I successfully defended my dissertation in 2001, consistently encouraging me to complete the biography. I am grateful for his, David Broder's, and Danny

Hayward's guidance on style, as well as for Ben Lewis's attention to copy-editing the manuscript. Simon Pirani read the manuscript several times and offered extensive, detailed and very helpful suggestions for improvements. Barbara Evans Clements, Rex Wade and Janet Rabinowitch read the entire manuscript and their advice improved it. I also appreciate having received constructive criticism from many others, including Thomas Allsen, Clayton Black, Sally Boniece, David Brandenberger, Beatrice Farnsworth, Donald Filtzer, Wendy Goldman, Malte Griesse, Anthony Heywood, Larry E. Holmes, Lisa Kirschenbaum, Anna Krylova, Lars T. Lih, Max Okenfuss, Alexis Pogorelskin, Roy Robson, Yngvild Sørbye, Lynne Viola, Robert Weinberg, Charters Wynn and La Salle University students in my spring 2013 'Stalin's Russia' course, all of whom read parts of the biography in various forms. Editors of the following journals gave permission to include in this book material published in article form: *Jahrbücher für Geschichte Osteuropas, Cahiers du Monde Russe, Revolutionary Russia, The Soviet and Post-Soviet Review* and *The NEP Era: Soviet Russia, 1921–1928*; anonymous reviewers for these and other journals offered vital advice for polishing the material. Other sections were previously published in *Russia's Century of Revolutions: Parties, People, Places*[1] and *A Dream Deferred: New Studies in Russian and Soviet Labor History*.[2] Joseph S. McCarthy's good humour carried me through later stages of this project. My sister, Patricia Rogers, offered invaluable assistance and support at home while I was away for research in Russia and at conferences. Any errors are my responsibility alone.

---

1   Melancon and Raleigh (eds.) 2012.
2   Filtzer, Kessler and Pirani (eds.) 2008.

List of Illustrations

1	Alexander Shlyapnikov's mother Khioniya Belenina with her cousin 14
2	Alexander Shlyapnikov's father Gavril Shlyapnikov 15
3	Alexander Shlyapnikov circa 1900 26
4	Alexander Shlyapnikov circa 1903 27
5	Khioniya Shlyapnikova (Alexander Shlyapnikov's mother) 28
6	Khioniya Shlyapnikova with her cousin's family 29
7	Alexander Shlyapnikov with workers in France, circa 1910–12 38
8	Alexander Shlyapnikov in Paris, 1911, among French workers of the *Département de la Seine* 39
9	Alexandra Kollontai, 1910 43
10	Alexander Shlyapnikov circa 1912 44
11	Alexander Shlyapnikov, Paris, 1913, holding the newspaper *L'Humanité* 48
12	Alexander Shlyapnikov circa 1914 53
13	Alexander Shlyapnikov with his mother and siblings, St. Petersburg, Russia, 1914 54
14	Maria Kovalenko (Alexander Shlyapnikov's younger sister), St. Petersburg, Russia, circa 1914 55
15	Alexander Shlyapnikov with Alexandra Kollontai and Scandinavian Social Democrats, Kristiania, Norway, summer 1915 60
16	Alexander Shlyapnikov's entry on the Kristianiafjord passenger list, summer 1916 73
17	Soviet Council of People's Commissars, 1917 100
18	Meeting of the Council of People's Commissars, circa January–March 1918 108
19	Sketch of Alexander Shlyapnikov by Yuri Artsybushev, circa December 1917–January 1918 109
20	Zoya Shadurskaya, 1910s 117
21	Portrait of Alexander Shlyapnikov in 1919 by the Murom artist, Ivan Kulikov 136
22	Alexander Shlyapnikov with family and a friend in Murom, Russia, circa 1920 149
23	Alexander Shlyapnikov with family in Murom, Russia, circa 1919–21 149

24	Murom, Russia, 1920	150
25	Murom, Russia, 1920	150
26	Murom, Russia, 1920	151
27	Alexander Shlyapnikov circa 1915–23	152
28	Alexander Shlyapnikov speaking with Clara Zetkin in Moscow, summer 1921	215
29	Alexander Shlyapnikov and Leonid Krasin in Paris, 1924	263
30	Sergei Medvedev, Mikhail Chelyshev and Alexander Shlyapnikov, November 1926	278
31	Maria Medvedeva, Antonina Tyutereva, Alexander Shlyapnikov, Sergei Medvedev, Klavdiya Chelysheva, and Mikhail Chelyshev, 1927	278
32	Alexander Shlyapnikov in the late 1920s	304
33	3/1 Spasopeskovsky Lane, Moscow, 1972	314
34	3/1 Spasopeskovsky Lane, Moscow, 2012	315
35	Donskoe cemetery, Moscow, 2012, common grave no. 1 for victims of Stalinist repression, 1930–42	364

List of Abbreviations and Acronyms

BBK	White Sea-Baltic Sea Industrial Complex
CC	Central Committee of the Russian Communist Party (trade-union central committees are not abbreviated)
CCC	Central Control Commission of the Russian Communist Party
GARF	State Archive of the Russian Federation
Glavki	VSNKh departments (literally 'chief committees') overseeing branches of industry
Glavmetall	Main Administration of Metals Industry
Gomzy	State Association of Machine-Building Factories
Gospromtsvetmet	Association of State Enterprises on Mining and Nonferrous Metalworking
GPU	State Political Administration
GUGB	Main Directorate of State Security
IWW	Industrial Workers of the World
Lenmashtrest	Leningrad Machine-Building Trust
Metalloimport	Metals Import Board
Mezhsovprof	International Council of Trade Unions
MOGES	Moscow Oblast Hydroelectrical Station
Mosmashtrest	Moscow Machine-Building Trust
Narkomindel	People's Commissariat of Foreign Affairs
Narkomprod	People's Commissariat of Food Supply
Narkomtorg	People's Commissariat of Trade
Narkomtrud	People's Commissariat of Labour
NEP	New Economic Policy
NKVD	People's Commissariat of Internal Affairs
OGPU	Consolidated State Political Administration
Orgburo	Russian Communist Party CC Organisational Bureau
Politburo	Russian Communist Party CC Political Bureau
Profintern	Red Trade Union International
Prombank	Russian Trade and Industrial Bank
RGAE	Russian State Archive of the Economy
RGASPI	Russian State Archive of Socio-Political History
RKP(b)	Russian Communist Party (Bolsheviks)
RSDRP(b)	Russian Social-Democratic Workers' Party (Bolsheviks)

RSFSR	Russian Soviet Federated Socialist Republic
RVS/Revvoensovet	Revolutionary Military Council
Sibbiuro	Siberian Bureau of RKP(b)
SNK/Sovnarkom	Council of People's Commissars
Sovnarkhoz	Economic Council (local body of VSNKh)
SPO	Secret Political Section
SDS	Russian Social Democrats
SRS	Socialist Revolutionaries
STO	Council of Labour and Defence
TsA FSB	Central Archive of the Federal Security Service
TsAODM	Central Archive of Social Movements of Moscow
Uralmet	Urals Metal Trust
VSNKh	All-Russian Council of National Economy
VTsIK	All-Russian Central Executive Committee [of the All-Russian Congress of Soviets]
VTsSPS	All-Russian Central Council of Trade Unions
Yugostal	Southern Metallurgical Trust

Introduction

Alexander Shlyapnikov's fate in many ways reflected the course of the revolutionary workers' movement in late-tsarist and early Soviet Russia. Born in 1885 into poverty in a Russian provincial town, he became captivated by the sophisticated new machinery of a rapidly industrialising Russia and, like many provincial youths, aspired to become a skilled metalworker. Impatient with repressive tsarist autocracy and the industrial capitalists' patriarchal treatment of workers, he fell under the sway of revolutionary Marxism and applied his talents to organising workers in trade unions and underground Bolshevik Party cells. As a skilled metalworker, he numbered among those revolutionary workers that Marxists prized as the most ideologically 'conscious' and 'advanced'. Revolution in 1917 elevated him and other workers into important leadership roles, while struggle against counterrevolution and foreign intervention during the Russian Civil War (1918–21) distracted them from consolidating worker power in the Russian Communist Party and trade unions. Shlyapnikov soon realised, to his chagrin, that militarisation had aborted his dreams of workers' initiative in building socialism. Mobilising those who shared his views, he led the Workers' Opposition (1919–21), which called on party and trade unions to facilitate workers' mastery over production. Vladimir Ulyanov (Lenin) and other Communist Party leaders resisted his proposals, arguing that workers had become declassed during the economic crisis of 1917–21 and needed many years of education before they could be trusted to collectively manage the economy. Lenin's position won the day, but Shlyapnikov continued to advocate distinct views on the Soviet socialist project. In the Great Terror of 1936–8, Iosif Stalin's regime executed him and other former oppositionists, simultaneously harnessing workers' organisations to raise production in the interests of the one-party state.

Many historians have examined how Russian workers radicalised, the extent to which they identified with the goals of the Marxist revolutionaries, the tensions between them and radical intellectuals [*intelligenty*] in party organisations and their lives under Soviet rule.[1] Although numerous biographers have studied Bolshevik *intelligenty* such as Lenin, Stalin, Lev Trotsky, Nikolai Bukharin and Alexandra Kollontai, there have been few life studies of

---

1 Wildman 1967; Zelnik 1995; Zelnik (ed.) 1999; Bonnell (ed.) 1983; Wynn 1992; Smith 1983; Aves 1996; Iarov 1999 and Rossman 2005.

the party's worker members.² Reginald Zelnik's works on Semyon Kanatchikov and Matvei Fisher, which set standards for Russian labour history, are outstanding exceptions. Unlike Shlyapnikov, Kanatchikov and Fisher grew up in agricultural villages.³ More recently, declassified archives have yielded tantalising material for two biographies of Nikolai Yezhov, who rose from metalworker to secret police (NKVD) chief under Stalin, who used him to orchestrate the Great Terror, then executed him. Yezhov cultivated in himself hatred of the upper classes, because of the poverty and cruelty he witnessed on an everyday basis in his youth in St. Petersburg. As a devoted Stalinist, his career ascended as that of the Old Bolshevik, Shlyapnikov, descended, although both met the same end.⁴ Shlyapnikov, who had studied Marxism more intensively than the younger man and, unlike him, had participated in Western-European unions and parties, possessed a more complex and nuanced perspective. Shlyapnikov's years in Western Europe also set him apart from Mikhail Tomsky, the worker who Stalin ousted from the Politburo and trade-union leadership in 1929 as a Right Oppositionist and who committed suicide in 1936, terrified by the prospect of arrest, torture, and public trial. Tomsky travelled abroad for party conferences, but did not spend extensive time in other countries.⁵

Shlyapnikov's actions and statements throughout the Soviet period provide a counterpoint to the recent Anglo-American consensus that Stalinist discourse, as the culmination of an eschatological dynamic that ran through Bolshevism, was hegemonic in the 1930s. Stephen Kotkin inspired this interpretation in his groundbreaking *Magnetic Mountain*, in which he proposed that Stalin and his ideologists had employed 'speaking Bolshevik' as the language of the new civilisation they created; however, his argument does not exclude the possibility of multiple Bolshevik discourses. Following Kotkin's findings, Jochen Hellbeck, a leading scholar of Soviet subjectivity, employed selected diaries to illuminate how their authors fashioned new self-concepts that conformed to Stalinist dictates in order to survive political terror and achieve upward mobility. In work that complements Hellbeck's, Igal Halfin has traced the discourse of the Russian revolutionary movement from the late-tsarist era through the Stalinist terror, locating it as the driving force behind political events.⁶ Unlike Hellbeck's subjects, Shlyapnikov strove to be a model prole-

---

2   Service 1991; Volkogonov 1991, 1994, 1996; Deutscher 1959; Deutscher 1966; Tucker 1973 and 1990; Wolfe 1960; Ulam 1973; Swain 2006; Cohen 1980; Clements 1979 and Farnsworth 1980.
3   Kanatchikov 1986 and Zelnik 1976.
4   Jansen and Petrov 2002 and Getty and Naumov 2008.
5   Wynn 2012.
6   Kotkin 1995; Hellbeck 2006; Halfin 2000, 2007, 2009; Ree 2010 and Krylova 2000.

tarian before the revolution. As an Old Bolshevik, he had the credentials and self-confidence to challenge the post-revolutionary reconceptualisation of the model. Moreover, as this biography will demonstrate, he mocked the Stalinist discourse that Halfin has portrayed as central to a party member's identity in the 1930s. Shlyapnikov belonged to a diverse Russian revolutionary culture harbouring potential for outcomes alternative to that course Stalin chose.

Because Stalinist historians declared Shlyapnikov's name anathema, both Russians and Westerners knew little about him during the Cold War era. Under Nikita Khrushchev, scholars cautiously used his works as historical sources, but were forced to describe his views as harmful. In the West, the Bolsheviks' moderate Socialist rivals (Mensheviks and Socialist Revolutionaries) long set the tone in Western historiography for interpreting Bolshevism. Many recalled Shlyapnikov as a hard-line Lenin supporter, with few independent views and dedicated, above all, to the triumph of the Bolshevik Party.[7] Most pre-1991 secondary works about Soviet history, or about early Communist Party history, have only scanty information about him. These brief accounts could not trace how he was transformed from a seemingly loyal follower of Lenin to leader of an opposition movement within the Communist Party. Due to lack of sources, many of these works failed to discern that he sometimes differed with Lenin before 1917.[8]

Yet fascination with Shlyapnikov and the Workers' Opposition persisted in the West. Shlyapnikov's books and articles, as well as published Russian Communist Party congress proceedings made some of his views accessible to historians who read Russian. Others perceived his views through the lens Kollontai provided in her booklet about the Workers' Opposition, printed for the Tenth Communist Party Congress in 1921, and translated into English, French, and German.[9] A popular audience would have become acquainted with him through Alexander Solzhenitsyn's *Red Wheel* series, which used Shlyapnikov's memoirs as a source, and in the writer's 1975 speech to an American Federation of Labor-Congress of Industrial Organizations audience. Lauding Shlyapnikov as having 'expressed the true interests of the workers within the Communist leadership', Solzhenitsyn made the exaggerated claim that 'before the Revolution it was Shliapnikov who ran the whole Communist Party in Russia – not Lenin, who was an émigré'.[10] The author appears to have employed Shlyapnikov to enable his anti-Communist agenda, portraying

---

7 Sukhanov 1962 and Tsereteli 1963.
8 Daniels 1988; Schapiro 1956 and Sorenson 1969.
9 Kollontai 1921b.
10 Solzhenitsyn 1972, 1976 and 1983–91.

the leader of the Workers' Opposition as an idealist with a true Russian soul, betrayed by Lenin and other cosmopolitan intellectuals. Before the collapse of the Soviet Union, Larry E. Holmes wrote on the Workers' Opposition and several postgraduate students defended theses on Shlyapnikov, but all conducted research without access to restricted archives.[11] Until Shlyapnikov's private correspondence and other archival documents became accessible, historians knew little about his personality and character, which infused his politics. In the late 1980s, under Mikhail Gorbachev, the floodgates of information finally opened.

As the Soviet Union collapsed, scholars mined previously restricted archives.[12] Post-Soviet Russian scholars used newly accessible sources to study Shlyapnikov or the Workers' Opposition, but some had a political or personal agenda, while all were uninformed by recent debates in Western historiography. In 1993, Vladimir Naumov published a brief biography of Shlyapnikov, which grew out of his work in the Soviet government committee on rehabilitating victims of Stalinist repression.[13] Thus, Naumov emphasised Shlyapnikov's devotion to Lenin and ignored his periodic strong criticisms of Lenin's views. Shlyapnikov's daughter Irina, a chemist by training, wrote an unpublished partial biography of her father, motivated by a desire to recapture his accomplishments from Soviet-era distortions. More recently, a Russian historian has demonstrated renewed appreciation for Shlyapnikov's historical memoirs, ranking them as among the most valuable of those by Russian socialists on the history of the Petrograd Soviet in 1917.[14] Among the new generation of Russian historians is a scholar of the Workers' Opposition, Tatyana Sandu, whose dissertation found important differences between provincial groups of the Workers' Opposition and its central leaders in terms of goals and methods. Arguing that conflicts between local party committees and trade unions arose from principled differences, she challenged a recent consensus among post-Soviet Russian historians that these disputes were mainly about access to power and privileges.[15] Nevertheless, her study was limited to a few years and did not include access to restricted materials I consulted during my research in the Central Archive of the Federal Security Service in Moscow (TsA FSB) and in the files of the Party Central Control Commission. The personal files of those investigated by the Central Control Commission in the 1920s–30s are

---

11   Holmes 1990; Spencer 1981; Glen 1973 and Peterson 1987.
12   Hagen 1993.
13   Naumov 1991.
14   Rachkovskii 2011.
15   Sandu 2006; other recent Russian theses are Kornilova 2008 and Rakov 2012.

no longer as accessible as they were when I conducted research in 1995, due to the expense of bringing them to Moscow either physically or in digitised format from their location in a closed military zone. The Central Archive of the Federal Security Service has never been officially open to researchers, so the opportunity for me and a few other foreigners to conduct research there in the 1990s was a rare one.

Central Control Commission (CCC) investigations of Shlyapnikov in the 1920s, his 1933 party purge, NKVD interrogations of him in 1935–6 and his strikingly candid personal correspondence reveal much about how Stalin expanded his control over the party and how oppositionists like Shlyapnikov manoeuvred in response. NKVD files I consulted included not only a complete set of original handwritten interrogation protocols of Shlyapnikov and his comrade Sergei Medvedev, but also thick files of letters, documents and diary entries confiscated from them. Other valuable documents mined for this book include Shlyapnikov's unpublished correspondence with Lenin and other Bolsheviks before and after the revolution, his published and unpublished reminiscences and diary entries, Kollontai's diaries, trade-union records, and notes from Workers' Opposition meetings. Thus, my research on Shlyapnikov contributes rich new detail on the formation of his principles, his political behaviour and the mechanisms of Communist Party politics and repression.

This biography examines Shlyapnikov's life chiefly through his political formation and positions, but it also attempts to relate important findings about him to recent historiographic approaches, such as the cultural and linguistic turn. Shlyapnikov wrote far less on political theory than did more prominent Bolshevik leaders with greater formal education (Lenin, Trotsky, Bukharin), so this study combines discussion of his ideas with how he attempted to implement them through his organising and administrative work. Following a chronological approach, the first chapter explores Shlyapnikov's upbringing among religious dissenters (Old Believers), education, early work experiences, and initiation into the revolutionary movement. His experiences in Western Europe (1908–16), covered in Chapter Two, demonstrate what he learned from trade unions and Socialist parties there and explore the formative influences of Lenin and Kollontai upon him. Chapter Three and Chapter Four examine his work establishing the Metalworkers' Union in Russia during the 1917 revolutions and his attempts as Soviet Commissar of Labour to establish the unions' role in government. Shlyapnikov's rising concern about disempowerment of workers and his steps to confront it, which culminated in the Workers' Opposition, are detailed in Chapter Five and Chapter Six. In chapters seven through nine, his initial struggle to retain control of the Metalworkers' Union and adjust his ideals to the conditions of the New Economic Policy shifts to his recognition that Soviet Russia did not provide the context for realising his vision. Refusing to distort his revolutionary past and steadfastly defending a Bolshevism that did not conform to Stalinist dictates, Shlyapnikov (chapters 10–12) absorbed himself in work to rebuild Soviet industry and preserve his memories of the revolutionary movement in the histories he wrote. Arrested during the Great Purges, he refused to confess to outlandish charges both under NKVD interrogation and when sentenced to execution in September 1937. Thus, his behaviour undermines the conventional view that Old Bolsheviks confessed for the good of the party.

Shlyapnikov's sense of self was formed by his family heritage of religious dissent, through the skilled factory work in which he took pride, by organising fellow workers, as a postrevolutionary leader, and as an oppositionist; at its core was a sense of individual autonomy that Stalin's ideological servants attempted, without complete success, to suppress. As Party leaders manipulated oppositionists and suppressed factionalism, compliance and resistance were not the only ways in which dissenting Bolsheviks responded to Stalin's pressure. Shlyapnikov carefully attempted to maintain an autonomous stance in Party politics while contributing his organisational talents to Soviet Russia's industrialisation. He hoped that industrial development under Communist guidance would improve workers' lives, but could not banish worries that flaws in Stalin's approach undermined the humanistic goal. His life story enriches our understanding of Soviet history and Russian political culture.

Note on Transliteration and Dates

Footnotes and bibliography employ the Library of Congress transliteration system (with exceptions made for Trotsky, Zinoviev and Russian imperial rulers), while names of people and places in the text are rendered in forms easier to read (for example, 'y' for 'ii'; 'ya' for 'ia'; and 'x' for 'ks'). Before 1918, Russia used the Julian calendar, which in the twentieth century was 13 days behind the Gregorian calendar employed in the rest of Europe and the United States. For events occurring and primary sources originating in Russia before March 1918, Julian dates are used and Gregorian for all other events and sources; in some cases, both dates are provided in citations. Citations conform to author-date style used by the *Historical Materialism* series, with the exception of archival citations, which are provided in longer form for researchers' convenience. Inquiries about sources may be addressed to the author.

CHAPTER 1

From the Old Belief to Socialism

In 1935, accused of political crimes, Alexander Shliapnikov sat in a remote prison in the Urals, separated from his wife and three young children in Moscow. His thoughts returned to childhood, when he and his siblings grew up in hardship, without a father. He began to write a memoir of childhood, as did some other victims of Stalin. Already a practised writer, he had composed lengthy historical memoirs of the revolutionary movement for a broad audience, but he wrote his prison memoir for his son Yuri to read, in a style accessible to an intelligent, well-educated nine-year-old boy and with age-appropriate content. His handwritten manuscript was preserved in secret police files and only released to the family after the collapse of the USSR. Because of the intended audience, it differs from worker-Bolsheviks' published recollections. Although he surely meant to transfer his memories to his children by means of this document, it also reflected his revised understanding of the environment that shaped him into a revolutionary, making it somewhat of a departure from the standard worker autobiographies published in the 1920s and a valuable source for this chapter. In simple language, Shliapnikov unfolded an interpretation of his upbringing as profoundly shaped by religious dissent. Detailing escapades, fears and dreams, he offered his son a model for masculinity and moral lessons emphasising education, sobriety and loyalty to family and friends. The source also reflects the changes Russia was undergoing in the 1890s, as large-scale industrialisation unfolded, facilitated by the policies of Finance Minister Sergei Witte; Russian commerce grew and its economy attracted capital for investment in industry. The rapid growth of a modern-industrial workforce encouraged Russian socialists to propagandise Marxist ideas among workers. The memoir culminated in a pivotal moment, Shliapnikov's first visit to Sormovo, a centre of advanced metalworking industry in Russia, in 1896, when he was 11 years old. His decision to become a metalworker exposed him to revolutionary socialism, which only intensified when he participated in the 1905 Revolution and suffered from subsequent harsh repressions. These experiences transformed his life's direction.[1]

---

1 Shliapnikov 1935; Bukharin 1998 and 2007; Kanatchikov 1986; Gambarov *et al.* (eds.) 1989; Wcislo 2011.

Early Childhood in Murom

Located on the Oka River, about three hundred kilometres east of Moscow, Shlyapnikov's birthplace of Murom was accessible by train from Moscow and St. Petersburg and by steamship from the trading centre of Nizhny Novgorod. An ancient city, with a rich heritage derived both from its original Finnic inhabitants and the Slavs who assimilated them around 1000 CE, the town's past was steeped in both legend and history. Not only was it renowned as the origin of the fabled Russian warrior, Ilya Muromets, but records attest that Tsar Ivan the Terrible built a cathedral in the town to celebrate his victory over the Kazan Tatars. In the late nineteenth century, Murom belonged to Russia's central industrial region; local industries included metalworking, textiles and a match factory. Its population of over fifteen thousand comprised gentry, clergy, townsmen and peasants, which were the four hereditary social estates into which Russia had been divided before the Great Reforms of the 1860s–70s.[2] Boundaries between social estates became more fluid in the late nineteenth century, as Russia modernised, but along with emerging categories of class, they still limited an individual's social trajectory.[3] The population was mostly Russian, with few national minorities, so local people had little opportunity to envision Russia as a multi-ethnic empire, unless they travelled to large cities or to the periphery. Well-educated elites and Russians in borderland areas were more aware of the empire's diversity.[4] Childhood in a small town set Shlyapnikov apart from Bolshevik workers such as Yezhov and Tomsky, who grew up in St. Petersburg or its environs, and Kanatchikov, who spent his early years in the countryside and first saw a factory when he went to work at one in Moscow at the age of 16.[5]

Since Russia was overwhelmingly peasant, townsmen like Shlyapnikov were a minority in the country as a whole, but in many ways, his childhood was typical. He was of Russian nationality, attended three years of primary school and went to work early. High intelligence and intense ambition distinguished him from many other poor boys. Factory Street, where he grew up, was a neighbourhood of mostly poor people, many of whom worked at local factories (hence the street name), but even so, his family and others lived in their own houses (not apartments), with kitchen gardens and fruit trees, which meant he was

---

2 Brokgauz and Efron 1897, vol. 20, pp. 216–18. The population included 232 gentry, 279 clergy, 2,134 merchants and honoured citizens, 9,376 hereditary townsmen and 3,235 peasants.
3 Clowes *et al.* (eds.) 1991.
4 Tolz 2011; Sunderland and Norris (eds.) 2012.
5 Wynn 2012, pp. 120–1; Kanatchikov 1986, pp. 7–8.

better fed than Tomsky and Yezhov, but less so than Kanatchikov.[6] In childhood, he remembered, he learned to value sobriety, hard work, compassion, honesty, studiousness and the natural world, but he also learned that many paths of social mobility were closed to him because of his class and religion.

Anger towards oppressive authorities and the desire for social justice flavoured Shlyapnikov's memories of childhood; these feelings emerged from his identity as an Old Believer of the priestless Pomortsy sect. The Russian Orthodox Church had split in the seventeenth century because Old Believers opposed reform of Russian church ritual and liturgy to make it consistent with practice in other Eastern Orthodox churches. Old Believers put great stake on hard work and adherence to a strict moral code, including abstention from alcohol and tobacco, and their faith often served as an ideology for opponents of increasing state power and centralisation. The Old Belief was the chief ideology of dissent in Russia before the arrival of Socialism from the West. One of its most stubborn martyrs, the Archpriest Avvakum, wrote the first autobiography in Russia, which inspired many generations of Old Believers to maintain their faith. One of the early founders of the Old Belief was Archpriest Loggin from Murom.[7] Since Old Believers hid their faith to avoid persecution, estimating their numbers is difficult, but there were likely millions of them in Russia in the late nineteenth century. Because they rejected the legitimacy and authority of the Russian Orthodox Church, Old Believers were frequently harassed and persecuted. Stories of exploitation and abuse of power by priests, police, and other authorities formed part of Shlyapnikov's early world view. Experience with religious persecution helped him develop critical thinking skills, powers of argumentation, and steadfastness in defending his beliefs. He later assessed his early experience with religious persecution as preparation for 'struggle and martyrdom'.[8] His roots in the Old Belief distinguished him from most other Bolshevik leaders.

Social conditions for poor families meant that many young Russian males, not only budding revolutionaries, had difficult or non-existent relationships with their fathers. This was true of Tomsky, who was illegitimate, Kanatchikov, whose father beat him, and Yezhov. At age three, Shlyapnikov lost his father Gavril, who drowned during an outing with friends. A mill owner's son, Gavril

---

6 Shliapnikov 1935, pp. 33, 40; Wynn 2012, p. 120; Getty and Naumov 2008, Chapter Two.
7 Robson 1995, Zenkovskii 2006; Avvakum 1979; Michels 1999, pp. 52–3. In 1896 there were 35 Old Believers in Murom town and 1,130 in the u″ezd, compared to 15,572 Orthodox in the town and 114,385 in the u″ezd (Brokgauz and Efron 1897, vol. 20, pp. 216–18).
8 Shliapnikov 1935, pp. 5, 14; Gambarov et al. (eds.) 1989, vol. 3, pp. 244–5, Shliapnikov's autobiography.

had held various unskilled and semi-skilled jobs. One of Alexander's earliest memories was accompanying his mother Khioniya when she retrieved Gavril's body from the riverside, and subsequently attending the funeral. That his father's friends were too inebriated to save him made a profound impression of the dangers of drunkenness. Moreover, Gavril's death brought to his dependants great hardship, which was only slightly alleviated by the financial aid for widows and orphans that they received as members of the urban estate [*meshchanstvo*]. Khioniya earned money by washing laundry, sewing, selling flour at the market, renting space to lodgers and scrubbing floors at a factory. Shlyapnikov recalled accompanying his mother to the factory where he admired metalworking forges and steam engines. But more often he was locked up at home with his younger sister Maria. Hungry and frightened of monsters in the dark, he worried that his mother and older siblings Anna and Peter would drown in the river where they had gone to wash linen.[9]

Shlyapnikov's memoir of childhood provides far more personal detail and emotional subtleties than sources on Tomsky's or Yezhov's early years. The memoir's pedagogical orientation offered Yuri lessons his father would not have the opportunity to teach in person. Tales of childhood play may have directed Yuri towards beneficial activities and away from harmful ones, but also served to entertain. Stories of poverty were leavened with more positive memories of treats on religious holidays and amusements at the annual fair [*yarmarka*], including rides on the carousel and the Petrushka puppet show. Circus themes from the fair seeped into imaginary play and seem to have shaped youthful perceptions of people in far-off lands. According to Shlyapnikov, he took a prominent leadership role among his peers, directing other boys in games of *lapta* (similar to baseball or cricket) and knucklebones, which served not only as marbles, but also as 'little men' in fantasy play. Another favourite game was captaining a 'steamship', which 'sank', requiring him to rescue passengers. Describing fights with boys from other streets, Shlyapnikov emphasised his disapproval of violent conflicts among adult men and the need for boys to avoid involvement in them. Given his later behaviour in strikes and demonstrations, it seems likely that in boyhood he led and initiated fist fights, but as a father would have wanted to direct his son away from trouble. When he occasionally misbehaved, he recalled, his mother threatened to whip him with a belt or birch rod, but his memoirs offer no evidence that an adult abused him in childhood, unlike the experiences of Kanatchikov, Yezhov or Tomsky (whose older brother psychologically abused him).[10] Historians of the revolu-

---

9   Shliapnikov 1935, pp. 1–3; Shliapnikova 1995; Wynn 2012, p. 120.
10 Shliapnikov 1935, pp. 3–19, 28, 47–8, 51–2, 64–5; Kelly 1990; Wynn 2012, p. 121.

tionary movement often find significant connections between revolutionaries' exposure to violence as children and their acceptance of it as a revolutionary tactic and method for implementing policy, but Shlyapnikov's childhood experiences with violence seem to have been relatively mild.

Work, another theme of play, very early became a necessity for poor children, but Shlyapnikov's mother tried to protect him and his siblings from its harsher aspects. During a summer break from school in 1891, Alexander and his older brother Peter picked pieces of iron from the slag heap behind the foundry, turning over their small earnings to their mother. The children made matchboxes at home until Khioniya decided the pay was too low. Shlyapnikov remembered that she warned them never to work at the match factory, because of the unhealthy environment. Children who worked in match factories developed edema, shortness of breath and a weak pulse. Sometimes they died of sulphur poisoning. In the summer, Shlyapnikov and his siblings gathered berries, potatoes and apples in the family garden. During the 1891 famine, flour was expensive and food aid from the *meshchanstvo* estate office did not suffice. Peter had to leave school to become a shoemaker's apprentice. When his mother heard that the shoemaker beat him, she transferred him to a different apprenticeship in her home village of Doschatoe.[11] Thus, Shlyapnikov remembered that despite hardship, his mother taught her children that they deserved respect and fair treatment.

Shlyapnikov's Old Believer relatives influenced him during the holidays he spent with them in nearby Doschatoe, reached by steamboat along the river. Grandmother Akulina took him to an Old Believer chapel, full of icons, to pray to God. Vividly describing heaven and hell, Akulina taught him to pray for his deceased father to reach heaven. He remembered that he then strongly desired to 'climb up to the sky' to discover if his father had reached heaven. She also told him stories about old times, when Doschatoe villagers were state peasants forced to work in iron mines, cut timber or gather peat. One tale was about her husband Nikolai, a miner, who had offended an overseer and been taken away in chains, never to return. Alexander vowed to find his grandfather and remove his chains.[12] Family stories may have fed in him a desire to become a liberator, which lay at the base of his more sophisticated adult world view.

One summer in 1894, an Orthodox missionary came to Doschatoe to convert the Old Believers. Such missionaries were often poorly educated and unable to employ sophisticated conversion techniques. After hiding their icons and books, the Old Believers gathered for a debate with the missionary, designating

---

11   Shliapnikov 1935, pp. 3, 5, 10–11; Gorshkov 2009, p. 81.
12   Shliapnikov 1935, pp. 5–7, 14–18.

a senior member of the community as their spokesman. Alexander argued for his right to attend, but children were not allowed. According to his uncle, the debate was brief. When the Old Believer representative compared the Orthodox sign of the cross to the gesture of pinching tobacco for snuff, a typical tactic, the priest angrily shouted threats to close their meeting house and send them all to Siberia. This incident inspired Alexander 'to learn how to dispute with the priests and defend the Old Belief'.[13]

Stories about good and evil shaped his early world view, but that outlook became more complex as he matured and embraced Marxism and atheism. Shlyapnikov's son Yuri had no memories of either parent ever discussing religion with him, but recalled only that his father always gave money to beggars outside churches. Yuri's sister Irina learned that their father did not forbid his mother-in-law from keeping icons in the family's apartment, for which his comrades criticised him.[14] Apparently not among those Communists who actively persecuted religious believers, Shlyapnikov modelled compassion for his children, but did not want them to become believers, because he regarded religion as an outmoded and defective belief system.

Shlyapnikov's adult Marxism seems to have shaped memories reflecting his perception of villagers' folk beliefs as superstition and caused him to conflate folklore with childhood fantasy. Tales he heard as a boy in Doschatoe ranged from the apocalyptic to the magical, leading him to perceive 'invisible monsters' in all natural objects and phenomena. As he returned by steamship from Doschatoe to Murom, he even imagined that the steamship was alive with animal-like noises. Rather than condemning villagers for ignorance, however, he seemed to realise that their stories and his village interludes had given him a lifelong love of wildlife and nature.[15] Fantasy also reinforced his childhood fascination with machinery, which many of the men he admired could manipulate with facility.

Since Shlyapnikov's father died young, the boy had to look to relatives and neighbours for models of masculinity, which varied greatly. Shlyapnikov remembered that some neighbours were drunken brawlers, while others were peaceful. His uncle Alexei, a rolling mill operator, served as an early male role model. Like many Russian men, Alexei did not attend church or pray. Instead, he enjoyed taking Alexander on walks through the forest and recounting stories of the enormous hammers and hard labour he had performed at a metalworking factory near St. Petersburg; he preferred lighter work in Doschatoe.

---

13   Shliapnikov 1935, pp. 34–5.
14   Iurii Shliapnikov 2007, interview, p. 7; Shliapnikova 1997, letter.
15   Shliapnikov 1935, pp. 13–17.

Nevertheless, Alexei did not dissuade his nephew from seeking a route to the city. Nor did Alexei's stories about powerful rich people intimidate Alexander, who boasted that in Murom he and his friends fought with boys from wealthy families. Adults told him that, in old times, those who were persecuted fled to the woods, where they attacked and robbed the wealthy, but did not molest the poor. His mother, from whom he may have acquired his sense of irony, offered the alternative explanation that some merchants in town were descended from robbers.[16] Thus, young Alexander was exposed not only to romantic tales about robbers but also to a perspective that linked them to exploitation. In this way, he differed from Iosif Djugashvili (Stalin), who was so inspired by the bandit 'Koba' in a novel, that he assumed the name in the revolutionary underground. Shliapnikov took the revolutionary alias 'Belenin', the surname of his Doschatoe relatives.

Male lodgers at his home in Murom also helped shape his concept of masculinity. Two were metalworkers, Karpych, a foundryman, and Sidor, a fitter from the Caucasus. The tattooed Sidor, who had been a machinist on a warship, captivated the children with stories of ocean travel, the revelation that the earth was not flat but round and tales of having worked in Baku with people of different nationalities and religions. Karpych found work in the foundry for Peter, who returned home to earn higher pay. In a common ritual, Peter had to drink and to treat his fellow workers to vodka on his first payday. Like other foundrymen, Peter fought with the tailors, cobblers and other artisans. Alexander remembered admiring the workers and enjoying their songs, but finding drunkenness repellent.[17] Warnings about alcoholism resounded in his memoirs, probably conveying his desire to discourage his son from drinking, but they also reflected his adult choices.

When Karpych argued with the foundry owner and left for Sormovo, where workers were being hired to work in new factories, his bold decisiveness stunned Alexander. From Sormovo, Karpych moved on to the Semyannikov factory (also known as the Nevsky Shipbuilding and Machine Plant) in St. Petersburg, where he offered to help Peter find a job. Workers in St. Petersburg factories often formed work units [artels] based on the town or village from which they had migrated. Khioniya worried but finally relented, since Peter was so eager. She must have feared that life in the city would tempt him away from Old Belief values. Nevertheless, she acquired a passport recording his age as 17, although he was several years younger, and he left by train. It was common practice for parents and children to hide children's true ages in order for them to obtain

---

16   Shliapnikov 1935, pp. 5–7, 15, 38.
17   Shliapnikov 1935, pp. 25–7. On Russian workers' drinking practices, see Transchel 2006.

work. Local authorities colluded in the deception.[18] Later Peter sent news that he was working at the Semyannikov factory. Thus, Alexander learned early that metalworking skills opened new horizons. He would follow a similar route to St. Petersburg.

FIGURE 1   *Left to right: Arisha Makhova (Khioniya's cousin), Makhova's husband, and Khioniya Nikolaevna Belenina (Alexander Shlyapnikov's mother) circa 1870 (provided by the Shlyapnikov family).*

---

18   Shliapnikov 1935, pp. 27–9; Gorshkov 2009, p. 152.

FIGURE 2   *Gavril Maximovich Shlyapnikov, Alexander Shlyapnikov's father (provided by the Shlyapnikov family).*

Schooling and Child Labour

Unlike Peter, who quit school, Alexander completed his primary education, at which he (like Tomsky and Kanatchikov, but not Yezhov) excelled. Schooling opened new horizons for him, but also reinforced tales of social injustice and oppressive authorities. Eager to learn, he begged his mother to send him to school a year early. In autumn 1892, she tried to enroll him, but the parish school rejected him because he was an Old Believer and the local government school because he was too young. Russian rulers Peter I (r. 1682–1725) and Catherine II (r. 1762–96) had introduced higher schools in Russia to educate a small percentage of their subjects. After the Great Reforms of the 1860s–70s, which ended serfdom and attempted to modernise Russia, primary schools expanded rapidly in Russia, as in the rest of Europe. The church, industrial enterprises, charities and local elected bodies of limited self-government [*zemstvos*] opened schools. The various school types reflect what Catriona Kelly calls the 'organisational chaos' of the Russian primary school system, with over twenty different types of school funded by a variety of government, church and private organisations.[19]

During the year before Alexander became eligible to attend school, his mother and older sister taught him his letters at home. Although literacy was very low among Russian women at this time, it was higher among Old Believer women. On the way to register him for school in late summer 1893, his mother reminded him that he should not partake in official Orthodox Church rites. Not only did the churches have some different icons, but the Old Believers crossed themselves with two fingers, as opposed to the Orthodox with three. Intertwining religious faith with a message about social justice, she emphasised: 'in old times our church was a defender of the poor, but now it has become a lackey of the rich'. Khioniya registered him at the *zemstvo* school, which was closer than others, and explained to the school official that since they were Old Believers, her son would not go to prayer service on the first day of school, but would come directly afterwards for lessons.[20]

---

[19] Shliapnikov 1935, pp. 11, 17–18; Wynn 2012, p. 121; Kelly 2007, p. 30. The best study in English of Russian rural primary schools is Eklof 1986, but there is no comparable study of town schools. Both rural and urban schools were subject to the same official policies, but operated in different socio-economic contexts.

[20] Shliapnikov 1935, pp. 11, 17–18. In Murom u"ezd in 1889 there were 30 *zemskie* schools, 15 *tserkovno-prikhodskie* schools, 10 *gramota* schools and some factory schools (Brokgauz and Efron 1897, vol. 20, pp. 216–18).

When Alexander arrived at school on the first day, he found that because he had not come to prayer service, he had been disenrolled, so, as he recalled, he ran home in tears. Khioniya, also upset, immediately left her work to seek advice from *meshchanstvo* officials, who directed her to the town primary school, on the other side of town. There, Alexander was immediately enrolled and quickly made friends. With more than seventy pupils, the teacher had little time for individual students; in fact, he sometimes applied corporal punishment to slow learners. But Shlyapnikov remembered enjoying the teacher's approval, because he had already learned his letters and could recite them according to the more difficult Old Church Slavonic method.[21]

Alexander's relations were much worse with the scripture teacher ('father deacon'), who threatened the pupils that if they did not attend church, he would 'strictly punish' them. When he told his mother about this, she had him read about the early Christian martyrs in *Lives of the Saints* (a source for the image of the 'ascetic hero' in Russian popular literature). Probably intending only to strengthen his faith, his mother nevertheless seems to have helped condition him to challenge authority. Enjoying the stories, he was inspired to follow their example and had the opportunity to do so when the deacon angrily announced one day that those who had missed Christmas church services should 'kneel and go without lunch'. In earlier autobiographies intended for a broad Soviet readership, Shlyapnikov wrote that the deacon intentionally targeted him. In his prison memoir, however, he clarified that he voluntarily submitted to punishment, for fear of being expelled from school if he ran away, and because he felt compelled to follow the example of Christian saints. Although sympathetic classmates appealed for mercy, the deacon ignored them; the 'martyr' remained on his knees for the rest of the day. Such punishment became regular.[22]

During school holidays, Alexander sought to earn income. When he turned age nine in summer 1894, he tried working at the spinning mill, over Khioniya's objections that it was too dangerous. The mill owner assigned him and two boys of similar age to pinch together string from lint in the carding room. Even with the windows open, lint and dust filled the air like fog, making the workers' eyes sting, their noses itch and throats hurt. Even their saliva became dirty. He and the other boys only quit work there when they found how little they earned. Their next job was collecting bits of iron which had fallen from train cars, also for low pay.[23] Factory work had been banned for children under age 12

---

21   Shliapnikov 1935, pp. 18–21.
22   Shliapnikov 1935, pp. 24–9; Morris 1993, p. 2.
23   Shliapnikov 1935, pp. 31–2.

in 1882, while children ages 12–15 were limited to eight hours of work per day. In 1884, children under 15 were prohibited from certain industries entirely. This and subsequent laws limiting child labour marked improvement over the early nineteenth century, when tsarist authorities had encouraged apprenticeships for children as young as ten. But as Shlyapnikov's work experiences attest, factory owners often turned a blind eye to the law.[24] His work did not last long, for Khioniya soon dispatched him to Doschatoe to holiday with her family.

Alexander and a friend sought work at the foundry in Murom in the summer of 1895. Lying about their ages, they claimed to be 12 and 13 rather than 10. The owner at first allocated them work in the yard sorting bits of iron and coke from discarded dirt. Rising at 6 a.m., they worked until 7 p.m., with two hours for lunch. Thus, the owner violated not only the law on minimum working age, but also on hours. After a few days, he told the boys to assist the furnace tender, who assigned them to bring clay and clean the pots into which molten iron was poured for carrying to the moulds. Casting took place on Saturday. While the furnace was hot, the boys pumped water onto the wooden beams and boards of the room to prevent them from igniting. To young boys at their first full-time job, the exhausting work marked a step into adulthood. Although accidents were frequent while they were smelting iron, Alexander avoided injury, except for broken blood blisters, which solicitous foundrymen showed him how to treat with coal dust to avoid infection. More seriously, aged 12, Tomsky injured a finger at his first job in a box factory, and was fired due to his disability.[25]

When workers were paid, the senior machinist departed from practice by paying the two boys individually and sending them home, not allowing them to join other workers who broke up large bills at the tavern. At the foundry, Alexander earned as much as his mother brought in, but she made him give notice early, so that he would have some holiday before school started. He had gained sympathy for ironworkers. The furnace tender told him that ironworkers had invented the 'myth about hell and devils', because the foundry was the very vision of hell and grimy ironworkers resembled devils. From his later perspective as a Marxist, Shlyapnikov came to interpret 'hell' as a condition 'created by wealthy people on Earth for the poor'.[26]

When Alexander returned to school, his work experience elevated his standing among classmates. Third grade brought more responsibility, as he was assigned to teach the alphabet to first graders. He remembered being a good student in all subjects, especially arithmetic, and that he enjoyed sharing his

---

24 Kelly 2007, p. 28; Gorshkov 2009, pp. 10, 26–7, 137.
25 Shliapnikov 1935, pp. 41–7; Wynn 2012, p. 121.
26 Shliapnikov 1935, pp. 45–8.

answers with other boys, which seems to have won him popularity. The teacher sometimes rebuked him for letting other boys copy his work, but never punished him. Unhappily for him, father deacon gave more frequent scripture lessons and continued to abuse Alexander. When Khioniya turned to a member of the district (*okrug*) court, a nobleman named Tolstoy for whom she washed clothes, for advice about her son's plight, she operated within a conjuncture of old and new Russia. After the Great Reforms, nobles had lost their patriarchal authority over those from lower estates, yet they often occupied influential positions in the post-reform courts and administration. Tolstoy advised her to warn school officials that she could take them to court for 'torture of a child'. After she did so, the deacon stopped abusing Alexander and even accompanied him home to apologise to his mother, explaining that he had only wanted to help the boy and save his soul. Khioniya accepted his apology.[27]

That the persecution ended with a nobleman's intervention, the threat of legal recourse and an apology, was never revealed in Shlyapnikov's official Soviet autobiographies. In those, 'father deacon' represented harsh and arbitrary tsarist and religious authority, but the same man became a more complex figure in his prison memoir. Perhaps Shlyapnikov's experience of Soviet purges and police interrogations had clarified his understanding of his earlier tormentor's psychology, or perhaps he had always been pressured to stereotype father deacon in his official autobiographies. In any case, he now realised that the deacon had aspired to convert him in order to send him to seminary, having recognised his intelligence and ambition. The church suffered from a shortage of priests after the Great Reforms released priests' sons from the clerical estate, yet the deacon miscalculated by employing abusive methods of recruitment.[28] Shlyapnikov may have wanted Yuri to understand the complexity of human behaviour that had not been apparent to him in his own youth. Moreover, sitting in a Soviet prison, he might have reflected upon how tsarist-era court officials had interceded on behalf of the oppressed, unlike those in Stalin-era courts. As later chapters will show, Shlyapnikov considered Soviet courts an important means of redressing grievances and supported the role of law in socialist society.

Emphasising that he never skipped school, because he loved his studies and feared expulsion, he surely meant to encourage Yuri to take education seriously. Having scored well on all his end-of-year exams, except scripture, Alexander passed third grade and completed his formal schooling, but he continued to read classic Russian literature, which helped shape his early outlook

---

27   Shliapnikov 1935, pp. 48–9.
28   On the parish clergy, see Freeze 1983.

on the world. From the library, he borrowed books by Alexander Pushkin and Mikhail Lermontov. With gift money, he bought books, including Nikolai Karamzin's sentimental story, *Poor Liza*,[29] about a peasant girl who, seduced by a noble, drowned herself. Recalling how it made him cry, Shliapnikov may have signalled to his son the acceptability of releasing sad emotions and of empathising with girls. This image might have contrasted with official portrayals of hardened metalworker heroes to which Yuri could have been exposed in the 1930s.[30] Shliapnikov's prison memoir had a didactic purpose, yet much of it rings true, based on the larger picture of his life that unfolds below.

Sormovo in 1896

Before the 1890s, Russian Populists aspired to stir revolution among peasants, while terrorists sought to topple the state by assassinating top officials. The industrialisation wave of the 1890s, however, gave revolutionaries the opportunity to educate and recruit urban workers. When a general strike of textile workers erupted in 1896 in St. Petersburg and other cities, Russian Marxists welcomed this as a sign of Russian workers' revolutionary potential.[31] Simultaneously, a rift deepened between the monarchy and nascent Russian civil society [*obshchestvo*], composed of *zemstvo* professionals (doctors, teachers, statisticians, journalists and charity organisers). Under Alexander III, the 1891 famine killed nearly half a million people in rural Russia. Russian educated elites believed many could have been saved if only the tsarist government had organised relief more competently. Then a tragedy cast an ill omen over the reign of Tsar Nicholas II. At his coronation in May 1896, more than one thousand people were killed in a stampede to receive presents at Khodynka field near Moscow. Informed society worried that the young tsar's government would be as insensitive to the people as his father's had seemed.

Such momentous events loomed in the background in the summer of 1896, as 11-year-old Alexander Shliapnikov travelled to Sormovo by steamship with his mother Khioniya and younger sister Maria to visit his older sister Anna, who had just given birth. Anna needed her mother's help to arrange a christening

---

29   Karamzin 1796.

30   In his memoir, Shliapnikov often referred to having cried as a child at numerous points (Shliapnikov 1935, pp. 50–2). Masculine tears throughout history have been interpreted variously, as markers of 'pleasure, sincerity, and heroism', or of 'self-indulgence, insincerity, cowardice' (Lutz 1999, p. 66).

31   Wildman 1967, p. 27.

according to Old Believer rites. Located near the large trading and industrial centre, Nizhny Novgorod, where the annual fair was the largest in Europe and attracted traders from all over the world, Sormovo arose independently as an industrial town, possessing technologically advanced machinery and attracting highly skilled labour. By 1899 it had thirty-three thousand residents, two-thirds of whom were male. With nearly eleven thousand workers at the shipbuilding plant and eight thousand five hundred employed at the steel works, the Sormovo industrial complex rivalled the large factories of St. Petersburg and the Donbas coal-mining region.[32]

Anna and her husband Ivan Tyuterev lived in a flat in a newly constructed building very close to the factory where he worked. As a turner in a steam engine mechanical shop, Ivan, like many Sormovo workers, considered himself more cultured than those in smaller towns. Alexander learned much from him about the life of highly skilled workers, who dressed well and discussed new technology. On pay day, they received wages in exact change and did not have to break large bills at the tavern, as workers did in his hometown of Murom. Having tasted new foods and admired new steel processing works, Alexander was eager to work in Sormovo, but the workers told him he had to turn 15 first, even though he had already worked in Murom. Owners of large, modern factories often supported child-labour laws, in order to remove the competitive advantage of small workshops.[33] Moreover, inspectors were more likely to visit Sormovo than Murom.

Alexander first heard about revolutionaries in Sormovo, which was located in a centre of labour unrest. One night while Ivan was at work, the women and children heard loud noises coming from the upstairs apartment. In the morning they learned that the gendarmes (political police) had arrested a worker and taken him away. The adults warned the children not to talk about it, but Alexander could not suppress his curiosity. Ivan finally revealed that a series of police raids had occurred over the previous several nights in Nizhny Novgorod, Sormovo, and other towns; many workers were arrested. The police were seeking 'anonymous letters' calling for the tsar's overthrow.[34]

Soon after the arrests, the family went to Nizhny to see Tsar Nicholas II arrive for the celebrated All-Russia Industrial and Art Exhibition, which Witte had arranged. With memories of the Khodynka tragedy still fresh, Khioniya carefully protected the children from the packed crowds. Hearing music, bells and shouts of 'Hurrah!', they glimpsed the tsar and tsaritsa in their carriages.

---

32 Evtuhov 2011, pp. 72–3.
33 Shliapnikov 1935, pp. 53–4; Gorshkov 2009, p. 103.
34 Shliapnikov 1935, pp. 56–7.

Despite grand displays of new machines and electric lights, Shlyapnikov recalled, workers complained that the tsar did not care how they lived and their conversations returned quickly to the recent arrests. Rumours circulated that the tsar had commanded that his enemies be 'destroyed' before his arrival. Alexander's relatives donated to a fund to aid wives and children of the arrested. Before they left Sormovo, Khioniya asked the Old Believers to help Anna if she were ever in need.[35] Alexander had already experienced and heard much about religious persecution, which after his experiences in Sormovo, must have merged with political persecution in his young mind.

Shlyapnikov recalled that upon returning to Murom, he thought much about becoming a turner like Ivan Tyuterev, a 'free and unrestricted master of metalworking', so that his mother and younger sister could have a better life. He later wrote a short story expressing his feelings: 'Sanka [a nickname for Alexander] had completed primary school and now dreamed of becoming a useful worker in a large family, to earn wages to bring to his mother and ease just a bit her cheerless labourer's existence, as "a widow with orphans" '. Only after two more years had passed would his mother allow him to work full-time in a factory. Shlyapnikov belonged to a slightly younger generation than his future comrades Kanatchikov and Tomsky. Tomsky had already, two years before, aged 14, participated in a strike at a metalworking factory in St. Petersburg, but labour unrest did not entangle the Moscow-based Kanatchikov until later.[36]

Youth in Factories and as a Revolutionary

Bribing clerks to falsify his documented age, Shlyapnikov began steady work in 1898 at the nearby Kondratov factory in Vacha. Having started as an office clerk, he soon got an apprenticeship in the mechanical shop. Metalworking offered the prospect of higher pay over time and fascinated him more. Shlyapnikov continued his education informally by reading Russian classical literature from the factory library in his leisure time. Later he recalled that these readings provided perspectives that 'liberated' him from religious influence. By 1899, when he went to work in Sormovo, he claimed he no longer attended church or believed in God. Nevertheless, his upbringing as an Old Believer must have

---

35 Shliapnikov 1935, pp. 57–8.
36 Shliapnikov 1935, p. 59; Gambarov *et al.* (eds.) 1989, vol. 3, pp. 244–51; Shliapnikov 1917f, p. 1; Wynn 2012, pp. 121–2. The prison memoir halted after Shliapnikov's return from Sormovo. The remainder of this chapter relies largely upon tsarist police records, Shliapnikov's memoirs published after 1917 and his 1933 purge testimony.

moulded his personality in ways that remained with him as an adult. His work ethic, sobriety, distrust of the authorities and stubbornness in defending his views resounded with Old Believer values.

Religious mysticism provided an initial interpretive framework for the appeal of a revolutionary's life. At the Kondratov factory, Shlyapnikov heard vague references to revolutionary literature, which the workers imagined as 'special black books which were kept hidden and in which the truth was written, but in disguised form'. Older workers told the youth that for this 'truth' people perished, ground up alive in special mills. Consequently, young workers acquired a reverence for the mysterious 'black books' and were eager to have revealed the truth said to be in them. When, at age 14, Shlyapnikov worked in Sormovo factories, he first read revolutionary Marxist literature. Social-Democratic workers gave him legal books to read and then showed him the local illegal newspaper.[37] They must have found him trustworthy and discreet in order to take such a risk.

At Peter's invitation, Shlyapnikov moved to St. Petersburg towards the end of 1900 and began working with his brother at the Semyannikov (aka Nevsky) factory. The opportunity to improve his vocational skills by learning from highly skilled and experienced Petersburg metalworkers excited him. His arrival coincided with the start of a long period of political unrest in the capital, in reaction to tsarist repressions in universities, the high prices of essential goods and low wages that were intended to promote industrialisation. Student protests erupted in February and March 1901, and in February the Minister of Education was assassinated. Unrest grew among the city's factory workers, including those at Nevsky, culminating in strikes around the time of the May Day holiday, and in violent confrontations between workers and police. For the first time, Shlyapnikov heard of May Day as a holiday for workers. Seeing police fire on demonstrating workers, he called it a 'colossal learning experience'. At the time, he recalled, he understood poorly the aims of the strike, but he was eager to show solidarity with his fellow workers. Therefore, with much 'zeal', he organised his fellow apprentices into squads that harassed strikebreakers and prevented them from working. At Nevsky, as well as at other factories, striking workers demanded the right to elect their own permanent representatives to

---

37 Rossiiskii gosudarstvennyi arkhiv sotsial'no-politicheskoi istorii (RGASPI), f. 589, op. 3, d. 9103, vol. 5: ll: 48–50, Shliapnikov's testimony at his 1933 party purge. Pagination was in reverse chronological order in many documents in f. 589, dela 9102 and 9103. I have cited the pages in the correct numerical order.

negotiate for them with the factory management. The Nevsky management granted this right, but later had the elected representatives arrested.³⁸

Because he participated in the Nevsky strike, Shlyapnikov was unable to find work at any major factories in Petersburg. Astonished by his turn of fate, he had 'never suspected collusion among capitalists or the existence of black lists'. That such a young worker (age 15) was blacklisted may attest to his effectiveness in organising fellow apprentices. Becoming increasingly desperate after working a series of low-paid jobs in Petersburg, he finally surrendered and returned to Vladimir province. Unable to get hired in Sormovo, where workers from Petersburg were automatically suspect as political radicals, he went home to Murom, his dreams deferred. This demoralising experience embittered him against tsarism and capital, heightening his receptivity to arguments that workers should organise. During his stopover in Sormovo, former comrades there had entrusted him with a cache of illegal literature to distribute in Murom. He later designated this as his initiation into the Russian Social Democratic Workers' Party (RSDRP), a meaningful rite of passage for the by then 16-year-old youth.³⁹

Among the illegal literature Shlyapnikov received for distribution were issues of *Iskra* (edited by the 'father of Russian Marxism', Georgy Plekhanov, and younger Marxists Yuli Martov, Lenin, and others) and a newspaper published by the RSDRP Nizhny Novgorod committee. He distributed some literature among co-workers at the Torsk factory in Murom, where he started working in January 1902, and pasted the remainder onto fences and walls around town. When he discovered that his first attempts caught the attention of *Iskra*, he must have been overjoyed. Its 15 June 1903 issue carried a report from a Murom correspondent describing the stir that the appearance of the leaflets caused in Murom society.⁴⁰

Russian Social Democrats (SDs) had a Marxist programme based on the inevitability of conflict between labour and capital and the eventual abolition of private property. They believed that capitalism was developing in Russia and that a revolution carried out by industrial workers could succeed, as opposed to older generations of Russian revolutionaries who had put their stake on the peasantry. The other major revolutionary party was the Socialist Revolutionary Party (SRs), who expanded the definition of an exploited class to include peasants as well as workers, and exploiters to include noble landowners along with capitalists. They advocated socialisation and equal distribution of the land to

---

38   Hogan 1993, pp. 51–2; Bonnell (ed.) 1983, p. 94.
39   RGASPI, f. 589, op. 3, d. 9103, vol. 5: 44–7; RGASPI, f. 70, op. 4, d. 387, l. 131.
40   Shliapnikov 1923c, pp. 38–9, citing *Iskra*, 42 (15 June 1903): pp. 39–40.

those who tilled it, while the SDs' agricultural plans were poorly developed. Among the SDs, there appeared in 1903 Bolshevik and Menshevik factions, the Bolsheviks led by Lenin and the Mensheviks by Martov. Lenin wanted only active revolutionaries to be party members, while the Mensheviks allowed that sympathisers could join. The factional division did not become permanent until 1914 and even then many SDs still sought unity. Unlike SDs, SRs had no central organisation, yet police reports indicate that the SRs had more support in Russia than did the SDs. SRs thought peasants had the potential to cooperate with one another in socialist projects, while Lenin disagreed, claiming to have discovered class divisions and conflict among the peasantry. SRs and SDs often collaborated in practical matters and many revolutionaries migrated between factions or remained independent.

Tainted by Shlyapnikov's need to prove his orthodoxy after the revolution, the question of when and why he became a Bolshevik does not have a simple or satisfying answer. News of the 1903 schism reached some workers very slowly, and others attached little importance to the differences between Bolsheviks and Mensheviks for some time after the split. Shlyapnikov remembered, with apparent embarrassment, that in 1903 he and his comrades 'distinguished poorly' among SD organisations and unwittingly distributed illegal literature by various political factions. It is more likely that he and his fellow activists sensed little importance in distinctions between SRs, SDs and other political radicals. At the time, it was enough for them to challenge the existing order; literature promoting the political role of industrial workers, irrespective of its source, appealed to them. By the end of 1905, however, Shlyapnikov had chosen to identify himself as a Bolshevik, likely under the influence of Bolsheviks he met in prison. To those who see Lenin's Bolsheviks as emphasising a centralised hierarchy dominated by *intelligenty*, and regard the Mensheviks as more democratic, Shlyapnikov's choice may seem puzzling, but the Bolsheviks before 1917 had a more flexible organisational structure than they did after coming to power. Shlyapnikov seems to have identified with Bolshevism because he perceived it as a movement led by workers versed in Marxist theory, with the ideological guidance of radical students, teachers, journalists and lawyers [*intelligenty*]. Among Bolsheviks, he encountered fellow workers, while among SRs and Mensheviks he perceived largely *intelligenty*, but memoirs by other workers sometimes indicate the reverse.[41] Lenin's close attention to worker-*intelligenty* as potential members of a vanguard skilled in

---

41   Shliapnikov 1923c, p. 39; Wynn 1992, p. 152; Bonnell (ed.) 1983, p. 32.

FIGURE 3   *Alexander Shlyapnikov circa 1900 (provided by the Shlyapnikov family).*

FIGURE 4   *Alexander Shlyapnikov circa 1903 (provided by the Shlyapnikov family).*

FIGURE 5   *Khioniya Shlyapnikova, Alexander Shlyapnikov's mother (provided by the Shlyapnikov family).*

FIGURE 6   *Khioniya Shlyapnikova pictured with the children and family of her cousin Arisha Makhova circa 1903–6 (provided by the Shlyapnikov family).*

underground organisation and his offering to them of 'a romantic self-image' probably garnered Shlyapnikov's trust as well.[42]

Shlyapnikov's perceptions notwithstanding, the revolutionary movement comprised a diverse array of people by class, gender and ethnicity. Although most revolutionaries were men, thousands of women also joined, distinguishing Russia as 'having by far the largest number of female revolutionaries of any country' at that time. Young noblewomen who became revolutionaries often did so out of the feeling that their mothers' and grandmothers' philanthropic efforts could not achieve the systemic change they felt Russia needed. Among Old Bolsheviks, the breakdown by occupation indicates that about one-third of men and two-fifths of women (mostly teachers) were intelligentsia or white-collar workers, while nearly half of men and almost one-third of women were urban workers. Less than one-tenth of men or women came from the nobility, while more than one-third of men had been born into the peasantry. More

---

42   For more on Lenin's appeal to workers, see Lih 2011a.

than one-quarter of men and women were hereditary workers, while a similar fraction of women and nearly one-third of men were from the intelligentsia, white-collar occupations or shop-keepers/artisans. Russians were the largest ethnic group among revolutionaries, although they did not seem to constitute a majority. More than ten percent were Jewish, while Poles, Latvians, Estonians, Georgians and Armenians were represented in smaller percentages.[43] In reality, revolutionary socialists were not united or divided so much by social origins or factional labels as by personalities and views on discrete issues.

Along with becoming a skilled political organiser, Shlyapnikov began to assume characteristics of a model proletarian. Revolutionaries regarded skilled workers, especially metalworkers, as natural leaders among workers. Although printers were better educated and informed, metalworkers manipulated the industrial machines and materials that had the productive potential to free humanity from material want. Highly trained workers often took pains to set themselves apart from unskilled labourers, to whom they referred simply as 'workers', while identifying themselves as members of particular professions, such as 'welders' or 'turners'. This deep-seated prejudice hindered Marxists' attempts to instil in skilled workers a sense of unity with the unskilled. Thus, as a Marxist, Shlyapnikov realised that he had to set an example for other workers in order to draw them into revolutionary activity. He had to stand up to management, work hard and defend fellow workers, even the unskilled. Moreover, he had to lead a 'clean life', which meant that he dressed well, read extensively, enjoyed cultural outings and abstained from alcohol. According to S.A. Smith, such workers defined masculinity in a new way, which privileged 'self-control, the assertion of reason over emotion, autonomy in personal relations, and a more respectful, but not necessarily egalitarian attitude toward women'.[44] Shlyapnikov's upbringing had in some ways prepared him to adopt this model.

Shlyapnikov continued to distribute literature when he received it (most frequently from the Nizhny Novgorod SDs). Early in 1903, he continued his education by enrolling in French language classes taught by Vera Yanchevskaya in a 'Sunday school' organised by *intelligenty* to educate workers. His choice of subject matter probably reflected intellectual aspirations. The Sunday schools existed throughout Russia and were a conduit for socialist *intelligenty* to

---

43   Clements 1997, pp. 14–15, 22–3, 32–7, 45. While only two percent of male Old Bolsheviks were peasants, nearly one-fifth were soldiers, many of whom could have been former peasants. About one-fifth of women listed no occupation. Clements's data on men are taken from Chase and Getty 1986 (no longer available). For data on the Socialist Revolutionary Party, see Perrie 1972.

44   Smith 2002, pp. 100–1.

propagandise amongst workers. Through them, Shlyapnikov organised SD circles at factories throughout Murom. Yanchevskaya, described by him later as a 'sentimental idealistic populist', lent him books and copied illegal literature using the hectograph of the Murom railroad administration where she worked. He wrote later that SRs tried to ally with his group through her, but that he and other SDs rejected their propositions.[45] Despite her history of association with SRs, he did not hesitate to write her a letter of recommendation in 1926, when her past carried a stigma.[46]

After leaving the Torsk factory in July 1903 for a more demanding, higher-paying job at the Valenkov machine-building factory, Shlyapnikov contacted a workers' group there which had established ties to Moscow and Nizhny Novgorod SD groups and to Murom *intelligenty*. When their organiser left for work in Moscow, Shlyapnikov assumed the central role in the group. Suspicious of two other members, a postal employee and a worker, he hid from them his own new contacts among workers. Later he discovered both were police spies. By January 1904, he had succeeded in creating an organisation isolated from the two provocateurs (a short time later he was arrested).[47] This organisation published its own leaflet and some verses in January 1904, signing off non-committally as the 'Murom Group of Workers'. When writing about this after the revolution, Shlyapnikov recalled that they had felt they could not call themselves an SD organisation since they had not been made part of the party structure. He emphasised: 'Only later did it become clear to us, that organisations are created, reinforced and achieve recognition through work and not from some higher authority'.[48]

Lines often blurred between revolutionary parties in the Russian provinces before the 1917 revolutions. According to a police informant, Shlyapnikov was in contact with SR students in Murom. Another revolutionary had said that Shlyapnikov joined the 'Murom Social Revolutionary Party', which consisted largely of students, because 'in this circle the programme was broader [encompassed more] than ours'. But the police arrested him in January 1904 on the case of the 'Murom organisation of the Russian Social-Democratic Workers' Party'. At first, he refused to talk. By summer 1904, however, he had devised a strategy. Accusing the informer of having given him illegal literature, he insisted that

---

45 Shliapnikov 1923c, pp. 41–7. Tsarist police records confirm that he studied French in 1904; see Gosudarstvennyi arkhiv Rossiiskoi Federatsii (GARF), f. 102 (DP), d. 299, l. 25.

46 Rossiiskii gosudarstvennyi arkhiv ekonomiki (RGAE), f. 8346, op. 1, d. 38, l. 11, December 1926 (copy).

47 Shliapnikov 1923c; GARF, f. 102 (DP), 1904, d. 299, ll. 16–40.

48 Shliapnikov 1923c, p. 48.

he had rejected both the leaflets and attempts to draw him into illegal work.[49] His testimony convinced the prosecutor that police had entrapped arrested workers and that there was insufficient evidence to detain them any longer. Shliapnikov was released on 30 September 1904.[50] On his way home, local Black Hundreds (reactionary ultra-nationalist monarchists who hated and attacked revolutionaries and Jews) set upon him and beat him brutally, probably having been alerted by police to his release. Neither his confinement nor the attack discouraged him from underground work; these experiences only embittered him more deeply against tsarist authorities. Having renewed ties to socialists, he obtained illegal literature through a network of Murom students in St. Petersburg.[51] In the capital, tensions between the autocracy and society were growing sharper, and soon a key event would increase sympathy for revolutionaries like Shliapnikov.

Revolution of 1905 and Reaction

In 1904–5, Tsar Nicholas II embroiled Russia in a disastrous war with Japan over territory in the Far East. Reform, industrialisation and greater access to education had stirred desires among Russian professionals and workers for participation in government and improvements in living conditions. Military defeat discredited tsarist authority and encouraged various groups in Russian society to mobilise to achieve their goals. In late 1904, liberal professionals gathered at banquets to discuss burning topics of the day, harkening back to the prelude to the 1848 revolution in France. The catalyst for revolution, however, emerged from a workers' movement led by a charismatic priest, Father Georgy Gapon, originally part of a police attempt to sponsor labour unions free of revolutionary elements that escaped police control. In January 1905, on 'Bloody Sunday', troops massacred peaceful demonstrators who, under Gapon's leadership, approached the Winter Palace in St. Petersburg with a petition for the tsar, requesting better working conditions, an eight-hour day, suffrage, and an end to the war. Protest strikes against the killings developed into full-scale

---

49 GARF, f. 102 (DP), 1904, d. 299, ll. 22, 24, and 39; ll. 60–3, July 1904; 7 d-vo, 1904, d. 299, ch. 3, l. 1.

50 GARF, f. 102 (DP), 1904, d. 299, l. 72, memorandum from Vladimir Okrug Court Prosecutor Danilov to Director of Vladimir Guberniia Zhandarmskoe Upravlenie, 25 September 1904.

51 Shliapnikov 1923c, p. 61. Police reports refer to the St. Petersburg Technological Institute student Aleksandr Serebrennikov, who had links to alumni of the Murom Real'noe Uchilishche and the Murom Women's Gymnasium (GARF, f. 102 (DP), 1904, d. 299, l. 49).

revolution that saw political parties emerge from the underground, the formation of civic organisations and trade unions, mutinies in the army and navy and peasant uprisings. By the end of the year, Nicholas II reluctantly accepted a constitution.[52]

The Revolution of 1905 unfolded across Russia, not only in the capital, but in other cities, towns and villages. Shlyapnikov's compassion, strong desire for justice and bitterness towards the authorities moved him to join with others to challenge tsarist power. Together with students from Moscow and a noblewoman from St. Petersburg, he led a large armed demonstration in Murom in July 1905 in commemoration of Bloody Sunday.[53] Because Shlyapnikov had helped take the Murom police chief hostage and forced the police to retreat, he was arrested and gaoled in Vladimir prison. Freed in October by a general amnesty, his militant intransigence led to another arrest in December 1905, whereupon he was held in prison until January 1907. This third arrest coincided with the beginning of harsh repression against worker demonstrations. Outside his prison, dramatic political changes unfolded in Russia, as the country transitioned to constitutional monarchy. Russians elected representatives to a legislative body, the Duma, which confronted an autocratic government resentful of having been forced to concede some of its power. Imprisoned together with more politically conscious and experienced workers from Ivanovo-Voznesensk, Shlyapnikov and his new comrades engaged in politics by electing delegates to party congresses and hearing reports about the congresses. He represented other prisoners as a *starosta* in dealings with prison officials.[54] This important formative experience must have cemented his allegiance to the Bolsheviks.

Harsh tsarist reaction in the wake of 1905 brought reprisals against peasant rebels and urban revolutionaries. One method was conscription. In January 1907, Shlyapnikov was drafted into the army. Refusing to take an oath of service to the tsar on the basis of his political convictions, he was sentenced to two years in a fortress. After being freed on bail with help from a sympathetic liberal lawyer, he went underground rather than risk imprisonment. After brief activism in the Lefortovo SD party organisation in Moscow, in which his cousin Yakov had earlier been a member, Shlyapnikov worked at the Electrical Station of 1886 in St. Petersburg. There he met Sergei Medvedev (1885–1937), a skilled metalworker born a peasant, who grew up near Moscow and St. Petersburg. Like Shlyapnikov, Medvedev had participated in the 1901 Obukhov strike. After

---

52   Sablinsky 1976; Ascher 1988–94; Bushnell 1985 and Shanin 1986.
53   GARF, f. 102, D7, 3861 (1905), ll. 3, 9, 13.
54   RGASPI, f. 589, op. 3, d. 9103, vol. 5: 40–1; Gambarov *et al.* (eds.) 1989, vol. 3, p. 248.

the strike, *Iskra* representatives recruited him and other workers to create a unified SD organisation with a leading centre. Medvedev played a central role in the reception and dispatch of weapons, including bombs, to revolutionary groups. He became Shlyapnikov's close comrade and shared his post-revolutionary political fate.[55] Their friendship underscores Shlyapnikov's acceptance of violent tools to overthrow state power.

By 1907, in the face of fierce tsarist repression, many Bolsheviks had left the party or had been arrested, which, along with Shlyapnikov's charisma, intelligence, organisational skills and leadership ability, could explain why, at the age of 22, he became a member of the Petersburg Committee of the RSDRP(b), the leading Bolshevik organisation in Russia. He attended party conferences, but there is little information on his activities in 1907. He surely was acquainted with Tomsky, who also became a member of the Petersburg Committee that year and attended the Fifth Party Congress in London in the spring. Shlyapnikov's growing prominence attracted police attention and made him more vulnerable to arrest. At the end of 1907, his friends advised him to emigrate. The Petersburg Committee gave him materials to deliver to Lenin.[56] While his comrades worked in the revolutionary underground within Russia, Shlyapnikov entered the world of Russian *émigrés* in Western Europe.

Shlyapnikov left Russia for Geneva in January 1908 under a false name, making his first stop in Austria, where he mailed a letter to his mother, exulting at having escaped the tsarist police's grasp. Briefly delayed due to misdirection by Bolshevik guides who sent him to Genoa rather than Geneva, he arrived in Switzerland by 6 February. After meeting with Lenin, Shlyapnikov proceeded to Paris. With excitement, he gazed upon the city he had known only from books and was awestruck by its standard of living and culture that were higher than in Petersburg. Lenin called Paris the 'foreign Petersburg' because after the 1906–7 reaction began in Russia, many Russian *émigrés* clustered there (at one time around eighty thousand). Most Russian revolutionary *émigrés* congregated in the cafes of the Latin Quarter, but Shlyapnikov also spent his years in France among workers, residing mainly in the northern, industrial suburbs of

---

55 RGASPI, f. 589, op. 3, d. 9102, ll. 173–88; RGASPI, f. 124, d. 2171 (Shliapnikov, Iakov Ermolaevich, 1876–1934), l. 2. Iakov reported that the police often dealt severely with him, associating or confusing him with his cousin Aleksandr (l. 6). For more on Medvedev's origins and life, see Allen 2007.

56 Gambarov *et al.* (eds.) 1989, vol. 3, pp. 246–9; Wynn 2012, pp. 125–6; RGASPI, f. 589, op. 3, d. 9103, vol. 5: 37–41; Shliapnikova 1991 and 1995.

Paris. Two months after his arrival, he found work at an automobile factory in the suburb of Asnières.[57]

By the end of 1907, Shlyapnikov had become a highly skilled metal turner and fitter, a crafty and conspiratorial underground activist and a steadfast Bolshevik. As such he belonged to an exclusive group of 'conscious' Russian proletarians. In Western Europe, however, he took a path that diverged from that of many other radicalised Russian workers. Life and work there gave him the opportunity to observe foreign trade unions' methods of organisation. Acquisition of fluent French and proficiency in German and English facilitated his education in Western-European labour organising and radical socialism, exposing him to a richer heritage of European socialist thought and practice than that available to Tomsky or Kanatchikov, not to speak of the much younger Yezhov, who did not learn foreign languages. Although Tomsky visited France in 1909,[58] Russia remained his base of activity, while Shlyapnikov formed close ties to French workers and to other Russians working in France. Shlyapnikov's record of illegal revolutionary activism in Russia and his association with violent methods made it unlikely the tsarist government could ever allow him a peaceful legal existence in Russia without a term in prison or forced labour in Siberia. Moreover the tsarist government continued to sharply limit the opportunities for civil society to develop in Russia. For these reasons, there was little chance Shlyapnikov would be tempted to moderate his stances while immersed in the Social-Democratic milieu of Western Europe.

---

57 Krupskaia 1970, p. 54; Shliapnikov 1926h, pp. 3, 7–8; Elwood 1974, p. 25; Shliapnikov 1908. Shliapnikov sent picture postcards to his mother on a monthly basis while he was abroad.
58 Wynn 2012, p. 128.

CHAPTER 2

Emigration and the Revolutionary Underground

From 1908 to late 1916, Shlyapnikov lived in Western Europe and Scandinavia, labouring in French, German and English factories and organising workers. During his years in Western Europe, party and trade-union organisations in Russia operated under severe restrictions, which only worsened with the outbreak of war in 1914. In Scandinavia in 1914–16, Shlyapnikov was the liaison between Petrograd Bolsheviks and Bolshevik Party CC members abroad, arranging the transport of literature, money and people. During World War I, he made three trips to Russia, where he consolidated a centre linked to the CC abroad and renewed and expanded ties with worker-Bolsheviks, many of whom later became his collaborators in the Workers' Opposition.[1] He also spent brief periods in England and the United States. Mentored by Lenin, Lenin's wife, Nadezhda Krupskaya, and the socialist feminist Alexandra Kollontai, he developed intellectually, writing short descriptive works on the metals industry in Europe, polemical articles and short stories. Although he respected Lenin's intellectual authority and usually agreed with his instructions on the direction of political struggle, unquestioning support did not accompany his devotion. He maintained a degree of autonomy, sometimes criticising Lenin's policies and tactics in correspondence. Moreover, he cultivated his own ties to European trade unionists and socialist leaders.[2] Burning issues among Western-European socialists included the trade unions' role in politics, whether violent revolution was necessary and whether socialists should support governments in war. Shlyapnikov took radical positions on all these questions.

---

1 His first trip occurred during the summer of 1914. His second trip placed him in Russia from October 1915 to February 1916. Shliapnikov returned to Russia in October 1916. Sources for this chapter include Shliapnikov's 1913–16 correspondence; Kollontai's diary entries; tsarist police reports; Shliapnikov's 1913–15 articles; his memoirs published after 1917; his testimony at his 1933 purge and Kollontai's diary entries.
2 RGASPI, f. 17, op. 1, ch. IV, d. 1398, letters from Shliapnikov to Krupskaia, 1914. His letters to Swedish socialists (in French and English) are in Arbetarrörelsens Arkiv och Bibliotek, Stockholm, in the files of Hjalmar Branting, Elin Lindley and Hannes Skölds. Wynn 2012 details several crucial episodes when Tomskii also pointedly disagreed with Lenin over important questions.

Becoming a Worker-*Intelligent*

A worker-*intelligent*, a category of Russian revolutionary analysed extensively by Reginald Zelnik and Mark Steinberg, was a person whose main profession was manual work, usually skilled, but who also engaged in writing polemical articles or fiction.[3] Tomsky and Kanatchikov belonged to this category, but Yezhov never did. Shlyapnikov quickly developed into one during his years in Western Europe, as attested to by an informer for the Russian political police [*Okhrana*], which kept extensive records on Russian revolutionaries living abroad. Its Paris office was particularly active, given the large number of Russians in the city. According to police records, Shlyapnikov at first led a rather solitary life in France, not entertaining any guests, but reading and writing in his spare time. Towards the end of 1908, however, he began giving speeches and wrote a number of articles and brochures on party matters, using the alias '*Metallist*' ('Metalworker'). In 1909 he continued to labour as a metalworker, moving to a job in a motor factory.[4] He cohabited with a French woman for an indefinite period and became more involved in French trade unionism and politics. Kollontai's son, Mikhail, later recalled Shlyapnikov as a very intelligent man who was fluent in French, and a scholar has assessed his written French as only 'slightly faulty'. A police report noted that his sartorial style, work skills and intelligence caused casual informers to mistake him for an engineer rather than a worker, but that he properly belonged to the category of 'worker-*intelligent*'. The report praised his skills: 'he is a very talented metalworker, who can also work well with wood, is very good at drafting, and can perform special assignments'. Although he was 'smart by nature' and spoke French and German, his 'superficial knowledge of Latin' revealed a lack of higher education. Another intellectual weakness, according to an informant, was to frequently 'reinforce' his papers and speeches 'with reference to one or another published work'. The police found him to be 'very careful and conspiratorial'.[5] Although condescending in tone, the report conveys the young metalworker's ambition, talents and intellectual orientation.

While improving his French-language skills and studying Marxism, Shlyapnikov participated in Russian *émigré* politics and French trade unions. Later he recalled that he and other Bolsheviks struggled with Mensheviks in

---

3   Zelnik 1995, pp. 225–6, judged worker-*intelligenty* to be a more exclusive group than 'conscious' workers. Steinberg 2002 comprehensively treats Russian 'worker-*intelligenty*'.
4   GARF, f. 102 (DP OO), op. 1915, d. 114, ll. 49–50.
5   Futrell 1963, p. 92; Vladimir Kollontai 2006, interview; GARF, f. 102 (DP OO), op. 1915, d. 114, ll. 50–1.

FIGURE 7   Alexander Shlyapnikov with workers in France, circa 1910–12 (provided by the family).

Paris over control of party organisations. Besides participating in Russian social-democratic factional struggles, he joined a regional committee of the Socialist Party of France and became a leader of the Parisian Mechanics' Trade Union, in which he was responsible for organising Russian metalworkers. Periodically blacklisted because he participated in strikes in France, he eluded detection by altering the transliteration of his name.[6] His work and revolutionary

---

6   RGASPI, f. 589, op. 3, d. 9103, vol. 5, ll. 36–7.

FIGURE 8   *Handwritten caption by Alexandra Kollontai: 'A.G. Shlyapnikov in Paris, 1911, among French workers of the Département de la Seine'. The workers are holding the newspapers,* La Bataille Socialiste *and* La Guerre Sociale *(provided by Vladimir and Ritta Kollontai).*

activism also led him into close collaboration with leftist German, Swedish and Norwegian metalworker trade unionists. Unlike many other Russian worker revolutionaries, Shlyapnikov absorbed the influence of autonomous socialist trade unions in France, Britain and Germany. His involvement with trade unions also made his *émigré* experience different from that of Russian party *intelligenty* such as Lenin, shaping the programme he later put forth as leader of the Workers' Opposition.

Nevertheless, Shlyapnikov became closer to Lenin in emigration. Lenin's ideas constituted only one strand of Bolshevism before the October Revolution in 1917, while Alexander Bogdanov put forth an important alternative. Lenin emphasised leadership, vanguard revolutionaries and centralisation, but Bogdanov elevated collectivism. Lenin's Bolshevism featured professional revolutionaries illegally conspiring to seize power through class war and communicating with one another through codes. Bogdanov, on the other hand, emphasised cultivating workers' minds in new ways and focused on propaganda as the means to do so. Some of Bogdanov's followers inclined 'toward syndicalism, the belief in the efficacy of the mass strike and direct action guided by useful myth'. They were also called 'god builders' for their belief in the necessity of creating a 'socialist religion of science'. In 1911, Bogdanov and Anatoly Lunacharsky, later Commissar of Enlightenment in the Soviet government, organised a party school in Bologna, Italy, intended to educate worker-Bolsheviks to better carry out organisational and propaganda work in Russia. Lenin responded by setting up his own school in Longjumeau, near Paris, summoning workers to leave Bogdanov's school for his. Many did so. Shlyapnikov was close to Alexei Gastev and Fyodor Kalinin, worker-Bolsheviks who followed Bogdanov. Nevertheless, there is little evidence that Bogdanovism influenced him. Already experienced in underground tactics and versed in Marxist writings, Shlyapnikov attended neither Bogdanov's nor Lenin's schools, but he frequently met with Lenin in Paris.[7]

Shlyapnikov's views, as expressed in letters and articles he wrote while he lived abroad, focus on tactics and do not explicitly compare Lenin's and Bogdanov's stances. Bogdanov's emphasis on the central role of the 'masses' in revolution should have appealed to him, but Shlyapnikov was not a partisan of creating a socialist 'religion'.[8] He had left religion behind him when he abandoned the Old Belief. Certainly, he numbered among Lenin's 'professional revolutionaries', especially during World War I. Lenin's practicality appealed to him. Lenin took extraordinary interest in conspiratorial tactics, which Shlyapnikov prided himself on carrying out skillfully, with Lenin carefully cultivating worker revolutionaries. However, Shlyapnikov was uncomfortable with what can now be perceived as Lenin's authoritarianism, as well as the 'heroic scenario' (Lih's phrase) that Lenin offered. Shlyapnikov's perspective is best encapsulated in the 'Internationale' verse that he often cited: 'Neither god, nor king nor hero will deliver us! We will achieve emancipation by our own hand'.[9] He believed that professional revolutionaries should inform and organise workers, but that workers should guide the political party by electing its leaders. Due to their distinctive personalities and interests, the workers Shlyapnikov and Gastev gravitated towards different Russian *intelligenty* for guidance.

---

7   Williams 1986, pp. 2–4, 158–9; Elwood 2011, pp. 3–15; GARF, f. 102 (DP OO), 1915, d. 114, l. 1; RGASPI, f. 304, op. 1, d. 12, l. 1, letter from Shliapnikov to an unidentified person about hosting Lenin and French workers on 21 May 1911.
8   Revolutionary socialists often referred to the 'masses', the meaning of which could vary. Sometimes it meant all those who engaged in manual labour. At other times, it meant only factory workers who were socialists.
9   Shliapnikov 1919c, p. 1.

While Shlyapnikov was becoming closer to Lenin politically, he romanced the socialist feminist, Alexandra Kollontai (1872–1952). From an aristocratic family, she was well educated, a popular and charismatic speaker and an author of works about socialism and women's issues. Having become a Marxist in the late 1890s, she turned to Menshevism after the Russian Social Democratic Workers' Party split in 1903. She had lectured at Bogdanov's school on the 'woman question'. As a part of the general project of women's social emancipation, she advocated a new type of relationship between men and women. The 'new woman' would conquer her own tendency towards submissiveness and would manage to reconcile her needs for autonomy and femininity. Kollontai struggled to achieve these goals in her own life, including in her romantic relationship with Shlyapnikov (1911–16). She came to Paris to write in spring 1911.[10] Since she was a Menshevik, she was not welcome to lecture at Lenin's school. However, she visited Lenin and Krupskaya and was well acquainted with Shlyapnikov's friend Gastev.

When Shlyapnikov and Kollontai first met, in Paris in late 1911, she was 39 and he was 26. Ivan Maisky, then a Menshevik and later a Soviet diplomat, had written of Kollontai the preceding year: 'She looked like a young girl. Beautiful, intelligent, energetic, full of a spring-like joy in life, Kollontai drew many people to her'. Although she was a Menshevik and Shlyapnikov a Bolshevik, such distinctions were not fatal before the revolution, as members of different revolutionary factions and parties often found common ground on which they could work. Physically fit, charming and kind, Shlyapnikov in 1911 cultivated the refined dress and manner of a worker-*intelligent*. The Finnish socialist, Karl Wijk, remembered him as 'quiet and good-natured, never boisterous, never gesticulating or gushing, always dependable, clear-headed and tireless... not like a Russian at all'.[11]

Kollontai and Shlyapnikov first became acquainted after one of her passionate speeches. They met again at the funeral of Paul and Laura Lafargue, prominent French socialists (Laura was the daughter of Karl Marx). When they met for a third time at Lenin's apartment, they decided to become better acquainted. After attending a play, they strolled around Paris and talked for several hours. Kollontai was impressed that Shlyapnikov, a worker, was capable of

---

10   Farnsworth 1980, pp. 40–1; Kollontai 1974, p. 32. Kollontai's personal *fond* 134 in RGASPI contains her handwritten diary entries about her relationship with Shliapnikov. A few letters from her to him are in the Shliapnikov family collection. From the late 1940s to her 1952 death, Kollontai prepared typed memoirs of her life, which were published in 2001 and 2004.

11   Clements 1979, p. 66; Futrell 1963, p. 106.

engaging her in debate. She described him as 'nice, cheerful, direct and strong-willed', a 'proletarian ... from a novel'. As they conversed that evening in Paris, she wrote later, 'a spark ignited' and she spent that night with him in Asnières.[12]

At the time, Kollontai was ending her two-year affair with the Menshevik agrarian specialist, Peter Maslov, who was married with five children. She had told him not to follow her to Paris. Yet when she returned by train from her tryst with Shlyapnikov, Maslov was waiting by the door of her boarding house. She told him of her new lover in order to convince him that their relationship was over. It seems that she did not expect her relationship with Shlyapnikov to endure. He, on the other hand, attributed more significance to the affair and, according to her, showered her with 'crazy' love letters in French and Russian. Because of his persistence and stubbornness, she sometimes referred to him ironically as Avvakum, a seventeenth-century martyr of the Old Belief. Although she felt affection for him, she resented the demands he made on her time.[13]

Kollontai left Paris in January 1912 for Berlin. Shlyapnikov joined her there, finding work in metals factories, but he could not adjust to life and the work regime in Germany. Although many socialists at the time held the German workers' movement in esteem for its scale and organisation, he was startled to find that he was the only worker at his factory to stay out on May Day. He later claimed that when his fellow workers encouraged him to say that he had been absent because he understood the German language poorly, he became disillusioned with German social democracy. Since he made this explanation in the 1930s, when he was undergoing the Party purge, it must be treated with scepticism. After only a few months, he returned to France, perhaps as much because of tensions in his relationship with Kollontai as due to his disillusionment with German labour. Nevertheless, he seems to have returned to Berlin several more times to stay with her for extended holidays. During December 1912 he was reunited with his friend Medvedev who, in his only trip abroad, spent several months working in Germany, then met with Lenin and other Party leaders in Cracow before returning to Russia.[14]

Although Kollontai called Shlyapnikov 'husband', they often lived apart and she expressed ambivalence about their quasi-marital relationship until

---

12   RGASPI, f. 134, op. 4, d. 4, l. 4.
13   RGASPI, f. 134, op. 4, d. 3, ll. 7–13, November 1911, Paris; l. 19, letter to Zoia Shadurskaia, 12 August 1912; d. 4, ll. 4–5; d. 22, l. 5; Clements 1979, pp. 68–9.
14   Kollontai 1974, pp. 32–5; RGASPI, f. 589, op. 3, d. 9102, ll. 173–88, Medvedev's autobiography for the purge, 10 February 1922; d. 9103, vol. 5, ll. 34–6; Shliapnikova 1991 and 1995, conversations; Ostrovskii 2002, p. 381.

FIGURE 9 *Alexandra Kollontai in 1910 (in Kolechenkova (ed.) 1989, unnumbered page).*

FIGURE 10   *Alexander Shlyapnikov circa 1912 (provided by the Shlyapnikov family).*

she broke it off in July 1916. He failed to understand the conflict she perceived between love and work, but she was reluctant to renounce her model proletarian. One illustrative episode occurred in summer 1913. Kollontai had left a note saying that she was going to a conference in London. He followed her, after telegraphing her the hour of his expected arrival. Disappointed not to find her waiting at the railway station, he then discovered that she had not even collected his letters. Moreover, none of his socialist comrades knew anything about the conference she had claimed to be attending. Shliapnikov suspected that she had made up the entire story in order to escape him, so he expressed his anguish to her:

> I still very much love you and want to keep you as a friend. I do not want to extinguish this beautiful feeling and I cannot bear to see and feel that you are now killing this love towards me, and only in service of some preconceived notion of 'inability to unify love and work'. How false now these words sound...[15]

Rarely did he express in writing such wounded emotions; his typical tone in letters to her was calm, slightly humourous and business-like. Often he broached politics and Party organisational matters. In her affectionate answers, Kollontai offered advice aimed towards facilitating his transformation into a worker-*intelligent*.

Before he met Kollontai, Shliapnikov had written brief articles for Russian and French newspapers. After their relationship began, his development as a writer accelerated, setting the stage for his post-revolutionary memoir histories of the Russian workers' movement. The years when he began writing, 1912–13, saw much discussion in the press of laws regulating factory labour; in 1913, the Russian government compiled all labour laws into a single Factory Law Code for the first time.[16] Inexpensive copies circulated among workers. Shliapnikov aired his views in the socialist and trade-union press.[17] He wrote in order to improve his capabilities as a worker-*intelligent* and, more practically, to garner income when no factory work was available. But his primary

---

15   RGASPI, f. 134, op. 4, d. 7, ll. 1–3, 15 June 1913.
16   Gorshkov 2009, p. 143.
17   His articles in *Prosveshchenie* were published under his real name, but in some articles for *Metallist*, he used a pseudonym. These articles (see the Bibliography below) were later incorporated into his book, *Po zavodam Frantsii i Germanii*. The book's description of the metalworking industry is highly technical and based on professional journals and statistical documents, which Shliapnikov gathered while in France and Germany.

goal was to communicate to fellow workers better methods of organisation. In addressing his Russian audience, he advocated some methods used by workers in Western Europe, such as organising industrial or production unions and labour exchanges.

American engineer Frederick W. Taylor's ideas on industrial efficiency, based on the standardisation of methods, were gaining currency in the early twentieth century. Criticising Taylorism for rewarding those workers who responded quickly but who showed little creativity or 'consciousness', Shlyapnikov wrote that its time-saving, production-increasing measures nullified achievements in shortening the working day. Because the new system put workers under more pressure, he wrote, those who worked 8.5 hour days suffered more accidents and nervous disorders than those who worked 10.5–11 hour days under the old system. Taylor opposed unions, while Shlyapnikov advocated the consolidation of trade and craft-based unions into industrial unions, which he saw as more progressive and stronger in the struggle with capitalists. Drawing on his experience as a member of the Council of the Union of Seine Mechanics, he represented this European development to Russian workers as the wave of the future. In an article on hiring practices, he explained to Russian metalworkers the practical advantages of a strong trade union, for in France the trade union assisted workers in finding a job. It kept track of vacancies and hiring needs at particular factories and was able to direct unemployed workers to factories in need of them. In Russia, on the other hand, because there was no 'stable and strong union of metalworkers, the search for work and conditions of acceptance at a factory are arranged ... by word of mouth ... or by haphazard [searches]'.[18]

Shlyapnikov's writings on revolutionary strategy were not published, perhaps because they did not accord with the views of party *intelligenty* who edited newspapers, or perhaps because his ideas were not sufficiently developed. Bolsheviks opposed sabotage, viewing it as a waste of revolutionary energy and as a product of a retrograde attitude towards industrial society. In a 1912 essay, however, he appeared ambivalent towards some types of sabotage, especially those that did not destroy property. Classifying acts aimed at decreasing the employers' profits as acts of sabotage, he found these acceptable means of struggle. About shop owners' practice of overcharging customers, he explained: 'A worker in a store can commit sabotage by not shortchanging customers, but still not exceed the law'. In so doing, the worker would reduce the

---

18   Shliapnikov 1913a, pp. 6–8; 1913c, p. 13; 1914a, p. 2.

shopkeeper's profits.[19] His analysis, if not theoretically developed, was at least not dogmatic.

When Shlyapnikov was in France, trade unionists argued fiercely over the unions' stance on politics. In the late nineteenth century, French trade unions had been weakened by their affiliation with socialist parties that suffered frequent splits. Strikes were even lost due to political bickering. The Guesdists called on trade unions to subordinate their economic struggles to serve party politics, while other trade unionists called for the repudiation of parties and politics altogether. Lack of unity at the top meant that French unions were particularly strong at the local level. By 1902 there was more national coordination, but the movement remained decentralised. Thus decentralisation and suspicion of politics were defining characteristics of French syndicalism. Nevertheless, workers were free to choose their own political affiliation, of which there was a variety. French trade unionists further disagreed over the structure of the trade-union movement; in the first decade of the twentieth century, they debated the advantages of industry-wide unions of workers, as opposed to craft-based unions working at cross purposes.[20]

Shlyapnikov stood with proponents of industrial unions and with advocates of a political role for unions. Criticising those French union leaders who tried to keep unions out of politics, he believed that this weakened unions and pushed workers towards anarcho-syndicalism, which he called 'trade unionism without membership dues, without paid secretaries'. Thus, he defined anarcho-syndicalism differently than his later opponents, who would fling the charge at the Workers' Opposition. Rejecting anarchism out of hand, he also displayed a negative attitude towards syndicalism, accusing syndicalists of condescension towards the masses and unwillingness to draw them into revolutionary work.[21] Finally, the French unions' vulnerability, due to their decentralised structure, would have led Shlyapnikov to agree with Lenin on the importance of centralised leadership of the party and the unions.

Thus, Shlyapnikov combined an emphasis on workers' initiative with a preference for unification and centralisation. A determined supporter of production unions, which were larger and more inclusive than craft-based unions, he nevertheless criticised trade unionists who exploited the trend towards unification in order to oust their rivals and seize common funds. His call for unity among trade unionists contrasted with the tactic he often supported

---

19 RGASPI, f. 28, op. 1, d. 441, ll. 1–7, 'O sabotazhe, kak metod bor'by', written in Berlin, April 1912. Shliapnikov submitted this article to *Sotsial'-Demokrat*, but it was not published.
20 Lorwin 1954, pp. 20–4, 30–1.
21 RGASPI, f. 28, op. 1, d. 441, l. 8; d. 445, 'K krizisu sindikalizma' (February 1913, Paris), l. 5.

FIGURE 11   *Alexander Shlyapnikov in Paris, 1913, holding the newspaper* L'Humanité (*provided by the Shlyapnikov family*).

of splitting political organisations to advance Lenin's agenda. He was also a strong proponent of mutual aid as a trade-union goal, in order to appeal to workers and meet their needs. French trade unionism's chief influence upon him was most likely its tendency to promote the leading role of working-class trade-union organisers, while confining middle-class intellectuals to theoretical work.[22]

Some Russian workers in France, such as Gastev and Kalinin, gravitated towards the creative intelligentsia by writing fiction and poetry, but Shlyapnikov showed less interest in creative writing. Only two stories by him are known. The semi-autobiographical 'To the Factory' was a sentimental account of a young boy's decision to enter factory work. 'Aviators', on the other hand, was a humorous story about a French worker who became a pilot, which encouraged his fellow workers to regard themselves as 'born aviators'. In attempting to form an 'aviators' club', they met with various misadventures.[23] Shlyapnikov's quick, dry wit and well-developed sense of irony ran through this story, the subtext of which may have been the formation of worker 'consciousness'. He conveyed that workers needed to study seriously in order to rise above their station.

Return to Russia in 1914

Shlyapnikov grew frustrated with his inability to garner income through writing, its passive nature and the lack of direct results. When he was living with Kollontai in Berlin in spring 1914, he complained that he could find no industrial work and was living mainly by selling Bolshevik literature and his own compositions. He yearned to return to St. Petersburg, where worker unrest was growing.[24] In April 1914 he entered Russia with the passport of a French citizen (Jacob Noé). When he returned to Russia, he had been away for so long that he already 'felt like a tourist' in his native land, indicating how strongly Western Europe had shaped his identity.[25] In Petersburg he met with Bolshevik

---

22 RGASPI, f. 28, op. 1, d. 445, ll. 17, 20; Lorwin 1954, pp. 35–6.
23 RGASPI, f. 17, op. 1, ch. 4, d. 1398, l. 5, letter from Shliapnikov to Krupskaia, 28 March 1914. According to Shliapnikov, 'Aviatory' appeared in *Pravda*, nos. 47–8. The name of *Pravda* changed eight times in 1912–14, circumventing tsarist censors. The story might have appeared in *Put' pravdy* in February or March 1914. It was republished in 1919.
24 RGASPI, f. 17, op. 1, ch. 4, d. 1398, l. 1, letter to Krupskaia, 26 February 1914.
25 RGASPI, f. 2, op. 5, d. 378, l. 1, letter from Shliapnikov to Lenin, 3 (16) May 1914. When writing to Lenin in the pre-revolutionary era, Shliapnikov dated his letters by the Gregorian calendar when he was in the West and by the Julian when he was in Russia. In the

Party leaders Lev Kamenev, Alexei Badaev and Grigory Petrovsky, but claimed later that he felt uncomfortable in the presence of Roman Malinovsky, who in 1918 was convicted of having been a police informer and shot. By keeping Malinovsky unaware of his whereabouts, Shlyapnikov unwittingly avoided the wave of arrests that decimated the ranks of Bolshevik leaders and activists in summer 1914. In 1914 many Russian socialists already suspected that Malinovsky was a police informer, but Lenin fiercely defended him. Lenin admitted that Malinovsky had grossly violated Party discipline and had been disciplined for doing so, but dismissed insinuations that he was a police agent as Menshevik 'slander'. In support of his position, Lenin cited a letter Shlyapnikov wrote (under an alias) to the Bolshevik Party newspaper, *Put Pravdy*. Shlyapnikov did write that workers found 'not a blemish' in Malinovsky's background, but the main thrust of his article, which Lenin bypassed, was to support a trial of Malinovsky and allow 'a word to the accused', rather than convicting him in the bourgeois and Menshevik press.[26] Thus he was concerned not only for minimising the case's damage to the Bolshevik Party, but also for ensuring due process.

Not long after Shlyapnikov arrived, Petersburg Bolshevik leaders offered him a post in the central Party organisation, due to his past membership in the Petersburg Committee and his leadership experience abroad. Instead, he chose to work in factories because he wanted to reacquaint himself with working-class life, make new contacts among workers and avoid police attention. He was first employed at the New Lessner Works and then he took a more highly paid job at the Ericsson factory. Because he was in Russia illegally, he told fellow workers that he was a Frenchman and guarded his contacts with Russian Social-Democratic *émigrés*. He believed that fellow workers never suspected that he was Russian, despite his occasional lapses into the dialect of the Vladimir region. He found his 'French' citizenship quite advantageous at times. As a foreigner in Russia, he reported, he enjoyed far more freedom and respect than he ever had as a native. Although Shlyapnikov was active in the Bolshevik underground, he hesitated to engage in activities that would have brought unwanted attention from the authorities. For example, he participated in May Day demonstrations, but refrained from speaking. He did not make direct contact with the editor of the Russian Metalworkers' Union journal, *Metallist*.[27]

---

twentieth century, the Julian was 13 days behind the Gregorian. Archival files include both dates for all letters.

26 RGASPI, f. 589, op. 3, d. 9103, vol. 5, l. 33; Cohen 1980, p. 18; Elwood 2011, chapters 6–7; Lenin 1999, pp. 131–4; Lenin 1914; Kaptelov *et al.* (eds.) 1992; Shliapnikov 1914e, p. 2.
27 Shliapnikov 1982, pp. 1–2, 7, 28.

Nonetheless, he was co-opted onto its editorial board and published articles under an alias.

Shlyapnikov's 1914 trip to Russia strengthened his conviction that workers had to take their fate into their own hands, not depend on *intelligenty* to accomplish their goals for them. Many worker socialists had become bitterly disillusioned with what they saw as the *intelligent* lack of commitment to the revolutionary cause. Shlyapnikov recalled in his memoirs that 'a typical feature of party work in the pre-war period was the absence of *intelligenty* ... The place of the petty-bourgeois *intelligenty* and student youth was taken by the intelligent proletarian with his callused hands and highly developed head who had not lost contact with the masses'. These workers gained organisational experience through insurance organisations and unions. The tsarist government had set up insurance groups in 1912 to administer a fund (financed by mandatory contributions from workers and factory owners) to provide for workers in case of injury or sickness. Workers and industrialists elected representatives to insurance-group councils. The insurance groups offered socialists a legal arena, in some areas the only legal arena, in which to operate and influence workers.[28]

The strike movement represented another side of the new wave of labour activism. The size and frequency of strikes had steadily grown since 1912, when at the Lena Goldfields in Siberia tsarist forces had killed or wounded several hundred workers who struck for shorter hours, higher wages and better food. The massacre shocked all of civil society. The increased activity of the workers in both legal and illegal forms of organisation raised Shlyapnikov's optimism about the Petersburg proletariat. In the first six months of 1914, about one-and-a-half million Russian workers went on strike; Shlyapnikov acclaimed the 'spontaneous [*stikhiinyi*] character' of a strike of Petersburg workers he witnessed in early July 1914. He enthused:

> I am in admiration of our proletariat. Since I last left Petersburg, it is as if it has been reborn. Real leaders have emerged from the deep cadres of the working class; despite exiles and arrests, the cause has moved forward.[29]

---

28   Shliapnikov 1982, p. 6; Bonnell (ed.) 1983, pp. 380–1; Elwood 1974, pp. 218–22. By 1914, there were more than two thousand eight hundred insurance councils throughout Russia, covering more than two million workers (Gorshkov 2009, p. 143). For more on the insurance movement, see Pate 2002 and 2005.

29   Melancon 2006; Shliapnikov 1915, pp. 161–7; RGASPI, f. 2, op. 5, d. 422, l. 1, letter to Lenin. Lih (Lih 2007) prefers 'elemental' for '*stikhiinyi*'.

Among those worker leaders in 1914 were Kirill Orlov and Alexei Kiselev, who later became his collaborators in the Workers' Opposition. Orlov had participated in the mutiny on the Battleship Potemkin in 1905. Kiselev, who had chaired the Metalworkers' Union in 1910 and had become a party CC member in 1914, helped Shlyapnikov make contacts among Bolshevik metalworker activists, many of whom he drew into the organisation of the CC's Russian Bureau in Petersburg. Kiselev was from the same province as he; thus, they shared a special tie (as *zemlyaks*).³⁰ Medvedev, a leader in the underground insurance movement, was hiding from the tsarist authorities near Moscow in 1914, so Shlyapnikov was unable to find him. In 1915, he was arrested and exiled to Siberia.³¹

Both Shlyapnikov's letters of the time and his later published histories convey his strong Bolshevik loyalties in 1914. While in St. Petersburg in summer 1914, he participated in factional struggle between the Bolsheviks, who advocated illegal methods of struggle, and the Mensheviks, who preferred legal means. He recalled that these battles disturbed workers, who found differences between the factions to be insignificant and objected to the 'acrimony' manifested in the struggle. Nevertheless, he was vested in convincing workers that there was a real difference of principle between the factions and that the Mensheviks were wrong. Optimistically assessing the workers' reception of Bolshevism, he reported several successes in convincing Menshevik workers to recognise 'the illegal form of workers' organisation'. Because he spoke French, Shlyapnikov also represented Bolsheviks at a June 1914 banquet to welcome Emile Vandervelde, president of the International Socialist Bureau, to Russia. Introducing himself as a Russian metalworker, he seems to have charmed Vandervelde. The episode revealed Shlyapnikov's professed view of the Mensheviks as representative only of the intelligentsia. He bragged to Vandervelde that Bolsheviks dominated organisations such as trade unions and insurance groups, which were representative of workers.³² The outbreak of World War I and then revolution, however, would provide the context for a realignment of factional identities.

---

30 RGASPI, f. 2, op. 5, d. 600, l. 2, letter from Shliapnikov to Lenin, 5 September 1915, Christiania. Kiselëv (b. 1879) began working, aged 14, as an apprentice metalworker in Ivanovo-Voznesensk and became a Social Democrat in 1898 (Gambarov et al. (eds.) 1989, vol. 1, pp. 191–4).

31 RGASPI, f. 589, op. 3, d. 9102, ll. 173–88, 10 February 1922.

32 Shliapnikov 1982, pp. 2–5; RGASPI, f. 2, op. 5, d. 422, l. 1, letter from Shliapnikov to Lenin, 19 June 1914.

FIGURE 12   *Alexander Shlyapnikov circa 1914 (provided by the family).*

FIGURE 13 *Standing are Alexander Shlyapnikov and his brother Peter Shlyapnikov; and seated are his sister Anna Tyutereva, his mother Khioniya Shlyapnikova, and his sister Maria Kovalenko, St. Petersburg, Russia, 1914 (photo by Maria's husband Iosif Kovalenko in his photography studio; provided by the Shlyapnikov family).*

FIGURE 14   *Maria Kovalenko, Alexander Shlyapnikov's younger sister, St. Petersburg, Russia, circa 1914 (photo by Maria's husband Iosif Kovalenko; provided by the Shlyapnikov family).*

World War I and the Revolutionary Underground

When World War I began, it raised questions that overshadowed prior conflicts among socialists. Socialists changed party or factional affiliations over their stance on the war; this seismic change shattered the Second International that had united socialists since 1889. Socialists who supported their countries' war efforts were called defencists. The most famous case was that of the German Social Democrats, who voted in the Reichstag for war credits. Many socialists, however, condemned the war as imperialist, as a war to gain territory and enrich capitalists at the cost of workers' and peasants' lives. Defeatists called for their own country's defeat; Lenin was a vocal defeatist, insisting that other CC members and Bolshevik Duma representatives support his line. Among Petrograd Bolsheviks were many who opposed the war, but who were reluctant to call for Russia's defeat. Moreover, Kamenev contested Lenin's attempt to force his views on the CC without discussion.[33]

The war also brought renewed repression against socialists who favoured illegal methods. A consummate conspirator, Shlyapnikov usually avoided group meetings with other Bolshevik leaders. As a result, he did not attend the meeting of the *Pravda* editorial board where the Okhrana arrested all of the editorial board's members. The arrests in summer 1914 decimated the ranks of skilled organisers and especially writers from the top ranks of the Bolshevik Party. He later recalled: 'After the raid on *Pravda* there was not a single person on the Petersburg Committee capable of writing a leaflet'. He also found the closure of trade unions and their publications disruptive to the cause. A leaflet he wrote was the first proclamation issued by the Petersburg Committee against the war. In addition, he spoke against the war at a number of meetings. During his 1933 purge from the Party, Shlyapnikov claimed, perhaps disingenuously, that he was unaware at that time of Lenin's call to turn world war into civil war.[34]

Although Shlyapnikov had hoped to stay in Russia indefinitely, the war's intervention forced him to leave. The French government was calling up all its citizens to return, so he could no longer remain in Russia on a French passport. In late September 1914 he left for Scandinavia, with a mandate from the Petersburg Committee and the Bolshevik Duma faction, as their representative abroad. Thus, as Futrell assessed, he became 'the key man in the northern underground' during World War I. Based on Lenin's published

---

33   Melancon 1990, pp. 175–6.
34   Shliapnikov 1982, pp. 19–20; RGASPI, f. 2, op. 5, d. 480, ll. 3–4, letter to Krupskaia, 28–9 October 1914; f. 589, op. 3, d. 9103, vol. 5, l. 32.

letters, Robert Service assumed that Shlyapnikov set up shop in Scandinavia on Lenin's orders. According to Futrell, Lenin had attempted to get other Bolsheviks to organise communications through Scandinavia, but nothing was accomplished until 'the energetic Shlyapnikov arrived in Stockholm'. In fact, Shlyapnikov proclaimed to Lenin that his assignment as liaison came from Bolsheviks in Petrograd (the city's newly Russified wartime name), not from Lenin and his immediate circle.[35] This important distinction illuminates how authority flowed among the Bolsheviks.

When Shlyapnikov came to Scandinavia, he expressed his approval of Lenin's 'internationalist' stance on the war, emphasising that he and other Petrograd workers had already taken an internationalist position before they heard of Lenin's views. Nevertheless, he worried that 'revolution at the rear' would only benefit Germany if accomplished just in one country. Thus, he expressed ambivalence towards defeatism, especially from the practical standpoint of how it would determine revolutionary tactics. Lenin explained that civil war was far different from 'individual acts of shooting at officers'. Strongly condemning Shlyapnikov's Swedish left-socialist friends, such as Zeth Höglund, who took a pacifist stance, Lenin pressured Shlyapnikov to come out unambivalently for the transformation of the war into a revolutionary struggle against imperialism.[36] Shlyapnikov made it plain that he did not challenge Lenin's theoretical stance, but only sought clarification in order to make the concept 'digestible for the masses'.[37]

Since Sweden was officially neutral, it was practically the Bolsheviks' only route for communicating with Russia. As it was, communications and transport were haphazard. Shlyapnikov arranged a route into Russia through Swedish transport workers, but no Russian party organisation would finance his activities. Nor could he find an industrial job in Sweden to finance the work. Taking loans from Swedish socialists, he sent material in a scattershot manner, smuggling issues of *Sotsial-Demokrat* inside hollowed boot heels. He placed much of the blame for his faltering plans on the Russian end. He had sent four packets of material to the Bolsheviks in Russia in the first half of October 1914, proposing several routes for smuggling operations, but had received no answer. Despite contributing little financially to his mission, Lenin worried that he would abandon his post. Shlyapnikov pointedly replied that he

---

35 Shliapnikov 1982, p. 28; Shliapnikov 1914f; Futrell 1963, pp. 85–6; Service 1991, vol. 2: p. 87; RGASPI, f. 2, op. 5, d. 474, l. 1, 11 October 1914, Stockholm. The city's Bolsheviks declined to change the name of the Petersburg Committee.
36 RGASPI, f. 2, op. 5, d. 474, ll. 1–2; Kamenev 1925, pp. 8–10 (17 October 1914).
37 RGASPI, f. 2, op. 5, d. 484, ll. 3–4, 6–7 November 1914, Stockholm.

would not leave 'the post entrusted to me earlier than the matter is settled or I receive a dismissal from Piter'. Nevertheless, the arrest of Bolshevik Duma deputies in Russia soon curtailed his activities.[38] The smuggling network lost too many links to continue successfully and needed time to be rebuilt. Moreover, Shlyapnikov was under increasing heat in Sweden, due to his camp's opposition to the war, in addition to the general suspicion of Russians as potential spies.

While in Scandinavia, Shlyapnikov not only busied himself with transport matters, but also participated in socialist politics. At the November 1914 Swedish Social Democratic Congress, he delivered a controversial greeting from the RSDRP(b), which a Swedish Social Democrat read in translation because it was considered too risky for Shlyapnikov to deliver in person. Containing harsh criticism of the German Social Democrats' stance on the war and labelling their approval of war credits as 'treason' to the international socialist movement, the greeting risked precipitating a split within the Swedish SDs, which was Lenin's intention. Karl Hjalmar Branting, leader of the Swedish Social Democrats, denounced the greeting and called for the congress to 'express regret' concerning its criticism of the Germans, which the congress voted to do.[39] Shlyapnikov privately urged Lenin to 'conduct polemics with Branting in a comradely manner' when writing about the congress, for Branting had helped him in practical matters. He insisted: 'It would be disagreeable to offend him; although an old opportunist, he is honest'. Shlyapnikov was not the only Bolshevik to object to Lenin's abusive attacks on fellow socialists, for this character flaw had already created tensions between Lenin and the editors of *Pravda* in 1912–14.[40]

Kollontai remained a pacifist for some time longer, but she continued to collaborate with Shlyapnikov on Bolshevik organisational matters.[41] Their working relationship facilitated the continuation of their romance and *vice versa*. She was arrested a few days before the congress for her anti-war activities. Although Shlyapnikov tried to mobilise Swedish socialists to appeal for her release, she was expelled from the country and sent to Copenhagen. His Swedish friends told him that he could not be far behind and that he should leave voluntarily. Lenin objected, insinuating that he only wanted to reunite

---

38 Shliapnikov 1982, pp. 37–8; RGASPI, f. 2, op. 4, d. 474, l. 4; op. 5, d. 480, l. 1, 28–9 October 1914, Stockholm; d. 484, ll. 1–4, 6–7 November 1914, Stockholm.
39 Shliapnikov 1982, pp. 42, 44; Shklovskii 1925, p. 145. In 1896, Branting (1860–1925) was the first socialist to be elected to the Swedish parliament and was Swedish Prime Minister in 1920, 1921–3 and 1925 (Futrell 1963, p. 225).
40 RGASPI, f. 2, op. 5, d. 517, l. 6, circa 23 January 1915; Elwood 2011, Chapter Three.
41 RGASPI, f. 134, op. 1, d. 83, ll. 26–8. She came out for Lenin's position on the war in summer 1915 (Farnsworth 1980, pp. 47, 50–1, 55).

with Kollontai, but Shlyapnikov indignantly assured Lenin that he did not move to Copenhagen for personal reasons. He explained that by leaving on his own volition he had preserved for himself the right to re-enter Sweden after things had settled down. Dismissing Lenin's suggestion to settle in the Swedish countryside, he described the mood in the rural areas as more suspicious than in the cities. Mollified, Lenin apologised for his presumption: 'If I've offended you, I'm ready to apologise in any way I can and I beg you, please, not to be hurt'.[42]

In need of funds, Shlyapnikov sought factory work in England. To Lenin's continued protests, he finally answered that not only was he unable to support himself and Bolshevik operations, but that he needed to help his mother in Murom. Having arrived in London in early April 1915, he established contact with Maxim Litvinov, the most prominent Bolshevik in England and later Soviet Commissar of Foreign Affairs.[43] Within four days of his arrival, Shlyapnikov found work as a turner at the Fiat automobile plant in Wembley, near London. Although he corresponded with CC members infrequently in the summer of 1915, he lectured at Russian clubs on the revolutionary movement in Russia and in Scandinavia. He spoke English well enough to discuss his opposition to the war and his political views with British workers. Moreover, he joined and participated in the Amalgamated Society of Engineers, a militant British union, and was proud of his membership. It was not easy for foreigners to join the ASE. Shlyapnikov's acceptance marked recognition of his advanced metalworking skills. Generally, English workers positively impressed him; he perceived them as less militarist or chauvinist than workers in 'semi-free' European countries.[44]

By August 1915, Shlyapnikov had earned sufficient wages and collected enough donations to re-establish Bolshevik illegal transport through Scandinavia. First, he personally investigated old smuggling routes from Norway into Finland and then he set up an organisational chart. Eventually he became convinced that he needed to go to Russia to set up operations from that end. Kollontai had already left for the United States to conduct propaganda and raise funds for the Bolsheviks, so he left Scandinavian Bolshevik operations in the hands of Bukharin (with whom Shlyapnikov had become

---

42 RGASPI, f. 2, op. 5, d. 489, l. 1, 21 November 1914; d. 495, l. 1, 27 December 1914; d. 496, 28 December 1914, l. 1; Kamenev 1925, p. 28 (3 January 1915).

43 RGASPI, f. 2, op. 5, d. 544, 4 April 1915; and d. 546, 9 April 1915, Christiania; f. 17, op. 1, ch. IV, d. 1635, 16 April 1915, letter from Litvinov to Krupskaia.

44 Shliapnikov 1982, pp. 54–5; RGASPI, f. 2, op. 5, d. 553, 25 April 1915; f. 351, op. 2, d. 78, l. 20, 7 August 1915 postcard from Shliapnikov in Holmenkollen to Iakov Bogrovskii in Stockholm.

FIGURE 15　*Alexander Shlyapnikov with Alexandra Kollontai and Scandinavian Social Democrats, Kristiania, Norway, summer 1915. The two men seated on the rocks below are Eugène Olaussen and Zeth Höglund. The woman to the left of Kollontai is Gunhild Höglund and to the right of Kollontai is the artist, Ruth Nyström (taken from Kollontai 2001, vol. 1, unnumbered page).*

acquainted in England), Evgenia Bosh and Yuri Pyatakov. These three had arrived in Scandinavia in the summer of 1915.⁴⁵

Before Shlyapnikov left for Russia, both Lenin and Zinoviev recommended that he gather a small bureau of the CC in Russia and recruit members only among workers. They preferred those workers who had been on the staff of the newspaper, *Pravda*, such as Kiselev and Vasily Shmidt (1886–1938). A Petersburg metalworker who had worked in Germany for several years, Shmidt became secretary of the Petrograd Union of Metalworkers in 1914 and was a Petersburg Committee leader. Further, Zinoviev instructed Shlyapnikov to persuade the Petersburg Committee to produce 'a detailed resolution about the war and the International'. Finally, Lenin and Zinoviev co-opted Shlyapnikov onto the CC in order to enhance his authority; the Bolsheviks' 1912 Prague Conference had legitimated co-optation of CC members.⁴⁶ Despite Shlyapnikov's later avowed preference for elections, he received this honour gladly at the time.

While Shlyapnikov prepared his trip to Russia, Lenin and other anti-war socialists met in September 1915 in Zimmerwald, Switzerland, to discuss the war. The Zimmerwald Conference issued a manifesto condemning the war and calling for peace without annexations or indemnities. The Zimmerwald Left consisted of socialists who actively supported struggling against the war. This group's coalescence set the context for further correspondence between Shlyapnikov and Lenin on the Bolshevik role in a future Russian revolution. In October 1915 Lenin outlined Bolshevik revolutionary strategy in *Sotsial-Demokrat*, proclaiming as slogans 'a democratic republic, confiscation of landowners' land, and the eight-hour workday'. Such slogans could appeal to radical democrats, poor peasants who wanted more land to farm and workers who wanted a shorter workday, but not to wealthy landowners or factory owners. In addition, he called on workers to demonstrate 'international solidarity' in opposing the war, seeking to overthrow warring governments and struggling for socialism.⁴⁷

At Lenin's request, Shlyapnikov sent his own thoughts concerning the role of the masses in revolution and Bolshevik tactics. Expressing general agreement with Lenin's proposals, he identified apparent contradictions in the details. Lenin had written that, when a revolutionary situation arose, the Bolsheviks

---

45   Shliapnikov 1982, pp. 61, 64.
46   Gambarov *et al.* (eds.) 1989, vol. 3, pp. 251–3; RGASPI, f. 17, op. 1, ch. IV, d. 1696, 29 September 1915; Lenin 1926–37, vol. 29, pp. 193–4, letter of early September 1915; Kamenev 1925, p. 57 [autumn 1915]; Elwood 2011, p. 34.
47   Gankin and Fisher 1940, p. 211; Lenin 1915, p. 2; Lenin 1960–70, vol. 18, pp. 356–8; 'Manifesto of the Zimmerwald Left' in Gruber (ed.) 1967, pp. 62–6.

could participate in provisional governments that included the 'democratic petty bourgeoisie' (shopkeepers and government employees). However, they could not cooperate with 'revolutionary social chauvinists' (socialists who had supported the war effort). Lenin envisioned a 'leading role' for the proletariat in a Russian bourgeois revolution, dependent on a leftward swing by the 'petty bourgeoisie'.[48] Shlyapnikov could not understand how such a development would ensure the 'hegemony' of the proletariat, since the 'petty bourgeoisie' would act only in its own interests, never in those of the proletariat. That is, its 'left' would be 'directed along a radical line against tsarism and the grand bourgeoisie' (capitalists). He explained that he imagined the Russian revolution would be 'a spontaneous process' giving rise to 'new revolutionary governments' all over Russia. He feared that if the Bolsheviks remained aloof from 'provisional governments supported by the masses', then they would alienate potential supporters. Instead, he proposed that the Bolsheviks should not only 'create' but also 'join the provisional governments wherever the masses nominate us'. Then they could implement their programme through these new governments. Significantly, he thought it possible that many so-called revolutionary social chauvinists could change their views during the course of revolution.[49] Not only did Shlyapnikov have misgivings about Lenin's factionalist methods of struggle, but he was more reluctant than Lenin to attach rigid labels to opponents that demonised them as enemies. He held out hope that contingency could lead some to change their views.

After entering Russia through Finland with a fake passport, Shlyapnikov arrived in Petrograd in late October 1915. His plan to set up a Russian Bureau of the CC in Petrograd met with opposition from Bolsheviks in the Petersburg Committee who were later revealed to be police agents (Leonid Stark and Miron Chernomazov). A Bolshevik centre set up in parallel to the Petersburg Committee would have taken revolutionary activities out of their view and out of their control. Shlyapnikov thought at first that egoism motivated Chernomazov, but he also suspected him of being a police spy. He was wary of Stark's persistent requests for the names of his contacts.[50]

Initially, the extent to which Chernomazov controlled the organisation and blocked Shlyapnikov's initiatives was frustrating. He wrote to Kollontai shortly after he had arrived, saying that he was able to see only a very limited circle of people and that 'people of our circle have greatly changed. Sound minds have

---

48   Lenin 1915, p. 2; Lenin 1960–70, vol. 18, pp. 356–8.
49   RGASPI, f. 2, op. 5, d. 614, ll. 2–3, 18 October 1915, Stockholm.
50   RGASPI, f. 2, op. 5, d. 618, l. 1, 12 (25) November 1915, Petrograd.

become rare'.⁵¹ Shlyapnikov found it suspicious that although he had covered his tracks very carefully, police agents began to follow him intensively within two weeks of his arrival in Petrograd. A police report confirms that agents kept him under surveillance. Factory-level organisers in Petrograd supported his suspicions that Chernomazov was a provocateur. Many of these organisers had set up cells independent of the Petersburg Committee, in order to avoid detection and arrest.⁵²

Despite handicaps imposed by police agents, Shlyapnikov contacted Orlov, who helped him liaise with other worker-Bolsheviks. Among these was Kliment Voroshilov, later Stalin's ally. Shlyapnikov acquired a new contact in Yuri Lutovinov, a Bolshevik worker at the Aivaz factory who was originally from the Donbas. After the revolution, Lutovinov would become a leading figure in trade unions and in the Workers' Opposition. At the district level, Shlyapnikov found many Bolsheviks who supported his plans. He succeeded in contacting Petersburg Committee members through district committees. The circuitous route acquainted him with grassroots organising. After meeting local organisers, he became more aware of the crisis in Petrograd Bolshevism, due to the lack of coordination between the Petersburg Committee's executive commission and the district representatives. In one extreme case, this resulted in workers disregarding the executive commission's appeal for a strike, which embarrassed and disheartened activists.⁵³

It was not only infiltration by police agents that weakened the Bolshevik organisation during the war. In his memoirs, Shlyapnikov wrote that, by late 1915, underground life had become largely depopulated of *intelligenty*. In attempting to organise teachers, he found them mostly unresponsive. When pursued by the police, he could find no refuge among *intelligenty*, only among workers. Since he found himself changing apartments on a nightly basis to avoid capture, refusing him quarters put him at risk of arrest and Siberian exile. Even those *intelligenty* who had not left the movement were, in his opinion, unprepared for practical work. Further, he faulted the *intelligenty* for limiting the work of factory circles to education, claiming that with workers in

---

51 RGASPI, f. 134, op. 4, d. 7, I. 11, 29 October 1915.
52 Shliapnikov 1982, pp. 94–8; GARF, DP, f. 102, 6 d-vo, 1914, d. 114, I. 52, 7 (20) March 1916 report to the director of the Russian Department of Police from the Okhrana chief in Paris, Aleksandr Krasil'nikov.
53 RGASPI, f. 2, op. 5, d. 661, II. 1–2, 11 March 1916, to Lenin from Shliapnikov in Stockholm; f. 74, op. 1, d. 1, I. 1; Shliapnikov 1982, p. 70. Lutovinov (b. 1887 in Lugansk) started working in metals factories in the Donbas as a teenager and joined the Bolshevik Party in 1904 (Gambarov *et al.* (eds.) 1989, vol. 1, p. 346).

charge, the circles were practical revolutionary organisations.⁵⁴ Shlyapnikov's retrospective evaluation coincided with his views in 1915 and reflected ongoing tensions between worker Social Democrats and the radical intelligentsia.

Some worker revolutionaries' suspicion of the *intelligenty* arose from the circumstances of underground work. Party cells, the smallest unit of party organisation, were constantly in danger of infiltration by police informers. Workers believed that the *intelligenty* lacked conspiratorial skills and were more vulnerable to police pressure, but *intelligenty* sometimes offered the same complaints about workers. Worker scepticism towards *intelligent* dedication to the cause was strengthened by the behaviour of many *intelligenty* during and after the 1905 Revolution. The violence of mass demonstrations and strikes during that revolution repelled some *intelligenty* from revolutionary social democracy. Others were discouraged by tsarist repression after 1905 that forced the revolutionary parties back into the underground. Also, some worker activists felt that *intelligent* leaders of Social-Democratic circles excluded workers from decision-making, especially when *intelligenty* called for appointing party committee members, rather than electing them. Some *intelligenty* reasoned that elections ran contrary to the interests of an underground party, for experienced leaders, who had to stay on the move to avoid arrest, often were too little known to the locals to win elections.⁵⁵

Shlyapnikov emphasised in his memoirs that Petrograd party organisations had a strong tradition of elections, even under the difficult conditions of underground existence. He thus differed from those who claimed that elections harmed the movement in illegal conditions. Moreover, he associated worker activism with signs of improvement in the revolutionary movement. In his opinion, longtime legal activity had 'diluted' underground organisations, but underground activism recovered in the context of wartime bans and police persecution. He thought that, in late 1915, underground organisations differed little in structure from those of 1902–7. Factory cells elected delegates to the districts and the districts elected the Petersburg Committee.⁵⁶ Shlyapnikov's strong professed belief in the elective principle would find a place in the programme of the Workers' Opposition in 1920–1.

Despite obstacles, Shlyapnikov created a working Bolshevik centre linked to the CC abroad. He formed his Russian Bureau of the Central Committee exclusively from proletarian activists, but they were not the ones Lenin

---

54 Shliapnikov 1982, pp. 94, 97, 104; RGASPI, f. 2, op. 5, d. 618, l. 1, letter from Shliapnikov to Lenin, 12 (25) November 1915, Petrograd; d. 661, l. 4, 11 March 1916, Stockholm.
55 Elwood 1974, pp. 52, 61; Wildman 1967, pp. 90–1; Ree 2010, p. 260; Wynn 1992, pp. 149–50.
56 Shliapnikov 1982, p. 95.

recommended, since all those had been arrested. The insurance groups were an important source. Tsarist police records confirm his success in mobilising workers of the Franco-Russian factory to carry out party work. In addition to worker activists, he coordinated his plans on transport and communications with Lenin's sisters, Anna Elizarova and Maria Ulyanova. Through them he recruited some student youth to help receive literature through Finland. Collection of dues from workers had been almost totally disrupted; he appealed to Maxim Gorky for funds. Aside from recruiting party activists, he directed party literature towards the important industrial and revolutionary areas of Kharkov, Ekaterinoslav, the Urals, the Volga region and the Caucasus.[57]

At the end of December, Shlyapnikov took a month-long tour of the provinces, surveying revolutionary work in Moscow, Vladimir and Nizhny Novgorod and visiting his mother in Doschatoe. Although the Old Believers warmly welcomed him, he felt he was in 'a distant, incomprehensible world', so far removed was he from the village after life in the cities of Western Europe. When he returned to Petrograd in January 1916, he found the Petersburg Committee facing a revolt from insurance organisers, who formed a rival centre for the co-ordination of Bolshevik workers' circles. Shlyapnikov aligned himself with the insurance organisers, which provoked Chernomazov to manoeuvre a rump session of the Petersburg Committee into condemning him. In a counter move, Shlyapnikov proposed Chernomazov's and Stark's expulsion from the Petersburg Committee. Perceiving Shlyapnikov's moves as a major threat, the Okhrana carried out 'devastating' arrests.[58]

Shlyapnikov prepared to try Chernomazov before a party court, but instead a full session of the Petersburg Committee rescinded its earlier condemnation of him. Chernomazov remained among party leaders, although his position had weakened. At the end of February 1916, Shlyapnikov returned abroad. Police observation had become too heavy for him to remain safely in Petrograd and carry out work effectively. He suggested to Lenin that someone from the foreign organisation go to Russia to continue his work, only in the 'area of theory and literature', in which he admitted his weakness. He claimed that Bolsheviks in Russia had adopted Lenin's slogan of 'civil war', but in fact support for

---

57   Shliapnikov 1982, p. 99; GARF, DP, f. 102, 6 d-vo, 1914, d. 114, l. 52, 7 (20) March 1916 report by Krasil'nikov; RGASPI, f. 2, op. 5, d. 618, l. 1, 12 (25) November 1915, Petrograd; d. 660, 11 March 1916, Stockholm. For more on Lenin's sisters, see Turton 2007.
58   Shliapnikov 1982, pp. 100–8; RGASPI, f. 17, op. 1, ch. IV, d. 1771, 14 (27) January 1916.

Lenin's position was tenuous. Many Bolsheviks remained defencists and those opposed to war were not 'overtly defeatist'.[59]

Despite the time and energy Shlyapnikov devoted to re-establishing the Russian Bureau, the police quickly arrested most of his recruits to it. Even the loss of one link in a chain of communications could take much time to recover from. When he returned to Sweden, he found as well that literature was no longer being smuggled through the route he had set up just a few months before, due to the discovery of a courier. He had to re-establish the smuggling network before returning to Stockholm.[60]

Nationalism Versus Internationalism: The *Kommunist* Affair

Even more exasperating to Shlyapnikov than transport failures was bickering among Bolshevik *intelligenty*. In Stockholm, Bosh, Pyatakov and Bukharin drew him into a fierce conflict with Lenin over the Bolshevik stance towards national self-determination. The differences arose while all four worked together as editors of the journal, *Kommunist*, which they founded in 1915 to provide a 'forum of Marxist intellectual discussion' among anti-war socialists from all over Europe. Many socialists had taken a principled stance against nationalism because of the role it played in igniting World War I. Bukharin, Bosh and Pyatakov numbered among those who called nationalism 'obsolete'. Bosh and Pyatakov believed nationalism to be terribly divisive in areas where the working class was composed of different nationalities (such as in Ukraine, where both had been in the revolutionary underground). Lenin, on the other hand, saw nationalism as a powerful force for bringing about revolution. He at first attempted to persuade Bukharin, Bosh and Pyatakov to share his position advocating self-determination, but all three resisted.[61] The historical literature shows that Lenin frequently encountered resistance to his views from fellow *intelligenty*, but less is known about how individual workers responded. Therefore, Shlyapnikov's role in the *Kommunist* affair is of interest.

---

59   RGASPI, f. 2, op. 5, d. 521, 20–3 January (2–5 February) [1916], from Shliapnikov in Petrograd to Lenin; d. 660, 11 March 1916, Stockholm; d. 661, l. 4, 11 March 1916; Shliapnikov 1982, pp. 104, 109; Melancon 1990, p. 178.
60   Service 1991, vol. 2, p. 124; Shliapnikov 1982, p. 112.
61   Service 1991, vol. 2, pp. 89, 109–10; Cohen 1980, p. 24; Clements 1997, p. 117. Bosh and Piatakov funded the journal. The Polish communist, Karl Radek, and the Dutch socialist, Anton Pannekoek, were also on the editorial board. *Kommunist* nos. 1–2 were published in a combined July 1915 issue. No further issues were published.

Not long after Shlyapnikov had left for Petrograd in October 1915, Bukharin asked Lenin and Zinoviev to allow his group to operate in the CC's name when communicating with the Bolsheviks in Russia. Lenin interpreted this as a power play and immediately broke off all relations with them. Consequently, mutual work on *Kommunist* ceased. Elizarova informed Shlyapnikov, while he was in Petrograd, of editorial disagreements. He in turn only told members of the CC's Russian Bureau of the falling-out. He did not inform other party members in order to avoid the appearance of dissension within the party leadership, which he thought would weaken the movement.[62]

Upon his return, Shlyapnikov severely chastised Lenin for having tried to bypass the Scandinavian route for communicating with him in Petrograd:

> First of all I am amazed. What moved you to contact me in Petrograd, requesting a 'direct' channel of correspondence? Indeed the organisation was set up 'directly' and even through people you recommended. It was already impossible to change it when I was in Petrograd. Clearly, you do not imagine the difficulties of arranging correspondence without people. In the future, refrain from making sudden changes, otherwise it will be impossible to organise anything.[63]

Shlyapnikov, who saw practical revolutionary work as more important than political intrigues, had no patience for Lenin's apparent caprice in demanding an overhaul of communications and transport just to isolate his political rivals. He emphasised to Lenin that he and all other CC Russian Bureau members decisively favoured continuing to publish *Kommunist*. Arguing that such conflicts 'sowed confusion' among workers, he pleaded with Lenin to compromise.[64]

The *Kommunist* editors' dispute disrupted practical work, which dismayed, alarmed and somewhat embittered Shlyapnikov. He considered the differences between Lenin and Bukharin not significant enough to require so much spite and pettiness. Moreover, he directly told Lenin that he considered Lenin's view on nationalism to be inconsistent with the views of the Russian proletariat. It bears noting that many Russian workers had little understanding of the problems of minority nationalities. However, Shlyapnikov respected Lenin's seniority. After his letter excoriating Lenin's interference in transport work, he wrote a more carefully worded missive, requesting that Lenin use evidence and

---

62   Service 1991, vol. 2, p. 112; RGASPI, f. 2, op. 5, d. 674, l. 2, 4 (17) May [March] 1916, Stockholm; Turton 2007, p. 72.
63   RGASPI, f. 2, op. 5, d. 674, l. 1, 17 March 1916.
64   RGASPI, f. 2, op. 5, d. 521, ll. 1, 3, 20–3 January (2–5 February) 1916; d. 674, l. 2, 17 March 1916.

reason to make his case, rather than abusive language. He noted that readers of *Kommunist* in Russia praised Bukharin's and Zinoviev's articles, but expected better from Lenin.[65]

Shlyapnikov objected to the dispute not only because he found it counterproductive, but also because he believed Lenin's promotion of national self-determination was contrary to the concept that all workers had common interests. He believed that many other Russian worker revolutionaries agreed with him and that Lenin should moderate his views when they clashed so sharply with the views of Bolshevik workers. He emphasised, moreover, that Zinoviev and Lenin alone could not be regarded as the entire CC and that their actions smacked of *'nepartiinost'* [lacked a party spirit].[66] Shlyapnikov complained to Krupskaya about the interruption in the supply of literature to him during the *Kommunist* crisis. He pointedly noted that his SR counterpart in Norway (P. Alexandrovich) received far more literature from SR Party leaders for smuggling to Russia than he did from the Bolshevik CC and that he was forced to help the SRs send literature to Russia for the sake of providing information to revolutionaries there.[67] Collaboration among organisers from different political parties was common in the revolutionary underground, but Lenin could not miss Shlyapnikov's intended rebuke.

In a letter to Zinoviev, Shlyapnikov objected that Lenin's tactics and vitriolic treatment of people not only disrupted transport and communications, but also affected the personal composition of the Bolshevik Party:

> Terribly harmful tales about Ilyich are circulating in Russia. His attempts to dissociate himself from any Bolshevik because of the smallest disagreement have made practical people shun us. Pawns, ready to carry out Ilyich's will, are not valued there and now under the noise of war they have all hidden away. Maybe they'll emerge when it will be profitable. Our party grows. The possibility of internal disagreements, with solidarity on basic questions, is fully permissible. I respect him. But this respect makes me (as well as many others in Russia) very demanding towards him. [Lenin] should not fly off the handle over trivia. He should support

---

65 RGASPI, f. 2, op. 5, d. 660, l. 2, 11 March 1916.
66 RGASPI, f. 17, op. 1, ch. IV, d. 1778, 1 March 1916 (or later), l. 2; d. 1786, l. 2, 22 March 1916; d. 1787, l. 1, 25 March 1916; f. 2, op. 5, d. 666, l. 1, 3–4 April 1916; d. 674, l. 2, 17 March 1916; Lenin 1926–37, vol. 29: p. 231.
67 RGASPI, f. 17, op. 1, ch. IV, d. 1813, 15 May 1916; Shliapnikov 1982, p. 114.

his proposals with evidence, not curses, and should not divide Bolsheviks into sheep and goats.[68]

Rejecting Lenin's attempt to lump other *Kommunist* editors and contributors together with social chauvinists, Shlyapnikov warned him that if *émigré* squabbles continued, he would leave Scandinavia. Yet he also tried to mollify Lenin, assuring him that none of his fellow editors had tried to form an organisation isolating him. He emphasised that they were 'not the heart of an "organisation" but the sum of individual persons'.[69] In attempting to smooth over tensions between the rivals, Shlyapnikov displayed tolerance towards heterodoxy among Bolsheviks and disagreed with Lenin on what constituted factionalism.

When Lenin refused a proposal for a 'compromise' edition of *Kommunist*, Shlyapnikov declared: 'From your wording only one thing is clear to me, that you don't want discussion ... I relayed your decision, but of course not in such a harsh form as your postcard. And I further refuse to be your intermediary in this affair'. Lenin dashed off a conciliatory message, convincing him to continue his role, at least temporarily. Bukharin was willing to compromise, but Pyatakov and Bosh were too deeply offended by Lenin's attempt to expel them from the editorial board of *Kommunist*.[70]

Lenin made one last attempt to appease Shlyapnikov, proposing to publish a collection of articles contributed by Lenin, Zinoviev and Bukharin's circle, but excluding Karl Radek, a Polish communist with whom Lenin had fallen out on the national question. However, Shlyapnikov objected that the exclusion of Radek was 'unacceptable', so he did not even bother to inform the others of this proposal. He found Lenin's 'political antipathy towards Radek' to be 'perplexing', since in the German press Radek supported the Russian Bolsheviks. He thus suspected Lenin of wreaking 'petty political vengeance'. He emphasised: 'We now need to value the leftists, to try to be a centre, around which the entire left congregates, and this demands from us great tact and some degree of patience'. In this controversy, his behaviour was far from that of a 'Lenin loyalist', much less a lackey of Lenin. On the contrary, he took Lenin to task for insufficient political maturity. Yet he also found fault with Bosh, Bukharin and

---

68 RGASPI, f. 17, op. 1, ch. IV, d. 1787, ll. 1–2, 25 March 1916. The Bolsheviks often referred to Lenin by his patronymic, 'Il'ich'. In a New Testament parable, Jesus compared separating righteous men from wicked ones to a shepherd separating sheep from goats (Matthew 25: 31–46).

69 RGASPI, f. 2, op. 5, d. 666, ll. 2–3, 3–4 April 1916; d. 669, l. 4, 14 April 1916; d. 784, ll. 1–2, 16 April 1916.

70 RGASPI, f. 2, op. 5, d. 677, ll. 1–2, 22 May 1916; d. 680, l. 1, 1 June 1916.

Pyatakov for incompetence as organisers. In his memoirs, he recalled that the *Kommunist* conflict undermined supplying Russian organisations with literature as well as contacts with Russia generally: 'I had imagined that you could keep your own opinion on this or that point of our programme and fight for its adoption, but I could not see the need for animosity and least of all for damaging the workers' cause itself with such animosity. This phenomenon is, however, endemic in our intelligentsia, which is so doctrinaire in defence of its "principles" that it will even abandon the work in hand'.[71] Although he came to support Lenin's position on the national question, he still did not consider it worth risking the party's unity. Abandoning European intrigues, he set out for America to realise a fundraising scheme he had devised.

To America and Back

In Petrograd Shlyapnikov had received some materials from the writer Gorky on the plight of Russian Jews, who had suffered terribly from atrocities inflicted on them by the Russian military. He had aimed either to sell them in Scandinavia or to use them to attract funds from European Jews to set up a publishing house. When this did not materialise, he fastened his hopes on American Jews.[72] No doubt, curiosity and the desire for adventure also propelled him to the New World. In summer 1916, he boarded a steamer for New York City. This journey marked an interlude that would see a great change in his personal life, as well as provide the means for him to return to Russia on the eve of revolution.

By spring 1916, Shlyapnikov's personal relations with Kollontai had entered a final crisis. She had fallen out of love with him, but found it difficult to tell him so. She still praised his qualities: 'dedication to the cause, the bravery of youth, courage'. However, she also perceived flaws in him: 'I feel that as a politician Al[exander] is helpless and clumsy ... He knows too little and is too little inclined towards intellectual work ... He can [identify and overcome] external obstacles, but he does not have enough self-discipline for systematic organisation of political work'. She based her evaluation chiefly on the lack of results

---

71 RGASPI, f. 2, op. 5, d. 687, l. 1, 28 June 1916; Shliapnikov 1982, p. 113.
72 Shliapnikov 1982, p. 115. Lenin had hoped to distract Bosh and Piatakov from *Kommunist* by persuading them to edit a collection of Jewish materials, but his hopes did not materialise (Lenin 1999, p. 187). On wartime atrocities against Russian Jews, see Lohr 2001. The materials Shliapnikov smuggled to New York might have belonged to a 'Black Book' project about Jewish suffering during World War I, of which many documents were lost during or after the war (see Zavadivker 2013).

from his trip to Russia in the winter of 1915–16, without understanding fully the obstacles he had faced from police infiltration of the party. Her intellectual disappointment with him contributed to her decision to end the relationship. Nevertheless, she worried about offending him, since she saw in him a 'personification' of the proletariat.[73]

While Shlyapnikov was in the United States, Kollontai wrote a letter terminating the relationship and left it for him to find upon his return (she had left her first husband in the same way). Thus, he wrote letters to her from the U.S. without knowing about her decision and must have felt humiliated when he only later realised she had already decided to break up with him. She and her son left for the United States before he returned to Scandinavia. Justifying her indirectness, she explained: 'To break Avvakum's will directly was impossible'. The next time they met was in March 1917 in Petrograd, when Shlyapnikov, as a member of the Petrograd Soviet, greeted Kollontai at the train station. Later, they had a long private discussion; she recalled that he 'rebuked' her for having broken off with him so 'rudely and hurtfully'.[74]

Transport across the Atlantic was hazardous due to wartime conditions and frequent storms. The Norwegian steamer, Kristianiafjord, on which Shlyapnikov travelled in 1916, wrecked off the coast of England one year later. Although Shlyapnikov came for a brief stay, he, like all third-class passengers, passed through the immigration facility at Ellis Island. Some immigrants were turned back, but he was easily admitted due to his metalworking skills and good health. He entered the United States on 8 July under his own name, using a French passport and his membership card in the Amalgamated Society of Engineers. A true conspirator, he named as his local contact the Russian consulate, rather than providing local socialists' names and addresses, as did Kollontai and Bukharin. After a few days in the city, he wrote to Kollontai: 'I like New York very much. In the port, when they held us all night, I fell in love with the skyscrapers, poking through the evening haze ... [S]uch strength, energy, enterprising spirit ... Much here pleases me and I feel that life in this country would not be so disagreeable as in Scandinavia'.[75]

Shlyapnikov's published memoirs subsequently gave a more negative impression. On his wait in the harbour, he wrote: 'The heat was unbearable ... like an

---

73   RGASPI, f. 134, op. 4, d. 10, ll. 36–8, 70.
74   RGASPI, f. 134, op. 4, d. 7, l. 15, 9 July 1916, letter from Kollontai to Shliapnikov; d. 22, ll. 1–6; Clements 1979, p. 22; Shliapnikova 1995, conversation; Ellis Island Immigration database at http://www.libertyellisfoundation.org (last accessed 11 October 2014).
75   Shliapnikov 1982, pp. 116–17; RGASPI, f. 134, op. 4, d. 7, l. 17, 14 July 1916, New York. The ship's passenger list names him as Alexandre Schlapnikoff (http://www.libertyellisfoundation.org/, last accessed 11 October 2014).

oven breathing fire'. Once in the city, he was disappointed in the American workers' movement, which he found to be 'primitive' in comparison to the European movement. While he was in New York, he witnessed a major strike of the Bronx tram workers, which was broken up by hired thugs working in collusion with the police. Repelled by the American factory owners' 'brutal' suppression of unrest and by the 'extreme selfishness' he found in the American way of life, he nevertheless noted: 'The New York worker dresses smartly and lives and eats considerably better than his European counterpart'.[76] He could share global admiration of higher living standards in the United States, even while he found fault with the excesses he perceived in American capitalism.

Although he had come to the U.S. partly to escape hostilities between Russian *émigrés* in Europe, in New York Shlyapnikov soon became immersed in local Russian socialists' factional antagonisms. Under his pseudonym, Belenin, which for conspiratorial purposes he used instead of his real name, he delivered a number of lectures in the New York region on the Russian workers' movement, one at the famous Beethoven Hall on East Fifth Street, the site of many gatherings of socialist, union and immigrant societies. His reports to *Novyi mir* socialists on the attitude towards the war in Russia and Europe intensified conflict between the Mensheviks and the Bolsheviks, who ran the publication, over what position to take on the war. He claimed that the Mensheviks 'waged a struggle in the American style, introducing personal and sensational issues, hysteria and abuse'. According to him, the Bolsheviks won the argument but could not oust Mensheviks from the paper because there were too few literate Bolsheviks to replace them.[77]

Shlyapnikov met with little success in selling the materials about Russian Jews. Upon arrival, he found that most potential buyers were on holiday. As in Scandinavia, he found some interested Jews who were Germanophiles, but he did not want the materials used as pro-German propaganda. After two months of waiting and negotiating, he finally received $500 from a group of Jewish scholars, half of which paid for his travelling expenses. He left for Scandinavia on 14 September. With his remaining funds, he renewed the transport of literature to Russia. He recommended that Bukharin come to the United States to provide an articulate Bolshevik voice for *Novyi mir*. Bukharin eagerly accepted the proposition but, according to Shlyapnikov, he badly bungled his travel arrangements by making reservations in his real name rather than the name on his passport (Moshe Dolgolevsky). Arranging travel in wartime conditions

---

76 Shliapnikov 1982, pp. 116, 118; Anon 1916.
77 RGASPI, f. 134, op. 4, d. 7, l. 20, 25 July 1916 letter to Kollontai; Anon 1916; Shliapnikov 1982, p. 117.

was complex, so Shlyapnikov had to spend much time and effort to correct his mistakes: 'Bukharin was the type of impractical Russian intellectual for whom I had to think out every detail of the trip'. This shot at Bukharin in his memoirs probably emerged from the bitterness he felt towards the man who helped remove him from leadership of the Metalworkers' Union in 1921, as well as broader resentment towards an 'impractical' party *intelligent* who was disdainful towards the workers' ability to manage the economy after the revolution. After seeing Bukharin off to America, Shlyapnikov eagerly returned to Russia to resume practical organisational work. His eventful journey in disguise through the Finnish underground included an accidental rendezvous with right-wing Finnish nationalists, who carelessly revealed to him a map of their entire organisation. Finally re-establishing contact with the Social-Democratic underground, Shlyapnikov arrived in Petrograd in the second half of October 1916.[78]

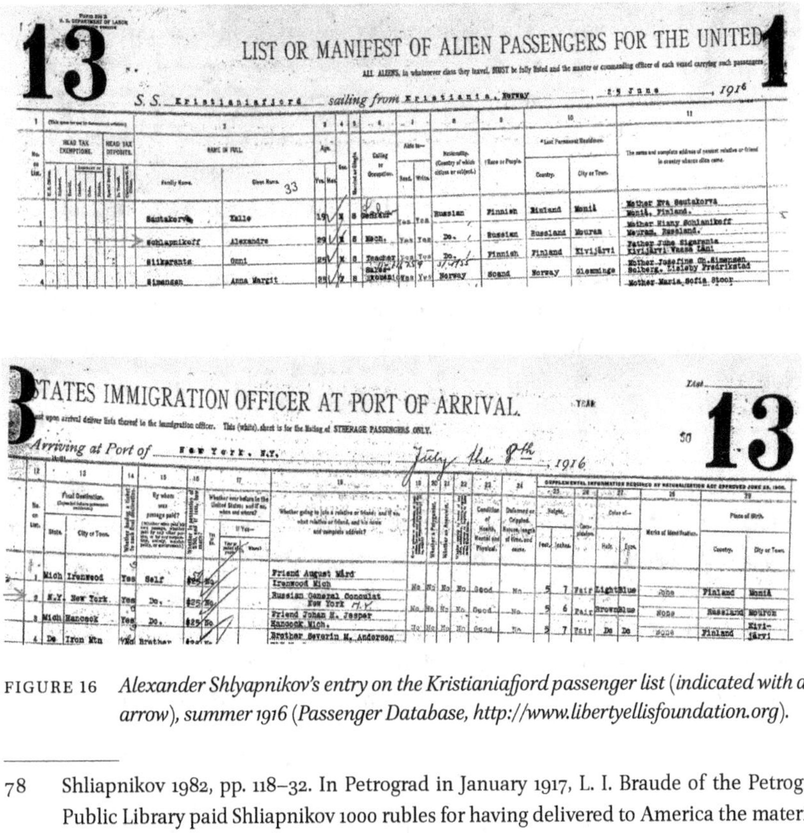

FIGURE 16   *Alexander Shlyapnikov's entry on the Kristianiafjord passenger list (indicated with an arrow), summer 1916 (Passenger Database, http://www.libertyellisfoundation.org).*

---

78   Shliapnikov 1982, pp. 118–32. In Petrograd in January 1917, L. I. Braude of the Petrograd Public Library paid Shliapnikov 1000 rubles for having delivered to America the materials about Russian Jews; this added to his funds for Bolshevik organisational work (Shliapnikov 1992, vol. 2, p. 58).

Conclusion

Shlyapnikov's political and organisational work in the revolutionary underground during World War I revealed much of his character, his principles, his strengths and his weaknesses. He considered himself a 'practitioner' [*praktik*], as opposed to a 'theoretician' [*teoretik*] and took great pride in his organisational work on behalf of the revolution. He also enjoyed his work smuggling literature and people and evading the police.[79] Friends, such as Kollontai, recalled his delight in conspiracy and his eagerness for illegally crossing borders, evading police agents and assuming other identities for underground work. His talent for storytelling probably enhanced the romantic image such pursuits conveyed to fellow revolutionaries and workers. His commitment to worker power ran consistently through his work during World War I. When he travelled to Russia, he either worked in factories or talked extensively with fellow workers to regain an understanding of their life. He enlisted workers to staff the Russian Bureau of the Bolshevik CC and to help him in other organisational work.

Shlyapnikov regarded leading Bolsheviks' arguments over theory and their struggles for control of party organs as sometimes detrimental to the cause. His effort to keep the *Kommunist* editorial board working together demonstrates this. Throughout the *Kommunist* conflict, he tried to convince the journal's editors of their responsibility to let practical work proceed unhindered for the sake of the workers' revolution. He also frequently reminded them of what the 'workers' thought about questions of nationalism.

Shlyapnikov's personal relationship with Kollontai reveals much about his personality and its intersection with his political beliefs. They shared faith in a revolution that would enable workers to take control of their own social and economic existence. Her emphasis on personal autonomy resounded with his devotion to the role of the working class *vis-à-vis* the radical intelligentsia in carrying out the revolution. Kollontai's role as intellectual mentor, first to Shlyapnikov and later to the Workers' Opposition, was exceptional for a woman and an aristocrat, but the tensions between the couple mirrored those between workers and *intelligenty* more broadly. She saw it as her duty to cultivate him, while he, although appreciative of advice, did not believe his own understanding of Marxism and analysis of revolutionary politics to be inferior to hers.

---

79   Shliapnikov 1982 and Futrell 1963 provide lively accounts of the ruses he used and the risks he took during his illegal border crossings.

Lenin forced other Bolsheviks to deal with him as a leader; he took over central organs and was the most active of the leaders in communicating with Russia. Shlyapnikov respected Lenin's seniority, his learning, his intellect and his dedication to international revolution. However, he addressed Lenin as a partner, not a lackey. Although he did not directly challenge Lenin on ideology, he persistently reminded him that 'conscious' workers were the leaders of the revolutionary effort. Often frustrated with Lenin's precipitation of intra-party polemics and squabbles, he did not hesitate to say that he found them detrimental to the cause of revolutionary organising. Nevertheless, Shlyapnikov's role as a 'practitioner', and perhaps his limited education, often blinded him to the importance that the resolution of theoretical disputes had for the role of workers in the party.

CHAPTER 3

Organising Workers in the Revolutionary Year 1917

Three years of total war, with attendant economic crises, exhausted Russian society and discredited Tsar Nicholas II's regime, which fell in February 1917 as a consequence of a mass protest in Petrograd against food and fuel shortages. After tsarist rule in Russia ended, an eight-month contest began between liberals, moderate socialists and radicals over the structure of government in Russia and important questions such as participation in the war and land redistribution. Freedom of speech, the press and organisation filled newspapers and the streets with a boisterous range of opinions. Hopes reigned high that Russia could follow Western Europe in establishing democratic, participatory constitutional government, but fears of anarchy and chaos also loomed large in the face of mounting economic disaster, growing war casualties, a crime wave, the aspirations of minority nationalities for self-rule and the fragility of the caretaker government that had replaced the tsarist regime. The power of the Provisional Government, composed of nominees from the Duma, the weak legislative body that had existed under tsarist rule, was challenged by soviets, bodies elected by workers, soldiers and peasants.

When the February Revolution began, Shlyapnikov was the most senior Bolshevik on the scene in Petrograd. Older, more experienced leaders were all abroad or in Siberian exile. Due to his metalworking credentials, experience abroad, intelligence, organisational skills and seemingly unlimited energy, he commanded the respect of lower-level activists in Russia and soon became a prominent member of the Petrograd Soviet. However, more moderate Bolsheviks, such as Stalin and Kamenev, who took control of the party's leading bodies and press until Lenin arrived in Russia in April 1917, edged him out of the central party leadership. Turning towards other forms of worker organisation, Shlyapnikov helped establish a workers' militia and the Red Guard, which played an important role in the October Revolution. A key figure in rebuilding the Petrograd Metalworkers' Union and transforming it into a strong national union, he later provided a valuable service to students of history by chronicling the revolution in his memoirs, which he wrote in the 1920s. Although his Bolshevik sympathies were evident, he used a range of sources and tried to represent revolutionary events honestly, acknowledging Bolshevik weaknesses and the role played by non-Bolsheviks.[1]

---

1   Rachkovskii 2011. Stalin banned Shliapnikov's memoirs, but they regained some degree of respectability as sources during the Khrushchev era. See Burdzhalov 1956a, 1956b and 1987.

The February Revolution

When Shlyapnikov returned to Petrograd in autumn 1916, his goals were straightforward and modest: to rebuild the Russian Bureau of the CC, to renew the transport of literature and to collect information about the revolutionary movement in Russia. These tasks were oriented towards maintaining the Bolshevik organisation in Russia, rather than preparing it for mass upheaval and revolutionary change. The organisation had suffered greatly since his last visit. Arrests had decimated leading party bodies, but local cells continued to operate. Trusting only their own, local cells avoided the central organisations and other parallel Social-Democratic groups for fear of police spies. Shlyapnikov attempted to harness local activists to work for the Russian Bureau.

The Petersburg Committee could not spare personnel to assist Shlyapnikov. To work with him in the Bureau, he recruited a student, Vyacheslav Molotov, and a worker, Peter Zalutsky. Shlyapnikov set up the organisation and conducted communications with the CC abroad, Zalutsky served as liaison with the Petersburg Committee and Molotov wrote and published CC materials. Shlyapnikov later wrote that he convinced other Bureau members to support Lenin's line on national self-determination, the pressing issue of the day, but with the stipulation that those who disagreed with Lenin should not be barred from contributing to CC publications or punished for expressing different views in independently published articles.[2] He did not want factionalism to undermine practical work.

In mid-December, Shlyapnikov went to Moscow to coordinate the calls of local Bolsheviks for street demonstrations on 9 January, the twelfth anniversary of Bloody Sunday. By leaving Petrograd, he escaped the web of police agents encircling him and was able to renew direct contacts with Bolshevik organisers in Moscow, Vladimir and Nizhny Novgorod. Through other Bolsheviks, he also set up communications with Bolshevik organisations in Kiev, Tula, Voronezh, the Donbas, the Urals and Siberia. He admitted in his memoirs, however, that scanty funds meant that communications with local organisations had to depend on 'chance visits... or strokes of luck'.[3] His candour regarding Bolshevik unpreparedness for revolution would become increasingly unfashionable in the early Soviet era.

Because of his trip to the provinces, Shlyapnikov was not in Petrograd to see the prelude to revolution there. First there unfolded an impressive strike of one

---

Chief sources for this chapter are secondary sources, reminiscences, including Shliapnikov's, and trade-union archives and newspapers.

2 Shliapnikov 1982, pp. 133–52, 201.
3 Shliapnikov 1982, pp. 141, 159, 214.

hundred and forty thousand (40 percent) of Petrograd's workers on 9 January. Workers blamed the war and the monarchy for the intolerable economic hardship. Although the strike's initiators were arrested in late January, the rebellious mood among Petrograd's workers did not dissipate. Workers engaged in labour protests almost constantly from 9 January through to 22 February, when directors of the Putilov factory, the largest plant in Russia, locked out workers. Then on 23 February, International Women's Day, women textile-workers, angered by long lines and high prices for bread, initiated an insurrection that brought one hundred thousand workers out on strike. Metalworker activists honed the rhetoric of the protestors' nascent political demands. Soldiers proved reluctant to disperse demonstrators. By the next day, two-thirds of the city's industrial workforce was on strike. On 25 February, middle-class citizens and students joined demonstrations. Workers attacked police and even some troops began to turn against them. By 27 February, soldiers were in full insurrection, crowds had freed political prisoners and criminals from gaol and the police melted away.[4]

During the February Revolution, events moved ahead of all socialist parties. None expected Women's Day to ignite a revolution. While moderate socialists tried to restrain strikes, more radical socialists came out in favour of them. Left socialists cooperated in issuing appeals and organising events. Printed leaflets had usually served as signals for mass actions, but issuing revolutionary propaganda was difficult given police harassment. A group of revolutionary Social Democrats called the Interdistrictites [*Mezhraiontsy*] was probably the major producer of socialist leaflets during the February Revolution. Bolsheviks in the Vyborg district of Petrograd were among the most radical. They wanted to arm detachments of worker guards, but Shlyapnikov refused to authorise this, for which other Bolsheviks criticised him then and later. He argued that worker guards could not stand up against trained military forces; therefore, it was crucial for workers to win over military units. Indeed, it appeared by 27 February that the revolution could descend into chaotic violence.[5]

The February Revolution culminated on 27 February. Tsarist ministers resigned. Socialists formed the Petrograd Soviet of Workers' and Soldiers' Deputies, a city-wide electoral body representing workers and soldiers through political parties and other organisations; its leading body was an Executive Committee. Liberal leaders of the Duma decided to create a temporary government. When, under pressure, Tsar Nicholas II abdicated on behalf of

---

4 Wade 2000, pp. 29–36; Hasegawa 1981, pp. 278–94; Burdzhalov 1987, p. 102; Thompson 1981, p. 21.
5 Melancon 1988 and 2009; Wade 2000, pp. 34–5; Burdzhalov 1987, pp. 86, 180; Shliapnikov 1992, vol. 2, pp. 62–5, 91–5; Hasegawa 1981, p. 296.

himself and his son on 2 March 1917, power quickly devolved to the Provisional Government, which was created on the same day by agreement between the leaders of the Duma and the Petrograd Soviet. Prince Georgy Lvov, a *zemstvo* liberal, was its head. Alexander Kerensky, a pro-war socialist, joined the new government as Minister of Justice, later becoming Minister of War. Shlyapnikov participated in the group of leftists that created the Petrograd Soviet and was elected to its Executive Committee; the Soviet appointed him commissar for Vyborg district, one of the main industrial areas of the city. Soviets would form in many Russian cities; within large cities there were district soviets. Although a majority of the Soviet Executive Committee had agreed to support the Provisional Government, this was the position of moderate Mensheviks and SRs who regarded the February Revolution as 'bourgeois'. They believed it unrealistic and contrary to Marxist theory to oppose the creation of a bourgeois government. Radical socialists were less willing to give the 'bourgeoisie' the opportunity to consolidate its power.[6]

The monarchist right having withered as tsarism collapsed, the political spectrum ranged from moderate right to far left. Centrist non-socialists, who were mostly liberal, cooperated with moderate socialists during the interval between the two 1917 revolutions of February and October. The most important liberal party was the Constitutional Democrats [Kadets]; their most prominent spokesman, Pavel Milyukov, became Minister of Foreign Affairs. Liberals desired to protect Russia from German conquest, resolve the economic crisis, create peace among social groups and prepare elections based on universal suffrage for a Constituent Assembly that would organise a new constitutional government for Russia. Many civic organisations had a liberal bent; these were organised by professionals for political, educational and cultural causes. As the crisis deepened, those who had seemed liberal came to be perceived as conservative.[7]

A range of opinions existed among Petrograd Bolsheviks over their stance towards the Provisional Government. Lenin's views were outlined in his 'Letters from Afar', which he wrote in early March 1917 while still in Switzerland. These consisted of opposition to the Provisional Government, a call for Soviet rule and opposition to the war. Most Bolsheviks in Petrograd agreed with Lenin's call for an end to the war, but their opinions varied widely on whether to cooperate with the Provisional Government. A majority of the Petersburg Committee

---

6 Hasegawa 1981, pp. 334–42, 356–7; Shliapnikov 1992, vol. 2, pp. 126–32; RGASPI, f. 70, op. 4, d. 387, l. 132; Wade 2000, pp. 91, 94. The Executive Committee was identical to an all-socialist group that had met in the weeks before the February Revolution (Melancon 2009).
7 Wade 2000, pp. 53–8.

advocated non-opposition to the Provisional Government, in line with the resolution adopted by the Petrograd Soviet. The far-left Vyborg District Bolshevik Committee called on workers to seize power. Shlyapnikov encouraged them to put a hold on their agitation for an uprising, arguing that it would be unwise to rise up without adequate preparation.[8]

Similarly to Lenin, Shlyapnikov and the Russian Bureau opposed the Provisional Government and called for the Soviet to form a provisional revolutionary government, which would have had an agenda of ending the war, establishing a democratic republic, the eight-hour day, confiscating landowners' estates, supplying the army and urban population with food and calling a Constituent Assembly. Some historians have assumed that Shlyapnikov merely implemented Lenin's orders.[9] Nevertheless, there was a subtle difference. The emphasis he placed on cooperation with other left socialists indicates that he did not aim merely to secure a dominant political position for the Bolsheviks.

The Russian Bureau membership expanded throughout March as Bolshevik leaders returned from prison or exile. Of these, Lev Kamenev was the most prominent. He led the moderate Bolsheviks, who included Stalin; these Bolsheviks were closer to the Petrograd Soviet majority's assessment of the Provisional Government than they were to Lenin's views. They claimed authority in the name of the former Bolshevik Duma delegation. The CC Russian Bureau struggled ineffectively with the moderates. Although the Bureau at first rejected Kamenev as a member, he circumvented it by taking control of the Bolshevik newspaper, *Pravda*. Kamenev's group also outmanoeuvred the Russian Bureau on the floor of the Soviet by supporting moderate positions in the name of the Bolshevik Party. Unwilling to reveal disunity, Shlyapnikov and his allies did not speak. That he was so easily outmanoeuvred lends credence to Nikolai Sukhanov's assessment of him: 'a party patriot ... an experienced conspirator, an excellent organiser and practical trade unionist, he was not at all a politician, capable of grasping the essence of the changing state of affairs and generalising from it'.[10] That Sukhanov's portrait of Shlyapnikov coincides with the one Kollontai wrote in her diary reinforces its aptness.[11]

---

8   Rabinowitch 1991, pp. 33–5 and Longley 1972, p. 67, have discussed in detail the differences between the Bolsheviks. For a different reading of these events, see Lih 2011b.
9   Shliapnikov 1992, vol. 2, pp. 65–6, 163–5; Longley 1972, p. 67; Schapiro 1956, p. 28; and Naumov 1991, p. 16.
10 Shliapnikov 1992, vol. 2, pp. 445–8; Sukhanov 1922, vol. 1, p. 79.
11 Quoted above. Kollontai's judgments can be found in: RGASPI, f. 134, op. 4, d. 10, ll. 36–8, 70.

When Kamenev's 15 March *Pravda* editorial supported continuing the war, consternation ensued among Bolshevik activists. The methods of the moderates, forcing through their own views without consulting rank-and-file members, were as much at issue as their policies, according to Shlyapnikov. Further, the content of *Pravda* was not so blatantly defencist, but it still did not publish a large part of Lenin's letters. Moreover, by 18 March, Kamenev had persuaded the Petersburg Committee to vote for 'conditional support' for the Provisional Government. Shlyapnikov long resented the moderates' steps; in his memoirs, he declared that Kamenev and Stalin had pursued a non-revolutionary policy. They had disunited the party in March by introducing 'into the leading bodies of the party disagreements and deep organisational frictions'. Attributing his troubles with the group to their *intelligent* origins, he argued that Bolshevik *intelligenty* often feared going too far in opposition to the government and bourgeois society.[12]

Shlyapnikov must have been relieved when Lenin arrived in Russia to take up the struggle against the 'bourgeois' Provisional Government. He had helped Bolsheviks in Europe arrange the 'sealed' train that transported Lenin and the other Bolshevik *émigrés* across Germany, Sweden and Finland to Petrograd and he was among those who greeted Lenin at the Finland station. The Mensheviks and Kamenev's Bolsheviks were on the verge of reunification when Lenin arrived in Petrograd. Lenin immediately and emphatically expressed his disagreement with Bolshevik moderates' positions on the war and towards the Provisional Government. His 'April Theses' called for the transformation of world war into international proletarian revolution, for opposition to the Provisional Government and for a total rejection of any efforts to heal the schism among Russian Social Democrats. Lenin placed first priority on 'a struggle for transfer of all power to the Soviets', control over which he hoped soon to wrest from the moderate socialists. Nevertheless, he did not endorse the radical Bolsheviks' appeals for an immediate seizure of power. He realised that more preparation was necessary before attempting to bring down the Provisional Government. Initially, most Bolsheviks rejected Lenin's positions, but this soon changed.[13]

Foreign Minister Milyukov, in assuring the Allies in a 20 April telegram that Russia would wage war according to the tsarist government's treaties with them, radicalised many leftists. By the Bolsheviks' Seventh Party Conference (24–9 April 1917), a large majority of delegates agreed with Lenin's positions on

---

12   Longley 1972, pp. 66, 72; Shliapnikov 1992, vol. 2, pp. 439, 452; Rabinowitch 1991, p. 36.
13   Service 1991, vol. 2, pp. 145–6; Rabinowitch 1991, pp. 36–45. The train was 'sealed' in that German officials agreed not to enter (Wade 2000, p. 73).

the Provisional Government and the war. Nevertheless, the conference did not agree wholly with his claim that Russia was undergoing a transition to socialist revolution, but leaned somewhat towards Kamenev's position that Russia was still in the process of a bourgeois-liberal revolution. Shlyapnikov played a minimal role in this sea change in the Party, because in April he suffered concussion in an automobile accident and was hospitalised for several weeks.[14] His incapacitation pushed him further from the centre of party activity.

Workers' Militia and Red Guard

As Shlyapnikov moved to the fringes of the party leadership, he assumed a more central role in non-party forms of worker organisation. His attitude towards the role of workers in the revolution is illustrated especially well in his conception of the tasks of the workers' militia and Red Guard, both of which he helped organise in spring 1917. The Petrograd Soviet officially created the worker militia of Petrograd on 28 February 1917, with the Soviet assigning Shlyapnikov the task of overseeing the arming and organisation of the militia. All over Russia, tsarist police forces disintegrated and were replaced by local militias. In spring and summer 1917, the Petrograd worker militias were superseded by the Red Guard, which in late August played an important role in defeating General Lavr Kornilov's attempts at counterrevolution.

Shlyapnikov's memoirs leave the impression that workers and activists at the local level played a greater role in organising the worker militias and Red Guards than he and other party leaders.[15] Certainly he operated without many staff at the central level, but in writing his memoirs, he intentionally emphasised workers' initiative. In reality, he probably expended more effort than he later acknowledged.

Shlyapnikov saw the purpose of the workers' militia as not only to police factory districts, but also to defend gains made for workers during the February Revolution. He revealed this to a 5 March meeting dedicated to forming a civil militia, under the Petrograd city administration. The Soviet sent him to the meeting as its representative. He spoke there of the need to broaden the militia's responsibilities to prevent a restoration of the monarchy and 'to ease the movement of the revolution forward'. This was his own opinion; the Soviet had not taken a stance. The militia's responsibilities were a sensitive question, as casting them too much in terms of class conflict could provoke opposition from

---

14   Rabinowitch 1991, pp. 40–6; RGASPI, f. 70, op. 4, d. 387, l. 132.
15   Shliapnikov 1992, vol. 2, p. 132; Wade 1984, pp. 43–4.

the non-worker social milieu. The Soviet, Provisional Government and city administration agreed that worker militias should unite with the civil militia of Petrograd in late April 1917, but many units continued to exist independently of the civil militia. According to Shlyapnikov, workers insisted that their militias report to district soviets, rather than to the city or regional administration, and that all administrative leaders in the militias be elected, rather than appointed. His emphasis on the workers' preference for elections consistently sounded in his memoirs.[16]

When the Petrograd Soviet created a section on militia affairs in mid-March, it removed from Shlyapnikov formal responsibility for links with militias. In late March and early April, he began to advocate a worker 'guard'. Shlyapnikov and Konstantin Eremeev, who in December 1917 became Petrograd Military District Commander, decided to organise the Guard in the most 'revolutionary' worker districts. Shlyapnikov authored the Vyborg District Soviet's 29 April decree on the organisation of the workers' guard. The Vyborg regulations restricted membership in the guard to workers who belonged to a socialist party or a trade union, or who were chosen by their fellow factory workers. The regulations defined the main tasks of the workers' guard as: '1) struggle with the counterrevolution, 2) armed defence of the working class and 3) defence of all citizens' life and safety'. Other districts modelled their Red Guard units on those of Vyborg. In August 1917 the Red Guard central staff was formed, with Shlyapnikov among its members. A Bolshevik memoirist historian credited him in particular for having 'worked indefatigably' to organise regional command centres for the Red Guard in all districts of Petrograd.[17]

When revolutionary socialists began organising the Red Guard, moderate socialists and liberals feared that the Bolsheviks would use the guard for partisan purposes. Defending the Red Guard against these charges, Shlyapnikov explained that it was necessary for several reasons. First, when the war ended, the radicalised Petrograd garrison would depart the capital, leaving workers vulnerable to repression by the Provisional Government and police. Second, the professional militia was 'cut off' from the people and had its own institutional interests. Workers therefore required their own militia, which would guard their interests. All guard units would be under the direction of their district soviets, which would eliminate any threat of spontaneous or independent action. Finally, workers would arm themselves no matter what. In order to avoid 'disorder', the soviets and parties should cooperate in forming

---

16   Wade 1984, p. 61; Shliapnikov 1992, vol. 2, pp. 389–91.
17   Shliapnikov 1992, vol. 2: pp. 392–3; RGASPI, f. 70, op. 4, d. 387, l. 132; Wade 1984, p. 97; Georgievskii 1919, pp. 66–7.

a network of militias under the control of the soviets.[18] This article demonstrated Shlyapnikov's continuing commitment to a broad revolutionary consensus that elevated the role of the organised workers.

Organising the Petrograd Metalworkers' Union

Shlyapnikov's actions as chair of the Metalworkers' Union in 1917 strengthened his conviction that the unions were of crucial importance to the workers' revolution. He spent a great deal of time and energy attacking the problems faced by the union, and his role as a trade-union leader would deeply influence his positions on political and economic questions. In summer 1917, he worked towards expanding and strengthening unions, with the goal of making them strong partners in negotiation with the heads of capitalist enterprise.[19] Day-to-day immersion in the details of negotiating wage rates and other matters of union organisation demanded much of his attention in the summer and autumn of 1917. However, political transformations and the sharpening economic crisis frustrated his efforts to improve workers' lives and encouraged him to support more radical measures.

Despite a high level of activism, metalworkers were among the last industrial workers to form a city-wide union in 1917. Reasons for this included individual metalworkers' political activism, such as leading demonstrations and organising soviets; the prominence in metalworking factories of elected factory committees, which had a stronger tradition in Russia as forms of workers' organisation than did trade unions; and the strong craft loyalty of many skilled workers, which made membership in a craft union more attractive than membership in a union of the industry in which they were employed. Finally, 'district patriotism' motivated some metalworkers, who worried that a central leadership could be less responsive than district-level leaders.[20]

Finally, on 23 April 1917, a constituent assembly of Petrograd district-level metalworker union representatives formally approved the Petrograd Metalworkers' Union's statutes. On 7 May, a citywide delegates' council elected

---

18   Anon 1917a; Shliapnikov 1917i, p. 5. Malakhovskii (Malakhovskii 1929) claimed that the Red Guard was revolutionary from the start (p. 5). In an unpublished article, Shliapnikov attacked Malakhovskii's claim, which in his opinion contradicted the party's actual goal of power through the soviets and through mass struggle (RGASPI, f. 70, op. 3, d. 896, ll. 5–6, '*Otvet eshche odnomu fal'sifikatoru istorii*').

19   RGASPI, f. 70, op. 4, d. 387, l. 132.

20   Smith 1983, pp. 104–5; Lepse 1927, p. 69.

a central board composed of Shlyapnikov, the unaffiliated socialist, Alexei Gastev, and the Menshevik, I.G. Volkov. Having recovered from injuries sustained in his car accident, Shlyapnikov chaired the first session of the central committee of the Petrograd Metalworkers' Union on 27 May. By 11 June, union leaders had begun to register the unemployed in labour exchanges and to find work for them. They had also set up a journal called *Metallist*. More importantly, they had begun to mediate conflicts between workers and industrialists, which was a major step towards boosting workers' confidence in the efficacy of a union.[21]

In many ways, the work of the Petrograd Metalworkers' Union laid the foundation for the All-Russian Metalworkers' Union, which worker delegates from all across Russia formed in late June/early July 1917.[22] Delegates elected Shlyapnikov and three other Bolsheviks to its central committee, which also included four Mensheviks. Shlyapnikov and the Menshevik Volkov tied for the largest number of votes. Gastev, the ninth member, soon aligned himself with the Bolsheviks.[23] Shlyapnikov was elected chair at the first meeting of the central committee, on 29 June 1917, perhaps due to Gastev's swing vote. Aside from making the Petrograd journal *Metallist* the all-Russian organ of the union, the committee could do little else at that time. All-Russian union leaders attended regional metalworker conferences, conferences of workers in the artillery department and soviet meetings, advised regional unions on organising and distributed literature to regional unions. Several members returned to work in their provincial unions. Those remaining in Petrograd became absorbed in tariff negotiations. Before the All-Russian Metalworkers' Union could fully function, many local problems had to be resolved, including the rivalry for members between the unions and factory committees.[24]

---

21   Anon 1917b, pp. 19–22; Bailes 1977, p. 385; GARF, f. 5469, op. 1, d. 33, I. 1, Metalworkers' Union board meeting, 27 May 1917. The union central committee included five representatives of each city district, elected by district assemblies.

22   The All-Russian Metalworkers' Union was formed simultaneously with the convocation of the Third All-Russian Conference of Trade Unions. The First All-Russian Conference of Trade Unions had been held in October 1905 and the second conference in late February 1906.

23   GARF, f. 5469, op. 1, d. 2, I. 4; Bulkin 1926, pp. 180, 190. Bulkin names Vladimirov instead of Volkov, but Vladimirov replaced Volkov only in mid-October 1917. Bulkin might have relied on the *Metallist*, 1–2 1917, for which the publication date is questionable.

24   GARF, f. 5469, op. 1, d. 4, II. 1–4; d. 33, I. 1; Gastev 1917, p. 24; Gol'tsman 1927, p. 66. Shliapnikov remembered attending the Moscow Oblast' Metalworkers' Union Conference in early October 1917 (Shliapnikov 1922a, pp. 11–12).

Shlyapnikov numbered among the moderate union leaders, including Bolsheviks and Mensheviks, who favoured the subordination of factory committees to industrial unions at the factory level. Bolshevik radicals, on the other hand, advocated an independent role for the committees. At the First Conference of the Petrograd Factory Committees, held on 30 May–5 June 1917, radical Bolsheviks won approval of a central council for the factory committees, thus unifying the factory-committee movement. The alarmed moderates saw this as a threat to trade unions, but the radicals held a stronger position. The radicals conceded that the Central Council of Factory Committees should coordinate its actions with the All-Russian Central Trade Union Council (VTsSPS), but there was no indication of any subordinate relationship. In addition, Shlyapnikov and some other moderate Bolsheviks won election to the Central Council of Factory Committees. When reporting the results to the Petrograd Metalworkers' Union, Shlyapnikov attemped to soften the blow by emphasising similarities and minimising differences between moderates and radicals, but his colleagues refused to surrender.[25]

The Metalworkers' Union did not accept the principle of factory-committee independence and quickly asserted that the trade union was to take priority over the factory committee in responsibility for workers' conduct. Furthermore, it declared that only the union could represent workers in negotiations with factory owners and the state, and in matters relating to workers' control ('control' usually meant 'supervision' of factory operations and working conditions, but the definition was not static, sometimes tending towards the more ambitious concept of worker administration of factories). Finally, it called for the complete subordination of the factory committees to the unions, which was a direct challenge to the authority of the Central Council of Factory Committees. Nevertheless, until the formal subjugation of factory committees to trade unions in early 1918, trade unions and factory committees continued to follow divergent policies.[26]

In the face of so many factors dividing metalworkers, Shlyapnikov and other union leaders searched for something to unite them. They found this in the struggle for a tariff, a system of wage rates for all categories of workers, upon which union leaders and industrialists would agree. This would address workers' dissatisfaction with working conditions and wages.[27] Factory committees

---

25   GARF, f. 5469, op. 1, d. 33, ll. 2–5; Shkliarevsky 1993, pp. 26–9.
26   Anon 1917b, p. 20; Shkliarevsky 1993, pp. xi–xiv.
27   Anon 1917c, p. 15. The Russian word *'tarif'* probably derived from the German word of the same spelling, meaning 'rates' (Zelnik 1995, p. 78, fn. 79). Shliapnikov usually used the word to mean wage rates.

had begun the fight for higher wages, but union representatives decided that a uniform standard was necessary. Uncoordinated efforts to achieve higher wages were paralysing and were fragmenting the labour movement. The union sought to create a more rational system of pay and working hours, to increase wages for unskilled workers, oversee hiring and firing decisions and 'to establish a procedure for the arbitration of disputes'. The tariff proved to be the most successful means of uniting metalworkers around their union, attracting workers away from factory committees and craft-based unions and building a strong organisation.[28]

As chair of the Metalworkers' Union, Shlyapnikov assumed primary responsibility for drawing up and negotiating the tariff. He was well-informed about tariffs already in place in Western industry as a result of his activity in French trade unions before World War I and his studies of unions in other Western-European countries. Gastev, who then worked alongside him, recalled later that Shlyapnikov's 'authority and competence' proved indispensable in this difficult struggle.[29] He and others in the commission based wage rates on the minimum cost of living, on professional qualifications, the difficulty and complexity of work and the danger of working conditions. With no pre-existing collections of statistics to guide them, commission members collected statistics on their own, factory-by-factory, and determined prices of essential groceries and goods. The union's contract categorised workers according to skill level and length of work experience.[30]

Before settling on a rates system, trade-union leaders and their tariff commission had to agree with leaders of unskilled metalworkers, who were especially militant in the spring of 1917. Their already low wages devastated by inflation in spring 1917, unskilled metalworkers formed their own union in early April to press for wage increases. In June they joined the Metalworkers' Union for greater negotiating leverage. In early June, the unskilled metalworkers of Vyborg District presented their wage demands to the leadership of the Metalworkers' Union. A strike of unskilled workers at the Putilov works briefly

---

28   Smith 1983, pp. 119–21.
29   Shliapnikov 1917g, p. 3; Gastev 1927, p. 67. It was no small gesture for Gastev to praise Shliapnikov, for in 1927 Shliapnikov was already under fierce attack for his memoirs' portrayal of the revolution and for his role in 1917. Other authors in this *Metallist* anniversary publication barely mentioned his role. For example, Ivan Lepse's article on the Petrograd Metalworkers' Union in 1917 did not name Shliapnikov at all (Lepse 1927, pp. 69–72).
30   Shliapnikov 1917g, pp. 3–4; Anon 1917b, p. 20 and Smith 1983, p. 122.

disrupted negotiations between union leaders and the unskilled, but also gave teeth to union demands in negotiations with factory owners.[31]

Shlyapnikov and other Petrograd Metalworkers' Union leaders entered tariff negotiations with the Society of Factory Owners and Manufacturers on 22 June. The Metals Department of the Provisional Government's Ministry of Labour (created in May 1917) mediated. Union leaders and representatives of the factory owners soon came to an initial agreement, but on 25 June the city-wide delegates' council of the Petrograd Metalworkers' Union presented obstacles to a compromise. Although the assembly approved 'guiding principles' for the tariff, it rejected all minimum-pay rates proposed by the Society of Factory Owners. Shlyapnikov believed that the great difference between the factory owners' proposed rates for the unskilled and for apprentices made a compromise difficult. Delegates especially fiercely objected to the factory owners' proposal that workers maintain a certain level of productivity in order to receive wages according to tariff rates.[32]

Shlyapnikov justified the guarantee of productivity by explaining that its acceptance gained credibility for the union in the eyes of 'bourgeois' society and the state, because it undermined capitalists' claims that workers wanted a guaranteed minimum wage without a guaranteed minimum of labour input. To allay the concerns of union delegates, the union's negotiators replaced the provision guaranteeing productivity with a provision on output norms, perhaps only a semantic difference. Before presenting the norms resolution to the delegates' assembly, Shlyapnikov had it approved not only by the Metalworkers' Union central board, but also by all regional boards and representatives of the Soviet and the political parties represented within it. Finally, union leaders threatened to resign if delegates did not cooperate. A delegates' assembly on 2 July caved in to their leaders' pressure and accepted the guarantee of productivity. Nevertheless, delegates made the caveat that such a guarantee made obligatory future discussion of implementing workers' control of production, which in their opinion was the only way to guarantee 'both labour productivity and the productivity of the enterprise as a whole'.[33] With the successful compromise, union negotiators calculated that they would soon agree with factory owners. On the next day, however, an abortive radical socialist uprising intervened, increasing friction between workers and industrialists and disrupting the tariff negotiators' timetable.

---

31   Smith 1983, pp. 121–4.
32   Shliapnikov 1917g, p. 4; Anon 1917b, p. 20 and Shliapnikov 1917b, p. 9.
33   Shliapnikov 1917g, p. 4; Anon 1917b, p. 20; Smith 1983, p. 125.

The July Days

In spring 1917, Russian military and political leaders prepared the last major Russian military offensive of World War I, aiming to force back German and Austrian forces, reinvigorate the morale of Russian troops and strengthen Russia's negotiating position in future peace talks. Conservatives, liberals and moderate socialists supported it, while Bolsheviks and Left SRs opposed it. Fearing high casualties, soldiers and workers believed the government should prioritise addressing economic problems over continuing the war. Their dissatisfaction was expressed in the protests of the 'June Days' in Petrograd, which culminated in an 18 June demonstration of nearly half a million people, most of them against the war. The offensive began impressively in Galicia that same day, but Russian troops soon fell back under the onslaught of a German counteroffensive.[34] The imminent collapse of the offensive, accompanied by a sharpened crisis in Petrograd's food and fuel supply, brought about a crisis of confidence in the government, which itself was in crisis after the 2 July resignation of Kadet ministers who opposed Ukrainian autonomy. The result was the July Uprising ('July Days').

Both workers and soldiers played important roles in the uprising. Unrest in each group fed dissatisfaction in the other. Soldiers, who feared being transferred to the front, began the uprising on 3 July. Members of the Bolshevik Military Organisation assisted the soldiers, despite the Bolshevik Party CC's orders to the contrary. Anarchists and Left SRs encouraged the soldiers. Workers, disgruntled over low wages and already on strike, joined the demonstrations. Despite the Soviet's condemnation, and the Bolshevik CC's opposition, soldiers and workers marched on the Tauride Palace, where the Soviet met. After tens of thousands of demonstrators surrounded the palace, the Bolshevik CC gave its support to the demonstrations and called for all power to the soviets. The Soviet majority, however, did not waver in its opposition to the uprising. As quickly as they had begun, the demonstrations subsided. This was due to 1) the Provisional Government's success in painting the Bolsheviks as German-sponsored saboteurs of the Russian war effort; 2) an upsurge in violence associated with the demonstrations and 3) news that loyal troops were on their way to Petrograd. The government quickly shut down *Pravda*, evicted the Bolsheviks from their party headquarters and arrested many of their

---

34 Wade 2000, pp. 172–80.

leaders. Lenin escaped arrest by going underground and fleeing in disguise to Finland in August.[35]

Shlyapnikov was aware that the tense mood in the capital could erupt into violence at any moment. When the uprising began, he was in tariff negotiations with representatives of the Society of Factory Owners. In a rash decision characteristic of the general mood, he commandeered a car belonging to one of the industrialists and immediately left for the Tauride Palace, where he witnessed demonstrations of workers and soldiers through the night of 3 July and the morning of 4 July. He spent the days of the uprising either at the Tauride Palace, in the Metalworkers' Union central offices or on the streets of Petrograd. All union work was suspended while he and other union leaders gave advice to workers.[36] Shlyapnikov understood the risks of a premature uprising. Neither encouraging nor attempting to halt the demonstrations, he merely informed workers who came to him of party resolutions (which either discouraged demonstrations, or later advocated only peaceful demonstrations), as he learned of them. In the unpredictable situation, he chose not to violate party discipline, but seemed prepared to let the 'masses' decide the course of events.

When the Provisional Government mustered loyal troops and cracked down on the Bolsheviks, the unions were also in the line of fire. A military patrol raided the central offices of the Metalworkers' Union on Fontanka, but Shlyapnikov's presence there, as a member of the Soviet's Executive Committee, saved the union from being shut down. The *Trud* publishing house, which printed much material for the Metalworkers' Union, was closed and some of its staff arrested. Its closure delayed by at least a month the publication of the first number of the union's journal, *Metallist*. Shlyapnikov attempted to use his authority as a member of the Soviet to get *Trud* staff released, but was unable to take them into his custody since he could not protect them from possible attack by pro-government soldiers. Having returned to the Tauride Palace, he demanded that the Soviet free them. Investigating the extent of the crackdown on the Bolshevik Party, Shlyapnikov found its headquarters in disarray and in the cus-

---

35 Rabinowitch 1991, pp. 135–214 and 1976, pp. 32–4; Wade 2000, pp. 181–4. For the role of the Kronstadt sailors, see Mawdsley 1978.

36 Shliapnikov 1992, vol. 3, kn. 4: pp. 592–5, 600, 621. Shliapnikov recalled seeing on 4 July armed detachments of the 'workers' guard' or 'factory militia' leading demonstrating workers on their way to the Tauride Palace, but other sources point to the Bolshevik Military Organisation as the moving force behind the July 1917 Uprising. Since membership in worker militias seems to have dropped precipitously during spring 1917, it is unlikely that they or the Red Guard played a significant role in the July Uprising (Shliapnikov 1992, vol. 3, p. 621; Rabinowitch 1991, p. 276, endnote 45). Some individuals, Kirill Orlov for one, belonged to both the Bolshevik Military Organisation and the Red Guard.

tody of soldiers. He could only hope that their occupation of it would prevent its restoration to its former owner, Madame Matilda Kshesinskaya (a ballerina rumoured to have had an affair with Tsar Nicholas II when he was in his youth). He and other Bolshevik trade-union leaders arranged for trade-union and factory-committee leaders to denounce the allegations against Bolshevik leaders of having been German agents.[37] There was little he could do to help the Bolsheviks further, for the popular mood had turned against them. Instead, his attention returned to resuming tariff negotiations, which the uprising had derailed.

Trade-Unionist Agenda

By the time tariff negotiations restarted on 12 July, the Society of Factory Owners, emboldened by the government's success in crushing the uprising, had decided not to compromise. The worsening economic crisis also hardened the industrialists' negotiating stance, as they feared that wage guarantees could threaten the survival of their businesses. Thus, the factory owners replaced 'liberal' negotiators with more conservative ones, who contested norms of wages by groups and categories. The industrialists' objection to rates was especially adamant in relation to unskilled workers, who made up the largest portion of the workforce.[38] Unable to agree on rates, union leaders and factory owners appealed to the Ministry of Labour to mediate. The Metalworkers' Union, under enormous pressure from unskilled members, prepared for a general strike of all workers in the industry. Shliapnikov and other union leaders took this step against the advice of Bolshevik Party leaders, who feared it was too extreme a step so soon after the July Days. On 22 July, the Ministry of Labour assigned wage rates to the unskilled and semi-skilled, which were less than what the union demanded, but more than what the factory owners offered. When the Society of Factory Owners refused to comply, an assembly of union delegates called a general strike. In response, the Ministry of Labour declared that it would compel factory owners to comply with the government's decision. Finding the Labour Ministry's offer acceptable, union leaders persuaded delegates to cancel their strike and to accept the offer as the best possible under existing conditions. Delegates expressed their dissatisfaction, however, in their final resolution, which stated that the workers' plight could

---

37 Shliapnikov 1992, vol. 3, kn. 4: pp. 620, 650–6, 669.
38 Flenley 1991; Shliapnikov 1917g, pp. 4–5. Shliapnikov's data on actual wages for unskilled workers came from his union's labour exchange.

only ultimately be resolved by social and economic legislation, the state regulation of industry and immediate peace. These preconditions, they believed, could only be fulfilled by a revolution that would bring workers to power. The Petrograd Metalworkers' Union and the Society of Factory Owners signed the tariff agreement on 7 August 1917.[39]

The Russian trade-union leaders' successful negotiation of a tariff in the midst of the revolutionary year 1917 was a remarkable achievement, even though inflation and the high cost of living rapidly outpaced its norms. It was a major accomplishment of the Metalworkers' Union to put the agreement into force in most Petrograd factories by October 1917, when the industrial economy was in complete crisis. Shlyapnikov admitted that Russian economic conditions in 1917 made the tariff agreement of limited immediate use. Moreover, he acknowledged that it had not addressed the exploitative relationship between capitalist and worker. On the other hand, he saw in the tariff a step towards unity for workers, for it set a standard and ceased the practice of pitting workers against one another. Once the tariff was in place, increases in rates could be negotiated. Unions and factory committees would cooperate in forming a rate commission, which would represent each major shop within the factory. All representatives had to be union members and had to be responsible both to their electorate and to the union, a provision that gave unions precedence over factory committees. If workers disapproved of their elected representatives' actions, they would present their grievances to the union rather than unilaterally recall representatives.[40] Commission members would be accountable both to their worker electorate and to union leaders. This set an important precedent for the broader programme that Shlyapnikov would present in 1920–1 as leader of the Workers' Opposition.

The tariff was only one way of strengthening the Russian unions. Another struggle in which Shlyapnikov played a central role was absorbing craft unions into industrial unions, which had a potentially broader base and were more relevant to an industry composed mostly of large factories. The craft-based unions' failure to join the industrial union greatly hindered its attempts to carry out negotiations or strikes involving all occupations in the metalworking industry.[41] The Petrograd Metalworkers' Union absorbed more than twenty craft-based unions in early 1917, but faced strong resistance from several groups. Much of Shlyapnikov's work on behalf of the Metalworkers' Union in

---

39   Smith 1983, pp. 125–6; Anon 1917b, p. 21.
40   Smith 1983, p. 129; Shliapnikov 1917g, pp. 3, 6.
41   Bonnell (ed.) 1983, p. 231.

1917 involved persuading, pressuring or coercing reluctant craft-based unions to join the larger unions.

Shlyapnikov argued that it was counterproductive for several different unions to exist in the same factory and encouraged his sympathisers to pressure reluctant craftsmen to join the industrial union. Providing specific examples of cases when the independent actions of craft-based unions had harmed other workers, he reasoned that workers in craft-based unions were not likely to achieve their own particular goals without the leverage created by the support of other workers. As a concession, he allowed that the crafts might preserve some autonomy once they were within an industrial union. As an example, he pointed to electricians who had joined the Metalworkers' Union while preserving for themselves a profession-based commission.[42] His approach indicated a willingness to compromise and to consider the sensitivities of workers who held different opinions to his own.

Shlyapnikov believed that the Metalworkers' Union, as the strongest union in Petrograd, had to take the lead in ending craft-based unions. He maintained that those who stubbornly remained in craft-based unions were among the minority. Neither highly qualified nor unskilled metalworkers objected to their integration into a production union. Both groups readily agreed to present their grievances to the union for arbitration. The more troublesome targets of unionisation included craftsmen with a strong guild mentality, such as stokers, welders, pattern makers and woodworkers, all of whom worked in the metals, textile and leather industries. However, because they were few in number (less than one thousand workers per profession), he believed that it would be easy to subject them to pressure.[43] The Woodturners' Union was actually quite large and its intransigent leaders refused calls from the metalworkers and other industrial unions to allow woodturners to join their ranks. The Woodturners' Union also rejected wage rates negotiated by the industrial unions on their behalf. In mid-October, they called a strike, which Shlyapnikov condemned.

Only after the October Revolution did the woodworkers end their strike. Nevertheless, compared to other countries, Russia made great strides towards industrial unionism in 1917.[44] Both the tariff negotiations and the absorption of craft unions brought many new workers into unions. For example, the Petrograd Metalworkers' Union membership went from seventy thousand in June to more than one hundred and forty thousand by October, perhaps

---

42 Shliapnikov 1917j, pp. 13–14.
43 Shliapnikov 1917c, p. 2. The unions of the stokers and welders only joined the Metalworkers' Union in 1918 (Smith 1983, pp. 106–7).
44 Smith 1983, pp. 107–9; Shkliarevsky 1993, p. 69.

even one hundred and ninety thousand (between one-third and one-half of all trade-union members in Petrograd).[45] Shliapnikov was only one of many union leaders who called for the amalgamation of craft-based unions into industrial unions, but he determinedly pursued this goal and it must be counted as a success that he and the other leaders of the Metalworkers' Union persuaded so many craft-based unions to join them.

Another very contentious issue that faced Shliapnikov and other union leaders was whether unions should take a stand on political questions, a conflict that probably reminded him of a similar one that had divided French trade unionists during his years in Paris. 'Internationalists' favoured intervention in political issues that affected workers' lives, such as the World War, while 'neutralists' believed that unions should limit themselves strictly to economic questions, such as pay rates and the length of the working day. Like most Bolsheviks, Shliapnikov favoured politicising the trade unions, which meant taking a stance against the war, against cooperation with liberals and for a world socialist revolution. Many Mensheviks were 'neutralists', fearing that involvement in politics would weaken the unions' ability to fight for the workers' economic rights. SRs could be found on both sides. Some neutralists thought that trade unions should push for greater social and political democracy, but that unions should not take stands on individual political questions. Most Menshevik trade unionists did not want unions to advocate the transfer of all power to the soviets, while most Bolsheviks did. In 1917, many Mensheviks and SRs worked within the Petrograd Metalworkers' Union. Shliapnikov was more patient with fellow workers who were Mensheviks or SRs than with the *intelligenty* of rival parties. But many positions were in flux in 1917 and a number of individuals switched positions and even parties during the course of that year.[46] Despite his deep commitment to Bolshevism, Shliapnikov was able to work with non-Bolshevik socialists in the Metalworkers' Union in 1917. His earlier trade-union activism in France may have conditioned him to attempt persuasion towards those with whom he disagreed.

Cooperation with other socialists was especially important in autumn 1917, as the All-Russian Metalworkers' Union, with Shliapnikov as its chair, expanded its activities. The Petrograd metalworkers presented their tariff as a model for other city and regional unions and as an important unifying measure. In fact,

---

45 Shliapnikov 1917h, p. 11; Smith 1983, p. 105. The higher number comes from Anskii 1928 and the lower number was an estimate by the Provisional Government's Ministry of Labour.

46 Shkliarevsky 1993, p. 71; Smith 1983, pp. 110–12. For a breakdown by district of each party's supporters, see Smith 1983, pp. 104–5, 113. For an elucidation of the complex political fluctuations in 1917, see Wade 2000, especially Chapter Three.

Shlyapnikov emphasised to those outside Petrograd that the tariff's main benefit in contemporary conditions was as an 'organising and mobilising tool'. In late September, work began on an all-Russian tariff and on a plan for workers' control of industrial enterprises. The union's plan presented financial control to the highest regulatory government institutions and called for a factory technical assembly to provide technical and administrative leadership of the enterprise. The assembly would consist of workers' representatives, technical supervisors and commercial managers of the factory. Union leaders also intended to push for union representatives to join state economic regulatory institutions. They resolved (on 13 October) to convoke a constituent congress in Petrograd or Moscow at the end of November.[47] But the October Revolution intervened, substantially altering the trade unionists' agenda.

Bolsheviks Come to Power

The Bolshevik Party had been hit hard by government repression and quite a bit of popular disapproval after the failed July Uprising, for which it was blamed. The Bolsheviks' opportunity for recovery came in late August 1917. Over the summer, the Provisional Government underwent a change in composition, losing some liberals and gaining socialists. Kerensky became Prime Minister. Yet strong political differences among parties represented in the government contributed to its increasing inability to stop the spiralling trend towards chaos in Russia. Those on the right reasserted themselves, seeking a strong man to restore order. They believed they had found him in General Lavr Kornilov, a Cossack with a heroic reputation but a weak comprehension of politics. The government's restoration of the death penalty in the army and measures to crush worker and peasant initiative were viewed by the radical left as ominous forebodings of counterrevolution. Even some liberals began to move towards the right. Meanwhile, the general population seemed to be radicalising in a leftward direction. On 27–31 August, the Kornilov Affair marked a watershed moment in 1917 politics, as an effort by Kerensky and Kornilov to prepare martial law in Petrograd collapsed in mutual suspicion. The Soviet, the socialist parties, the Red Guards and the railway workers cooperated to prevent what they perceived as an attempted coup by Kornilov. Kerensky was discredited, but the Bolsheviks were redeemed, along with the rest of the radical left.[48]

---

47 Gol'tsman 1918, p. 3; Shliapnikov 1917h, p. 10; GARF, f. 5469, op. 1, d. 4, ll. 28–9.
48 Wade 2000, pp. 194–205. I found no record of Shliapnikov playing a prominent role in the Bolshevik response to the Kornilov Affair.

The popular mood had grown more radical in Russia over the summer. A peasant rebellion had gathered steam, as state power in the countryside dissipated and peasants seized control of land that they had long desired. Socialist Revolutionaries had established peasant soviets, but peasants often acted through land committees they constituted themselves and grew increasingly frustrated with the Provisional Government's hesitation to implement land reform. Along the borderlands, minority nationalities that at first had sought autonomy increasingly began to seek independence from the collapsing Russian Empire. While liberals and moderate socialists were reluctant to accommodate national self-determination, Lenin's already developed stance on national autonomy allowed Bolsheviks and other radical leftists to ally with minority nationalists. Worker discontent grew over factory closings and, as the supply crisis grew sharper, urban residents generally struggled to feed themselves and heat their homes.[49]

Lenin and other radical Bolsheviks began to urge an armed insurrection to wrest control from the Provisional Government. Moderate Bolsheviks, on the other hand, called for the transfer of power to a government formed from socialist parties represented in the Soviet. Fears were growing among government officials, and in other parties, of a Bolshevik-led insurrection that would result in a dictatorship. Suspicion of the Bolsheviks was voiced at the Democratic State Conference, held in Petrograd in September. Shlyapnikov, who at this time considered himself a moderate Bolshevik, sat on the conference presidium. He remembered later how Nikolai Avksentev, an SR who served as Interior Minister in the Provisional Government, goaded him: 'Take power, the masses are behind you'. Shlyapnikov jokingly asked if Avksentev would voluntarily relinquish power to the Bolsheviks. Laughter ensued, and the delegates did not press him further.[50] Shlyapnikov was no longer a party CC member after it was re-elected in April 1917; his injuries in a car accident had deprived him of the opportunity to stand for election. Although he rarely attended its meetings in autumn 1917, his position as Metalworkers' Union chair made his support for an uprising crucial.

The radicals' attempts were initially rebuffed within the Bolshevik Party. In late September 1917 the Bolshevik CC held a strategic session at which its members dismissed Lenin's proposal for a mass uprising. Moderates, as well as those leftists sympathetic to Lenin's appeals, were aware that the Bolshevik Party did not have enough influence among Russian industrial workers to rouse them to insurrection. They also felt that Lenin did not appreciate the workers'

---

49   Wade 2000, pp. 140–9, 188.
50   Shliapnikov 1922a, pp. 8, 10.

deep desire for a revolutionary, but broad-based and democratic government founded on the soviets. Finally, they saw Lenin's plan as unwarranted in its desperation. There was no immediate threat from the right. Moderates looked to the October Congress of Soviets to take power in the name of all socialist parties in the Soviet.[51]

In late September and early October, Lenin cajoled and bullied to get his way, arguing that the European proletariat was on the verge of revolution, the initiation of which depended on Bolsheviks taking power in Russia. Gathering behind him more militant Bolsheviks who composed a majority in the Petersburg Committee, he revealed to them that the CC had censored his articles in late September, cutting the most radical parts. This revelation brought even the holdouts to his side in sympathy. Radical Bolsheviks gained more support when they accused the Provisional Government of planning to surrender Petrograd to the Germans and thereby 'crush' Russia's revolutionary centre. By the time Bolshevik leaders met on 10 October, Kamenev and Zinoviev were the only two moderates who voted against Lenin. The CC voted 10–2 to organise an armed uprising. A number of moderates such as Alexei Rykov and Viktor Nogin, who would have supported Zinoviev and Kamenev, were not present. Shlyapnikov was in Moscow in early October, attending the Moscow Oblast Metalworkers' Union Conference. There he heard metalworkers demand, with immediacy in their tone, soviet power, nationalisation of large industry and transport and the implementation of workers' control (supervision) over production.[52]

Moderate parties began to get wind of Bolshevik intentions and newspapers began warning of a Bolshevik coup attempt. A simultaneous shake-up in the leadership of the All-Russian Union of Metalworkers may have been linked to revolutionary politics. At a meeting on 15 October, Ershov (a Bolshevik) became a full member of the central committee. When committee members re-elected their leading bureau, only three votes were cast for Volkov (a Menshevik), who consequently quit the central committee.[53] Mikhail Vladimirov (a Bolshevik)

---

51   Rabinowitch 1976, pp. 170, 187.
52   Rabinowitch 1976, pp. 193–6, 201–6; Shliapnikov 1922a, pp. 11–12. It seems that Shliapnikov did not attend the 10 October meeting. When he wrote his memoirs of these days, his memory was not precise regarding the dates of secret meetings. The meeting he recalled attending was probably on 16 October (Shliapnikov 1922a, p. 13).
53   Rabinowitch 1976, p. 215; GARF, f. 5469, op. 1, d. 4, ll. 29–31. Busy in the Petrograd Metalworkers' Union and Sovnarkom, Shliapnikov missed the 15 October meeting and subsequent ones through 28 December. Volkov may have been arrested in a Bolshevik repressive action against the Mensheviks in July 1918 (Brovkin (ed.) 1991, p. 122).

replaced him as treasurer.[54] By this time, most of the Mensheviks had stopped working in the central committee anyway, but the vote gave the Bolsheviks an official majority. Therefore, Shlyapnikov did not have to contend, even formally, with Menshevik opinions when deciding what stance the Metalworkers' Union should take towards the October Revolution. Nevertheless, Bolshevik metalworkers hesitated.

On 16 October there was a meeting of Bolsheviks from all revolutionary organisations – the Petersburg Committee, the party CC, the Bolshevik Military Organisation, the Petrograd Soviet, the trade unions and the factory shops. They were divided over whether and when to seize power. Many participants, including Shlyapnikov and other trade-union leaders, spoke of a lack of resources and a lack of commitment by workers and soldiers to exclusive Bolshevik rule. Vasily Shmidt, from the Petrograd Council of Trade Unions, warned that union members could not be relied upon to take direct action towards seizing power in the name of the soviets, for they 'fear[ed]...dismissals and layoffs'. Shlyapnikov supported Shmidt, explaining that even in the mostly pro-Bolshevik Metalworkers' Union recent 'rumours' of 'a Bolshevik coming-out...had even triggered panic'.[55]

Shlyapnikov later asserted that before the 16 October meeting he had been unaware of disagreements within the party CC. Once in attendance he was confronted with majority support in the CC for Lenin's position on taking power. He recalled that he believed at that time that the party had not sufficiently elaborated its position on vital economic questions. At the meeting, he asked the CC to take a definite position on economic questions in Petrograd, but party leaders could only offer 'the abstract slogan of "workers' control"'. He concluded that the party's decision to take power was based primarily, if not purely, on political calculations, not economics. Emphasising that trade unions were left to figure out economic problems on their own, he implied

---

54 Anon 1917b, p. 23. Strangely, Vladimirov's elevation was reported in an article supposedly published two months before the event. Perhaps the issue's publication was delayed until October, which would make other content equally suspect. Vladimirov (1880–1938), an RSDRP member since 1899, worked in metals factories in Sormovo, Moscow and Petersburg. He was arrested and exiled to Siberia several times. From 1917 to 1922, he was secretary and treasurer of the Metalworkers' Union's central committee (Vilenskii-Sibiriakov et al. (eds.) 1974, pp. 10–11; Eremina and Roginskii (eds.) 2000). This is not Miron Konstantinovich Vladimirov, who worked in the People's Commissariat of Food Supply [Narkomprod] and died of natural causes in 1926.

55 Rabinowitch 1976, pp. 218–19, 221.

that the defence of workers' economic interests was always a top priority with unions, if not with the party.⁵⁶

A significant minority of those who voted on 16 October were unwilling to approve an 'immediate insurrection'. How Shlyapnikov voted is not clear; if he voted with the majority, it was probably with reservations. Lenin and the Bolshevik Military Organisation wanted to make the government takeover an accomplished fact before the Second Congress of Soviets began on 25 October. Events proceeded quickly. Having won over the garrison on the night of 21–2 October, on the next day the Bolsheviks organised large demonstrations at which their speakers warned of surrender of the city to the Germans. On 24 October, Kerensky closed Bolshevik printing presses. Trotsky responded by calling the Bolshevik Military Revolutionary Committee (MRC), formed on 20 October, to arms.

By the morning of 25 October, the Military Revolutionary Committee and troops loyal to the left had won major strategic points in the city. Kerensky fled the capital for the city of Pskov, in order to rendezvous with loyal troops and prepare a counteroffensive. When the Congress of Soviets opened late in the evening on 25 October, the Bolsheviks had the largest representation, but in order to form a majority they had to ally with Left SRs. Incensed by the Bolsheviks' coup, the Mensheviks and SRs withdrew from the congress, leaving the Bolsheviks free to form a government, which moderate socialists did not think would last. Early on the morning of 26 October, Bolshevik forces seized the Winter Palace and arrested the government ministers meeting there. On 27 October, the Congress of Soviets confirmed the Council of People's Commissars [*Sovnarkom*], which replaced the old cabinet of ministers. Shlyapnikov became Commissar of Labour; he was one of only two commissars who could claim a proletarian background.⁵⁷

Despite his doubts, Shlyapnikov aided the October Revolution at its most crucial points. On 25 October, he convened a special session of the leadership of the Petrograd Metalworkers' Union, which approved his resolution appealing to metalworkers 'to unite behind the slogan of the Petrograd Soviet'. The union also gave the Petrograd Soviet fifty thousand rubles from its funds. (Mensheviks later accused Shlyapnikov of having bought the post of Commissar of Labour). Shlyapnikov organised fighting and medical brigades

---

56   Shliapnikov 1922a, pp. 13–14.
57   Rabinowitch 1976, pp. 222–306. The other was Viktor Nogin (1878–1924), who, although the son of a salesman, had worked in Petersburg factories. Commissars Pavel Dybenko and Aleksei Rykov were from the peasantry; Rykov had a university education and Dybenko was a sailor.

FIGURE 17   *Soviet Council of People's Commissars, 1917;*
Shlyapnikov is second-from-right in the top row.
Lenin is in the centre. Others pictured include Iosif
Stalin, Alexei Rykov, Pavel Dybenko, Anatoly
Lunacharsky and Lev Trotsky.

of metalworkers, gathered weapons at the Putilov factory for the Red Guard and collected barbed wire for defence of the approaches to Petrograd. Trade-union leaders had found the Ministry of Labour unable or unwilling to enforce the unions' agreements with industrialists and they hoped that soviet power would 'end political and economic instability and…enhance the unions' economic role'.[58] Thus, Shlyapnikov worked for the success of the October Revolution in the interests of the trade-union movement and offered allegiance to the Petrograd Soviet.

---

58   Shliapnikov 1922a, pp. 21–2; RGASPI, f. 70, op. 4, d. 387, l. 134; Shkliarevsky 1993, 96–7.

Conclusion

Shlyapnikov reacted to the revolutionary events of 1917 with both caution and radicalism. He numbered among those politically radical Bolsheviks who opposed the Provisional Government, promoted a coalition government of revolutionary socialist parties and called for an end to the war. By late March 1917, Bolshevik moderates had presented their position as that of the party majority, circumventing the Russian Bureau of the CC, which Shlyapnikov led. With the return of Lenin and other CC members from abroad in April 1917, the role of the Russian Bureau diminished even more. Nevertheless, Shlyapnikov found a vital calling in his work as a trade-union leader and tariff negotiator. For him, the economic struggle of summer 1917 was at least as important as the political struggle on the streets and in the soviet. His trade-union work may have brought him closer to the position of Bolshevik moderates, who had edged him out of a central role in party politics in March.

It is not entirely surprising that Shlyapnikov's involvement in tariff negotiations in summer 1917 moderated his political stance somewhat. Union leaders not only had to restrain the union members' radical impulses, but also had to work together with other trade unionists of varying political persuasions. During the summer of 1917, Shlyapnikov came to better understand how volatile the revolutionary situation was and to believe it necessary to form a relatively broad coalition to take power. In the summer of 1917, his statements accorded with the (moderate) Bolshevik programme that called for soviet power and a socialist coalition government, until a constituent assembly could create a new political system.

Due to their commitment to improving workers' everyday lives, expressed most visibly in tariff agreements, the unions acquired the respect and loyalty of many workers. Nevertheless, the frustrations of tariff negotiations and the inability to address fundamental inequities made Shlyapnikov more determined in his belief that only revolution could accomplish real change. Difficulties in extracting concessions from industrialists and the weakness of the Provisional Government seem to have frustrated him to the point that he was eager for the triumph of soviet power. He hoped that a soviet socialist government would bring about the passage of social legislation and elevate unions to the management of the economy and the regulation of production.[59] In August 1917, the leaders of the Metalworkers' Union began to call more

---

59 Smith 1983, p. 217. The Petrograd Metalworkers' Union led the campaign for these goals, even though the All-Russian Trade Union Conference had explicitly rejected a role for the unions in managing the economy.

insistently for a Soviet government. Neither Shlyapnikov nor other leaders of the Metalworkers' Union considered a Bolshevik seizure of power as appropriate. After the experience of the July Days, they were uneasy about revolutionary outbursts that could set back the movement. In October he and other Metalworkers' Union leaders helped bring the Bolsheviks to power, but in the name of the Soviet. Shlyapnikov recalled the days of the October Revolution as a time of optimism. Workers' initiative was at its zenith and the Bolshevik programme was closer to the spirit of the masses than at any time after the revolution. He never forgot that both non-Bolshevik and Bolshevik metalworkers ensured the success of the October Revolution.[60]

---

60   Avilov 1917, p. 3; RGASPI, f. 70, op. 4, d. 387, l. 134; f. 589, op. 3, d. 9103, vol. 5, l. 22.

CHAPTER 4

Labour Commissar

The realities of holding power contrasted sharply with the emancipatory dreams of 1917. In the early months of Soviet rule, as counterrevolutionary armies formed and German troops surged into Russian territory, the Bolsheviks faced a fierce fight for the survival of their regime. Rapidly issuing decrees to mollify diverse leftist constituencies, they acquiesced to peasants seizing large estates, proclaimed workers' control of factories, nationalised banks, transport and communications, and began peace negotiations. While organising a government and army, they also aspired to craft a socialist society. Despite their increase in membership over the course of 1917, they were still a small urban party with no control over large swathes of the collapsing empire. To cope with developing crises and multiple agendas, the Bolsheviks often occupied multiple party, state and military posts and carried out divergent assignments in various parts of the country, shifting rapidly from one work assignment or geographic area to another. Shlyapnikov regarded the work of the trade unions as crucial to the foundation of socialism and attempted to utilise his new power as Commissar of Labour to increase their role in economic management and government. Nevertheless, other demands on his time, including overseeing the early stage of the evacuation of industry from Petrograd and transporting food from the south to cities in the north, distracted him from the commissariat's work. The contrast between his ideals and his disappointment with the flaws that developed in the Soviet system surfaces in this chapter and develops in the next.

Shlyapnikov's political behaviour fluctuated in late 1917 and early 1918, illustrating the fluidity of moderate and radical positions in the revolutionary context. Not only did revolutionaries migrate between moderate and radical views across time, but they sometimes held moderate and radical positions on different issues at the same time. Initially a moderate on the question of a coalition government, Shlyapnikov then followed Lenin's radical line towards the Constituent Assembly. Nevertheless, he took some moderate economic positions that conflicted with Lenin's short-term political goals. Shlyapnikov's policies were oriented towards including workers in economic policy-making and planning, provided that these workers were socialist, even if they were not Bolshevik. Assuming that the Bolsheviks would take over the trade unions by political persuasion, out of political considerations he would not have undermined the role of the union. Nevertheless, his attempts to give economic power to the unions may actually have contributed to undermining their independence and their ability to defend workers. The economic power of the union was closely tied to Bolshevik decisions on how to hold onto political power.

The Question of Power

The question of maintaining power confronted the Bolsheviks as soon as they had wrested control from the Provisional Government. Party moderates, led by Zinoviev and Kamenev, believed that the Bolsheviks were too weak to stay in power alone and favoured a coalition government including representatives of other socialist parties. Shlyapnikov was among those moderates who objected to the exclusively Bolshevik composition of the government formed at the Second Congress of Soviets. On 3 November the Soviet's Central Executive Committee (VTsIK) voted in favour of Kamenev's and Zinoviev's resolution to bring other socialist parties into the government. Lenin reacted furiously, threatening to 'expel' the opposition from the party. In response, most moderates resigned from their CC and government posts. The subsequent inclusion of the Left SRs in the government appeased many of the moderates, however.[1]

Although Shlyapnikov signed Zinoviev's and Kamenev's statement in support of a coalition socialist government, he refused to resign as Commissar of Labour because he did not want to abandon work. Although the moderates had explicitly called for an agreement with all the parties represented in the Soviet, Shlyapnikov later claimed that when he signed the statement he only wanted Left SRs included. Under pressure from Lenin, he reneged on support for a coalition socialist government:

> When this document appeared, Lenin said to me, 'So you're stepping down'. I said, 'Nothing of the sort, I wrote that I'm not resigning'. He took me by the arm and before the [Bolshevik] fraction of the VTsIK I declared my support for an agreement with the SRs, but stated that I oppose an agreement with the Mensheviks.[2]

Nevertheless, Shlyapnikov continued to act moderately in the early days of the Bolshevik Revolution. When the Bolsheviks seized power, most government-ministry employees went on strike to hinder the efforts of the new commissars to establish control of the ministries. Each commissar coped in different ways.

---

1 Rabinowitch 1976, pp. 309–10.
2 RGASPI, f. 589, op. 3, d. 9103, vol. 5, ll. 19–21.

Some, such as Trotsky, responded with massive arrests. Shlyapnikov proudly recounted securing the Ministry of Labour with tact and persuasion, rather than force. Because he had visited the premises often during tariff negotiations, guards and other lower-level personnel already knew him. He recalled: 'Without the slightest violence, without any threats at all, even without raising my voice, with simple comradely explanation I won over the lower-level personnel of the Ministry of Labour'. He issued an appeal to the mid-level and senior bureaucrats on strike, which simply stated that if they did not return to their posts by the next workday, he would replace them. A month later, the senior staff was ready to capitulate. Shlyapnikov responded that he had filled their positions, but that their petitions for employment would be reviewed.[3] His pride in peacefully accomplishing his goals may have had more to do with the emphasis he placed on self-discipline and professional skills as a revolutionary than with a principled objection to violent tactics.

Yet Shlyapnikov even seemed willing to take a moderate position towards 'enemies of the revolution'. On 19 November 1917, Sovnarkom approved Trotsky's recommendation to arrest generals Alexei Manikovsky and Vladimir Marushevsky, because Manikovsky (the War Minister) ordered that elected commanders should not replace appointed ones and Marushevsky interfered with armistice negotiations. Sovnarkom resolved to purge the military ministry and to obligate each People's Commissar to conduct and report daily on purges among their commissariat staff. At a Sovnarkom meeting two days later, Shlyapnikov, Nikolai Podvoisky and Kollontai called for Manikovsky to be freed from arrest and allowed to occupy a 'responsible position'. However, in the face of Trotsky's opposition, the suggestion was defeated. Further, as the protocols stated, 'moderates' were warned 'to deepen efforts to purge counter-revolutionary nests and not to raise again the question of changing the policy of the dictatorship of workers and peasants, directed against leading counter-revolutionaries'. A week and a half later, Sovnarkom resolved to release the two generals on bail. The motives behind the objections of the three Sovnarkom members are hard to define. Podvoisky, Commissar of Military and Naval Affairs, was probably disturbed by the disruption that the arrests had caused among the staff of the commissariat he led.[4] Kollontai often interceded on behalf of the arrested and Shlyapnikov preferred alternatives to arrests.

Shlyapnikov's opposition to a campaign of arrests was probably limited to its harmful impact on the work of the institutions. There is no record that he was

---

3   Shliapnikov 1922a, 25, 41; GARF, f. 130, op. 1, d. 110, 27 October 1917.
4   GARF, f. 130, op. 1, d. 1, ll. 8, 12, 22, 19–30 November 1917; Lenin 1960–70, vol. 42, pp. 38–9; Clements 1979, p. 123; Molodtsygin 1991, pp. 381–2; Voitikov 2007, pp. 3–12.

concerned about the fate of 'bourgeois' politicians. Around this time, the liberal Kadet party was disbanded and its leaders arrested. On 28 November, the day the Constituent Assembly was scheduled to meet, Sovnarkom approved Lenin's proposal to arrest Kadet leaders and directed that they be turned over to a revolutionary court. Stalin was the only member to vote against the proposal.[5] Shlyapnikov was not present at this session and his stance is unknown. Likewise, it is not known how he initially responded to the creation of the Cheka, the Soviet secret police led by Felix Dzerzhinsky, which was founded to combat currency speculation, sabotage and counterrevolution.

Despite Shlyapnikov's moderate stances on particular issues and perhaps as a way of radicalising his position, the CC entrusted him with Bolshevik preparations for the Constituent Assembly. His exemplary organisational skills were needed. Kamenev and a group of Bolshevik moderates had taken over the provisional bureau of the Bolshevik delegation to the Constituent Assembly in early December, hoping to have it adopt their stance, which accepted the assembly's authority in forming a new government. They were thwarted by the Bolshevik CC, which arranged a meeting of selected Bolshevik delegates on 12 December 1917, who approved Lenin's proposals on the Constituent Assembly and formed a new provisional bureau, with Shlyapnikov as chair. Shlyapnikov later insisted that he took a hard-line view of the assembly and wholeheartedly endorsed its closure because he believed that the soviets were a higher form of democracy than the Constituent Assembly, which in his view was more suited to a bourgeois government. Thus he accepted the Bolshevik line that elections conducted for the assembly in early October did not reflect the views of the masses by the time it convened, and that the assembly had become the 'bourgeoisie's' last hope of creating a conservative government to preserve private property.[6]

Shlyapnikov's stance on the Constituent Assembly, therefore, was not at all moderate, but coincided exactly with the evaluation of the assembly by Lenin and other radicals. The CC must have trusted that, when faced with moderate arguments, he would remain firm and would convince others to remain firm. Menshevik delegates to the First Trade Union Congress, which opened shortly after the Bolsheviks had dispersed the Constituent Assembly and shot demonstrators, jeered Shlyapnikov during his opening address and remonstrated against him chairing the congress. Voicing the opinion that in a situation verging on civil war it was impossible not to have innocent victims, he nevertheless expressed doubts that the demonstrators were innocent, perhaps disingenu-

---

5   GARF, f. 130, op. 1, d. 1, l. 20, 28 November 1917.
6   Rabinowitch 2007, pp. 88–91; Shliapnikov 1924b, pp. 9–10.

ously giving credence to false rumours that they were carrying bombs and guns. In later reminiscences, he still did not express any regrets at the shooting of demonstrators who supported the Constituent Assembly.[7]

Shlyapnikov believed that it was important to work with proletarians of different political views, but he was not devoted to the principle of political pluralism. Perhaps the election results that showed widespread support for Bolsheviks in urban areas, and among factory workers, were decisive in determining his view of the Constituent Assembly. Another factor was absorption in his work as Commissar of Labour, for he likely began to see the commissariat's economic work as far more crucial than the question of fair political representation. Shlyapnikov was surely optimistic that he could use his new powers to improve the lives of workers. A newsreel film depicting more than a dozen Soviet leaders in early 1918 shows Shlyapnikov smiling broadly at the film crew, then feigning a serious expression as he shuffles through papers. Breaking into a wry smile, he poked fun at the dignity of his position, while enjoying its authority.[8]

Commissariat of Labour

The Bolsheviks struggled to establish a government of an entirely new type while their enemies mobilised against them and the economy collapsed around them. In this unpredictable and rapidly evolving context, Shlyapnikov aspired to a broad role for the Commissariat of Labour [*Narkomtrud*]. Rather than simply mediating between workers and management (as the Provisional Government's Ministry of Labour had done), Narkomtrud would promote workers' welfare and collaborate with trade unions to organise and regulate industry. Nevertheless, Narkomtrud faced tremendous challenges: the ambitions of the factory committees, the workers' interpretations of the state's responsibilities towards them, the need to ensure labour discipline and the intransigent leaders of non-Bolshevik unions. There were dissensions internal to Narkomtrud, for some in its leadership disagreed with Shlyapnikov on the relationship between trade unions and the government, such as the Mensheviks, SRs and a number of Bolsheviks. The threat of counterrevolution overshadowed the Bolsheviks' new political, social and economic experiment, making their struggle more desperate.

---

7 VTsSPS 1918, pp. 2, 5, 7; Shliapnikov 1924b, pp. 9–10.
8 https://www.youtube.com/watch?v=czIjQIBlaEc&feature=player_embedded#! (06:00–06:12).

FIGURE 18   *Meeting of the Council of People's Commissars, circa January–March 1918. Alexander Shlyapnikov is sixth from the left. Others pictured include Lenin, Stalin, Kollontai and Pavel Dybenko.*

FIGURE 19 *Sketch of Alexander Shlyapnikov by Yuri Artsybushev, circa December 1917–January 1918, in Artsybushev 1918, p. 21 (New York Public Library Digital Gallery).*

Shlyapnikov filled key Narkomtrud positions with trade-union staff, because he believed that their expertise in the regulation of wages and working conditions qualified them to perform these duties in the government. Pursuing a partisan approach, he invited Bolsheviks and Left SRs to work, but held members of other parties at arm's length. The metalworkers', textile workers' and leather workers' unions (all controlled by Bolsheviks) contributed the most staff to Narkomtrud and had representatives in the commissariat's board (collegium). VTsSPS was controlled by the Mensheviks in late 1917, so Shlyapnikov did not request staff from it. Hoping to ensure the continued strong influence of the unions within government, he encouraged trade unionists to enter into other commissariats and government bodies, for example the All-Russian Council of National Economy (VSNKh), which he helped to establish by Sovnarkom order. In its first several months of existence, VSNKh was run by Left Communists like Valerian Obolensky (N. Osinsky), who favoured worker administration of factories, but when the Left Communists resigned from government in March 1918, VSNKh (under Lenin's direction) revised its stance to advocate appointed factory boards supervised by workers' organisations.[9]

Other socialists perceived flaws in Shliapnikov's strategy. In January 1918, at the First Trade Union Congress, chaired by Shliapnikov, the debate over trade-union participation in government flared up dramatically. E.H. Carr wrote that the congress 'virtually settled the principle of the subordination of the trade unions to the state, which now remained uncontested ... for nearly three years'. Menshevik delegates regarded the introduction of trade unionists into state institutions as syndicalist. Due to his experience in France, however, Shliapnikov defined syndicalism differently, namely as a decentralised movement that isolated unions from political power. In his opening speech, he declared that the unions should be equal to other governing bodies and should assume a primary role in the organisation of industry, as well as the economy as a whole. The congress declared 'organising production' to be one of the unions' major tasks, but seems to have left unresolved the exact relationship of the unions to government economic bodies.[10]

Lack of clarity in the congress decisions probably reflected dissension among Bolsheviks, some of whom sided with Mensheviks on trade-union independence from government, such as David Ryazanov, who had played a leading role in organising trade unions in St. Petersburg in 1905 and after the 1917 revolutions. In the 1920s he would help organise the Marx-Engels Institute in Moscow and serve as its director until 1931, when he was exiled to Saratov; he was executed in 1938. When the Bolshevik Party CC nominated Shliapnikov for membership of VTsSPS, Ryazanov voiced disagreement, both because Shliapnikov held a government post and because Ryazanov disagreed with some of his policies at Narkomtrud.[11] Other Bolsheviks saw no need for unions under a socialist regime. Questions about the role of the unions in the

9   GARF, f. 130, op. 1, d. 1, l. 1, 15 November 1917; f. 382, op. 1, d. 17, ll. 1–4, 34; Shliapnikov 1922a, p. 35; Obolenskii 1918, pp. 11, 14; Oppenheim 1973, p. 15.
10 VTsSPS 1918, p. 3; Smith 1983, p. 217; Carr 1950–3, vol. 2, p. 111.
11 RGASPI, f. 17, op. 1a, d. 119, l. 8, letter from Shliapnikov to the CC, 11 January 1918; Gambarov et al. (eds.) 1989, vol. 2, pp. 230–2; and Beecher and Fomichev 2006, p. 143.

transition to socialism would simmer until the trade-union debate of 1920–1. Under Shlyapnikov's direct guidance, Narkomtrud would follow his policies. As soon as he redirected his attention to other areas of work, however, dissension would surface.

Many of the questions Narkomtrud decided on in its first months of existence were related: the tariff, workers' control over industry, the nationalisation of enterprises and worker productivity. Shlyapnikov and many other Bolshevik trade unionists were deeply committed to organised workers' control of industry under centralised coordination. To them, the nationalisation of industry would ease the implementation of workers' control. For workers' control to succeed, and for nationalised industry not to bankrupt the state, labour productivity had to be guaranteed.

Of all the projects on Narkomtrud's agenda, the tariff was perhaps the easiest to negotiate but one of the more difficult to implement. Faced with the factory owners' obstinate disinterest in working out a new tariff, Narkomtrud simply revised existing tariff rates to account for inflation and published them as a decree. Shlyapnikov thought that the tariff would attract workers from small industry to large nationalised enterprises, thus concentrating labour and resources in large enterprises and raising production to a higher level.[12] Nevertheless, rapid inflation made the tariffs impractical and Narkomtrud was unable to enforce tariff rates under conditions of economic collapse and the flight of both capital and capitalists.

The deteriorating economy and conflicting political priorities undermined other Narkomtrud projects. Shlyapnikov later recalled that he worked closely with Lenin on the first decree on workers' control and that it reflected Lenin's aim that as many workers as possible participate in economic management. Nevertheless, there were crucial differences in their views on workers' control, which were reflected in the two different draft decrees. Radical Bolsheviks aligned with the factory committees and moderate socialists in trade unions disagreed on workers' control. Lenin perceived a danger that the moderate Bolsheviks would join forces with other moderate socialists in trade unions. He tried to undermine them by throwing his support to the radicals, so his draft decree on workers' control reflected the wishes of factory-committee activists. The Narkomtrud draft decree reflected the views of moderate Bolshevik trade unionists, including Shlyapnikov and Shmidt.[13]

Lenin envisioned only including representatives of the soviets and factory committees in economic regulatory institutions, but Narkomtrud placed equal

---

12   Shliapnikov 1918, p. 14; GARF, f. 382, op. 1, d. 17, l. 4.
13   Shliapnikov 1922a, p. 33; Shliapnikov 1924c, p. 4; Shkliarevsky 1993, pp. 119, 160.

emphasis on the role of the trade unions. In Lenin's draft, factory committees would supervise the day-to-day work of the factory, while trade unions would merely serve as higher institutions of appeal. Narkomtrud's draft assigned the formulation of regulations to councils of workers' control, with only an executive role for the factory committee. Another key difference was that Narkomtrud allowed participation in workers' control by workers who held various political views, while Lenin's draft was designed to ensure that his confederates would dominate. Although the final decree incorporated most of Narkomtrud's proposals and was confirmed by Sovnarkom and endorsed by the soviets, Lenin conspired with factory-committee leaders to circumvent it. With Lenin's encouragement, in practice the factory committees ignored the soviets' legislation. Thus the Central Council of Workers' Control (composed of Petrograd Trade Union Council members) had no real power and was supplanted by VSNKh. Lenin, however, soon abandoned the factory committees. By March 1918, the Bolsheviks had largely captured the trade unions from the Mensheviks, so the factory committees were no longer of use. Lenin readily agreed to the factory committees being subordinated to the trade unions.[14]

Shlyapnikov and his colleagues in Narkomtrud hoped that the nationalisation of industry would facilitate the centralised coordination of workers' control of industry, halt Russia's economic collapse and rationalise the economy to make it stronger and more productive. The Bolsheviks had nothing more than a vague commitment to nationalising industry when they came to power. Banks and important industrial sectors, such as oil, coal, sugar, metallurgy and transport, would be nationalised. However, no plan existed for how to accomplish nationalisation, or how quickly. Narkomtrud played a crucial role in recommending which factories to nationalise. One of the challenges included convincing workers to turn profits over to the state. Shlyapnikov admitted to the First Congress of Labour Commissars that Narkomtrud had made mistakes, including the hasty nationalisation of enterprises that turned out to be unprofitable. In some cases, he thought, factory committees had conspired with employers to defraud the government by seeking aid for factories that could not turn a profit. Consequently, Narkomtrud appointed commissions to determine the profitability of enterprises before nationalising them.[15]

The decline of industry threatened to derail Shlyapnikov's plans for workers' control and the nationalisation of industry. As Commissar of Labour, he took some steps that appeared to contradict his views on workers' control. For example, in a report he gave to VTsIK on 20 March 1918, he raised alarm about

---

14   Shkliarevsky 1993, pp. 119–23, 128–9, 160.
15   Smith 1983, pp. 220–3; GARF, f. 382, op. 1, d. 17, l. 3.

the decline in labour productivity in the railroad industry. He had found that workers at railroad-car plants were transforming cars into residences for themselves. Stationmasters told him that the cars were dirty and in disrepair because of a lack of supplies, but he determined that railroad employees were stealing supplies. Engineers and conductors, he noted, often did not work, although they were paid. Shop committees, elected by employees, found it impossible to impose discipline and remain in office.[16] Here he showed the railroad employees little of the sympathy that he had shown industrial workers; perhaps his frustration stemmed from the perception that white-collar employees were syphoning off resources meant for workers.

In response to the railway workers' intransigence, the government reintroduced one-man management for railways on 26 March 1918, replacing colleges (boards) composed of two or more men, including union representatives. Railway unions could still send representatives to sit on commissariat boards, but their candidates had to be confirmed by Sovnarkom and VTsSPS. Although this was one of the first steps in limiting workers' responsibility for the economy, Shlyapnikov seems not to have objected. Since socialists who opposed the Bolshevik government controlled the All-Russian Executive Committee of Railwaymen [*Vikzhel*], which had pressured the Bolsheviks to form a coalition government after their seizure of power, some Bolshevik leaders accepted coercion against them. Shlyapnikov's prior record was to favour soft tactics towards railwaymen.[17] Nevertheless, he considered local trade-union subordination to VTsSPS important for regulating the economy and for strengthening the workers' movement. Notably, he had not supported this principle when the Mensheviks controlled VTsSPS. Thus, politics had created inconsistencies in his commitment to union power. Still a young man aged 32, he was not an experienced politician; moreover, multiple work commitments distracted him.

In another case, Shlyapnikov decried the lack of discipline among those involved in production. He ascribed this problem to 'the syndicalist tendencies of the workers who look upon whole branches of industry as belonging to the trade, forgetful of the fact that it is the state which owns the industries'.[18] Nevertheless, he continued to maintain that trade unions should collectively influence industrial policy, only criticising trade unionists who attempted to control their own industry without coordinating their actions with other unions and state regulatory agencies.

---

16   Bunyan 1967, p. 20.
17   Sorenson 1969, p. 53; Browder and Kerensky 1961, vol. 2, p. 763.
18   Bunyan 1967, pp. 383–4, Shliapnikov's address to the Second All-Russian Congress of Labour Commissars on 19 May 1918.

Shlyapnikov and other government and union leaders hoped to help reverse economic decline by requiring workers to guarantee that they would turn out products.[19] Guarantees of productivity had been contentious before the revolution and continued to be so. The chief question was enforcement. Some officials called for tighter discipline and harsher punishments, including dismissal, to encourage workers to work harder. Others insisted that weakness from hunger, rather than lack of discipline, was to blame for the decline in productivity. The solution, they insisted, lay in 'higher wages, greater workers' control and moral suasion'. Shlyapnikov called for the revival of piece-rates, as an incentive for workers to work harder.

The proposal to revive piece-rates was very controversial. Piece-rates had largely been abolished after the February Revolution and had not returned since then, even though unions had allowed for them in their 1917 tariff agreements. The Petrograd Metalworkers' Union was in favour of piece-rates, but the Petrograd Council of Trade Unions was not. Ryazanov, an influential member of the council, deemed piece-rates an exploitative practice 'incompatible with socialism'. Practices such as piece-rates and Taylorism, however, were compatible with the views of Gastev and some other prominent members of the Metalworkers' Union, who composed the 'Platform of Labour Industrialism' group in early 1918. They imagined that socialist production would not only ensure a comfortable life for workers, but would also create a culture of labour and foster innovation. They were thus open to some capitalist methods designed to encourage innovation. In the 1917 wage-rates agreement between the Metalworkers' Union and factory owners, piecework pay had not been intended to replace tariff-designated wages, but to supplement them, accounting for no more than 25 percent of pay beyond normal wages.[20] Productivity was important to Shlyapnikov because on it hinged the survival of industry and of the industrial working class. His concept of workers' control was heavily imbued with the idea of central direction through worker-based organisations; he tried to justify the revival of piece-rates and a guarantee of productivity by arguing that workers' control would ensure that exploitation would not occur. Indisputably, however, piece-rates were a means of squeezing surplus value from workers. Shlyapnikov's excessively optimistic support for them may have lacked foresight, but rested on desperation to restore a ruined economy.

Far from assuming a dictatorial attitude towards workers or ignoring their desperate plight, Shlyapnikov was preoccupied with the struggle to aid industrial workers. For him, ensuring the success of the workers' revolution meant

---

19 GARF, f. 382, op. 1, d. 17, l. 3.
20 Smith 1983, pp. 132–3; Sh[liapnikov] 1917k, p. 3.

giving first priority to the survival of the industrial working class and of Russian industry. To prevent workers from abandoning industry for other professions and trades, he requested that Sovnarkom issue to Narkomtrud 30 million rubles to fund cafeterias, rations and work projects for the unemployed. He also asked Sovnarkom to issue 500,000 rubles to fund trade unions, insurance committees and other workers' organisations, as well as to publish works on 'questions of workers' politics'. When Lenin reviewed Shlyapnikov's request, he noted that if Sovnarkom approved any funds, it should distribute them through VSNKh, not through VTsSPS. In early April, Alexei Rykov had become chair of VTsSPS and he gradually clarified its structure and chain of command. Lenin seems to have trusted him to carry out party leaders' policies without divergence.[21]

When Sovnarkom refused both of Shlyapnikov's requests, he resolved to resign from Narkomtrud in protest. Threats to resign were not rare among Bolsheviks, but government members usually only did so over policy matters, not budget decisions. In November 1917 Shlyapnikov had not considered the Bolshevik CC's rejection of a socialist coalition as important enough to warrant his resignation. He thought that the refusal to grant funds to workers' organisations, however, represented a significant orientation of government policy away from the interests of the working class. In his resignation letter, he implied that the government purposely assigned little importance to the support of workers' organisations. Sovnarkom's decision to grant aid to a provincial bureaucrats' union, at the same meeting at which it denied one of Shlyapnikov's requests, must have bolstered his suspicions.[22] He may also have felt that Sovnarkom's decision reflected distrust towards him personally, but his resignation was not accepted. He remained Commissar of Labour until October 1918, although other assignments removed him from Moscow for the entire summer.

Assignments that took Shlyapnikov away from Narkomtrud in 1918 may have intensified his frustrations with its inability to facilitate workers' control of the economy. He spent much time travelling between Petrograd, Moscow, Vladimir and southern Russia that year. Due to German military advances and the rise of counterrevolution, the Bolsheviks had decided to move Russia's capital to Moscow and to evacuate industry from Petrograd. Because of his organisational abilities and familiarity with Petrograd factories, Shlyapnikov became chair of the commission to oversee the evacuation of industry from the former capital. This meant dismantling and relocating many of the factories that had attracted him and other metalworkers to Petrograd years before.

---

21   RGASPI, f. 19, op. 1, d. 100, ll. 4, 12, 20 April 1918; Oppenheim 1973, pp. 6–8.
22   RGASPI, f. 17, op. 4, d. 180, l. 5.

Having planned the commission's work and assigned responsibilities to staff, Shlyapnikov appointed assistants to oversee practical details but remained on the board and available for consultation.[23]

Although some close comrades and relatives came from Petrograd to Moscow to work with him, his personal networks of comrades, friends and family were disrupted due to evacuation, the transfer of the capital, demands of governing and rising military action. It is difficult to determine the emotional impact these events had on him, for information on his personal life during the October Revolution and the Civil War is fragmentary. He may have had an affair in 1918 with Kollontai's friend, Zoya Shadurskaya, which she ended because she was dissatisfied with his unwillingness to be more open about it. Shadurskaya worked as his secretary in the Commission on the Evacuation of Petrograd Industry in 1918 and would come to his aid in 1922, in support of a petition to the Comintern.[24] Personal relationships among Bolsheviks facilitated the formation of networks in government, trade unions and industry.

Intrigues and Departure from Narkomtrud

The intrigues within Narkomtrud in the summer and autumn of 1918 provide an example of how clashes over policy merged almost indistinguishably with bureaucratic and personal intrigues. Shlyapnikov's assistant at Narkomtrud was by then Viktor Nogin, who disagreed sharply with Shlyapnikov's policy of promoting the role of unions in government. In November 1917 Nogin had resigned his position as Commissar of Trade and Industry after he signed Zinoviev's and Kamenev's protest against the exclusion of other socialists from the Bolshevik government. Subsequently Shlyapnikov, who also signed the protest but did not resign his position, replaced Nogin as head of the commissariat. To add insult to injury, Nogin became Commissar of Labour for Moscow, making him Shlyapnikov's subordinate.[25]

Furthermore, Nogin numbered among the Left Communists (the Bolsheviks renamed themselves the Russian Communist Party in March 1918), led by Bukharin, who opposed the March 1918 Treaty of Brest-Litovsk with Germany, ending Russia's participation in World War I, while Shlyapnikov supported it. The treaty represented a great sacrifice, as Russia had to surrender (until the

---

23   GARF, f. 3842; RGASPI, f. 5, op. 1, d. 1469, l. 1, note from Shliapnikov to Lenin, prior to 3 May 1918.
24   Shliapnikova 2000; GARF, f. 3842.
25   GARF, f. 382, op. 1, d. 17, l. 1.

FIGURE 20   *Zoya Shadurskaya, 1910s (in Kolechenkova (ed.) 1989, unnumbered page).*

November armistice) one-third of its European territory and population. It also meant that, at least temporarily, Russian Communists would postpone their dreams of inciting revolution among German soldiers. Disagreement with the treaty drove the Left SRs out of the coalition government and provoked several Communists, including Kollontai, to resign from Sovnarkom.[26] Shlyapnikov later recalled that many of the party's left wing reproached him for not having joined them.

When the Bolsheviks transferred the capital of Russia to Moscow, Narkomtrud moved into the offices of the Moscow Commissariat of Labour and the staff of the two bodies merged. Nogin became Shlyapnikov's assistant. Their staff did not cooperate harmoniously. During Shlyapnikov's frequent trips to Petrograd to oversee evacuation, Narkomtrud's internal frictions worsened. He heard complaints from his relocated Petrograd staff that Nogin was trying to edge them out, but he did not take time to confront his assistant. After having overseen the evacuation commission's most important work, he spent no more than a month at work in Narkomtrud in Moscow before he left for the south of Russia. Therefore, he had little time to re-assert control over Narkomtrud. In early June 1918 Sovnarkom sent him on a mission to the North Caucasus to gather food for the population of central Russia (see next chapter). While he was away, Nogin replaced his appointees.[27]

Nogin covered his actions by reference to a summer 1918 Sovnarkom decree outlawing nepotism. Consequently, all state bodies were required to dismiss relatives who worked in direct subordination to, or in the same department as, other family members.

There were several reasons why nepotism became widespread in the early months of the Soviet government. Most of those who could have passed civil-service exams in the past did not qualify for posts in the revolutionary government due to their social background. The Bolsheviks were in a hurry to staff institutions and selected those whom they felt they could trust and those they knew best, who sometimes were relatives. In addition, people who assumed positions of power were expected to take their relatives and friends with them to provide for their needs. In some cases, however, these principles were followed in the extreme and entire departments consisted of relatives, who ended up serving their own interests more than those of the institution in which they worked.

---

26 RGASPI, f. 589, op. 3, d. 9103, vol. 5, l. 82; Rabinowitch 2007, p. 207; Clements 1997, p. 155. For more on the Left Communists, see Kowalski 1991.

27 GARF, f. 130, op. 2, d. 1, ch. 3, l. 233; ch. 4, l. 317; d. 2 (ch. 1), l. 142; f. 382, op. 1, d. 19, l. 114; RGASPI, f. 589, op. 3, d. 9103, vol. 5, ll. 173–4.

Among those people Shlyapnikov hired to work in Narkomtrud were his niece, Tyutereva, who served as chief accountant, and his brother-in-law, Iosif Kovalenko, who supervised the preservation of the Marble Palace. Originally built by Catherine the Great's lover, Grigory Orlov, and an important cultural centre on the eve of revolution, the palace had housed the Ministry of Labour under the Provisional Government. Shlyapnikov trusted his relatives, who had aided him while he worked in the revolutionary underground during World War I. There is no evidence that they abused their positions. Nogin also had a relative in Narkomtrud; his brother-in-law, Viktor Radus-Zenkovich, was a department head. On 2 August the Narkomtrud board fired Shlyapnikov's relatives without severance pay, but it used a loophole in Sovnarkom's decree to designate Radus-Zenkovich 'essential' personnel and retain him.[28]

When Shlyapnikov returned to Moscow in late August 1918, he was taken aback by the replacement of his appointees and immediately restored them to their positions. When the Narkomtrud board objected, Shlyapnikov insisted that, as commissar, he had the right to annul decisions of the board and of his assistant (Nogin). His consternation increased upon realising that Nogin had replaced the entire Narkomtrud board in his absence. The dismissal of Shlyapnikov's relatives was part of Nogin's broader campaign to replace Shlyapnikov's appointees (all from Petrograd) with Muscovites loyal to him. Shlyapnikov believed that the personnel changes served Nogin's goal of distancing Narkomtrud from the trade unions. Nogin's supporters denied that the conflict was between Muscovites and Petrograders and raised the question of whether the board could work normally with Shlyapnikov countermanding its decisions. They asked the CC to expel Shlyapnikov and his relatives from Narkomtrud. In addition, both VTsIK and VTsSPS were asked to give an opinion on the legality of the actions of Shlyapnikov and the board. Perhaps it is significant that many of Nogin's appointees had Jewish surnames, while Shlyapnikov's seem to have been Russian. According to Mawdsley, well-educated Jews who had been excluded from the tsarist bureaucracy provided a 'pool of talent' for the new Soviet regime (still, a majority of Soviet officials seem to have served in the old bureaucracy).[29] Although documents do not reference ethnic antagonisms in this case, it is possible that perceived bias exacerbated personal hostilities.

---

28 GARF, f. 382, op. 1, d. 19, ll. 89–91.
29 GARF, f. 382, op. 1, d. 19, ll. 64–6; RGASPI, f. 17, op. 4, d. 128, l. 12; Mawdsley 1987, pp. 78–9. Charges of nepotism against Shliapnikov surfaced six years later (Gindlin 1924); he refuted the charges in a letter to the CCC Presidium (RGASPI, f. 589, op. 3, d. 9103, vol. 5, l. 173, 24 October 1924).

VTsSPS refused to make a judgment of guilt in the conflict, dismissing it as 'a minor practical disagreement' that should not be allowed to hinder important work on the tariff. Mikhail Tomsky, one of the VTsSPS representatives to Narkomtrud, argued that the constitution stipulated that the board could not cancel the decree of the commissar. Implying that Narkomtrud had not shown the worst instances of nepotism, Shmidt, also from VTsSPS, noted that the nepotism decree 'was worked out on account of careerists and we had in mind VSNKh, where a whole family worked in one department'. Tomsky emphasised that the commissar's primary concern should not be the trust of his staff, but that of the working masses. Since the First Congress of Labour Commissars had unanimously elected Shlyapnikov chair, he said, Shlyapnikov clearly had the masses' support, whereas mass opinion of Nogin had not been gauged.[30] VTsSPS leaders thus confirmed their trust in Shlyapnikov.

Finally, the CC decided to remove both Shlyapnikov and Nogin from the Commissariat, which became a typical Bolshevik practice in situations involving personal conflict. At the same time as it was reproving the board for having exaggerated the importance of the conflict, the CC was also urging Narkomtrud to cooperate closely with VTsSPS, acknowledging that differences (over primary responsibility for the tariff) had emerged between the two bodies during the conflict. This illustrated the difficulty of separating personal clashes from institutional and political conflicts. When the Narkomtrud board reconvened, trade-union representatives and Narkomtrud board members still proved unable to agree. Unease in relations between Narkomtrud and the trade unions persisted after the departure of Shlyapnikov and Nogin. Radus-Zenkovich, making no secret of his desire to subordinate the activities of the trade unions to Narkomtrud, attempted to stack the board with personnel from Narkomtrud's departments. Trade unionists objected vehemently to this threat to their numerical superiority.[31] Although tensions over the roles of government and unions persisted, Shlyapnikov had to remove himself from the debate for a time.

---

30 GARF, f. 382, op. 1, d. 19, ll. 56–60. In 1918, Tomskii was a member of the VTsSPS Presidium; in October, he became its chair (Gorelov 1989: pp. 3, 32).

31 GARF, f. 382, op. 1, d. 19, ll. 50–3, September 5, 1918. RGASPI, f. 17, op. 4, d. 128, ll. 3 (13 December 1918), 14; Anikeev 1974, p. 426. Shliapnikov continued to chair board meetings through 1 October (GARF, f. 382, op. 1, d. 19, l. 34). On 8 October, Nogin announced he was leaving Narkomtrud for work in VSNKh. Shmidt became Commissar of Labour and began chairing board sessions on 12 October (GARF, f. 130, op. 2, d. 2, ch. 1, l. 268; f. 382, op. 1, d. 19, l. 31).

In summary, there were at least three opinions within the Narkomtrud board concerning the unions' relationship to the commissariat. Nogin favoured subordinating the unions to the commissariat. Shmidt and Tomsky wanted to preserve the unions' decision-making power while making Narkomtrud an executive body. Shlyapnikov hoped that the unions would combine their work with that of Narkomtrud in such a way that unionists would dominate the government body. During the trade-union debate two years later, Nogin would defend the authority of the state bodies and the relegation of the trade unions to a subordinate role. During one debate, Tomsky would remind Nogin that Lenin had rebuked him (Nogin) in 1918 for favouring the destruction of trade unions.[32] Shlyapnikov's and Nogin's personal conflict thus merged with an institutional one between VTsSPS and Narkomtrud; running through both were fundamental political disagreements over the role of the one-party state and unions in directing the economy.

Conclusion

Not long after Shlyapnikov endorsed Zinoviev's and Kamenev's statement advocating a socialist coalition government, Lenin convinced him to accept a Bolshevik-Left SR government. Immersed in his work as Commissar of Labour, he became a reliable member of the majority in the party leadership, backing Lenin on the question of political power. But the exigencies of power sometimes drove a wedge between him and Lenin on economic questions. His trade-union work in 1917 strengthened his commitment to trade unions as a channel through which workers could acquire the capability to govern, which strongly influenced the policies he enacted as Commissar of Labour. His reputation as an efficient, practical and tireless worker, as someone who could get things done, resulted in his appointment to various urgent tasks during the course of 1918, many of which distracted him from his goals and undermined his work at Narkomtrud.

---

32   GARF, f. 5451, op. 42, d. 3, l. 60, VTsSPS fraction stenographic report, 20 December 1920.

CHAPTER 5

Defending Soviet Power and Unions in the Civil War

During the Russian Civil War, millions died from violence, disease and famine. Not only was combat brutal, but both sides perpetrated atrocities upon the civilian population. Organised, armed hostilities began in May 1918 when the Czech Legion, attempting to leave Russia via the Far East in order to join forces fighting Germany on the Western front, began an uprising on the Trans-Siberian Railway. In summer, former tsarist officers formed counterrevolutionary (White) armies along the periphery of the Russian Empire and Right SRs created governments in Siberia. Allied governments introduced troops into Russian ports and directed aid to White armies, hoping that a Bolshevik collapse would bring Russia back into the war against Germany. In organising a 'Red' Army, Communists faced the dilemma of attempting to create a new type of revolutionary military force while depending on former tsarist officers for expertise, since the Bolsheviks had little experience as military commanders. Improvising policies to cope with a whirlwind of crises, they were forced to utilise inherited tsarist structures and personnel.[1]

Suffused with militarism during the Civil War, the coercive and centralising variant of Bolshevism achieved ascendancy. Only later called 'War Communism,' Bolshevik economic policies in 1918–21 were often inconsistent and based on contingency, but usually entailed food requisitions, rationing, forced labour and state control of the economy and transport. Effective leadership became synonymous with being 'firm' [*tverdyi*], yet this result was not preordained. Bolsheviks could have chosen from divergent paths in laying the foundation of their rule. Russian Communists felt they were fighting for the survival of their regime and of the socialist dream, the unfolding and expansion of which they believed hinged on their success. Preferring negotiation and persuasion, Shlyapnikov selectively authorised force to achieve Bolshevik goals, but was unwilling to apply indiscriminate violence. When workers were

---

1 Rabinowitch 2007 examined how objective circumstances shaped Bolshevik decision-making, while Raleigh 2002 showed how the Civil War set the stage for Stalinism to prevail over Bolshevik alternatives to it. For a survey of Civil War military operations, see Mawdsley 1987, who argues that the Russian Civil War began upon the Bolshevik usurpation of power in October 1917.

massacred in Astrakhan, a troubled Shlyapnikov demanded investigations. His experiences on the front increased his frustration with the Soviet state's policies towards workers and more sharply defined his conception of the role of the trade unions *vis-à-vis* the Communist Party. When he returned from the front in 1919, he promoted unions as natural organisers of the economy. Many other Bolsheviks, especially those in unions, had similar ideas; the Workers' Opposition would emerge from their criticisms.

'For Bread and Oil'

Anxious to feed hungry urban residents in the north and thus stave off potential uprisings in cities, the Communists directed loyal personnel to obtain food from fertile agricultural zones in the south; Stalin and Shlyapnikov were assigned to the important transportation hub, Tsaritsyn (renamed Stalingrad in 1925 and Volgograd in 1961), on the Volga River. While Stalin remained in Tsaritsyn, he agreed that Shlyapnikov should venture into the dangerous North Caucasus region. Shlyapnikov's original mission naturally evolved into different military assignments, for obstacles to the transport of food and fuel included not only White General Anton Denikin's control of railways in southern Ukraine, but also violent conflicts between Cossacks and mountaineers over land redistribution in the North Caucasus. His most perilous assignments included procuring supplies for the Eleventh Army, tightening its discipline and implementing Sovnarkom's order to destroy the Black Sea Fleet.[2] Intense battles were fought in the territory where he and his personnel travelled. Cossacks clashed with Soviet forces; Chechen and Ingush mountain peoples attacked Cossacks. While Baku changed hands between the British and the Turks, battles raged around Grozny and Vladikavkaz. Because loyal Soviet forces were few in number, isolation often bred desperation and arbitrariness.

Stalin-era historians and memoirists were under exceptional pressure to elevate Stalin's role and omit or denigrate those like Shlyapnikov, who became his opponents, but Shlyapnikov defended his July–August 1918 food-requisition work in a manuscript, 'For Bread and Oil'. Unfashionably for the early 1930s, when he wrote it, his manuscript did not slander Trotsky, but only criticised some of his decisions as Red Army commander. While condemning Left SR views, he incorporated in his manuscript entire texts of documents originating from them, violating the standards of the time by conveying their views

---

[2] Naumov 1991, pp. 20–1; Lenin 1958–65, vol. 50, p. 82; RGASPI, f. 2, op. 1, d. 6287, d. 7584; f. 5, op. 1, d. 1470 and Svechnikov 1926, Appendix.

in undistorted form. Although his published works had already been attacked for failing to conform to Stalinist dictates on writing history, he persisted in combatting myths developing around the Civil War. Emphasising that open clashes and hostilities were harmful to the cause, he wrote that he preferred behind-the-scenes negotiations.[3] In reality, peaceful means often failed, given the high stakes involved.

Food-requisition brigades, usually composed of urban workers and soldiers, were infamous for violent, coercive tactics. Shlyapnikov recruited industrial workers and trade-union members for his requisition brigades. Feeling that he relied too much on workers, Lenin instructed him to recruit among broader sectors of the population, but he seems to have ignored the instruction.[4] According to a brigade member, Shlyapnikov used non-violent measures to ensure cooperation whenever possible, resorting to force only as a last resort. In Tsaritsyn, he persuaded railway workers to speed up the dispatch of grain-loaded train cars to the centre (which was effective while he was present). Further down the line, he dismissed a recalcitrant depot chief from his position (rather than shoot him). Reportedly, he 'soothed' Mineralnye Vody residents who feared that the Red Army would 'take away their bread, money and horses'. Shlyapnikov even attempted to negotiate with rebellious Cossacks, but when talks failed he agreed with the local Soviet military commander (Alexander Egorov) that force was needed in order to 'clear the path to move grain'.[5] According to one historical account, the Cossacks fired first, after Shlyapnikov had given them 12 hours to 'lay down arms and disperse'.[6]

Shlyapnikov's brigades, like many others, brought manufactured items with them to trade for food. When brigades ran out of barter items, they often resorted to theft and violence, but some commanders saw such actions as undisciplined and counterproductive. Shlyapnikov numbered among those who dispatched numerous telegrams to Moscow, pleading for cash in small denominations and manufactured goods (household items, cloth) to exchange for livestock. He planned to set up food-processing plants to send food to the north and help develop industry in the south. At the same time, he requested newspapers and other pro-Soviet literature for distribution, hoping to use them to persuade locals to cooperate. Optimistic that showing concern for the

---

3   Shliapnikov 2002 and 2003.
4   Figes 1989; RGASPI, f. 2, op. 1, d. 7584, l. 1, Shliapnikov's handwritten letter to Lenin and Lenin's handwritten notation (photocopy).
5   Rossiiskii gosudarstvennyi voennyi arkhiv (RGVA), f. 1, op. 1, d. 265, ll. 79–82, N.I. Nazarov, 'Report of A.G. Shliapnikov's produce brigade,' 16 August 1918. Nazarov wrote that the brigade left Moscow on 8 July 1918. Mauricio Borrero provided me with a photocopy of the report.
6   Svechnikov 1926, p. 37.

needs of the local population would win them over, he asked for medicines to combat epidemics among local people and livestock.[7] What little that the centre could deliver, however, was held up because hostile forces blocked rail lines. The break in communications and his delayed return led many in Moscow to conclude that he had been killed.

Civilian suffering impressed upon Shlyapnikov the need to instil discipline. Reporting to Sovnarkom that when Soviet forces (Grozny workers) defeated and disarmed Cossacks, their Chechen allies burned Cossack villages and massacred inhabitants, his tone conveyed strong disapproval. He creatively improvised to bypass dangers, such as sending runners across mountains to carry messages when communications were cut off. But there was little hope for victory without supplies. Due to a lack of ammunition, Soviet forces at Kizlyar were barely holding out under siege by Cossacks. Worried that the English were arming Cossacks, Shlyapnikov pleaded that Sovnarkom turn attention to this front. He argued that with sufficient material and men, coordination and discipline, railway transport across Chechnya could be restored and the pipeline made to work again in order to supply the north with fuel.[8]

With Stalin's consent, Shlyapnikov went to Ekaterinodar (now Krasnodar) to convince local Bolsheviks to cooperate with the central party leaders' decision to destroy the Black Sea Fleet in Novorossiysk rather than allow it to fall into the hands of the enemy. Due to mistakes by the previous emissary, Nikolai Glebov-Avilov (former Commissar of Post and Telegraph), misunderstandings had created opposition to the decision. Blaming Glebov-Avilov for lacking 'self-control, good sense and tact', Shlyapnikov claimed that with patient explanations, he convinced local Soviet leaders and fleet delegates of the logic behind the decision and the urgency of carrying it out. He left its implementation in the hands of Fyodor Raskolnikov, a Kronstadt revolutionary and Red Fleet commander.[9] Confirming Shlyapnikov's version in a report to the centre, Raskolnikov harshly condemned Glebov-Avilov as deserving of 'severe military punishment' for having abandoned his post.[10] Barely escaping before

---

7   RGASPI, f. 5, op. 1, d. 1470, ll. 2–7, copies of telegrams from Shliapnikov to Lenin and others.

8   GARF, f. 130, op. 2, d. 170, ll. 29–32, report from Shliapnikov to Sovnarkom, 20 September 1918.

9   RGASPI, f. 2, op. 1, d. 6287, l. 1, Sovnarkom telegram to 'Stalin or Shliapnikov', 13 June 1918; f. 5, op. 1, d. 1470, l. 1, undated letter from Shliapnikov to Lenin. Soviet historians later smeared Shliapnikov with opposition to the fleet's destruction (Kozlov 1985, p. 172, for example).

10 'Statement of F. Raskol'nikov to CC RKP(b)', from RGVA, f. 33987, op. 1, d. 572, ll. 1–3 (copy), Dmitry Volkogonov Papers, Library of Congress, Washington, DC. Raskol'nikov's 1918 report differs from his 1934 published memoirs, in which he conformed to the Stalinist

Ekaterinodar was taken by the Whites, Shlyapnikov could not deliver to central Russia the one million poods of grain he had collected.[11]

Immediately upon his return to Moscow at the end of August, Shlyapnikov appealed for aid to the North Caucasus. He requested five thousand troops and equipment to revive the railroad and oil pipeline across Chechnya. A commission comprising representatives of the Produce Commissariat, the Military Commissariat and VSNKh approved his proposals, but the Military Commissariat offered only one thousand one hundred troops. Neither the Produce Commissariat nor VSNKh offered to develop the region as a source of raw materials and produce. Bitterly disappointed, Shlyapnikov assessed their lack of support as 'a crime before the working class'.[12] Increasingly, party leaders and military commanders employed inflammatory language against those who were unable or unwilling to fulfil their requests. Concerned with crises in their own realms, local commanders could not perceive, as the centre did, the dangers pressing in from all sides. Difficult decisions to prioritise one front meant likely failures on another.

In part due to his experience in the south and advocacy for it, in late October Shlyapnikov was appointed to membership of the Revolutionary Military Council [*Revvoensovet*, or RVS] of the Southern front, chaired by Stalin in Tsaritsyn. Given their divergent party history and personalities, it seems likely that both men realised that they would have an incompatible working relationship. Perhaps for this reason, in addition to genuine strategic needs, Shlyapnikov quickly proposed to organise a Caspian-Caucasian section based in Astrakhan, a southern port city located on the Volga River near the Caspian Sea. When the Caspian-Caucasian section became an independent front on 8 December 1918, Shlyapnikov was appointed chair of its RVS.[13] From November 1918 to February 1919, he oversaw the Eleventh and Twelfth Armies. The military commander of the Caspian-Caucasian front was Mikhail Svechnikov, a former tsarist officer sympathetic to Soviet power. He and Shlyapnikov quickly found common ground and maintained a close friendship until both perished in Stalin's terror.

---

line by claiming that Shlyapnikov was against the destruction of the fleet. After openly defying Stalin in 1939, Raskol'nikov died in a mysterious accident in France.

11   Naumov 1991, p. 21. A pood [pud] is equal to 16.38 kilogrammes. The USSR abolished the measurement in 1924.

12   Svechnikov 1926, Appendix, letter to Svechnikov from Shliapnikov, Moscow, 22 June 1925; GARF, f. 130, op. 2, d. 170, ll. 29–31. Nazarov had advised that fifteen thousand troops were needed (RGVA, f. 1, op. 1, d. 265, l. 82).

13   Naumov 1991, pp. 21–2.

The chief obstacle Shlyapnikov faced to his work as chair of the Caspian-Caucasian RVS was a lack of material support from central political and military authorities, about which leaders on all fronts complained. In telegrams to Sovnarkom and the Military and Produce Commissariats, he pleaded with central authorities to send troops, uniforms and ammunition.[14] The centre did not have enough resources to send everything that was requested and much seems to have been diverted along the way due to corruption and dire need. With the revolution's survival apparently at stake, many actors looked for guilty parties among social groups deemed hostile to the revolution, or scapegoated fellow commanders.

Clashes between political and military leaders became common on all fronts. Upon the appointment of Evgenia Bosh as head of the political department of the RVS on the Caspian-Caucasian front, conflicts began between, on the one hand, Shlyapnikov and his RVS military commanders, and on the other hand, militant local party leaders led by Bosh. Ignoring orders from RVS leaders, Bosh allied with the Astrakhan gubernia party committee in asserting the local party organisation's authority over Red Army commanders.[15] Confident in her abilities, owing to her prior command experience, she tried to appoint commissars to military units without RVS permission and in contradiction of RVS decisions. Complaining to the chair of VTsIK, Yakov Sverdlov, that her actions were insubordinate and harmful, Shlyapnikov warned that he would order her trial by a party court if she was not recalled. Confirming the political department's subordination to the RVS, Sverdlov requested that the two sides come to a peaceful agreement. Bosh proved intransigent, refusing to subordinate party work to the leadership of a 'non-party organisation' (the RVS). Furthermore, she encouraged Astrakhan party officials to ignore Sverdlov's order for her to return to Moscow.[16]

After Shlyapnikov travelled to Moscow in early January to speak with Sverdlov, the VTsIK chair forced Bosh to resign, but she did not do so quietly. While Shlyapnikov was in Moscow, she had convinced Astrakhan party officials to order the arrest of his local Cheka allies for 'counterrevolutionary actions'. In addition, an anonymous denunciation sent to Moscow demanded his dismissal for 'betraying all Communists into the hands of unreliable

---

14   RGASPI, f. 5, op. 1, d. 2436, l. 3, telegram from Shliapnikov to Lenin, 11 November 1918.

15   The *guberniias* were territorial subdivisions of the Russian Empire, which the Soviets replaced with oblasts by 1929. A smaller territorial unit was the *u"ezd* (divided into *volosts*); the *u"ezd* was replaced with the *raion* or *okrug*.

16   Naumov 1991, p. 24; Sverdlov 1976, pp. 107–10 (RGASPI, f. 86, op. 1, d. 52, ll. 6, 18, telegrams, December 1918–January 1919). On Bosh, see Clements 1979, pp. 184–8.

military specialists'.[17] Western historians have accepted Soviet historians' assertions that both Shlyapnikov and Bosh were disgraced in this affair, but Shlyapnikov left the front a month later than she did – and for a different reason. He emerged from this conflict convinced that regional party bodies too often expanded their powers to the detriment of practical work (in this case the military effort).

This explains why he did not join the 'Military Opposition', which was formed by Bolsheviks opposed to the role of tsarist officers in the Red Army. Trotsky promoted the employment of tsarist officers in the Red Army and introduced other measures intended to strengthen discipline and a centralised chain of command, while many other party leaders feared that this would undermine the revolution. Lenin eventually sided with Trotsky, whose position prevailed at the Eighth Party Congress in March 1919.[18] Many historians have not understood why Shlyapnikov aligned himself with former tsarist military officers (or even that he did so), given that he later decried the role of 'specialists' in industry, but from his perspective the two situations were different. He valued the specialists' expertise both in military campaigns and in industrial enterprises, but workers had direct knowledge of production that many party politicians did not have of military tactics and strategy. In wartime, a reliance on military specialists was essential to victory. In industry, however, an excessive reliance on specialists threatened to block workers' initiative in transforming production.

Shlyapnikov's conflicts with Sergei Kirov (later Leningrad party secretary) and Grigory 'Sergo' Ordzhonikidze (later Commissar of Heavy Industry) only increased the number of his personal enemies on the Southern front. By temperament, personality and experience, Shlyapnikov differed from Kirov and Ordzhonikidze, who belonged to Stalin's circle of rowdy drinkers. Kirov's abandonment of underground work in 1909, his legal work as a journalist during World War I and his support for the Provisional Government in 1917 also set him apart from Shlyapnikov. At first, all three jointly sought more resources for the North Caucasus. Their first conflict occurred in mid-January when Kirov, returning to the North Caucasus from Moscow with supplies and 50 million rubles in cash, disobeyed an order from the Caspian-Caucasian RVS not to cross the Volga, where the ice was already melting, by truck. When the truck, with all the money, sank into the river, Shlyapnikov arrested the infuriated

---

17   Anikeev et al. 1971, pp. 15–16; RGASPI, f. 2, op. 1, d. 8190, 7 January 1919, telegram to Shliapnikov in Moscow from Grasin, an Astrakhan Cheka official; RGASPI, f. 17, op. 66, d. 42, I. 62.
18   Mawdsley 1987, pp. 178–9.

Kirov for 'misappropriation of government funds'.[19] That he would place Kirov in custody awaiting trial conveys his deep concern with Kirov's lack of discipline and flouting of military orders.

When tragedy struck the Eleventh Army in January 1919, its commander, Ordzhonikidze, together with Kirov, blamed Shlyapnikov. Stricken by typhus and forced to retreat across the steppe in winter, most of the army's soldiers died *en route* to Astrakhan. Trotsky held North Caucasus military authorities and local commanders responsible, while Shlyapnikov and Svechnikov blamed central political and military authorities for their lack of support. Shlyapnikov reminded Trotsky of the many requests that he and other local commanders had made for supplies and reinforcements, which either were denied or came too late. Svechnikov continued to defend Shlyapnikov in his 1926 memoirs: 'by the time comrade Shlyapnikov turned over his position as RVS chair to Mekhonoshin, the fleet was nearly ready for operations... [and] the units of the Twelfth Army were to a significant degree formed in Astrakhan'.[20]

In February 1919, Shlyapnikov left his post and returned to Moscow. He asked to be relieved of his duties, because (as he later said) he had contracted Ménière's syndrome, an inner-ear disorder which caused dizziness, severe headaches and periods of hearing loss (he would suffer episodically from this disease for the rest of his life). Because his departure from the front occurred so soon after the Eleventh Army's collapse, some assumed that he was in disgrace. In fact, Ordzhonikidze (an extraordinary commissar of southern Russia since spring 1918) had accused Caspian-Caucasian RVS staff of diverting, delaying and even stealing supplies destined for the Eleventh Army. Shlyapnikov offered to submit himself to a military tribunal, but all charges were withdrawn after an investigation. Nevertheless, Soviet biographers of Ordzhonikidze and Kirov maintained that Shlyapnikov was dismissed for incompetence or even 'treasonous' acts.[21] Post-Soviet historians found that Stalin diverted and hoarded

---

19   Knight 1999, pp. 42–4, 60, 68, 73–4; Khlevniuk 1995; TsA FSB, R27744, vol. 1, d. 3257, l. 79, 15 January 1935. Knight's sources suggest that Kirov was unaware the river ice was thawing, and that he sent divers to recover the money, while Shliapnikov claimed that Kirov violated a ban on crossing the river and that the RVS called in divers. Efimov 2009 dispels myths surrounding Kirov's service in the Civil War.

20   Naumov 1991, p. 23. Svechnikov 1926, pp. 182, 204–31, and telegrams in Appendix, (13 December 1918) telegram from Shliapnikov to Trotsky, Lenin and Vatsetis.

21   RGASPI, f. 589, d. 9103, v. 5, l. 16, 17 June 1932; Ordzhonikidze 1956, vol. 1, pp. 69–92; Naumov 1991, p. 26; Kondrashev 1947, pp. 3–23; Verigo 1986, p. 111 and Razgon 1941. The novelist, Kholopov, (Kholopov 1955) perpetuated negative caricatures of Shliapnikov, which were echoed by Knight 1999, p. 75 and Biggart 1976, p. 238.

many supplies in Tsaritsyn.[22] The widespread shortage of troops and supplies meant that the centre probably could not have mobilised more than it had already dedicated to this front in 1918–19. Nevertheless, in addition to his poor health, the accusations were a heavy burden on Shlyapnikov.[23]

A Massacre of Astrakhan Workers

When he returned to Moscow, Shlyapnikov became better informed about the Communist repression of workers throughout Russia's central industrial region. Displeased with the Bolsheviks' repressive turn, workers in Tula, Sormovo, Yaroslavl and other cities demanded the right to strike, free elections to soviets, and independent unions. Having elected responsive Menshevik and SR candidates, workers saw the Communists disperse oppositionist soviets. In August 1918, workers rose up in Izhevsk and Votkinsk, centres of the armaments industry. Petrograd workers, upset about restrictions on trade and elections, went on strike in summer 1918, for which some were locked out of their plants. Discontent also simmered in Moscow factories. Worried Communist leaders pursued an inconsistent line in early 1919 against their socialist opponents, at first allowing free speech, then rescinding it and ordering mass executions. Needing the backing of the workers as the Civil War entered a crucial stage, they feared losing that support to rival socialist parties.[24] As the Civil War raged furiously in the borderlands, Communist leaders felt compelled to apply extreme coercion.

Astrakhan was one such place; the city suffered from severe famine in winter 1918–19 due to the ban on the free trade of food (any available produce was requisitioned for the army and for the inhabitants of central Russia). Shlyapnikov may have considered lifting the ban. An SR writing in 1920 speculated that he was replaced as commander of the Caspian-Caucasian RVS because central Communist leaders objected to his 'concessions' to starving workers. While Shlyapnikov served as Caspian-Caucasian RVS chair, he had worked closely with trade unions. The former officer turned military historian, Svechnikov, credited him with winning over unionised workers, emphasising: 'With the slightest inability to maintain contact with them [the workers] they

---

22 Kuromiya 2005, p. 40.
23 Dazhina (ed.) 2010, p. 188. In her published diaries, Kollontai blamed Shliapnikov's troubles on Trotsky, without mentioning Ordzhonikidze or Kirov.
24 Brovkin 1990, pp. 350–73; Rosenberg 1985, pp. 213–39; Pirani 2008. Aves 1996 discusses worker unrest in 1920–2, after Shliapnikov had developed a critical stance.

would have become a great opposition to the authorities'. Svechnikov, who was in Astrakhan in March 1919, must have been alluding to events surrounding the massacre. Having examined Russian State Military Archive documents, a recent Russian biographer of Kirov confirms the picture of Shlyapnikov as one who 'did not act like a dictator'.[25]

After Shlyapnikov's departure, local Bolshevik authorities demanded greater productivity from workers, dispersed worker assemblies and arrested their leaders. In response, Astrakhan workers turned against the regime. After electing new officers to the local Metalworkers' Union in late February 1919, the workers declared a strike. A worker assembly of ten thousand people had hardly agreed on tentative demands when Bolshevik forces fired on them with machine guns and hand grenades, yielding an estimated two thousand victims. In the wake of the shootings, the local Cheka executed hundreds of workers and threw their bodies into the Volga. Some were drowned by having rocks tied around their necks. Konstantin Mekhonoshin (Shlyapnikov's replacement as RVS chair) and the local Cheka head gave the orders – Trotsky telegraphed his approval. Bolshevik leaders justified this large number of executions by concocting charges that the workers were counterrevolutionaries. Kirov claimed the uprising was an English-funded 'White Guard conspiracy' and called for the rebels to be destroyed by all means available. By April 1919 more than four thousand people were executed, including several local leaders of the Metalworkers' Union. Communist leaders may have been particularly harsh in Astrakhan because of its strategic location as a place where White armies could unite.[26]

Shlyapnikov seems not to have objected to arrests of priests, nobles or merchants, but he did not think that Civil War conditions justified coercion against workers. His response to the Astrakhan massacre illustrates the gulf between him and Communists who were more hardened by their Civil War experiences. Having learned of it from the chair of the Astrakhan Council of Trade Unions, Shlyapnikov requested that the CC determine who was 'guilty' of having issued orders to shoot. Informing the CC that the Metalworkers' Union would send its own representative to investigate, he signalled that the unions were equal partners with the party in matters pertaining to the workers. Finally, he advised that the government smooth over relations between local officials and workers. The

---

25   Silin 1922, p. 249; Svechnikov 1926, pp. 130, 134; Efimov 2009, p. 28.
26   Silin 1922, pp. 251–2; Knight 1999, p. 76; Brovkin (ed.) 1991, pp. 368–9; Efimov 2009, pp. 34, 39, citing a figure of one thousand five hundred executions. Efimov 2009, p. 40, lays responsibility on 'Kirov's *protégé*' Georgii Atarbekov, head of the Eleventh Army 'Special Section', for the executions; Atarbekov was later a secret police chief in Baku.

Metalworkers' Union investigator, A. Babitsyn, concluded that the Astrakhan workers supported Soviet power, with only a few anarchists voicing anti-Soviet slogans. Pay delays, reduced rations, the division of military industry workers into a privileged group receiving higher pay for piecework and overtime and another group earning little as day labourers, and finally the authorities' high-handed, threatening treatment of workers gave rise to resentments that flared up in the uprising. The Astrakhan shootings must have intensified the concern Shlyapnikov had begun to feel over the growing alienation between the Soviet officialdom and industrial workers. In January 1919 Kollontai had expressed to him her discomfort with the relative comfort in which Soviet higher-ups lived, compared to the 'people's sufferings', but he had dismissed her pangs of conscience as 'intellectualism' [*intelligentshchina*].[27] Upon his return to Moscow a month later, he must have begun to revise his perspective. He failed to perceive, however, that coercion against workers was rooted in its application towards formerly privileged classes.

Trade Unions Should 'Master the Entire Economy'

When Shlyapnikov returned to work in Moscow in February 1919, he was dismayed by what he saw around him. The best workers had left industry, which was in collapse. 'Bureaucracy' had taken hold in government institutions, of which VSNKh now asserted its ability to manage the economy. VSNKh's responsibilities had markedly expanded since spring 1918. With about six thousand personnel (most of whom were not Communists), it oversaw more than two thousand nationalised enterprises through its constantly growing *glavki* (chief committees), each of which oversaw a branch of industry. By 1920 there were 179 *glavki*, subdivided into trusts, which were most concentrated in the textiles, metals, woodworking and the food-processing industries.[28] The state and party relied on 'specialists', who usually came from the pre-revolutionary intelligentsia, to run industry and staff governmental bodies. Clearly, the goal of worker management of industry was seriously endangered. He especially worried about a new pessimistic attitude towards the proletariat in leading government and party institutions: a belief in the need to control and coerce workers. Like many others, he feared that the Communist Party, striving to

---

27 RGASPI, f. 17, op. 66, d. 42, l. 63, 8 April 1919; Efimov 2009, pp. 31–2; Dazhina (ed.) 2010, p. 180.
28 Oppenheim 1973, pp. 5, 9–11.

raise production, establish its power and win the Civil War, had abandoned the ideal of emancipating and empowering the proletariat.

An opportunity to redirect the party's attention towards the organised workers' ability to manage the Soviet economy came at the Eighth Communist Party Congress, held in March 1919, where a new party programme was adopted. For Shlyapnikov, the most significant passage of the programme was paragraph five of the economic section, which became the linchpin of the programme of the Workers' Opposition. Paragraph five read, in part, as follows:

> By Soviet law and established practice, trade unions already participate in all local and central bodies for managing industry. Trade unions should further concentrate in their hands management of the entire economy as a single unit. In this way, they will secure an indissoluble link between the central state administration, the economy and the labouring masses. Trade unions should, to the greatest extent possible, attract the masses into directing the economy. Mass participation through the trade unions in directing the economy is the chief means of struggle with the bureaucratisation of Soviet power's economic system. Moreover, it will make possible actual popular control over the results of production.[29]

Ryazanov criticised paragraph five for being 'syndicalist and industrialist'. Marxism, he argued, gave trade unions no management role in production.[30] Further passages in the programme emphasised the unions' responsibility to mobilise labour and to ensure the productivity of the workforce. Thus on the role of trade unions, the new party programme reflected the position of the moderate Bolshevik trade unionists of 1917–18. It is puzzling why Lenin and other party leaders made this concession, given their later opposition to such power in the hands of trade unions. Perhaps it was a cynical tactic to get the consent of union leaders to direct their staff and resources towards the military effort. It could have also reflected the more idealistic strain of Lenin's thought, or perhaps there was a dimension of international propaganda to the programme's intended appeal.

Encouraged by the results of the party congress, Shlyapnikov began criticising the actual situation in industry and in the trade unions, which he believed to be in stark disparity with the party programme. First he attacked the practice of relying on technical and managerial specialists to run industry, which

---

29 RKP(b) 1959, p. 403.
30 Tsentral'nyi arkhiv obshchestvennykh dvizhenii goroda Moskvy (TsAODM), f. 3, op. 2, d. 34, l. 56.

he saw as evidence of an unhealthy chasm between state economic bodies and workers. Arguing that specialists of non-worker origin had neither the incentive nor enthusiasm necessary to socialise industry, he insisted that workers should be trained as managers. Next, he joined in opposition to those who wanted to impose harsh discipline on industrial workers in order to bring production back on track. Blaming bottlenecks in the supply of fuel and raw materials for work stoppages that had lowered workers' pay and impelled skilled workers to seek other jobs, he called on the state to free workers' hands to initiate orders and coordinate the delivery of raw materials for their factories. To increase production and attract skilled workers back into industry, he proposed eliminating caps on pay and basing wages on piecework. To those who feared exploiting the workers, he replied that if workers were in control, they would 'not allow' themselves to be exploited. His other demands included increasing requisitions of 'unrationed products' in order to feed workers, greater specialisation by factory and a greater division of labour within factories, along the lines of Henry Ford's innovations in the United States. Criticising the Commissariat of Enlightenment for having done little to establish evening schools for workers, he called for trade unions to control worker education.[31] Not since 1917 had Shliapnikov argued so forcefully that trade unions could be more effective in economic policy than state bodies.

The March 1919 congress also saw the rise of the Democratic Centralists, who carried the banner of democratic reform within the context of a one-party state. Led by Timofei Sapronov and N. Osinsky (Valerian Obolensky), the Democratic Centralists wanted 'democratic centralism and proletarian democracy' to replace the bureaucratic centralisation they perceived in the party. Specifically, they urged more frequent party committee meetings and party conferences at all levels. Because the CC had become large and many of its members had duties that made it impossible for them to frequently meet in Moscow, the Eighth Party Congress created the Politburo from among their number, a smaller body that could hold more manageable discussions of important policy matters.[32] The Orgburo and Secretariat, also formed from the CC, would manage mundane organisational business. In reality, there was much overlap. At the very top, the Democratic Centralists insisted that the CC should be the main decision-making body, while the Politburo and Orgburo

---

31 Shliapnikov 1919c, p. 1; Kii 1919, p. 8; Shliapnikov 1919d, pp. 1–2; TsA FSB, R33718, d. 499061, vol. 37, I. 203–5, 19 April 1919; Shliapnikov 1919e, pp. 2–3.
32 Lenin, Trotsky, Stalin, Kamenev and Krestinskii were full Politburo members in 1919; Bukharin, Zinoviev and Kalinin were candidate members.

should only implement those decisions. The party would provide political leadership to soviets and trade unions, but should not interfere in their everyday work or in their preparation of draft proposals. The Democratic Centralists desired more open discussion of party matters in the press (without violating party unity), more workers in party committees and the revival of the party cell (the smallest unit of party organisation) as a forum for discussion of vital questions.[33]

Shlyapnikov was therefore only one of many critics of party policies, but Lenin and other leaders began to view with apprehension his remarks about the role of unions in workers' lives. For example, in spring 1919 he presented a controversial resolution to a VTsSPS communist fraction meeting. Tomsky later cited as dangerous the resolution's call for trade unionists to 'stand at the head of the masses' increasing discontent'. Placed in context, Shlyapnikov's demand was for unions to meet the needs of the workers by all means possible, while explaining to them the 'pernicious' nature of wildcat strikes.[34] However, some soviet and party leaders interpreted his call as a threat to the party's role, as well as a dangerous incursion on the powers of state economic bodies.

Given the shortage of capable organisers, party leaders offered Shlyapnikov many assignments in spring 1919, such as work in the State Control Committee [*Goskontrol*]. He rejected them, however, because they could distract him from his work as chair of the Metalworkers' Union, to which he gave priority. (He had the right to refuse a government appointment, whereas he could not have refused a party assignment without violating party discipline.) Conflicts over the role of trade unions and his own position, however, seem to have taken a toll on Shlyapnikov's health. In late May he requested and received several months' medical leave due to physical and emotional strain brought on from a 'head contusion' he had suffered in his 1917 automobile accident and from 'overstrain of the nervous system'.[35] During his holiday, he wrote his memoirs of the revolutionary underground during World War I. He also used the time to evaluate the role of workers and unions in Soviet economy and society and to consider a strategy for enhancing the role of the working class in politics.

---

33   RKP(b) 1963, pp. 656–62; Pirani 2008 pp. 55–6; Priestland 1997, no. 2, pp. 37–61.
34   RKP(b) 1963, p. 367. The text of Shliapnikov's resolution is in RKP(b) 1933, pp. 869–70, fn. 137; see also *Pravda*, 27 March 1919.
35   Fomichev (ed.) 1984, vol. 7, pp. 47, 52; RGASPI, f. 17, op. 66, d. 42, ll. 64–5, 20 May 1919. f. 589, op. 3, d. 9103, vol. 5, l. 16.

FIGURE 21   *Portrait of Alexander Shlyapnikov in 1919 by his old acquaintance, the Murom artist, Ivan Kulikov (provided by the Murom History and Art Museum).*

While Shlyapnikov was on leave, other leaders of the Metalworkers' Union raised the alarm about the decreasing role of the unions in industry. Complaining that local economic councils [*sovnarkhozes*] and local soviets edged unions out of economic activities, they wanted to subordinate sovnarkhoz metals departments to metalworkers' union organisations. Another grievance was that the trade unions had little authority over large factories, which were subordinated directly to VSNKh departments [*glavki*]. Key party leaders sided with VSNKh. Zinoviev, for example, warned trade unionists not to seek national economic leadership. Perceiving their ambitions as a threat to the Communist Party, he insisted that the party was 'the highest synthesis of all forms of struggle by the working class for its emancipation from capitalist slavery'.[36]

Still, party leaders tried to reconcile with Communist trade-union leaders who they perceived to be overly assertive. Returning from leave in the autumn of 1919, Shlyapnikov not only resumed his duties as chair of the Metalworkers' Union, but party leaders approved his election to the VTsSPS communist fraction bureau.[37] Having obstinately used his new responsibilities to seek a larger role for the Russian trade unions, he was removed in a re-election after only a month in the leadership of VTsSPS.[38] Probably frictions arose between him and Tomsky; Politburo or Orgburo pressure was most likely involved too. None of them, however, managed to dampen Shlyapnikov's enthusiastic advocacy of the unions' authority.

The Civil War reached its critical point in the autumn of 1919, when counter-revolutionary armies were at their height, numerically and organisationally, all along the periphery of the former Russian Empire. Renewing their offensive from the south, White forces captured Kursk and Orel, taking many prisoners. Welcoming deserters from the Red armies, White commanders hoped that the closer their armies came to Moscow, the more they would demoralise its defenders. The Reds were also alarmed by a small White army's surge out of Estonia towards Petrograd. While the effective leadership and control of

---

36 Sandu 2006, p. 47, on the Second All-Russian Metalworkers' Union Conference, July 1919; *Pravda* (18 September 1919), pp. 2–3, contains Zinoviev's address to a Petrograd trade-unionist assembly.

37 As was usual with Soviet organisations, there were several leading bodies of VTsSPS. The VTsSPS presidium was the 'official' leading body of all trade-union councils. Its non-party members were a small minority, who had no real influence over the organisation's decisions. The VTsSPS communist fraction held real power and it elected (usually under the party CC's direction) a bureau as its leading body. Bureau members usually held dual posts in the VTsSPS presidium, so communists made up the majority of the presidium.

38 RGASPI, f. 95, op. 1, d. 1, l. 8, 26 September 1919 and l. 10, 29 September 1919; RGASPI, f. 17, op. 3, d. 37, ll. 1, 5, 16 October 1919.

railway and telegraph hubs have been cited as factors in the Communists' victory, the Whites' political weaknesses seem to have been paramount. Not only could former tsarist generals not agree on a common political programme, they could not establish effective government in the areas they conquered. By January 1920 it was clear that the Whites' chances of victory had been lost.[39]

Perceiving that a crucial turning point in the Civil War had been reached, some Communists raised criticisms of the militarist party regime. The Democratic Centralists, for example, convinced the Eighth Party Conference in December 1919 to support their proposals to strengthen the soviets as independent institutions. Shlyapnikov promptly offered an assertive vision of the role of trade unions that presaged many points in the later programme of the Workers' Opposition. Addressing a trade-union audience in print and speeches, he argued that the unions would become major actors as the country's tasks shifted from military struggle to rebuilding the economy. The party should prepare trade unions for their new role, but its fitness for this task was questionable, in his view, for many of the most dedicated revolutionaries had either fallen at the front or become military officers. In their stead, he warned, 'hostile' elements had infiltrated the party and had set up bureaucratic barriers between central party and soviet leaders and local bodies. Accusing the party and soviet leaders of breaking up party organisations and deliberately reassigning non-conformist party activists, he proposed to remedy the situation by increasing the participation of lower-level party and soviet staff in decision-making through frequently convening soviet and party assemblies at all levels. Candidates to party and soviet posts would need to have been in the party for a certain number of years and their promotions to be confirmed by meetings of local soviet and party members. Finally, he criticised party and soviet leaders for ignoring the instructions of the Eighth Party Congress on bringing more workers into all bodies of the republic. On the scale he envisioned, trade unions would take over government and party institutions at the highest levels. Portraying unions as having been consistently more progressive than soviets in promoting workers' interests, he wrote that the unions' organisational structure and their huge staff of proletarians would soon be capable of 'mastery of the entire national economy'.[40] His championing of the unions distanced him from the Democratic Centralists, who promoted the role of the soviets.

---

39   Mawdsley 1987, pp. 194–6, 210–11, 219; Kenez 1977, p. xiii.
40   Pirani 2008, p. 56; Shliapnikov 1919b; TsA FSB, R33718, d. 499061, vol. 37, ll. 210–12, a 12-point speech notated as having been delivered at an autumn 1919 meeting of the Metalworkers' Union central committee with VTsSPS; TsA FSB, R33718, d. 499061, vol. 37, l. 205.

Worried about Shlyapnikov's assertiveness, party leaders decided to remove him from Moscow, but found few takers. Neither the Third International (led by Zinoviev) nor leaders of the Southern front (Stalin, Leonid Serebryakov and Ordzhonikidze) wanted him. This was most likely due to his obstinate advocacy of the role of trade unions and to his reluctance to use coercion against workers, which ran contrary to the priorities of Lenin, Zinoviev and Stalin. Finally, he was assigned to the RVS of the Sixteenth Army, which was based in Smolensk on the Western front. At the time he was assigned there, the Western front was not a crucial military staging area. After spending some time at his new post, he wrote a letter to Lenin, in which he expressed exasperation with a post that had no significant duties. He requested either a more demanding post or that he be allowed to return to the Metalworkers' Union. The 'time spent in idleness', he revealed, had 'a thoroughly bad effect not only on my morale but also on my nerves, which have been in bad shape'. During his forced idleness, he sat on the sidelines while the role of the trade unions diminished. With no pressing military duties, Shlyapnikov assisted local unions. For example, he appealed to VTsSPS to satisfy a hospital union's requests for regular wages for sick members and the restoration of freely hired staff to regular and field hospitals.[41] His solicitousness towards a non-industrial union may have stemmed from the priority he placed on helping unions and from his own need for medical care.

While Shlyapnikov was absent from Moscow, Trotsky's December 1919 proposals for organising the post-Civil War economy, which he sent to the CC for discussion, were published by accident or intent in *Pravda* (edited by Bukharin). His proposed 'labour armies', which would be 'run in military fashion', caused a stir within the party and trade unions, because they implied that the state would subsume the unions. Very many prominent Communists opposed Trotsky's ideas. Shlyapnikov offered his opinions when he returned to Moscow in late December to meet with other leaders of the Metalworkers' Union. Developing an argument for a greater role for the trade unions in reviving the economy, he aired his views in such a way that these ideas left the confines of Moscow and circulated in the provinces. This prompted strong criticism from the Politburo.[42] Despite the Politburo's response, he persisted, because he was

---

41   RGASPI, f. 17, op. 3, d. 37, ll. 1, 5; Deutscher 1966, pp. 210–11; Meijer (ed.) 1964, p. 763; RGASPI, f. 17, op. 66, d. 42, l. 67, Shliapnikov's telegram to the VTsSPS communist fraction, copy to the CC, Smolensk, 24 November 1919.

42   *Pravda* (17 December 1919): p. 1; Sorenson 1969, p. 94; RGASPI, f. 2, op. 1, d. 12106, l. 1, telegram from Shliapnikov to Trotsky, copy to Lenin, 17 December 1919; RKP(b) 1960, pp. 591–2.

convinced that his ideas were sound and that there was strong support for his views among Communist metalworkers and other trade unionists.

In January 1920, Shlyapnikov sent to Lenin and to VTsSPS leaders his response to Trotsky's project. His proposals were not hastily concocted, but grew out of his earlier statements from autumn 1919, which meant that he had reached these conclusions long before Trotsky's initiative.[43] According to CC secretary, Nikolai Krestinsky, Shlyapnikov's ideas were known throughout much of Russia and Ukraine, presumably because the arguments he presented in December had been personally carried by representatives of the Metalworkers' Union to their local organisations. Sandu writes that N.V. Kopylov, chair of the Tula Metalworkers' Union, defended Shlyapnikov's views at the February 1920 Tula gubernia party conference. She also found support for Shlyapnikov's views in spring and summer 1920 in the Urals, Nizhny Novgorod, Samara and Perm.[44] In a more extensive analysis of the problems facing Soviet Russia than in his earlier papers, Shlyapnikov argued that Trotsky's plan for the militarisation of the economy would destroy workers' initiative. Acknowledging that only military commissariats could effectively implement the mobilisation of workers for industry, he stipulated that the unions should guide mobilisation, a position that nevertheless reflected the growing acceptance of militarist methods. From his point of view, union guidance would prevent the kind of disaster that had occurred in Astrakhan in March 1919. Party leaders must have been alarmed by the prospect of unions having military forces at their disposal.

Shlyapnikov emphasised that only the 'organised proletariat', workers represented by their trade unions, could successfully overcome the current 'ruin in industry and transport'. Unions should make practical plans to revive transport and increase the supply of fuel and raw materials, and should decide how many workers each branch of industry required, with first priority going to industries that processed raw materials. Then unions should register all skilled and unskilled workers and summon them back to work as needed, from the countryside, the army and government institutions. (The registry would be compiled from union-membership rosters and industrial enterprises' personnel lists for the entire post-revolutionary period.) To ensure that workers were supplied with basic goods, he recommended that local produce commissariats

---

43 RGASPI, f. 2, op. 1, d. 12562, ll. 1–5, '*Zadachi ekonomicheskikh organizatsii rossiiskogo proletariata*'. GARF, f. 5451, op. 42, d. 6, ll. 17–19, draft sent to VTsSPS. Shliapnikov signed and dated the proposals in Smolensk on 15 January 1920. Sorenson 1969 wrote that Shliapnikov formulated his proposals hastily, in response to Trotsky, without thinking through their implications for the role of the party (Sorenson 1969, p. 94).

44 RKP(b) 1960, p. 81; Sandu 2006, pp. 52–61; Pavliuchenkov 2008, pp. 56–9.

cooperate with the unions and factory management to arrange a barter system. In off-hours, factory workers would use their skills and facilities to repair and manufacture agricultural equipment for local peasants in return for food and other daily necessities that peasants could supply. His proposals for supplying workers by means of horizontal economic relationships with peasant producers ran contrary to the trend promoted by the party of the centralised direction of the economy.[45]

The most controversial passage of Shlyapnikov's January proposals was point 10, which read, in part: 'For realising their production programmes, unions should wholly have at their disposal the state apparatus, organising and regulating the economy'. Designating VTsSPS as 'the responsible organiser of production', he called for VSNKh to be composed solely of trade-union leaders. Unions would take over state economic bodies at all levels, direct state policy and implement it within enterprises. Enterprise management would report regularly to workers with the goal of 'drawing the whole proletarian mass into the process of economic construction'.[46] Such was to be the ideal management of the Soviet economy, in his eyes. Aware of his proposals' implications, he carefully considered the role he desired for the party. He strongly believed in the significance of the party's ideological guidance, but he demanded that worker-communists prevail in party committees and central party institutions. Valuing the learning and insights of party *intelligenty*, he regarded them more as mentors than as effective organisational leaders.

Trotsky's ideas on post-Civil War economic reconstruction prevailed in early 1920 because they were supported by Lenin. Simultaneously, Lenin pressed a plan for one-man management of industry to replace the collegial system, in which trade-union representatives had participated alongside bureaucrats from state economic bodies. Both leaders found support among trade-union leaders. Abram Goltsman in the Metalworkers' Union, for example, saw the potential of militarised labour to create a class of managers from the working class 'without impairing efficiency'. For him, union participation in management was not necessary as long as management was composed of individuals from the working class. Most union leaders, however, were aligned against Trotsky and many also were alarmed by Lenin's plan for one-man management.

---

45 RGASPI, f. 2, op. 1, d. 12562, ll. 1–4; Aves 1996, p. 9. Kollontai wrote in her diary that Shliapnikov believed the peasantry had gained much more from the revolution than had industrial workers (RGASPI, f. 134, op. 3, d. 34, l. 4, 5 February 1920).
46 RGASPI, f. 2, op. 1, d. 12562, ll. 4–5.

According to Kollontai, Trotsky carried on a 'very lively debate' with trade-union leaders at a January 1920 'party meeting'.[47]

Union leaders opposed to Trotsky were divided. Tomsky favoured the collegial management of industry but thought it premature to give workers control over production. His authority as VTsSPS chair and his moderate position won over many trade-union leaders. Unlike Shlyapnikov, Tomsky argued that the typical worker could not handle the 'extraordinary nervous strain' accompanying administrative duties that would wear out even an *intelligent*. He claimed that workers were 'exhausted, fed up with War Communism'. Although Tomsky believed Trotsky's plan of forced labour was unrealistic, he also painted Shlyapnikov as naïve, which was an unlikely trait, but a kinder label than 'syndicalist', which VSNKh leaders used against him.[48] Less willing to challenge party leaders than Shlyapnikov, Tomsky also seemed more pessimistic than he about the workers' potential.

Standing behind Tomsky, the VTsSPS communist fraction accepted his moderate proposals to continue collective management but to accept one-man management in certain cases. Moreover, VTsSPS leaders reined in Shlyapnikov, as they planned the upcoming Third Congress of Trade Unions. Assigned to speak on the narrow topic of 'professional-technical education' for workers, Shlyapnikov stubbornly insisted on delivering an ambitious speech on the unions' 'cultural-educational activity', which seems to have addressed the relationship between unions, soviets and the party and which called for the party not to interfere in union organisational matters. Only Shmidt supported him, while the majority voted to limit him to the narrower topic. The vote reflected disagreement with his position, as well as fear of the Politburo's likely reaction. Despite their caution and tact towards party leaders, VTsSPS leaders soon found that the CC insisted on asserting its leadership over the unions by postponing the trade unions congress until after the party congress. In this manner, the party could present communist trade-union leaders with decisions they would have to accept. Fearing a confrontation, VTsSPS leaders asked and received the Politburo's permission to push Tomsky's proposals at individual trade-union congresses, but party leaders took steps to ensure that their line would prevail among trade-union leaders by sending CC members Bukharin and Radek to work in VTsSPS.[49]

---

47 Sorenson 1969, p. 95; RGASPI, f. 134, op. 3, d. 34, l. 1, 13 January 1920.
48 RKP(b) 1972, pp. 179–81; Sorenson 1969, pp. 95, 97.
49 RGASPI, f. 95, op. 1, d. 5, l. 1, 23 January 1920; l. 89, 21 January 1920 VTsSPS communist fraction bureau meeting; f. 17, op. 2, d. 27, l. 1; op. 3, d. 66, ll. 2–3; op. 2, d. 28, 6 February 1920; d. 30.

Nevertheless, discord continued between party and trade-union leaders. While party leaders such as Zinoviev asserted that the party was superior to all other worker organisations and that in time the state would take over trade unions [*ogosudarstvlenie*], Tomsky called for party leaders to trust trade unions and exercise party authority only through communist fractions of unions. He supported the subordination of trade-union representatives to economic council staff [*sovnarkhozists*] in economic bodies, but called for a delineation of duties between unions and sovnarkhozes. Refusing to pipe down, Shlyapnikov insisted that trade-union representatives in economic institutions should be responsible to the unions that sent them there and boldly proposed that unions elect VSNKh, with CC confirmation.[50]

Party leaders endeavoured to remove Shlyapnikov from the scene during the discussion of Trotsky's plans for labour armies and one-man management. Obligating him to remain in the Sixteenth Army RVS, they denied his request for medical leave. Then, in March 1920, he was sent to Western Europe on a trade-union mission, which removed him from Moscow until well after the Ninth Party Congress. His absence was a matter of speculation. Konstantin Yurenev, a Democratic Centralist who had served with Shlyapnikov on the Western front and seemed sympathetic towards him, charged that the CC had intentionally diverted him from participating in the congress, to which Kamenev retorted that the party had exiled him for 'syndicalist tendencies'. Both Lutovinov and Krestinsky asserted that he went on the trade-union mission willingly, although Lutovinov claimed that in the past the CC had sent Shlyapnikov to jobs away from Moscow for political reasons. Privately, Kollontai noted that it was Lenin's tactic to dispatch stalwart dissenters to work abroad or to highly difficult assignments in Russia, where they would become targets of the 'masses' dissatisfaction'.[51] The controversy over Shlyapnikov's absence thus reflected a climate of concern over the treatment of dissenters.

Shlyapnikov most probably placed high priority on his trip abroad, for he deeply desired to strengthen ties between Russian and Western-European trade unions in the interests of furthering international revolution. He had already begun to plan such a trip in autumn 1919, but had encountered CC resistance to the far-reaching goals he envisioned for it.[52] Just as Lenin had

---

50   Sandu 2006, pp. 50–1, on a 7 March meeting of trade-union leaders, CC members and Moscow party officials.

51   RGASPI, f. 17, op. 3, d. 61, 6 February 1920; RKP(b) 1960, pp. 47–80; RGASPI, f. 134, op. 3, d. 34, l. 5, 23 February 1920 diary entry.

52   RGASPI, f. 95, op. 1, d. 1, ll. 8–14. VTsSPS had given in to party pressure by only sending trade unionists on a fact-finding mission in the winter of 1919–20.

seen the Russian Revolution as inseparable from a broader European political revolution, Shlyapnikov understood the importance of the trade unions' international ties to the revolution's economic and social base. His appearance at the party congress, therefore, could have seemed less important to him than establishing links with trade unions abroad.

Shlyapnikov's Metalworker Allies

Many of Shlyapnikov's closest allies were from his pre-revolutionary circle of close comrades. They were trade-union leaders and most had served in the Civil War. Sergei Medvedev and Yuri Lutovinov were Metalworkers' Union leaders and Lutovinov worked in VTsSPS. Lutovinov had also been a leader of the Communist Party of Ukraine. Ivan Kutuzov was chair of the Moscow Textileworkers' Union. Both Medvedev and Alexei Kiselev, the chair of the Miners' Union, had served on the VSNKh Presidium.[53] Such experienced revolutionaries were well-prepared, in Shlyapnikov's absence, to struggle for their common goals. First, they attempted to reconstitute their unions' staff in the wake of severe losses suffered during the Civil War, but party and government officials tenaciously held onto personnel who had left union work for military and administrative posts. Although leaders of the Metalworkers' Union complained of a policy bias against unions, the Politburo deflected their complaints to the Orgburo, deeming the issue an organisational matter unrelated to high policy. Likewise, the CC Secretariat refused the union's request that it route new work assignments for demobilised metalworker-union staff through the union's central committee. Further, Shlyapnikov's allies denounced the political sections that Trotsky advocated creating in industrial administration. Instead, they called on the party to support political work by key industrial unions. In industry represented by weaker unions only, they called on the party to only form political sections through consultation with union leaders.[54]

---

53   Gambarov et al. (eds.) 1989, vol. 1, pp. 191–4, 253–5, 346; RGASPI, f. 589, op. 3, d. 9102, ll. 173–88; f. 2, op. 1, d. 8, l. 90, 7 January 1919. Kollontai identified the leaders of the Workers' Opposition as Lutovinov, Shliapnikov, Medvedev and two others whom she named only by initials ('T' and 'M'), all former workers (RGASPI, f. 134, op. 3, d. 34, l. 5, 23 February 1920 diary entry). 'T' was probably the artillery industry leader Alexander Tolokontsev. Lutovinov identified himself to Lenin as a founder of the Workers' Opposition (Lenin 1960–70, vol. 45, pp. 160–5).

54   RGASPI, f. 17, op. 3, d. 66, l. 1, 17 March 1920; f. 99, op. 1, d. 4, l. 2, 28 January 1920; l. 3, 21 February 1920; d. 14, l. 7, March 1920 Metalworkers' Union central committee communist fraction bureau letter to Trotsky.

At party and union meetings in March, Shlyapnikov's supporters echoed his call for a separation of powers between the unions (economic power) and the party and soviets (political power). Kamenev chided them for aiming to limit the party's power. CC members confronted Shlyapnikov's allies at a VTsSPS meeting scheduled to discuss one-man management versus the collegial management of industry. Although Tomsky and his supporters claimed to represent mainstream trade-union opinion, Krestinsky and Radek from the CC chose to attack Shlyapnikov's views, which they insisted carried more weight among trade unionists. Warning that workers feared that the 'old order' (pre-revolutionary) was being re-established, Kiselev bluntly declared that he had seen 'lords' [*gospoda*] occupying the highest party posts in the provinces. He asserted that the revolution would fail if workers were not allowed to speak their minds.[55] Recalling that no one had attacked the unions when they were needed to fight the Civil War, Kutuzov bitterly complained that the trade unions became weak because they gave up much to defend the revolution. He asserted that the trade unions and factories were deprived of their best personnel, who were sent to fight on the front and perish, while the less trustworthy remained in the centre to put their stamp on policy directed towards destroying unions. Medvedev called for the promotion of qualified workers to management positions, adding that worker hostility was growing towards specialists and administrators appointed from above. The responses of CC members were extreme and scathing. Bukharin criticised Shlyapnikov's proposals to hand over the management of the economy to the trade unions as heretically non-Marxist, arguing that there would be no trade unions in communist society.[56]

Either convinced by the arguments of CC members, intimidated by their attacks or persuaded by Tomsky's moderation, Lutovinov diverged from his fellow oppositionists and moved closer to Tomsky. Conceding that trade unions could not take control of production as it was then organised, he listed preconditions that included raising the masses' cultural level, introducing discipline into factories and unions, enforcing the tariff and workers' inspection. Nevertheless, he envisioned greater worker participation not only in the management of factory production but in all aspects of life in the Soviet republic.

---

55   Sandu 2006, p. 52, on the 13–14 March 1920 Moscow guberniia party conference; GARF, f. 5451, op. 42, d. 3, l. 205; ll. 213–14, 7 March 1920 VTsSPS communist fraction meeting. Both GARF and RGASPI contain records of VTsSPS fraction meetings, but the GARF records are better organised and more complete than those in RGASPI.

56   GARF, f. 5451, op. 42, d. 3, ll. 169, 171–4, 15 March 1920, VTsSPS communist fraction session; l. 178.

Finally deciding in favour of presenting a united front by union leaders at the party congress, Lutovinov praised Tomsky's position as one around which most trade unionists could rally. Tomsky discouraged anyone from comparing his and the VTsSPS position with that of Shlyapnikov, which he implied had caused party leaders to suspect 'that trade unionists want to create a party within the party'. Ryazanov also blamed Shlyapnikov's 'sharp criticism' of the CC for having 'exacerbated' the misunderstanding between the party and the unions. On the eve of the Ninth Party Congress, VTsSPS and the Moscow city trade-union council expressed nearly unanimous support for Tomsky's position over that of Shlyapnikov.[57]

Ninth Party Congress

Despite Lutovinov's vacillations (he supported the separation of functions, but not of power, between party, unions, and soviets), he presented Shlyapnikov's proposals to the Ninth Party Congress, which met 29 March–5 April 1920 in Moscow. In these proposals, Shlyapnikov addressed the relationship between the party, soviets and trade unions. Repeating his earlier calls for union management of industry, the proposals adopted an openly hostile and arrogant tone towards intellectuals, peasants and artisans, which may have reflected his and allies' incensed reaction to their treatment by CC members. Declaring that only the 'proletariat' could be relied upon to support socialist goals, he characterised most of the privileged intelligentsia as hostile to the proletariat. Neither craftsmen, nor poor or middle-strata peasants were fully committed to socialism, in his view, and would hardly have supported the 'proletarian revolution' but for the more distasteful alternative of a revived autocracy. Acknowledging the party's leading role in both economics and politics, Shlyapnikov stressed that this leading role should not be exclusive, for unions and soviets also had important roles to play.[58]

Blaming the CC for meddling in the work of the unions and the soviets, and in his opinion thereby exceeding the responsibilities assigned to it in the party

---

57 GARF, f. 5451, op. 42, d. 3, ll. 116–17, 123–4, 142, 178; RGASPI, f. 95, op. 1, d. 5, l. 15, 20 March 1920 joint meeting of VTsSPS and Moscow city trade-union council communist fractions. One vote was cast in opposition.

58 RKP(b) 1960, p. 235; GARF, f. 5451, op. 42, d. 6, 1920, ll. 17–21, Shliapnikov, 'K voprosu o vzaiimootnosheniiakh R.K.P., sovetov i proizvodstvennykh soiuzov'. His proposals were not published in the Ninth Party Congress stenographic report.

programme, he complained that the CC made policy towards workers without even consulting VTsSPS. Raising an objection that many others had voiced, he accused the CC of not following the true spirit of the resolutions passed by party congresses and conferences regarding the 'workerisation of state-management bodies'. Instead of 'bringing mass worker organisations into bodies of management', the CC had only included individual workers. Declaring the CC to be incompetent, he called for the CC to be 'workerised', which according to his interpretation would have meant a CC composed largely of union leaders.[59] Shlyapnikov's call for a wholesale turnover in CC membership was a declaration of war, but one that resounded with those Communists who favoured a greater role for workers in leading party bodies.

Refusing to engage Shlyapnikov's criticisms, Bukharin, who gave the main report on trade unions at the congress, simply denounced the proposals as 'rot'. Lenin encouraged this abusive style of party discourse, which would only turn nastier. In effect, the response of the party congress to Shlyapnikov's proposals was its decision to revise the section on unions in the party programme adopted at the Eighth Party Congress. Dropping the suggestion for the unions to manage the entire economy, the new programme specified that unions could organise but not manage production and would educate workers. Moreover, the communist fractions of the local union committees would be subordinated to local party committees rather than to the communist fractions of their unions' central committees, as the communist fraction of VTsSPS would be subordinated to the CC. Finally, the congress resolved to flood unions with new staff composed of the 'most reliable and hardiest Communists', decisively rejecting Shlyapnikov's wish that the most reliable worker Communists should inundate leading party and state bodies.[60]

Lured by a strategic offer of compromise from Lenin, trade-union critics quickly retreated from their support for the collegial management of industry. The compromise allowed trade unionists to have a role in management either as assistants to a specialist director or as directors with specialist assistants. Tomsky did little to defend his own proposals. Even Lutovinov, while expressing disagreement with the party's policy, promised to support its implementation. Union leaders appeared to be swayed by assurances that one-man management would not exclude workers from management; rather, it would allow the limited number of qualified worker administrators to be assigned to a

---

59 GARF, f. 5451, op. 42, d. 6, 1920, ll. 17–21.
60 Naumov 1991, p. 28; KPSS SSSR 1954, pp. 490–4; Schapiro 1956, p. 233.

large number of factories, rather than congregate in collegia at a few factories.[61] Effectively, they traded balance of powers for upward personal mobility.

VTsSPS was offered several places on the CC elected at the Ninth Party Congress.[62] These were filled by Tomsky (who proved his loyalty at the congress), Jan Rudzutak (a government man) and Andrei Andreev (aligned with Trotsky).[63] An alternative list proposed by the Metalworkers' Union, comprising its representatives Lutovinov, Andreev, Lepse and Vladimirov – an obvious challenge to Tomsky – was rejected. Lutovinov was nominated separately, but not confirmed by the CC. Subsequently, the CC changed the leadership of various trade unions, even subjecting the leadership of the Miners' Union to a wholesale reorganisation. In a move against Shlyapnikov and an attempt to split his supporters, Lutovinov and Andreev were nominated as joint chairs of the Metalworkers' Union. Rejecting the nominations, the Metalworkers' Union retained Shlyapnikov as chair. Finally, the CC sent several high-ranking members (Bukharin, Radek, Stalin and Kamenev) to guide the Third Congress of Trade Unions. Joined by Tomsky, Andreev and Rykov, they edited resolutions of both the communist fraction and the congress and confirmed VTsSPS leaders.[64] The decisions of the Ninth Party Congress on trade unions thus prepared the way for the defeat of, and ban on, the Workers' Opposition that would take place at the Tenth Party Congress in 1921.

---

61 KPSS SSSR, pp. 483–4; Aves 1996, p. 27; Schapiro 1956, pp. 231–2.
62 After March 1920, and until the Tenth Party Congress, the CC consisted of: Andreev, Sergeev (Artëm), Bukharin, Dzerzhinskii, Kalinin, Kamenev, Krestinskii, Lenin, Preobrazhenskii, Radek, Rakovskii, Rudzutak, Rykov, Serebriakov, Smirnov, Stalin, Tomskii, Trotsky and Zinoviev. Petrovskii, Iaroslavskii, Muranov, Miliutin, Stuchka, Nogin, Gusev, Piatnitskii, Beloborodov, Zalutskii, Molotov and Smilga were candidate members. The increasingly important CC Secretariat was headed by Krestinskii, Serebriakov and Preobrazhenskii, who also were Orgburo members (Schapiro 1956, pp. 262–4).
63 Ian Rudzutak (b. 1887), from a working class family in Latvia, joined the VSNKh presidium in 1917, the CC and VTsSPS presidium by 1920 and the Politburo in 1926 (Gambarov *et al.* (eds.) 1989, vol. 2, pp. 213–22). Andreev (1895–1971), born in Smolensk guberniia, completed two years of village school, worked in a Moscow restaurant and then Petrograd factories. He belonged to the Petersburg Committee in 1915–17. After the revolution, he chaired the central council of factory committees of the Urals and was a leader of the Ukrainian Metalworkers' Union. In 1920-2 a secretary of VTsSPS, he was a party CC member in the 1920s and a Politburo member from 1932 to 1952. See Zen'kovich 2002, pp. 18–20.
64 RGASPI, f. 17, op. 2, d. 29, ll. 1, 3; d. 30; f. 95, op. 1, d. 5, l. 144.

FIGURE 22   *Valentina Ostroumova (family friend), Nikolai Plastinin (Maria's husband), Alexander Shlyapnikov, and his sister Maria, Murom, Russia, circa 1920 (provided by the Shlyapnikov family).*

FIGURE 23   *Maria (Shlyapnikova) Plastinina, Alexander Shlyapnikov, and unknown child, Murom, Russia, circa 1919–21 (provided by the Shlyapnikov family).*

FIGURE 24 *Murom, Russia, 1920 (provided by the Shlyapnikov family).*

FIGURE 25 *Murom, Russia, 1920 (provided by the Shlyapnikov family).*

FIGURE 26   *Murom, Russia, 1920 (provided by the Shlyapnikov family).*

In Scandinavia and Germany

While important negotiations and power plays unfolded between the Russian Communist Party and the unions in spring 1920, Shlyapnikov headed a Soviet trade-union delegation to Scandinavia and Germany, where he spoke to metalworkers about the achievements of Soviet socialism and campaigned for a united international metalworkers' union. The International Federation of Metalworkers had last met in 1913 and metalworker organisations were scheduled to meet again in August 1920. A major obstacle to unity was the Russian Communist Party leaders' desire to control the international workers' movement through the Communist International (Comintern), which was founded in March 1919 in Moscow as a replacement for the Second International. In 1919, communists assumed that world revolution was imminent, so the Comintern's chief goal was to 'hasten international socialist revolution'. The Comintern and its Executive were to be the supreme bodies of the international communist movement and their decisions were to take precedence over those of any member organisation. In practice, because the Comintern was based in Russia and Zinoviev, a Politburo member, chaired it, Russian party leaders held much sway over the body. The Amsterdam International of Trade Unions opposed joining the Comintern because of Russian Communist Party leaders' tight control of it, and pressured European metalworker unions to resist unity with Russian communist metalworkers. Nevertheless, Shlyapnikov was optimistic

FIGURE 27 *Alexander Shlyapnikov circa 1915–23.*

that the upcoming Eighth International Congress of Metalworkers' Unions, which he helped organise during his spring 1920 trip, would establish a powerful international federation of metalworkers' unions.[65]

---

65 Chase and Staklo (eds.) 2001, pp. 11–19; Kan 2007, p. 167, 18 April 1920 letter from Shliapnikov to Zinoviev; International Labour Office 1920, p. 1.

Shlyapnikov gave this mission his full attention and energy. While abroad, he gave no public indication of his dissatisfaction with Soviet policy towards Russian workers. His speeches lauded the revolution's accomplishments and he claimed that the workers' unions held real power in the management of industry. He blamed the Civil War for poor living conditions, but claimed that Russian workers tolerated these because they knew that they were masters of state and industry. His chief goal was to convince European workers that socialism in Russia was working and that it was necessary to join with Russian metalworker unions to create a unified international organisation of metalworkers. As a result, he did not hint at dissension within Russian communist ranks, but instead extolled the achievements of the Russian unions and promoted industrial unionism.[66] Since he saw revolution in Europe faltering, he probably was even more reluctant to hint of the true position (as he saw it) of workers in Russia.

Shlyapnikov's first-hand view of the political situation in Germany dampened his earlier optimism regarding imminent revolution in Western Europe. Confronted with the fact that the workers' 'class enemies' were much better armed, he decided that Comintern policy towards Germany was wrong. From abroad, between April and June he wrote letters to party and trade-union leaders that the Comintern mistakenly attempted to propel Germany along the exact lines followed by the Russian revolutions of 1917, since neither the German nor international situation was the same as in Russia in 1917. Then he urged the CC to replace Comintern representatives in Germany, advice that could not have endeared him to Zinoviev. Complaining that the Russian telegraph agency [*Rosta*] only printed news about prominent leaders and ignored workers' initiatives, he urged: 'It's time to discard this bourgeois habit of a cult of personality!' He saw little short-term hope of winning major European trade unions to the Comintern's side, although he hoped to convince some of their members to support it. In Germany, for example, he gave speeches to German factory committees and the metalworkers' union, which were controlled not by communists but by the 'left faction' of the Independent Social Democratic Party (USPD). Shlyapnikov valued the cooperation of the USPD members, because German communists failed to organise meetings with German workers for him.

---

66 Shliapnikov 1920d, pp. 5, 27–8; Kan 2007, pp. 162–71; RGASPI, f. 2, op. 1, d. 13570, ll. 2–3, '*Rosta*' *Bulletin*, 68, Stockholm, 13 April 1920, translation into Russian of Shliapnikov's speech in French (through a Swedish interpreter) to an 11 April Swedish metalworkers' meeting.

When Shlyapnikov returned to Russia in mid-July, trade unionists were preparing for the First International Congress of 'Red' Trade Unions. The congress was organised by the International Council of Trade Unions [*Mezhsovprof*], whose Russian members (Solomon Lozovsky, Nogin, Rykov and Grigory Tsyperovich) were selected by the CC without consulting Russian trade-union leaders. The congress created the body that later became known as Profintern (Red Trade Union International). There is no record that Shlyapnikov participated in these efforts, and it is unlikely that party leaders would have welcomed his participation, since his views on trade unions differed from theirs.[67] The contrast between Shlyapnikov's high profile at trade-union gatherings abroad and his absence from the first international congress of communist trade unions at home was striking. His pre-revolutionary contacts with European trade-union and socialist leaders still offered him possibilities to pursue his goal for trade unionists to independently manage the international trade-union movement, although it seems he had not thoroughly thought through the implications of bringing trade unions into a Comintern with whose policies he disagreed, or perhaps he was optimistic about changing Comintern policy.

The Eighth International Congress of Metalworkers' Unions was to begin on 20 August in Copenhagen, Denmark. Shlyapnikov, who headed the delegation of the Russian Metalworkers' Union to the congress, believed he had convinced left-leaning Swedish and Norwegian metalworkers' unions to help the Russians seize control of it from those who were opposed to participation in the Comintern.[68] With the cooperation of the Danish and Norwegian authorities, J.A. Hansen, the chair of the congress, put obstacles in the path of the Russian delegation. While the Danes forbade the Russian delegation from entering Denmark, Norwegian police arrested Shlyapnikov and other delegation members several times on their trip through Norway. Despite adventurous attempts to escape the net of police interference, which he detailed in a captivating report, Shlyapnikov was unable to reach Copenhagen for the congress. When he informed all delegations by telegraph that Hansen had barred his attendance, consternation ensued at the congress. A French delegate (Merrheim) repeatedly pressed congress leaders to justify their decision and other delegates worried that the congress was weaker by being so unrepresentative.[69]

---

67   RGASPI, f. 17, op. 84, d. 175, l. 78. Lozovskii (Solomon Abramovich Dridzo) became VTsSPS secretary in 1917. He often spoke as a trade-union representative at Comintern and Profintern world congresses (Gambarov et al. (eds.) 1989, pp. 333–6).

68   GARF, f. 5667, op. 5, d. 226, l. 5; RGASPI, f. 5, op. 1, d. 1472, l. 1; f. 95, op. 1, d. 5, l. 159.

69   RGASPI, f. 304, op. 1, d. 11, ll. 1–7; GARF, f. 5667, op. 5, d. 226, ll. 99–104, August 1920 report by Shliapnikov, presented on 30 September 1920; International Labour Office 1920,

Aside from calling to enforce the eight-hour working day, agreeing to transfer the federation's seat to Switzerland (a neutral country) and issuing a blanket condemnation of war, the congress had few results. The federation remained associated with the Amsterdam International of Trade Unions. Even many delegates who were sympathetic to the missing Russian delegation did not want to follow the Russian path towards socialism, because they believed it would mean civil war. Some expressly equated Communism with militarism. Most, however, refused to pass judgement on the Russian Revolution in the absence of the Russian delegation.[70] After several weeks in Scandinavia, Shlyapnikov returned to Russia in late September 1920.

Conclusion

Shlyapnikov in 1918–20 represented and advocated the views of a significant number of communist industrial trade-union leaders and activists that communist workers must prevail within the party and should manage the economy through trade unions. The convictions that drove him grew out of his past as a worker revolutionary, but the Civil War lent urgency to his cause. His conflicts with Bosh and Kirov stemmed not only from turf wars or clashing personalities, but from different approaches to consolidating power and implementing policy. While Kirov's brash voluntarism would become a cornerstone of the 1930s Stalinist economy (expressed in the exhortation, 'Bolsheviks can storm all fortresses!'), Shlyapnikov's brand of caution and pragmatism would bring prison sentences. He believed it was both necessary and possible for workers to take an active role in building a socialist society, but by 1919 he recognised that something had gone wrong. He blamed the influence of bureaucratic and reactionary 'elements' over state policy. Party leaders felt that rule from the centre was more expedient than mass participation and that dictatorship was vital to military victory. To Shlyapnikov, the resulting 'disempowerment' of workers was an unfortunate departure from the original goals of the October Revolution.

---

pp. 4–6. Delegates came from Germany, Austria, Hungary, Norway, Sweden, Switzerland, Czechoslovakia, Belgium, France, Denmark and Holland (International Labour Office 1920, p. 2); the Russians, British, Italians, Luxembourgers and Americans were missing for various reasons (International Labour Office 1920, p. 3). The French delegate was probably Alphonse Merrheim. Shliapnikov's journey lasted from 7 August to 19 September (3 October report in *Pravda*).

70   International Labour Office 1920, pp. 5–8.

Urgently seeking correctives, Shlyapnikov and those who shared his views mounted a concerted campaign to restore workers' influence over party and state policy. Trade unions, he believed, were the institutions least likely to exclude workers from positions of power. According to his proposals, reflected in major speeches, papers and published articles (1919–20), trade unions would replace state economic bodies as managers of the economy. Moreover, the CC would stop interfering in the everyday affairs of local party, trade-union, and factory-committee organisations. He believed that the active, voluntary participation of the workers was essential for economic development and in building the new socialist society. At first, like other Communist dissenters, Shlyapnikov saw bureaucracy as the chief enemy. In considering how to combat it, and when confronted with a 'dictatorial' stance towards workers among party and soviet leaders, he turned his thoughts towards creating a structure which would ensure control over the economy by elected trade-union bodies.

There was no contradiction between Shlyapnikov's allegiance to the party and his proposed division of power between the unions, the party and the soviets. At a time when party discipline did not yet equate with uncritical adherence to a Marxist-Leninist ideology still under development, his determination to pursue worker empowerment through party and communist-dominated trade-union bodies reflected his belief in the necessity of both these branches of the workers' movement. Although he strongly believed in the power of the party's ideological guidance and its authority as a 'worker' organisation, he understood that the party could not force workers to imbibe its principles. The views he professed represented a version of Bolshevism that was most representative of the hopes and ambitions of those skilled and self-educated worker-Bolsheviks who had belonged to the movement from its beginning.

CHAPTER 6

The Workers' Opposition and the Trade-Union Debate

Even as the Civil War was coming to an end, Russian Communist Party leaders faced many challenges. The policies of War Communism, especially grain requisitions, were becoming unsustainable and increasingly difficult to justify. Just as the Whites were defeated, peasant rebellions seemed to threaten the Communist hold on power and discontent among workers and soldiers weakened the Communists' support base.[1] While the population chafed at requisitions and goods shortages, tensions grew between party leaders and rank-and-file members over apparent elite privileges, as well as a lack of 'democracy' in the party. When a CC consensus over Trotsky's approach to rebuilding industry evaporated, the discussion of the role of the trade unions could no longer be contained within the confines of the leadership of the party and the unions. With debate opened in late December 1920 to include all party members, Shlyapnikov and his comrades resolved to struggle (as the 'Workers' Opposition') for acceptance of their programme at the 1921 Tenth Party Congress. The congress was held as Kronstadt sailors and Petrograd workers, who had been among the most militant forces of the revolution, rose up in rebellion against party policies. Party leaders used this rebellion to tar dissenters belonging to the Workers' Opposition, the Democratic Centralists and other groups. Not only was the Workers' Opposition defeated and censured at the Tenth Party Congress, but factionalism was banned, which also had implications for groups like the Democratic Centralists. The ban on factionalism was not such a crucial turning point as is sometimes supposed, for it only changed the terms of intra-party struggle. More significantly, the new economic policies adopted at the congress radically changed the debate over the role of the trade unions.

Assessing the Programme of the Workers' Opposition

The history of the term 'workers' opposition' in the Russian Social Democratic Workers' Party dated as far back as 1900, when *intelligenty* used it to refer to

---

1 Malle 1985; Figes 1989; Aves 1996.

uncooperative groups of workers in Ekaterinoslav and Kharkov. It also was applied to Urals workers who in 1918 supported the anti-Bolshevik All-Russian Constituent Assembly Committee [*Komuch*] in Samara. As a hostile term, the name drove a wedge between worker and *intelligent* socialists.[2] It may be that Shliapnikov and his supporters did not choose this name for themselves, but that Lenin foisted it upon them. Accused by party leaders of having created a dangerous faction, members of the Workers' Opposition came to emphasise the movement's informality and short life. There is no precise date on which the group coalesced. No conference or congress marked its founding. Scattered by the Civil War, Petrograd metalworkers at the forefront of Bolshevik organising in 1917 only began to reunite in the All-Russian Metalworkers' Union in late 1919, whereupon Shliapnikov's proposals of autumn 1919 galvanised their support. His supporters arranged meetings by word of mouth. Attendance at the meetings fluctuated, which makes it difficult to tally the group's membership. Arguing that the Workers' Opposition was built upon currents of 'critical thought' that circulated among the 'masses' in the summer of 1920, Alexandra Kollontai emphasised its popular roots, yet she claimed that it formed a faction only after party leaders had done so. Shliapnikov later gave the impression that the Workers' Opposition came into being only after the Fifth Trade-Union Conference in November 1920.[3]

By December 1920, the group's programme had been signed by 38 leaders of the trade unions and industry. Hundreds of party members voted in favour of it, especially at trade-union conferences. The Workers' Opposition came to incorporate groups of Communist workers that arose independently, such as the Bauman group in Moscow and followers of Efim Ignatov.[4] The Democratic Centralists and the Workers' Opposition attempted to unify on the basis of a common platform, but they could not agree on the exact relationship between the party and the unions. While the Democratic Centralists talked of the degree to which the party should influence unions, the Workers' Opposition saw the question in terms of union influence over the party.

---

2   Wildman 1967, pp. 107–8; Pavliuchenkov 2008, p. 59.
3   Kollontai 1921b, pp. 8–9; RGASPI, f. 589, op. 3, d. 9103, v. 5, l. 16, 17 June 1933, Shliapnikov's party purge session.
4   For more on the Bauman and Ignatov groups, see Pirani 2008, pp. 50–69, 117–26, 195, 237–52. Pirani maintains that the groups 'had their own political identities' (Pirani 2008, p. 61), whereas I see less rigid boundaries between workerist groups in the party, with movement of individuals between groups and joint action at important moments, much as socialist activists of various parties behaved before the revolution.

The Workers' Opposition emphasised that its programme was based on principles laid out in earlier all-Russian trade-union congresses, but that it stemmed in particular from the economic section of the party programme, which was passed at the Eighth Party Congress in March 1919. The oppositionists complained that the militarisation of industry during the Civil War had forced trade unions into a role not accorded to them by party resolutions. In practice, the role of the trade unions in production had been relegated to that of 'an office of inquiry and recommendation'.[5] The Workers' Opposition blamed the marginal role of the unions in production on growing bureaucratisation. The only remedy for this unfortunate state of affairs was for unions to implement economic policy. Following the 1919 party programme, the plan called for trade unions to 'concentrate in their hands management of the entire economy as a single unit'. Reform had to begin at the lowest level and extend upwards to the central leadership. First, trade unions would immediately receive more staff and resources. Then, unions and factory committees would supersede state economic bodies in the organisation and management of the economy. Finally, unions would nominate, install and recall economic managers without interference from VSNKh.[6]

On all levels, union representatives would be elected, in order to ensure mass participation in economic management. Within the trade unions, higher levels would be accountable to lower ones through direct elections and periodic reporting, and lower levels would report to higher ones. Union representatives would assemble in all-Russian producer congresses for each branch of the economy and for the economy overall. To facilitate such representation, management of industries would be rationalised 'according to production feature' (such as metalworking, mining, textiles, etc). A factory-level worker assembly, elected by 'organised producers', would be the basic organisational unit of the union. The proposals made clear that both manual workers and white-collar employees would elect management bodies. All separate leading bodies, including factory committees, wage-rates committees, shop committees and so on, would come together into one factory assembly to meet two or four times per month and decide all important questions facing the factory. The primary allegiance of each factory organisation, therefore, would be to the factory assembly rather than to higher organisations outside the factory. Finally, in order to improve the workers' standard of living and to raise their productivity, the Workers' Opposition recommended banning all payments-in-kind. Necessities, including clothes, food, transport and housing,

---

5 Shliapnikov *et al.* 1921f, p. 2.
6 Shliapnikov *et al.* 1921f, p. 3.

would be provided for workers, but would not be distributed in place of actual regular wages.⁷

Having developed a well-organised and theoretically based attack upon the Workers' Opposition, Lenin undercut its claim to legitimacy by arguing that point five of the party's 1919 economic programme would indeed be implemented, but not until trade unions were ready. He, Zinoviev and Bukharin promoted the accusation that the Workers' Opposition fostered syndicalism, that it was 'an anarcho-syndicalist, petty-bourgeois deviation'. Party leaders also associated the Workers' Opposition with anti-Bolshevik forces, warning that it would allow non-party workers to manage production. By this time, Communists often understood 'non-party' to mean former Mensheviks, SRs or anarchists. Bukharin claimed that a congress of non-party metalworkers, mainly Mensheviks and SRs, had passed a resolution 'nearly the same as' that of the Workers' Opposition. Focusing on the Workers' Opposition's call for a 'congress of producers', party leaders claimed that a producers' congress would have meant allowing non- and semi-proletarian producers (that is to say, peasants and artisans) to exert influence over economic decisions. Insinuating that Shlyapnikov's years of work in French trade unions had contaminated his Marxism, Bukharin scoffed that the 'Proudhonist' term 'producer' emerged from French syndicalism. Describing the 'mass' of the working class as 'peasant-oriented', Bukharin insisted that a congress of producers could not avoid channelling peasant perspectives into management of the economy.⁸

Forced onto the defensive, Shlyapnikov insisted that the Workers' Opposition was not anarcho-syndicalist because it did 'not repudiate political struggle, the dictatorship of the proletariat, the party's leading role, nor the significance of the soviets as bodies of power'. Moreover, it did not advocate decentralised ownership of production, which was at the core of syndicalism, as he pointed out. He tried to explain that by a congress of producers the oppositionists essentially meant 'an all-Russian congress of trade unions'. By 'producers' they meant 'factory and plant workers, white-collar staff, and all personnel necessary for production'. Peasants could not be included, he insisted, for at that time there were no peasant unions in the RSFSR. Furthermore, Shlyapnikov claimed Marxist legitimacy for the term 'producer', for it originated with Engels. Lenin deftly retorted that Engels was speaking of communist society, not a society in transition, while class war was ongoing. Zinoviev asserted that the Workers'

---

7 Shliapnikov *et al.* 1921f, p. 3; RKP(b) 1963, p. 366.
8 Lenin 1960–70, vol. 32, p. 50; *Pravda*, 27 January 1921, pp. 2–3; TsAODM, f. 3, op. 2, d. 2, ll. 3, 10, 15, sixth Moscow guberniia party conference, 19–21 February 1921; McNeal 1974, vol. 2, p. 122; RKP(b) 1963, pp. 222–3.

Opposition had employed the term cynically or carelessly 'in order to give their pro-worker platform a broader appeal'. Shlyapnikov maintained that he only desired an inclusive term that would apply to all those who contributed to industrial production, whether through manual or intellectual labour. Unable to refute party *intelligenty* on theoretical grounds, he could only conclude with irony that no matter what term he used, his opponents would have twisted its meaning to exaggerate his alleged departure from orthodoxy.[9] Later in life, he seemed to have accepted that he had erred in the use of 'producer'.[10]

Russian syndicalists did not recognise the Workers' Opposition as kindred to them, merely regarding it as part of a Bolshevik family feud. A strict definition of syndicalism truly did not fit the Workers' Opposition, because it accepted the Communist Party as equal to the trade unions and because its proposals depended on a centralist, rather than federalist structure. According to Wayne Thorpe, Western-European syndicalists were 'nonpolitical socialists' who 'repudiated political activity and organisation in favour of revolutionary action channelled through the workers' primary organisations, the trade unions, themselves organised ideally on a decentralised or federalist basis'. The Workers' Opposition shared the syndicalists' optimism about the potential of workers. Yet this only marked both groups as workerist [*ouvriériste*]. This meant that they had a working-class background, were active in trade unions and advocated the direct participation of the workers in creating a socialist manner of work and life.[11] A representative assembly based on delegates elected by vocation was not unique to syndicalists. This had been a component of corporatist theory. The idea was especially popular directly after World War I, although the leftist variant died out by the late 1920s. The congress of producers advocated by the Workers' Opposition had no political role, which their programme allocated to soviets. Moreover, the type of representation proposed by the Workers' Opposition for the congress and its scope of activity

---

9   RKP(b) 1963, pp. 359–67, 380, 526–31; Sandu 2006, pp. 50–1. He said that if he had used the term 'workers', rather than 'producers', he would have been charged with Makhaevism.

10 At his purge in 1933, Shliapnikov said: 'When Lenin said to me that "producer" could be understood as "commodity-producer", I was indignant, but of course I cannot deny the fairness of such a rebuke' (RGASPI, f. 589, d. 9103, vol. 5, l. 13). Shliapnikov's daughter Irina possesses a 75-page manuscript about the Workers' Opposition that her father wrote in the mid-1920s; the NKVD confiscated it upon his arrest in 1935 and the Central FSB archive only returned it to the family in the 1990s. I have not had access to this document and have not seen references to it anywhere in the archives I consulted for my research.

11 Voline 1974, p. 437; Thorpe 1989, pp. xiii, 15, 165. Thorpe, whose definitions are rooted in the context of French syndicalism, admits that syndicalists varied by country and region (Thorpe 1989, p. 28).

was significantly different from producer congresses proposed by many corporatists and syndicalists. Nevertheless, the anarcho-syndicalist label persisted, both in Soviet historiography and in many Western studies.[12]

Tsektran, the Ninth Party Conference and the Trade-Union Commission

Shlyapnikov's determined campaign to promote the role of workers' initiative was, in his opinion and that of his supporters, the only acceptable means for redressing the dire economic straits in Russia towards the end of the Civil War. They believed that rival programmes would necessitate abandoning the emancipatory goals of the revolution. Trotsky disagreed. Having identified the transport crisis as the main reason for food and fuel shortages and inadequate supply of the army, he advocated militarisation and compulsion to make railways work efficiently and smoothly. The CC's creation of Tsektran, which merged the unions of railway workers and water-transport workers, in late August 1920, was his initiative. As Tsektran chair, he planned to use it to implement his ideas on labour conscription. He chose to amalgamate the railway and water-transport unions and appoint their leadership because he did not trust elected union leaders to use compulsion against workers.[13] As the most controversial example of CC interference in union matters at this time, his measure inflamed discussion over the role of the trade unions in the post-Civil War economy. Shlyapnikov and other union leaders feared the precedent Tsektran set for amalgamating unions, absorbing them into a centralised state administration and appointing leaders willing to follow CC orders. They suspected that Trotsky was preparing to extend militarisation of transport to all industry.

Until the Ninth Party Conference, which took place in Moscow on 22–5 September 1920, Trotsky and his supporters had great influence within the CC. Due in part to increasing worry in the party about conflicts between party leaders and activists, however, his influence began to wane on the eve of the conference. Thus the conference presidium proposed by the CC included Lenin, Zinoviev, Tomsky and Bukharin, but neither Trotsky nor any of his more

---

12   Landauer 1983, pp. 1, 69; Shukman (ed.) 1988, p. 152; Sorenson 1969, p. 94; Ruble 1981, p. 10, and Ruble 1983, p. 3.

13   Bunyan 1967, pp. 188–9, 26 August 1920 decree; Sorenson 1969, p. 107; Rosenberg 1989, pp. 349–73. The actual implementation of the Tsektran merger began only in October 1920, due to opposition from high-ranking members of the water-transport union.

adamant defenders. Trotsky's supporters managed to add him and Radek to the presidium.[14] The focus of the conference was Russia's military situation, especially the Red Army's defeat in Poland, but intense debate ensued over the state of 'democracy' within the party and over Trotsky's plans for the militarisation of the economy.

An important watershed in the debate over the role of the trade unions and over party democracy, the Ninth Party Conference featured fierce exchanges between leaders of the Workers' Opposition and higher party leaders. Shlyapnikov returned from Scandinavia only in time for the last part of this conference. Changes in how some CC members viewed Trotsky's policies impressed him, although he remained sceptical of their motives. For example, Zinoviev undercut many of the opposition's demands by calling for greater criticism of party decisions, for more tolerance towards differing opinions among party members and for more frequently convened assemblies of party members. Due to growing concern over discord between party leaders and the rank-and-file, he and some other party leaders saw a need to tone down the harsh impression created by the policies Trotsky initiated and to extend a hand towards dissenters.[15]

Having been in Scandinavia during the creation of Tsektran, Shlyapnikov was not prepared to speak about it. Instead, Lutovinov was the main speaker for the Workers' Opposition. Having adopted a more radical position since the Ninth Party Congress in March, he delivered a speech so replete with criticism of party leaders that it was never published in its entirety. Calling for 'radical treatment' for 'all the cancers [*yazvy*] eating away the body of our party', his demands for reform included: 1) restoring leadership of the party to the CC rather than (as he implied) leaving it to the Politburo, 2) allowing soviets, party committees and trade unions to work without interference from higher party bodies and 3) ending the practice of appointments of party and soviet officials by central bodies.[16] Perhaps he was angered by the failure of the CC elected at the last congress to redress grievances.

---

14 RKP(b) 1972, p. 3. In June 1920, CC secretary, Evgenii Preobrazhenskii, warned of the danger posed by conflicts between the 'rank-and-file' [*nizy*] and the 'higher-ups' [*verkhi*] in the party and in early September the CC issued a circular on the topic (Sandu 2006, p. 79).
15 RGASPI, f. 95, op. 1, d. 10, I. 202; Sandu 2006, pp. 71–2; Pirani 2008.
16 Zorkii (ed.) 1926, p. 16; RKP(b) 1972, pp. 63–4. The Ninth Party Conference protocols were first published in a shortened version in 1920. The version published in 1972 was based on the full stenographic report preserved in party archives, but it contained only a brief summary of Lutovinov's speech.

In unpublished parts of his speech, Lutovinov insisted that the party should stop dispersing elected bodies and should step up efforts to include workers in party committees, soviets and trade unions. Even the Politburo and CC should hold a worker majority. Central officials who behaved in an authoritarian way would be sent to the provinces and replaced by 'fresh forces from the local level'. Workers, under party leadership, should discuss all policy matters. He warned that if such measures were not taken, workers would rise up against the party. Rumours arose that he advocated 'a third proletarian revolution'.[17] Indeed, Evgeny Preobrazhensky, a CC secretary and Trotsky supporter who responded to Lutovinov's speech, perceived a veiled threat in his words. From his perspective, the CC had insufficient staff to exert leadership, much less interfere in the work of other bodies.[18] Lutovinov's position, and the reaction to it, harkened back to the controversy over Shlyapnikov's 1919 proclamations.

Others echoed Lutovinov's criticisms. Questioning Zinoviev's sincerity, Medvedev, Kutuzov and Kollontai demanded guarantees that workers would take up at least half of the places on regional party committees and that those who criticised would not be transferred from their positions. Their complaints provoked the wrath of Lenin, who retorted that in times of military danger there could be no question of discussion.[19] Nevertheless, the CC consensus of supporting Trotsky's policy on the militarisation of industry was breaking down. Shlyapnikov and other dissenters thus had the opportunity to contribute towards building a new consensus.

In autumn 1920, the major factions in the debate over the role of the trade unions took formation in broad outlines; there were supporters of Lenin's position, those who stood behind Trotsky's proposals and the Workers' Opposition, led by Shlyapnikov. Both Trotsky and Lenin were in the CC, which split in support for their platforms, while the Workers' Opposition had no CC presence. Lines between Trotsky's supporters and his opponents in the CC were drawn more definitively in early November 1920. At the 8–9 November CC plenums, Lenin and Trotsky submitted separate proposals on the role of the trade

---

17   RGASPI, f. 17, op. 71, d. 79, ll. 1–2, 23 October 1920, a copy of Lutovinov's letter to Ukrainian comrades. In the letter, Lutovinov urged his Ukrainian comrades to oust specific leaders of the Communist Party of Ukraine (Rakovskii, Iakovlev, Epshtein and Kassior), which brought his letter to the attention of party leaders in Moscow. According to Trotsky (RGASPI, f. 5, op. 2, d. 288), Zinoviev delivered Lutovinov's letter to the CC. The Orgburo investigated the letter after leaders of the Communist Party of Ukraine complained about it (RGASPI, f. 17, op. 112, d. 100, l. 6).

18   RKP(b) 1972, pp. 172–3.

19   RKP(b) 1972, pp. 175–6 (Medvedev), pp. 186–7 (Kutuzov), pp. 187–8 (Kollontai), and pp. 188–90 (Lenin).

unions. Sharp debate followed. While Trotsky wanted to subsume the trade unions into the state, Lenin's more moderate proposal opposed labour armies and allowed trade unions to be organisationally separate from the state, while strictly limiting their role to educating and preparing workers for their role in a socialist society. In the absence of several key Trotsky supporters, Lenin won a narrow CC majority.[20] Given the close vote, some CC members called for a public discussion, but the majority sought consensus.[21]

Several other viewpoints in the CC gradually merged with Lenin's or Trotsky's position. Bukharin, for example, called for trade unions both to educate workers and to be gradually absorbed as an equal partner into the state system for administering industry, but by January 1921, he and Trotsky had agreed on common proposals. Tomsky and Rudzutak, representing the majority of the VTsSPS Presidium, favoured a greater role for the unions in economic management than under Lenin's plan, but rejected forceful subordination to state bodies, proposed by Trotsky. They accepted the party CC's sole right to make policy regarding workers, but advocated that it consider the opinions of the trade-union leaders. Representing VSNKh, Rykov favoured Nogin's proposal to eliminate all trade-union activities in areas already supervised by the state (such as in culture, tariffs, education and finances). It is hard to imagine that any role would have remained for unions under such a plan. By late January, VTsSPS and VSNKh leaders had aligned themselves with Lenin. This faction, forming a slight majority in the CC, was then referred to as the 'Ten'.[22] The Ten called for trade unions to educate workers in communism and mobilise labour for raising the level of production, but they deemed the absorption of the trade unions into the state to be unwise, for it would interfere with their task of educating workers. The remaining eight minority CC members supported

---

20   Eight voted for Lenin's proposals, while seven voted for Trotsky's. The CC created a commission composed of Lenin, Trotsky, Zinoviev, Bukharin and Tomskii to rework Lenin's proposals (RGASPI, f. 17, op. 2, d. 37, 8 November 1920). Those attending were Lenin, Trotsky, Zinoviev, Kalinin, Tomskii, Krestinskii, Serebriakov, Bukharin, Artëm, Preobrazhenskii, Dzerzhinskii, Andreev, Kamenev, Rudzutak, Rykov and Radek. Only four of Trotsky's supporters came out against Lenin's theses; the rest abstained.

21   RGASPI, f. 17, op. 2, d. 38, 9 November 1920. Kamenev, Tomsky, Bukharin, Serebriakov, Sergeev, Dzerzhinskii, Radek, Krestinskii, Rykov and Zinoviev called for renewed discussion in the hope of creating a consensus. These 10 members, who included some supporters of Trotsky, were not identical with the 'Ten' who supported Lenin's platform on unions.

22   Cohen 1980, pp. 103–5; Lenin 1960–70, vol. 32, p. 47; GARF, f. 5451, op. 42, d. 3, l. 43. The Ten were Lenin, Zinoviev, Stalin, Tomskii, Rudzutak, Artëm, Kalinin, Kamenev, Petrovskii and Rykov. Their platform is in Zinoviev 1921, pp. 9–32.

Trotsky's proposals.[23] Because representatives of absorbed factions gave minority papers at debates on the role of trade unions, Medvedev argued that the Ten attempted to sow confusion and create the impression that only they represented stability.[24] The Workers' Opposition, which continued to stand on its own platform, suffered from appearing to be one of many minor platforms, rather than the major alternative to Trotsky and the Ten.

The communist fraction of the Fifth All-Russian Conference of Trade Unions (2–9 November 1920) offered a major forum for a discussion of the role of the trade unions. Many trade-union leaders attacked Trotsky's proposals. In his first major speech on behalf of the Workers' Opposition since returning to Russia from abroad, Shlyapnikov spiritedly defended the Workers' Opposition and skewered his rivals. Perhaps rashly, he accused Rykov and Trotsky of attempting to increase their personal power in the government by hoarding rights, prerogatives and resources for their bureaucratic power bases in VSNKh and Tsektran. Some applauded him, but others accused him of 'infamy' from the floor. Blaming Rykov for bureaucratic obstacles that seemed intended to exclude metalworkers from organising the metals industry, he also accused him of employing representatives of pre-revolutionary firms in influential positions. Alluding to Trotsky and Bukharin, Shlyapnikov proclaimed that 'lawyers or journalists, who have just joined up' could never manage at the level of union administrators with three years of crisis-management experience in industry. He found it ironic that Trotsky, who 'has become an inveterate trade unionist only in two months', tried to teach delegates the history of trade unions and their purpose. He warned that if Trotsky managed industry as he had railroads, workers guilty of minor infractions would be gaoled. Extolling workers for their heroism, he concluded that in order to become true managers of production, trade unions had to seize control of the Communist Party. In the final accounting, however, he laid the blame for the weakness of the unions at the feet of the CC secretary. Somewhat contradictorily, Shlyapnikov called both for unions to have more of an institutional link with the CC, so that their influence would not depend upon the personality of the party secretary, and for the party to 'leave us alone'.[25]

---

23   Trotsky's CC supporters were Krestinskii, Preobrazhenskii, Serebriakov, Andreev, Dzerzhinskii, Bukharin and Rakovskii (RGASPI, f. 17, op. 2, d. 56, l. 5). Piatakov, Larin, Sokol'nikov, Iakovleva, and Gol'tsman (none of whom belonged to the CC) also signed (Daniels 1988, pp. 132–4).

24   TsAODM, f. 3, op. 2, d. 34, l. 54, 21 January 1921, Moscow party committee session.

25   RGASPI, f. 95, op. 1, d. 10, ll. 1–44, ll. 113–17, 202–4.

In the wake of so much criticism within the closed communist fraction, Trotsky's supporters in Tsektran brazenly (and atypically) aired his views to non-party delegates and characterised his critics' speeches as 'demagogic'. Communist Party members usually conducted serious debate only within the communist fraction, but did not air their disagreements in open forums, where reports on benign topics were given. Therefore, Shlyapnikov, Tomsky and others appealed to the CC to prosecute (in a party court) those who had violated discipline. Relations between Trotsky's trade-unionist supporters on the one hand, and those who supported Tomsky and Shlyapnikov on the other, became so contentious that the party CC invited trade-union leaders into the commission it had already established to iron out differences among CC members on the trade-union issue. Party leaders often used semi-formal commissions to resolve conflict outside full CC sessions. Original members of the commission were Zinoviev (chair), Tomsky, Trotsky, Rudzutak and Rykov, while Shlyapnikov, Lutovinov, Andreev and Lozovsky were added as union representatives.[26]

The trade-union commission quickly unravelled. First, Trotsky resigned before it even started to meet, as he had realised that its composition put him at a disadvantage. With Trotsky absent, the commission quickly took stances diametrically opposed to his. Shlyapnikov seems to have hoped that the Workers' Opposition would be included in a consensus, but his distrust of Tomsky and frictions between him and Lutovinov undermined any such possibility. When Shlyapnikov's suggestions (in his absence) were not incorporated in the commission's draft proposals, he resigned. Although Lutovinov remained, the commission's final proposals, formulated by a subcommission composed entirely of Lenin's supporters, reflected only the point of view of the Ten.[27] The surprised Lutovinov, frustrated by the commission's lack of practical results and by the way in which he had been manipulated, announced his intention to leave his leadership posts to resume factory work, but VTsSPS forbade him to do so. Trotsky agreed with Lutovinov that Lenin had employed the commission to bolster support for the platform of the Ten. Victor Serge,

---

26   RGASPI, f. 5, op. 2, d. 334, l. 5, memo to the CC (copy) dated 6 November 1920 and signed by Tomskii, Lozovskii, Lutovinov and Shliapnikov; RGASPI, f. 17, op. 2, d. 37, 8 November 1920; RGASPI, f. 95, op. 1, d. 10, 9 November, ll. 145–6; RGASPI, f. 17, op. 2, d. 41, 10 November 1920; *Pravda* (13 November 1920), p. 2.

27   RKP(b) 1963, p. 379; Trotsky 1921, pp. 15–21; RGASPI, f. 5, op. 2, d. 288; f. 95, op. 1, d. 23, ll. 4–13; GARF, f. 5451, op. 42, d. 3, ll. 19–20, 25, 41–4. The final proposals were published under the initial 'Iu', creating the impression that Iurii Lutovinov was responsible for the final formulation. Subcommission members were Zinoviev, Lozovskii, Tomskii, Tsyperovich, Stalin and Kamenev.

who saw Shlyapnikov around this time, recalled him as 'a very bitter man'.[28] If Shlyapnikov felt he had been manipulated, this would explain his resentment and anger. It remained for the Workers' Opposition to wage a campaign for support of its platform during elections to the upcoming Tenth Party Congress. But there was little time.

The Metalworkers' Union was potentially a powerful instrument for the advocacy and implementation of the Workers' Opposition's programme. It was led by a central committee, which elected a presidium and a chair (Shlyapnikov). In addition, the union's central committee included a communist fraction, which was led by a bureau. Shlyapnikov chaired the bureau, which actually guided the union. Most members of the bureau belonged to the Workers' Opposition, but the Workers' Opposition had only a slight majority in the Metalworkers' Union's central committee (the minority was split between supporters of Trotsky and Lenin). After 38 leaders of trade unions and industry endorsed the proposals of the Workers' Opposition on 18 December, the bureau of the Metalworkers' Union central committee prepared a bulletin to mobilise support for these proposals among the union's regional branches. Of the five bureau members, four (Shlyapnikov, Vladimirov, Lavrentev and Skliznev) belonged to the Workers' Opposition. Gurevich, a supporter of Trotsky, cast the lone vote against the dissemination of the circular and contested the bureau's decision to appeal to regional committees for support, without first seeking agreement within the union's central committee.[29]

In the bulletin, the bureau emphasised that communist workers should define the role the party would take within the state and urged that metalworkers participate more actively in party affairs, especially in the selection of delegates to the Tenth Party Congress. Scoffing at the platforms of Trotsky and the Ten on the role of trade unions, the bureau endorsed the platform of the Workers' Opposition as that closest in spirit to the section on the role of trade unions in the party programme adopted at the Eighth Party Congress. Carrying out economic policy through production unions, the bureau declared, would eliminate bureaucracy and draw workers back into production. Moreover, putting unions in charge of VSNKh would eliminate confusion sometimes caused

---

28 RGASPI, f. 95, op. 1, d. 23, ll. 1, 4, 8; d. 5, l. 172; TsAODM, f. 3, op. 2, d. 34, l. 33; Serge 2002, p. 123. Zinoviev, Tomskii, Rudzutak and Lozovskii signed the final proposals, but Andreev, Shliapnikov, Lutovinov, Rykov and Trotsky did not. For Serge's biography, see Weissman 2001.

29 RGASPI, f. 99, op. 1, d. 11, l. 20, Metalworkers' Union central committee communist fraction bureau session, 27 December 1920 (misfiled among Metalworkers' Union central committee party cell [*iacheika*] protocols).

by contradictory orders issued by the unions and by state economic bodies. To achieve acceptance of these goals, the bureau urged regional unions to elect supporters of the Workers' Opposition to the party congress.[30]

Nevertheless, the union was not prepared to carry out the bureau's assertive line, for at the end of 1920 trade unionists were still struggling for the return of staff that had been diverted to other work during the Civil War.[31] Considering that only a few months remained before the party congress, the bureau had hardly given its local committees time to do the type of work that would win them political domination of local party organisations. The fact that the Metalworkers' Union was only beginning to systematically attempt to muscle its way into local party leadership roles did not bode well for the chances of the Workers' Opposition in the coming struggle over the trade-union question.

The Grassroots Workers' Opposition

Leaders of the Workers' Opposition tried to mobilise grassroots support among communist trade-union members, but the evidence of how much support they received is fragmentary. Although the Workers' Opposition enjoyed a majority in few party organisations, support for it was considerably stronger in industrial trade unions. Many well-known members of the Workers' Opposition had the support of local union organisations that they led. Certain local party and union organisations had made reputations as hotbeds of dissent and were associated, in one way or another, with the Workers' Opposition. Among these were industrial areas of Kharkov, the Donbas, Odessa, Nizhny Novgorod, Samara, Omsk, Ryazan, Krasnodar, Vladimir and Moscow. Still, support in the unions for Lenin's views was also strong and Trotsky had some followers there as well.

In Ukraine, Kharkov showed significant but uneven support for the Workers' Opposition. A party conference held there in November 1920 witnessed a fierce conflict between advocates of the Workers' Opposition, such as Ivan Perepechko, and Zinoviev, who represented the Russian party CC.[32] After

---

30   GARF, f. 5469, op. 17, d. 6, ll. 1–2, 16 December 1920 bulletin, signed by Shliapnikov, Vladimirov, Lavrent'ev and Skliznev.
31   RGASPI, f. 95, op. 1, d. 5, l. 176, 13 December 1920 VTsSPS communist fraction bureau meeting.
32   Zorkii (ed.) 1926, p. 89. The main speakers at the conference were Rakovskii and Kassior, who were members of the CC of the Communist Party of Ukraine (in his letter to Ukrainian comrades, Lutovinov had urged that they be ousted).

Zinoviev castigated them for repeating allegedly 'Menshevik' criticisms, the resolution of the Workers' Opposition received only 23 of the 316 votes cast.[33] Conversely, the communist fraction of the Kharkov regional Metalworkers' Union voted in favour of the Workers' Opposition's proposals, without even considering those of the Ten. Trotsky had a few supporters. Nevertheless, the union's chair viewed with pessimism the metalworkers' prospects for taking over the party, since his organisation had frequently changed leadership and lost many staff during the Civil War. Once union leaders gathered their forces in November 1920 and urged metalworkers to be more active in party organisations, they met with hostility from local party leaders, who branded them as 'syndicalists'. Metalworkers prevailed among party members in the district of Petinsky, where the union was centred, and party leaders there feared being overwhelmed. The union chair was forced onto the defensive, insisting that his organisation never intended to challenge 'the party's ideological leadership'.[34]

According to Anton Mitrevich, an Old Bolshevik who worked in Kharkov in 1921–2, the Workers' Opposition even found support among Kharkov sovnarkhozists.[35] Mitrevich attested that the sovnarkhozists were all highly skilled metalworkers, mostly from Petrograd, and they were 'closely bound together by personal friendship'. All but a handful supported the Workers' Opposition. They were powerful because they constituted almost the entire Kharkov regional committee of the Communist Party of Ukraine. Some *intelligenty* who worked at the sovnarkhoz 'flirted' with the Workers' Opposition, but its worker members did not fully accept them, said Mitrevich, who questioned the degree to which some Kharkov members of the Workers' Opposition were devoted to its principles. He noted that several prominent members quickly abandoned the opposition when it no longer benefited their careers.[36]

---

33 Zorkii (ed.) 1926, p. 88. My dissertation discusses a subsequent exchange of letters between Zinoviev and Perepechko regarding their remarks at the Communist Party of Ukraine conference.

34 GARF, f. 5469, op. 17, d. 10, l. 82, 13 or 18 January 1921; l. 85, 24 January 1921.

35 TsA FSB, R33718, d. 499061, vol. 36, ll. 20–1, 36–8, Mitrevich's draft memoirs. Medvedev's friend, Mitrevich, was assistant secretary of the Petersburg Metalworkers' Union and a member of the Bolshevik Petersburg Committee in 1913. He contributed articles to *Pravda* under the pseudonym '*Staryi Putilovets*'. Mitrevich claimed that he took no part in the 1920–1 trade-union debate because he had only recently arrived in Kharkov.

36 TsA FSB, R33718, d. 499061, vol. 36, ll. 36–8, 44. As an example, he cited Vakulev, a worker who later 'made of himself a fervent Leninist and toady of our party leadership'. The CC appointed Vakulev to the 'tamed' central committee of the All-Russian Metalworkers' Union in 1922.

In other regions of Ukraine, there was a more typical pattern of divergence between union organisations and party committees. For example, in the Ekaterinoslav region, where Mitrevich worked in November 1920, he found polarisation between party and union organisations in worker districts and those in the city centre and at the gubernia level, where other social groups predominated. According to him, worker districts viewed members of the gubernia party committee as 'products of the bourgeois intelligentsia ... alien to the working class'. Although he was an outsider, local workers welcomed him as a 'Petersburger and veteran party member'.[37] Mitrevich's memoirs highlight the importance of Petrograd metalworker networks to the spread and rise of the Workers' Opposition. There was enormous cachet in having been a Petrograd metalworker, especially among industrial workers.

Samara, where Yuri Milonov led the party organisation, was one of the few areas in which the Workers' Opposition had a majority among party members. In late January, its provincial party committee voted by eight to four for the Workers' Opposition's programme over that of the Ten. By late February, the Ten had gathered their forces. A majority of provincial party-conference delegates voted for the platform of the Ten. Nevertheless, delegates elected a provincial party committee, of which two-thirds were supporters of the Workers' Opposition. Thus, prominent adherents of the Workers' Opposition still enjoyed much trust among communists in Samara. Milonov asserted that the Workers' Opposition had constituents in largely working-class districts, not those populated by peasants or soviet staff.[38]

If the Workers' Opposition could not win a majority for its platform in Samara, where it had the support of local party leaders, it faced an uphill struggle winning in other areas, where it did not have the local party's support. It came close to winning a majority at a party conference in the Krasnodar oblast, where it collected 30 votes but was edged out by the Ten's 33 votes (nine delegates voted for Trotsky's platform). The Workers' Opposition assembled 15 votes at the Ryazan uyezd party conference, but the Ten prevailed with 30. Even in Ivanovo-Voznesensk gubernia, which had a long tradition of working-class unrest, the party conference resulted in an overwhelming win for the platform of the Ten, which secured 99 votes, against 12 for Trotsky and nine for the Workers' Opposition.[39]

---

37 TsA FSB, R33718, d. 499061, vol. 37, l. 425.
38 Holmes 1990, p. 15; RKP(b) 1963, p. 84. Milonov became Samara province party chair in late 1920.
39 Spencer 1981, p. 169.

In the Uralsk Metalworker Union's communist fraction, a majority of 13 against four approved the platform of the Workers' Opposition. (One member opposed the transfer of production to unions because he feared workers would regard unions as bosses.) The Workers' Opposition scored another victory in the communist fraction of the Orenburg-Turgaisk regional section of the Metalworkers' Union, where 10 members backed 'comrade Shlyapnikov's proposals', as opposed to five voting for 'comrade Lenin's proposals'. In Ekaterinburg in the Urals, the trade-union debate prematurely opened in early December, when the newspaper *Uralskii rabochii* aired support for Trotsky's views. But on 18 December, trade unionists in Ekaterinburg responded publicly with support for the Workers' Opposition.[40]

A discussion of the role of the trade unions also opened early in Nizhny Novgorod, an old Russian industrial centre and a source of the strength of the Workers' Opposition. Shlyapnikov travelled there in late 1920, apparently in an attempt to rally support, although published records reveal nothing about speeches he might have made for the Workers' Opposition. Andrei Chernov-Greshnev, director of the Sormovo factory, had endorsed the programme of the Workers' Opposition. The Workers' Opposition won a large majority at the party fraction of the Nizhny Novgorod provincial trade-union council in early March. The communist cell of an important artillery factory there unanimously approved its programme. It also found backing in the industrial areas of southern Russia.[41]

The most extensive records about support for the Workers' Opposition at the local level are from Moscow. As elsewhere, the Moscow party was polarised between activists in worker districts and city and district leaders. Moscow party-committee leaders favoured the Ten, but Trotsky also commanded very strong support among Moscow communists. The Workers' Opposition inspired intense devotion in worker districts, especially the Bauman district, where in August 1920 tempers flared over a rift between party leaders and rank-and-file activists. Trade unionists had tried to put a new district party committee in place, headed by Kutuzov. At a November 1920 Moscow gubernia party

---

40 RGASPI, f. 99, op. 1, d. 12, ll. 33, 47; Sandu 2006, pp. 84–5.
41 Holmes 1990, pp. 15, 24–5; Sandu 2006, p. 86; RGASPI, f. 99, op. 1, d. 12, ll. 27–9, communist cell meeting, Kovrovsk Pul'zavod, 18 January 1921. The most support for the Workers' Opposition in Nizhnii was in the Beregovoi, Sormovo and Gorodskoi districts. There was also strong support for the Workers' Opposition in artillery factories, which were under Tolokontsev's direction, in areas of armaments production, such as Tula and Izhevsk, and in the Armavir Metalworkers' Union in the southern Krasnodar region (Sandu 2006, pp. 72, 81).

conference, the Workers' Opposition formed a bloc with other opposition groups, including followers of Efim Ignatov, who favoured a role for the soviets, as well as the trade unions, in managing production. The bloc proposed its own list of candidates for the Moscow party committee and even met separately 'in an adjoining hall'. When the opposition bloc got a large minority of delegate votes, it requested proportional representation. At this point, the CC intervened to ensure that only supporters of Lenin were selected. Consequently, delegates from several worker districts of Moscow expressed a lack of confidence in the Moscow party committee. Arguments over proportional representation were endemic during debates leading up to the Tenth Party Congress. All factions accused their rivals of rejecting or supporting proportional representation for motives of self-interest, but Lenin's faction manipulated representation most effectively.[42]

The Bauman case also highlights the reprisals against oppositionists. Having received reports that Bauman party leaders and activists held illegal assemblies and broached the topic of armed struggle, the Moscow party committee resolved to expel many of them from the party. When informed that direct threats of armed struggle had not been made, Moscow leaders decided only to remove the accused from their posts until they changed their behaviour. When the accused attended delegate assemblies in defiance of the Moscow party leadership, they were tried before a party court and deprived of membership in district party committees. Representatives from worker districts accused the Moscow party committee of having overreacted to rumours and being out of touch with the districts and with trade unions.[43]

The Moscow case shows how support for the Workers' Opposition was sometimes rooted more in communist workers' dissatisfaction with local party leaders than with national party leaders. This undermined the attempts of Shlyapnikov and the Workers' Opposition to galvanise opposition to national party leaders, especially to Lenin, who enjoyed much respect among communist workers across Russia and who controlled more resources than did Shlyapnikov and his allies. In the Sokolniki district of Moscow alone, Lenin supplied fifty agitators with literature and a car in order to propagandise the views of the Ten. He met personally with oppositionist workers to persuade them to abandon the Workers' Opposition. Lenin appeared on short notice at the Congress of the Miners' Union to attack the Workers' Opposition as a 'syndicalist deviation' from communism. This discredited Shlyapnikov, who in his

---

42 Sandu 2006, pp. 66–7, 74–6; Spencer 1981, pp. 136–7; Shliapnikov 1921b, no. 1, p. 13; TsAODM, f. 3, op. 1a, d. 2, I. 5, Moscow guberniia party conference, 20–6 November 1920.
43 TsAODM, f. 3, op. 1a, d. 2, ll. 16–17, 25.

keynote address had just defended the proposals of the Workers' Opposition as a fulfilment of the party programme written by Lenin. Lenin's intervention brought an overwhelming victory for the Ten. Andreev remarked later that the Ten had brought out the 'heavy artillery' (Lenin) against Shlyapnikov at this congress.[44] Lenin's charisma and tactics undermined the oppositionists' mobilisation of supporters in preparation for the Tenth Party Congress. Yet the oppositionists did not give up hope that Lenin might be convinced to support their views, especially if they could demonstrate the depth of their support through open debate and through the election of congress delegates.

Although Shlyapnikov showed sympathy for those oppressed national minorities who were also workers, the programme of the Workers' Opposition had no provisions on the nationality question. Other than advocating equal pay for women workers, Shlyapnikov paid little attention to combating entrenched misogyny. The Workers' Opposition was primarily a movement of ethnically-Russian male metalworkers, whose leaders assumed that class-based priorities overrode ethnic and gender questions and that proposals to promote workers' decision-making would resolve the problems of women and national minorities. A sense that they were oblivious to the grievances of minority nationalities probably limited their programme's appeal to non-Russians and may have even raised suspicions that they were insensitive or even hostile towards some non-Russians. For example, both the Democratic Centralist leader, Rafail, and Emelyan Yaroslavsky, later a party historian and leader of anti-religious propaganda, insinuated that the Workers' Opposition employed anti-Semitic rhetorical devices to stir up working-class anger against party intellectuals. In the wake of the Kronstadt uprising, Radek and other party ideologues linked members of the Workers' Opposition to Black Hundreds and White counter-revolutionaries, but these charges were patently ludicrous.[45]

My examination of Worker-Oppositionist rhetoric did not reveal anti-Semitism. In Shlyapnikov's speeches and publications he took pains to emphasise his lack of ethnic chauvinism. For example, he wrote in his memoirs that in a Petrograd streetcar confrontation with a Black Hundredite as World War I was beginning in 1914, he had spoken up for Russian Jews and given 'a proletarian box on the ear' to his anti-Semitic opponent. The only contrary evidence consists of brief remarks in a letter from Shlyapnikov to Krupskaya on Anatoly

---

44   Sandu 2006, p. 92; Shliapnikov 1921d, no. 1, p. 4 and no. 2, p. 3; RGASPI, f. 95, op. 1, d. 24, l. 20. The Miners' Union Congress was held in Moscow from 22 January to 2 February 1921. The Ten received 137 votes over 61 for the Workers' Opposition and 8 for Trotsky.

45   Fitzpatrick 1988, pp. 599–613, citing RKP(b) 1963, pp. 105, 263, 274; and Fitzpatrick 1992, p. 28; TsAODgM, f. 3, op. 2, d. 36, l. 1, Radek's speech to Moscow party activists.

Lunacharsky's arrest in 1913 by the German police, where he wrote that the Jewish students who had invited Lunacharsky 'took such a fright' at his arrest, 'that it was a pity, it was disgusting to see'. Both his sentiment and the ethnic term he used [*evreichiki*] were insulting and insensitive and, if known in party circles, could have created distrust towards him and his comrades. Negative feelings could have been compounded by the conflict within the Narkomtrud board (discussed above). Nevertheless, when a worker named I. Makh (possibly Jewish), under investigation for illegal factionalism in 1923, was asked if he ever encountered anti-Semitism among members of the Workers' Opposition, he answered that he had not and that in his opinion they were far too ideologically 'conscious' Marxists to fall sway to such prejudice.[46] Nevertheless, such powerful rumours probably helped to discredit the Workers' Opposition among non-Russian and *intelligent* party members.

Trade-Union Debate Opened

Not only had the efforts of party leaders to resolve differences privately failed by mid-December 1920, but all factions had actually begun debating at the local level even before the CC officially opened debate on 24 December and Trotsky immediately addressed a meeting of trade unionists and delegates to the Eighth Congress of Soviets. The major factions first clashed openly in the communist fraction of the Eighth Congress of Soviets on 30 December. Zinoviev gave the main speech for the Ten, arguing in favour of limiting the role of trade unions to organising and educating workers, and against the unions managing production. Shliapnikov forcefully declared that the trade-union debate boiled down to whether, during the transition to socialism, the Communist Party would put 'canonised bureaucrats and specialists' in charge of implementing economic policy or whether the party would implement economic policy directly through the workers, organised into unions. He asserted that to make unions into disciplinary bodies, as Lenin intended, was unnecessary because 'comrade courts'[47] could perform this role. Most radically, he concluded that the trade-union crisis was part of a broader soviet and party

---

46 Shliapnikov 1982, p. 27; RGASPI, f. 17, op. 1, ch. IV, d. 1398, l. 1, letter to Krupskaia, 26 February 1914; RGASPI, f. 82, op. 2, d. 179, l. 86, testimony of I. Makh, member of the Workers' Group, 1923.

47 'Comrade or party courts irregularly considered violations of party discipline between purges, but they functioned poorly.... The most frequently made charges concerned breaches of party discipline, malfeasance, drunkenness, counterrevolutionary activities,

crisis, the resolution of which demanded a purge of the CC at the Tenth Party Congress.[48] No doubt, his chief goal was to rid the CC of those like Trotsky who supported the militarisation of industry. Nevertheless, many high-ranking party members must have realised that a 'shake up' of the CC was inevitable, due to the deep and close split growing within it.

Soon the Ten, working through staunch Zinoviev supporters in the Petrograd party organisation, attempted to take control of the trade-union discussion. Towards this goal, the Petrograd organisation sent a letter to the CC offering to 'organise' the party-wide discussion on trade unions. Although the Moscow party committee immediately objected, Lenin endorsed the Petrograders' step as a healthy sign of lower-level initiative to heal the party from factional struggle. The party's Central Control Commission (CCC) did not agree. Created at the Ninth Party Conference in September 1920, the CCC's role and responsibilities would be defined at the Tenth Party Congress in 1921. Among its early leaders were Dzerzhinsky and Yaroslavsky. Both were Old Bolsheviks who had spent much time in prison and exile. Although one of the CCC's chief responsibilities was to try ethical infractions by party members (drunkenness, nepotism, physical abuse, sexual harassment etc), it also became an important tool to discover and punish intra-party factionalism. (Local and regional control commissions were also formed.)[49]

The CCC warned that the Petrograd organisation's appeal threatened a party split, but it also criticised the CC for its avoidance of a leadership role, which created the impression 'that we do not have a party but only separate political groups which will struggle among themselves at the party congress'. The CCC recommended that the CC take control of the trade-union discussion and conduct it 'only in the form of comradely principled explanation and not factional struggle accompanied by elements of a split'. Implicitly, this was strong criticism of the CC and Lenin for declaring the debate 'open'. Nevertheless, the CC ignored the CCC's advice when it marginally approved voting for congress delegates by platform.[50] The CCC's pronouncements conveyed its leaders' sup-

---

and desertion. The comrade courts frequently did nothing more than issue reprimands where drinking was concerned' (Raleigh 2002, p. 138).

48 RGASPI, f. 17, op. 2, d. 48; f. 95, op. 1, d. 5, l. 46; d. 19; Naumov 1991, p. 32. A verbatim report of the 30 December speeches is in Zinoviev 1921a.
49 TsAODM, f. 3, op. 2, d. 23, l. 6; Lenin 1960–70, vol. 32, p. 48; David-Fox 1997, pp. 115–16.
50 RGASPI, f. 5, op. 2, d. 150, ll. 1, 3, 5 January 1921; f. 17, op. 2, d. 55, 12 January 1921. Lenin, Zinoviev, Stalin, Tomskii, Rudzutak, Artëm, Kalinin and Kamenev voted for Zinoviev's proposal. Voting against were Trotsky, Bukharin, Krestinskii, Dzerzhinskii, Serebriakov, Preobrazhenskii and Andreev.

port for top-down management of the party, rather than broader democratic decision-making.

As the trade-union debate developed, Shlyapnikov tried to dispel insidious rumours about the radical nature of the proposals of the Workers' Opposition, assuring his audiences that the group's platform was based on the party programme and was the product of practical experience. Dismissing other proposals as 'office reflections', he painted the supporters of Trotsky as being remote from workers. Rather than attacking the Ten directly, he attacked those VTsSPS leaders who had joined it, as unreliable proponents of strengthening trade unions. His strategy was to capture supporters from their camp. As an example of the ineffectiveness of the VTsSPS leaders, he cited long delays in publishing union journals, which rendered obsolete their news and advice to workers. Moreover, the attempts of VTsSPS to ensure a role for the unions in production had so far amounted only to the delegation of union representatives as 'hostages' to state-regulatory bodies. Union representatives, who were a minority in the state bodies, had no real decision-making power and so lost touch with the workers.[51]

Shlyapnikov's opponents could be found even among communists in the Metalworkers' Union, some of whom leaned towards Trotsky. Shlyapnikov formally presented the proposals of the Workers' Opposition at the 21–3 January Metalworkers' Union central-committee plenum. Its communist fraction formally discussed the role of the trade unions on 24 January 1921. While 11 voted for the proposals of the Workers' Opposition, seven came out for proposals based on Trotsky's and two stood for 'Lenin's theses'.[52] The slight majority for the Workers' Opposition was hardly auspicious, considering that this union was its anchor. Shlyapnikov and his allies had thus not managed to win the support of an overwhelming number of their own union members on the eve of the Tenth Party Congress.

Although the platform of the Workers' Opposition was signed on 18 December 1920, *Pravda* editor, Bukharin, and other party leaders delayed its publication in *Pravda* until 25 January 1921, later than the proposals of any other

---

51   TsAODM, f. 3, op. 2, d. 25, ll. 1, 35–7, Moscow party committee session, 17–18 January 1921. The Moscow party committee voted for the Ten.
52   Fomichev 1984, vol. 10, p. 3; RGASPI, f. 99, op. 1, d. 8, l. 1, 24 January 1921. Those for the Workers' Opposition were: Vladimirov, Shliapnikov, Lavrent'ev, Skliznev, Rozental', Budniak, Solov'ev, Pleshkov, Kariakin, Medvedev and Tolokontsev. Medvedev, Tolokontsev and Solov'ev were candidate members. In favour of Trotsky's proposals were: Gol'tsman, Gurevich, Andreev, Lutsuk, Denisov, Tarygin and Veinberg. Gorbachev and Lepse voted for the Ten's theses. Lepse became union chair in 1922.

faction. This postponed the VTsSPS communists' discussion of the trade-union question. When the VTsSPS communist fraction finally took a stand in the trade-union debate, it was anti-climactic. Only representatives of the Ten and of Trotsky spoke.[53] There was no report from the Workers' Opposition. Shlyapnikov was supposed to have spoken but was absent. By then, he must have realised that he had little chance of success in this arena. Lutovinov flatly stated his expectation that the assembly would vote for the platform of the Ten, but he urged delegates to hold a 'real debate' anyway. The majority voted not to debate, with one delegate insisting that he had heard enough at the local level. The Ten received 70 votes, Trotsky 23 and the Workers' Opposition 21. Supporters of the Ten dominated a commission selected to rework the platform. Ryazanov and Lutovinov refused to fill the minority positions, with Lutovinov exclaiming: 'I cannot be a puppet in someone else's hands'. At the end of January, VTsSPS accepted his resignation from its leadership and approved his request to work abroad.[54]

Unlike Lutovinov, Shlyapnikov continued the struggle by addressing communists in Tula and other cities outside of Moscow, with steadily declining results.[55] Other comrades of his also fought against the current, but they were increasingly pessimistic. When Kiselev spoke to a Moscow gubernia party conference, he assessed the role of the workers in the Soviet economy as not significantly better than their role under capitalism. He suffered a heavy loss.[56] Unsuccessful in winning over VTsSPS and Moscow gubernia, the Workers' Opposition faced gloomy prospects. Meanwhile, unrest grew among workers. In early February in Moscow a conference of Bolshevik, SR, and politically unaffiliated (non-party) metalworkers convened. Delegates decried unequal rations that privileged 'higher-ups' and demanded the end of grain requisitions. Many regarded the party's increasing concentration of power in its hands as detrimental to the interests of the workers. Resentment was also high

---

53 RGASPI, f. 95, op. 1, d. 23; d. 24, l. 1, 4, undated stenographic report of VTsSPS communist fraction session, chaired by Lutovinov and probably occurring on 28 January (despite a delo label of 23 January), given Tomsky's reference to Kollontai's 28 January *Pravda* article as having been published that same day.
54 RGASPI, f. 95, op. 1, d. 22, ll. 35–6, 208; d. 24, ll. 22–8.
55 *Pravda*, 27 January 1921, p. 4. He, Kamenev and Trotsky spoke to Tula party representatives on 25 January. Kamenev won 587 votes for the Ten, while Trotsky gathered 272 and Shliapnikov only 16.
56 TsAODM, f. 3, op. 2, d. 2, ll. 3, 14–16, 18, 19–21 February. The Ten received 217 votes, the Trotsky-Bukharin group 52 votes, the Workers' Opposition 45 votes and the Democratic Centralists 13.

against *glavki* and specialist management of industry.⁵⁷ In the increasingly tense climate, leaders of the Workers' Opposition faced dissatisfaction from workers who identified them with Communist Party policy, pressure from VTsSPS leaders to bring rebellious metalworkers into line and efforts by party leaders to smear them by association with workers who had SR and anarchist sympathies.

One final anecdote from the campaign is instructive. Communists working in the artillery industry represented a significant source of support for the Workers' Opposition. Alexander Tolokontsev, chair of the Central Board of Artillery Factories, was a prominent member of the Workers' Opposition. He had been a metalworker in the Izhorsk factory in Petrograd before the revolution, distinguished himself during 1917 in the factory-committee movement and belonged to the Presidium of VSNKh and the leadership of the Metalworkers' Union.⁵⁸ Nevertheless, among artillery-industry communists, the vote was very close. The Workers' Opposition, represented by Shlyapnikov, garnered 25 votes and the Ten, represented by one of its less prominent members, Mikhail Rykunov, received 24. Although members of the Workers' Opposition dominated the commission elected to write a resolution, it could not agree.⁵⁹ This failure represented a marked turnaround from Shlyapnikov's angry and determined speeches at the opening of the debate in December 1920.

Tenth Party Congress

The Tenth Communist Party Congress was in session in Moscow from 8–16 March 1921. As the first party congress since the end of the Russian Civil War, it marked the transition from War Communism to the era of the New Economic Policy, of which the cornerstone was a tax-in-kind on grain to replace requisitions. Featuring stormy debates on internal party democracy

---

57 Pirani 2008, pp. 74–8 on a conference that took place on 2–4 February 1921.
58 Aleksandr Tolokontsev (1889–1937) joined the party in 1914. In a 10 August 1921 memo to Lenin, P.A. Bogdanov of VSNKh described him glowingly: 'To the highest degree an energetic worker, quick at making decisions, capable of displaying great strictness and being demanding, accompanying this with great tact in relation to his subordinates, including specialists ... one of the most interesting people who I have met during the October revolution' (RGASPI, f. 5, op. 1, d. 910, l. 3). Tolokontsev continued to carry out high-level economic work into the early 1930s, but was executed in 1937.
59 RGASPI, f. 99, op. 1, d. 12, l. 45, Third All-Russian Conference of Artillery Factories, 21 February 1921. Gurevich spoke for the Trotsky-Bukharin group, for whose platform nine delegates voted. One delegate did not cast a vote.

and the relationship between the party, the soviets and the trade unions, the congress culminated in the passage of resolutions condemning the Workers' Opposition and putting a lid on the future expression of dissent within the party. Nevertheless, such harsh results were not preordained in the minds of Shlyapnikov and his supporters. By the time the congress met, the Workers' Opposition had reached a consensus on the importance of working strictly within party institutions to achieve its goals.[60] Of 694 voting delegates, the Ten held the majority. Approximately 45 were from the Workers' Opposition.[61] This small number decreased even more during the congress, but Shlyapnikov and key comrades stubbornly persisted. The congress provided an important forum for their views, which they hoped would eventually prevail. More practically, the opposition hoped to gain some concessions for its platform in the resolutions adopted by the congress.

Desperate to seize the attention of congress delegates, Shlyapnikov appealed to Kollontai. Admiring her passion and skill at swaying audiences, he and other members of the Workers' Opposition asked her to write something about the group. The result was her famous booklet, *Rabochaya oppozitsiya*, published only for delegates to the Tenth Party Congress, but eventually

---

60   TsA FSB, R33718, d. 499061, vol. 42, l. 297, Medvedev's notes from a private meeting of the Workers' Opposition, where it was proposed to introduce Shlyapnikov and Perepechko into the congress's presidium and other members into the congress's secretariat, mandate commission and editorial commission. Shlyapnikov received 46 votes as a candidate for the congress presidium, Perepechko 33, Kollontai 30, Ignatov 24, Milonov 17, and Kiselëv 15. Kiselëv received 27 votes to the mandate commission, and Burovtsev 14. Kollontai was chosen unanimously as the representative of the Workers' Opposition in the editorial commission. To the commission on the trade-union movement, those assembled voted unanimously for Shlyapnikov (TsA FSB, R33718, d. 499061, vol. 42, l. 299). Congress delegates accepted all these nominations at their first session. The Workers' Opposition offered no separate list. Rather, its nominees were included among nominations made in the name of the Moscow, Urals, Siberian and Ukrainian delegations (RKP(b) 1963, pp. 3–6). Shlyapnikov was the only representative from the Workers' Opposition elected to the trade-union commission (RKP(b) 1963, p. 765).

61   At least 46 delegates belonging to the Workers' Opposition attended a meeting of it on the eve of the congress (TsA FSB, R33718, d. 499061, vol. 42). Kollontai wrote in her diary that there were 60 members of the Workers' Opposition at the congress, all of whom were workers. 45 were full delegates and 15 had a consultative vote (RGASPI, f. 134, op. 3, d. 37, l. 1). In 1931 Shlyapnikov informed the Marx-Engels-Lenin Institute (upon its query) that up to 60 supporters of the Workers' Opposition were initially present at the Tenth Party Congress, but he declined to name them (TsA FSB, R33718, d. 499061, vol. 43, l. 142, 14 January 1931).

translated into many languages.[62] This has been treated as the chief document of the Workers' Opposition. Yet the group's leaders did not endorse the booklet; they only signed the proposals of the Workers' Opposition that were published in *Pravda*. Shlyapnikov in fact emphasised that Kollontai's publication was not authored or endorsed by the Workers' Opposition; rather, it was a tract about the Workers' Opposition. He consistently refused to answer for it before the party.[63]

An early confidante of members of the Workers' Opposition, Kollontai was an *intelligent*, not a trade-union leader or worker, but the views of the Workers' Opposition accorded with her values. In private meetings of the Workers' Opposition, she assumed a role rather like that of a mentor. Shlyapnikov also prevailed upon her to agitate for them. Due to illness and her work in the Women's Department [*Zhenotdel*], she only began to speak out in late 1920. In her view, the spirit of Bolshevism, based on worker creativity, had decayed since 1917. Her language in print was stirring yet incendiary, more inflammatory than Shlyapnikov's proposals. She emphasised the grassroots of the Workers' Opposition. Her claims that the membership of the Workers' Opposition was growing rapidly, especially in major industrial centres, and that it was rooted among 'broad worker masses', were provocative. In hyperbolic prose, she asserted that the Workers' Opposition was 'organically' linked to widespread mass discontent present in the country, thus enhancing its vulnerability to accusations of collusion with 'counterrevolutionary forces'.[64] Shlyapnikov had been careful to insist that the Workers' Opposition attempted to calm unrest among workers and redress their complaints within the framework of party regulations.

Kollontai's propositions for reform mostly repeated those enumerated by the Workers' Opposition, but she placed a greater emphasis on reducing 'bureaucratisation'. Calling bureaucracy 'a direct negation of mass activity', she explained that the greatest defect of a large bureaucracy was the extent to which it hindered local initiative and made all activity dependent on receiving orders from the centre. Enlivening Shlyapnikov's call for drawing the working masses to directly participate in management of the economy, she wrote: 'the task is clear: to stir the masses' initiative and self-activity' and then not to frustrate this initiative by means of red tape and bureaucracy. Implying that

---

62 Only fifteen hundred copies of her booklet on the Workers' Opposition were originally published in Russian, but it fell into the hands of foreigners and was published in English, German and other languages (RKP(b) 1963, pp. 100 and 866, note 66).

63 RGASPI, f. 589, d. 9103, vol. 5, ll. 12–13.

64 RGASPI, f. 134, op. 3, d. 34, l. 4, 5 February 1920; Kollontai 1921a, p. 1 and 1921b, p. 5.

the current ruling elite had betrayed the principles of the revolution, she concluded by paraphrasing Marx and Engels: 'building communism can only be the affair of the working masses themselves'.[65] Her concrete proposals differed little from those of the Workers' Opposition, but her publication was far more severely attacked. Her brochure quickly fell into the hands of non-communists, and its language conveyed much harsher criticism of the party and CC than did Shlyapnikov's language. Most significant in making Kollontai and the Workers' Opposition vulnerable to charges of irresponsibility and of aiding counterrevolution, however, was the Kronstadt mutiny, which unfolded simultaneously with the 1921 party congress.

Located on an island in the Gulf of Finland, Kronstadt was the base for the Baltic Fleet and it guarded access to Petrograd. Its sailors had been at the forefront of revolution in 1917. Influenced more by the SRs than by the Social Democrats in 1917, they supported soviet power. By 1921, Kronstadt sailors were angered by Bolshevik grain requisitions and the repression of workers and peasants. A large strike had started in Petrograd in February 1921, on the eve of the Kronstadt revolt in March. Neither workers nor sailors were opposed to socialism; rather they were dissatisfied with the policies of the Communist dictatorship. Workers decried food and fuel shortages. The Kronstadt sailors sympathised with them and with peasant uprisings across Russia. They called for new elections to the soviets by secret ballot; freedom of the press for socialists, workers, and peasants and other measures to end Communist repression against those who made the revolution and in whose name it was made. Fearing that the uprising could lead to their loss of power, leaders of the Communist Party ordered that it be suppressed; they had already imposed martial law on Petrograd. The Red Army and Cheka stormed the fortress, crushed the uprising and killed more than one thousand rebels.[66] Party leaders spread propaganda that SRs, reactionaries and foreign agents had instigated the uprising, knowing full well this was not true. Opponents of the Workers' Opposition discredited the movement by linking it to the events in Kronstadt.[67] The revolt and its suppression loomed large against the background of the March party congress.

Opening the attack on the Workers' Opposition at the congress, Lenin dismissed it as 'a syndicalist deviation' and belittled the significance of the trade-union debate. Depicting the party of the proletariat as besieged in a country mostly populated by peasants, he declared that the programme of the Workers' Opposition threatened party unity and the party's hold on power. Shlyapnikov

---

65 Kollontai 1921b, pp. 36–47.
66 Avrich 1970; Getzler 1983; Iarov 1999.
67 TsAODgM, f. 3, op. 2, d. 36, l. 1, Radek's speech to Moscow party activists.

responded vigorously, shifting the blame for disrupting party unity onto the party leadership; this in turn gave rise to the Workers' Opposition. He insisted that the party had lost the 'organic link between party members and their leading bodies', because the centre did not trust local organisations to make decisions. Challenging Lenin to recall the enthusiasm and comradeship in the party during the underground years and the revolution, he advised that hurling insults at the Workers' Opposition could not create unity nor prevent workers from leaving the party. He warned: 'Do not go too far in the direction of struggle with us. Here, perhaps, you will suppress and smash us; but from this you will only lose'.[68] Delegates applauded him.

Kollontai also charged that the CC had not tried sufficiently to resolve the crisis confronting the country and the party. Turning the tables on Lenin, she admonished him for not discussing the Kronstadt uprising in his report. Lenin again took the floor and crashed hard upon the Workers' Opposition, constructing a link between it and petty-bourgeois, anarchist counterrevolution. He lambasted Kollontai's booklet as the best example of this link and accused the Workers' Opposition of irresponsibility and of violating party unity in submitting it to the printers, even as they were aware of the outbreak of the Kronstadt mutiny. Fulminating that a person who would present such a booklet to the congress was 'playing games with the party', Lenin challenged the Workers' Opposition to produce a defence solidly grounded in theory. Referring to the Moscow gubernia party conference, where adherents of the Workers' Opposition had broken off and met separately, he intimated that the Workers' Opposition was bent on fracturing the party. Returning to Kollontai's booklet, he exclaimed that it contained the same slogans as did the speeches of Kronstadt rebels.[69]

Kollontai had thought that her 'hastily published' brochure initially met with much favour among delegates. But she observed how Lenin 'leafed through' it and 'disapprovingly shook his head'. Lenin castigated her, accusing her of writing 'the platform of a new party'. He threatened that: 'For this you should not only be excluded, but shot, as well!' Simultaneously he promised to 'place your brochure before a court of the International!' Lenin's remarks, overheard by a number of nearby delegates, had an immediate effect. Those who had previously eagerly reached for copies of her brochure now shunned her. Even Shlyapnikov and Medvedev distanced themselves from her. In a private meeting with Lenin and his supporters, they renounced her brochure, Medvedev acknowledging that he had not even read it. The members of the Workers'

---

68 RKP(b) 1963, pp. 27–40, 8 March 1921; RKP(b) 1963, pp. 71–6, 9 March 1921.
69 RKP(b) 1963, pp. 100–3; pp. 112–24.

Opposition seemed unsure and divided as to how they should evaluate the Kronstadt uprising and worker unrest in Petrograd. Certainly, Shlyapnikov's defence of the Workers' Opposition was thrown into disarray by Lenin's vitriolic attack on Kollontai's brochure, which, inexplicably, Shlyapnikov was not prepared to defend.[70]

On the evening of 9 March, when a majority of delegates accepted a CC resolution on Lenin's report, 45 delegates still voted for the alternative resolution of the Workers' Opposition. The resolution, which Medvedev presented, criticised the CC for having failed to carry out resolutions of prior party congresses on the rejuvenation of the party and on worker democracy, to take measures against bureaucracy and to implement workerisation. The rhetoric of the party leaders became fiercer. Bukharin made the astonishing accusation that the Workers' Opposition 'was complicit in peasant opposition to the Soviet regime'. Just because Shlyapnikov had been a worker, he proclaimed, did not mean that his politics were correct.[71]

The Workers' Opposition soldiered on. After Bukharin gave the majority report on party organisation and the Democratic Centralists responded with their views, an ally of the Workers' Opposition, Ignatov, made several proposals, with which Shlyapnikov agreed. Attributing the crisis within the party to an influx of careerist elements during the Civil War and to the 'transfer of military methods of rule into everyday practice of the party', Ignatov saw the solution partly in a party purge, with automatic expulsion of all non-peasant/non-proletarian members who entered after mid-1918. Further, he recommended the imposition of a one-to-two year wait before non-proletarian party members could hold party posts. On the other hand, he would have exempted workers from needing a recommendation to be admitted into the party. Finally, he would have required party members to carry out 'no less than three months of physical labour' annually and to show proficiency in some peasant or proletarian job or skill. The point was for communists not of working-class origin to understand the 'labouring proletarian psychology'. When the vote on party organisation was taken, only 23 votes were recorded for the Workers' Opposition, which represented a marked drop in the number of delegates voting for the group's proposals. Some of its supporters went to Kronstadt to battle

---

70 RGASPI, f. 134, op. 3, d. 37, ll. 1–2, 23 March 1921; RKP(b) 1963, p. 125. Kollontai was not invited to attend the meeting, which took place after the eleventh session, during the evening of March 13 (RKP(b) 1963, pp. 336, 882).

71 RKP(b) 1963, pp. 136–7, 222–3.

rebels (which did not redeem them in the eyes of party leaders), while others may have left for home.[72]

Shlyapnikov attempted to salvage what he could from the programme of the Workers' Opposition. Defiantly rejecting the charge of syndicalism, he nevertheless conceded that the programme of the Workers' Opposition could be implemented in stages, the first of which should ignite workers' initiative by allowing voting on major questions of economic management at factory assemblies. The last stage would have to await the mechanisation of agriculture. He stubbornly asserted: 'no matter what platform you accept here, life will dictate not what is written by you, but what is fixed in our platform'.[73]

Despite his retreat (or perhaps because of it), his opponents continued to flog him mercilessly. Asserting that a party congress would decide that trade unions had sufficiently prepared themselves to take over the economy, Lenin nevertheless reached out a hand to the Workers' Opposition, requesting the assistance of its members in fighting bureaucracy. In the end, the party congress resolved that the unions would be considered 'ready' for the administration of the economy when they were free of a 'narrow guild outlook' and when all workers were unionised, a slight but significant rewording of the paragraph on trade unions in the 1919 party programme. The position of the Ten on the trade-union question won a large majority. Only 18 voted for the proposals of the Workers' Opposition. Despite the low vote for the Workers' Opposition, the congress included Shlyapnikov in the commission responsible for writing the final version of the resolution, but he could not have any influence on it in isolation.[74]

---

72 RKP(b) 1963, pp. 234, 243, 334, 652–4. On a list of those who left the congress for Kronstadt were at least four Worker Oppositionists, including Mikhail Chëlyshev (RKP(b) 1963, pp. 765–8). (According to Irina Shliapnikova, her mother pronounced Chëlyshev's name with an 'ë', although I have only seen it written as 'Chelyshev', which is how the name is currently pronounced in Russian.) Shliapnikov later requested that Medvedev, Kiselëv and other Old Bolsheviks with pre-revolutionary experience in Petrograd enter a commission to investigate the February–March events in Kronstadt and Petrograd; he did not trust one composed of people who did not know Petrograd workers. He also challenged Zinoviev to prove his allegations that Worker Oppositionists, instead of suppressing the Kronstadt rebels, had attempted to win over workers to the platform of the Workers' Opposition (RGASPI, f. 82, op. 2, d. 173, l. 13, 7 April 1921).

73 RKP(b) 1963, pp. 359–67, 14 March session.

74 RKP(b) 1963, pp. 369–71, 380, 399; 'On the syndicalist and anarchist deviation in our party' see McNeal 1974, vol. 2, pp. 121–3. The total number of votes (404) was far less than the total number of delegates attending the congress (694). By this time, around two hundred

The final business of the congress included laying the foundations for party unity by inhibiting future organised criticism within it. Lenin and Bukharin worked together to accomplish this goal. Despite Lenin's harsh rhetoric, he had been cajoling his supporters behind the scenes to include a few oppositionists in the CC. Lenin also seems to have conducted private negotiations with leaders of the Workers' Opposition. Bukharin, meanwhile, initiated the proposal to ban factions, which would become the basis for persecuting dissenters within the party. Floored by Bukharin's proposal, Shliapnikov announced that the Workers' Opposition would not make any nominations from its group to the CC unless the leaders of the congress majority would renounce a ban on factions.[75]

Meeting privately on the eve of the congress's final session (16 March), the Workers' Opposition understood that there would be a censure of the opposition but were not yet sure what form it would take. Some members wondered if oppositionists should join the CC and other leading party bodies. Some thought it possible to work fruitfully with party leaders from other factions, while others feared a swindle, and still others questioned the motives of those who would enter the leadership. Given such disagreement, Shliapnikov offered the option of personal refusal. Kollontai asked whether the opposition would disband after the congress. Shliapnikov firmly stated: 'There is no reason for us to disband,' and said that the Workers' Opposition would 'conduct work on a new basis'. Others agreed, with varying levels of enthusiasm, to continue work, but not under the name of the 'Workers' Opposition'. Some were enthusiastic that their views would eventually prevail.[76] It seems that they did not expect a resolution specifically aimed at them.

Two anti-factionalist resolutions passed easily at the final session. The resolution on party unity did not explicitly attack the Workers' Opposition, but its concluding clause (which Stalin made public only in 1924, at the Thirteenth

---

of the congress delegates had left for the Kronstadt front. Even so, around 90 delegates must have abstained from voting, if they had not left the congress for other reasons.

75 According to Cohen 1980, Bukharin supported the resolution because of the danger that the Kronstadt uprising posed to the regime (Cohen 1980, p. 106). Shliapnikov, Medvedev, Perepechko and Ignatov declared they would not send representatives to the CC if Bukharin's resolution condemning the Workers' Opposition passed (RKP(b) 1963, p. 790). According to Mikoian 1970, Lenin exhorted 'a closed meeting of his supporters' to vote to include 'Shliapnikov, Kutuzov, and perhaps Kiselëv' in the CC (Mikoian 1970, pp. 139–43). In a private meeting, members of the Workers' Opposition referenced 'private negotiations' between their own leaders and those of the Ten (TsA FSB, R33718, d. 499061, vol. 42, l. 285).

76 TsA FSB, R33718, d. 499061, vol. 42, l. 285, Medvedev's notes.

Party Conference) allowed the CC, by a two-thirds vote, to demote or expel CC members who conducted factional activity or who violated party discipline. The second resolution, condemning the 'syndicalist and anarchist deviation in our party', was aimed directly at the Workers' Opposition. It hinged on Shlyapnikov's use of the term 'producer' as a non-Marxist term. The resolution explicitly underlined that the Communist Party could 'unify and organise' the avant-garde of the proletariat and lead 'all parts of the proletarian movement, including all labouring masses'. This was one of Lenin's contributions to Marxism. The resolution made further advocacy of the basic tenets of the Workers' Opposition's programme impossible.[77]

Responding with outrage to the two resolutions, Shlyapnikov characterised the resolution on the anarcho-syndicalist deviation in the party as unprecedentedly 'demagogic and slanderous'. Strongly objecting to 'the proclamation of punitive measures' in the resolution on party unity, he and his supporters offered an alternative resolution, which stipulated that the congress reject the 'leading party bodies' [policy of] distrust of the creativity of the working class'. They repeated their call for a purge of 'careerist groups and socially alien elements' from the party and the 'workerisation' of the party and soviets. Further, all party members should be required to struggle against the suppression of dissent within the party. Only under such conditions would it be appropriate to abolish party factionalism. A mere 26 delegates voted for this final resolution, evidence that the Workers' Opposition was haemmorhaging members.[78]

Lenin presented the inclusion of members of the Workers' Opposition in the CC as a peace offering. Shlyapnikov was elected to the CC as a full voting member.[79] He was also appointed to lead a commission on improving workers' living conditions and to the Central Purge Commission; other members of the Workers' Opposition joined regional purge commissions. Their inclusion was a message from party leaders that the purge should rid the party of 'petty-bourgeois elements'. Lenin even suggested that Shlyapnikov, as a member of the commission on editing the resolutions, might find a way of softening their language. Finally, he proposed that the congress not accept any resignations. Agreeing with him, a majority passed a resolution obligating all members of

77 RKP(b) 1963, pp. 573–5, 773–4, 778; KPSS SSSR 1954, vol. 1, pp. 529–33; RKP(b), pp. 573–5. 25 delegates voted against the resolution 'On the Unity of the Party' ['*Ob edinstve partii*'] and 30 delegates voted against 'On the Syndicalist and Anarchist Deviation in our Party' ['*O sindikalistskom i anarkhistskom uklone v nashei partii*'].
78 Zorkii 1926, pp. 27–9; RKP(b) 1963, pp. 526–7.
79 RKP(b) 1963, p. 402. Shliapnikov received 354 votes out of 479. Medvedev and Kiselëv were made candidate members of the CC.

the Workers' Opposition to remain in their posts. Moreover, the CC delegated Zinoviev, Bukharin and Kutuzov to write a letter to local party organisations, instructing them to smooth over differences and work together with members of former factions.[80]

Shlyapnikov was not willing to risk exclusion from the party by disobeying the congress's decision. Moreover, he desired the power he thought he would have as a CC member and in overseeing the party purge, which he thought offered a good chance to reform the party. Perhaps he also trusted promises that there would be no reprisals. Despite his willingness to enter the CC, Kollontai knew that Shlyapnikov and his comrades continued to gather in the evenings in his room in the Hotel National, where many party and Soviet leaders resided, to 'criticise' and 'crack jokes' in a dissenting manner. She thought he was 'intoxicated' by his CC membership.[81] Although she regarded his behaviour as hypocritical, her observation demonstrates that he and other leaders of the Workers' Opposition expected to continue their campaign at upcoming trade-union congresses. They were optimistic that, through the unions, they could still win the party. Years later, Shlyapnikov reminisced that the Workers' Opposition had learned that when one conducted factional politics, and the debate ended, no room was left for manoeuvre.[82] This statement would explain much about his behaviour after 1922, when he continued to criticise party policy without joining any faction.

Conclusion

Through the Workers' Opposition, a number of Communist trade unionists sought to address problems of economic management that caused discontent among industrial workers. The group's core consisted of skilled Petrograd metalworkers who had been union and party organisers before the revolution. They assumed that workers had valuable knowledge and experience that could help in resolving economic problems and that industrial workers and engineers should work together, through the trade unions to revive the economy and to ensure worker mastery over production, rather than worker

---

80 RKP(b) 1963, p. 538; KPSS SSSR 1954, vol. 1, p. 533; RGASPI, f. 17, op. 2, d. 62, l. 2. According to Naumov 1991, Lenin convinced Shliapnikov to withdraw his resignation (Naumov 1991, p. 39).
81 TsA FSB, R33718, d. 499061, vol. 41, l. 158, letter from Shliapnikov to a supporter; RGASPI, f. 134, op. 3, d. 37, ll. 3–7; RGASPI, f. 2, op. 1, d. 14615, l. 1.
82 RGASPI, f. 589, d. 9103, vol. 5, l. 14, Shliapnikov's 1933 purge hearing.

subordination to production. By 1920, trade unions were in Communist hands and included far more workers than were party members. Shlyapnikov and his colleagues therefore regarded the unions as more worker-oriented and revolutionary than many party committees. The party, they thought, needed a new influx of worker members and leaders in order to restore its revolutionary character. Their approach was neither syndicalist nor anarchist, but was rooted in the Bolshevik Party's multi-faceted tradition.

Trade unionists had diverse views on the role of unions. Many trade unionists, even in the Metalworkers' Union, worried that the proposals of the Workers' Opposition were too ambitious, for unions had only recently begun to recover from their loss of staff during the Civil War. Some were die-hard supporters of Trotsky. Others preferred for unions not to become bosses of industry, for they might no longer be willing to protect workers. Despite some support in the trade unions for Shlyapnikov and the Workers' Opposition, the party controlled material resources, directed state policy and determined the fate of the unions. Trade unions had large memberships, but they did not command the resources necessary to overcome the party. Moreover, Lenin led the party and he had often proven effective at charming and browbeating supporters and opponents in order to get his way. Finally, all decisions regarding the appointment or transfer of personnel who were communists had to be routed through the Orgburo. To defy the Orgburo would have violated party discipline.

During the crucial period of November–December 1920, Shlyapnikov put a great stake on negotiations with other faction leaders in the commission on trade unions. When negotiations failed, Lenin and his backers acted quickly to appropriate the commission's authority to promote their own programme. Too little time remained to rally sufficient support for the platform of the Workers' Opposition. Lenin's political strategy was more effective than that of the Workers' Opposition in gathering delegates for the party congress. Finally, the Kronstadt rebellion and worker protests in Petrograd on the eve of the congress made the Workers' Opposition vulnerable to the party leaders' accusations of unorthodoxy. Perhaps Shlyapnikov could have found support among non-party workers, but he chose not to do so. An essential dilemma of his strategy was its dependence on party officials voluntarily relinquishing their powers.

Shlyapnikov was optimistic that he and his supporters could use their new influential positions in the party to achieve some goals of the Workers' Opposition. The CC secretaries, Krestinsky, Preobrazhensky and Leonid Serebryakov, to whom Shlyapnikov had objected, were replaced by Molotov, Yaroslavsky and Vasily Mikhailov. Furthermore, in the wake of the congress, the CC appeared to be committed to creating 'peace' in local party organisations.

Thus the party congress's resolutions directed against the Workers' Opposition seemed less dangerous. Shlyapnikov could hope that, through elections, his supporters would gain control of local party committees and eventually of higher party institutions. When Shlyapnikov was asked to renounce the Workers' Opposition during his 1933 party purge, he refused to do so. He allowed that its chief errors had been to show excessive haste in attacking the remaining bourgeois elements in the country and to ignore the peasantry in its plan for economic management. Without repudiating its ideals, he conceded that its programme could not be fulfiled in Russia in the early 1920s.[83]

---

83   RGASPI, f. 589, d. 9103, vol. 5, ll. 14–15.

CHAPTER 7

Early NEP and the Trade Unions

After eight years of world war, revolution and civil war (1914–21), Russia's economy was exhausted and its urban population reduced. Communist leaders therefore reluctantly resolved to retreat from War Communism and compromise with the peasantry in order to restore the economy and repopulate the cities. Lenin's announcement at the Tenth Party Congress, that Civil War-era agricultural requisitions would be replaced with a tax-in-kind, led to a series of economic and social changes, which resulted in a mixed economy with small private enterprise allowed. Under the New Economic Policy (NEP), which unfolded in the months after the congress had ended, the tax on grain was set at a sufficiently low level to ensure that peasants had a surplus, which they could sell at market prices. Because most peasants could not easily travel to markets, intermediaries (derisively called 'speculators') were allowed to transport produce to cities for sale. Later changes allowed private traders to sell consumer items to peasants. Reassessment of prior Soviet economic policy also led to a reversal of the nationalisation of industry. The state retained control of banking, foreign trade, transport, communications, and large industry (the 'commanding heights'), but it denationalised small-scale manufacturing, retail, handicrafts and services, which could be held in private hands.[1] Shlyapnikov numbered among those communists who feared that NEP would facilitate the bourgeoisie's revival and so undermine the revolution. He voiced concerns on early NEP initiatives as they developed and offered proposals to modify discrete aspects of NEP. VSNKh, which initiated many of the new policies, was an early target of his ire.

NEP fundamentally changed the debate over the role of organised workers in economic management. Shlyapnikov still believed that trade unions should dominate government and the party, as they were best suited to protect and empower workers. Throughout 1921, he was preoccupied with political struggle over the relationship between party and unions. The decree of the Tenth Party Congress banning factions did not make them disappear. Despite creating an impression of unity at the top by promoting Shlyapnikov and other oppositionists to key positions, party leaders transferred and removed individual oppositionists from leadership positions and dispersed entire party and union organisations. Lenin guided this policy of administrative reprisals,

---

1 Koenker 1985, pp. 424–50; Carr 1950–3, vol. 2, pp. 269–357.

which nevertheless stopped short of criminal prosecution or even the purging of leading figures from the party. Party leaders removed Shlyapnikov as chair of the Metalworkers' Union and packed its leading bodies with more tractable men. Shlyapnikov responded in a variety of ways: negotiation, appeal, evasion and confrontation up to the point of violating party discipline, but not beyond it. He carefully attempted to avoid charges of factionalism while promoting trade unions. In the summer of 1921, his mood changed. Angry over the party leaders' takeover of the Metalworkers' Union, unable to prevent retaliation against his supporters and frustrated by the failure to accomplish reform, he lashed out with harsher criticism of NEP. Lenin responded by bringing him up before the CC and CCC for violation of party discipline. Struggles at the top took place in a context of widespread confusion about the implications of the New Economic Policy, worry about the workers' low living standards and famine in rural Russia.

Shlyapnikov and VSNKh

As the Tenth Party Congress ended, Workers' Opposition members charged Shlyapnikov with composing a critique of NEP. Nevertheless, for several reasons he was slow to develop it. First, he had to be careful not to violate party discipline. In addition, he wanted to make the analysis a collegial effort. Finally, the main features of NEP developed gradually. Shlyapnikov therefore reacted to NEP decrees in a piecemeal way. He said little about the tax-in-kind on peasant production, not only because the party congress had backed it, but also because he likely understood that taxation could facilitate rational economic planning more than could arbitrary, coercive requisitions. His greatest ire was directed towards the revival of private trade and the privatisation of small enterprises, which came as an unpleasant shock to him, since he had guided many of the decrees on the nationalisation of industry in early 1918. When VSNKh decided in principle to allow the leasing of large enterprises ('concessions') to private individuals, including foreigners, Shlyapnikov and many other communists feared that capitalists would regain a dangerous foothold in Soviet politics and society. Also resentful at what he perceived as VSNKh's failure to give workers a significant role in implementing new policies, he expressed his views orally and in writing to trade-union and party organisations, as well as to individual comrades.[2]

---

2   TsA FSB, R33718, d. 499061, vol. 41, ll. 153, 157, early July 1921 letter from Shliapnikov to F. Mitin; Nove 1984, pp. 83–5. The decree on the nationalisation of small-scale industry was

By April 1921 NEP was beginning to take shape in broad outlines. Initially airing his views to an audience of fellow trade unionists, Shlyapnikov addressed NEP as it pertained to foreign concessions. Careful to avoid the appearance of principled opposition to party policy, he offered indirect criticisms. Drawing on history, he recalled that tsarist concessions, such as the Electrical Enterprise of 1886, had increased productivity.[3] He recalled, however, that factories under lease had acquired a 'most conservative' system of management and production relations, which still existed in those factories in 1921, four years after the revolution. Moreover, he warned that concession contracts always included a guarantee of some profit for the lessee, whether or not the enterprise would or could be made to work efficiently. Beneath his 'practical' objections lay a worry that concessions would endanger the socialist project of worker emancipation. Shlyapnikov admitted that Soviet Russia needed foreign investment to put enterprises in working order and to supply workers with enough food and clothes to work productively. Nonetheless, he proposed to exclude the largest enterprises from lease to foreigners and instead offer them for lease to collectives of Soviet industrial workers. Giving workers this experience, he thought, would ultimately be more valuable than receiving fees and investment from European capitalists. Demanding that the unions have final approval over all concession contracts (to safeguard worker interests), he continued to promote unions as economic managers. In fact, few foreign concessions came to fruition because few foreigners trusted the Soviet government to protect their investments.[4] The problem of how to find capital to develop Soviet industry plagued the USSR through the 1920s. Imposed after 1928, Stalin's solution, one that until then had never seriously been contemplated by any Bolshevik leader, would wrench capital forcibly from peasants and cause tremendous loss of life and damage to health among peasants and workers to achieve rapid, large-scale industrialisation.

By early May, Shlyapnikov's concerns had grown. He requested a special Politburo session on economic issues, which was held before the trade-union

revoked on 17 May 1921. On 5 July a VSNKh decree allowed the leasing of enterprises and a 7 July decree allowed the privatisation of handicraft production and small manufactories.

3   The Electrical Enterprise of 1886 was a joint-stock company, founded by Karl Siemens as a subsidiary of the German company, Siemens & Halske; it opened power stations in St. Petersburg, Moscow and other Russian cities. After the Russian Revolution, the Moscow plant was renamed the Moscow oblast' hydroelectrical station (MOGES). Shlyapnikov was its party mentor in 1921 (Myllyntaus 1997, p. 542).
4   GARF, f. 5451, op. 42, d. 29, ll. 60–3, VTsSPS communist fraction session, 11 April 1921; Nove 1984, p. 89. Of 42 concession agreements, 31 actually operated, and most of those were in the timber industry.

congresses and the Tenth Party Conference met that month. In proposals he prepared for it, he heavily criticised VSNKh's plan for the denationalisation of industry. Arguing that nationalisation was not at fault for the unprofitability of enterprises, he asserted that the method of management was to blame. If it had oriented their production towards 'the broad mass of consumers' (presumably peasants), the Soviet government could have managed them as profitably as their former capitalist owners had done. Worried that 'bourgeois' attitudes lay behind VSNKh threats to withhold food and clothing from workers unless they were more productive, he maintained that the Soviet state had provided very few necessities to workers, which had forced them to support themselves through moonlighting and 'disorganised barter with the countryside'. Their work had suffered due to shortages, not because they were lazy.[5] Regarding workers as people dedicated to producing quality products in the face of terrible deprivation, he sorely resented implications that they would shirk their responsibilities when guaranteed a minimal level of supply. For Shlyapnikov, the fate of communism in Russia was bound to the well-being of the industrial working class. Changes wrought by NEP intensified his fears for workers and for the fate of Russian communism.

Shlyapnikov's charitable attitude towards the proletariat did not extend to other social classes. He insisted that workers had borne the chief burden of obligations to the state during the Civil War years, while the peasantry and petty bourgeoisie had received national resources 'free-of-charge'. He stubbornly insisted on the allocation of national resources to the working class as the chief priority. VSNKh leaders found his assessment of the peasantry's situation ludicrous, considering the ruinous expropriations visited on the peasantry during the Civil War. Ludwig Martens, chair of the VSNKh Metals Department, pointed out that peasants had owned thirty-seven million horses on the eve of war, but only fifteen million in 1921.[6] Moreover, in 1921 famine raged across the agricultural regions of Russia. Shlyapnikov's concern for labour partially blinded him to peasants' suffering, but he may have regarded their acquisition of the land as a long-term benefit that outweighed temporary loss of livestock and mortality due to famine. Unlike Stalin's 1928–9 policies, however,

---

5 RGASPI, f. 2, op. 1, d. 20219, ll. 1–2; f. 17, op. 3, d. 160. Shliapnikov's proposals for the 11 May meeting, '*K voprosu o nashei khoziaistennoi politike i praktike*', are in RGASPI, f. 2, op. 1, d. 20219 and TsA FSB, R 33718, vol. 38. Kutuzov, Medvedev, and Kubiak endorsed them.

6 RGASPI, f. 2, op. 1, d. 20219, ll. 3; f. 99, op. 1, d. 9, l. 7. Martens (1874–1948) became a Marxist while studying at St. Petersburg Technological Institute in the early 1890s and lived in exile in Germany, Britain and the United States from 1899 to 1919. He joined VSNKh and became its Metals Department chair in 1921 (entry in Prokhorov (ed.) 1969–78, vol. 15).

Shlyapnikov's ideas inclined more towards cooperation and voluntary agreements between workers and peasants than towards coercion. His views were thus compatible with the 'worker-peasant alliance' [*smychka*] of NEP.

Although Shlyapnikov carefully avoided the appearance of opposition to party policy, his conjecture upon the nature of NEP and how it accorded with the party's professed goals hit at the core of what Lenin considered to be a necessary retreat. For example, he questioned how the implementation of NEP corresponded to the party's promises to expropriate the bourgeoisie and to transform the means of production into the 'common property of all labourers'. He conceded that such constituent features of NEP as the tax-in-kind, support of small industry and handicrafts, cooperatives and private leasing were consistent with the party's directive to increase production of items that were of greatest importance to the population. Nevertheless, he warned against relying on small industry and handicrafts to rescue the economy, since their role in the Russian economy was 'insignificant' in comparison to that of large industry. Moreover, he argued that leasing small enterprises to entrepreneurs would not aid the consolidation of the 'proletariat's power'. He proposed instead that the state subsidise the lease of state enterprises by workers' cooperatives. Workers would compensate the state with their own labour, or with a percentage of goods produced by them.[7]

Shlyapnikov was most worried that concessions to foreign capitalists would deprive Russian workers of the opportunity to develop heavy industry themselves. He therefore insisted on government control of key industrial sectors, including 'all large enterprises, mining and processing industry' and all power plants. Most importantly, he proposed that the state rely on organised workers' initiative to rebuild industry. He called for trade unions and collectives of workers and staff to operate large enterprises, certain that workers, as private owners had done before the revolution, would find the necessary resources to maintain their workforce and make their enterprises profitable. As proof he pointed to how workers employed in nationalised enterprises, even though erratically and insufficiently supplied by the state, had managed to survive through barter and toil on the land. Moreover, he argued, if production were oriented towards serving the demands of agriculture, enterprises could become profitable.[8] His emphasis on workers' initiative showed continuity with the ideas he had voiced as leader of the Workers' Opposition.

Not limiting his ideas on cooperation to individual factories, Shlyapnikov saw a greater reliance on trusts and industrial combinations both as a useful

---

7 RGASPI, f. 2, op. 1, d. 20219, ll. 3–5.
8 RGASPI, f. 2, op. 1, d. 20219, ll. 4–5.

means to revive the most vital branches of industry and as the next step in building a socialist economy. He believed that such associations would rationalise the supply of industry with necessary raw materials, cash and supplies for workers. Less important enterprises, which produced agricultural and light consumer products, would supply the needs of their workers by making a certain percentage of the enterprise's products available for barter and sale. The proceeds would be devoted exclusively to supplying the enterprise's workers with clothing and food. Calling to expand the territory of state farms [*sovkhozes*], he recommended organising mutual supply networks between individual sovkhozes and industrial enterprises. In that way, the proletarian state would become independent of smallholder peasants. Because he emphasised horizontal, rather than vertical, links between economic units, his ideas ran counter to the Soviet trend towards centralisation of economic management. In response to Shlyapnikov's recommendations, the Politburo asked him to elaborate several of his more promising proposals (which ones were unspecified) and instructed VSNKh to assist him.[9]

Shlyapnikov's anxiety was aggravated by changes he witnessed in the party, from which there was a heightened exodus of members due to the introduction of NEP. Workers asked party leaders when the tax-in-kind would be applied to them. Commissar of Agriculture, Osinsky, after a trip round the provinces, reported to the CC that many people perceived NEP as a departure from socialism, while others suspected that it was a political ruse that would soon be abandoned. He called for an extraordinary party conference to clarify NEP tasks. At the ensuing Tenth Party Conference in late May, Lenin explained the theoretical basis for NEP as rooted in the variegated social structure in Russia that had existed even before civil war had weakened the proletariat. In his view, the tax-in-kind, industrial concessions and cooperatives would restore the peasant economy, revive industrial enterprises and improve workers' living conditions. Asserting that Communists could learn much from 'bourgeois specialists', he warned that the Mensheviks and SRs, in 'non-party' guise, were attempting to mislead workers about NEP and spread demoralisation. Only partially mollified, delegates aired concerns about early NEP initiatives; they especially worried that leaders, in their 'haste', had not sufficiently 'thought through' the implementation of their policies. Osinsky assured them that NEP would require 20–5 years to unfold (Lenin revised this to 5–10 years) and that the transition from 'bourgeois relations' to socialism would take place not by

---

9 RGASPI, f. 2, op. 1, d. 20219, ll. 5–6; f. 17, op. 3, d. 162, 11 May 1921.

means of 'order and compulsion' but by means of 'enterprise directed towards the general good'.[10]

The response of VSNKh to criticisms and doubts was to accelerate its planned economic changes. Despite the Politburo's instruction, VSNKh did not incorporate any of Shlyapnikov's proposals into its own plan for resolving Russia's economic crisis. Instead, in early July VSNKh issued several decrees that supported small industry and the lease of enterprises to entrepreneurs.

Unrelenting, Shlyapnikov responded to the new decrees with a scathing letter of protest to the Politburo and VTsSPS. This reflected his state of mind after he had been ousted from the leadership of the Metalworkers' Union in May 1921. VSNKh's focus on the peasant producer as the main figure in the economy greatly disturbed him; he suspected that this elevation of the peasant concealed a bias in favour of the peasantry as a social class. Asserting that the resolutions revealed a disdain towards workers, he angrily complained: 'There is no one poorer and hungrier than that industrial proletarian seemingly well-supplied by nearly all bodies of the Republic'. Moreover, he alleged that supplies meant for workers never reached them, but instead were plundered or misappropriated by peasants, townsmen and petty-bourgeois elements in Soviet institutions. Finally, he found the decrees profoundly neglectful of the need to preserve the industrial work force, revitalise industry and ensure the success of the workers' revolution, concluding: 'The entire decree is full of anti-proletarian tendencies indicating that the VSNKh Presidium is influenced by proprietary desires and petty bourgeois interests'.[11] With this letter, Shlyapnikov vented his outrage at the turn that state economic policy was taking.

Fourth All-Russian Congress of Trade Unions

Despite the attempts of party leaders to clarify the nature and time span of NEP, much confusion persisted – particularly over what the role of the unions should be in the mixed economy that was developing. The Fourth All-Russian Congress of Trade Unions, which met on 17–25 May 1921 in Moscow, faced contentious issues such as party-union relations, the competition between production unions and gubernia trade-union councils for the direction of VTsSPS and whether the supply of workers should be tied to productivity. Discontent from below, and the Politburo's dissatisfaction with trade-union leaders, threatened

---

10 Tsakunov 1994, pp. 52–7. Lenin's report echoed points he had made a month earlier in a brochure on the tax-in-kind (Lenin 1960–70, vol. 32, pp. 329–65).
11 RGASPI, f. 5, op. 2, d. 340, l. 81; f. 17, op. 84, d. 175, ll. 94–6. Medvedev co-signed the letter.

a shake-up of the VTsSPS leadership. Production-union congresses were usually held immediately before the All-Russian Congress of Trade Unions. Rumours circulated that the Workers' Opposition would first consolidate its strength at production-union congresses, then attempt to take control of the All-Russian Congress of Trade Unions. To outmanoeuvre Shlyapnikov, the Politburo brought forward the date of the all-union congress so that it would fall before individual union congresses. The Metalworkers' Union opposed the change to no avail. From the perspective of VTsSPS leaders, the Politburo's step was inconvenient and worrisome, for it gave them little time to plan for the all-union congress.[12]

Animosities among trade-union leaders and their divergent opinions on party-union relations prevented them from presenting a united front against party interference in their affairs. Shlyapnikov agreed with party leaders that Trotsky's supporters should be ousted from the VTsSPS leadership, while Tomsky was reluctant to displace them. While Tomsky feared that Shlyapnikov and the Politburo were colluding to replace him, Shlyapnikov blamed Tomsky for having helped remove supporters of the Workers' Opposition from their posts and for inadequately defending the interests of unions and workers in CC plenums.[13]

Shlyapnikov led a group of production-union delegates, who were the best organised group at the congress. Representing eight production unions, they included many former members of the Workers' Opposition who shared Shlyapnikov's views on the role of trade unions and on NEP. Union leaders who had supported Lenin in the trade-union debate also joined. The most prominent of these was the chair of the Miners' Union, and CC member, Artyom (Fyodor Sergeev).[14] Aiming to increase the influence of production unions over VTsSPS, these union leaders were particularly angry about recent VTsSPS attempts to centralise trade-union administration by giving trade-union councils greater authority over production unions at all levels. Shlyapnikov feared

---

12 TsA FSB, R33718, d. 499061, vol. 41, l. 195; RGASPI, f. 99, op. 1, d. 9, l. 1. Daniels 1988 errs in the order he assigns to the congresses and in identifying Medvedev as the leader of the Metalworkers' Union (Daniels 1988, p. 157). Communist fraction sessions ran from 16–24 May. For details of the confusion resulting from the Politburo's decision, see Allen 2002.

13 TsA FSB, R33718, d. 499061, vol. 41, ll. 195–6, 200–1.

14 An Old Bolshevik with a long history of underground revolutionary work, Artëm (b. 1883) spent six years before the 1917 revolutions working and organising Russian workers in Australia, where he became a citizen. Having returned to Russia in 1917, he became a member of the Ukrainian government in 1919. He died in 1921 in a bizarre train accident, involving a rocket-powered locomotive (Gambarov *et al.* (eds.) 1989, chapter 1, pp. 19–22). Stalin fostered his son.

that VTsSPS would weaken production unions by diverting their staff to trade-union councils. He believed that this would lead to trade unions becoming a branch of government. The production-unions group proposed a list of candidates for the congress leadership which included many former members of the Workers' Opposition.[15] By wresting control of VTsSPS, Shlyapnikov's group would seek to extend the influence of production unions over state economic policy and to preserve some degree of proletarian democracy in production unions.

While production unions had a pre-revolutionary history in Russia, the gubernia trade-union councils, the delegates of which constituted a rival interest group, were creations of the Soviet era. These delegates felt that production unions and profession-based unions had too much influence over VTsSPS. They wanted central trade-union leaders to show greater sensitivity to their concerns, which meant extending more authority and resources to them. They were not united behind any one leader and seemed to differ quite a lot on specific policies. Some appeared to follow the Tsektranist line, represented by Efim Bumazhny, which favoured a military-style administration of industry, the appointment of trade-union leaders and the incorporation of the trade unions into the state system of administering industry. Tsektranists (or Trotsky supporters) could be found in a broad array of bodies: trade-union councils, various union central committees and in the central staff of VTsSPS. Other gubernia trade-union council delegates were weary of factional infighting and intrigues that had occupied top party and union leaders. In an unintentionally ironic twist on the political term 'opposition', these delegates were referred to as a 'business-like opposition' [*delovaya oppozitsiya*].[16]

Given the Politburo's dependence on Tomsky to carry out a shake-up of the VTsSPS leadership he had put in place, preparations could not go smoothly. Unexpected developments included Ryazanov's election to the congress's temporary presidium. Ryazanov was well regarded by Russian communists for his command of Marxist theory, for his historical writings on the socialist movement and for his extensive experience working in the trade unions. Nevertheless, he had a troubled history with party leaders, who had expressly told Tomsky that he should not be elected to the presidium. When Ryazanov's

---

15 TsA FSB, R33718, d. 499061, vol. 41, ll. 201, 208.
16 TsA FSB, R33718, d. 499061, vol. 41, ll. 205, 213–15. Bumazhnyi was one of the board members of *Narkomtrud* who had tried to oust Shliapnikov from his position as Labour Commissar in autumn 1918.

resolution criticising both VTsSPS and the Politburo passed through the communist fraction, party leaders became alarmed.[17]

Tomsky's report to the communist fraction revealed the strain that he was under. Maintaining that the VTsSPS bureau had to 'indisputably obey' party leaders, he channelled the party leaders' distrust of workers and union leaders when he voiced the view that trade unionists' daily work with factory workers made them susceptible to the same 'vacillations' that plagued the deprived 'working masses'. Both Shlyapnikov and Ryazanov fiercely criticised VTsSPS leaders, but Ryazanov also attacked the CC (unlike Shlyapnikov, who was now a member of it). Blaming VTsSPS leaders for their lack of leadership ability, which led to excessive dependence on the CC and allowed regional party committees to disrupt trade-union work, Shlyapnikov proposed that participation of trade unionists in party organisations should be increased, that the roles of the party and the unions should be clearly demarcated and that the control of the production unions over VTsSPS and the trade-union councils should be strengthened. Lashing out at Tomsky for allowing the CC to hold VTsSPS in a stranglehold, Ryazanov complained that party leaders did not take unions seriously, failed to consult them except in the most peremptory way and ordered them to sign off on decrees that were obligatory regardless of whether they approved. Moreover, he said, VTsSPS leaders did not resist when party leaders actively quashed the attempts of unionists to strengthen their organisations.[18] Ryazanov thus staked out the clearest position on proletarian democracy, which motivated an overwhelming majority of delegates to vote for his resolution. Attributing the poor work of VTsSPS to the CC's excessive and 'petty' interference, he called on the party to end its meddling in the 'routine' work of VTsSPS. Most importantly, he called for the election of union leaders by communist trade-union members themselves, free of party interference.[19]

Ryazanov's past year of tense relations with party leaders set the mood for his tempestuous outburst. In 1920 the communist fraction of the Third Congress of Trade Unions had adopted his resolution that all *Narkomtrud* functions should be transferred to VTsSPS (effectively abolishing *Narkomtrud*),

---

17 RGASPI, f. 17, op. 3, d. 157, l. 3; TsA FSB, R33718, d. 499061, vol. 41, ll. 199, 202, 213–15.
18 RGASPI, f. 17, op. 84, d. 217, ll. ll. 6–10, 30–3, 48; and f. 95, op. 1, d. 23.
19 TsA FSB, R33718, d. 499061, vol. 41, ll. 208, 214. He also wanted to end non-party conferences of industrial workers because he thought they disrupted trade-union work. I could not find an exact vote count in the stenographic report of the congress. Riazanov later claimed that his resolution passed by 1500–30 votes (RKP(b) 1961, p. 262). He also referred to a 945–500 vote to keep him in the trade-union movement. A vote taken at another session shows that at least 856 communist delegates were in the fraction (RGASPI, f. 17, op. 84, d. 217, ll. 203–4). The discrepancies may reflect flaws in the congress's organisation.

instead of the CC's resolution. Considerably embarrassed, the CC resolved not to bring Ryazanov's resolution to the Third Congress of Trade Unions plenum and to exclude him from trade-union work on account of his 'undisciplined speeches' at the congress. He was only re-admitted to work in the unions in December 1920. Ryazanov blamed Tomsky and the rest of the VTsSPS leadership for failing to appeal against his exclusion.[20]

The vote for Ryazanov's new resolution forced party leaders to take control of the Fourth Congress of Trade Unions and to investigate how his resolution passed.[21] The investigative commission was made up of CC members Mikhail Frunze (chair), Stalin, Kiselev and Dzerzhinsky. Frunze had commanded the Eastern front during the Russian Civil War and was renowned for his brutality in Turkestan. A rising star in party politics, he died in 1925 while undergoing an operation ordered by Stalin. He and Stalin were aligned with Lenin on trade-union matters. Kiselev, former chair of the Miners' Union, had belonged to the Workers' Opposition; in spring 1921 he was a candidate member of the CC, a member of the CCC Presidium and chair of Little Sovnarkom (which handled prosaic matters unrelated to policy). Dzerzhinsky, head of the Cheka, had been aligned with Trotsky during the trade-union debates.[22] The unpublished transcript of the commission's investigation illuminates personal rivalries and policy differences among trade-union leaders, as well as evolving methods of control over communist assemblies.

Under questioning, both Shlyapnikov and Artyom harshly criticised Tomsky for ineptly organising the congress and for showing greater concern with his personal reputation than with creating a strong organisation. Shlyapnikov aspired to remove Tomsky as chair, but he agreed with other witnesses that Tomsky had not conspired against party leaders. Having concluded that there was no evidence of 'conscious cooperation' between Tomsky and Ryazanov to pass Ryazanov's resolution, the commission nevertheless recommended Tomsky's removal as VTsSPS leader due to his mistakes.[23] Stalin and Frunze were perplexed as to why no one took the 'usual' measures to ensure that

---

20   RGASPI, f. 17, op. 2, d. 30.
21   RGASPI, f. 17, op. 2, d. 65, 18 May 1921; TsA FSB, R33718, d. 499061, vol. 41, I. 215. At this point, the congress's stenographic report becomes unclear. My information on the passage of Riazanov's resolution comes from the records of the CC's commission on investigating this affair (TsA FSB, R33718, d. 499061, vol. 41, II. 195–216).
22   Gambarov et al. (eds.) 1989, chapter 1, pp. 191–4 and chapter 3, 191–3; TsA FSB, R33718, d. 499061, vol. 41, II. 195–216, stenographic report of the commission's interviews with trade-union leaders, 19 May 1921.
23   RGASPI, f. 17, op. 84, d. 217; TsA FSB, R33718, d. 499061, vol. 41, II. 215–16. Only Stalin, Kiselëv and Frunze signed the decision, raising doubt as to whether Dzerzhinskii agreed with the commission's conclusions.

Ryazanov's resolution did not pass; these included halting the proceedings and excerpting and combining the three resolutions offered. When Tomsky claimed, in his defence, that he did not perceive the CC's disapproval of Ryazanov's candidacy as a 'directive', Frunze pointedly replied: 'But you had the definite opinion of the [CC] commission. And I think it's the same with us as with the military – opinion is equal to directive'.[24] This told of the Civil War's influence on party politics.

There was so much discontent with central party and union leaders among delegates, the source of which few of the leaders seemed to understand, that unexpected events were inevitable. Perhaps all factional leaders, including Shlyapnikov, were so immersed in the politics of their causes that they did not understand how deeply dissatisfied delegates were with factionalism and how strongly delegates felt that their leaders did not understand the challenges of carrying out everyday work at the regional and local level. The party's decision to rush the congress had not only made the work of VTsSPS leaders more difficult, but had rushed the delegates' preparations as well.

During the remainder of the congress, Shlyapnikov cooperated with party leaders to diminish Tsektranist influence over VTsSPS. When the communist fraction of the trade-union congress reconvened without Tomsky in charge, party leaders had already constituted a new congress presidium, which included Shlyapnikov and at least four others from the former Workers' Opposition, as well as Artyom. As a presidium member, Shlyapnikov enforced CC decisions that were rejected by a majority of the communist fraction of the congress. One such matter concerned wage rates and the supply of workers with food and other goods. The communist fraction had approved a resolution linking pay and provisions to worker productivity, despite being aware that the CC had already rejected this Tsektranist approach. The fraction majority remained steadfast, despite the Politburo revoking its decision and its approval of alternative proposals that did not tie the provision of food to worker productivity.[25]

Shlyapnikov, who favoured the alternative proposals, announced that he and other presidium members would vote against the fraction's decision at the congress's open session. His declaration emerged from genuine conviction, since he strongly opposed basing the provision of food and clothing to

---

24 TsA FSB, R33718, d. 499061, vol. 41, ll. 198–9.
25 RGASPI, f. 17, op. 84, d. 217, l. 214, Politburo protocol excerpt, 22 May 1921. Vlas Chubar's resolution 'established that, where possible, the supply of rations should continue and called for the introduction, as an experiment, of collective supply in some enterprises. It also stressed the growing role of bonuses to workers in their own production and the creation of enterprise-level goods funds' (Aves 1996, p. 163).

workers on their productivity. Nonetheless, his decision directly contradicted his overall stance against party leaders dictating to communist fractions. Bumazhny sarcastically rejoined that Shlyapnikov should 'learn the party statutes'. Molotov, speaking for the CC, offered a compromise. To preserve the appearance of party unity, individual communists could abstain from voting. Shlyapnikov instead proposed that the fraction meet again to reconsider its vote. Delegates accepted his proposal.[26] In the meantime, he and other presidium members convinced a majority to change their minds.

After delegates' positions shifted, the communist fraction voted to decouple worker productivity from the supply of workers with food and other goods. Key delegations speaking in favour of these proposals were those of the Miners' Union and the Donbas region trade-union delegations, over whom Shlyapnikov had much influence. Blaming Shlyapnikov for their defeat, the Tsektranists pointedly proposed to replace him with Trotsky in the new VTsSPS leadership. Ostensibly, they objected to him because he had 'intrigued' against Tomsky. Nevertheless, a large majority (582–274) voted in his favour. Shlyapnikov must have been satisfied with the (temporary) removal of Tomsky as VTsSPS chair and the reduction of the Tsektranists' influence over VTsSPS. His own position was enhanced by his appointment to the VSNKh Presidium, which appeared to offer him real influence over the making of NEP.[27] However, these were ephemeral victories. If Shlyapnikov believed that the new CC was more sympathetic to his own views on the role of the unions, he was clearly misguided.

Fourth Congress of the Metalworkers' Union

The Politburo next turned to weakening Shlyapnikov's influence over the Metalworkers' Union by replacing his supporters in the leadership with new men who were loyal to the CC majority. At the Fourth Congress of the Metalworkers' Union in May 1921, the union's communist fraction resisted the Politburo's changes and re-elected all those rejected by the Politburo. This set the stage for a direct confrontation. There was little indication before the congress that its proceedings would degenerate into a stand-off between the union's communist fraction and the party Politburo. In fact, Shlyapnikov skirted sensitive political issues when writing about the congress's agenda. Even when the communist fraction of the union's central committee

---

26   RGASPI, f. 17, op. 84, d. 217, ll. 164–7, 183.
27   RGASPI, f. 17, op. 84, d. 217, ll. 184–5, 190–1, 203–4, 212; f. 5, op. 1, d. 231, l. 4. Shliapnikov was appointed to VSNKh on 25 May 1921.

met to prepare for the congress, its discussion seems to have been non-political.[28] As a consummate conspirator, Shlyapnikov could have conducted preparations out of his opponents' direct view, or perhaps he was confident that his union backed him.

Despite the innocuous nature of the metalworkers' recorded statements on the eve of the congress, tensions must have been high when the communist fraction of the Metalworkers' Union Congress first met on 26 May. Almost all those elected to the important bureau and presidium were former members of the Workers' Opposition. On the same day, the Politburo organised a commission to lead the congress. Attending that Politburo session were Lenin, Zinoviev, Bukharin and Molotov; they set the terms of the struggle against Shlyapnikov's supporters. The commission they constructed included only Shlyapnikov from the former Workers' Opposition. All other members, including Bukharin, supported the line of the Politburo.[29] Thus the battle lines were drawn in the struggle for control of the Metalworkers' Union.

The first conflict came over the union's leadership. Shlyapnikov's supporters and those of the party leaders presented separate lists of candidates for the new central committee of the Metalworkers' Union. Henceforth termed the 'Moscow list' for the sake of brevity, Shlyapnikov's list was endorsed by major regional organisations of the Metalworkers' Union, including Moscow, Nizhny Novgorod, Kharkov, Tula and the Urals. The Petrograd Metalworkers' Union, which was manipulated by Petrograd party secretary Zinoviev, offered a rival list. As was standard practice, the standing leadership of the Metalworkers' Union had to approve a list of candidates before presenting it to the communist fraction. The recent All-Russian Trade Union Congress, however, had not followed this procedure.

Communist fraction leaders on the central committee of the Metalworkers' Union discussed the lists. Shlyapnikov chaired the meeting, which other members of the party CC commission (except Bukharin) attended. Nearly all metalworkers in attendance were former members of the Workers' Opposition. Only the leader of the Petrograd Metalworkers' Union (Grigory Fyodorov) supported the Petrograd list. CC commission members immediately pronounced the Moscow list unacceptable because it was so heavily skewed towards the Workers' Opposition. Nevertheless, nearly all metalworker leaders present demonstrated their independence by accepting it. Later that day, Bukharin announced to the communist fraction of the Metalworkers' Union congress

---

28   Shlyapnikov 1921a, p. 1; RGASPI, f. 99, op. 1, d. 8, l. 4, 25 May 1921. The account of the proceedings by Sorenson 1969, p. 169, appears to be based on a 6 August 1921 *Izvestiia* article.
29   RGASPI, f. 99, op. 1, d. 7, ll. 7–8; f. 17, op. 3, d. 170, 26 May 1921.

that the Politburo wanted the list of the Petrograd delegation to be passed. Nevertheless, the fraction voted for the Moscow list.[30]

The Politburo promptly ordered the fraction to endorse the Petrograd list. In protest, Shlyapnikov resigned his membership of the CC's commission on the congress. He also demanded to withdraw his name from the Petrograd list. The Politburo rejected his resignation and refusal. Instead, it authorised the commission to reconcile the two lists. This created the appearance of compromise. The commission met later that day with the bureau of the communist fraction of the Metalworkers' Union. The majority (minus Bukharin) rejected the former members of the Workers' Opposition as union central committee members, but Shlyapnikov voted for them. The majority of the CC commission did not hide the fact that candidates were unsuitable precisely because they had been in the Workers' Opposition, which moved Shlyapnikov to object that this violated the' ban on factional struggle passed by the Tenth Party Congress. He managed to salvage a few candidacies from certain large industrial areas. Under his influence, the fraction's leaders refused to endorse the commission's modifications.[31]

Faced with such determined resistance, the Politburo allowed many former members of the Workers' Opposition to be nominated for the union's new central committee. At the union's communist fraction, Bukharin announced that a majority of the union's central committee must consist of those who followed the CC's line, but that a minority of seats could go to former Worker Oppositionists. Thereupon, a delegate defended 'democratic' methods of election in the union by interjecting that the fraction had no right to go over the heads of union organisations that had nominated candidates to the Moscow list. Attempting to preserve the pretence of democracy, Bukharin persistently urged the fraction to discuss the list. A majority of delegates refused to discuss it, rejecting Bukharin's political game. Abandoning any pretence, Bukharin declared that discussion would be held 'as a party directive'. Shlyapnikov could not actively resist a party directive, but he could refuse to participate in a political charade. Feeling that he personally had been 'systematically discredited', he requested to remove his candidacy from the commission's list and a number

---

30 RGASPI, f. 17, op. 84, d. 220, l. 3, 28 May 1921. Attending the fraction's 28 May session were 164 delegates with a deciding vote, 30 with consultative vote and three members of the CC's commission on the congress – Chubar', Shmidt and Uglanov. The fraction accepted the Moscow list over the Petrograd list 122–40. Two delegates abstained from voting (RGASPI, f. 99, op. 1, d. 7, l. 10). I could not find a complete stenographic report of the debate.

31 RGASPI, f. 17, op. 3, d. 171, 28 May 1921; op. 84, d. 220, ll. 1–3; f. 99, op. 1, d. 7, ll. 12–13.

of other candidates demonstrated solidarity with him. Bukharin insisted that the party CC would not accept any resignations.[32]

Many impassioned comments by Shlyapnikov's supporters ensued. Most of these reflected a sincere feeling that the Metalworkers' Union was being intentionally and permanently disempowered. One delegate scoffed at the idea that the Petrograd delegation had drawn up a list of candidates for the union's leadership; he described its members as 'standing on Zinovievist graves', insinuating that Zinoviev had removed earlier leaders of Petrograd trade unions and had replaced them with his own supporters. Tolokontsev also rejected the pretence, suggesting (probably sarcastically) that the party should openly declare that it would not allow elections and appoint union leaders instead. Vladimirov broke down in tears as he expressed how he was 'sorry to the core that our organisation, to which I gave all my strength, as did many others, now could collapse and completely die'. Only the Petrograd delegation leader called for obeying the party's directive and 'getting to work'.[33] Emotions ran so high that the fraction postponed discussion until the next day. In the meantime, Shlyapnikov appealed to the Politburo.

Unsurprisingly, the Politburo confirmed Bukharin's order. The union's communist fraction had to accept the Petrograd list as a party directive, but it rejected the directive to 'discuss' the list. Fraction members instead wanted to debate the legality of the Politburo's directive, but this was not allowed. The CC commission offered dissident metalworkers the possibility to appeal, through their new leadership, to the party CC, the CCC or the next party congress. Distrusting their new leaders' commitment to this right to appeal, the majority resolved to obligate them to complain both to the CC and to the CCC that the Politburo had violated the decree of the Tenth Party Congress. If leading bodies rejected the complaints, then they would have to appeal to the Eleventh Party Congress. A member of the CC commission attempted to dilute the content and soften the language of the resolution, which delegates rejected. Upon the commission's demand for a roll-call vote, Shlyapnikov resisted this obvious attempt to bully the fraction. He allowed fraction members to choose whether they would go on record by writing a note to the union secretariat.[34] Commission members dropped their demand.

---

32   RGASPI, f. 17, op. 84, d. 220, l. 4, 29 May 1921. Medvedev, Vladimirov, Pavlov, Chernov, Lobanov, Tolokontsev, Mitin, Bruno and some others also requested to resign.
33   RGASPI, f. 17, op. 84, d. 220, l. 4; f. 99, op. 1, d. 7, l. 14. The transcript records Vladimirov's emotional reactions. Semkov's statement is only recorded in the transcript in f. 99, not f. 17.
34   RGASPI, f. 17, op. 84, d. 220, ll. 5–7, 30 May 1921; f. 99, op. 1, d. 7, l. 22, 30 May 1921. Only Chubar', Shmidt and Uglanov attended from the commission (Bukharin was absent).

The Politburo confirmed the union's new central committee (as composed by the commission). Neither Shlyapnikov nor any of his supporters were allowed to resign. The next step was to eliminate Shlyapnikov's influence over the union, of which he had been chair since late 1917. To marginalise him, the Politburo resolved to replace the position of chair with a 'secretariat' (a secretariat had just been introduced in VTsSPS). Molotov was appointed to carry out the Politburo's instructions.[35] Such a significant modification inevitably met resistance at the communist fraction meeting of the union's new central committee.

In the presence of communist fraction members and Molotov, Shlyapnikov regretfully intoned that it would be the last time he would serve as chair.[36] Before proceeding, he asked Molotov whether the CC wished to make any announcements.[37] Molotov replied that he would introduce 'modifications' to the fraction's decisions as became necessary.[38] Thus, he conveyed the fraction's reduced status from the outset. As soon as the election of leaders was brought up, a few fraction members immediately proposed to replace the chair and presidium with a secretariat, as in VTsSPS. Shlyapnikov retorted that the Metalworkers' Union had set the precedent of having a chair, and that it should be directed not only by VTsSPS statutes but also by its own decrees and directives. Molotov interjected that since the party CC favoured a secretariat, the metalworkers should organise one. Shlyapnikov's supporters continued to resist, offering a resolution to retain the old leadership structure. Molotov countered with a motion for a three-person secretariat. While only 10 voted for Molotov's solution, a majority of 14 voted for the old system.[39] This was startling, since Bukharin was supposed to have assured a majority of 14 loyalists against 10 Shlyapnikov supporters. Molotov, perhaps taken aback and unsure how to proceed, did nothing.

Despite this small victory, Shlyapnikov knew his tenure as leader was over. Although Lenin's supporters, led by Ivan Lepse, favoured retaining Shlyapnikov in the presidium, he would have been in a minority, together with his

    According to the record, Medvedev's resolution passed 132–53, with three abstentions. On the next day, Shliapnikov gave a slightly different breakdown: 134 for; 39 against and nine abstentions (RGASPI, f. 99, I. 1, d. 8, I. 4, 31 May 1921).

35 RGASPI, f. 17, op. 3, d. 172, 31 May 1921.
36 RGASPI, f. 99, op. 1, d. 8, I. 4. The session began on 31 May 1921 at 8 p.m. According to Molotov's report to the CC, dated 6 June, 18 full members and a majority of candidates attended (RGASPI, f. 17, op. 65, d. 21, I. 205).
37 RGASPI, f. 99, op. 1, d. 8, I. 5.
38 RGASPI, f. 17, op. 65, d. 21, I. 205.
39 RGASPI, f. 99, op. 1, d. 8, I. 5; RGASPI, f. 17, op. 65, d. 21, I. 206.

supporters, Vladimirov and Tashkin.⁴⁰ Shliapnikov asked to withdraw, declaring that he was 'not in the condition to work' in the presidium; Vladimirov and Tashkin joined him in resigning. While Tashkin claimed insufficient experience at the national level, Vladimirov, his voice faltering, said he was suffering physically and needed time to recuperate. Lepse flatly declared: 'Tashkin's and Vladimirov's declarations have no foundation'. Shliapnikov intervened sharply, declaring: 'He who does not want to kill comrade Vladimirov, must accept [his] declaration'. Genuine concern for his comrades created a sympathetic bond cementing their personal loyalty to him, as they also supported his views.

Having recovered his composure, Molotov declared that no one, especially not a party CC member (meaning Shliapnikov), could withdraw his own candidacy. Shliapnikov, with an air of exasperation, replied: 'I must declare that we have one refuge remaining, one right – this is the right to refuse and no one can take this away from us'. Chastising Shliapnikov for putting factional interests over those of the party, Molotov ordered him and Vladimirov to enter the new presidium, but conceded that Vladimirov could take sick leave (he did not require Tashkin to serve). Shliapnikov retorted that Molotov should not lecture him, but should remember how they both 'helped build the party together'. Molotov should know from this, Shliapnikov insisted, how devoted he was to the party. Shliapnikov's outburst, directed at Molotov, underscores the sense of humiliation he must have felt at his looming subordination, in the Metalworkers' Union, to leaders who refused to recognise his role in organising it. Shliapnikov concluded: 'Personally, I have neither the moral nor the physical strength to work and you will not see me either in VSNKh or in the Metalworkers' Union'. Despite Molotov's order, a majority voted to allow the three men to resign. Complaining of factionalism, Molotov declared that the Politburo would examine the vote.⁴¹

---

40   Ivan Lepse (head of the Petrograd Metalworkers' Union) proposed to elect Shliapnikov, Fëdorov, Tashkin, Ianson, Sergeev, Vladimirov and Bukhanov (RGASPI, f. 99, op. 1, d. 8, l. 5). Lepse (1889–1929) joined the party in 1904, worked in machine-building factories in Riga and Petrograd and was conscripted into the army in 1914. In 1917 he held posts in the Bolshevik Party and the Metalworkers' Union. He served in the Civil War and, in 1921–9, led the Metalworkers' Union central committee (Lane 1995, vol. 1, pp. 563–4; Zen'kovich 2002, p. 312–13).

41   RGASPI, f. 99, op. 1, d. 8, l. 5. On 16 June 1921, the Politburo fulfilled Shliapnikov's formal request to resign from VSNKh (RGASPI, f. 17, op. 3, d. 176). In letters to supporters, Shliapnikov confirmed that his own response to the leaders' 'factional intrigues' was to refuse to take on work. That was one of the reasons why he rejected his assignment to VSNKh; another was the incompatibility of his views with those of its leaders (TsA FSB, R33718, d. 499061, vol. 40, l. 124 and vol. 41, l. 157).

When the communist fraction of the Metalworkers' Union central committee reconvened, Molotov announced that the Politburo had decided to retain a presidium, but to create a secretariat to lead it. The Politburo acquiesced to Shlyapnikov's refusal to serve in the presidium, but retained in it Vladimirov, who was highly valued for his administrative and organisational skills. Shlyapnikov then orchestrated a vote in the faction to appeal to VTsSPS and to the party CC concerning the Politburo's 'persistent violations' of party unity (it passed 14–10). Molotov cut discussion short, declaring that the new presidium would discuss all further questions on the agenda, due to the fraction's 'accidental composition'. Medvedev had the last word, sarcastically questioning how the fraction could be 'accidental' when the Politburo had selected it.[42] Since the fraction had proven unreliable, the secretariat and presidium handled the union's business until a new central committee could be elected.

Lenin and other Politburo members had thus removed Shlyapnikov from his longstanding position as elected chair of the Metalworkers' Union. This was a decisive defeat. According to Shlyapnikov, Lenin had regarded the Metalworkers' Union as 'the party organisation of the Workers' Opposition'. Lenin worried that there were more workers in the union (five hundred thousand) than in the party, so he resolved that Shlyapnikov could not remain as chair. Nevertheless, Shlyapnikov did not concede that his cause was lost, merely that it had suffered a major setback. He advised a supporter that because of events at the trade union congresses, it was necessary to start organising again from the ground up. Believing that Lenin's factional politics violated the directives of the Tenth Party Congress, he was determined to resist. He was optimistic that methods such as the party purge still offered the opportunity to reform the party and bring it closer to workers.[43]

Shlyapnikov Responds to Reprisals Against the Workers' Opposition

In animated exchanges with Molotov over changing the leadership of the Metalworkers' Union, Shlyapnikov had blamed top party leaders for persecuting

---

42 RGASPI, f. 99, op. 1, d. 8, l. 7, 1 June 1921; RGASPI, f. 17, op. 3, d. 173; op. 65, d. 21, l. 208. Fëdorov, Ianson and Gurevich comprised the secretariat. The new presidium was finally composed of Fëdorov, Ianson, Gurevich, Sergeev, Bukhanov, Vladimirov, Vasil'ev and candidate members Tarygin, Lepse and Rozental'.

43 TsAODM, f. 88, op. 1, d. 168, l. 66, Khamovnicheskii district party conference, Moscow, January 1924; TsA FSB, R33718, d. 499061, vol. 40, l. 124; vol. 41, l. 158, letter to a supporter.

the former Workers' Opposition. In all, he received 26 letters of complaint about reprisals against workerist-oriented communists, about which he registered protests to the Politburo, Orgburo and the CC in April, May and June 1921. At first the Politburo asked the CCC to investigate the incidents and include Shlyapnikov in the investigation. Shlyapnikov and key supporters were also included in the deliberations on how to attract both party and non-party workers to work in the soviets. Finally, the Politburo instructed the CC Secretariat to re-emphasise to local party organisations their obligation to observe the CC's memorandum on party unity.[44] These attempts were made in April 1921, before the trade-union congresses discussed above were held. Valuing Shlyapnikov's organisational skills and his stature in the party, Lenin attempted to retain him in the leadership while depriving him of an independent power base.

Shlyapnikov's harassed appellants saw few results from his petitions or from the Politburo's attentions. Several – Vasily Panyushkin, Ivan Perepechko and Flor Mitin – took extraordinary initiatives to combat reprisals. Shlyapnikov's responses to their efforts reveal his attitude towards dissent and opposition. Panyushkin, who in mid-March 1921 had renounced his Communist Party membership due to the decisions of the Tenth Party Congress, formed a splinter group called the 'Worker-Peasant Socialist Party', which called for 'power to soviets, not parties'. Describing the Communist Party as 'full of non-worker elements', Panyushkin and his supporters agitated for the election of more workers to the soviets in April 1921; they also supported political participation by non-Bolshevik left socialists. Shlyapnikov understood Panyushkin's mood, but he strongly opposed his decision to form a new party, which Shlyapnikov compared to the SRS. Panyushkin castigated Shlyapnikov for political 'indecisiveness', but later was grateful to him for having 'categorically curs[ed] me in a comradely fashion'. Having come back into the fold after the Cheka crushed his own party, Panyushkin confirmed that Shlyapnikov valued party unity.[45]

Panyushkin was not the only former oppositionist to air grievances against Shlyapnikov and to call for active resistance to the persecution of workerist

---

44 RGASPI, f. 99, op. 1, d. 8, l. 5; f. 48, op. 1, d. 14, ll. 52–3, Eleventh Communist Party Congress closed session stenographic report, 2 April 1922; f. 17, op. 3, d. 156, 28 April 1921. Sandu 2006 discusses in more detail reprisals against provincial oppositionists.
45 TsA FSB, R33718, d. 499061, vol. 40, ll. 124, 234–5; vol. 41, l. 22, letter from Paniushkin, perhaps published in *Rabochii*, no. 11; Aves 1996, p. 179; Pirani 2008, pp. 105–6. Vasilii Paniushkin (1888–1960) joined the Bolshevik Party in 1907, served in the Cheka during the Civil War, and worked in the CC apparat. After returning to the party, he worked in VSNKh and in the Soviet trade mission in Germany. See Vinogradov *et al.* (eds.) 2007, p. 696. Paniushkin was 'renowned' for having ordered the execution, without trial, of seven young aristocratic students in March 1918 (Aleksandrov 2005; Dan 1922, p. 210).

Communists. Ivan Perepechko (separately from Panyushkin) may have authored a letter to members of the former Workers' Opposition in late spring or early summer 1921. The letter lambasted Shlyapnikov for failing to resist the party leaders' reprisals and called on oppositionists to respond to these reprisals in kind. Shlyapnikov objected strongly to the accusation that he had not resisted reprisals, calling it 'superficial and frivolous' and the result of misinformation. By the time former members of the Workers' Opposition re-assembled in early 1922, Shlyapnikov and Perepechko had reconciled.[46] Shlyapnikov valued all workers in the Communist Party no matter how misguided he thought them to be, hoping to teach them to correct their various 'mistakes'.

In contrast to his disapproval of Panyushkin's and Perepechko's actions, Shlyapnikov endorsed Mitin's initiative in circumventing the reprisals. Mitin's method involved transferring those targeted to a low-level position in a different geographical area, and then to a higher-level position in yet another geographical area. In so doing, he had preserved his comrades' ability to continue working in responsible positions. Mitin avowed that his long-term plans including placing 'our people' in key factory committees, getting control of factory cells, then regional party committees and so on, up the hierarchy. Nevertheless, Mitin expressed uncertainty as to what 'our ideological world view' was and what route to take 'out of our dead end'. He concluded: 'All oppositions seem to be a game in comparison with that tragedy which is being played out here, at the local level, among industrial workers'. Shlyapnikov expressed his firm approval of Mitin's tactics, which met his goal of retaining former oppositionists in important positions where they could influence party and trade-union policy.[47] Party leaders were appalled by Mitin's tactics, which struck at the heart of their attempts to manipulate cadres to serve political purposes, and excluded him from the party at the Eleventh Party Congress in 1922.

Shlyapnikov's own methods to defend his supporters, through petitions to higher party bodies, produced few positive results. More ominously, the reprisals extended, by association, to worker-communists who were not oppositionists. Alexander Medvedev reported that in Bryansk gubernia many trade-union

---

46 RGASPI, f. 17, op. 71, d. 77, ll. 1–3, unsigned, undated, verified typed copy of a letter likely from Perepechko; TsA FSB, R33718, d. 499061, vol. 40, l. 145; vol. 41, l. 157.

47 TsA FSB, R33718, d. 499061, vol. 41, ll. 153–7, Mitin's mid-1921 letter and Shliapnikov's response. Mitin (b. 1882), a skilled worker in Petrograd and Ekaterinoslav factories before the revolution, had chaired (at various times) the Donets, Tula, Kharkov and Ekaterinoslav Metalworkers' Union branches. An RSDRP member since 1902, he was likely a Menshevik until he joined the Communist Party in March 1920 (GARF, f. 5667, op. 5, d. 226, ll. 199–200).

leaders and staff were transferred to other posts. Those who replaced them, he said, were completely discredited among union members and consequently were unable to carry out useful work. Mitin agreed that retaliation caused widespread disillusionment among worker-communists, who ceased to participate in elections after seeing their elected bodies dispersed. When, for example, the gubernia conference in Mitin's area was disbanded because it had selected Shlyapnikov as a delegate to the Metalworkers' Union congress, workers were so disillusioned that they did not vote in the elections for a new gubernia conference. Such cases caused Shlyapnikov worry that acts of vengeance against the opposition undermined the authority of the trade unions among workers. To convey the seriousness of his concern about the leaders' 'factional intrigues', he requested (and received) Politburo permission to resign from his recent appointnment to work in VSNKh (he also held views incompatible with those of VSNKh leaders).[48]

Yet Shlyapnikov still attempted behind-the-scenes negotiations with Zinoviev and Lenin. In late June, he met with Zinoviev to ascertain the possibility of an agreement to empower workers, develop industry and return the Metalworkers' Union to its former leadership. In what was likely an empty threat, he warned of a split from the party if 'the official course' continued unchanged.[49] Zinoviev acted amenable to negotiations and reported that 'the old man' (Lenin) was 'tired of quarrelling'. Shlyapnikov made five conditions for a 'ceasefire'. These included: 1) a special party instruction to end attacks on the former 'Workers' Opposition'; 2) the easing of the repression of workers; 3) the convention of a conference of the Metalworkers' Union and the validation of all the decisions made by the communist fraction of the union's congress; 4) the inclusion of 'worker representatives' in VSNKh and other leading state economic bodies; and 5) the reorientation of economic policy towards intensive investment in heavy industry and the assignment of a certain percentage of industrial products to workers for barter with the peasantry. Lenin and Zinoviev delayed talks, ostensibly because the Comintern congress was meeting.[50]

While Shlyapnikov negotiated with party leaders, he pressed Kollontai to inform the Third Comintern Congress (meeting in Moscow, 22 June–12 July 1921) about dissent within the Russian Communist Party over NEP. Although

---

48   RGASPI, f. 589, op. 3, d. 9103, vol. 3, ll. 99, 102; f. 17, op. 3, d. 176, 16 June 1921; TsA FSB, R33718, d. 499061, vol. 40, l. 124; vol. 41, l. 157.
49   TsA FSB, R33718, d. 499061, vol. 42, l. 128, letter from Shliapnikov to Medvedev, 28 June 1921.
50   TsA FSB, R33718, d. 499061, vol. 42, l. 128; TsA FSB, R33718, d. 499061, vol. 41, ll. 157–8, letter from Shliapnikov to Mitin.

she had given him the cold shoulder after he disappointed her at the Tenth Party Congress, she was now more cooperative. Addressing the Comintern congress on 5 July, Kollontai warned, on behalf of a small minority in the party, that NEP threatened to disillusion workers, to strengthen the peasantry and 'petty bourgeoisie' and to facilitate capitalism's rebirth. Like Shlyapnikov in his private speeches and reports to the Politburo, she complained that NEP ignored the 'creative energy of our working class' as an instrument to resolve economic problems. In a conclusion that invited a fierce counterattack, she declared that the only recourse was to maintain within the party a 'strong core' of Bolshevik stalwarts, who in the case that NEP killed communism in Russia, could undertake a second worker revolution. In her words, this legion 'would take the red banner of revolution into their hands, in order to secure the victory of communism in the whole world'. Almost certainly, she was stating aloud Shlyapnikov's private opinions. Even so, he criticised her for delivering 'too hasty' and unpersuasive a speech. Kollontai realised as much as soon as she had finished speaking (even though she had noticed 'faint applause'). In retrospect, she felt that her speech was quixotic.[51]

In their replies, Trotsky and Bukharin devastated Kollontai, as Shlyapnikov's surrogate, using gender-coded language in their attack on her. Trotsky painted her as an individualist, denying her claim to represent others' views. He derided her as an 'Amazon', his acolyte Radek helpfully translating this to 'Valkyrie' for German-speaking delegates. Finally, Trotsky ridiculed the notion that a simple worker communist could build communism on his own or take up an engineer's work without help. Bukharin attacked her Menshevik past, ignoring Trotsky's similar background, and compared her threat of another revolution to the calls for one from the Mensheviks and SRs, except that their arguments were 'more logical' and more coherent. In the end, the congress expressed its approval of NEP. After her speech, other Bolsheviks accused Kollontai of having violated party discipline and many were outraged that she had involved foreigners in Russian party affairs. When she objected that these 'foreigners' were 'delegates of fraternal parties' who 'should know the truth', one of her interlocutors rudely replied: 'We'll give them the truth, but what you and the shitty Workers' Opposition think is harmful to distribute. It plays into our enemies' hands'.[52]

---

51 Kommunisticheskii internatsional 1922, pp. 367–9; Carr 1950–3, vol. 3, p. 381; RGASPI, f. 134, op. 3, d. 37, ll. 21–4, 2 August 1921.
52 RGASPI, f. 134, op. 3, d. 37, ll. 15, 23; Kommunisticheskii internatsional 1922, pp. 370–3, 379–83.

The only effect of Kollontai's speech on foreigners was to lead some foreign communists, who resented the Russian Communist leadership's iron hold over the Comintern, to think that they had potential allies in the Workers' Opposition. In late August, a prominent member of the Communist Workers' Party of Germany (KAPD) wrote to Shlyapnikov soliciting the participation of the Workers' Opposition in the foundation of an 'international union of all revolutionary leftist political groupings', which would be an alternative to the Comintern.[53] In reply, Shlyapnikov insisted that the Workers' Opposition had never been a 'special party'. He denied that it continued to exist after the Tenth Party Congress and wrote that he frowned upon a split in the Third International.[54] Despite his grievances, he did not want to leave the party. Shlyapnikov found it suspicious that when he reported the solicitation, the CC was uninterested; he concluded that the proposal was a Russian Cheka attempt at entrapment. When he accused the Cheka of organising a fourth international, party leaders just laughed.[55] Shlyapnikov's suspicions were heightened after his trial for violating party discipline and after he had received information about the actions of the Cheka against other dissenters in the party.

After the Comintern congress ended, Lenin scheduled a meeting with Shlyapnikov's ally, Sergei Medvedev, on 19 July. It must have had few results. By mid-summer 1921, Shlyapnikov had demonstrated that he would continue to criticise the policies of party leaders, who then paid far less attention to his complaints about harassment and demotion of his supporters. Although CCC

---

53   TsA FSB, R33718, d. 499061, vol. 41, l. 1, Levit's letter dated 30 August 1921. The KAPD split from the Communist Party of Germany (KPD) in autumn 1919. At the Third Comintern Congress in summer 1921, the KAPD called for the Comintern to be autonomous 'from the Russian state policy system' (Carr 1950–3, vol. 3, pp. 145, 393). Although I found archival references to a 'fourth international' envisioned by dissident European communists in the early 1920s, the actual Fourth International was founded by Trotskyists in 1938.

54   TsA FSB, R33718, d. 499061, vol. 41, l. 2, Shliapnikov's signed response, dated 31 August 1921. RGASPI, f. 2, op. 1, d. 24625 contains an unsigned copy of the letter, which Shliapnikov sent to Lenin on 31 August. Ruth Fischer, who was expelled from the Communist Party of Germany in 1926, claimed in her memoirs that Shliapnikov, Lutovinov and Gavriil Miasnikov, on early 1920s trade missions to Germany, had attempted to convince German leftists to split from the Communist Party of Germany (Fischer 1982, pp. 181–3, 311–12). But Fischer was not in direct contact with any of the three and was most probably mistaken, at least in regards to Shliapnikov.

55   RGASPI, f. 48, op. 1, d. 14, l. 59, September 1921 CC plenum. On 9 March 1922, someone who purported to represent the KAPD again asked him to participate in the formation of a fourth international (RGASPI, f. 17, op. 3, d. 280, l. 15, Shliapnikov's letter to the Politburo). Shliapnikov suspected that this was also a Cheka provocation.

FIGURE 28   *Alexander Shlyapnikov (left) speaking with Clara Zetkin (second from left) during the Third Congress of the Communist International in Moscow, summer 1921. Photo taken by Agence Meurisse (provided by Bibliothèque nationale de France).*

members visited a number of gubernias, repression continued in most cases. Shlyapnikov envisioned taking further appeals to the party conference and congress, but he could not imagine leaving the Communist Party or encouraging others to do so.[56] Nevertheless, party leaders feared that he was prepared to take his struggle to a broader audience within Russia.

Shlyapnikov Goes to Trial

There was a long tradition of holding party courts to judge party members.[57] Party members had been tried on suspicion of being police informants before the revolution. Both before and after the revolution, party courts were held to settle charges of defamation by one party member against another or to

---

56   RGASPI, f. 2, op. 1, d. 19867, 19 July 1921 meeting (Kiselëv acted as intermediary); TsA FSB, R33718, d. 499061, vol. 40, l. 124.

57   Non-Communists were tried in judicial trials for political offences. The first large-scale judicial political trial would be that of the SR leaders in June 1922.

determine whether a party member was guilty of violating party discipline. Shlyapnikov's trial in August 1921, however, differed from most previous trials of party members, in that the 'court' was composed of the CC and CCC, which would decide whether to expel an elected member of the CC from that body. The trial would send a significant political message, for this was the first case in which a CC member would be tried on charges of having violated the Tenth Party Congress directive banning factionalism. Shlyapnikov's conviction would cast a pall on the discussion of political and economic issues among party members and would set an example for reprisals against supporters of minority views within the party.

As Russian Communists consolidated their one-party dictatorship, they gradually created party cells in most workplaces. While the party 'fraction' had helped decide important policies, the cell increasingly served to educate and mobilise the rank-and-file. Prominent communists often served as mentors for party cells. Appointed by the Moscow party committee to mentor the party cell of the Moscow Hydroelectrical Station (MOGES), Shlyapnikov later recalled having had good relations with both party members and non-party workers at MOGES. When the station's communist cell met in late July 1921 to discuss rumours that the station was to be 'let out for concessions', its members resolved to invite Shlyapnikov, their party 'mentor', to advise them. Unfortunately, no protocol survives from the 26 July meeting where he spoke, but a cell member (K. Frolov) was moved to denounce him to the CC for having uttered the phrases: 'they are guilty for leading the workers to thievery' and 'our entire party – with the exception of the Workers' Opposition, has become petty bourgeois'. Shlyapnikov later admitted that he had spoken impulsively at the cell but denied having criticised the party's policy or leadership. Rather, he had spoken against VSNKh's proposals, which in his opinion were 'capitalist' and 'deeply anti-party'. The informer's motives are unknown, but could have included concern for party discipline or careerism. The denunciation passed through the hands of Gleb Krzhizhanovsky, who at the time chaired both the State Committee for Planning (Gosplan) and the State Commission for Electrification of Russia (and thus had jurisdiction over MOGES). An old comrade of Lenin, Krzhizhanovsky forwarded the document to party leaders (Shlyapnikov suspected Krzhizhanovsky of having set him up).[58]

Still unaware of the denunciation, Shlyapnikov spoke on 29 July to a communist assembly in Bauman district, which was heavily populated by textile workers and whose administration contained many supporters of the Workers'

---

58   RGASPI, f. 2, op. 1, d. 20251; f. 589, d. 9103, vol. 5, ll. 12, 77; TsAODM, f. 267, op. 1, d. 4, ll. 29, 32; Gambarov et al. (eds.) 1989, ch. 1, pp. 234–6.

Opposition. In response to his call for a greater role for the unions in production, a majority of 20–10 voted in favour (with five abstentions). Earlier that month, party leaders had attacked Kollontai at the Comintern congress for defending Shlyapnikov's views. Nearly two weeks had passed since his comrade, Medvedev, met with Lenin to discuss his proposals. Shlyapnikov still hoped to come to create accord with Lenin; perhaps he hoped the Bauman district vote would demonstrate that workers supported his views. But Lenin preferred other methods. Upon receiving Frolov's charges, the CC scheduled a special session to try Shlyapnikov for having violated party discipline and the directives of the Tenth Party Congress banning factionalism.[59]

Determined to vindicate Shlyapnikov, his supporters scrambled to refute the accusations against him. At the request of S.P. Vasilev, secretary of Zamoskvoretsky district Metalworkers' Union, the MOGES communist cell met in special session just hours before Shlyapnikov's trial to discuss whether the allegations carried any weight. Representing the Zamoskvoretsky district party committee, Rozaliya Zemlyachka, who had a well-deserved reputation as a harsh and rigid defender of the party line, attempted to guide the cell in determining the depth of Shlyapnikov's guilt. Disregarding her, the cell sided with Vasilev and, in a 'lively debate', proceeded to assess the veracity of the charges.[60]

Cell members conceded that Shlyapnikov had called VSNKh's draft proposals anti-proletarian. They acknowledged that he had said that the 'leading bodies' created the circumstances under which workers were reduced to stealing. Cell members also agreed that he argued that the economic crisis was due to an economic imbalance, in that the proletariat had 'serviced' the far more numerous 'petty bourgeoisie' (meaning mostly the peasantry) and had received little in return. Finally, they recalled, he urged them to question what they would hear from all sides on discussion of the 'economic question'. Nevertheless, cell members denied the claim that Shlyapnikov had laughed at VSNKh's assessment that the nationalised economy 'was conducted thriftlessly'. Instead, he had only spoken 'with a smile'.[61] Finally, they rejected the most serious charge, namely that Shlyapnikov had made anti-party statements.

When Vasilev requested that the cell assess whether Shlyapnikov's speech in any way promoted factionalism, Zemlyachka objected to his involvement. She insisted that party matters were the business of the district party committee and echoed the line of the party leaders that the Metalworkers' Union

---

59   Sandu 2006, pp. 148–9; RGASPI, f. 5, op. 2, d. 320, l. 1, 31 July 1921; f. 17, op. 2, d. 67, l. 93; f. 589, op. 3, d. 9103, l. 266, 8 August 1921 (morning).
60   TsAODM, f. 267, op. 1, d. 4, l. 32, 9 August 1921; RGASPI, f. 589, op. 3, d. 9103, vol. 3, l. 104.
61   TsAODM, f. 267, op. 1, d. 4, l. 32.

should only be concerned with 'production work'. Despite her objection, cell members concluded that Shlyapnikov had made no factional statements in his speech.[62] His good relationship with most cell members no doubt favourably disposed them towards him. Despite his popularity with cell members, the real determination of whether he had violated party discipline was up to the CC and the CCC.

The CC and the CCC met on the afternoon of 9 August 1921 to decide Shlyapnikov's fate. These bodies resolved to allow him to remain in the CC but to reconsider his expulsion if he were to make any more statements, outside of CC sessions, that criticised either party policy or specific decisions reflecting the 'opinion' of the party congresses. Significantly, the second stipulation expanded the definition of factionalism and gave him less room in which to express dissent. Those present voted unanimously for this decision, with three abstentions. Despite the decision to retain him in the CC, those assembled voted to remove him from his work in the Central Purge Commission, to which he had been appointed at the Tenth Party Congress in March 1921. Shlyapnikov's election to this commission had been one of the more significant concessions made to the Workers' Opposition. Seven CC members voted for his exclusion from the commission, but three opposed it. A CCC majority (four against two) voted to keep him in the purge commission, probably so as not to disrupt its work. This disagreement caused concern among Politburo leaders, but the plenum resolved to table the differences between the two bodies for later discussion.[63] Shlyapnikov retained nominal membership in the commission.

Although Shlyapnikov avoided expulsion from the CC, his opponents took advantage of his disgrace to intensify attacks on his supporters, which was most evident in Moscow. In autumn 1921 some communists complained to the Moscow party committee that district party committees had taken advantage of Shlyapnikov's 'trial' and censure to 'commence rabid persecution' of former members of the Workers' Opposition. The Moscow party committee did not restrain the district committees but encouraged them and even enforced the purge of oppositionists from the Bauman district of Moscow.[64] In the

---

62   Ibid.
63   RGASPI, f. 17, op. 2, d. 69; f. 589, op. 3, d. 9103, l. 267. The trial protocol was not available to me. Mikhail Chëlyshev, a former member of the Workers' Opposition who still shared many of Shliapnikov's views, must have voted to keep him in the purge commission. Shliapnikov later said that Sol'ts had not voted against him (RGASPI, f. 589, d. 9103, vol. 5, l. 12).
64   TsAODM, f. 3, op. 2, d. 18, ll. 23–5; RGASPI, f. 589, op. 3, d. 9103, vol. 3, l. 104; Pirani 2008.

context of 1921, this meant the removal of individuals from leading positions and possibly from party membership, but not yet execution, criminal exile or imprisonment.

Commission on Improving Workers' Living Conditions

As chair of the CC commission on improving workers' living conditions, Shlyapnikov could take practical steps towards preserving the working class. On the eve of the Tenth Party Congress, Russian workers had been restive due to inadequate food, clothing and fuel. The purpose of the commission was, at least temporarily, to centralise the provision of workers and to take quick measures to address their most urgent needs. Party leaders strictly limited the commission's role to rendering material aid, including housing, to workers, offering no mandate for broad reform. They made Shlyapnikov chair for several reasons: 1) as a famous worker communist he was an important symbolic figure for the Soviet government; 2) he was a capable organiser; and 3) the job was a useful diversion for him without offering him much real influence over policy. Nevertheless, Shlyapnikov welcomed his assignment as important and endeavoured to use it not only to improve the material conditions of workers but also to achieve the other goals of the Workers' Opposition.

In early April 1921, the commission started work both in the centre and on the gubernia level. Despite the party's instruction to use either soviet or Sovnarkom personnel as staff, Shlyapnikov chose chiefly trade unionists. His justification was that they had more experience in meeting workers' needs. In defining its main goal, the commission expected to meet hostility from 'soviet institutions' and to have to 'force' those institutions to 'adapt themselves to the thorough service of working-class needs'.[65] This reflected his bias against soviet bodies as staffed by largely non-proletarian elements, which put priority on their own bureaucratic interests rather than on the interests of workers.

The commission quickly achieved some practical results in providing workers with housing, medical care, food and household items and in authoring a decree that sanctioned the registration of workers' housing under the administration of factories. This was significant because it would allow factory committees and trade unions to finance the construction and repair of workers' housing without needing permission from the State Construction

---

65 RGASPI, f. 17, op. 3, d. 142, 28 March 1921. Shliapnikov reported that he had found party and military channels essential in overcoming obstacles presented early on by Soviet bureaucrats (RGASPI, f. 2, op. 1, d. 19039, l. 1, 30 May 1921).

Committee [*Komgosor*]. Shlyapnikov thus asserted that progress had been made in 'awaken[ing] local initiative' and in redirecting the attention of 'soviet bodies' towards workers' needs. He concluded that workers' living conditions could be improved only by comprehensive economic renewal, but that the latter depended on the improvement of workers' living conditions.[66] This rather circular observation suggests he had convinced himself that his work in the commission furthered his more fundamental goals.

In summer 1921, Shlyapnikov tried to institutionalise the commission's function by means of 'a minimal fund' to supply workers with consumer goods. The party CC endorsed his request to this effect. Despite CC support, Sovnarkom rejected his proposal on the grounds that further study was required to determine whether such a fund was feasible and necessary. Angered by this vote of nonconfidence in his argument and evidence, Shlyapnikov charged that Sovnarkom was violating the Tenth Party Congress decree on relieving the material plight of workers.[67] Both Sovnarkom's delay and VSNKh's decrees on NEP released earlier that month heightened his fears that the state, under NEP, was abandoning the working class. His concerns for workers' material needs coincided with his worry about party reprisals against former members of the Workers' Opposition, provoking him into making criticisms of NEP that, in Lenin's view, exceeded the bounds of party discipline.

Shlyapnikov's trial in August 1921 distracted him from the commission's work, but by October–November 1921, he had gathered strength for another battle to expand its mission. He submitted a project that boldly asserted the state's obligation to provide for workers under NEP but far exceeded the limits of the commission's assignment. Lenin seems to have been amenable to Shlyapnikov's proposal for a watchdog role for the commission, in particular as an advocate for the unemployed to receive government relief. Nevertheless, Lenin objected strongly to Shlyapnikov's proposed abolition of all taxes on workers. Lenin found most controversial his proposals on the role of the trade unions in the commissions and the extent of resources he demanded. Consistent with his intent to empower trade unions, Shlyapnikov instructed the commissions to support and defend 'all trade union directives on labour questions'. Considering that he had also called for state bodies to implement the commission's decisions, this was a thinly veiled method of forcing the state to execute trade-union policies. Given Shlyapnikov's obstinacy and

66 RGASPI, f. 2, op. 1, d. 19039, ll. 2–4; d. 18858, ll. 1–2.
67 RGASPI, f. 17, op. 3, d. 179, l. 5, 25 June 1921; d. 184, l. 3, 7 July 1921; op. 84, d. 175, l. 88, 27 July 1921; f. 2, op. 1, d. 20012, l. 1, 27 July 1921, decision signed by Lidiia Fotieva.

Lenin's dissatisfaction, it is not surprising that the Politburo reassessed the need for the commission while Shlyapnikov was away from Moscow on a work assignment.[68]

In Shlyapnikov's absence, government representatives, especially those from the Commissariat of Social Security [*Sobez*], attempted to dissolve the commission, because they claimed its philanthropic mission had gone as far as it could. Trade-union representatives advocated its continued existence, because state institutions would ignore the unions' complaints on behalf of workers, if not for the commission as an advocate. Under NEP, many state agencies and enterprises had to finance their own operations [*khozraschet*]. Although the commission continued to exist until spring 1922, it had no means of paying for its own operating costs, so VTsSPS eventually dissolved it. Having already recognised the futility of its work, Shlyapnikov no longer actively defended it.[69]

Autumn of Discontent

Shlyapnikov remained committed to unions. After a September 1921 holiday, during which he wrote a section of his memoirs, he resumed work in the Central Purge Commission and the commission on improving workers' living conditions. Desiring greater outlets for his energy, he requested more work in Moscow, but the Orgburo assigned him to food-procurement work in Gomel gubernia in Belorussia instead. Not only was this assignment not urgent, but also it removed him from work in the party purge commission at the most crucial time, when recommendations from local commissions were arriving in the centre for validation.[70] He thus had little influence over the purge. Moreover, the posting would have required him to miss important sessions of the central committee of the Metalworkers' Union. With good reason, Shlyapnikov concluded that the Gomel assignment was meant to isolate him from political

---

68   RGASPI, f. 2, op. 1, d. 22298, ll. 1–5, project dated 9 November 1921, with Lenin's notations. The Politburo discussion was on 1 December 1921.

69   RGASPI, f. 304, op. 1, d. 3, ll. 1–16, 28 January 1922; TsA FSB, R33718, d. 499061, vol. 40, l. 158, letter to the Orgburo, 7 October 1921.

70   CCC member Chëlyshev objected to the CCC's decision to confirm Shliapnikov's assignment to Gomel' (RGASPI, f. 17, op. 84, d. 206, l. 22, 22 October 1922). In a 1922 speech at Sverdlov University, CCC chair Sol'ts discussed aspects of the party purge (see Rosenberg (ed.) 1984, pp. 42–54).

decision-making in Moscow. In protest, he threatened to seek factory work rather than comply.[71]

The appeal process gave Shlyapnikov just enough time to attend the mid-October meetings of the central committee of the Metalworkers' Union. He and his supporters had hoped to convene an extraordinary congress of the Metalworkers' Union in autumn 1921 to recapture their union, but VTsSPS refused their request.[72] Rather than violate party discipline by calling an extraordinary congress without permission, they turned to the October plenum of the union's central committee and especially to its communist fraction. The communist fraction met for the first time since the May 1921 congress, where the Politburo had replaced Shlyapnikov as chair with a more compliant secretariat.

Seizing the floor at the communist fraction meeting, Shlyapnikov and his allies heaped criticism on the union's new leaders for neglecting important questions such as the role of the workers and the unions under NEP and for becoming too greatly immersed in administrative minutiae. The new leaders blamed former members of the Workers' Opposition for hindering their work, but a neutral member (Yakov Rozental) confirmed that some presidium members had been unwilling to work together with Shlyapnikov's supporters. When he said that the Metalworkers' Union was weak because it had insufficient staff at lower levels, a VTsSPS representative (Andreev) implicitly rebuked Shlyapnikov's supporters for having abandoned work. Vladimirov, the only former member of the Workers' Opposition in the union's presidium, declared that the new leadership was paralysed. In his view, when it appointed the unions' leaders, the party CC had destroyed both the authority of the union central committee and its organisational links with the regions. Vladimirov recalled with nostalgia a time when the central committee of the Metalworkers' Union had been 'a seething stream, to which all metalworking Russia was drawn as if to a magnet'. He called for the election of new leaders who 'could firmly carry the metalworkers' banner and disperse the fog of appointmentism'.[73]

---

71 TsA FSB, R33718, d. 499061, vol. 40, l. 158, Shliapnikov's letter to the Orgburo, Moscow, 7 October 1921; RGASPI, f. 17, op. 3, d. 215, 14 October 1921.

72 RGASPI, f. 17, op. 84, d. 219, l. 24, 6 October 1921.

73 RGASPI, f. 99, op. 1, d. 8, ll. 1, 11–13. The communist fraction met on 17–21 October 1921. Rozental' was a metalworker from the Urals and chaired the railroad transport repair commission under the VSNKh Metals Department. P.A. Bogdanov of VSNKh characterised him as 'an energetic worker and capable organiser', but faulted him slightly for being 'very hot-tempered and sometimes tactless towards his specialist coworkers, who are rather afraid of him' (RGASPI, f. 5, op. 1, d. 910, l. 3, memo to Lenin dated 10 August 1921).

Shlyapnikov's supporters complained that the new leadership had not implemented resolutions passed by the Fourth Congress of the Metalworkers' Union. These had included taking control of gubernia trade-union councils and formulating a position on the leasing of state enterprises, leading ultimately to 'the seizure of control over production'. One of the new leaders insisted that the union did not need its own line, but should hew strictly to the party line. Another interjected that NEP had rendered moot the congress's directives. A vote on the work of the union's presidium demonstrated that a majority (13–9) of fraction members remained defiant towards their union's Politburo-appointed leadership.[74]

After the vote had shown support for his views, Shlyapnikov scathingly criticised union leaders for failing to influence the work of the VSNKh Metals and Electric Departments. Faulting the Metals Department for having failed to find working capital to finance factories, he contended that capital could be found within production if VSNKh were not so determined to centralise the administration of industry. He called on the plenum to assign the Metals Department specific tasks. He had thus not given up on exerting union influence over government economic bodies. In turn, the new union leaders complained that because Shlyapnikov had refused to work in the Metals Department, it was hypocritical of him to criticise its weaknesses and that the plenum should force him to work there. His response, worded carefully, conveyed that he could not work there as long as the party and unions disagreed on major issues affecting the metals industry. He did not want to give the impression that he supported policies, which he actually saw as harmful to workers. Agreeing with him, a majority of fraction members resolved to form a commission to make proposals regarding the Metals Department.[75]

Despite their disagreement over the relationship between union, party and state, leaders of the Metalworkers' Union found common ground in their opposition to foreign concessions. The focus of discussion was whether to allow a group of American workers to lease the Nadezhdinsky factory in Kuzbas coal-mining region. The Council of Labour and Defence (STO) supported the project, which had been endorsed by well-known labour leaders Bill Haywood and Tom Mann, but the Metalworkers' Union and the VSNKh Metals Department objected to it as 'utopian'. In 1920 Shlyapnikov had taken a very different position, having expressed support for a proposal by Swedish metalworkers to come help rebuild Russian industry. Then the only problem he foresaw was that more experienced Swedish workers might out-earn Russian

---

74 RGASPI, f. 99, op. 1, d. 8, ll. 11–14.
75 RGASPI, f. 99, op. 1, d. 8, ll. 15–18.

workers, giving rise to tensions.[76] Likewise, in the spring of 1921 Shlyapnikov had, in the spirit of internationalism (he said), supported inviting foreigners to work in Russia. He even called for foreign workers to be covered by the same trade-union regulations as native workers. He had feared then that exempting foreigners from the protection afforded by Russian unions set an 'extraordinarily dangerous' precedent.[77]

By the fall of 1921, Shlyapnikov had become more pessimistic, perhaps due to negative results from past 'colonisation attempts', as he put it. The isolated nature of the Americans' project worried him. Furthermore, he believed that American workers should work for revolution in their own country. He feared that if they came to Russia with unrealistic hopes, only to be disillusioned, they would turn 'counterrevolutionary', as he believed other foreign workers had. Besides, he argued, capital investment was needed far more than foreign expertise. Foreign comrades, he insisted, should 'buy up shares from capitalists who take our concessions', rather than come to work in Russia. Both supporters and opponents stood solidly behind him. Unanimously, they rejected an American workers' colony in Kuzbas.[78] Shlyapnikov probably tapped feelings of wounded national pride, as well as worries about NEP.

Despite this momentary agreement, discord resurfaced in the vote for a new presidium. A majority (13–9) endorsed a list composed almost entirely of former members of the Workers' Opposition, while a VTsSPS-proposed list that gave a minority of seats to the former Workers' Opposition was defeated. This meant that a majority in the union's central committee still supported Shlyapnikov's line on the role of the trade unions. The Politburo promptly annulled both the vote for a new presidium and the vote against the American workers' colony; instead, it approved a presidium not dominated by former members of the Workers' Opposition. In response, fraction members voted unanimously against the Politburo's decision to approve the American project, demonstrating that this issue could drive a wedge between party leaders and their most loyal supporters in the trade unions. Fraction members acquiesced to the Politburo's directive on their leadership, but a majority refused to support those leaders. In effect, Shlyapnikov and his supporters accepted the limits to which they could take political struggle without violating party discipline,

---

76   RGASPI, f. 99, op. 1, d. 8, I. 18; GARF, f. 5667, op. 5, d. 226, I. 6, Shliapnikov's letters to VTsSPS and to the Metalworkers' Union central committee, 19 April 1920, and I. 10, 15 April 1920.

77   GARF, f. 5451, op. 42, d. 29, ll. 44–6, 62, VTsSPS communist fraction session, 11 April 1921. Tomskii had wanted to limit the number of foreigners allowed to work in Russian industry and to exclude them from Russian unions.

78   RGASPI, f. 99, op. 1, d. 8, ll. 18, 24. See also Zhuravlev 2000.

but they had not yet submitted. They would attempt to retake control of the Metalworkers' Union at its March 1922 congress. With the adjournment of the Metalworkers' Union central committee and Shlyapnikov's appeals to stay in Moscow exhausted, he was forced to depart for Gomel, where he remained for almost three months.[79]

NEP had ended grain requisitions and in some areas encouraged peasants to sow more land. Nevertheless, the enduring consequences of Bolshevik policies, Civil War conditions and drought had led to poor harvests and famine, which especially afflicted the Volga region. Despite aid from abroad, most notably via Herbert Hoover's American Relief Administration, millions died of starvation and more than twenty million people suffered from malnutrition. In the winter of 1921–2, the party mobilised all available personnel to organise the next campaign for the harvest. Provinces with successful harvests were offered cash and material incentives.[80] Shlyapnikov's food-procurement work in Gomel must have differed both from his 1918 assignment in the south and from simultaneous work carried out by Communists in other parts of Russia. Because he was not sent to a region hard hit by famine and because he completed his work before the Communist campaign to seize church valuables (ostensibly to aid famine victims) began, it cannot be determined how he might have implemented policies in those contexts. Perhaps party and government leaders preferred not to employ him in work that demanded harsh methods. In some circumstances they may have found his preference for persuasion and tact preferable to the militarist, coercive tactics of Civil War 'heroes'.

Conclusion

As the NEP era commenced, Shlyapnikov's chief concerns were ensuring the protection of workers' rights and promoting organised workers as viable managers of denationalised enterprises. His ideas for economic reform centred on intensive investment in heavy industry and horizontal trading relations between workers' organisations and peasants. As Russian industry recovered after the Civil War, trusts and industrial combinations assumed an important economic role and many of Shlyapnikov's comrade metalworkers played roles in administering them, but this was after they had lost their leadership positions in trade unions.

---

79 RGASPI, f. 99, op. 1, d. 8, l. 19, 23; d. 9, l. 12; f. 17, op. 3, d. 220, 21 October 1921; and d. 223, l. 8, 27 October 1921. I was unable to consult files on his work in Gomel'.
80 Carr 1950–3, vol. 2, pp. 284–6; Long 1992, pp. 510–25.

Party leaders promoted developments in the unions that paralleled those in the party: centralisation and the devolution of authority to higher bodies. Under Lenin's direction, the party's replacement of trade-union leaders in 1921 prepared the way for the elimination of local autonomy and initiative and harnessing the population to achieve the goals of the state and party leadership. In a different context, perhaps Shlyapnikov's optimistic strategy for taking control of the party through the trade unions would have been effective. During the Civil War, however, the trade unions had lost the personnel, resources and independent leadership they needed to challenge the party. The dramatic resistance of Shlyapnikov and his compatriots to the Politburo notwithstanding, they did not have enough supporters to take over party organisations. Non-communist trade-union members, who were not allowed to participate in the most vital decisions affecting unions, had little incentive or means to support Shlyapnikov's proposals, nor did Shlyapnikov seem interested in appealing to them.

Shlyapnikov's two chief weaknesses that contributed to his movement's failure after the Tenth Party Congress were that he could not resolve the dilemma of trying to wrest unions from the party's dictatorial grip while observing party discipline, and that he did not possess sufficient material resources or supporters to take over party organisations at the local level. His two greatest strengths were his organisational base in the Metalworkers' Union and his reputation as a worker communist who rose to a high rank within the party and trade unions based on his own natural talents and hard work. When the former was taken away from him at the May congress and the latter was besmirched by the August trial, he was left on shaky ground.

CHAPTER 8

Appeal of the 22 to the Communist International

After the Tenth Party Congress, divisions grew between former oppositionists at the centre and at the local level, between advocates of the trade unions and proponents of the soviets as bodies better suited for the democratisation of Soviet life, and between those who thought it necessary to remain within the Communist Party and those who wanted to create a new, improved workers' party. Significantly, there was even disagreement over the relative merits of the Soviet courts versus the unions in defending workers under NEP. Yet all were united by their perception that the role of workers within the Communist Party was diminishing and by their dissatisfaction with this situation. Ironically, given the frictions within the Russian Communist Party, a December 1921 CC plenum announced a campaign to create a united front of revolutionaries with non-revolutionary European workers to struggle against the bourgeoisie.

In the wake of his August 1921 trial, Shlyapnikov's political tactics became increasingly cautious. Nevertheless, he and his allies felt that a February–April 1922 political conjuncture offered the opportunity to air their grievances against some features of NEP and to convey their sense that party-worker relations were troubled. The meetings, rather close to one another in time, of the Comintern Executive, the Fifth Congress of the Metalworkers' Union and the Eleventh Party Congress meant that a small group could obtain the attention of a large audience (Russian and foreign communists and Russian metalworkers) for its views. In addition, it was legitimate, within the framework of party statutes, to appeal to these forums. Shlyapnikov and his allies therefore chose this time to act, but members of the Comintern Executive proved resistant to their message and party leaders undertook to punish them for their bold move. The methods used by party leaders reflected their increasing intransigence towards comradely dissent within the party, to which party members reacted in a range of ways. Debates at open and closed congress sessions and political manoeuvring behind the scenes revealed much about the evolving meaning of party discipline and the limits of internal political discussion and disagreement.

Private Meetings

Shlyapnikov and his supporters decided to appeal to the Comintern only after much discussion. In February 1922 he held several private meetings with comrades in the Metalworkers' Union to discuss their tactics, goals, and a course of action at the upcoming Fifth Congress of the Metalworkers' Union and the Eleventh Party Congress.[1] Participants held diverse views, but were closely connected to the former Workers' Opposition. Eight had signed the Workers' Opposition programme, while nearly all had supported it.[2] The chief exception was Gavril Myasnikov, a Russian metalworker from Perm in the Urals, whose ideas departed significantly from those of Shlyapnikov. Myasnikov had polemicised with Lenin regarding the former's call for freedom of speech and press for all from 'monarchists to anarchists'; later, he qualified these freedoms as only for workers and peasants. He differed from Shlyapnikov in advocating soviet control of production and peasant unions.[3] Because Myasnikov was a worker, Shlyapnikov engaged in dialogue with him, despite their differences, and often interceded on his behalf with higher party leaders.

The first meeting in mid-February 1922 was devoted to discussing workers' political opinions as expressed at the local level, the role of unions under NEP, the proposed workers' united front and the group's further plan of action. According to all participants, a dismal mood had settled upon communist and non-party workers. Party and union life was dead, discussion was often forbidden and many communists and unionists no longer tried to make proposals or discuss important questions because they felt it did not matter. In Perm, reportedly, everyone was afraid of the Cheka and in Ekaterinburg unionists were afraid of publishing anything. Entire cells of communists were leaving the party, some enticed back only by gifts of boots from party leaders. Apathy prevailed among Moscow worker communists and many were indignant at the Soviet government for ordering industrial products from abroad rather than subsidising their production within Russia.[4]

The oppositionists blamed one another for missed opportunities. Supposedly in Ukraine, oppositionists could have taken over the Metalworkers' Union leadership if only their most prominent spokesmen had rallied and spoken. Local representatives blamed Shlyapnikov and others in the 'centre' (Moscow) for not showing enough direction and for allowing a gulf to develop between

---

1 TsA FSB, R33718, d. 499061, vol. 41, ll. 68–9, Sergei Medvedev's handwritten notes, dated 10 or 16 February 1922; and vol. 40, ll. 127–8. Medvedev organised the meetings and took notes.
2 RGASPI, f. 17, op. 71, d. 3, ll. 1–2.
3 Gavriil Miasnikov (1889–1945), a Bolshevik underground activist since 1906, had served seven years of hard labour in Siberia before the revolution and was infamous for having murdered in 1918 Tsar Alexander III's youngest son Grand Duke Mikhail, who had rejected the throne in March 1917. In 1923 Miasnikov formed an opposition faction called the 'Workers' Group of the Russian Communist Party'. See Avrich 1984, pp. 1–29; Miasnikov 1995, pp. 137–91; Alikina 2006.
4 TsA FSB, R33718, d. 499061, vol. 40, ll. 68, 127.

leaders of the opposition and potential supporters. The situation in Nikolaev, where purportedly an already existing 'underground' organisation existed, was instructive. An overwhelming majority of delegates (84 out of 100) to a local trade-union congress had voted for the Workers' Opposition. When the congress's oppositionist majority clashed with the majority in the gubernia union committee supporting the Ten, central party leaders sent CC member, Dmitry Manuilsky, to Nikolaev; he transferred about 90 prominent supporters of the Workers' Opposition elsewhere. Some in Nikolaev continued to organise, but they reportedly resented Shlyapnikov for not taking a lead or rendering aid. He refused to consider providing leadership for the Nikolaev group, although he found it acceptable to organise such groups.[5] He thus tacitly encouraged his supporters to form groups at the local level, but refused to set up a centralised network of leadership as it would bring charges of factionalism from party leaders.

Responding to criticism that he was a weak leader, Shlyapnikov responded that he had sensed no support from the regions. He rebuked his supporters for not working closely enough with factory workers, for providing insufficient material for a political platform and for offering little concrete information about the moods, desires and life of workers at the local level. The problem lay not only at the local level. He admitted that the opposition itself had to a certain extent become demoralised.[6] Despite their dejection, Shlyapnikov and his supporters attempted to explore where their perspectives coincided and to develop the group's future tactics. The most important issue was the role of the unions under NEP.

Myasnikov's views on the role of the unions and the soviets in the management of production sounded a discordant note. Like Shlyapnikov and his supporters, he had suffered at the hands of party leaders for his outspoken criticism of the diminishing role of workers in the party and in managing the economy. But they had disagreed on precisely how to manage production: Myasnikov advocated soviets, the Workers' Opposition advocated unions. Shlyapnikov harshly criticised Myasnikov's plan for management through soviets, saying that, in essence, it meant the 'organisation of peasant unions'. He concluded: 'The working class should not organise a unit hostile to it'. Most

---

[5] TsA FSB, R33718, d. 499061, vol. 40, ll. 128, 143; vol. 41, ll. 68–9. Dmitrii Manuil'skii (1883–1959) joined the party in 1903, participated in the 1905 revolution, was a *Vperëdist* in 1907, an internationalist during World War I, a *Mezhraionets* in 1917, and in 1920–1 Ukraine Commissar of Agriculture, Communist Party of Ukraine CC secretary and *Kommunist* newspaper editor (RKP(b) 1961, p. 834).

[6] TsA FSB, R33718, d. 499061, vol. 40, ll. 127–8.

of Shlyapnikov's supporters agreed with him that Myasnikov's proposal to give management of production to the soviets could further strengthen the peasantry's influence over state policy. Later in the meeting, Shlyapnikov expressed the fear that the Communist Party was degenerating and falling into the hands of 'a peasant element aspiring to become the complete master of Russia'.[7] His inclusion of Myasnikov, whose views he opposed, reflects the respect he held for others of worker origin, regardless of their views.

A dialogue about the management of production led to a more general conversation on what role the unions should assume in the face of their exclusion from an important supervisory role in production (whether by soviets or by state economic bodies). One participant was perplexed by the proletariat's removal from the administration of a proletarian state, because for him it threw into question the relationship between workers and the Communist Party. All participants saw NEP as a setback for the revolution. One point of view was that if unions were not allowed to manage production then they should resume their pre-revolutionary role as defenders of workers' rights in the workplace. Nevertheless, they acknowledged the harsh reality that without strike funds, trade unions could not carry out strikes, the ultimate method of pressure against employers.[8]

The final question on the meeting's agenda concerned further tactics. Views ranged from the creation of a new 'worker' party to unspecified 'strong means' to heal the party. Between the two extremes was a proposal to create 'circles with a leading group' within the Communist Party. Some wanted Shlyapnikov and Medvedev to prepare a platform for discussion, but Medvedev objected that a platform had to be the product of collective work. He did not think there was enough agreement within the group to write a platform. Further, he commented sardonically that some of those demanding a platform feared to 'write anything that would diverge from CC decrees'. Shlyapnikov flatly called a platform 'impossible'.[9] Not only would it violate the ban on factionalism passed by the Tenth Party Congress, but his supporters had not provided enough information about workers to include in a platform.

Nevertheless, against Shlyapnikov's protests, his supporters voted to assign him and Medvedev to elaborate a political platform that they would discuss at a future meeting and present to the Eleventh Party Congress. Archival records indicate that the two men did not formulate a platform but a set of proposals. These were discussed at a subsequent meeting, but never presented to

---

7 TsA FSB, R33718, d. 499061, vol. 40, ll. 127–8.
8 Ibid.
9 Ibid.

the party.[10] The fact that Shlyapnikov's colleagues would instruct him and Medvedev to prepare a platform and that they would ignore that order and write a different type of document, perhaps even for an audience different from the one that the others at the meeting had in mind, testifies to the chaotic relationship between Shlyapnikov and those who shared his concern about a role for the workers in socialist society. While his supporters sought inspiring leadership, Shlyapnikov wanted to know that workers truly mobilised behind his efforts.

Appeal to the Comintern

In the end, Shlyapnikov and 21 others decided to appeal to the Comintern, as the highest court in the international communist movement, about the persecution of dissenters within the Russian Communist Party.[11] Kollontai could be effective in that setting. Although there is no evidence that she attended any meetings of the original signatories in February 1922, she shared Shlyapnikov's concerns, as well as his hopes, about the Comintern's impartiality and his sense that appealing to it was the only route that remained. Shlyapnikov had always valued her talents as a persuasive speaker and hoped that she might sway an international audience. Moreover, she was scheduled to speak on the 'woman question' at the Comintern conference and so there was the possibility that she, more easily than others of the 22, could interject with some words on behalf of the appeal.

Lenin and Zinoviev had authored the guiding 21 Points (or conditions), adopted by the Comintern in 1920. One of the points stipulated that individuals belonging to any member party had the right to appeal to the Comintern as the highest body of the international Communist movement, either separately or collectively, if their grievances were not satisfied by the leading bodies of their national party.[12] If Shlyapnikov sincerely believed that the appeal had a chance of consideration by the Comintern, he was blind to the influence of the leaders of the Russian party in the Comintern, which was so strong that realistically his tactics were hopeless.

---

10   TsA FSB, R33718, d. 499061, vol. 40, l. 128, ll. 133–9.
11   RGASPI, f. 17, op. 71, d. 1, l. 10.
12   Chase and Staklo (eds.) 2001, pp. 11–19. Lars Lih argues that the use of the term rarefaction [*razzhizhenie*] in the '21 conditions' highlights how Zinoviev was the main author of the document (Lih 2011c, p. 52).

Nevertheless, an appeal to the Comintern was 'legal', according to its founding document. An expanded Comintern Executive was to meet from 24 February to 4 March 1922 to discuss the proposal for a 'united front', which was to unite all revolutionary socialists (including anarchists and syndicalists) and Social-Democratic workers in the struggle against international capital and reformist socialist leaders.[13] In fact, the leadership of the Russian-dominated Comintern intended to centralise the international communist movement under its leadership. The efforts of the 22 to reveal deep disagreements within the RKP(b) thus undermined Russian party leaders' campaign for a united front.

The 22, joined by Kollontai and Zoya Shadurskaya, presented their petition to the Comintern Executive on 26 February 1922. Before approving the Russian party leaders' plan for a united front in Western Europe, the petitioners called on the Comintern to 'heal the rift' between workers and party leaders in Russia. They found it unlikely that the Russian Communist Party could lead an international effort for a 'united workers' front' when there was so much disunity and a reduction of the role of the workers within the Russian party itself. The signatories complained that 'bourgeois' elements had flooded into the party, diluting the influence of 'proletarian' members and fostering the suppression of dissent among worker Communists. The trend away from participatory democracy within trade unions and towards unilateral decision-making by the 'party and trade union bureaucracy' had disillusioned communist workers, who were leaving the party. Finally, the signatories expressed their support for an international workers' united front, but first asked that the Comintern intervene to 'eliminate the threat of a schism hanging over our party'.[14]

When Kollontai attempted to speak before the Comintern Executive on 26 February on behalf of the views expressed in the appeal, Russian party leaders (most notably Trotsky and Zinoviev) on the presidium of the Comintern conference removed her name from the list of orators. In a private meeting with Kollontai, they urged her not to speak. Zinoviev insisted that support for

---

13 Humbert-Droz 1967; Tivel and Kheimo (eds.) 1967.

14 The original signatories were: M. Lobanov, N. Kuznetsov, A. Polosatov, A. Medvedev, G. Miasnikov, V. Pleshkov, G. Shokhanov, S. Medvedev, G. Bruno, A. Pravdin, I. Ivanov, F. Mitin, P. Borisov, M. Kopylov, Zhilin, M. Chëlyshev, A. Tolokontsev, A. Shliapnikov, I. Barulin, V. Bekrenev, A. Pavlov, and A. Tashkin (RGASPI, f. 17, op. 71, d. 3, ll. 1–2). Zoia Shadurskaia (1873–1939) was a close friend of both Kollontai and Shliapnikov; she shared their ideals and their concern that the revolution was taking a wrong course. Located in RGASPI, f. 17, op. 71, d. 3, ll. 1–4, the letter was published in RKP(b) 1961, pp. 749–50, and in Anon 1922, p. 16.

the united front was a party directive that the entire Russian delegation had to pursue without reservations. When she proved recalcitrant, Trotsky forbade her to speak and issued a decree, in the name of the CC, that ordered all members of the Russian delegation to 'obey party directives'.[15] Both Trotsky and Zinoviev thus stifled criticism in the name of party discipline.

The Politburo delegated Zinoviev and Trotsky to convince the Comintern Executive that the 'Letter of the 22' contained distortions and was a factionalist statement of the former Workers' Opposition.[16] To investigate the letter, the Comintern created a commission, the members of which either knew little about Russia or were malleable.[17] The most prominent member of this commission was Clara Zetkin, who, according to one historian, was then 'old, upset over the death of Rosa Luxemburg, and easily flattered and manipulated by RCP leaders'.[18] According to Kollontai, the commission only 'hastily' questioned her and Shlyapnikov. Then it sat in a long session with Trotsky and Zinoviev, after which it roundly condemned the letter and its signatories. Kollontai suspected that Radek had authored an 'accusatory, prosecutorial' speech by one commission member. Disappointed by Zetkin's silence, she exclaimed: 'To what degree has Zinoviev developed lackeyism, cowardice!' The commission censured the 22 and warned them not to make such an appeal in the future.[19] Zinoviev and

---

15 RGASPI, f. 134, op. 3, d. 37, ll. 33–5. Other presidium members were Radek and Bukharin (Russia), Brandler (Germany), Souvarine (France), Terracini (Italy), Kreibich (Czechoslovakia) and Carr (née Ludwig E. Katterfield, USA). For more on Carr, see Haynes et al. 1998, pp. 19, 360.

16 RGASPI, f. 17, op. 3, d. 273, 27 February 1922. The Executive, as elected at the July 1921 Comintern Congress, consisted of: Zinoviev, Bukharin, Radek, Lenin, Trotsky (Russia), Gehert and Frohlich (Germany), Souvarine (France), Burian and Kreibich (Czechoslovakia), Terracini and Gennari (Italy), and seventeen other members. The extended session in late February–early March 1922 was attended by 105 participants from 36 countries (Tivel and Kheimo 1929, p. 160). For biographies of leading Comintern members, see Morgan et al. (eds.) 2005.

17 Members were Clara Zetkin, the French Communist Marcel Cachin, Jakob Friis of Norway, the young Italian Communist Umberto Terracini, Arthur MacManus of Great Britain, Kreibich of Czechoslovakia, and Vasil Kolarov of Bulgaria (RGASPI, f. 17, op. 71, d. 3, l. 13). The syndicalist, Alfred Rosmer, and the anarchist-turned-Bolshevik, Victor Serge, recalled Frossard as one who would change his views according to the prevailing wind (Rosmer 1971, p. 152; Serge 2002, p. 104).

18 Farnsworth 1980, pp. 262–3.

19 RGASPI, f. 134, op. 3, d. 37, ll. 36–8, 12 March 1922. No protocol was recorded at the 3 March session when the Comintern commission interviewed Kollontai and Shliapnikov, but one of the commission members later restored it from memory (RGASPI, f. 48, op. 1, d. 14, ll. 15–16).

other leaders of the Russian Communist Party held the Comintern so tightly in rein that it could only be a 'court of appeal' for those whose goals coincided with the interests of Russian party leaders. Shlyapnikov's and his supporters' recourse to it signified that they had already been backed into a corner. Yet Shlyapnikov's strategy required taking a principled stand.

The Fifth Congress of the Metalworkers' Union

A few days after the 22 Russian communists had presented their appeal to the Comintern, the Fifth Congress of the Metalworkers' Union convened. Before the congress began, Shlyapnikov and those who shared his views had determined to wage, in the union's communist fraction, a campaign to reassume the leadership of their union. But since the last session of the union's central committee in October, some of them had vacillated in their support. In addition, the Politburo had intervened in the selection of congress delegates. As the fraction convened, it appeared doubtful whether Shlyapnikov's supporters would command a majority of delegates.

On the eve of the congress, Shlyapnikov and his allies were uncertain of their strength. Vladimirov had apparently withdrawn from the struggle. Those who remained decided that their primary goal at the congress would be to give 'rebuff' to the 'coalition of fools and careerists' in the union leadership. If they could win a majority of the fraction, they would demand the implementation of their decisions. If half of the fraction were with them, they would push for proportional representation in the union's leadership. If they had a 'resolute' large minority, they would carry the struggle to 'lower bodies' of the union.[20] They did not address the question of what to do if they had a majority, but the CC (or Politburo) struck down their decisions, as had occurred at the last congress, when Shlyapnikov and many of his supporters submitted to party discipline.

Meanwhile, the Politburo prepared for a confrontation at the congress. On Lenin's initiative, it created an Orgburo commission to compose the new central committee of the Metalworkers' Union and instructed guberina-level party committees to select union leaders at their level. In preparation for the congress, only CC-endorsed proposals were presented (by Lepse) to the communist fraction of the Metalworkers' Union's central committee. Of 16 voting members present, eight had formerly supported the Workers' Opposition. Nevertheless, 11 of the 16 voted for Lepse's proposals, indicating that several of

---

20 TsA FSB, R33718, d. 499061, vol. 43, l. 148.

Shlyapnikov's supporters had shifted allegiance.[21] When the communist fraction of the congress convened, conflict immediately surfaced over who would lead the congress. The Orgburo had approved one list of nominees for the congress presidium, while another originated from Shlyapnikov's supporters. Although the names of a few nominees were on both lists, they quickly asked to be removed from the rival list, attesting to the intractable nature of the dispute within the union over its leadership and direction. Shlyapnikov urged delegates not to be influenced by accusations swirling around the 'Letter of the 22'. Yet, perhaps recognising that he did not have majority support, he even withdrew his name from the list put forward by his supporters. This signified his resignation from the struggle to resume control of the union. When voices from the floor rang out in support of him, Nikolai Yanson, a loyal member of the union's 'new' leadership, rejected their calls and disparaged Shlyapnikov. He scoffed: 'It is possible to bandy one's name about, to be a noisy cart, but to do little in everyday work'. Yanson put forth Vladimirov's name as an example of a diligent and hard worker.[22]

In refusing his nomination to the presidium, Vladimirov spoke as passionately as he had at the previous congress. He declared that he had never yearned for high-ranking posts, but had worked hard 'because I sensed the vibrancy of this work'. Nevertheless, he said, for the preceding six months, he had suffered more at his job than he had in tsarist prisons. Furthermore, he maintained that he would refuse to hold a post in the union's central committee, even if he were to be charged with violating party discipline. Vladimirov concluded: 'I am thankful for your trust in me for four years, but this time I ask you to leave me in peace'. Lepse questioned Vladimirov's loyalty to the party, but the fraction allowed him to resign. By a small majority (85–76), the fraction endorsed the Politburo-approved list. These proceedings showed disarray among Shlyapnikov's supporters. Some (Skliznev and Kiselev) still put up a fight, but others (Shlyapnikov, Vladimirov, Tashkin, and G.F. Tarasov) refused to participate in such a charade.[23]

The debate on the role of the Metalworkers' Union under NEP revealed subtle differences between Shlyapnikov and his comrade Medvedev. Addressing

---

21   RGASPI, f. 17, op. 3, d. 271, l. 4; f. 99, op. 1, d. 8, l. 33. The Orgburo commission comprised Tomskii, Andreev and S. Syrtsov, who led CC agitation and propaganda work.

22   RGASPI, f. 99, op. 1, d. 2, ll. 1–6. The congress and its communist fraction met 2–8 March 1922, with 161 delegates attending the fraction.

23   RGASPI, f. 99, op. 1, d. 2, l. 5; d. 7, l. 24. Schapiro 1956 assumed that Kiselëv 'had broken with the opposition' (Schapiro 1956, pp. 332–3), since he did not sign the Letter of the 22, but he still actively attempted to regain control of the Metalworkers' Union.

the role of the unions in defending workers under NEP, Medvedev called for the right of workers in capitalist enterprises to strike and for the union to create strike and unemployment funds; for without these, the capitalists would not abide by collective agreements. Significantly, he wanted to extend this discussion to consider the unions' defence of workers not only in capitalist enterprises, but also in state enterprises, alluding to his doubts that the 'proletarian state' actually ruled in the interests of the 'proletariat'. Although he clarified that he was not calling for the independence of the unions from state power, as did the Mensheviks and the SRs, one of the new Politburo-approved leaders labelled his proposals 'anti-Marxist' and declared that it was no longer necessary to use 'antiquated methods' of trade-union work. Shlyapnikov retorted that pre-revolutionary methods would not be necessary only if 'everything in our government had changed'. Unfortunately, he continued, the current policy was not new in relation to capitalism. Nevertheless, he differed with Medvedev on strikes, advocating instead that 'state laws and courts' be used to enforce collective agreements between concessionaires and unions.[24] Aware that no funds would be available for strikes, Shlyapnikov staked his hopes on the law and Soviet judges.

Attempting to influence the delegates' vote for the new central committee of the union, both sides highlighted controversial issues. Tomsky (restored to VTSSPS leadership) informed them of the Politburo's highly critical view of the 'Letter of the 22', which prepared the way for Yanson's proposal of a list for the union's new central committee that excluded those who had led the appeal to the Comintern. Shlyapnikov then accused Tomsky of provoking a split. Contrary to Yanson's proposal, Medvedev urged delegates to elect a 'strong, authoritative central committee' that would exert influence on such vital questions as the 'necessity to stop orders abroad for equipment that could be made at home'.[25] Foreign orders stirred the emotions of the delegates, because it was a concrete example of the Soviet economic leadership's distrust of the Russian workers' capabilities.

During the debate over the elections to the new central committee, the history of party and trade-union relations came into play. Shlyapnikov's sympathisers criticised the central committee that had existed between the fourth and fifth congresses for having accomplished nothing, because, as appointees, its members had no credibility. Arguing that 'appointmentism' was a legitimate tradition in the history of Communist (or Bolshevik) relations with the

---

24 GARF, f. 5469, op. 17, d. 3, ll. 1–11; RGASPI, f. 99, op. 1, d. 2, ll. 23–5, 76; d. 7, l. 42. Medvedev was only allowed to address the congress after 42 delegates signed an appeal.
25 RGASPI, f. 99, op. 1, d. 2, ll. 26, 35–7.

trade unions, Lepse erred in referring to Shlyapnikov as an appointee in 1917. Shlyapnikov rejected this attempt to revise party history, recalling that when the CC assigned him to win over the Metalworkers' Union in 1917, he was the sole Bolshevik in the bureau leading the union. When he and his comrades won the union, he insisted: 'We consistently did so by means of elections'. His response drew applause from the delegates.[26]

Predictably, this applause for Shlyapnikov notwithstanding, the Politburo-approved list for the union's new central committee won, by 99 votes to 84, over that proposed by his supporters.[27] Given this small margin of victory, the Politburo moved to consolidate its victory by engineering a vote in the fraction on the 'Letter of the 22'. Surprisingly, the fraction voted unanimously (with five abstentions) to 'caution' those who signed the appeal 'from further such acts'. Thus, nearly all of those delegates who supported Shlyapnikov voted in favour, perhaps finding it necessary to recognise the Comintern as the highest party court. Refusing to surrender, Shlyapnikov's allies proposed proportional representation in the union's central committee. Unable to decide, the fraction asked the CC to rule. The Politburo, in the CC's name, rejected proportionality, characterising the majority's list as sufficiently representative. Moreover, it cast aspersions on the rival list as composed of people who had been censured by the Comintern.[28] The Fifth Congress of the Metalworkers' Union thus ended without a single victory for Shlyapnikov and those who shared his views. The new leadership of the union had managed to eke out a majority among delegates. Nevertheless, the large minority of votes received by Shlyapnikov and his fellows at this late date testifies to the depth of their support among rank-and-file metalworker unionists and to the difficulty the party and new union leaders had in extinguishing it.

Many of the questions raised at the Metalworkers' Union Congress were decided by the Politburo and Narkomtrud in spring 1922 and announced as policy at the Fifth All-Russian Congress of Trade Unions in September 1922. Trade unions were not to strike in defence of workers, for they should support the goal of the party and the state to rebuild the economy, which required increased productivity from workers. The 1922 Labour Code had been prepared by Narkomtrud without consulting the broad trade-union movement, only

---

26 RGASPI, f. 99, op. 1, d. 2, ll. 49–52, 148. Appointmentism [*naznachenstvo*] would be a prominent theme in the party discussion of late 1923.

27 RGASPI, f. 99, op. 1, d. 2, ll. 104–7. This total exceeds the number of 161 delegates attending the congress; I cannot explain the discrepancy.

28 RGASPI, f. 99, op. 1, d. 7, ll. 28–31; f. 17, op. 3, d. 277. These events occurred on 6–7 March 1922.

VTsSPS, which was bypassed when the final revisions were made. Trade-union critics, such as Ryazanov, censured the code for weakening the enforcement of collective agreements between management and workers, for allowing employers to arbitrarily refuse employment to workers hired through labour exchanges, for failing to protect workers who were not paid on time or at all and for failing to enforce the maximum working day and holiday time. With Tomsky's support, however, the code took effect by the end of 1922. In the meantime, the Eleventh Party Congress had already approved Lenin's resolution clarifying that trade unions could not aspire to a management role, but should serve as mediators between workers and managers of state industry.[29]

The Party Leaders' Campaign Against the 22

Some party leaders wanted to go further than the Comintern's decision and to prosecute the 22 for factionalism. There was real concern that pressure from the former Workers' Opposition, together with widespread economic grievances, would lead to a split in party ranks.[30] The Soviet press thus used the Comintern's decision as fodder to attack the signatories and other former supporters of the Workers' Opposition for factionalism and violating party discipline. The party press impugned the signatories as ideologically tainted by Menshevism, anarchism and all other political associations especially repugnant to Russian communists at that time. Forced on the defensive, the 22 had to explain repeatedly in writing and in person what had compelled them to appeal to the Comintern. As the Eleventh Party Congress drew nearer, Shlyapnikov and other prominent figures among the 22 faced the prospect of exclusion from the Communist Party.

Bukharin, who edited *Pravda* in 1917–29, must have helped lead the press campaign against the 22. Lenin could not have been actively involved in it, since for much of March 1922 he was outside of Moscow, recuperating from illness. Although Bukharin would not have undertaken the campaign without Politburo approval, he had his own reasons to press it. He was strongly opposed to factionalism within the party, was increasingly identified as a chief advocate of NEP and finally had developed an argument to justify the party's dictatorship, claiming that the proletariat was incapable of generating an 'intellectual elite' from its own ranks with the ability to organise 'all of society'. In his opinion, the proletariat had been unable to do this because of 'bourgeois' control

---

29   Sorenson 1969, pp. 174–6; Pirani 2008, p. 156.
30   Kvashonkin *et al.* (eds.) 1996, p. 243, March 1922 letter from I.N. Smirnov to Lenin.

over education in capitalist society.³¹ Shlyapnikov and his comrades undermined Bukharin's interpretation both because of what they stood for and who they were: self-educated proletarians who had proven to be capable organisers and administrators during the Civil War and early NEP.

Despite furious accusations against him in the press, Shlyapnikov still received letters of encouragement from individual worker communists and party cells scattered across Russia. These letters, no doubt, boosted his morale in the trying month of March 1922. Support came chiefly from old party members who knew him well. In expressing their solidarity with the 22, those defenders overcame enormous pressure from party leaders to condemn the appeal to the Comintern; but as one informed Shlyapnikov, there were few like them left. Many oppositionist workers had left or been hounded out of the party; most of those who remained readily participated in ritual condemnations of the appeal of the 22. In his diary, a detached observer wrote of apathy among Moscow workers towards the appeal, but acknowledged that at higher levels in the party there was a large measure of sympathy for the 22, even among their opponents.³²

Shlyapnikov's opponents not only used the letter to condemn him and his associates, but also made allegations regarding what Shlyapnikov and Kollontai had said to the Comintern commission. In a letter to the CC, Shlyapnikov decried distortions in the press of his statements to that commission, denying that he had threatened 'worker uprisings', insisting that he had only pointed out that worker dissatisfaction was so deep that sometimes it 'erupted in the form of strikes'. The party press had derided him for alleging that the Cheka had subjected him to a search. He explained that a person bringing him a letter had been searched and relieved of that letter, about which he had complained to the Comintern commission. He clarified that many other letters to him had been 'lost' in the mail, which to him demonstrated 'the absence of mutual trust' between him (a prominent worker communist) and leading party institutions.³³

The party-press campaign also utilised any flaws, real or apparent, in the political background of Shlyapnikov's supporters. For example, Shadurskaya's signature on the 'Letter of the 22' did not include the year in which she joined the Communist Party. This served as a pretext for party leaders to portray her

---

31 Pipes 1994, p. 457; Cohen 1980, pp. 142, 156. Kollontai named Radek as another principal author of the press campaign to 'smear' the 22 (RGASPI, f. 134, op. 3, d. 37, l. 36).
32 TsA FSB, R33718, d. 499061, vol. 41, ll. 22–4, 84–5; Pirani 2008, pp. 120–4; Koval'chenko (ed.) 1993, vol. 4, pp. 108–9.
33 RGASPI, f. 17, op. 71, d. 1, ll. 5–8, March 1922.

as politically suspect, which tainted the rest of the 22 and their appeal. In fact, as Shadurskaya wrote to the Politburo, she was a longtime party member, as she was sure party leaders were well aware.[34] Myasnikov, who had also signed the 'Letter of the 22', was expelled from the Communist Party by the Politburo on 20 February for 'repeated violations of party discipline' and for attempting to create a faction within the party. Shlyapnikov's opponents used Myasnikov's exclusion and his signature on the 'Letter of the 22' to discredit the letter and those who had signed it.

Shlyapnikov claimed that he learned of Myasnikov's expulsion only after Myasnikov had signed the appeal to the Comintern, whereupon Shlyapnikov immediately appealed to the Politburo to reconsider its decision. The Politburo refused. Shlyapnikov, however, did not back away from Myasnikov's defence. He again asked the Politburo to review his case, but the Politburo refused. Insisting that Myasnikov would not have been among the 22 if his expulsion had been known, he nevertheless openly disagreed with the Politburo's decision. Calling Myasnikov 'a proletarian that has given his whole life for the party', Shlyapnikov argued that the party should not 'throw him over the side'.[35]

Given the press campaign's limited effectiveness, party leaders applied other measures at their disposal. Stalin used his new powers as CC secretary against Shlyapnikov's supporters in the provinces. For example, in Omsk, communists who supported the 22 had taken over the gubernia party committee. The Siberian party bureau [*Sibbiuro*], the Omsk gubernia Cheka and the Orgburo cooperated to remove the oppositionists from power. Stalin, as CC secretary, sent a 'threatening telegram' in which he accused them of factionalism. He authorised the Sibbiuro to conduct a re-registration of the entire Omsk gubernia organisation and to expel from the party those who had 'conduct[ed] agitation for leaving the party'. In May and June, members of the party, the soviets and the trade unions were verified in Omsk, resulting in a few expulsions, reprimands and about twenty transfers. By the end of 1922, Sibbiuro transferred more than one hundred party functionaries to establish firm control over the Siberian organisation.[36] Nevertheless, such methods were still a far cry from the criminal prosecutions that would be applied against dissident Communists in 1923.

---

34   RGASPI, f. 17, op. 3, d. 280, l. 15, 8 March 1922.
35   RGASPI, f. 17, op. 3, d. 270, 22 February 1922, d. 278, 8 March 1922 and f. 48, op. 1, d. 14, l. 61. Shliapnikov's speech to a closed session of the Eleventh Party Congress, 2 April 1922.
36   Olekh 1994, pp. 107, 115–18; Demidov 1994, pp. 8–9. S.V. Kossior served as Sibbiuro secretary from November 1922.

Political pressure became so great that some of Shlyapnikov's comrades considered relinquishing their party-appointed positions and returning to manual labour. Medvedev for example drafted a letter to the Orgburo (which was perhaps not sent) in which he stated that due to the party leaders' lack of trust in him, he would not accept future CC work assignments but instead would work in a metals factory.[37] Some of their nervous tension emerged from the belief that party leaders were resorting to provocation. For example, Shlyapnikov reported to the Politburo that a woman who claimed to represent the KAPD personally invited him and the 'Workers' Opposition' to participate in a conference of a fourth international. When he denied the existence of the Workers' Opposition and disagreed with attempts to split the Third International, she allowed that a faction within the KAPD also disapproved of the creation of a new international. Reinforcing his suspicion, she then asked him to write out an answer to her invitation and to discuss the position of the Workers' Opposition in the German press. Shlyapnikov refused.[38] Her methods mirrored those of secret-police provocateurs.

Party leaders used not only the press (and possibly the Cheka) but also the CCC against the oppositionists. The first step in the CCC's investigation was a formal letter from Timofei Krivov, CCC secretary, to Shlyapnikov, as the presumed leader of the 22, requesting that he present in writing his evidence for accusing party centres of a 'struggle against proletarians with their own opinions'. Krivov also required Shlyapnikov to explain why he did not present his evidence to the party before submitting it to the Comintern and, more provocatively, if he thought that his accusations could 'lead to a party split'. Suggesting ominously that the 'Letter of the 22' violated the Tenth Party Congress's resolution on party unity, Krivov asked whether Shlyapnikov would comply with the Comintern commission's ban on future appeals.[39]

Shlyapnikov prefaced his answers to Krivov with the comment that he considered it 'unusual' for the CCC to become involved in an exclusively political matter. Moreover, since the Comintern, as the highest court in the communist

---

37 RGASPI, f. 589, op. 3, d. 9102, 9 March 1922 letter (copy). This copy found its way to Medvedev's CCC file after a party member accidentally discovered it in a library book he borrowed in December 1922.

38 RGASPI, f. 17, op. 3, d. 280, l. 15. The woman, who gave her name as Goldstein, visited Shliapnikov on 10 March 1922. Together with Dutch and Bulgarian oppositionists, the KAPD formed the Communist Labour International in April 1922 (Schapiro 1956, pp. 330–1).

39 RGASPI, f. 17, op. 71, d. 1, l. 9. Krivov (1886–1966) joined the party in 1905 and served as CC Urals bureau secretary after the revolution (RKP(b) 1961, p. 828). In 1922 he was a CC instructor and CCC member.

movement, had already made a decision on the affair, he considered it inappropriate for the CCC, as a lower court, to re-examine it. Nevertheless, he cited numerous examples of persecution and then added wryly: 'I have no doubt that in your files there is rather more material than I have in my memory'. In reply to Krivov's second question, Shlyapnikov wrote that he had tried unsuccessfully to convince the CC to discuss his grievances. As to whether his accusations could weaken the party, he declared forcefully that in the past the Bolsheviks had never feared discussing their faults. Rather, the elimination of the causes of these faults would strengthen the party. He declared emphatically that the appeal had not violated the Tenth Party Congress's ban on factionalism, but that he did not intend to violate the Comintern's ban on future appeals.[40] Moreover, he rejected the CCC's designation of him as the 'leader' of the 22, insisting that he did not speak for others who had signed. He thus avoided confessing to factionalism but enhanced the probability that others of the 22 would be interrogated.

When the CCC met with the 22, its investigators assured the signatories that their only goal was to ensure healthy 'party life'. Nevertheless, they could not guarantee that criminal prosecutions would be avoided. After all, the 'Letter of the 22' had fallen into the hands of enemies of the revolution. Medvedev responded that the fault for this lay with those party leaders who had published it in *Pravda*. Ignoring for the moment his ironic jibe, the CCC proceeded to question each signatory individually, but in the presence of all. This saved time and was less formal than individual interrogations. Yet the presence of a stenographer made some of them uncomfortable. Each emphasised his own particular reasons for signing. Genrikh Bruno had become disillusioned when he witnessed central bodies restore to the party 'alien elements' purged by the gubernia purge commission in which he worked.[41] Tolokontsev claimed that agreements made to buy locomotives abroad, rather than to produce them in Russia, drove him to sign the 'Letter of the 22'. Despite his high positions of authority, he said, he could not remain silent in the face of 'actions that kill the proletariat'.[42] Kollontai was most concerned, she said, with the 'mass

---

40 RGASPI, f. 17, op. 71, d. 1, l. 10.
41 Genrikh Bruno (1889–1945) joined the party in 1906. During the Civil War he held important posts on the front and in the Cheka and chaired the artillery industry board (RKP(b) 1961, p. 812 and RGASPI, f. 5, op. 1, d. 910, l. 3). He was reputedly an 'energetic, efficient' and 'versatile' administrator, despite having 'a few Chekist approaches' that were 'gradually diminishing' (RGASPI, f. 5, op. 1, d. 910, l. 3, 10 August 1921, P.A. Bogdanov's memo to Lenin).
42 Several years later, Tolokontsev still complained that the decision to buy locomotives abroad rather than build them in the RSFSR had delayed the recovery of the metals industry (Anderson *et al.* (eds.) 2007, vol. 2, p. 45, Politburo session, 14 June 1926.

departure of workers from the party'. Acknowledging that she would obey the Comintern's directive, she added that she would not remain silent if nothing changed. Mitin stated that he too would continue to air grievances as an individual, although perhaps not in a collective appeal again.[43]

CCC members responded with condemnation rather than comradely discussion. One urged the signatories to recant; another warned them that they were on the road to factionalism. The level of tension was high. When Medvedev was asked bluntly if he thought that current CC and CCC members had no right to sit in these bodies, he replied tersely: 'The [Tenth Party] Congress elected you; I did not vote'. His answer only annoyed the questioner. At this point, the stenographer was dismissed and the rest of the meeting was not recorded. The CCC either desired less formality or wanted no record of defiant remarks. As a result of its investigation, the CCC recommended that those members of the 22 who had been 'guilty of frequent, systematic violation of the Tenth Party Congress's decree on party unity' be expelled, but it did not specify whom, perhaps indicating disagreement within it.[44] This investigation set the stage for a commission of the Eleventh Party Congress to make specific recommendations on whom to ask the Congress to expel.

The CCC's recommendation threw into question Shlyapnikov's recent appointment as a member of the Russian delegation to the Genoa economic conference. To be held on 10 April–19 May 1922, the conference would bring representatives from Germany and the USSR together for the first time with representatives of 32 other European nations to discuss trade and financial questions, including tsarist-era debt. True to his views and character, Shlyapnikov had dissented with some key decisions made by the party's commission on the conference. He doubted its assumption that large loans would be forthcoming from European capital; instead of seeking these, he thought it more realistic to form industrial associations in mining and processing with only a 'partial participation of foreign capital'. Rather than negotiating with individual capitalist firms over pre-revolutionary contracts, he proposed the organisation of a giant trust.[45] Given that his party membership was in jeopardy after the CCC's recommendation, the CC officially put on hold his work as

---

43   RGASPI, f. 589, op. 3, d. 9103, vol. 3, ll. 97–106, 17 March 1922. CCC members present were Krivov, A.A. Sol'ts, Z.Ia. Litvin-Sedoi, K.A. Ozol' and S.N. Smidovich (a Zhenotdel leader). Sol'ts, Sedoi and Smidovich had been party members since 1897–8. Most of the 22 were present. At least one, Polosatov, had been questioned earlier and was not present. This text appears to be incomplete.

44   RGASPI, f. 589, op. 3, d. 9103, vol. 3, ll. 97, 103; f. 48, op. 1, d. 14, l. 3.

45   TsA FSB, R33718, d. 499061, vol. 40, ll. 154–7, a paper Shliapnikov presented to the Politburo in February 1922.

a member of the Genoa conference delegation.[46] He did not attend the conference, which in any case had few results for Soviet Russia. Nevertheless, his ideas would resonate as the NEP economy developed trusts and syndicates to manage industry.

The Eleventh Party Congress

At the Eleventh Party Congress (27 March–2 April 1922), Shlyapnikov and his supporters defended themselves against charges of having violated party unity with their appeal to the Comintern. Their opponents accused them of having continued to organise themselves as the 'Workers' Opposition' and of having pursued a line contrary to party policy. Because of the party leadership's campaign in the winter of 1921–2 to remove supporters of the former Workers' Opposition from their organisational bases, only a handful of those who had signed the programme of the Workers' Opposition had returned as voting delegates at the Eleventh Party Congress. Nevertheless, many delegates were dissatisfied with some features of NEP and with the expanding powers of the party control commissions. The 22 thus stood some chance of benefiting from the delegates' mood, especially since two high-ranking leaders were absent or had a reduced presence at the congress. Lenin, whose charisma and persuasive powers could sway delegates, missed a number of sessions due to his poor health and Bukharin, a highly effective speaker and critic of the 22, was in Berlin for talks on the united front.[47] Because the congress's open proceedings were published and have been analysed in secondary literature, my discussion of it will emphasise what is to be learned from the unpublished records, including the record of the closed session where delegates discussed and voted upon the exclusion of Shlyapnikov and others.

Aware of his supporters' numerical inferiority at the congress, Shlyapnikov attempted to appeal to a broad range of delegates. He aimed, at the very least, to convince them that the party's relationship with workers was truly troubled and in need of repair. In open session, he denied that the Workers' Opposition had continued to function as a group. He asserted that party leaders would rather blame the party's troubles on a scapegoat, on a conspiracy of malcontents, rather than address genuine problems. He warned that worker discontent posed a real threat to the party because workers were saying that it was 'better

---

46 RGASPI, f. 17, op. 2, d. 77, l. 2, 25 March 1922.
47 Schapiro 1956, pp. 334–8; Sorenson 1969, pp. 171–2; Daniels 1988, pp. 163–5. Bukharin and Radek had travelled to Berlin at the head of a Comintern delegation (Cohen 1980, p. 151).

to lose power now, in order to take it anew in 10 years'. Contesting Lenin's claim that the Russian proletariat had ceased to exist as a class in the Marxist sense, Shlyapnikov, with customary irony, congratulated congress delegates 'on being the vanguard of a non-existent class' (the proletariat). In a more serious vein, he insisted that Communists needed to work with the industrial proletariat that existed. He did not share the view that the Russian proletariat had degenerated; rather, he thought that this perspective was a 'justification for political manoeuvres, searches for support in other social strata' (such as soldiers who emerged from the peasantry). He insisted: 'Another and "better" working class we will not have, so we should accept the one we have'.[48]

Ever fond of militaristic metaphors, Lenin had accused the 22 of having created panic in the party ranks with their appeal. Expanding the metaphor, he reminded delegates that in a real army those who created panic during a retreat were shot 'and correctly so'. Gamely retorting that the Comintern was 'not a manoeuvreing army', Shlyapnikov also questioned the basis for prosecution, since all of those who signed had already accepted the decision of the Comintern. He uttered the opinion that comradely relations among party members were fading and that this posed a danger to the party's very existence. If the party turned its back on its core constituency of workers, he believed, it would lose its right to rule. He warned that the atmosphere in the party reminded him of that in 1907 when *intelligenty* abandoned the workers and showed apathy towards the cause of revolution. He reminded delegates that he and his supporters were not alien political elements weakening the Communist Party but belonged to the party's core constituency. At the congress, Zinovy Litvin-Sedoi had smeared Medvedev as a Menshevik. Defending his comrade, Shlyapnikov remembered that in 1914, when Sedoi enlisted in the French army as a volunteer, Medvedev was on his way to Siberian exile for organising a protest against the arrest and trial of anti-war Bolshevik deputies in the Duma. 'That is the irony of fate', Shlyapnikov drily added. He concluded dramatically: 'Do not forget that we came from [the working class] to this tribune, and back [to the working class] we will return'.[49]

Certainly some party leaders wanted to exclude Kollontai, Shlyapnikov and Medvedev from the party and perhaps even prosecute them criminally. But other party leaders hesitated to risk such a step for fear of stirring up congress delegates who, although they did not approve of the appeal to the Comintern,

---

48 RKP(b) 1961, pp. 103–4.
49 RKP(b) 1961, pp. 24, 187–8. Litvin-Sedoi disputed Shlyapnikov's accusation (RKP(b) 1961, p. 190), but his autobiography does not clearly define his stance towards the war (Gambarov et al. (eds.) 1989, chapter 3, pp. 30–1).

sympathised with the grievances expressed in it. Kollontai sensed 'vacillation' and a 'wait-and-see attitude' at the top. She was aware that the congress's commission appointed to investigate the 22 had no members sympathetic to the opposition, yet she believed that even they hesitated to vote for exclusion.[50] Lenin did not take a firm stand, as subsequent party investigations of Shlyapnikov made clear. When, in 1926, one CCC member asserted that in 1922 Lenin had favoured Shlyapnikov's exclusion from the party, another allowed only that Lenin had never spoken against it. Shlyapnikov claimed that not only had Lenin opposed his exclusion, but that in retrospect Stalin had recognised that its proposal had been a mistake and had confirmed that it was not Lenin's initiative. Shlyapnikov later argued that if Lenin had spoken in favour of his exclusion, then it would have passed. During his 1933 purge, he claimed that Kamenev had introduced the 1922 resolution to exclude him and others who had signed the 'Letter of the 22'.[51] This raises questions, since Kamenev was not a member of the commission. He was out of favour in 1933 and a convenient scapegoat. Shlyapnikov generally did not make charges he believed to be false, but he sometimes relayed information uncritically. Perhaps Stalin named Kamenev, or perhaps Shlyapnikov's memory confused Kamenev with Zinoviev, who was a member of the commission.

The Eleventh Party Congress met in a special closed session on 2 April 1922 to consider the recommendations of the congress' commission, which had been formed to investigate whether members of the 22 had violated the Tenth Congress's ban on factionalism. The commission's report determined that there were ideological and organisational links between the former Workers' Opposition and meetings of those who signed the 'Letter of the 22', but the appeal alone did not constitute factionalism. The commission did find evidence of 'constant long-term factional work' in Mitin's July 1921 letter, in which Mitin referred to meetings of the former Workers' Opposition after the Tenth Party Congress and to his tactics (discussed earlier) for taking over the Donbas party organisation.[52]

---

50   RGASPI, f. 134, op. 3, d. 37, l. 37. The commission had 19 members, among whom the most prominent were: D.Z. Lebed', G.I. Petrovskii, E.M. Iaroslavskii, S.M. Kirov, L.M. Kaganovich, Z. Ia. Litvin-Sedoi, G.E. Zinoviev, I.V. Stalin and F.E. Dzerzhinskii (RKP(b) 1961, p. 178). For its report, see RKP(b) 1961, pp. 702–10.
51   RGASPI, f. 589, op. 3, d. 9103, vol. 1, ll. 149–68, CCC Presidium session, 23 October 1926; vol. 5, l. 358, 18 June 1933, Shlyapnikov's letter to Gosplan RSFSR purge commission chair Ivanov.
52   RGASPI, f. 48, op. 1, d. 14, ll. 3–7. This session's proceedings were not published in the stenographic report of the congress, but were preserved in party archives. Mitin's letter was published in Zorkii 1926, pp. 51–3.

Singling out Shlyapnikov, Medvedev, and Kollontai as those most guilty of having continued 'factional work', the commission recommended their expulsion for an indefinite period for having violated the Tenth Party Congress's directives on unity and against factionalism. Of the remaining signatories, the commission recommended to expel only Mitin, for the actions described in his July 1921 letter and for having hidden his Menshevik past, and Nikolai Kuznetsov, for misrepresenting his social origins and length of party membership.[53] Those signatories who were not targeted for exclusion proclaimed their solidarity with Shlyapnikov, Kollontai and Medvedev (but not with Mitin and Kuznetsov), announcing their intention to resign from the party if those three were expelled. The CCC warned that they were in possible violation of party discipline.[54]

Shlyapnikov, Kollontai and Medvedev were permitted to speak in their own defence. Kollontai, who spoke first, steadfastly denied that the 22 had formed a faction. She deplored the party leaders' growing tendency to make a 'faction' out of any group of communists meeting informally. She noted pointedly:

> When two of us are together, we can talk, but when the third comes (laughter), we drop silent. We fear one another. We think that this third communist can suppose that we two are the Workers' Opposition.

The party, she insisted, could only gain from friendly meetings of its members discussing issues of vital importance to the party. Gently mocking charges that she and Medvedev were particularly unrepentant, she recalled that the nineteenth-century Russian satirist, Mikhail Saltykov-Shchedrin, had written about peasants who were asked why they were exiled:

> They answered, because we were unrepentant. The landowner taught us what was good, intelligent, and reasonable. He even dragged us by our hair. Still, we were unrepentant and were exiled.

---

53 An Old Bolshevik commission established that Kuznetsov had entered the party during World War I (not in 1904, as he claimed) and before the war had worked as a grocer, not a metalworker. Kuznetsov joined Miasnikov's 'Workers' Group' in 1923.

54 RKP(b)1961, p. 710; RGASPI, f. 48, op. 1, d. 14, ll. 9–13. D.Z. Lebed' (1893–1939) came to the Bolsheviks from the SRs in 1909, after the October Revolution edited the journal, *Vestnik Narkomvnudel*, and later became Communist Party of Ukraine CC secretary and control commission chair (RKP(b) 1961, p. 830).

Emphasising her party loyalty, her devotion to the workers' leading role in the Soviet state and to the implementation of the Tenth Party Congress's decree on worker democracy, she dramatically concluded: 'If there is no place for this in our party, then exclude me. But even outside of the ranks of our party, I will live, work and fight for the Communist Party'.[55]

Shlyapnikov, speaking next, denied the charge of factionalism and scoffed at the presentation of Mitin's single letter as proof of 'systematic contact' between leaders of the former Workers' Opposition and their followers. Meetings of those who signed the 'Letter of the 22' were not formal meetings of a group, but of 'old friends'. He insisted: 'To make a faction out of this is just as difficult to do as from a tea party or pancake suppers which take place in Moscow, even in the Kremlin'. Party leaders possibly then did not know, or have proof, that the meetings were chaired, that there was an agenda, a vote at the end and a record of the discussion. Nevertheless, the form of the meetings was consistent with longstanding practice in the party and did not violate party discipline as it had been understood before the Tenth Party Congress. In this sense, Shlyapnikov was truthful when he declared that the meetings were not of a factional nature. He emphasised: 'Party unity is for me higher than anything'. Developing a counterattack, he charged his opponents with factionalism. Complaining that party cells were not allowed to invite him to speak to them, he declared that his election by four factory party cells as a delegate to their gubernia conferences proved that communist workers supported him. He concluded: 'if you find ... that our thoughts and worries about the fate of the working class are alien to you, then, all right, exclude us'.[56]

Medvedev, the last of the three to speak, could not restrain his customary sarcasm when he pointed out the contradiction between Molotov's proclamations in open sessions of the congress that party unity had been established and 'groupings' dissolved, and the claim in closed session that the Workers' Opposition continued to exist. He expressed ironic surprise at Molotov's lack of diligence in failing to notice such a large and active group as that described. Like Shlyapnikov, Medvedev referred to his support among workers. Workers at the Radio Morse factory had elected him to the congress of the Moscow Metalworkers' Union, even after it was known that he might be excluded from the party. Medvedev thus declared he had survived trial before 'a court of the working class'. Unlike Shlyapnikov, he spoke defiantly, declaring that even if he

---

55   RGASPI, f. 48, op. 1, d. 14, ll. 14–24.
56   RGASPI, f. 48, op. 1, d. 14, ll. 50–64.

were excluded: 'I do not think you will fatally wound me'. He did not fear the delegates' decision, he said.[57]

Following the three oppositionists' speeches, four well-respected and long-standing party members debated the proposal to exclude them. Two, Nikolai Kubyak and Vladimir Antonov-Ovseenko, opposed exclusion and two did not take a clear position. Dmitry Manuilsky spoke for 'strong measures' against the oppositionists and Grigory Petrovsky criticised the oppositionists for poor judgment, but neither came out for exclusion. A former Workers' Opposition supporter, Kubyak reminded delegates of the long history of 'struggle' between *intelligenty* and workers in the party. He recalled how students edged workers out of party-leadership posts because, students claimed, workers were illiterate and could not make speeches. There had been a 'workers' faction', of which Kubyak was a member, at the Third Party Congress in London in 1905, where the question of elevating the role of workers in the party was discussed and the first worker entered the CC. Kubyak also referred to the 1906 Fourth Party Congress in Stockholm as having been 'called by the workers' party'. Presenting party history in this light, he legitimised the efforts of Shlyapnikov and others to provide a 'worker' perspective on party policy and to increase the role of workers in the party leadership. He argued that the party leaders' acknowledgement that the 22 had the right to appeal to the Comintern contradicted their simultaneous condemnation of its appeal. Regarding Mitin's letter, Kubyak maintained that if individual letters sufficed to prove the existence of an anti-party faction, then one could find equally damning letters on Lenin's desk and the authors of such letters sitting among the congress's delegates. There was no evidence that Shlyapnikov and his supporters 'prepared for a split', he insisted. Finally, Kubyak asserted that, with their party history, it was 'the purest nonsense' to insist that Shlyapnikov and Medvedev prove their 'dedication to the working class'. He was not so charitable towards Mitin and Kuznetsov. Kubyak agreed that Mitin and Kuznetsov should be expelled from the party, but he proposed that delegates simply confirm the Comintern's decision pertaining to Shlyapnikov, Medvedev and Kollontai.[58]

Petrovsky rejected Kubyak's argument that Shlyapnikov's, Medvedev's and Kollontai's history of service on the party's behalf warranted a lighter

---

57 RGASPI, f. 48, op. 1, d. 14, ll. 126–31.
58 RGASPI, f. 48, op. 1, d. 14, ll. 65–7. Kubiak (1881–1937) was born into a working-class family in Kaluzhskaia guberniia. He worked in a steam-engine factory and joined the party in 1898. In 1920 he chaired the Northern oblast' forestry workers' union and in 1921–2 was a CC instructor. In 1922 he was CC Dal'biuro secretary and later CC secretary (RKP(b) 1961, p. 829; Zen'kovich 2002, pp. 284–5).

punishment for them. In his opinion, senior members of the party should show more discipline than should newer members. He thought that Shlyapnikov and the others had unwisely surrendered to the panicked mood created among some party members by 'rumours about the imminent "sale" of Russia at the Genoa conference'. Recalling his own initial participation in the Workers' Opposition, Petrovsky said he still supported the goal of bringing more workers into the CC, but that he found this single goal an inadequate basis for forming an 'entire opposition'. He abandoned the group, he said, when Kollontai began attracting 'former Mensheviks' into the opposition. Nevertheless, Petrovsky did not think that Shlyapnikov's and Kollontai's mistakes warranted severe punishment (significantly, he omitted mention of Medvedev). Concerning the evidence of Mitin's letter, Petrovsky concluded that one could not 'look at all documents from a gendarme's point of view'. Rather than analysing 'each letter of a word', one had to consider whether true factional activities had occurred.[59] Petrovsky did not call explicitly for the exclusion of anyone from the former opposition.

Antonov-Ovseenko assured delegates that he had not sensed any underground, anti-party work when he had worked with members of the former Workers' Opposition in Samara. Noting that some of Shlyapnikov's, Kollontai's and Medvedev's statements met with 'applause' at the congress, he said that one could not deny that there was a 'hidden illness' in the party. Dismissing the commission's case as 'contrived' and 'unfounded', he argued that the party congress could not call for greater punishment than had the Comintern without discrediting the latter as the highest body of the international Communist movement. He suggested a ritual condemnation of the 'Letter of the 22', abiding by the Comintern's decision on the matter. Furthermore, he offered a resolution to exclude Shlyapnikov, Medvedev and Kollontai from the party if they would violate party discipline in the future.[60]

Speaking far more harshly, Manuilsky charged that the 22 had worked towards the formation of a liberal workers' party and that the Mensheviks had exploited their appeal in order to discredit the Communist Party. In juxtapo-

---

59 RGASPI, f. 48, op. 1, d. 14, ll. 70–1. Petrovskii (1878–1958) joined the party in 1897 and was a Bolshevik deputy to the Fourth Duma in 1912–14. In 1918–19 he served as People's Commissar of Internal Affairs, and from 1919 to 1938 chaired the Ukrainian Soviet and then the All-Union Soviet. In 1922 he was a CC member. No other sources attest to Petrovskii's membership in the Workers' Opposition, aside from his acknowledgment of it at the Eleventh Party Congress.

60 RGASPI, f. 48, op. 1, d. 14, ll. 72–3. Antonov-Ovseenko (1884–1939), a tsarist officer's son, had been a revolutionary from 1901, a Menshevik while in emigration and a Bolshevik since 1917. During the Civil War he was a Ukrainian front commander and an NKVD RSFSR collegium member (RKP(b) 1961, p. 809).

sition to Shlyapnikov's and Medvedev's claims of worker support, Manuilsky cited scores of resolutions by party assemblies across Ukraine, unanimously demanding to exclude the offenders from the Communist Party. He nonetheless stopped short of recommending such an expulsion, but only emphasising the need 'to act severely in regard to frequent offenders'.[61] Manuilsky's phrase left open the door for letting the oppositionists go with a warning.

Following the debate there ensued a complicated series of resolutions, amendments and votes, reflecting evolving opinions within the party on how to treat dissent. Two resolutions on whether to exclude five members of the 22 were presented to this closed session of delegates to the Eleventh Party Congress: one, from the commission, to exclude Shlyapnikov, Medvedev, Kollontai, Kuznetsov and Mitin; a second, from Antonov-Ovseenko, to support the Comintern's resolution, but to go no further. An initial hand vote was too close to call, but a majority of delegates rejected going on record with a roll-call vote. Another hand vote resulted in 215 votes for Antonov-Ovseenko's resolution and 227–45 votes for the commission's resolution. After this, the Petrograd delegation (under Zinoviev's control) offered an amendment to the commission's resolution which would allow the excluded comrades to rejoin the party after one year, if they maintained good behaviour and showed dedication to the party. A majority of the delegates accepted the amendment. Then P.A. Kin proposed a correction to the resolution which called for the exclusion of Kuznetsov and Mitin and for the acceptance of the Comintern's decree only in relation to Kollontai, Shlyapnikov and Medvedev. Delegates accepted Kin's correction by a vote of 225–35 against 215. Upon the chair's objection that the combination of the original resolution with the amendment and correction would confuse 'Russian and foreign workers', Tomsky added another correction, allowing the CC to exclude Shlyapnikov, Medvedev and Kollontai if they violated party discipline in future. An overwhelming majority of the delegates passed the commission's resolution after it was edited to take into account Tomsky's and Kin's corrections.[62] Kuznetsov and Mitin were thus excluded from party membership, but Shlyapnikov, Kollontai and Medvedev were allowed to remain in the party pending further violations of party unity.

Conclusion

During the episode of the 22, Shlyapnikov's actions and statements remained consistent with his past political behaviour and views. He took care to avoid

---

61   RGASPI, f. 48, op. 1, d. 14, ll. 75–8.
62   RGASPI, f. 48, op. 1, d. 14, ll. 78–84.

actions that smacked of 'factionalism' because he sincerely desired a party unity based on responsiveness to workers' initiative. In his opinion, 'comradely' meetings to discuss important issues were firmly rooted in party tradition. He emphasised that building an organisation had to occur through local initiative. This was not anarchism, for he accepted a hierarchy that culminated in central leadership, but it ran counter to the militarist Bolshevism that had evolved during the Civil War.

The controversy around the 'Letter of the 22' to the Comintern was crucial to the process by which the party defined the meaning of party discipline and the limits of political discussion. The Eleventh Party Congress delegates' narrow vote in a closed session to allow Kollontai, Shlyapnikov and Medvedev to remain in the party 'until further outbursts' signified that many within the party still supported the right to air critical views. Lenin's reluctance to call outright for their expulsion may have emboldened other delegates to resist that option. Many congress delegates wanted to observe communist 'legality', according to which the Comintern's decisions prevailed over those of member parties. Delegates, many of whom were experienced party activists, declined to expel the 22, but were sufficiently concerned about retribution to resist a roll-call vote. Rather than risking defeat, party leaders allowed delegates to choose lesser measures, yet by 1922 the possibility of criminal prosecution for dissent had entered the party's political discourse. Most old party members probably understood that Lenin was speaking figuratively when he referred to using 'machine guns' against opponents within the party. As newer members recruited during the Civil War increasingly replaced 'Old Bolsheviks' at party congresses, the intensely violent language of the leaders came to be understood more literally.

Crucial policy matters also led congress delegates to sympathise with the 22 and to resist the proposal to exclude Shlyapnikov, Kollontai and Medvedev from the party. Many in the party felt guilt and discomfort over the ideological compromise that NEP entailed and they feared that concessions to the peasantry posed a danger to urban and industrial worker hegemony. Nevertheless, this very compromise with the peasantry and the consequent vulnerability of the 'proletarian party' drove hardliners to insist that the party close ranks and stifle heterodoxy in order to survive the transition to socialism through NEP. Events surrounding the 'Letter of the 22' were thus a defining moment in the transitional stage between an era of relatively open discussion within the party and one in which party members could be vilified, stigmatised and isolated for expressing opinions that differed from the Politburo's line.

CHAPTER 9

Factional Politics in the NEP Era

With its first phase completed by the end of 1922, NEP entered a second, when monetary taxation began to play a significant role in state revenue and banking was revived. A plentiful harvest in 1922 offered prospects for recovery from the deprivations of War Communism, yet it hardly assured stability.[1] Free to sell much of their crop on the open market, peasants could hold back their goods in order to force up prices, thus threatening Soviet workers with famine. With industry recovering more slowly than agriculture, an imbalance arose between industrial and agricultural prices, culminating in the October 1923 'scissors' crisis, when peasants withdrew from the market. Workers, who continued to suffer from unemployment in 1923–4, could hardly afford the food, clothing and services that had become widely available. They were not paid wages for months at a time, effectively lacked unemployment or sickness insurance and suffered frequent injuries in the workplace. Early NEP crises related to market phenomena set the context for strikes and oppositionism.

The years 1923–6 saw furious internal party debates on the course of NEP and on building socialism. Many party members worried that, under NEP, opponents of socialism would overwhelm the party. They saw the rapid industrialisation as the only hope, while others believed that the triumph of socialism was dependent on NEP's continuation. Lenin intervened less often in party politics, as he suffered several strokes in 1922–3. Mute and paralysed through 1923, he died on 21 January 1924. The question of who would lead the party after his death was inseparable from debates over political and economic policies. Trotsky jousted with the ruling triumvirate of Zinoviev, Kamenev and Stalin until 1925, when political alliances and positions realigned. Trotskyists, Zinovievists and other politically active factions attempted to enlist former members of the Workers' Opposition for their own efforts, while Stalin and Bukharin pressured them to conform. Although the Workers' Opposition had disbanded, its leading figures held important positions in government and industry, cultivated union-wide networks of supporters and met to discuss politics and economics. The ghost of the Workers' Opposition haunted the rhetoric of party control bodies and the political police.

Shlyapnikov's political views continued to evolve in the 1920s in dialogue with contemporary events, but he gradually came to realise that factionalism

---

1 Carr 1950–3, vol. 2, pp. 353–7.

was a dead-end. After his near-expulsion from the party, he was not re-elected to the CC at the Eleventh Party Congress. No longer did he have a base in the Metalworkers' Union. Instead, he turned to writing his memoirs in order to convey his views on worker-*intelligent* relations in the party and the role of unions. In autumn 1922 he began work in the Commission on the History of the October Revolution and of the RKP(b) [*Istpart*]; the first volume of his memoir, *Semnadtsatyi god*, was published in 1923. This and subsequent volumes were important records of revolutionary history, which conveyed messages to workers to organise themselves, not to depend passively on party *intelligenty*. Despite his increasing distance from top leadership positions, he continued to enjoy the personal sympathy of many high-ranking party members due to his charm and the reminder he provided of the revolutionary romanticism of their youth. Other leaders, however, resented his critical stance.

Shlyapnikov's Relationship with the Workers' Group

By late 1922, Shlyapnikov and his close comrades from the former Workers' Opposition appeared to have bowed to the party's decisions on trade unions and reconciled with the need for NEP as a general policy, yet they continued to be troubled by their perception that workers did not prevail in the party, unions, higher education or the army. They claimed to stand steadfast in their desire for workers 'to hold all levers of management, in the party as well as in the government'.[2] Shlyapnikov's concern for the role of workers in the party and industry resonated with the views of other oppositionists, especially Gavril Myasnikov's 'Workers' Group' and another group called 'Workers' Truth'. Nevertheless, key differences remained. Myasnikov elevated the soviets above the unions as economic managers, which Shlyapnikov opposed, because he feared peasant influence in the soviets. While Shlyapnikov aimed to achieve greater worker influence within the party, Myasnikov seemed prepared to create a new party dominated by workers. Although 'Workers' Truth' claimed to be a Bogdanovist group that emerged from the Workers' Opposition, there is actually little evidence of close personal ties between 'Workers' Truth' and former members of the Workers' Opposition. Moreover, Alexander Bogdanov denied any connection to it. With a membership mainly composed of student youth of proletarian origins, its programme pertained more to culture than to

---

2 TsA FSB, R33718, d. 499061, vol. 13, ll. 1–12, letter from Medvedev to Shlyapnikov, 26 September 1922, describing conversations with German metalworkers in Berlin, where he was on a work assignment.

economic management. Despite these differences, party leaders feared that workerist groups might link up.³ Therefore, the OGPU (formerly Cheka) kept them under close surveillance.⁴

OGPU head Dzerzhinsky suspected the Workers' Opposition of maintaining a faction, collaborating with the Workers' Group and Workers' Truth and using their administrative posts in the metals industry in order to attract worker support for their positions.⁵ Informants told Dzerzhinsky of several meetings of Shlyapnikov's and Myasnikov's supporters in the first half of 1923. Among attendees were former members of the Workers' Opposition such as Vladimirov, Chelyshev, Alexander Pravdin, Orlov, Lutovinov and Tolokontsev. Allegedly, they discussed whom to elect to the CC and CCC, supporting a CC with Stalin, Zinoviev and Trotsky, but rejecting Kamenev, Dzerzhinsky and Molotov. They would have nominated Medvedev and Orlov to the CC and Shlyapnikov to the CCC.⁶ Participants also discussed Myasnikov's manifesto, which he wanted to present to the Twelfth Party Congress. Mutual recriminations arose against Myasnikov 'for organising a new party' and against Shlyapnikov for succumbing to the dispersal of the Workers' Opposition. Both informer reports and participant accounts confirmed that the majority sided with Shlyapnikov, not Myasnikov. The two men thus came to no agreement. On the contrary, their circles competed for members, with some overlap between them.⁷

---

3   Pirani 2008, pp. 126–7; Bordiugov *et al.* 1995, kn. 1: 204–22; RGASPI, f. 82, op. 2, d. 181, 4; d. 182. Upon Medvedev's 1935 arrest, the NKVD found in his apartment old copies of Workers' Group and Workers' Truth materials, including the Workers' Truth newspaper (TsA FSB, R33718, d. 499061, vol. 40), indicating he and Shliapnikov were familiar with its proposals.
4   In February 1922, the State Political Administration (GPU) replaced the Cheka, then became the OGPU in 1923 with the creation of the USSR. Lower-level political police administrations were still called GPU. See Hagenloh 2009, Glossary and pp. xvii–xviii. The term GPU was often used interchangeably with OGPU.
5   RGASPI, f. 82, op. 2, d. 175, l. 12, copy of memo from Dzerzhinskii to the Politburo, 28 February 1923.
6   RGASPI, f. 76, op. 3, d. 296, ll. 25–50, an informant's report to Dzerzhinskii. The report that attendees found Kamenev's and Dzerzhinskii's CC membership unacceptable, while accepting Stalin's and Zinoviev's presence, departs significantly from the allegation of a speaker at the Twelfth Party Congress, who claimed that the Workers' Opposition wanted the entire triumvirate removed from the CC (Deutscher 1959, p. 96). Informants often poorly understood the content of political discussions or had self-interested motives to distort it, but this informant seems to have been a highly placed and well-informed party member.
7   RGASPI, f. 589, op. 3, d. 9103, vol. 3, ll. 41–3, M.F. Mikhailov's letter to Shliapnikov describing his OGPU interrogation, [October] 1923; TsA FSB, R33718, d. 499061, vol. 37, ll. 29–36, copies of correspondence between Kuznetsov and Miasnikov and excerpts from Workers' Group members' testimonies.

Because he encouraged workers to strike, Myasnikov was arrested in May 1923. Forcibly dispatched to a diplomatic post in Germany, he struck up ties with German communists who were dissatisfied with Comintern policy. His supporter, N.V. Kuznetsov, attempted to carry on efforts to draw into their group former members of the Workers' Opposition. Myasnikov warned him that Shlyapnikov was a hypocrite, kowtowing to party leaders and trying to hinder genuine efforts to organise on the part of Myasnikov and his supporters. According to Kuznetsov, circles led by Lutovinov, Ignatov and Shlyapnikov met with Myasnikov's followers in July but did not come to an agreement. Lutovinov objected to the plans of the Workers' Group to organise non-party workers and warned them that Dzerzhinsky had unsuccessfully attempted to recruit him (through Tomsky) to attack the Workers' Group.[8] Medvedev seems to have admitted to an informer that he met in the woods with Workers' Group organisers, but scoffed that the Workers' Group programme only got two votes. Both he and Shlyapnikov acknowledged having known of the Workers' Truth newspaper, but denied having seen it before the informer showed it to them. Denying any harm in their familiarity with workerist oppositional groups, Shlyapnikov and Medvedev apparently criticised the OGPU's tactics and stance towards the Workers' Group and Workers' Truth, but they reluctantly agreed to condemn them in the press, if the CC so instructed.[9]

Without success, the Workers' Group attempted to bring Kollontai into its struggle, which came to the attention of party authorities. Upon a brief return to Moscow from her diplomatic posts abroad, she noted how tense Shlyapnikov and Medvedev had become in late summer 1923. Accusing her of enjoying her 'honorary exile' and of not having time for old friends, both addressed her in an ill-natured ironic tone, for which she blamed Medvedev more than Shlyapnikov. By the time she returned to Moscow in December 1923, however, she had 'good, comradely' relations with them.[10] Perhaps this was because party leaders had, by then, opened debate on crucial issues of

---

8 TsA FSB, R33718, d. 499061, vol. 37, ll. 29–36, testimony by Makh. Lutovinov committed suicide in May 1924, disillusioned with NEP and distraught over marital tensions. See Gurevich 1927, p. 5; RGASPI, f. 17, op. 2, d. 30 and op. 3, d. 71; and f. 593, op. 1, d. 9, ll. 23–4, and d. 10, ll. 2–3, 10–11, 18.

9 RGASPI, f. 76, op. 3, d. 296, ll. 1–2, Dzerzhinskii's 27 July 1923 notes from the report of an informer ('Foma'), apparently a high-ranking party member. Foma was the underground name of at least four prominent Old Bolsheviks: Pëtr Zalutskii, Dmitrii Manuil'skii, Aleksandr Smirnov and Nikolai Kozyrev.

10 RGASPI, f. 82, op. 2, d. 175, ll. 45–53, Kollontai's answers to Kuibyshev's questions in his report (copy), December 1923; RGASPI, f. 76, op. 3, d. 296, l. 41; Kollontai 2001, vol. 1, pp. 156–7, 182–3.

economics and intra-party relations. The party institutions' treatment of communists, such as those in Workers' Group, disturbed even many party members who viewed Myasnikov negatively.

With Politburo sanction, the OGPU arrested key members of the Workers' Group in 1923, but Shlyapnikov and other Worker Oppositionists emerged unscathed from the case. After Dzerzhinsky reported on the Workers' Group and Workers' Truth to the Politburo on 19 September 1923, Molotov told him to strike the names of Shlyapnikov, Medvedev and Lutovinov from the version to be circulated.[11] Apparently, the Politburo was not convinced of a link between the groups and preferred not to divulge methods used to drive apart the oppositionists. Myasnikov was arrested only in the autumn, after Dzerzhinsky convinced him to return from Germany to Russia by insincerely guaranteeing his protection from arrest. Unaware of the arrest, Shlyapnikov and another former oppositionist dropped by Myasnikov's apartment on the morning after he was taken, intending a visit, only to be caught in a Cheka 'ambush'. Although they were released within a few hours, Myasnikov was imprisoned until spring 1927 and was then sent into internal exile in Yerevan. He escaped from there to Iran in 1928, making his way to Paris, where he worked in factories. After the end of World War II, he was repatriated to the USSR, tried secretly and executed.[12]

Although Shlyapnikov disapproved of the Workers' Group's programme and methods, he (like many others) criticised the OGPU's method of fighting such groups. At an October 1923 CC plenum, he accused the OGPU of using Okhrana methods, as well as its former agents, against party members. His evidence included letters from communist workers complaining of OGPU bodies gathering criminal evidence against dissenters and from former oppositionists who had asked him to intercede for them after they were arrested, imprisoned and interrogated by the OGPU. Interrogators charged them with belonging to the Workers' Group, asked them about links with Shlyapnikov and Medvedev and if the Workers' Opposition was active. In party cells Shlyapnikov and Kollontai were even accused of 'links with foreign counterrevolution'. He concluded that the OGPU was trying to artificially link dissenters who wanted to work only within the party to those who organised outside of it. An investigation of his charge that the OGPU used former tsarist agents revealed only that a former Okhrana general had served as a military spy and that the OGPU had never used non-party agents to investigate party members. Although there was no evidence that Shlyapnikov was disingenuous, party leaders rebuked

---

11 RGASPI, f. 76, op. 3, d. 296, ll. 25–50.
12 RGASPI, f. 17, op. 162, d. 1, ll. 9–31, 6 September–22 November 1923; Alikina 2006, pp. 158–60.

him for making false charges and compelled him to apologise to Dzerzhinsky. Labelling his accusations 'maliciously philistine, Menshevik', the CCC initiated an investigation of his and Medvedev's behaviour during meetings with the Workers' Group, charging that they had 'conduct[ed] their own directives at illegal assemblies'. This constituted a warning not to contest the party's use of the OGPU against intraparty dissenters. Party committees relied increasingly on the secret police throughout the 1920s to monitor oppositionists and interpret their activities to party leaders. A Russian historian has argued that the party 'oligarchy' used the secret police in the 1920s to serve factional interests, but that the police sometimes 'fabricate[d] reports to force the party nomenklatura to act under the Cheka's dictate'.[13] Despite use of police and party control bodies against dissenters, discontent continued to percolate in the party.

Trotsky's Left Opposition Opens Debate on Industrialisation and Democracy

As Lenin's illness worsened and limited his role in the leadership, discontent grew within the party over its domination by Zinoviev, Kamenev and Stalin (the '*triumvirs*') and in reaction to their policies. Some party members regarded Trotsky as Lenin's natural successor, but Lenin's choice was by no means clear, nor was it his right to designate a successor. Although Stalin, of all party leaders, saw Lenin most frequently in 1923, he and Lenin had recently sparred on nationalities policy and the formation of the USSR, with Lenin favouring federalism and Stalin centralism. Having dictated notes (later called his 'Last Testament'), in which he evaluated his potential successors as all lacking in some way and made proposals to enlarge the CC, restructure Gosplan and merge the CCC with the Workers' and Peasants' Inspectorate [*Rabkrin*], Lenin subsequently added the proposal to remove Stalin as General Secretary of the party because he was 'too rude'. This characterisation emerged partly from crude words Stalin spoke to Krupskaya and partly from his and Ordzhonikidze's intimidation of Georgian communists who sought their own republic within the USSR (Ordzhonikidze struck one of them). Lenin sought to enlist Trotsky to present his proposals to the party, but Trotsky agreed with the *triumvirs* not to attack them at the April 1923 Twelfth Party Congress in return for their

---

13 RGASPI, f. 17, op. 2, d. 104, ll. 1–26; f. 589, op. 3, d. 9103, vol. 3, ll. 1–28, 38–46; Vilkova (ed.) 2004, p. 103, CCC presidium secretariat session protocol excerpt, 31 October 1923; Olekh 1999, p. 89.

permission to air his views on industrial planning and the concentration of industry within the context of NEP. By 'concentration of industry', he meant to close many unproductive factories and concentrate production in a few large ones, but this alarmed workers who were already suffering from unemployment and low wages.[14]

By autumn 1923, Trotsky's agreement with the *triumvirs* had disintegrated. In a letter to the Politburo in early October, he attacked party economic policy and appointmentism, and faulted the lack of intra-party democracy. Forty-six Russian communists subsequently signed the 'Declaration of the 46', echoing his views and calling for an extraordinary conference of the CC.[15] On 25–7 October 1923, the CC and CCC discussed these documents, ultimately deciding to censure Trotsky. Passions were high on all sides. Krupskaya later wrote to Zinoviev that he, Stalin and Kamenev were as guilty as Trotsky and his supporters for inflammatory statements and false accusations. She and Shlyapnikov were the only people invited to the plenum who were not directly involved in the affair (many others unsuccessfully petitioned to attend). Given increasing agitation in party cells over the declaration, party leaders decided to open the debate in early November, but Trotsky, laid low from malaria, could not engage in it until December.[16]

Meanwhile, foreign affairs intruded into the discussion. Soviet communists, including Shlyapnikov, paid close attention to German leftist politics in 1923, the year of the famed hyperinflation in Germany. They had high hopes for a German revolution, so the failure of a Communist Party of Germany uprising in Hamburg in late November 1923 provoked debate in the circles of the Russian Communist Party. In December 1923 a German communist spoke to Shlyapnikov and his comrades. Declaring that it made no sense to conduct revolution in Germany as it was carried out in Russia, he pointed to contextual differences including the absence of war, a more formidable and better-organised bourgeoisie, a robust Social-Democratic party, a weak communist party and a

---

14   Lewin 1968, chapters 4, 6, 7; Deutscher 1959, pp. 92–102. Sakharov 2003 disputes the testament's provenance, arguing that there is no evidence that it originated with Lenin, citing circumstantial evidence that Lenin's secretaries may have manufactured or tweaked it in order to aid Trotsky in the succession struggle.

15   Deutscher 1959, pp. 112–13; Day 1973, pp. 87–8. Deutscher 1959 claims that members of the Workers' Oppositionists figured among the 46, but I did not recognise any of their names (Deutscher 1959, p. 114).

16   Vilkova (compiler) 2004, pp. 272–3, letter from Krupskaia to Zinoviev, 31 October 1923; RGASPI, f. 17, op. 2, d. 104, ll. 1–26; Deutscher 1959, pp. 116–18.

fierce fascist movement.[17] His interpretation likely influenced views expressed by Shlyapnikov and members of his circle during the ongoing party debate.

With Trotsky's return to action and rising levels of criticism of domestic and foreign policies, the debate in party cells reached a fever pitch in December 1923. The Trotskyists and Democratic Centralists decried the government's neglect of heavy industry and the lack of 'democracy' within the party. Trotsky tried to harness the energy of young party members and Komsomolists, claiming that a generational divide existed in the party. Although some historians have claimed that in this debate Shlyapnikov sided with the triumvirate, he actually criticised both sides. Calling for an acceptance of intra-party criticism, state subsidies and orders for heavy industry and for more workers to join the party, Shlyapnikov participated in the debate in several ways. Firstly, he and his circle wrote and promoted a resolution in party cells. Secondly, he spoke at party meetings, most visibly at the Khamovniki party conference in Moscow in January 1924. Thirdly, he wrote an article, which was published in *Pravda* in January 1924.[18]

The resolution that Shlyapnikov and his allies circulated complained of 'careerists' replacing workers in the party's leading bodies and called for an influx of factory workers into the party. They wanted 'intra-party democracy', which to them meant elections to infuse the party with 'new forces' and 'general meetings of party members' to decide more questions. They also insisted on the equalisation of senior bureaucrats' pay with that of skilled workers and on ending the system of keeping 'secret characteristics on party members'. The Metron factory party cell endorsed the resolution. Trotsky also called for a surge of workers into the party and criticised the 'bureaucratic degeneration' he saw within the party. Yet Trotsky regarded mobilising not only the workers but also the youth as twin solutions to this crisis.[19]

At the Khamovniki party conference in Moscow, leading oppositionists spoke. Sensitive to Trotsky's complicity in persecuting the Workers' Opposition in 1921, Shlyapnikov outlined his agreements and disagreements with Trotsky. Nevertheless, he supported freedom of criticism for all party members, including Trotsky. He emphasised that freedom of criticism did not lead inevitably to

---

17 Albert 2011, pp. 111–42; TsA FSB, R33718, d. 499061, vol. 42, ll. 232–7, Medvedev's notes, dated 6 December 1923.

18 Sorenson 1969 concluded from Shliapnikov's published article that he supported the troika by criticising the Trotskyists (Sorenson 1969, p. 232), but I believe that in the original manuscript he criticised both sides equally.

19 RGASPI, f. 589, op. 3, d. 9103, vol. 2, l. 2; TsA FSB, R33718, d. 499061, vol. 37, l. 27, 19 December 1923; Deutscher 1959, p. 122.

factionalism and that general party discussion would help to prevent factionalism. Unlike Trotsky, he did not perceive a generational division within the party, but a social division, and insisted that it was necessary to change economic policy in order to attract more workers into the party. Characterising CC policy towards heavy industry as 'criminal', he expressed fear that heavy industry under NEP would die out, but he opposed Trotsky's plan to revive industry by closing small enterprises and concentrating industry in a few large ones. His own ideas on funding large-scale investment in heavy industry were limited to more efficient use of resources and using Soviet gold to build up domestic industry rather than to buy foreign manufactures.[20]

Shlyapnikov expressed disappointment with the speeches of proletarian party members he heard at the conference. Calling them 'backward', he regretted that the party's demands for obedience rather than initiative made the 'outstanding developed workers' he regularly met in the factories reluctant to join the party. Turning his criticism to NEP, he insisted that industry could not thrive by depending solely on the peasant market and argued that heavy industry should be expanded in order to create a market for peasant bread. In the countryside, he said, poor peasants should unify into collective farms and receive machines and equipment on credit. Addressing once more the poor state of internal party democracy, he asked the CC majority not to falsely accuse others of factionalism in order to discredit them. Finally, he disagreed with Trotsky's assertion that bureaucracy should be destroyed, instead arguing that it had to be strengthened by electing its members.[21]

Shlyapnikov's *Pravda* article elaborated upon his speech and added some nuances. In it, he equally criticised both the CC majority and the Trotskyists for weakening intra-party democracy. Recalling, with some nostalgia, a more unified pre-revolutionary party, he attributed this to what he remembered as its largely proletarian social composition. In the party of 1924, he perceived too much social heterogeneity and too few proletarians to build unity. Addressing those who feared his proposals were anti-*intelligent*, he insisted that 'worker democracy' would not deprive non-proletarian party members of their rights. A shake-up of the bureaucracy, as Trotsky advocated, would not bring in more workers, only a change in policy would. The concentration of industry was not such a policy, for it threatened the survival and growth of the working class.[22] Of the programme of the Workers' Opposition, trade-union hegemony had

---

20   TsAODM, f. 88, op. 1, d. 168, ll. 65–83, 7–10 January 1924.
21   TsAODM, f. 88, op. 1, d. 168, ll. 29–42.
22   Shliapnikov 1924a, pp. 4–5; Zorkii 1926, pp. 144–57; RGASPI, f. 17, op. 71, d. 82, ll. 7–22, original manuscript '*O propavshei gramote, po povodu diskussii*', dated 21 December 1923.

fallen away, but Shlyapnikov still promoted the thorough workerisation of the institutions of power, elections and the development of heavy industry. Pride and faith in the capabilities of Russian workers ran through his desire to produce domestically rather than to import complex machinery from abroad.

The debate ended with the Thirteenth Party Conference, 16–18 January 1924, during which Trotsky again was weakened by malaria and forced to evacuate the stage. Few supported his views at the party conference, elections to which the triumvirate had manipulated in its favour. Trotsky was condemned, the triumvirate prevailed and Trotsky went south to recuperate. On the way, he heard of Lenin's death on 21 January, but did not return to Moscow for the funeral, which seems to have struck a blow to his prospects for the succession. Little concerned with Trotsky's health or his chances at the leadership, Shlyapnikov and his comrades were more preoccupied with the conference's decision to admit a massive number of workers into the party. The number of one hundred thousand recommended by the conference was increased after Lenin died (the 'Lenin levy') – in February to May, two hundred and forty thousand workers joined.[23] In time, however, the Old Bolsheviks would come to understand the political illiteracy and careerist ambitions of many new entrants.

Diplomacy and Family Life

After the period of open debate ended, Shlyapnikov returned to writing his memoirs. In 1924, more than four hundred thousand workers entered the party. In view of the transformative effect he thought this could have on the party, Shlyapnikov probably considered it vital to publish his memories of the role of workers in the party before and during 1917, while others in his circle sought a more immediate effect by circulating copies of their resolution, his speech and his *Pravda* article to sympathisers in the provinces. Due to his general silence and his posting to France in late 1924, however, some of his allies thought he had submitted to the Politburo. Ukrainian sympathisers started to believe rumours, spread by the chair of the Soviet Central Executive Committee, Mikhail Kalinin, and others, that Shlyapnikov shared the Politburo's views on all issues. The rumours had a demoralising effect, but Medvedev did his best to refute them in Shlyapnikov's absence.[24]

---

23   Deutscher 1959, pp. 132–5.
24   TsA FSB, R33718, d. 499061, vol. 13, ll. 29–40, letter from Medvedev to Shliapnikov, 27 December 1924.

FIGURE 29 *Alexander Shlyapnikov and Leonid Krasin, Paris, 1924. Photo taken by Agence Meurisse (provided by Bibliothèque nationale de France).*

Speculation regarding his trip to Paris annoyed Shlyapnikov. He had agreed to conduct negotiations over outstanding tsarist-era Russian debts to France, but came to regret having accepted the assignment. First, there was not enough work for him to do; second, he clashed with Leonid Krasin over policy (Shlyapnikov argued that the Soviets should conclude a friendship treaty with France before seeking economic concessions), so the staff of the Commissariat of Foreign Affairs [*Narkomindel*] gave him the cold shoulder. He claimed to have realised too late that party leaders had only wanted to remove him from Moscow. Nevertheless, he enjoyed renewing old friendships with French socialist comrades and former co-workers in Parisian factories. He discovered that his old metalworker friends had left the Communist Party of France and were working exclusively in the trade unions. They told him that they resented the party's attempts to graft Russian methods of organising onto French workers; he found their views similar to those of his German metalworker comrades.[25] No doubt he also enjoyed life in Paris after his long absence from the city.

25 TsA FSB, R33718, d. 499061, vol. 13, ll. 41–8, letter from Shliapnikov to Medvedev, 7 January 1925; Adibekov *et al.* (eds.) 2001, pp. 60–2.

Shlyapnikov's wife, Ekaterina, (*née* Voshchinskaya) accompanied him to France. Fifteen years younger than her husband, she was born in western Russia to a father from the landowning gentry and a peasant mother. Her father was indebted, so her gymnasium education in Moscow was initially financed by a governor's grant for impoverished gentry children. After the governor died and his support vanished, she worked as a tutor and typist to pay for the remainder of her schooling in Samara. After the revolution, she held a variety of secretarial positions for the Soviet government and the Communist Party. Her first husband was shot in 1918 for speculation. She and Shlyapnikov met in 1919–20 while she was working as Tolokontsev's secretary in the Central Artillery Board. In 1921 Shlyapnikov brought her to work for him in the CC commission on improving workers' living conditions.[26]

The Russian Revolution had created fluidity in marital relations, as laws restricting divorce were abolished and revolutionary culture encouraged freer relations between men and women. Thus, according to the family, Ekaterina did not realise she and Shlyapnikov were 'married' until 1924, when in preparation for their trip to France he brought her a passport confirming it. That he did not consult her beforehand may convey his confidence that she would not refuse. During the early 1920s, Ekaterina recovered from tuberculosis, contracted during the Civil War, and studied law until her first child was born. She and Shlyapnikov shared a large apartment with Medvedev and his wife Maria for about four years (1925–9), until Shlyapnikov's family moved into cooperative housing. Common living arrangements thus facilitated Shlyapnikov's and Medvedev's 1920s political partnership. The Medvedevs had two daughters, Aida (born in 1922) and Irina (born in 1926), while the Shlyapnikovs had Yuri in 1926, so the apartment was well-populated. Home life may have been a welcome distraction for Shlyapnikov during his political troubles.[27]

Views on the Turn to the Countryside and to the East

Upon his return from France, Shlyapnikov again took up commentary on party policies. In a draft manuscript that probably circulated among Moscow friends, he disagreed with Stalin's and Bukharin's policy formulations at the Fourteenth Party Conference in May 1925. On Stalin's theory of socialism in one country,

---

26   TsA FSB, R33718, d. 499061, vol. 43, l. 328; RGASPI, f. 589, op. 3, d. 9103, vol. 4, l. 1, 14 April 1949 autobiography of Ekaterina Shliapnikova; Shliapnikova 1995 and Medvedeva 1995.

27   TsA FSB, R33718, d. 499061, vol. 13, ll. 41–9; vol. 42, l. 209; vol. 43, l. 328; RGASPI, f. 589, op. 3, d. 9103, vol. 4 (E.S. Shliapnikova), l. 1, 14.

he wrote: 'Stalin refuses to accept that socialism as an economic system cannot be contained by the borders of one country'. Moreover, he declared that the USSR was not yet socialist, because the prevailing economic form was small commodity production, with a range of other structures, 'from peasant barter, to small-scale handicraft production, minor private capital, and finally state capitalism as a transitional step towards socialism'. Rather than perceiving, as Stalin did, 'contradictions' between foreign capital and Soviet socialism, Shlyapnikov saw the main difference between the USSR and the capitalist countries to be found in the fact that Soviet leaders did not freely allow foreign capital to operate in the USSR.[28]

Addressing the 'turn to the countryside' announced at the conference, Shlyapnikov declared it a continuation of earlier pro-peasant policy, only without socialist pretence. Arguing that coming to terms with the peasantry was not sufficient to build socialism, he criticised Bukharin's interpretation of Lenin's 1923 stance on the cooperative movement, saying that Lenin meant strictly cooperation among workers of the Central Union of Consumer Cooperatives [*Tsentrosoyuz*], and that he did not intend for it to be extended to agriculture. Moreover, he scoffed, peasant agriculture could not be improved significantly just by offering horses and by bringing poor peasants into cooperatives. Calling for the voluntary concentration of agriculture, he proposed that the state should buy out poor peasants or lease their land. He favoured legalising hired labour in the countryside (another change made by the conference) in order to protect hired labour. He insisted that the real answer to the countryside's problems was to quickly and intensively develop heavy industry, which he did not think was growing as much as official figures indicated.

Shlyapnikov found the Soviet Communist Party leaders' assessment of the Western-European proletariat too pessimistic. The war had exhausted and diluted the Western-European working class, but in his opinion it would recover. He therefore derided the theory of the 'worker aristocracy', which posited that highly skilled, better-paid workers develop an interest in the maintenance of capitalist exploitation. He insisted that it was not wages, but their role in production that determined workers' consciousness. This theory, he believed, was an excuse for the communists' failures to recruit highly skilled workers, which he said was due to the errors of the Communist leaders. Their first mistake was to struggle with the trade unions instead of working within them to persuade workers that moderate Social-Democratic goals were only bandages to temporarily cover up the wound, not a long-term

---

28   TsA FSB, R33718, d. 499061, vol. 38, ll. 22–74. The manuscript, '*O nekotorykh chertakh sovremennogo momenta*', was dated May 1925. As far as I know, it was never published.

solution. A second fallacy, he wrote, was to expect the 'petit bourgeois' to serve the interests of proletarian revolution. A third misstep, according to him, was the effort to graft Russian revolutionary experience onto other countries, which led only to a 'caricature' or 'adventurism'. The final error was to look eastward for revolution, for he believed that the people of Asia were far behind those of Europe on the path towards proletarian revolution. Moreover, the liberation of the Eastern peoples from feudalism and imperialism would 'not essentially change the correlation of class forces in the west'. Calling for a policy of persuasion to win over the Western-European proletariat, he requested that the Soviet Communist leaders should not isolate the Soviet trade unions from the Western-European ones.[29] His time abroad had thus not reconciled him to the leadership's policies.

Nevertheless, Shlyapnikov's commitment of his views to paper did not mean that he was ready to engage in political struggle. Victor Serge, a supporter of Trotsky at that time, recalled that in spring 1925: 'The militants of the old Workers' Opposition proved to be non-committal, since they believed us to be too weak and, as they said, distrusted Trotsky's authoritarian temper'.[30] Upbraiding Shlyapnikov for passivity, one comrade outside Moscow expressed disappointment with him for being 'indecisive' and for failing to give directions.[31] In addition, Ivan Nikolaenko, the administrator of the Ukrainian Tobacco Trust in Kiev, wrote of his concern at having seen a photo in *Izvestiya* of Shlyapnikov standing next to members of Stalin's circle. Worried that this meant he was politically close to them, Nikolaenko complained that Stalin's circle suppressed dissent and initiative. Specifically, he disparaged Lazar Kaganovich, secretary of the CC of the Communist Party of Ukraine, as possessing the 'boorishness of a shop clerk'. Replying that his positioning in the photo was accidental and had no political significance, Shlyapnikov noted that he had tried to enrol in the list of speakers at the congress, but Valerian Kuibyshev had told him that he would not be allowed to speak 'for your own good'.[32]

---

29   TsA FSB, R33718, d. 499061, vol. 38, ll. 22–74.
30   Serge 2002, p. 210.
31   TsA FSB, R33718, d. 499061, vol. 13, ll. 101–3, undated [perhaps late 1925] letter from Mariia Trifonova. She corresponded with Shliapnikov and Medvedev in the second half of the 1920s and the first half of the 1930s. In 1924, she and her husband, Ivan Pivon', had belonged to the 'workers' list' of delegates at the Eniseisk guberniia party conference. The guberniia party control commission voted to exclude them from the party for factionalism (Demidov 1994, pp. 36–7).
32   TsA FSB, R33718, d. 499061, vol. 14, ll. 5–10; vol. 12, l. 21, 12 May 1926.

Not only did Shlyapnikov's sympathisers outside of Moscow feel disconnected from him, but he also felt isolated from important party work. He complained to Kollontai in late 1925 that the party gave him no work in trade unions or party organisations, which limited his 'circle of social life' as well as his work. He immersed himself in writing historical memoirs, despite continued attacks of vertigo, headaches and periodic deafness as a result of Ménière's disease.[33] Shlyapnikov strongly desired to be useful to the party in a practical way. Before that would happen, however, the CCC subjected him to intense grilling during the 1926 party debates.

The 'Baku Letter' and Investigation

Despite Zinoviev's 1924 call to purge Trotsky from the party and to exert pressure on him to recant his views, Zinoviev and Kamenev moved closer to his evolving position on industrialisation and further from Bukharin's encouragement of peasant consumerism. In late 1925, Stalin's 'socialism in one country' doctrine finally drove Zinoviev and Kamenev to join Trotsky in the 'United Opposition'. As Shlyapnikov and his circle had developed their own fairly comprehensive critique of party policy independently of Zinoviev, Kamenev and Trotsky, these more prominent oppositionists attempted to sway the former members of the Workers' Opposition to their side. Stalin used various methods to divide and subdue the oppositionists, including CCC investigations. Shlyapnikov and his comrade Medvedev became CCC targets due to a January 1924 letter Medvedev had sent to Valeryan Barchuk, a former metalworker employed by the Commissariat of Enlightenment [Narkompros] in Baku, a major centre of the oil industry on the Caspian Sea and a pre-revolutionary nexus of revolutionary activity (Stalin had organised cells there). In response to Barchuk's inquiry about Shlyapnikov's views on NEP, workers and international revolution, Medvedev's so-called 'Baku letter' reiterated points that Shlyapnikov had made in public discussion, but in more incendiary language. That he wrote on behalf of a group of people (Mikhail Mikhailov, Chelyshev, Nikolaenko, Bruno, Pravdin and Shlyapnikov) was conveyed through his signature 'from all of us'.[34] This letter, as well as the 1926 CCC investigation of it, are important for what they reveal about Shlyapnikov's evolving views on NEP and

---

33   RGASPI, f. 134, op. 1, d. 437, l. 1, 23 November 1925 letter from Shliapnikov to Kollontai.
34   Deutscher 1959, p. 138; Fel'shtinskii (ed.) 1990 vol. 1, pp. 90–101 (Medvedev's 'Baku letter'). The original version was probably written in late January 1924; Fel'shtinskii reprints the version that Medvedev presented to party leaders in July 1926 and claimed to be

the CCC's role in redefining key political concepts such as oppositionism, party loyalty, party discipline, bloc and faction.

Medvedev's letter expressed his and Shlyapnikov's fear that NEP was becoming established economic policy and voiced their objections to the development of private agriculture and the stimulation of peasant consumerism. He called for the expansion of heavy industry, but to acquire capital for this he could suggest only eliminating waste in the budget and imposing higher taxes on the peasantry. In international policy, he criticised the Comintern for applying the Russian model of centralised control to other European socialist and worker movements and for assuming that revolution in Western Europe would unfold according to the Russian pattern. He opposed the departure of communist minorities from trade unions, soviets and factory committees dominated by Social Democrats. With typical bluntness, he called the existing Western-European 'communist' parties and organisations 'a horde of petty-bourgeois minions, supported by Russian gold, depicting themselves as the proletariat'. Finding it natural that workers would trust Social-Democratic leaders who looked out for their everyday interests more than communists offering them 'red pipedreams', he argued that in order to win over the Western-European workers, communists needed to patiently and skillfully defend basic needs of workers. Only after doing so could they disillusion workers of the belief that 'the satisfaction of such necessities will essentially change their social and material situation'.

The letter and materials from the 1923–4 party discussion only reached Baku in early June 1924. The Azerbaijani Cheka, which had been keeping Communist Party members under surveillance since at least mid-1922, became aware of the letter in July 1924, when they infiltrated informers into the so-called 'Baku group of the Workers' Opposition'. Police reported that most of the group's dozen members were former workers who were employed in soviets, although a few were industrial workers at the time. The group had only two or three meetings. In October 1924 Baku party officials sent a copy of Medvedev's letter to the CCC, where it was greeted with mockery, yet was kept on file in case of future need.[35] There were hundreds, perhaps thousands, of such 'cases' in CCC

---

authoritative. Under NKVD interrogation in 1935, he named others who had read the letter in Moscow in 1924 (TsA FSB, R33718, d. 499061, vol. 5, ll. 28–31).

35 RGASPI, f. 589, op. 3, d. 9103, vol. 1, ll. 286–7, letter to CCC RKP(b) from L. Mirzoian, Baku Party Committee secretary, 2 October 1924; and ll. 293–300; Knight 1993, p. 23. In Transcaucasia, Chekas remained in place until mid-1926, when they were replaced by GPUs (Knight 1993, p. 29).

files, but this letter became a weapon of Stalin's party leadership against the oppositionists.

The version of Medvedev's letter that Baku officials sent to the CCC was distorted. Uncharacteristic spelling mistakes and grammatical errors were not the only features that distinguished it from his original. The second version made it appear as if he sought large-scale industrial concessions and large foreign and internal loans as a means of gathering capital for intensive industrialisation. Moreover, it conveyed the impression that he had given up on the Western-European workers as revolutionary and proposed that the Western-European communist organisations dissolve and rejoin Social-Democratic parties. Bukharin, Stalin, Yaroslavsky and others based their attacks on the falsified version of the letter. References to the letter in secondary literature have been based on inaccurate information originating from these opponents.[36]

When Zinoviev (on Politburo assignment) discussed the letter with Medvedev in December 1924, he did not show him the version received from Baku, but Medvedev sensed that it diverged from the original. Expressing concern that the OGPU had doctored it, he requested its publication, explaining that the rumour mill had roused curiosity among many who were eager to read it. The Politburo considered demanding that Zinoviev write a denunciation of Medvedev's letter but Zinoviev did not do so. Nevertheless, that was not the end of the matter. The Azerbaijani Party Control Commission took up investigation of the 'group' in Baku in 1925.[37] Further developments were tied to intra-party political struggles, as Zinoviev and Kamenev went into opposition against Stalin.

In December 1925, at the Fourteenth Party Congress, Stalin proposed his theory of 'socialism in one country', which Zinoviev and Kamenev openly opposed. At this congress, Zinoviev and Kamenev employed Lenin's 'Last Testament' in an attempt to undermine Stalin. Also, evidence of Stalin's personality cult first began to appear. Kollontai attended. Surprised to see Zinoviev in opposition, she found that many of her old comrades supported Zinoviev and Kamenev. She, on the other hand, praised Stalin as the 'personification' of the party 'as Lenin was', as 'stronger and more courageous' than Zinoviev and Kamenev. Noting that Shlyapnikov and Medvedev 'lean towards the Leningraders' (Zinoviev and his supporters), she did not place them solidly in that camp.

---

36 Daniels 1988, p. 279; Day 1973, pp. 158–60; Deutscher 1959, pp. 274, 277, 307. The version party leaders received from Baku is located in RGASPI, f. 589, op. 3, d. 9103, vol. 2, ll. 226–33.

37 TsA FSB, R33718, d. 499061, vol. 13, ll. 29–36, letter from Medvedev in Moscow to Shliapnikov in Paris, 27 December 1924; RGASPI, f. 589, op. 3, d. 9103, vol. 1, ll. 293–300.

To her the factional struggle appeared motivated by personal rivalries between Zinoviev and Stalin. Although she recognised discontent among the 'masses of workers', she thought that none of the factions had the masses' support; moreover, she confessed that did not know what the masses wanted.[38]

Trotsky was opposed to 'socialism in one country', but did not immediately ally with Zinoviev and Kamenev. Nevertheless, Stalin feared that the oppositionists would join forces, so he took pre-emptive measures, beginning with removal of Zinoviev, Kamenev and their allies from important positions. Political tensions also increased at the local level, which had implications for former members of the Workers' Opposition. In January 1926 Shlyapnikov received a letter from a comrade outside Moscow who reported that local officials in his area sharply criticised the 'Leningraders' and would not allow him and his associates to speak, charging that they were the 'Workers' Opposition' and were 'ganging up with the Leningraders'.[39] This letter set the tone in which Shlyapnikov received news of the Baku case.

When the newspaper, *Bakinskii rabochii*, revealed the Baku affair in early February 1926, it described the group as a cell of the Workers' Opposition that had links with other oppositionist groups, had conducted work outside the party and included former Mensheviks and SRs. The newspaper warned that 'freedom of criticism' led inexorably to the formation of factional groups, and finally to 'direct counterrevolution'. In early February 1926, the Azerbaijani Party Control Commission found the 'Baku oppositionists' guilty of underground anti-party organisation and agitation. Four were excluded from the party, six were reprimanded or warned and six others were 'rehabilitated'. The investigation reportedly included physical abuse and intimidation. Zemlyansky, who had hidden Stalin from the tsarist secret police in Baku, wrote to Stalin charging that the Azerbaijani Cheka had not only beaten him but had kidnapped his wife and kicked her. He alleged that interrogators threatened other suspects with revolvers.[40] Communist Party leaders in Baku accused Shlyapnikov and Medvedev of having directed the group's activities.

After Shlyapnikov and Medvedev saw the Baku newspaper article, they accosted Yaroslavsky and Bukharin in the Bolshoi Theatre and then tried unsuccessfully to see Stalin. Although 'very courteous', he kept postponing their

---

38 RGASPI, f. 134, op. 3, d. 44, ll. 6–10, 3 February 1926, Oslo. These short notes were not included in Kollontai 2001.
39 TsA FSB, R33718, d. 499061, vol. 39, l. 31, 12 January 1926, a letter from 'B'.
40 RGASPI, f. 589, op. 3, d. 9103, vol. 1, ll. 290–300; TsA FSB, R33718, d. 499061, vol. 39, l. 333, 3 March 1926; RGASPI, f. 589, op. 3, d. 9103, vol. 2, ll. 143–4, 19 May 1926 letter from Shliapnikov to the Politburo and CCC.

appointment with him. Finally, they sent a letter of protest to the Politburo and the CCC. Framing the affair in terms of provocation (a 'timely denunciation', a repentant criminal, leaders and seduced workers), they insisted there was no Workers' Opposition in Baku, only mutual acquaintances meeting to discuss politics. Mounting an offensive, they accused party leaders in Baku of intent to frame 'old and meritorious party members' as counterrevolutionaries. Finally, they requested the publication of their protest in *Pravda* and in Baku newspapers, as well as the publication in *Bolshevik* of all the materials Medvedev had sent to Barchuk in 1924.[41] They aimed not only to reveal the documents' true contents, but also to provoke an open discussion of the issues raised in them.

Yaroslavsky fired off a memo to other CCC members expressing consternation that the Azerbaijani Party Control Commission had not coordinated its investigation with the CCC, especially since such an important figure as Shlyapnikov was involved. Tensions between central and local party control bodies were a persistent problem in the history of the CCC and of its successor, the PCC (Party Control Commission, 1934–8). The *de facto* subordination of local control commissions to local party committees, rather than to the CCC, exacerbated frictions. Despite Yanson's attempt to maintain the investigation's focus on Shlyapnikov and Medvedev, Yaroslavsky insisted on upbraiding the Azerbaijani and Transcaucasian party control commissions, to which the chief of the Transcaucasian control commission responded that he had not known about the case. Regardless of the appearance of local initiative and administrative confusion, Stalin's inspiration cannot be ruled out. Sergei Kirov, who had been first secretary of the Communist Party of Azerbaijan in 1925, had an 'old friend' in the editor of *Bakinskii rabochii*, Peter Chagin.[42] Since Stalin had recently orchestrated Kirov's promotion to Leningrad party chief, perhaps Kirov returned the favour by arranging an attack on his old nemesis Shlyapnikov, or locals could have curried favor with newly promoted Kirov by dragging in Shlyapnikov's name.

After having sent a commission to conduct an on-the-ground investigation in Baku, the CCC initially concluded that there had been no oppositional group in Baku, despite an unsuccessful attempt to form one, and that group members met 'accidentally, to drink together, as acquaintances, or at family gatherings'. Consequently, the CCC changed expulsions to stern rebukes with warnings or reprimands. Changing expulsions to milder punishments had become customary for control commissions at all levels. Nevertheless,

---

41   RGASPI, f. 589, op. 3, d. 9103, vol. 1, ll. 75–115; vol. 2, ll. 33–4, 20 February 1926.
42   RGASPI, f. 589, op. 3, d. 9103, vol. 1, ll. 301–4; vol. 2, l. 36; Getty 1997, p. 2; Antonov-Ovseenko 1981, p. 48.

Shlyapnikov and Medvedev were forced to confront CCC investigators Aaron Solts, Yaroslavsky and Maria Ulyanova at the end of March. The meeting was tense, as Shlyapnikov refused to believe that this case could have gone forward in Baku without someone in the leadership giving instructions, while the CCC investigators claimed to feel insulted by his implications.[43]

Questions to both concerned whether Shlyapnikov and Medvedev held the views expressed in the letter, what was the purpose of the letter and exactly who had been involved in its drafting and dispatch. The investigation's subjectivity was underscored by a question characterising the letter's content as 'organisational and propagandistic directives'. Shlyapnikov's demand to publish all the documents, his insistence on answering CCC questions in writing (contrary to usual CCC procedures of oral examination) and his request to take investigatory materials home for examination all roused suspicions that he wanted to use the investigation for factional politics. Finally agreeing to submit questions in writing, CCC investigators allowed Shlyapnikov and Medvedev to leave without answering questions. Nevertheless, they refused to allow the men to take investigatory materials home, justifiably fearing that the two would duplicate and distribute them. They could only examine the materials in CCC offices.[44]

Through spring and summer 1926, the investigation was postponed. In late May, Stalin wrote to Molotov that he should press Bukharin to accelerate writing an article directed against the Workers' Opposition. Stalin recalled that Zinoviev had been assigned to write it, but had not done so and therefore had 'sabotaged the assignment from the Politburo'. Inferentially connecting Trotsky and Zinoviev to Shlyapnikov, Stalin wrote to Molotov in mid-June: 'I think pretty soon the Party will punch the mugs of Trotsky and Grisha [Zinoviev] along with Kamenev and turn them into isolated splitters, like Shlyapnikov'. In the meantime, more pressure was applied, including a corollary investigation of Medvedev, based on allegations that he had engaged in factional politics in Moscow oriented towards 'linking' with Zinoviev, who would 'give directives', although it is ludicrous to imagine Medvedev seeking 'directives', especially from Zinoviev. Finally, a 10 July *Pravda* editorial ('On the Right Danger in the Party', probably written by Bukharin) accused Medvedev of giving up on international revolution and favouring the lease of large-scale Soviet industry to foreign capitalists. Shlyapnikov, who was on holiday in the south when the *Pravda* article appeared, declared to Medvedev his intention to appeal

---

43 RGASPI, f. 589, op. 3, d. 9103, vol. 1, ll. 127–214; vol. 2, ll. 95–117; Getty 1997, p. 2. Mariia Ul'ianova supported Stalin and Bukharin in 1925–6 (Turton 2007, pp. 114–15).

44 RGASPI, f. 589, op. 3, d. 9103, vol. 2, ll. 102–17, 136–8, 8 April 1926.

against 'Bukharinist distortions' and print the response he had composed as a pamphlet.[45]

At an important party plenum on 15 July 1926, Stalin called Medvedev's letter 'Menshevist' and accused Zinoviev of 'sabotage' in having delayed criticising it. Further, he accused Trotsky and Zinoviev of having formed a bloc with the Workers' Opposition. Objecting that the Politburo never 'assigned' him to write an article, Zinoviev claimed that he had thought the letter should be published and critically analysed in the journal, *Bolshevik*, and that he had thought Stalin and other Politburo members had agreed with him on this in 1924–5.[46] For his part, Medvedev objected that accusations made against him in the press and at the plenum were based on statements not even in his original letter, that his views on foreign leases had coincided with those of Lenin and that his opinions were very different from those cited in the article. Shlyapnikov joined him in sending a letter of protest to *Pravda* and the CCC, requesting the publication of Medvedev's original 1924 letter and a manuscript by Shlyapnikov, both of which were attached.[47]

Without waiting for an answer, Shlyapnikov circulated copies of his manuscript among party members on holiday with him in the southern resort of Kislovodsk. The sanatoria were sometimes arenas for discussions among communists who could not rest from politics and who had the opportunity to meet comrades there who they otherwise might not see. A scandal erupted when a Moscow party raikom instructor seized a copy of Shlyapnikov's manuscript and forwarded it to the CCC. A sanatorium administrator was particularly concerned that the public outcry against the informer threatened to draw holidaying Donbas workers, some of whom were not party members, into the affair.[48] There was thus a genuine worry that oppositionist views would spread to workers.

---

45 RGASPI, f. 589, op. 3, d. 9103, vol. 1, ll. 149–214; vol. 2, ll. 139–40, 147–8, 154–5; Lih *et al.* (eds.) 1995, pp. 104–5, 114–15; TsA FSB, R33718, d. 499061, vol. 43, l. 204. Lih *et al.* (eds.) 1995 also believed that Bukharin wrote the 10 July editorial in *Pravda* (Lih *et al.* (eds.) 1995, p. 104).

46 Lih *et al.* (eds.) 1995, pp. 104–5, citing RGASPI, f. 17, op. 2, d. 246, vyp. 1, ll. 75–6; and d. 696, ll. 46–7. Lih *et al.* (eds.) 1995 wrote that they found no Politburo decision assigning Zinoviev to write an article criticising Medvedev's letter.

47 RGASPI, f. 589, op. 3, d. 9103, vol. 2, ll. 186–91, l. 250. The CCC promptly conducted a comparative analysis of the two different versions of the 'Baku letter' (RGASPI, f. 589, op. 3, d. 9103, vol. 2, ll. 192–233). *Bol'shevik* published Shlyapnikov's manuscript in September 1926, but Medvedev's letter was only published in Russia in 1990.

48 RGASPI, f. 589, op. 3, d. 9103, vol. 1, ll. 22–7; TsA FSB, R33718, d. 499061, vol. 12, l. 23.

Shlyapnikov's manuscript eventually reached an even broader audience, for the United Opposition distributed copies of it. The agreement to do this might have occurred in Kislovodsk, where Trotsky and Kamenev were on holiday and met with Shlyapnikov. Trotsky was giving political talks in the sanatoria. Aware of their collaboration, Stalin wrote to Molotov in late September that the question of Medvedev could not be 'glossed over'.[49] Stalin's repeated badgering of Molotov may indicate that the latter was reluctant to press charges of factionalism against the former members of the Workers' Opposition.

In his manuscript, which was finally published in *Bolshevik* in September 1926, Shlyapnikov delivered a sharp rebuttal to *Pravda*'s charges, a spirited defence of Medvedev's views and an attack on the motives of party leaders. He insisted that Politburo members were raising a political scandal around the letter merely in order to carry out reprisals against 'growing oppositional moods in the party'. Next he complained that the political slander of oppositionists had become a weapon of party struggle and a means of rapid promotion for party careerists. Supporting Medvedev's accusation that the worker-peasant alliance [*smychka*] was turning into an alliance with wealthy peasants [*kulaks*], he concluded by calling for the 'triumph of workers' democracy' and for an end to the internal party system of 'criminal investigations, denunciations, public defamations, and threats'.[50]

Despite Shlyapnikov's spirited defiance, the Opposition had already lost this round due to Stalin's reliance on 'rowdies' to 'disrupt' oppositionist meetings, his successful depiction of the Opposition as anti-peasant and the apparent appeal of the 'socialism in one country' doctrine to the rank-and-file. Trotsky, Zinoviev, Kamenev and other leaders of the United Opposition acknowledged their defeat and pledged to dissolve their opposition. The Politburo required them to denounce Shlyapnikov's and Medvedev's 'Menshevik platform'.[51] In late October, Trotsky was expelled from the Politburo, after *The New York Times* published Lenin's 'Last Testament' and Trotsky hurled at Stalin the insult, 'gravedigger of the revolution', at an expanded Politburo meeting. The high tensions within the CC over this affair helped shape the context in which Shlyapnikov and Medvedev had also come to terms with the CCC. Isaac

---

49   RGASPI, f. 82, op. 2, d. 185, ll. 59–60; f. 589, op. 3, d. 9103, vol. 1, ll. 127–33, 149–214; Lih *et al.* (eds.) 1995, p. 129.

50   Shliapnikov 1926e, pp. 62–73. It closely follows the draft, which is in RGASPI, f. 589, op. 3, d. 9103, vol. 1, ll. 7–21 and 41–62. Shlyapnikov's article in *Bol'shevik*, the 10 July *Pravda* article and the *Bol'shevik* response were all republished in book form (Slepkov (ed.) 1926).

51   Deutscher 1959, pp. 282–6; RGASPI, f. 17, op. 3, d. 592, 7 October 1926. Bukharin, Rykov and Tomskii signed the Politburo resolution.

Deutscher portrayed theirs as an abject submission, writing in error that both were expelled from the party and only re-admitted after making an 'exemplary recantation'.[52] On the contrary, they struggled determinedly to resist charges of anti-party factionalism.

Shlyapnikov and Medvedev met 20–9 October in almost daily long sessions with the CCC and finally the Politburo. Initially defiant, Shlyapnikov reiterated his suspicion of a provocation: 'nothing like the Baku affair can go on in our party on the initiative of the regions. If you [the CCC] did not know, then that means Stalin knows'. His chief evidence was ephemeral, a memory of having seen among investigatory materials a telegram from Moscow to Baku in late 1925, a document that later could not be found. Both sides acknowledged that mutual suspicion and heated exchanges had created misunderstandings. As Shlyapnikov retreated, Medvedev continued to mock the CCC's suspicions:

> Alexander Gavrilovich and I live in the same apartment. Of course we exchange opinions. It's absurd to conceive that we could live in the same apartment, sit at the same table and say no, I won't talk with you, because I'm afraid that Solts will call me a factionalist'.

Solts interjected that writing down political views gave them an entirely different character than talking about them privately. Medvedev eventually admitted to carelessness, but Shlyapnikov added, in his defence, that he did not write for distribution or publication. Becoming conciliatory, Solts and Ulyanova accepted Shlyapnikov's premise that the letter was private, but Solts asserted that factionalism arose when the Baku workers gathered and analysed the letter. Shlyapnikov retorted, 'There were only 10 of them, but you made this letter accessible to the whole country and even beyond'.

Pressured to renounce the views in the letter, Shlyapnikov maintained that only the interpretation of these views had been mistaken. Then he turned negotiations to his and Medvedev's 'abnormal' party situation. The Moscow party committee refused to assign him to a party cell, the party did not assign him work and he could not seek work independently without violating party discipline. (As his wife had given birth to their first child Yuri in February, he needed a steady and dependable income; he also desired an outlet for his organisational energies and a sense that he was making a practical contribution to the revolution.) The CCC refused to guarantee work for him. Warning

---

52 Deutscher 1959, pp. 295–6; Deutscher 1966, p. 309. The testament travelled through oppositionist networks to Boris Souvarine in Paris and from him to the American socialist, Max Eastman.

that they were 'hanging by a thread', Yaroslavsky insisted that they denounce their 'Menshevik' political views in order to avoid exclusion from the party. He allowed that they did not have to admit to having been in a bloc. Medvedev agreed to make a statement but angrily added: 'even if five commissions threatened me, if they threatened to put me in the GPU's basement, they won't convince me that I'm a Menshevik'. Shlyapnikov also refused to abase himself, still denying that he had been in a bloc with other oppositionists. Solts admitted that the views of Shlyapnikov, Zinoviev and Trotsky could not be reconciled coherently but thought there was some sort of organisational bloc, since all of them spoke against a 'ruling faction'. Finally answering in writing the CCC's initial questions, Shlyapnikov and Medvedev characterised the 'Baku letter' as a personal letter written during a period of authorised debate within the party. Reiterating their disapproval of factionalism, they merely admitted that the letter contained some mistaken and crude formulations that permitted its misinterpretation. Apologising for polemical excesses, they asked for a 'normal existence' within the party. Shlyapnikov let it slip that he and Medvedev were conceding just to relieve the pressure on them.[53]

Dissatisfied with these answers, CCC members composed a text requiring them to completely reject their previously-held views on all important questions and to recognise that the accusations brought against them in the party press were justified. Significantly, the CCC required them to acknowledge that neglecting to distance themselves from the United Opposition was sufficient evidence of a bloc. Finally, the CCC demanded that they express regret that Medvedev's letter was used against their wishes as the basis for an anti-party attempt to organise a group. Shlyapnikov and Medvedev did not do all that the CCC required. Their next letter declared simply that they were not in a bloc and did not consciously violate party unity; they promised to implement all party decisions, but insisted that the 'Baku letter' was misinterpreted. Expressing regret that it was characterised as a political platform and became widely accessible, they did not assume responsibility for these results.[54]

Increasing its pressure, the CCC's investigatory commission subsequently contradicted its earlier findings by concluding that Medvedev's letter did spur several Baku party members in 1924 to organise a faction and that their new platform was 'even more anti-party' than the old one of the Workers' Opposition. Although arguing that Medvedev's exclusion was justified, the commission advised to issue him a stern reprimand with a warning and to sternly reproach Shlyapnikov for having failed to prevent Medvedev's

---

53 RGASPI, f. 589, op. 3, d. 9103, vol. 1, ll. 72–115, 20 October 1926.
54 RGASPI, f. 589, op. 3, d. 9103, vol. 1, ll. 70–1, 140–1, 21 October 1926.

activities, about which he knew, for not distancing himself from Medvedev's views and for defending them.⁵⁵

The case then went to the full CCC Presidium. Shlyapnikov, perhaps expecting sympathy, noted that many presidium members had supported the Workers' Opposition before 1922. Some edgy jokes were directed towards Medvedev before Solts and Yaroslavsky commenced to impress upon the two men (and perhaps fellow presidium members) the serious nature of the charges: struggling with the CC, joining an ideological bloc with the opposition and reluctantly renouncing their errors. Shlyapnikov insisted that they had to defend themselves against *Pravda* charges 'which depicted us as freaks'. Unfavourably comparing their intransigence to Trotsky's and Zinoviev's recognition of their errors (they in fact had also tried to negotiate), Kuibyshev objected that Shlyapnikov 'thinks that he enjoys some kind of special moral authority in the party'. Indeed, some presidium members seemed sympathetic towards Shlyapnikov, leading to a suggestion to punish him less harshly than Medvedev.⁵⁶

Consequently, the CCC resolved to expel Medvedev from the party and to give Shlyapnikov a stern rebuke and warning. Dismayed, the two men appealed to the Politburo. Still, they did not acknowledge mistaken views or condemn their allies. The Politburo assigned Ordzhonikidze and Yanson to 'make a last attempt to work out with comrades Shlyapnikov and Medvedev a text that could satisfy the party's interests'. The final product of this exchange was an unsigned letter, which fulfiled much of the CCC's request, stating that Medvedev's letter contained crudely erroneous views, that attacks in *Pravda* and *Bolshevik* were justified and that their previous statements to the CC and CCC regarding the Baku case were wrong. The letter acknowledged that they used methods of factional struggle and condemned these methods. It called on their allies to disperse any factional underground groups they might have formed. But it still did not acknowledge that they were in a bloc with Trotsky, Zinoviev and Kamenev, nor did it repudiate all their past views. Thus, they did not simply submit abjectly. After Ordzhonikidze and Yanson forwarded the letter to Stalin, the CCC rescinded its warning towards Shlyapnikov and conceded that Medvedev could remain in the party.⁵⁷

---

55 RGASPI, f. 589, op. 3, d. 9103, vol. 1, ll. 127–37, commission's conclusion and protocol of its 22 October 1926 session. Iaroslavskii, Sol'ts and Ul'ianova signed the conclusion.
56 RGASPI, f. 589, op. 3, d. 9103, vol. 1, ll. 149–214; Anderson *et al.* (eds.) 2007, vol. 2, pp. 345–415, 427–52.
57 RGASPI, f. 17, op. 162, d. 599, protocol 65, 29 October 1926, p. 2; f. 589, op. 3, d. 9103, vol. 1, ll. 148, 215–30, 241–2, 247, 25–30 October 1926. The final text was published in *Pravda*, 31 October 1926.

FIGURE 30   Sergei Medvedev, Mikhail Chelyshev and Alexander Shlyapnikov, November 1926 (in Ioffe (ed.) 1990, p. 151).

FIGURE 31   Top (left to right): Maria Medvedeva, Antonina Tyutereva (Alexander Shlyapnikov's niece), Alexander Shlyapnikov; and bottom (left to right): Sergei Medvedev, Klavdiya Chelysheva and Mikhail Chelyshev, 1927 (provided by the Shlyapnikov family).

Shlyapnikov avoided factionalist intrigues after October 1926, but he still found much to criticise about party policy. When the Soviet-supported Chinese Nationalist Party crushed the Chinese Communists in April 1927, and when British trade unionists withdrew from the united front in September, the revived United Opposition disparaged Stalin's and Bukharin's apparent miscalculations in foreign affairs. Although members of the opposition may have tried to entice Shlyapnikov to declare support for it, by signing its May 1927 declaration (the 'Declaration of the 83'), which criticised a broad range of foreign and domestic policy measures, he maintained an autonomous stance in intraparty discussions. Some of his own supporters pressured him to speak out. One (perhaps Maria Trifonova) wrote to him inquiring as to where he stood in the looming political struggle within the party. She scorned the programme of the United Opposition for incorporating 'too much democratic honey' and for weak 'formulas on workers and the economy'. Taking Shlyapnikov to task for following 'old tactics of silence and inactivity', however, she warned that if he did not act, she and her confederates might join 'the left wing of the opposition'.[58]

Chiding his comrade for allowing 'emotions' to cloud her 'cold Marxist analysis' (a hint of gender-coded language), Shlyapnikov acknowledged that many Communists were 'surprised' that he did not come out in public support of the United Opposition. Assuring her that he remained a revolutionary Marxist, he explained that he supported the new opposition but without 'merging with it, not losing our political identity'. He did not sign its programme because he was not invited to help draft or revise it and because its leaders had not repudiated their 1926 condemnation of the Workers' Opposition. Although six thousand communists signed the Declaration of the 83, Shlyapnikov seemed sceptical of its validity, concluding: 'Remember that "programmes" are elaborated during struggle that can last years'. Thus, he continued to elevate the initiative of workers above the direction of leaders. Shlyapnikov afterwards confirmed sympathy for the leftist opposition, but denied ever having joined it. He was loathe to become a victim of provocation or to lend his name without any real influence. His comrades from among the most prominent members of the

---

58   TsA FSB, R33718, d. 499061, vol. 40, ll. 168–74, unsigned letters from June 1927. Pëtr Zalutskii may have asked him to consider signing the 'Declaration of the 83' (TsA FSB, R33718, d. 499061, vol. 5, ll. 42–3, 4 March 1935 interrogation of Medvedev). Somewhat confusingly, the 'Declaration of the 83' is occasionally referred to as the 'Declaration of the 84', but for consistency I have used 'Declaration of the 83'. Daniels 1988 wrote that Shliapnikov and Medvedev made peace with the regime after 1926 (Daniels 1988, p. 309), but this was not so.

Workers' Opposition probably agreed with him. A CC statistical analysis shows that only one former member of the Workers' Opposition signed one of the United Opposition's petitions.[59]

When party leaders allowed oppositionists to publish in an official discussion supplement to *Pravda* in November 1927, Shlyapnikov utilised this sanctioned means of expressing his views. In his contribution, he decried unemployment and long lines for food as symptoms of exacerbated 'class struggle' in the country. Complaining that the party press overlooked the true 'Right danger' of 'petty-bourgeois private-property owners' in favour of scapegoating the Workers' Opposition and other tendencies, he urged workers to examine documents of the party congress and not to listen to just one side. Defending the Workers' Opposition as an advocate of heavy industry, he disputed claims in the party press of industrial recovery, asserting instead that in the metals industry 1913 levels had not been reached. Disputing the party leaders' distortion of the positions of the Workers' Opposition, he asserted that it had always advocated a stronger role for workers in the party and the improvement of their working and living conditions. As evidence, he cited passages from the 'Letter of the 22' to the Comintern. Blaming disagreements within the party on the presence within it of 'an enormous number of petty-bourgeois elements' and their 'ideology and policies', he called for an influx of industrial workers into the party. If the party was largely proletarian, it would not be harmful to have disagreements and debates within it. Finding it 'completely intolerable and deeply defective to have years of hidden struggle and outward silence followed by weeks of discussion reminiscent of the most vulgar attacks in bourgeois election campaigns', he appealed for 'worker democracy' to replace the existing political culture.[60]

The United Opposition was defeated at the Fifteenth Party Congress in December 1927 and 75 opposition leaders were expelled from the party. Zinoviev and Trotsky had been expelled earlier. In total, around eight thousand oppositionists were expelled in 1927–8. Nevertheless, some oppositionists continued to air criticisms into 1928.[61] Unknown persons continued attempts to involve Shlyapnikov in oppositional politics, but he was increasingly

---

59 TsA FSB, R33718, d. 499061, vol. 12, ll. 28–35, typed letter from 'Aleksandr' to 'Dear comrade', 19 July 1927; RGASPI, f. 82, op. 2, d. 186, l. 47.

60 RGASPI, f. 82, op. 2, d. 195, ll. 117–25, 'Lessons of intra-party struggle', copy dated 9 November 1927.

61 Daniels 1988, p. 320; Gusev 2008, p. 153; Halfin 2007, chapters 5–6.

suspicious of OGPU provocations.⁶² One might compare his stance to that of Kollontai. When she published an article in *Pravda* in 1927 attacking the United Opposition, Shlyapnikov chastised her. Troubled by his disapproval, she sought solace in nostalgia, holidaying in the same hotel room in Holmenkollen, Norway, where he had resided in 1915, and remembering his pre-revolutionary kindness that had won him the nickname 'golden heart' [*zolotoe serdechko*].⁶³

Conclusion

Shlyapnikov's political and economic views in 1923–6 were in some ways consistent with those he had held before the Eleventh Party Congress, but his views also evolved due to changing circumstances. While he sought the inclusion of more workers within the party and its leading bodies, he advocated freedom of criticism within the party for all its members. Continuing to demand an end to the CC's meddling in lower-level elections, he also warned of the danger he thought OGPU methods posed to party members. He advocated the development of heavy industry through increasing state orders of industrial goods, with capital to come from Soviet gold reserves; he called for the promotion of voluntary collectivisation or state leasing of poor peasants' land. Fearing that NEP entailed too many concessions to the peasantry, he worried that a failure to develop heavy industry would allow the subversion of the revolution within Russia and that the revolutionary movement abroad would be derailed by Russian communist leaders alienating advanced Western-European workers.

Shlyapnikov attempted to conform to party discipline, but party leaders in the CC, CCC and secret police constantly redefined permissible conduct in terms of party discipline. Shlyapnikov did not follow Myasnikov's course towards the formation of a new workers' party, nor did he allow Trotsky and Zinoviev to manipulate him to serve their purposes in intra-party factionalism. He insisted that Medvedev's communication with Baku communists was healthy political discourse, but many party leaders and members already viewed such activities as dangerous and contrary to the party's interests. Shlyapnikov defined factionalism narrowly as central leadership giving formal

---

62   TsA FSB, R33718, d. 499061, vol. 40, l. 1, 9 November 1928 letter to Shliapnikov and Medvedev from the Temporary Central Bureau on Organisation of Worker Communist (Bolshevik) Parties of the Union. The letter alluded to 'rumours ... that supposedly Stalin and the GPU inspired our newspaper'.

63   Kollontai 2001, vol. 1, pp. 182–3, and 328–9, 20 December 1927.

directions to organised groups at the local level and sharing with them a common formal written programme (such as Myasnikov's effort). He did not consider private political discussion to constitute factionalism. While he insisted on the right to freedom of criticism within the party, local authorities in Baku (in conformity with Stalin's line) firmly maintained that freedom of criticism inexorably led to factionalism and counterrevolution.

The CCC was a crucible for forging new political definitions; moreover, it constituted a closed forum for debate on these definitions and their underlying concepts. As the CCC investigation evolved, its definition of factionalism changed from actual organisational work to the attempt to form an oppositional group and to disseminate views contrary to those of the Politburo majority. Nevertheless, some differences of opinion remained within the CCC. Did political disagreements have to be written down to constitute factionalism or was oral discussion of them sufficient? How strictly should a 'bloc' be defined? Must it include only those who signed an oppositionist document or could it loosely include all who used a particular phrase in describing party leaders, or their policies, or those who refused to renounce the oppositional views of others? Stubbornly maintaining that a formal bloc consisted of people who jointly wrote and advocated a political programme, Shlyapnikov insisted upon his own interpretation of proper political behaviour within the party, even as standards changed around him. Yet attempts to evade the control of party leaders only tempted those leaders to expand their definitions of politically unacceptable behaviour.

CHAPTER 10

Late NEP, Industrialisation and Renewed Repression

Stalin turned against NEP in the late 1920s, claiming that it put the USSR at risk of being overtaken by external enemies and undermined by internal ones. Having defeated the Right Opposition of Bukharin, Tomsky and Rykov, who wanted to continue the gradualism of NEP, Stalin and his men imposed forced collectivisation and rapid industrialisation on the Soviet Union. Stalin's 'revolution from above', or 'Great Break', was an often unspeakable personal tragedy for millions of Soviet citizens. So-called 'wealthy peasant' [*kulak*] families were abruptly and forcibly exiled to remote regions, many of them dying *en route* or at their destinations, while famine devastated the lives of, and brought untold suffering to, huge numbers of Ukrainians and Kazakhs. Stalin's policies not only starved the countryside, but put pressure on workers. Many inexperienced new workers lost their lives in workplace accidents on construction sites, in mines and in factories. The Stalinist economy born of the new five-year plans was deeply flawed, with bottlenecks, spoilage, statistical manipulation and neglect of the consumer sector becoming systematic. Nevertheless, Stalin's revolution created entirely new industries, new industrial centres and drastically increased the urban population and industrial workforce.[1]

Many former Left Oppositionists hoped that Stalin's drive for industrialisation, despite its flaws, would realise their goal of creating a highly productive and egalitarian economy and society that would assure a better quality of life for all Soviet citizens. They yearned to participate in the project for, as Deutscher wrote: 'It was a galling thought for the Trotskyists also that the great change, this "second revolution", might be carried out without them'. Although Stalin undertook to put his own men in control of the Soviet Union's economic and industrial administration, he was still forced to rely upon many former oppositionists to help carry out his policies. The continued high profile of former oppositionists in industrial and other posts troubled him, especially when labour unrest erupted in various regions as a result of food shortages, workplace injuries, long hours and pay delays. Many Trotskyists and Democratic

---

1 On Stalin's break with Bukharin and his revolution from above, the many important works include Tucker 1990; Cohen 1980; Fitzpatrick 1983; Kuromiya 1998; Lewin 1975 and Viola 2007.

Centralists had not reconciled with Stalin's policies, but maintained an underground political network. For them, the lack of intra-party democracy and the harnessing of workers to production tasks seriously flawed efforts to industrialise and collectivise.[2] Fearing that oppositionists might capitalise on worker unrest, Stalin directed renewed police attention to them.

Like many other Oppositionists, Shlyapnikov enthusiastically supported Russia's industrialisation, to which he contributed as chair of a metals-import board in 1926–9 and of a metalware-industries association in 1931; he even published an article in the Soviet press praising Stalin's industrialisation policy in 1929. Nevertheless, Stalin and many of his supporters continued to distrust Shlyapnikov and exert pressure on him. Political attacks intensified on his memoirs, which he wrote during periods of unemployment. Moreover, the CCC and OGPU entangled him and Medvedev in an investigation of oppositionism in Omsk. Crossing from late NEP into the era of Stalin's revolution from above, this chapter illuminates the politics and economics of this transitional period as they affected Shlyapnikov's life.

Metals Import

When the case of the Baku Opposition was settled, Shlyapnikov received a new work assignment. After consulting with Stalin in November 1926, he was assigned to lead the import of metals into the USSR to supply a slowly reviving industry. The organisation of industry had changed greatly since Shlyapnikov had left Narkomtrud and been forced out of the Metalworkers' Union. It continued to evolve while he led metals imports. Under NEP, industry was organised in trusts. Most metals trusts were subordinated to VSNKh, but trusts often ignored its orders and even competed with one another. In fact, in 1924 the chair of VSNKh, Dzerzhinsky, had complained of the resulting arbitrariness: 'We have almost every trust doing just what it pleases ... and if anything does not work out right it hides behind the backs, and receives the support, of local institutions'. Trusts told factories what and how much to produce, provided funds for wages and coordinated sales of products. They needed permission to import machinery, but they determined what kind of machines were needed and employed their own specialists to go abroad and study the techniques of foreign industry. The trusts created syndicates to oversee sales of items produced by factories under the trusts, but by 1926–7 syndicates had begun to compete with trusts for control over distribution and production. Eventually syndicates

---

2 Deutscher 1959, p. 411; Rossman 2005; Gusev 2008, p. 154.

even challenged the authority of VSNKh. For the most part, trusts operated without much guidance from the planning bodies, the chief one of which was Gosplan, which was under the Council of Labour and Defence (STO). VSNKh also had a planning division. In addition, the Commissariat of Internal and External Trade [*Narkomtorg*] was an actor in Soviet metals imports. There was a great demand for metals in 1926–7 due to new construction projects like the Dnieper Dam and Hydroelectric Station and the Turkestan-Siberian Railway [*Turksib*]. The Gosplan Presidium made these priorities on 6 November 1926. Already in August 1926, Narkomtorg proposed to reorient imports for 1926–7 towards a greater percentage of raw materials and a smaller percentage of fully manufactured goods and consumer items. This was in line with the goal of orienting Soviet industry towards producing more finished goods.[3]

Shlyapnikov's appointment as chair of Metalloimport was thus an important assignment.[4] He reported to Kuibyshev, head of VSNKh, and to Anastas Mikoyan, who led Narkomtorg. Metalloimport was a joint-stock company founded in May 1926 by Narkomtorg and the following state trusts: Southern Metallurgical Trust [*Yugostal*], the State Association of Machine-Building Factories [*Gomzy*], the Leningrad and Moscow Machine-Building Trusts [*Lenmashtrest; Mosmashtrest*], the Urals Metal Trust [*Uralmet*] and the Association of State Enterprises on Mining and Nonferrous Metalworking [*Gospromtsvetmet*]. Its mission was to purchase and import into the USSR 'metals industry equipment, ferrous and nonferrous metals, semi-processed materials and tools'. Tolokontsev, a former member of the Workers' Opposition and Shlyapnikov's close comrade, was the first chair. But his other responsibilities, a death on the board and personal conflicts meant little work was done before Shlyapnikov came on board. As a CC and VSNKh member who met sometimes with Politburo members, Tolokontsev may have facilitated Shlyapnikov's employment as chair of Metalloimport. A determined advocate of the rapid development of the metals industry and iron imports, he favoured forms of industrial and economic organisation based on share-holding by state-controlled organisations.[5] Shlyapnikov also supported these goals.

---

3 Chernobaev (ed.) 2008, p. 761; Shearer 1996; Nove 1984; Gregory and Stuart 1986; Carr and Davies 1976.
4 RGAE, f. 8346, op. 1, d. 10, l. 2, Orgburo protocol 71 (excerpt), 16 November 1926, signed by Molotov.
5 RGAE, f. 8346, op. 1, d. 4, ll. 1–7; d. 38, l. 1, memo from board member Klyshko to Shliapnikov; Anderson et al. (eds.) 2007, vol. 2: pp. 45–6, Politburo session on *Glavmetall* report, 14 June 1926.

State trusts controlled three-quarters of the shares in Metalloimport, while Narkomtorg possessed only one-quarter. A majority of stockholders elected the chair and other members, who had to be confirmed by Narkomtorg. Metalloimport opened departments in Soviet foreign-trade missions, but its operations abroad were not clearly defined. Metalloimport could set up bank accounts and pay bills, but its operating funds were subsumed under the Soviet foreign-trade representatives' 'general balance'. Moreover, foreign-trade representatives could appoint heads of Metalloimport offices abroad, although they were supposed to coordinate appointments with the board of Metalloimport. Metalloimport departments could earn commissions on work for other organisations but not on Metalloimport assignments. Foreign-trade representatives and Metalloimport determined the size of commissions, according to Narkomtorg instructions. Commissions went 'to cover the departments' expenses'.[6] Metalloimport was thus self-financed, although the trusts for which it worked were largely financed from the state budget.

Since much Soviet trade was conducted with Germany, Metalloimport's most important department abroad was in Berlin. German economic policy was oriented towards coaxing the Bolsheviks to abandon communism and accept free enterprise. In 1921 many German government officials and business leaders saw NEP as evidence of the Bolsheviks' tendency towards moderation, but by 1926–7 they were far more pessimistic about the Bolsheviks' potential to abandon communism. Pragmatism prevailed over theory in Soviet foreign trade, unlike internal trade. Nevertheless, some Soviet pragmatism stemmed from a cautious attitude towards capitalist markets, which the Soviets posited would undergo 'increasingly severe crises'. Soviet-German trade was in principle governed by an economic agreement signed in 1925, but the Soviets and Germans interpreted the agreement differently. Germany issued a 300-million gold ruble (400 million Reichsmark) credit to the USSR in 1925–6 in the hope of linking the Soviet market more closely to Germany's, in order to assert Germany's importance internationally and to alleviate unemployment. The so-called 'great German gold rush' led to widespread purchases of unnecessary equipment by trusts, especially Yugostal. From 1927, Narkomtorg sought to create 'international competition' for Soviet orders in order to buy products more cheaply. The Soviets therefore increasingly sought to order directly from the English and Americans, rather than going through Germany as an intermediary. Narkomindel resisted the policy, because it sought to prioritise trade relations with Germany, but the policy went ahead. Second only to Britain in

---

6 RGAE, f. 8346, op. 1, d. 4, ll. 1–5.

machinery imports in 1927, the Soviet Union carried a favourable balance of trade with the UK, unfavourable with the US and about equal with Germany.[7]

Shlyapnikov had to overcome resistance from Soviet trade representatives and diplomats in Germany in order to accomplish Metalloimport's goal of achieving more advantageous terms for Soviet metals and machinery imports. One of his first challenges as chair of Metalloimport was a conflict with the Narkomtorg representative in Germany. Before Shlyapnikov assumed command, the anarchist and former IWW activist, Vladimir 'Wild (or Big) Bill' Shatov, who was serving as assistant chair of Metalloimport, went to Berlin to set up a Metalloimport department called Tekhnoimport. In appointing as the head of Tekhnoimport a communist of proletarian background named Libet, Shatov clashed with the Narkomtorg representative in Berlin, K.M. Begge. Begge preferred another communist named Finkel, who was an engineer, fluent in German and had worked in the Berlin trade mission for two years. Shatov appointed Finkel as Libet's assistant.[8] Begge complained to Mikoyan that Shatov's appointees were 'inexperienced comrades ignorant of the business'. Shatov protested that trade representatives shifted their operating costs onto Tekhnoimport. Complicating the matter was that Shatov reportedly had travelled abroad against Tolokontsev's orders. Shlyapnikov recalled Shatov, but the controversy over Libet continued.[9] Moreover, the Soviet ambassador to Germany, Krestinsky, Shlyapnikov's old political rival, became involved. The affair bore the stamps of personal and institutional conflicts, with a veneer of social prejudice.

To clarify Metalloimport's relationship with Soviet trade missions, Shlyapnikov rewrote the Metalloimport statutes to make it more autonomous and less subordinate to Narkomtorg. Apparently he went too far, for Mikoyan weakened some of his language so as not to give Metalloimport exclusive rights to trade in metals and metals equipment. Shlyapnikov's statutes were criticised for having 'defined the tasks' of Metalloimport more broadly than the October CC plenum and STO had described. The party had assigned Metalloimport to obtain machines from abroad only for union-level metals

---

[7] Cameron 2005, vol. 40, no. 1, pp. 7–24; Carr and Davies 1976, vol. 1, part 2, pp. 706, 711, 716; Gregory and Stuart 1986, p. 62; Kashirskikh 2006, vol. 9: pp. 35–48; Shearer 1996, pp. 47–8.
[8] RGAE, f. 8346, op. 1, d. 10, l. 5, Shliapnikov's 15 December 1926 complaint; d. 26, ll. 30–48, Shatov's report on his June–November 1926 trip abroad; also referenced in d. 18, l. 6, and d. 19, ll. 133–4. Vladimir Sergeevich Shatov had lived for ten years in the United States; in the 1920s, he directed Turksib Railway construction (Avrich 1968, pp. 296–306; and Payne 2001).
[9] RGAE, f. 8346, op. 1, d. 5; d. 11, l. 24, Begge's letter to Mikoian (excerpt), 24 November [1926]; d. 38, l. 1.

industries, but Shlyapnikov claimed for Metalloimport the right to supply all industrial branches. Moreover, he attempted to subordinate foreign departments directly to Metalloimport rather than to Narkomtorg representatives, omitting any role for trade representatives in Metalloimport's organisational structure abroad.[10] He may have intended to increase his own power, as well as to delineate clearer boundaries between Metalloimport and Narkomtorg. In so doing, he trod on Narkomtorg's toes.

Shlyapnikov journeyed abroad in January 1927 to sort out the personnel conflict in Germany. At a party meeting, Libet and the VSNKh representative sided with Shlyapnikov, while Begge and representatives of Narkomtorg accused him of trying to break up the 'foreign-trade monopoly'. Shlyapnikov criticised the trade missions for being bureaucratically isolated from industry and not taking its interests into account, while Krestinsky accused him of advancing the programme of the Workers' Opposition. When confronted with documents signed by Kuibyshev (VSNKh) and Mikoyan (Narkomtorg) that supported Shlyapnikov's position, trade representatives delayed recognising them, because they found them to contradict the STO decree on import societies. Moreover, they hoped Mikoyan would change his mind and return to former practice. No agreement was reached.[11] Policy differences, personal rivalries and entrenched bureaucratic interests all interfered.

Shlyapnikov postponed resolving the problem, for he had to leave Berlin in order to carry out Metalloimport business elsewhere. He met with fewer obstacles to his work in Denmark, where firms were eager to sell high quality machines to the USSR and offered good terms, in his opinion. There was no Soviet trade representative in Copenhagen; the assistant trade representative, who was 'non-party', gave him no trouble. Moreover, he was on good terms with the Soviet ambassador to Denmark, who was an old acquaintance. Another old comrade, who was trade representative in Norway, helped him negotiate an even more favourable agreement. Kollontai, serving as ambassador to Sweden and Norway, also helped him with trade agreements. Writing to him, she mused wryly that if anyone had told them in 1911, during their romantic stroll in Asnières, that 16 years later they would be corresponding about the

---

10   RGAE, f. 8346, op. 1, d. 4, ll. 14; 15–16, 30 November 1926 letter from an unknown person to Shliapnikov.

11   RGAE, f. 8346, op. 1, d. 26, ll. 53–7, 4 January 1927 letter from Shliapnikov to the Metalloimport board, copies to Mikoian at Narkomtorg, Kuibyshev at VSNKh, Valerii Mezhlauk at Glavmetall and Lepse at TsK VSRM. Other interdepartmental conflicts are discussed in dd. 18–19.

quality and price of iron, they would have considered it to be mad ravings.[12] The romanticism of revolution thus surrendered to the realities of power.

After his successes in Scandinavia, Shlyapnikov returned to Berlin with renewed determination that Tekhnoimport had to be 'fully under control' of the Metalloimport board in order to compete effectively with autonomous buyers of metal on the European market. He faulted Narkomtorg for inaccurately gauging the supply of nonferrous metals in Germany and thus failing to obtain favourable terms. Warning that agreement by German trusts and syndicates to control the nonferrous metals market in Germany raised the danger of speculation in nonferrous metals purchased through the trade missions abroad, he pressed VSNKh and Narkomtorg to support the centralisation of Soviet purchases of nonferrous metals through Tekhnoimport. Georgy Pyatakov at VSNKh supported his proposals, but Begge continued to throw up obstacles. Narkomtorg instructed Begge to negotiate with Shlyapnikov and allow the Narkomtorg board to decide any matters upon which the two men could not agree.[13]

Krestinsky added fuel to the fire by refusing to confirm the Tekhnoimport staff recommended by the trusts, instead recommending the wives of the senior staff of the trade mission and embassy. Shlyapnikov and Tekhnoimport engineers deemed the women unqualified; the engineers emphatically declared that they did not come to Berlin to set up an 'almshouse for wives of senior staff'. In turn, Krestinsky labelled several trust nominees with SR and Menshevik pasts as insufficiently 'soviet', as 'alien people'. Moreover, he accused Shlyapnikov of blindly following the dictates of the trusts and of protecting his own bureaucratic interests. To Shlyapnikov and the trusts, their nominees' proletarian experience and engineering studies superseded in importance their tainted political backgrounds.[14] The conflict reflected unresolved perspectives in the 1920s of who exactly was 'soviet' and who was 'alien'.

Without resolving the dispute, Shlyapnikov travelled from Berlin to London on Metalloimport business. Another Metalloimport representative assumed

12   RGAE, f. 8346, op. 1, d. 26, ll. 74–8, 8 January 1927, letter from Shliapnikov to the Metalloimport board; ll. 92–3; Kollontai 2001, vol. 1, p. 310, 15 May 1927, letter 'to an old comrade'.
13   RGAE, f. 8346, op. 1, d. 26, l. 90; ll. 139–45, letter from Shliapnikov in Berlin to the Metalloimport board, dated 25 January 1926 [should be 1927]; ll. 147–50, 27 January 1927; ll. 58–62, letter from Krumovits to Shliapnikov, 15 January 1927. For more on Piatakov and VSNKh, see Graziosi 1991, vol. 32, pp. 539–81.
14   RGAE, f. 8346, op. 1, d. 26, ll. 135–7, 25 January 1927; d. 31, ll. 18–23, letter from Krestinskii to Shliapnikov, 26 January 1927.

that he would find in the London and Paris trade missions the same excessive red tape as in Berlin. Shlyapnikov's impressions differed. In England he was awestruck by the large factories of Saville, Jessop and Vickers in Sheffield. First in London, then in Paris, he succeeded in arranging orders through Soviet trade representatives.[15] His problems with establishing Metalloimport work abroad lay only in relations with Krestinsky and Soviet trade representatives in Germany, while everywhere else his work went smoothly. This disparity highlights the clashes that sometimes occurred between diplomatic and trade priorities, but also underscores how important were personal relations to conducting the business of the Soviet agencies.

While in Paris, Shlyapnikov carried out a personal mission that further illustrated his flexibility towards individuals' political pasts. His close friend, Svechnikov, in 1927 a professor at the Red Army Academy, had been separated during the Civil War from his then 10-year-old son, who along with other military cadets was evacuated from Russia to France by the Whites. Svechnikov asked Shlyapnikov to find him. Locating the youth quickly, Shlyapnikov first vetted his politics and associations through French communists. Svechnikov's son had continued to associate with counterrevolutionaries in Paris, without telling them who his father was. After meeting him, Shlyapnikov was positively impressed by his 'sensitivity to his father's fate' and his lack of 'White Guard moods'. The unemployed young man agreed to reunite with his father in Russia, whereupon Shlyapnikov helped him obtain a Soviet passport.[16]

Institutional politics proved more difficult to resolve. In support of Shlyapnikov, Tolokontsev, VSNKh's director of military industry and a CC member, wrote to Narkomtorg that its trade representatives purchased faulty and incompatible equipment for Soviet industry. A factory director complained of equipment from abroad that was missing parts, wore out quickly, was packaged incorrectly and lacked blueprints, blaming this on the incompetence of trade-mission staff and German desire to unload inferior goods onto Russia. A representative of Metalloimport, while praising the competence of trade-mission staff in Berlin, offered the opinion that they were 'caught in their own snares', perhaps a reference to office intrigues. Shlyapnikov attempted to lessen Narkomtorg's influence over Metalloimport by rebalancing the board's

---

15   RGAE, f. 8346, op. 1, d. 26, ll. 147–50, 27 January 1927; d. 23, ll. 9–20, 9 February 1927, report by Khrennikov; d. 26, ll. 174–9, 4 and 11 February 1927, letters from Shliapnikov to the Metalloimport board.

16   RGAE, f. 8346, op. 1, d. 38, ll. 12–13, letter (copy) from Shliapnikov in Paris to M.M. Lomovskii of the Soviet trade mission in Paris, 11 February 1927; l. 22, letter from Davtian to Shliapnikov, 3 May 1927. The younger Svechnikov's subsequent fate is unknown.

membership to include more representatives from trusts. But Narkomtorg representatives in Germany remained a thorn in his side, even though he was backed by VSNKh and the Metalworkers' Union. Through most of 1927, Begge continued to bypass Libet by having Finkel handle the work of Tekhnoimport. Despite Libet's lack of experience in technical matters and in commerce, Shlyapnikov supported him. Alleging that opposition to Libet emanated from class prejudice, he pressured Begge, a former metalworker, to accept Libet as a fellow proletarian who could grow in his job. Maybe Shlyapnikov regarded Begge as Krestinsky's client. Finally, after Shlyapnikov met with Stalin about the impasse, Mikoyan urged Begge to smooth things over.[17]

Apparently, no further conflict occurred between Narkomtorg representatives in Berlin and Metalloimport. In 1928 Narkomindel lost its power to place candidates in Soviet trade-representative posts abroad. Krestinsky's backing was thus no longer as important for Begge, who in 1928 supported the policy of stimulating competition among capitalist countries for Soviet orders, which Shlyapnikov had pursued in 1927. By winter 1928–9, the proportion of Soviet imports from England and the USA increased, while German firms began accepting lower prices for their goods. The Soviets also ordered materials and equipment from Denmark and Czechoslovakia. The shift in foreign-trade policy, away from dependence on Germany, may have been connected to Stalin's campaign against the Right Opposition, led by Bukharin, Rykov and Tomsky.[18]

Stalin's turn against Bukharin's alliance with the technical intelligentsia surfaced during the Shakhty Trial, which took place in 1928 in the Donbas region of southern Russia. Employing methods later applied more effectively in the Great Terror of 1936–8, this show trial falsely charged Soviet and German engineers with industrial sabotage ('wrecking') and with being class enemies. Subjected to pressure and intimidation, some succumbed by making false confessions, but others resisted. Those on trial were sentenced to execution or imprisonment; following the trial, thousands more engineers were arrested. This trial threatened to derail trade with Germany, but Krestinsky worked together with Narkomtorg to smooth over relations. Shlyapnikov left no opinion of the case, but probably was sceptical of the charges and critical of the

---

17   RGAE, f. 8346, op. 1, d. 22, ll. 56, 62; d. 23, ll. 9–20, Khrennikov's 9 February 1927 report; d. 10, l. 16, Metalloimport fraction meeting protocol, 8 March 1927; d. 6, ll. 21–8, correspondence between Shliapnikov and Begge, 13–28 May 1927; d. 11, ll. 150–1, 17 September 1927 letter from Shliapnikov to Mikoian; Chernobaev 2008, pp. 26, 773, 19 September 1927; RGAE, f. 8346, op. 1, d. 11, l. 146, 22 September 1927 letter from Mikoian to Begge (copy to Shlyapnikov).

18   Kashirskikh 2006, pp. 39–47.

process. His views may have mirrored those of his close comrade, Tolokontsev, who, even after the Shakhty affair of 1928, remained an 'outspoken' defender of his managers.[19]

Shlyapnikov made another trip abroad on behalf of Metalloimport in autumn 1928, visiting France, Germany, Czechoslovakia and Austria, returning to Moscow in mid-December. Accompanying him were his wife Ekaterina and son Yuri, who long remembered his first sight of the sea in southern France and a luxurious hotel in Germany, where the small child became disoriented in a corridor lined with mirrors. Ekaterina later told their children that she had pleaded for the family to remain in France, but Shlyapnikov could not abandon Soviet Russia to live alongside counterrevolutionaries in Paris. He may have also feared that his defection would discredit comrades who still held leading positions in Soviet industry. This was his last trip abroad before a new campaign began against him. In early 1929 he was accused of 'Rightist deviation' for unspecified remarks he had made in the Metalloimport party cell.[20] At the same time, Shlyapnikov's strong supporter (and perhaps patron), Tolokontsev, entered troubled waters, when in March 1929 the OGPU claimed to have discovered 'a counterrevolutionary organisation' that had long existed in the military industry. Submitting his resignation, Tolokontsev simultaneously pointed out logical inconsistencies in the accusations, which he argued disrupted work and thus constituted 'wrecking'. Although Tolokontsev's resignation was not accepted, he lost his STO seat and consequently some authority at the top level of policy making. Tolokontsev's weakened leadership surely made Shlyapnikov's position less tenable. By spring 1929, Shlyapnikov expressed dissatisfaction with his Metalloimport work, which he left in early September 1929. Perhaps the rise of the syndicates and the decline of the trusts also impeded his work, since the trusts were major partners in Metalloimport. Although he sought further employment in the metals industry, he was instead offered work at Ekonombank. Increased centralisation of banking in 1929 demanded the redirection of personnel to that sector, but he did not feel comfortable working in banking. He therefore resumed work on his memoirs.[21] Nevertheless, he came under increasing attack, both for his memoirs and for his alleged ties to oppositionists.

---

19   Kashirskikh 2006, p. 36; Shearer 1996, p.102. Documents on the Shakhty case were published in Krasil'nikov et al. (eds.) 2010–11.
20   RGASPI, f. 134, op. 1, d. 437, ll. 2–5, Shliapnikov's letters to Kollontai, October 1928–January 1929; interviews with Iurii Shliapnikov and Irina Shliapnikova; RGASPI, f. 589, op. 3, d. 9102, ll. 69–70. The cell's records were not available to me.
21   Sokolov 2012; pp. 101–4; RGASPI, f. 134, op. 1, d. 437, ll. 6–8, letters from Shliapnikov to Kollontai, April–September 1929; Shearer 1996, p. 70.

The Case of the Omsk Group of the Workers' Opposition

By 1929 Stalin perceived the need to break with NEP and commence intensive industrialisation, for which he would acquire capital by forcing the peasants to turn over more grain to the state. To mobilise the party to support his policies, he conducted a widespread campaign against former oppositionists and supporters of Bukharin. Having expelled Trotsky from the USSR in February 1929, in April Stalin defeated Bukharin's opposition to his industrialisation plan, yet many party members were still reluctant to abandon the worker-peasant alliance of NEP.[22] Stalin needed to neutralise potential opponents in the party. Despite Shlyapnikov's efforts to remain apart from political struggle, he was dragged into an investigation of an alleged group of oppositionist workers in Omsk, a city in south-western Siberia which had served as a capital for the Whites during the Civil War. In contrast to the Baku case, that regarding Omsk featured a far more visible OGPU role, yet at times played out with comical errors.

Omsk party officials and the CCC constructed a history of the 'Workers' Opposition' in that city; Shlyapnikov disputed their narrative. A protracted dispute had unfolded in 1922 between groups in the Omsk party organisation, one of which was labelled the 'Workers' Opposition', and advocated elevating workers to party-leadership posts, while the other was loyal to the Sibbiuro.[23] A Trotskyist detained and interrogated by the OGPU tried to deflect the attention of the authorities away from himself by providing evidence about a new 'Workers' Opposition Group' in Omsk in 1926–7. After the Trotskyists ceased opposition, he claimed, the Omsk Workers' Opposition continued it, by creating parallel party organisations, distributing a leaflet, obtaining a press to print Lenin's 'Last Testament' and seeking support among workers of the Anzhero-Sudzhensk and Kolchuginsk coal mines. This 'Workers' Opposition', however, consisted of office staff who, in their criticism of the 'intra-party regime', may have been motivated by career-related grievances. Earlier informers had reported on them, but the authorities ignored them until transport police arrested N.S. Krylov for drunken brawling at a railway station in mid-May 1927 *en route* from Omsk to Moscow. A search of him revealed letters allegedly of a political nature addressed to Nikolai Maximov, an oppositionist who left Omsk after the 1922 conflict and then worked in Moscow in VSNKh. Conveyed to Moscow, Krylov was interrogated by Yakov Agranov, a prominent OGPU official, who coaxed him into confessing that he belonged

---

22 Cohen 1980, pp. 304–14.
23 Olekh 1994, pp. 101–23. Olekh concludes that the 1922 group was not truly kindred with the Moscow Workers' Opposition, but Sandu 2006 disagrees (Sandu 2006, pp. 156–9).

to an 'underground' organisation linked to Shlyapnikov through Maximov. The centre's attention to this case led to the arrest of 15–20 Omsk 'oppositionists', all of whom acknowledged having read and distributed oppositionist literature, but who denied accusations of having formed an 'underground organisation'. The investigation was halted due to insufficient evidence.[24] Despite the transfer of some accused conspirators away from Omsk, oppositionist texts continued to circulate in Siberia.

With Stalin's renewed struggle against his intra-party rivals in 1929, the 'poorly educated but fanatically devoted' first secretary of the new Siberian krai committee, Robert Eikhe, brought attention to alleged oppositionism by Trotskyists and members of the Workers' Opposition in Omsk. On his initiative, thirteen people, including some accused of being members of the Workers' Opposition in 1922 and in 1926, were arrested in late August 1929 for having possessed illegal literature, printing moulds and for having tried to link up with workers in other industrial centres. Given the allegation of long-term activity, the OGPU and CCC, now led by Ordzhonikidze, resolved in autumn 1929 to investigate the Omsk group of the Workers' Opposition. Based in the Omsk railway workshops, the organisation reportedly had attempted, without success, to organise workers in the Anzhersk mines. The flimsy evidence consisted of Krylov's 1927 confession, letters to Maximov that were found on him then and 'illegal leaflets' from 1927–8, criticising the doctrine of socialism in one country and party policy towards the peasantry. The OGPU alleged that five members of the Omsk group met several times in 1928–9 with Maximov, Medvedev and Shlyapnikov, who gave 'directives'.[25]

The OGPU weakly defined Shlyapnikov's directives as advice to meet 'as if to drink tea' (the workers preferred harder drinks) and 'to use only legally published literature about the "Workers' Opposition"'. Even Shlyapnikov's and Medvedev's recommendations 'not to issue underground leaflets, not to participate in strikes and not to link up with Trotskyists in the underground', were cast as particularly subversive attempts to avoid coming to the attention of the authorities. Shlyapnikov allegedly said that enterprise directors in Moscow belonged to the Workers' Opposition and gave it funds, and Maximov

---

24 Demidov 1994, pp. 77–82.
25 Demidov 1994, p. 122; RGASPI, f. 589, op. 3, d. 9102, l. 13, list of those implicated in Omsk case, signed by Agranov, OGPU secret section assistant chief; ll. 34–7. Allegedly, the group had 62 members. Testimonies were attached to the original, but copies of those were not in this CCC file. The report appears to have been authored by Agranov and Iagoda, then assistant OGPU chair, and directed to Iaroslavskii, who, with Ordzhonikidze and Shkiriatov, approved further CCC investigation of the case.

told them that groups of the Workers' Opposition existed in other Soviet cities. Medvedev's gift of money to several of the visitors for return tickets to Omsk was depicted as conspiratorial. The OGPU report also named Chelyshev, at that time chair of the Moscow regional court, and Nikolaenko, a former Chekist working in the Nonferrous Metals Syndicate, as being at the the centre of the Workers' Opposition.[26]

Most of those arrested in 1929 were quickly released. Unemployed, most soon recanted their views. The few who did not were exiled. One of these was an Old Bolshevik, Mikhail Vichinsky, who had been taken prisoner and tortured by the Whites during the Civil War, and was toughened by this experience. Recantations were sent 'for correction' to Moscow, where central authorities, guided by Yaroslavsky, created a revisionist history of consistent and intensifying oppositionist factionalism in Omsk from 1922 to 1929, with links to Shlyapnikov and Medvedev, who allegedly 'gave directives', were 'ideological leaders', 'supplied literature and money' and told workers to rejoin the party and 'conduct destructive work within it'.[27]

With Politburo endorsement, the CCC turned to investigating the role of Shlyapnikov and Medvedev in the Omsk case.[28] In late November 1929 CCC investigators Krivov and Kaganovich interrogated them in separate sessions, a departure from past CCC investigations, when they were questioned together.[29] While Medvedev was sarcastic, combative and acerbic, Shlyapnikov more carefully contested the charges. Of the Omsk workers who allegedly visited them, Medvedev recalled only Vichinsky, already ill and old, coming to Moscow in

---

26   RGASPI, f. 589, op. 3, d. 9102, ll. 34–5. I did not have access to Chëlyshev's CCC and NKVD files and was allowed to consult only some of Nikolaenko's materials.

27   Demidov 1994, pp. 130–1; RGASPI, f. 589, op. 3, d. 9103, vol. 3, l. 54, protocol no. 84 (excerpt – copy) of 22 October 1929 OK VKP(b) Omsk Bureau closed session, received by the party CC information section, and directed to Iaroslavskii, who on 5 November 1929 sent a copy to Agranov.

28   RGASPI, f. 17, op. 162, d. 8, l. 2, Politburo decision, 30 October 1929, stamped with Stalin's signature and directed on the same day to Ordzhonikidze, who assigned Krivov and Kaganovich to interview Shliapnikov and Medvedev. Iaroslavskii and Shkiriatov were to be kept informed (RGASPI, f. 589, op. 3, d. 9103, vol. 3, l. 55). Demidov 1994 incorrectly wrote that Shliapnikov and Medvedev were only investigated after L.M. Kaganovich made a trip to Siberia in April 1930 and became aware of the Omsk case (Demidov 1994, p. 131).

29   RGASPI, f. 589, opis 3, d. 9102, ll. 67–106, 25 November 1929. On 3 December 1929, Shkiriatov sent the uncorrected stenographic records, marked 'urgent' and 'top secret', to Ordzhonikidze, Stalin, Molotov, Kaganovich and Smirnov (RGASPI, f. 589, opis 3, d. 9102, l. 107, 3 December 1929). Medvedev was promised a copy of the stenographic report for corrections, but this transcript appears to be uncorrected.

1929 to appeal for a pension and asking for his and Shlyapnikov's help in interceding with the CCC for one. Asked why he did not report this to the party, he asserted that he had no need to report his visitors, because those who kept him under surveillance were well aware of who he saw and under what circumstances.[30] Shlyapnikov also claimed that he and those close to him were under OGPU surveillance during these years, about which he often complained to the OGPU.[31]

Attempting to explore the evidence, Shlyapnikov received only vague answers and concluded that this was an old case, already resolved, but his interrogators were not dissuaded. He therefore obligingly related that in 1927 several workers from Omsk had come to Moscow to appeal against their exclusion from the party. He recalled having strictly advised them not to engage in factionalism or to create a new party, or to attribute to him views that 'Trotskyists sowed under the guise of a united opposition'. Finally, he cast doubt on the possibility that Vichinsky, 'a very serious person', could have said and done as the CCC depicted. When asked why he received these men, he answered that it would have been rude to turn away a visitor or inquire as to his reasons for visiting. Moreover, he could not control how the other person interpreted the meeting. Regarding links, Shlyapnikov found it natural that fellows from Omsk would visit their comrades who had been transferred to Moscow, including Maximov. He declined to cast judgment on what Maximov said to them, but only insisted that he himself gave no directive.[32]

Either in jest or feigned *naïveté*, Shlyapnikov pointed out that these Omsk workers did nothing wrong in opposing 'Rightist' ideas and policies and he doubted that they had conducted any illegal work. When the interrogator suggested that Shlyapnikov's 1926 articles could have been interpreted as 'directives', he objected that they were published by the party and had opposed factionalism. Moreover, he mischievously asserted, his proposals in 1924–6 differed little from 1929 party policies on industrialisation.[33] Humour and language emphasising his adherence to proper party conduct had become his chief means of defence against false accusations. Yet both CCC and OGPU officials

---

30 RGASPI, f. 589, op. 3, d. 9102, l. 104–5. Shliapnikov and Medvedev spoke on his behalf with Sol'ts and Iaroslavskii, who said that Vichinskii did not go through the proper channels to request his pension.
31 RGASPI, f. 589, op. 3, d. 9102, l. 41, letter from Shliapnikov to the CCC Presidium, 14 August 1930.
32 RGASPI, f. 589, op. 3, d. 9102, ll. 77–84.
33 RGASPI, f. 589, op. 3, d. 9102, ll. 75–6.

were determined to fit his open, 'legal' forms of dissent into a uniform oppositionist framework.

Shlyapnikov found it ludicrous that anyone could think that he and Medvedev would 'make a base of our illegal organisation somewhere in Siberia, the devil knows where'. When Krivov inquired as to whether he had expressed any 'doubts about the party line' to his visitors from Omsk, Shlyapnikov drily replied that he would not have had such a subtle conversation with strangers. Despite Shlyapnikov's conciliatory posture, Kaganovich doubted that he had only told supporters to work within the party. In fact, to him even this sounded subversive. Persistently, Krivov argued that Shlyapnikov and Medvedev were to blame because they had 'not actively conducted the party line' in speeches or in the press. Krivov emphasised the importance of 'sincerity' and Kaganovich warned: 'The time is coming, when one can't be silent'. Shlyapnikov offered that he could use as the basis for a new article his 1925 manuscript, in which he had criticised Bukharin's and Zinoviev's proposals on agriculture. He found it relevant to the situation in 1929, a not-so-subtle reminder that he had been more consistent than Stalin in promoting industrialisation. The interview concluded with Shlyapnikov's promise to write an article and his assurance that wanted to preserve 'good relations'.[34]

In mid-December 1929, Shlyapnikov published in *Pravda* an article supporting intensive industrialisation.[35] This did not mean that he approved of Stalin's approach to collectivisation, which was poorly planned and implicitly encouraged excesses, resulting in horrible human tragedy and enormous damage to agriculture. More than five million people from successful farming families (called '*kulaks*' and presumed hostile to Soviet power) were deported to Siberia and the far north as forced labour. Many died of hunger, cold or disease; children and elderly people were particularly vulnerable. Peasants killed over half their livestock rather than relinquish their animals to the collective. Even spring planting was threatened.[36] In his 2 March 1930 'Dizzy with Success' article in *Pravda*, Stalin condemned excesses, cautioning that collectivisation should be voluntary and suit local conditions. Shlyapnikov then remarked privately that Stalin's article would have been timelier in October or November.[37] Such irony was hardly in keeping with the horror that had been visited upon the peasantry. For his part, Stalin disapproved of Shlyapnikov

---

34   RGASPI, f. 589, op. 3, d. 9102, ll. 67–74.
35   Shliapnikov 1929.
36   Viola 1996 and 2007; Fitzpatrick 1996.
37   TsA FSB, R33718, d. 499061, vol. 43, l. 207, letter to Medvedev from Shliapnikov, Kislovodsk, 6 March 1930. The letter was sent through an acquaintance, to be mailed in Moscow.

being published in *Pravda*, even when he was writing in favour of party policy. He faulted the editors of *Pravda* for allowing Shlyapnikov's article to 'slip through' and assured Molotov, who was on holiday, that he would '*straighten out the Shlyapnikov affair today*' (Stalin's emphasis).[38] Shlyapnikov and Medvedev had just written a letter to the CC in which they expressed disapproval of factionalism and denied having engaged in underground work.[39] Unsurprisingly, however, it was not published.

Maximov's arrest, around the time of Shlyapnikov's and Medvedev's questioning by the CCC, had further implications for them and casts light on the methods of the OGPU at that time. In early December an OGPU employee tried to deliver to Maximov's wife a parcel for Shlyapnikov or Medvedev. Shlyapnikov appealed on her behalf to the OGPU but he received only denials. The 'persecutions' of agents continued. On the advice of his old comrade, Voroshilov, at Revvoensovet, and CC secretary Alexander Smirnov, Shlyapnikov appealed in writing to the chair of the CCC, Ordzhonikidze. Subsequently, Maximov's wife was no longer bothered by OGPU agents.[40]

In his letter to Ordzhonikidze, Shlyapnikov asserted that the scanty materials he had been allowed to study on the Omsk case convinced him that the case had been conducted 'abnormally', that there was nothing new in it and that neither he nor Medvedev had violated party statutes. However, the authorities had interpreted their 'friendly party advice' as a 'directive' issued by a 'centre'. In his opinion, the resulting picture was a 'contradictory hodgepodge'. Further, he was offended that the OGPU and CCC had 'worked up' this case secretly since spring 1928, in violation of party regulations. Reminding Ordzhonikidze of his earlier assurances that the CC did not consider this matter important, Shlyapnikov objected that the case was indeed being pursued seriously. As confirmation, he pointed not only to Maximov's imprisonment for more than a month, but also to visits to Maximov's wife at home and work by an OGPU

---

38 Lih *et al.* (eds.) 1995, pp. 185–6, 25 December 1929 letter to Molotov. The Bukharinists had been purged from *Pravda*'s editorial board in early autumn 1929; Iaroslavskii numbered among the replacements (Cohen 1980, pp. 297, 450, fn. 120).

39 I did not find a copy of this letter, supposedly sent on 24 December 1929, but saw a reference to it in RGASPI, f. 589, op. 3, d. 9102, l. 4, letter from Shliapnikov and Medvedev to CCC, 28 April 1930, copy to the Politburo.

40 RGASPI, f. 589, op. 3, d. 9103, vol. 3, ll. 50–1, letter from Shliapnikov (signed) to the Politburo and CCC, 2 January 1929 [surely 1930; he probably mistakenly wrote the old year]; stamped at top as received either 21 February 1930 or 2 March 1930 (barely legible). Shliapnikov addressed Ordzhonikidze with the familiar 'you' [*ty*]. See also RGASPI, f. 589, op. 3, d. 9102, l. 41, signed letter from Shliapnikov to the CCC Presidium, 14 August 1930, explaining circumstances around his involvement in Maksimov's case.

employee identifying himself as 'Stolypin'. This OGPU employee tried to give her a package for Shlyapnikov or Medvedev, despite her protests that she did not know them or where they lived. 'Stolypin' persisted, on one occasion even trying to slip the package into her boots in a tram car. Shlyapnikov wrote that 'the poor woman' was 'terrorised' and could not understand why the OGPU wanted her to act as a 'courier'. He requested that Ordzhonikidze help free Maximov and halt 'provocational work'. Shlyapnikov seems to have considered his old comrade Molotov a potential intercessor with Stalin and the OGPU, for when updating Medvedev, who was on holiday in the same resort as Molotov, Shlyapnikov requested that he 'try to negotiate with Molotov regarding the case'.[41]

In mid-January 1930, not having heard from Ordzhonikidze, Shlyapnikov went to visit him at the CCC but found him away. After that he dropped in on Yaroslavsky to discuss the case. After consulting with OGPU personnel by telephone, Yaroslavsky claimed that the person who approached Maximov's wife was not an OGPU agent named Stolypin, but was instead a former factory worker and supporter of the Workers' Opposition named Salygin, who served as a prison guard and attempted to convey a letter from Maximov. Then Yaroslavsky 'half-jokingly' taunted Shlyapnikov that the latter had revealed and surrendered his 'own agent within the OGPU'. Shlyapnikov concluded that 'they intended to use this "Salygin case" against me'. Yaroslavsky placed Shlyapnikov's protest on the agenda of the CCC party collegium (board), but then it was postponed until Medvedev returned to Moscow.[42]

When Medvedev finally returned from holiday in early February, he found in his mail a handwritten letter signed 'Maximov', but not in Maximov's handwriting. Postmarked in December, the letter was improperly addressed. Consequently, it was delivered to a neighbour's address. Only after a few days, and after having been opened, was it dropped at Medvedev's building. Shlyapnikov insisted that a construction fitter and plumber such as Maximov was incapable of having written a letter in such delicate, tiny script. Besides, Maximov would have known Medvedev's correct address and that he was on holiday. Maximov's wife agreed that the letter was not in his handwriting, yet

---

41   RGASPI, f. 589, op. 3, d. 9103, vol. 3, ll. 50–1; TsA FSB, R33718, d. 499061, vol. 43, l. 138, letter from Shliapnikov to Medvedev, 3 January 1930. Molotov was on holiday during December 1929, but returned to Moscow by mid-January (Watson 2005, p. 92).

42   RGASPI, f. 589, op. 3, d. 9102, ll. 40–1, letter from Shliapnikov to the CCC Presidium, 14 August 1930; TsA FSB, R33718, d. 499061, vol. 43, unnumbered page, postcard from Shliapnikov to Medvedev, 21 January 1930. Shliapnikov had just seen CC and CCC members at the Bol'shoi, where he and they had attended a commemoration of Lenin's death.

she did not recognise it as the letter offered by the mysterious intermediary.[43] On 23 February 1930, the CCC again delayed deciding the Omsk case until it received the disputed letter from Medvedev.[44]

On that same day, CC and CCC members urged Shliapnikov to write a statement about the Omsk case. Responding promptly, with a document entitled 'About a big mistake by a small group in Omsk', Shliapnikov repudiated factionalism and denied that the Workers' Opposition had 'led underground work'.[45] Instructing Medvedev to deliver the statement, attempt to see Stalin about the case and stay in touch by mail, Shliapnikov left for holiday in Kislovodsk and Gagry, where he spent March and part of April. Perplexed by the party institutions' treatment of the case, Shliapnikov jested that party-appeal processes were as difficult to comprehend as quantum mechanics.[46] Accustomed to seeing members of the Stalinist leadership at public functions and speaking with them on relatively polite terms, he was unable to foresee the terror that would be directed against Old Bolsheviks.

While Shliapnikov was on holiday in the south, he learned about Cossack uprisings there, resulting from collectivisation and dekulakisation. Following these events with great concern, he worried that the press was not rebutting unspecified 'absurd rumours' that had spread about the events. He hoped that 'political tact' could help restore 'peaceful mutual understanding' in the wake of numerous arrests.[47] There must have been a large measure of self-delusion in his assessment of the events unfolding around him, as it seems that he

---

43 RGASPI, f. 589, op. 3, d. 9102, l. 40, letter from Shliapnikov to the CCC Presidium, 14 August 1930. The CCC preserved in its files the original letter that Maksimov claimed was a forgery, along with enlargements of Maksimov's own letters and a 30 June 1930 NKVD handwriting analysis, which concluded that the disputed letter was in Maksimov's handwriting (RGASPI, f. 589, op. 3, d. 9102, ll. 30–1, 53). In my opinion, the handwriting samples appear markedly different.

44 RGASPI, f. 589, op. 3, d. 9103, l. 52, excerpt from CCC protocol, no. 116, point 1, 23 February 1930, with Iaroslavskii's signature stamp. Present: Krivov, Agranov, Iaroslavskii, Medvedev, Shliapnikov, A.P. Smirnov and Shkiriatov.

45 RGASPI, f. 589, op. 3, d. 9102, ll. 2–3, typed manuscript 'About a big mistake by a small group in Omsk', signed by Shliapnikov, 28 February 1930. See also RGASPI, f. 589, op. 3, d. 9102, l. 4, letter from Shliapnikov and Medvedev to the CCC, 28 April 1930. Shliapnikov sent the statement to Omsk in early April.

46 TsA FSB, R33718, d. 499061, vol. 43, ll. 80–1, 207, 211, letters from Shliapnikov in Kislovodsk to Medvedev in Moscow, 6, 22 and 26 March 1930 (6 March letter sent through an acquaintance).

47 TsA FSB, R33718, d. 499061, vol. 43, l. 210, letter to Medvedev from Shliapnikov in Kislovodsk, 27 March [1930].

did not comprehend the full tragedy of forcible collectivisation at that time. Deeply immersed in writing his historical memoirs and preoccupied with avoiding prosecution on the Omsk case, perhaps he was not fully able to assess the meaning and impact of Stalin's radical new policies. Despite his failure to employ the language of class warfare in his private reflections on collectivisation, he surely saw it as a necessary and objectively 'progressive' measure, the only way to accomplish Soviet industrialisation in the existing domestic and international context of limited capital for investment and increasing hostility from the Soviet Union's neighbours.

While on holiday, Shlyapnikov wrote to Omsk party leaders, asking them to print his statement about the Omsk case, which had not yet appeared in the party press. Instead, Omsk party leaders published in the newspaper, *Rabochii put*, a 'Letter of 10 Oppositionists' that implicated Shlyapnikov and Medvedev in factionalism. The CCC, expressing dissatisfaction with Shlyapnikov's and Medvedev's earlier statements, called on them to write another one. Nevertheless, Shlyapnikov and Medvedev continued to complain that they could take no responsibility for people misunderstanding their views. Combatively, they argued that the CCC's logic would make even Yaroslavsky an accomplice of Omsk workers, because they had read his book about the Workers' Opposition.[48]

On 13 March 1930, the CCC voted to expel Maximov from the party. Released from prison, he appealed against his purge from the party and three-year exile to Central Asia. Denying that he or the Omsk workers had been in the Workers' Opposition, he insisted that the only reading material he had given them was that approved by the CC, including Yaroslavsky's book and party-congress protocols. Complaining about OGPU threats to keep him in jail until he would confess to anti-party work, Maximov wrote that he had refused to confess because he did not want to 'deceive myself, you, the party and history'.[49]

---

[48] RGASPI, f. 589, op. 3, d. 9102, l. 1, letter from Shliapnikov in Gagry to Omsk RKP(b) okrug committee bureau, 4 April 1930; l. 4, letter from Shliapnikov and Medvedev to the CCC, 28 April 1930, referring to a 13 April 1930 letter to them from the CCC (received by them on 25 April 1930).

[49] RGASPI, f. 589, op. 3, d. 9102, l. 57, CCC party collegium protocol (excerpt), 13 March 1930; ll. 15–19, Maksimov's handwritten letter to the Politburo and CCC, 24 May 1930. Among OGPU methods of which he complained were transfer to a cold cell and deprivation of exercise, parcels, books and mineral water Essentuki no. 17 to treat his 'attacks of liver disease'. Such measures were, of course, mild compared with those of 1937–8. A decision regarding Salygin awaited Krivov's further investigation.

He asked Shlyapnikov and Medvedev for assistance in his appeal.[50] They were in a weak position to do so, yet they tried.

On 28 May the CCC concluded that Shlyapnikov and Medvedev had been aware that people in Omsk had created 'an underground group of the Workers' Opposition' and were at fault for having failed to stop them and for having failed to tell party leaders. Despite this rebuke, Yaroslavsky, on 29 May 1930, confirmed their verification by the party purge that the Sixteenth Party Congress had ordered in 1929. On the same day, however, someone (perhaps Yaroslavsky) attempted to re-open the Omsk case and to ratchet up the charges. Depicting an evolution of the Omsk affair that linked worker opposition to peasant uprisings, the accusation now was that a counterrevolutionary group discovered in March 1930 in Omsk had sought to lead kulak uprisings to overthrow Soviet power.[51]

In the new narrative, oppositionists turned to the peasantry because they had become disillusioned in the working class, as if they were reverting from Marxism to Populism, except that they were linked to kulaks. Describing unsuccessful attempts to obtain arms, the unknown author wove unrelated groups and incidents into a narrative that purported to show an unbroken line of opposition that had evolved into counterrevolution. Resistance to collectivisation in Siberia had indeed grown rapidly. Hundreds of armed bands in Siberia attacked collective farms [*kolkhozes*]. In 1930 the number of bands in Western Siberia alone had grown to eight hundred and eighty. Transit camps for kulak deportees in Omsk, Tomsk and Achinsk held people who had cause to be embittered against the Soviet regime.[52] Whether or not Omsk workers had sought to collude with peasant bandits, someone in the party and/ or secret police intended to demonstrate links between intra-party opposition and counterrevolution. Rather than apply the 'tact' that Shlyapnikov preferred in dealing with peasant disturbances, Stalin and his allies opted to scapegoat oppositionists.

It is not clear whether this report was used, but Yaroslavsky did introduce a resolution to the CCC Presidium calling for harsher measures against Shlyapnikov. On 3 August, the CCC sternly reprimanded Shlyapnikov for having 'support[ed] anti-party elements leading factional struggle against the party', of having 'covered up' the Omsk group's work, and of having slan-

---

50 TsA FSB, R33718, d. 499061, vol. 43, ll. 162–7, letters from Maksimov to Shliapnikov and Medvedev, 22 June and 2 August 1930.

51 RGASPI, f. 589, op. 3, d. 9103, vol. 3, ll. 56–61, 109; d. 9102, l. 5. Alleged leaders of the new organisation included that same Krylov arrested in 1927 for drunken brawling at the train station.

52 RGASPI, f. 589, op. 3, d. 9103, vol. 3, ll. 56–60; Werth 2007, pp. 37, 86.

dered the OGPU. Formally disputing all the charges, Shlyapnikov argued that Yaroslavsky had introduced no new evidence. He interpreted the latest charges as a response to his appeal on Maximov's behalf and to his criticisms of the OGPU for having applied 'methods of provocation' in regard to Maximov's wife. He clarified that his accusations were against individuals, not the OGPU as an institution, and were not universal, but pertained to the Omsk case specifically. Refusing to apologise for having defended Maximov, he declared: 'I considered it my duty to stand up for him'. The CCC let stand the reprimand and all the other decisions on the Omsk case. Moreover, Yaroslavsky continued to scour not only the USSR, but also peripheral regions, for evidence damning former members of the Workers' Opposition. On 3 September 1930, for example, he informed higher-ups that a communist in Mongolia had denounced Medvedev. The denunciation was based on brief information provided during the party purge from a communist named Antonov, whose 'deep agitation' and 'ill state of health' made it impossible to coax more detail from him.[53]

Shlyapnikov and Medvedev must have been relieved to put the Omsk case to rest, for in 1930 their personal lives had taken new turns. While Medvedev lost his wife, Maria, to tuberculosis, Shlyapnikov and Ekaterina had a baby, Irina, who was born in July. Shlyapnikov's letters to Kollontai during this period provide glimpses into his family life. Although they talked politics on her brief visits to Moscow, his letters treated safer topics, such as his books, the children's development, and his family's health. On teaching his son to shoot from his rifles, he employed Marxist terminology with light irony, joking that Yuri was 'experiencing the stage of "primitive militarism"'. Kollontai's grandson, Vladimir, was near Yuri in age, so she easily shared Shlyapnikov's joy and concerns. He asked her to send him French and German newspapers, from which he gathered perspectives on international affairs which were unavailable in the Soviet press. Underscoring the Stalinist economy's low priority on consumer goods, he often prevailed on her to send or bring items from abroad that he could not find in the USSR.[54]

---

53 RGASPI, f. 589, op. 3, d. 9102, l. 39, 3 August 1930; l. 62, 8 August 1930; ll. 40–1, letter from Shliapnikov to the CCC Presidium, 14 August 1930; ll. 44–56; ll. 108–9, letter to CCC VKP(b) from an Ulan Bator party purge commission chair (illegible signature), with two dates – 25 November 1929 and 24 March 1930. For more on Iaroslavskii's attitude towards oppositionism, see Dahlke 2008.

54 RGASPI, f. 134, op. 1, d. 437, ll. 11–27, nine letters from Shliapnikov to Kollontai, 15 May– 24 October 1930. His requests included medicines and medical supplies, a typewriter, baby food, a camping tent and a Swedish motor for a boat. Selecting the motor caused Kollontai some frustration, leading to some comical exchanges between them.

FIGURE 32 *Alexander Shlyapnikov in the late 1920s (provided by the Shlyapnikov family)*.

Nevertheless, political dangers would continue to haunt Shlyapnikov. Omsk figured among the cities where the NKVD would in 1935 accuse him of having organised counterrevolutionary groups. For the Omsk workers, however, final consequences would arrive even earlier. The NKVD alleged that in 1933 Omsk oppositionists had raided a collective farm, killed four collective farmers and stolen *kolkhoz* property. In July 1934 several Omsk oppositionists returned from prison camp and exile only to be accused of new counterrevolutionary work. They, along with nearly 40 other workers, were arrested and some were shot.[55]

Rosmetizprom

Having condemned factionalism and expressed support for intensive industrialisation, Shlyapnikov still enjoyed some sympathy from highly placed former comrades. This, and the party's need for experienced administrators during the First Five-Year Plan, eventually brought him new employment. In June 1931 VSNKh RSFSR entrusted him with leadership of the metalware-industries association [*Respublikanskoe obedinenie metiznoi promyshlennosti – Rosmetizprom*]. Although republic-level assignments were less significant than all-union positions, Shlyapnikov had the opportunity, as chair, to turn metalware production in a new direction. Since the revolution, Rosmetizprom factories had abandoned samovar production but still made thermoses, lye washers, hinges, clamps, bolts and castings, so they still had far to go in the transition to manufacturing precision instruments and parts needed in the aviation, auto and tractor industries, as demanded by the First Five-Year Plan.[56]

Along with several other associations, Rosmetizprom had, in April, separated from the RSFSR metals-industry association (ROMP). Both Shlyapnikov and VSNKh RSFSR leaders criticised ROMP and Rosmetizprom (in its first months) for weak leadership and lagging plan fulfilment. Shlyapnikov was to meet deadlines in constructing new factories, eliminating bottlenecks, hiring personnel and supplying them with housing, communal services, food and manufactured goods. Setting to work with his customary energy, Shlyapnikov immersed himself in his duties as he went on site to inspect construction sites in Nizhny Novgorod, Pavlovo, Murom and other towns. In Vladimir he insisted on revising plans for converting a spinning mill into a factory for the production of precision mechanical instruments, due to the poor soil in the original location that would not only interfere with proper construction, but also with

---

55   Iakovlev (ed.) 1991, pp. 105–6; TsA FSB, R33718, d. 499061, vol. 5, ll. 28–31, 15 February 1935; Papkov 1997, p. 105. The secret police and CCC collaboration to present a unified narrative has influenced not only Soviet-era accounts but also post-Soviet historiography. Papkov designated the Workers' Opposition as 'one of the most united organisations, a symbol of revolutionary steadfastness and unity of workers in the struggle with the authorities' (Papkov 1997, p. 104). This positive depiction of the group turned the Stalinist narrative on its head, but was no more accurate.

56   RGAE, f. 4088, op. 1, d. 6, l. 146; d. 39, ll. 32–3, 49, 57.

the production and storage of raw materials and finished goods. His instructions to managers included collecting trustworthy data, creating priority lists and investigating the non-fulfilment of orders. Locals honoured him by naming a factory in his hometown of Murom after him, a common mark of deference to the Stalinist elite.[57]

Shlyapnikov's reports and decisions demonstrated his commitment to improving the Russian metalwares industry by reorienting it from manual to mechanised labour, rationalisation, improved transportation, greater specialisation of factories, more cooperation with other factories and new types of production. He also emphasised the need to provide decent working and living conditions (ventilation, sewage, food and clothing and cultural opportunities) for workers. Yet the limited resources available for industrialisation meant that the needs of workers became subordinated to the demand for production. Shlyapnikov was forced to approve construction projects that did not budget for 'heating, plumbing, ventilation and sewage disposal'. Although he insisted that administrators should present estimates for such safeguards as soon as possible, he must have known that workers would long suffer primitive conditions before improvements would be provided. He was also surely aware of high injury rates on work sites, for he called for increased technical supervision of workers and for better maintenance of equipment (preventative repair). Nevertheless, he also supported the goal of increasing production, signing proposals calling for piecework for new workers, time-saving studies and bonuses to workers who discovered time-saving measures.[58]

Shlyapnikov faced increasing frustrations as chair of Rosmetizprom, which was bleeding factories as they were reassigned to other associations. Ascertaining flaws in the industrialisation strategy, he argued that it was 'inexpedient' to concentrate the production of particular items at one factory. Such specialisation would be a chronic problem in the Soviet economy. Shlyapnikov was not the only one to detect it, for the prominent engineer, Peter Palchinsky, educated in the tsarist era and arrested in the 1930 Industrial Party Case, had pointed out this weakness, among others. Continuing the campaign against 'bourgeois specialists' begun by the 1928 Shakhty Trial, the Industrial Party Case involved around two thousand engineers arrested as scapegoats for Soviet industrial failures and culminated in a show trial that convicted leading technology experts of working with foreign governments to overthrow the Soviet

---

57 RGAE, f. 4088, op. 1, d. 6, ll. 34–7, 153; d. 7, ll. 11–12; d. 9, ll. 26, 32; d. 39, ll. 43–6, 55–6, 62, 133; op. 2, the summary of archivist M.V. Mironova.

58 RGAE, f. 4088, op. 1, d. 9, ll. 2–5, 29 September 1931; ll. 32–9; d. 39, ll. 11–13, 25 October 1931; ll. 133–4, 160.

government.⁵⁹ Shlyapnikov's opinions of it are not known, but his thoughts on organising Soviet industry, providing for workers' everyday and cultural needs, setting realistic goals for production and collecting valid data mirrored the outlook of engineers like Palchinsky.

Yet in other ways, Shlyapnikov adapted to Stalinist methods. Unable to meet plan targets, he placed blame on suppliers' delays and insufficient funding by the Russian Trade and Industrial Bank [*Prombank*] and resorted to coercive methods common at the time. In one case, he recommended that the prosecutor's office [*prokurora*]⁶⁰ investigate a factory's construction delays and 'make the guilty responsible'. He must have been aware that his request could have ominous consequences. Perhaps he regretted it, for in a later case he called on VSNKh RSFSR to fine the Moscow oblast sovnarkhoz and the chairs of the Moscow metals department for dragging their feet in approving paperwork. It seems likely that the nervous strain he experienced in attempting to meet unrealistic goals set by the leadership, as he witnessed the harm this did to workers, worsened the symptoms of Ménière's disease and led to his decision to leave active leadership of Rosmetizprom at the end of October 1931 for one and a half months of medical leave.⁶¹ The intensifying criticism directed at his books also increased his anxiety. He did not return to Rosmetizprom, which was abolished on 1 December 1931.

Conclusion

Shlyapnikov's work in Metalloimport in 1926–9 and in Rosmetizprom in 1931 seemed to offer him the opportunity to contribute to the cause that concerned him most – rebuilding Soviet industry and, with it, a more ideologically 'conscious' proletariat that would one day take control of production into its own hands. As the chair of Metalloimport, he worked closely with the Metalworkers' Union and with former union staff who had come to work in VSNKh, trusts and syndicates. He clashed with old rivals like Krestinsky and still suspected

---

59 RGAE, f. 4088, op. 1, d. 9, l. 52; d. 12, ll. 1–2; d. 13, ll. 39–41; d. 39, l. 14; d. 40, ll. 1–6; Bailes 1978, pp. 95–121; Graham 1993.

60 According to Getty and Naumov (Getty and Naumov 1999, p. 119), a procurator, by definition of the term in Continental and Russian law, not only prosecutes criminal cases, but also reviews the work of state institutions to ensure that they function according to the laws.

61 RGAE, f. 4088, op. 1, d. 9, l. 42; d. 10, l. 1; d. 12, l. 3, 26 October 1931; l. 10, 18 October 1931; l. 35, 8 August 1931.

that obstacles in his way were placed by *intelligenty* who wanted to impede the advancement of workers. Yet his attitude towards Svechnikov's son and students in Germany with politically variegated pasts revealed a certain tolerance and flexibility. At the same time, his autonomous views and continuing contacts with former comrades in the Workers' Opposition aroused the suspicion of party leaders and brought him under investigation for oppositionism.

The CCC, with OGPU assistance, cynically manipulated the Omsk case to construct a conspiracy that involved a centre in Moscow. There was initiative both from below and from above in the fabrication of the Omsk case, with the centre playing a guiding role. Shlyapnikov contested the labels that central party authorities foisted upon him and his close comrades. He denied that they had been a 'centre' and rejected the label 'directive' for his 'friendly party advice'. Furthermore, he refused to characterise as 'links' his ties to old acquaintances within the party accused of oppositionism. Finally, he insisted that the 'case' of the Omsk oppositionists was a 'provocation'. Moreover, he actively contested, even mocked, the CCC's attempt to paint him into an ideological corner. The *naïveté* he projected may have been his defence and a mechanism for continuing to transmit his views. The Omsk case was a half-baked attempt to subdue him and his close comrades, which did not result in punishment that went beyond a reprimand. Shlyapnikov did not pursue a line of resistance, but instead attempted to work within the party in the right party spirit [*partiinost*]. His views and language differed from the apocalyptic vision of Yaroslavsky and, ultimately, Stalin, who was behind the campaign against him and his comrades. Attempting to keep alive an alternative party spirit, he operated in a system that denied basic individual liberties, a system that he had helped to construct. Although, during his tenure at Rosmetizprom, Shlyapnikov had to some extent succumbed to Stalinist pressures to raise production regardless of the costs, this took a physical toll on him and forced him onto the sidelines for a time.

CHAPTER 11

Purged from the Party

Stalin's policies of forced collectivisation and breakneck intensive industrialisation were deeply flawed, causing death and suffering for millions and giving rise to unrest among workers, peasants and even party members, which challenged and at times seemed to present overwhelming threats to the party's dictatorship. Party leaders thus found it urgent to compel unity in the party and justified their measures by exaggerating the party's historical unity and role in the revolution. Despite carrying out his work competently, Shlyapnikov could not escape the attention of those in the party who wanted to eradicate vestiges of critical thinking. His departure from Rosmetizprom coincided with a new, more aggressive turn in Stalin's persecution of heterodoxy in the historical profession. During his medical leave, while he recuperated from aggravated symptoms of Ménière's syndrome, Shlyapnikov had to defend himself against attacks on his books for their failure to glorify Stalin and the role of the Bolshevik Party in 1917. Not only were his books condemned and suppressed, but he was harried by petty charges. After he submitted to pressure to condemn errors in his books, he was assigned new work in the Gosplan RSFSR Presidium, but soon he was harassed for having allegedly made an anti-party speech in his party cell. Like many other former oppositionists, in 1933 Shlyapnikov was excluded from the Soviet Communist Party, a long and arduous process which took its toll on his nerves and health. His dialogue with purge-commission members reveals precisely how they perceived his words and behaviour to be incompatible with the Stalinist ideal. He defended himself by demanding material evidence for the charges and by employing humour to subvert them, but the absurd and irrational process proved difficult for him to comprehend and drained his energy.

The Case Against Shlyapnikov's Memoirs

Shlyapnikov's memoirs in article and book form had seen publication since the early years of Soviet power. His memoir of 1917 [*Semnadtsatyi god*] was printed in four volumes from 1923 to 1931. Historians of 1917 value his memoir histories for their extensive reliance on a broad range of primary sources from that year, for he included long excerpts and, on occasion, even entire documents in his texts. He also consulted non-Bolshevik memoirs, even those published abroad. Although he was biased against non-Bolshevik politicians, he did not demonise them, nor did he distort the sources in order to exaggerate the Bolshevik Party's role in 1917. Instead, Shlyapnikov provided evidence of the collaboration between the Bolsheviks and other radical socialists in the revolutionary underground and during the February Revolution.[1]

Until 1927, Shlyapnikov's books were only criticised harshly by those who thought he had unfairly depicted their own roles and views in the revolutionary events. Reviewers used typical 'scholarly standards' in evaluating the books. Yet in 1927 several historians published articles in the party journals, *Bolshevik* and *Istorik-marksist*, calling on him to revise *Semnadtsatyi god* to base it more on Marxist theory and less on the documents he had used. The very significant changes for which they called included glossing over the differences among Bolsheviks in early 1917 to make it seem as if all agreed with Lenin and forcefully distinguishing Stalin's views from those of Kamenev. At the same time, Shlyapnikov's role in 1917 came under attack, as critics accused him of rejecting the proletarian revolution. Taking umbrage at his critics for failing to produce evidence for their assertions, Shlyapnikov was astounded by their insistence that he 'falsify...events of which I was a participant and eyewitness'. The attacks on him were part of a general shift in the historical profession after 1927, in which 'bourgeois' historians were dismissed, arrested and imprisoned. Remaining historians had to glorify Stalin's role in the party's history and present it as consistently united. By 1930 many other Bolshevik memoirs were also dismissed or attacked.[2]

Nevertheless, Shlyapnikov's fourth volume of *Semnadtsatyi god*, published in October 1931, was document-based. Moreover, he did not surrender to the trend towards glorifying Stalin and demonising figures such as Trotsky, Zinoviev and Kamenev. At the end of October 1931, Stalin crashed hard on the historical profession, condemning those who relied on documents as 'archival rats' and 'hopeless bureaucrats'. In a letter to editors of the historical journal, *Proletarskaya revolutsiya*, he insisted that the party's interpretation of revolutionary history was not to be questioned or disputed. Subsequently, in December 1931 in the journal, *Bolshevik*, a team of scholars from the Institute of Red Professors extensively vilified all Shlyapnikov's writings on revolutionary history, calling their publication a mistake. His histories were deemed a

---

[1] Holmes 1979, p. 229.
[2] Holmes 1979, pp. 232–8; Shliapnikov 1927a, p. 84. Critics included D. Kin, A. Divil'kovskii and A. Lomakin.

'Menshevik falsification' and the editors who allowed their publication were guilty of 'rotten liberalism' (Stalin's term).[3]

For those who did not read party historical and theoretical journals, in January 1932 *Pravda* published an article by historians condemning Shliapnikov's memoirs for paying insufficient attention to Stalin's role in 1917 and incorrectly analysing Stalin's role and that of other actors in the revolutionary events. Insisting that the charges had not been proven, Shliapnikov accused his critics of not understanding what they had read.[4] In February, however, the Orgburo summoned him to attend a meeting at which his books and his own role in history were excoriated by members of the Orgburo, the CCC, the OGPU and by guests from the Institute of Red Professors. His attempt at self-defence was received as further confirmation of his guilt. The Orgburo resolved to stop publishing and distributing his works and to require that he acknowledge his errors in them or be expelled from the party.[5]

Shliapnikov appealed against the Orgburo's decision to the Politburo. Asserting that Lenin had not objected to his books, he was certain that many of his critics had not read them and pointed out that some of them had not even been Bolsheviks in 1917. Despite his request that the Politburo allow him to eliminate from his books passages that allowed 'incorrect interpretation', the Politburo confirmed the Orgburo's decision and gave him five days to comply.[6] Subsequently, Shliapnikov acknowledged mistakes in his memoirs of 1917, but in language that made his errors appear less grievous. For example, instead of the Orgburo's assertion that he had 'denied the hegemony of the proletariat', he wrote that he had poorly formulated his ideas, which had led some to conclude that he had denied the proletariat's hegemony. Nevertheless, the 'confession' as it appeared in *Pravda* on 9 March changed his claim of having been

---

3 Stalin 1931, p. 12; Holmes 1979, pp. 239–40; Barber 1976, pp. 21–41; Shliapnikov 1992, vol. 1, pp. 22–3; Holmes 1979, p. 241; Shcherbakov et al. 1931, p. 123.
4 Pospelov et al. 1932; Zlokazov 1994, no. 3, pp. 196–211, Shliapnikov's January 1932 letter to the *Pravda* editorial board. The 6 February 1932 letter of the *Pravda* editors to the Orgburo is preserved in RGASPI, f. 589, op. 3, d. 9103, vol. 3, ll. 88–96, and has been published in Demidionova and Shliapnikova (eds.) 1997, pp. 123–4.
5 Demidionova and Shliapnikova (eds.) 1997, pp. 103–25, Shliapnikov's notes from this 19 February meeting; RGASPI, f. 17, op. 3, d. 874, l. 15, 19 February 1932.
6 RGASPI, f. 589, op. 3, d. 9103, vol. 3, ll. 82–7, letter from Shliapnikov to the Politburo, 26 February 1932, published in Demidionova and Shliapnikova (eds.) 1997, pp. 114–18; RGASPI, f. 17, op. 3, d. 874, 3 March 1932, p. 2 (published in Getty and Naumov 1999, pp. 105–6). He asked for permission to continue publishing new works; these included his Civil War memoirs and his World War I-era correspondence with Lenin (RGASPI, f. 134, op. 1, d. 437, l. 12, letter to Kollontai, 20 May 1930).

misunderstood to a cruder and more thorough repentance. Kaganovich may have dictated this 'confession'.[7] Secondary and tertiary literature has gone so far as to interpret the March 1932 statement as a repudiation of all his former oppositional stances in party discussions. In fact, the original statement Shlyapnikov wrote and signed was not even a complete repudiation of his memoirs.

Kollontai tried to console Shlyapnikov, telling him that in Sweden his works were still popular. Expressing ironic surprise, he replied that in the USSR, interest in his books was two-sided: 'some zealously seek them out and don't find them, since they apparently are sold out', while others subjected both the memoirs and the author to 'medieval' forms of criticism. He nevertheless continued to write, despite knowing that his books were 'already out of fashion' and 'without any real hope that [they] will see light anytime soon'.[8] His books were no longer issued and were destroyed or confined to restricted access in libraries (accessible only to highly trusted party members). Shlyapnikov's career had been disrupted by the attacks on his memoirs, but he needed work to feel useful and support his growing family (a third child, Alexander, was born in 1932). In June 1932, several months after his books were banned, he was appointed to membership in the Gosplan RSFSR Presidium, as director of the construction sector. Although this was not a position of great responsibility, it attested that party leaders wanted to employ him in some capacity. There was still sympathy towards him at the highest levels and respect for his organisational and planning skills.

The Ryutin Affair

Nevertheless, Shlyapnikov like all former oppositionists, was vulnerable due to Stalin's increasingly paranoid insecurity in the face of resistance to collectivisation, widespread famine that killed millions and dissatisfaction within the party over problems related to intensive industrialisation. Shlyapnikov was to some extent aware of these problems. In an April 1932 diary entry, he referenced rumours about 'ferment among workers' in the Donbas, Vychuga and Ivanovo-Voznesensk. He had heard stories about Ukrainians fleeing

---

7 Demidionova and Shliapnikova (eds.) 1997, pp. 104, 123–4 (Shliapnikov's 6 March statement to the CC); Naumov 1991, p. 59.
8 RGASPI, f. 134, op. 1, d. 437, ll. 30–1, Moscow, 21 February 1932 (his last surviving letter to Kollontai).

across the border: 'over there horses neigh, cows moo, and sheep bleat; roosters crow in the morning; at night the youth have fun, sing songs... but on our side?... dead silence'.[9] These briefly jotted notes must have signified his perception that Stalin's policies were deeply flawed. Other party members knew more and were deeply agitated. In 1932 three oppositional groups were discovered (the Ryutin group, the Eismont-Tolmachev-Smirnov group maintaining Bukharinist views and another group allegedly associated with Trotsky) that expressed discontent within the party over collectivisation. Stalin's irrational fears magnified the threat he perceived from 'enemies' within and outside the party and contributed to determined efforts to root out and punish dissent.

In autumn 1932 Martemyan Ryutin circulated a treatise criticising collectivisation and attacking Stalin's leadership, about which the CCC questioned former oppositionists, including Medvedev. The press had reported a dubious link between Ryutin's supporters and the Workers' Opposition. Shlyapnikov, who was in Kislovodsk on holiday, wrote that the Ryutin affair had created a sensation there. No one in Kislovodsk had seen Ryutin's platform, but diverse rumours about it were circulating. Shlyapnikov doubted that Ryutin and his supporters were united closely in views and suspected they had poorly prepared their act. He nevertheless recognised that Ryutin's criticisms reflected a general state of dissatisfaction within the party and government over important policies. He had observed that in Kislovodsk, senior and mid-level bureaucrats talked about 'reform' during walks in the park, where they were less likely to be overheard and informed upon.[10] Party leaders feared that private expressions of discontent would lead to factionalism. Although Stalin called for the death penalty for Ryutin and his allies, CCC and Politburo majorities voted instead to strip them of their party membership and transfer them to work outside of Moscow. Before the opening of Soviet archives, many historians thought that this and other disagreements between Stalin and Politburo members signified that there were moderate and radical wings within the leadership in the early 1930s. The Russian historian, Oleg Khlevnyuk, has cast doubt on this interpretation, arguing instead that any differences emerged from bureaucratic politics and turf wars.[11]

---

9   TsA FSB, R33718, d. 499061, vol. 14, Shliapnikov's diary entry for 21 April 1932 (the original handwritten diary is now in the family's possession).
10 TsA FSB, R33718, d. 499061, vol. 42, ll. 203–5, Medvedev's notes about a 25 October 1932 meeting with Iaroslavskii; vol. 43, l. 205, letter from Shliapnikov to Medvedev, 16 October 1932.
11 Cohen 1980, pp. 343–4; Wynn 2008, pp. 97–117; Khlevniuk 2008.

Housing Scandal

Not only high-level political unrest, but even minor disputes between neighbours brought Shlyapnikov to the CCC's attention. A minor housing dispute in the residential cooperative where he lived, and in which he was an elected

FIGURE 33   *3/1 Spasopeskovsky Lane, Moscow, 1972. Alexander Shlyapnikov, his wife, and their children lived in an apartment in this building in the 1930s (provided by the Shlyapnikov family).*

FIGURE 34   *3/1 Spasopeskovsky Lane, Moscow, 2012 (photo by Barbara Allen).*

administrator, entangled him in late 1932 and early 1933. This incident conveys both the importance Shlyapnikov placed on 'legality' and how the CCC attributed political significance to seemingly mundane matters. After a member of the cooperative, who as a physician had belonged to the pre-revolutionary intelligentsia, was arrested on political charges, two rooms in his apartment were given to a party official, outside of the formal process and by means of the CC members' intervention. When the physician returned with permission to live in Moscow, he appealed for the return of the rooms. Shlyapnikov and other cooperative administrators, as well as court officials, attempted to follow cooperative guidelines and established legal procedures in settling the matter, whereupon the party official who occupied the rooms accused Shlyapnikov of defending a counterrevolutionary element. The CCC, in a decision guided by Yaroslavsky, rebuked Shlyapnikov for committing a political mistake.[12] Before the affair ended, it became so tense that a courtyard dispute between Shlyapnikov and a drunken guest of the party official, concerning the guest's illegally parked car, also came before the CCC. Despite the character references Shlyapnikov presented not only for himself but also for his German shepherd puppy (accused of menacing the party official's guests), Yaroslavsky assigned him primary responsibility for the dispute.[13] In defending even his dog from prosecution, Shlyapnikov poked fun at the CCC, but his humour was not appreciated there, especially in the wake of the Ryutin affair.

Scandal Over a Speech in Gosplan RSFSR

On the eve of the 1933 purge, distrust and hysteria over dissent grew within the party and individual members began to fear exclusion from its ranks. Shlyapnikov came under attack not only in his housing cooperative, but, more significantly, at his workplace. In January 1933 he was pilloried for remarks he allegedly made at a Gosplan RSFSR party-cell meeting. The affair began when the Gosplan RSFSR party cell met on 27–8 January to discuss the results of the January CC plenum.[14] Mikhail Rogov, the chair of Gosplan RSFSR, gave the main report. With no stenographer to type a complete transcript of everyone's speeches, a cell secretary took notes and composed a protocol (summary)

---

12   RGASPI, f. 589, d. 9103, vol. 5, ll. 214–29. Shlyapnikov lived at 3/1 Spasopeskovskii pereulok, Arbat.
13   RGASPI, f. 589, d. 9103, vol. 5, ll. 146–76. A female neighbour testified that she had never witnessed the dog behaving in a hostile manner.
14   TsAODM, f. 390 (Gosplan RSFSR), op. 1, d. 8, l. 1. The cell had 109 members and 12 candidates. Of those, 86 members and six candidates attended on 27 January and 83 members and eight candidates on 28 January. In the presidium were Rogov, Solov'ev, Golikov, Chuprakov, Kartashev and Kuliabichev. In addition, Mosgorkom and Bauman *raikom* personnel attended on 28 January. Total numbers of cell members may also include staff from the RSFSR Economic Accounting Board (UNKhU).

of the meeting, the accuracy of which Shliapnikov would later contest.[15] Shliapnikov's remarks were impromptu, made on the urging of a cell member, M.N. Smirnov, who probably was setting him up. After speaking, he immediately left to attend a meeting of the Astrakhan Civil-War Fellowship [*zemlyachestvo*] at the Red Army House, so he was not present to rebut the criticism of his speech.[16] If he sought solace in recalling past adventures with old comrades, however, nostalgia did not permit him to escape efforts to scapegoat him for intra-party dissension.

Among Shliapnikov's alleged controversial statements were: 1) that his discussion of political questions would provide an instructive example to younger party members; 2) that the October Revolution gave nothing to the poor peasant [*bedniak*]; and 3) that discussion within the party was acceptable. After Shliapnikov left, Smirnov condemned him, claiming that he approved of individual disagreement with party decisions. Another cell member also criticised him and called on others to join in, but subsequent speakers either did not answer the call or only did so half-heartedly. At that point, the chair, Golikov, postponed the meeting until the following day.[17]

On that day, 28 January, Shliapnikov had left his office in mid-afternoon to run errands. As he made his way home in the evening, a Gosplan RSFSR party organiser caught up with him and asked him to return to Gosplan, since there were speeches against him in the party cell. At the cell he was presented with a version of his speech from the day before, which he insisted was incorrect. In his presence, eight speakers harshly criticised him, while eight criticised him mildly and ten said nothing at all about him. Meteletskaya, a hardline Stalinist from the Moscow city party committee [*Mosgorkom*], criticised him especially harshly and attempted to rouse others present to do so as well.[18] Shliapnikov denied having said what was attributed to him. Asserting that he had had no differences with the party since 1927, he challenged his critics to provide

---

15 RGASPI, f. 589, op. 3, d. 9103, vol. 5, ll. 371–5. Shliapnikov later alleged that the speech attributed to him at the January 1933 Gosplan RSFSR party-cell meeting was composed by a cell technical secretary who, as a former tsarist officer, feared expulsion and who indeed was purged. (RGASPI, f. 589, op. 3, d. 9103, vol. 5, ll. 56–9; and TsA FSB, R33718, d. 499061, vol. 14, ll. 92–9, both copies dated 20 July 1933.)

16 TsAODM, f. 390, op. 1, d. 8, l. 88 and RGASPI, f. 589, op. 3, d. 9103, vol. 5, ll. 366–7, 3 February 1933 letter from Shliapnikov to the Gosplan RSFSR party-cell bureau, the Bauman raikom and the Mosgorkom.

17 TsAODM, f. 390, op. 1, d. 8, ll. 1–5.

18 TsAODM, f. 390, op. 1, d. 8, ll. 1–5, 88 and RGASPI, f. 589, op. 3, d. 9103, vol. 5, ll. 366–7, 3 February 1933 letter from Shliapnikov to the Gosplan RSFSR party-cell bureau, to Bauman raikom and to Mosgorkom.

evidence that he had doubted party policy on collectivisation or the five-year plans. When asked whether the party could trust him, he responded that party members should be trusted in the absence of proof that they had conducted anti-party work.[19] His interpretation of party regulations thus countered that advanced by Stalin and was a threat to it.

Those present unanimously condemned Shliapnikov for making 'anti-party assertions', for 'not giving full criticism to his former mistakes' and for not providing an unambiguous condemnation of groups within the party that criticised Stalin's policies. Further, the cell removed him as leader of his study circle on the January CC plenum's decisions. Meteletskaya reported indignantly to the CCC that Shliapnikov had made even more anti-party errors, some party members did not denounce him and cell members had not responded adequately to her call to condemn all those who did not comment on his speech. Moreover, the cell's final resolution was far milder than she desired. She thus concluded that the cell was rotten with 'Philistine conciliationist moods'.[20] Employing the rhetoric needed at that time to survive and advance, she also voiced party leaders' concern with the challenge that strong patron-client relations [*semeistvennost*] posed to the party's control over other institutions.[21]

Having reconstituted from memory his 27 January speech, Shliapnikov sent it to the Gosplan RSFSR party cell. In it he expressed support for party policy on collectivisation and industrialisation and condemned groups led by Ryutin and Alexander Smirnov. When referring to his past oppositional struggle, he insisted that he did not violate the spirit of party statutes [*partiinost*]. He furthermore agreed that party members must implement plenum decisions like military orders. He nevertheless emphasised that he preferred to discuss doubts within a party assembly rather than hold critical conversations in the corridor, as some cell members carried on. He must have meant to imply that pressure to conform did not create true unity within the party. Clarifying his thoughts on the poor peasants, he explained that the aid they had received from the Soviet government before collectivisation did not help them emerge from poverty, but that collectivisation offered more promising results. When he compared the political sections being created under collectivisation to those that were created during the Civil War, he said, he had specified their creation under 'different conditions'. He thus refuted allegations that he had

---

19 RGASPI, f. 589, op. 3, d. 9103, vol. 5, ll. 378–82. Shliapnikov personally verified and signed the 28 January stenographic report. His corrections included striking out the phrase, 'I have waged factional struggle since 1906'.
20 TsAODM, f. 390, op. 1, d. 8, ll. 1–5; RGASPI, f. 589, op. 3, d. 9103, vol. 5, ll. 371–7.
21 Fitzpatrick 2005; Rigby 1990; Gill 1990; Getty 2013.

accused the party of intending 'to wage civil war with the whole peasantry' by means of political sections.²²

In his attempt to overturn the cell's condemnation of him, Shlyapnikov objected that those who had spoken most sharply against him had not even been present when he made his first speech, while many fellow cell members had been reluctant to attack. Subverting Stalinist discourse, he asserted that when Meteletskaya engaged in distortions, she was 'unmasked' – the cell 'rebuffed' her. He usually avoided such language, but employed it sardonically here. Insisting that he had been condemned on the basis of an incorrect protocol, he added for corroboration the cell secretary's recognition that the protocol had been 'conducted inattentively'. Finally, turning the tables on his accusers, he suggested that they might have attributed to him 'their own thoughts' in order to offer them for consideration 'in the guise of struggle with them'.²³

Rejecting Shlyapnikov's written recounting of his original speech, the bureau of the Gosplan RSFSR party cell unanimously resolved to request that he revise it to include the phrase, 'anti-Marxist conversations and thoughts [are] not dangerous for the party at assemblies'. He instead continued to ridicule the distortions. Anyone who knew his past positions, he said, would realise that he was usually criticised for saying the opposite of what had been ascribed to him. He also rebuked his accusers for not having a sense of humour. Insisting that his correction should replace the distorted one in the official record, he exclaimed: 'This is the established right of each party comrade and until now, nowhere has it been called into question'. He argued that it had always been custom in the party to allow speakers to verify and approve their remarks before they were entered into the record: 'Even a stenographic record can only serve as a document after it has been signed'. He professed not to understand why his 1921–2 mistakes were being dredged up: 'What do you want to achieve by working over these things now? ... I was sent here for work and not for an ordeal'.²⁴ He thus gave determined battle against changes in party procedures that served Stalin's interests by transforming the party into his personal vehicle for holding onto power. The final battle still lay ahead, during the upcoming party purge.

---

22   RGASPI, f. 589, op. 3, d. 9103, vol. 5, ll. 366–70; TsA FSB, R33718, d. 499061, vol. 14, l. 16; TsAODM, f. 390, op. 1, d. 8, l. 88.
23   TsAODM, f. 390, op. 1, d. 8, l. 88 and RGASPI, f. 589, op. 3, d. 9103, vol. 5, ll. 366–7.
24   RGASPI, f. 589, op. 3, d. 9103, vol. 5, l. 360, protocol (excerpt) of a Gosplan RSFSR 15 February party-cell bureau meeting with party activists; ll. 361–5, personally verified transcript of Shliapnikov's speech.

Shlyapnikov's Purge from the Party

The 1933 party purge took place against the backdrop of horrifying, large-scale famine in the countryside, resistance among rural communists to the 1932 grain collection and a rise in worker unrest that posed a potential danger to the party's claim to rule in the name of the proletariat. In a panicked atmosphere, Stalin worried that his old intra-party rivals could take advantage of disorders to mobilise resistance to his rule. At the January 1933 CC plenum he therefore called for 'vigilance' towards those who could facilitate 'a revival of the activities of defeated groups of the old counter-revolutionary parties', among which he included the Trotskyists and 'Right deviationists'.[25] His warning set the tone for the 1933 purge, in which party members were only subject to expulsion, not execution as in the Terror of 1936–8, but which nevertheless foreshadowed it in some ways.

According to April 1933 guidelines, the purge was to target 'double-dealers', 'alien elements' and other categories. Almost one-fifth of party members were eventually excluded as a result. The largest single group targeted consisted of 'inactive' party members, while former oppositionists supposedly were a small minority. Official categories, however, most likely failed to reveal the extent of the purge's political character. The party had already established a pattern of using purges to cull dissenters. In the 1920s purges and quotas were assigned and categories devised in order to 'camouflage the charge of Trotskyism'. It was therefore difficult to determine the actual reasons for individual expulsions based on the statistical categories provided by the party.[26] For example, Shlyapnikov had helped oversee the 1921 purge but could not prevent the purging of his political supporters, under cover of other charges.

After the Gosplan RSFSR party cell purged Shlyapnikov in June 1933, he appealed directly to Stalin, indicating where he saw ultimate authority resting, but the leader deflected his request and forced him to make three separate applications to successively higher commissions. In all, he met with four levels of purge commissions (cell, district, region and central). To each commission, he recounted in detail his work on behalf of the party; he refused to make a wholesale condemnation of his previous stands or to characterise them as linked. Demanding evidence for the charges against him, he employed sarcasm and irony. His dialogue with purge-commission members reflected an

---

25 Kuromiya 2005, p. 110; Rossman 2005.
26 McNeal, (ed.) 1974, vol. 3, pp. 124–9; Getty 1985, p. 51; Getty and Naumov 1999, pp. 127–8 (depending on a 1971 Soviet source); David-Fox 1997, p. 158. Central Purge Commission members included Rudzutak, Kaganovich, Kirov, Ezhov, Iaroslavskii and Shkiriatov.

alternative understanding of the spirit of party regulations [*partiinost*] and a stance that lay somewhere between resistance and compliance.[27] He wanted to remain within the party, but not at the cost of smearing his political past. During these months, he suffered 50 percent hearing loss, which limited his ability to respond to charges against him and contributed to his obvious exhaustion by the end of each purge session.

In Shlyapnikov's case, members of higher-level commissions participated in the proceedings of lower-level commissions and *vice versa*. As was customary, some of the proceedings were open to spectators (almost certainly the cell-level purge session was), including people who were not party members, for purge hearings were supposed to provide lessons to a broader party and sometimes non-party audience.[28] Shlyapnikov and commission members thus spoke not only to one another, but also addressed a broader audience.

In Gosplan RSFSR, the party purge began on 8 June 1933. According to Ivanov, the chair of the purge commission, Shlyapnikov appeared for his purge that day and tried to teach commission members how earlier purges had been conducted, but then he left early and did not appear on the second day. Providing a doctor's note, he asked to postpone his purge due to illness. Reportedly, he said that the CCC would purge him, not the cell. Nevertheless, his Gosplan RSFSR purge session was held on 17 June 1933.[29] Those carrying out the purge intended for him to discuss moments when he had held minority views in party discussions and to prove his devotion to the party in 1933. Insisting that there was more to his party history than those moments of opposition, he spoke for almost two hours, with surprisingly few interruptions, about his childhood, youth and pre-revolutionary party activism. Recounting his childhood, he emphasised experiences of oppression even more strongly than in earlier autobiographies. Twice he compared tsarist oppression of

---

[27] For essays on the suitability of the term 'resistance' to characterise the views, stances and behaviour of individuals and groups in Russian and Soviet political history, see David-Fox *et al.* (eds.) 2003.

[28] Pirani 2008 noted audiences of non-party workers at cell purge meetings in 1921. Shearer 1996 noted that in 1930 'purge hearings were public spectacles and officials were required to attend' (Shearer 1996, p. 203).

[29] RGASPI, f. 589, op. 3, d. 9103, vol. 5, ll. 1–51, stenographic report of the Gosplan RSFSR party cell assembly on the purge of Shliapnikov, 17 June 1933; ll. 353–5, undated letter (copy) from Gosplan purge commission chair Ivanov to Knorin, oblast' purge commission chair. Antropov and Shillert were other members of the Gosplan purge commission. Peters and Sol'ts from the Moscow region (oblast') commission participated. Vil'gel'm Knorin was director of the Institute of Red Professors in the 1930s, a *Pravda* editorial board member and chief editor of a 1935 textbook on party history.

him as an Old Believer and revolutionary to tsarist-era anti-Semitism and to pogromist violence. Emphasising his own consistent loyalty to the Bolsheviks, he noted that some of those purging him had been in other parties before the revolution.

Shlyapnikov was determined to run the purge hearings as much on his own terms as possible. When the chair impatiently interrupted to remind him that he should describe how he 'struggled with the party', he objected that he 'struggled more with the capitalists'. As he recounted numerous adventures in the wartime revolutionary underground, Yakov Peters (from the Moscow region purge commission) grew indignant: 'You are talking history, telling all kinds of stories; this is not what a purge demands'. Purge-commission members pressed him to acknowledge that he had rejected the dictatorship of the proletariat in late 1917, when he joined the call for a coalition government of socialist parties represented in the soviets. Disagreeing, he pointed out that he did not resign from his post then. Confronted with a demand to characterise his mistake as 'panic' in a political sense, he jokingly parried that he was not a person who was easily frightened. In another assertive moment, he scolded Peters for having a weak grasp of history.[30]

When the chair insisted that Shlyapnikov confine himself to the topic of his 'struggle with the party', he drolly complained: 'You are only interested in the negatives, but not in the positive things that I contributed to our party'. He vaunted his military leadership during the Civil War and his international trade-union work. Refusing to vilify the Workers' Opposition, he maintained that its proposals derived from the 1919 party programme and asserted that its only mistake had been failure to realise that trade-union management of production was premature in the early 1920s. Reiterating that its vision was just not realistic at the time, he further explained that he and his comrades had learned a lesson from the Tenth Party Congress: 'The logic of factional struggle is that having orchestrated it, you cannot freely manoeuvre once it has ended. Therefore we learned a lesson, not to repeat factional groupings in the future'.[31] Fraught with meaning, this statement may have signified that all his political actions after 1921 were oriented towards pursuing a different means than factional struggle for disseminating his ideas.

The purge commission pressured Shlyapnikov to designate the 'Letter of the 22' an act of factionalism, but he denied this, insisting it was only 'group work'. As those present discussed the definition of factionalism, the chair Ivanov opined that a faction did not have to be large, that only three people

---

30   RGASPI, f. 589, op. 3, d. 9103, vol. 5, ll. 17–24, 33.
31   RGASPI, f. 589, op. 3, d. 9103, vol. 5, ll. 12–16.

could constitute one. Defending himself, Shlyapnikov pointed out that, at the Eleventh Party Congress Solts, (present at that session) did not vote to exclude him for factionalism. Ivanov was disturbed. When Shlyapnikov insouciantly continued: 'I do not want to compromise comrade Solts due to his goodwill towards me', noise ensued among participants. Although Shlyapnikov seemed to be tiring, he did not let up on Solts. When Solts badgered him about misrepresenting his early 1920s activities, Shlyapnikov retorted that Solts also knew how to conduct factional work in the 1920s.[32]

Commission members tried to link him with Trotsky, Zinoviev and Kamenev in the United Opposition, but Shlyapnikov denied any connection. Other episodes, such as his dealings with Myasnikov in 1923 and Medvedev's 1924 'Baku letter' were reviewed, as were Shlyapnikov's own political articles in intra-party discussions in 1924–6. Finally, the charge of double-dealing [dvurushnichestvo] was introduced; this meant that one continued to struggle against the party line while paying formal lip service to it. Defiantly, Shlyapnikov insisted that it only appeared so if selected episodes were examined, but not if the entirety of his work were considered. The commission only touched upon his work in Gosplan RSFSR near the very end of the session. He admitted that he worked 'very little' in Gosplan because of his deafness. Indeed, his hearing worsened during the course of the purge session. Despite his deafness and weariness, when requested to present a document 'that would actually and fully criticise severely your position for the whole period of your struggle', Shlyapnikov retorted: 'No one has assigned me such literary work'. In exasperation, someone asked: 'Didn't you think of it yourself?' When the commission called for criticism of his work in Gosplan, Shlyapnikov asked to be excused because he felt ill and could not hear.[33]

The Gosplan RSFSR purge commission excluded Shlyapnikov from the party for double-dealing. It found him guilty of having diverged from the party ever since the October 1917 Revolution, asserted that he had 'spoken together with Trotskyists and Right opportunists', and accused him of having worked poorly at Gosplan RSFSR. In purges of the NEP era, party members purged for political reasons were often charged with 'incompetence' in work; by 1930, one historian has argued: 'there were no longer any clear distinctions between professional and political behaviour'.[34] Shlyapnikov was charged with political errors and poor work, but of all charges, the party-cell purge commission spent the

---

32   RGASPI, f. 589, op. 3, d. 9103, vol. 5, ll. 4–12.
33   RGASPI, f. 589, op. 3, d. 9103, vol. 5, ll. 1–10.
34   RGASPI, f. 589, op. 3, d. 9103, vol. 5, l. 52; David-Fox 1997, p. 158; Shearer 1996, p. 203.

least time developing that of malfeasance in his work, perhaps due to lack of corroboration.

Shlyapnikov read of his purge in *Pravda* before he received the official notification necessary for appeal. A campaign in the party press depicted him as a 'consummate double-dealer'. After finally receiving formal notification, he appealed in writing directly to Stalin, requesting that the Politburo reconsider his case. Explaining that deafness had interfered with his ability to defend himself, he also reminded Stalin that Kaganovich and Stalin himself had assigned him to work in Gosplan RSFSR, despite the reservations of its chair, Rogov, that there was not enough work to do. Shlyapnikov defended his work as construction-sector chief, as having placed that sector fifth among 17 Gosplan RSFSR sectors according to quality of work. Moreover, no one had criticised his work until the purge campaign began. Stalin forwarded his appeal to the Central Purge Commission, which forced him to appeal to the next highest commission.[35]

Within a few days, Shlyapnikov appealed to the Bauman district (*raion*) purge commission. Disputing the commission's assertion that he had 'conducted struggle against the party' since October 1917 'without interruption', he detailed everything he had done to help the party. Denying charges of factionalism, he argued: 'I committed all my mistakes within the party and resolved them through the party'. He thought the fact that the party had continued to assign him work in the 1920s indicated its trust in him. Defending his work in Gosplan RSFSR, he insisted that the Bauman commission misunderstood the nature of his work there, which was strictly related to planning and not at all to 'operative' work. Finally, he urged that purge-commission members verify his good work in Gosplan RSFSR by consulting the records.[36]

Before the Bauman district purge commission, Shlyapnikov did not repeat the life story he had recounted at the cell purge session, but dwelled on the period after 1917. Again, he had difficulty hearing. He made a concerted effort to refute the charges of continuity in his political struggle, pointing out that he only spoke out during times of political discussion within the party, and that factions were not even formed around some of the documents he signed, such as that of the People's Commissars in 1917. Moreover, he rejected any links between his views and those of the *kulaks* or 'capitalist elements', for even when he had erred, he had done so in the sincere belief that he was trying to

---

35   RGASPI, f. 589, op. 3, d. 9103, vol. 5, ll. 53–4; TsA FSB, R33718, d. 499061, vol. 14, l. 17, 15 July 1933.

36   RGASPI, f. 589, op. 3, d. 9103, vol. 5, ll. 56–72; TsA FSB, R33718, d. 499061, vol. 14, ll. 92–9, 20 July 1933.

'defend workers'. Surely, he argued, the fact that the party accepted the Workers' Opposition's proposals on improving workers' living conditions attested that he had not consistently been at odds with the party. Investigations of him in the 1920s failed to find him guilty of factional struggle, he reminded those judging him. Despite his efforts, the district purge commission confirmed the cell purge commission's decision to exclude Shlyapnikov, added charges pertaining to his memoir-histories and declared that he had 'decisively broken with Bolshevism and stays in the party because it is the only party and is in power'.[37]

Obstinately, Shlyapnikov appealed to the Moscow region (*oblast*) purge commission. He accused Bauman district commission members of incompetence, 'malicious desire and personal enmity'. Relying on documents to refute the accusations, he expressed indignation that the commission did not consult the documents when it accused him. Disavowing any links to the Trotskyists or the Rightists, he also refused to accept the commission's conflation of the two groups. Regarding his memoirs of 1917, he found it unnecessary to condemn him for these, as he already had acknowledged his mistakes in public. The commission, he wrote, engaged in 'fortune-telling' when it interpreted his earlier admissions of errors as 'double-dealing' undertaken in order to allow him to continue 'attacks against the party'.[38]

Shlyapnikov's meeting with the Moscow region purge commission in early September 1933 began confrontationally, with his declaration that he was 'especially upset' by the district purge commission's depiction of him as if he were 'still engaging in factional work'. Commission members attributed this to a typographical error, but added that they did regard him as still in 'divergence' from party policy. Shlyapnikov demanded documented proof of his divergence. His interrogators replied variously: that it was up to him to prove he was not in divergence (P.N. Karavaev) and that the purge commission was not a court (Peters). Shlyapnikov disagreed, calling it a 'party court'. As before, he insisted: 'I struggled inside the party, not against the party'. Solts intoned that it was not necessary 'to prove by some juridical route' whether a member should be purged. Instead, the matter 'is decided on the basis of party conscience'. Konstantin Gei faulted him for holding 'juridical' rather than 'political' conversations with the purge commissions, for defending himself rather than 'disarming'. For Gei, self-defence signaled that Shlyapnikov still held to

---

37   RGASPI, f. 589, op. 3, d. 9103, vol. 5, ll. 60–84. Gei chaired; other members were Varlen and Leonov.
38   RGASPI, f. 589, op. 3, d. 9103, vol. 5, ll. 85–92; TsA FSB, R33718, d. 499061, vol. 14.

his old views.[39] Molotov had likewise accused Tomsky of acting like a 'cunning lawyer' when he defended himself in 1932 against charges of forming a faction.[40] Such ironic charges against esteemed proletarians reflected the hysteria and irrationality of the time.

Shlyapnikov asserted that if there were no documents proving the charges, then 'personal enmity' must lie behind them. Calling him a degenerate [*pererozhdenets*] for thinking so, Peters assured him that any enmity he felt was 'only according to party regulations'. Shlyapnikov drily replied: 'That is very pleasant'. Solts admitted to 'extraordinary interest' in Shlyapnikov's purge because he had a long party history, continuing: 'We live in such a grandiose period that if a party member does not manifest his commitment, he is not a party member ... In such a time, in such a great time, about which we have dreamed so many years, comrade Shlyapnikov strikes an ironic pose'. Shlyapnikov still had trouble hearing at this session, but Solts deemed his complaints of illness and 'weakened emotions' to be 'trifles'. Addressing Shlyapnikov, Solts proclaimed: 'your heart is empty ... each time I meet you, I become more convinced that you are hopeless and this worries me'.[41]

Escalating the charges, Vilgelm Knorin proposed to designate Shlyapnikov a Menshevik and 'enemy of the party' outright, rather than 'an inoffensive Philistine [*meshchanin* and *obyvatel*]', as some 'comrades' preferred. Moreover, he wanted to declare Shlyapnikov's very appeal to be 'an anti-party document'. Understanding that some favoured a measure of leniency, Shlyapnikov offered to be more active in the Moscow party organisation. Spurning his offer, Filatov declared he had 'entered a dead-end street'. Shlyapnikov obstinately maintained:

> I have been in the party 33 years. Half of them I have not had a party card. If I am deprived of a party card, then this will alter nothing. I won't be different. I have no convictions that are not of the working class.

When Filatov told him that he was already transformed, Shlyapnikov retorted: 'If I have changed, then at least I am not like you, but am true to myself'. At this point, he was told to leave. Then Solts insisted that the decision emphasise that he was being purged not only for past offences, but also for the present.

---

39 RGASPI, f. 589, op. 3, d. 9103, vol. 5, ll. 110–19; 4 September 1933. Knorin, Peters, Karavaev, Sol'ts, Filatov and Ivanov attended.
40 Wynn 2008, pp. 110–11.
41 RGASPI, f. 589, op. 3, d. 9103, vol. 5, ll. 103–8, 114–15. Halfin has explored the 'eschatological' party mindset in many publications.

PURGED FROM THE PARTY 327

The others agreed. The final decision proclaimed that Shlyapnikov 'continues double-dealing' and 'continues to defend the Workers' Opposition, which was born of trade-unionist Menshevism', that his 'appeal is a deeply anti-party document'. Nevertheless, it did not designate him as a Menshevik outright.[42]

The final court of appeal was the Central Purge Commission; Shlyapnikov met with its secretariat on 29 September 1933. As the meeting began, he set the tone by asking with irony why the CC and CCC had not noticed earlier that he 'conducted anti-party work for 16 years'. Yaroslavsky held forth: 'Shlyapnikov still doesn't understand what is demanded of him ... He says he was sick ... It's no misfortune if Shlyapnikov lives one year less, if he would live as a true party member [*partiets*], having corrected his behaviour in the eyes of party members'. The chair of the Gosplan RSFSR party-cell purge commission, perhaps defensively, asserted that his commission had not treated Shlyapnikov unfairly, that unlike all others, he was allowed to talk about his life for two hours. Regretting that Shlyapnikov's assistant, Shcherbakov, had refused to criticise Shlyapnikov's work in Gosplan RSFSR, he noted that Shcherbakov was 'raked over the coals' for this. Shcherbakov's honesty and loyalty to Shlyapnikov was thus punished by those responsible for setting up the case against him. Members of the Central Purge Commission all rebuked Shlyapnikov for having insufficiently criticised his past mistakes and for behaviour unsuitable for a party member. Continuing to object, Shlyapnikov admitted that some of his mistakes arose from 'pride'. Finally, however, he humbly requested that they help him 'get onto the path'.[43] Multiple hearings had worn down his resistance.

At this point, Nikolai Yezhov, who led the party purge, intervened and spoke at length. Emphasising that recognition by Shlyapnikov of past errors had always been followed by new ones, he condemned the older revolutionary for having insufficiently 'fought for the party's general line'. The party had been 'patient' with him because he was 'an old party member, a worker, a cultured worker', on whose 'upbringing' the 'party spent a lot'. Acknowledging that Shlyapnikov had also worked hard ['*svoim gorbom*'] and had accomplished feats, such as writing books, that were beyond many workers, Yezhov nevertheless accused him of 'constantly abusing' the party's patience by using his talents and strength 'only in struggle against the party'. For Yezhov, the need to 'bring up young party members in the correct spirit' clinched Shlyapnikov's exclusion from the party. Yezhov allowed that he might enter the party again

---

42 RGASPI, f. 589, op. 3, d. 9103, vol. 5, ll. 93–100; l. 120, 10 September 1933.
43 RGASPI, f. 589, op. 3, d. 9103, vol. 5, ll. 122–44, 29 September 1933. Besides Shliapnikov, those who spoke were Shkiriatov, Iaroslavskii, Stasova, Ivanov, Shillert, Sol'ts, Ezhov and Knorin. I did not find a written appeal from Shliapnikov to the Central Purge Commission.

in the future.⁴⁴ Shliapnikov's final words revealed the toll the purge had taken on him:

> If you think that I possess any capabilities needed by the party, that I am not ballast, then I ask you to help me to get onto the path. My nerves are shattered. Do you think it is easy to endure this nervous strain? I am losing my hearing. You know about my moral state ... I believe that I am not at all the person that you are exposing me as ... I do not regard myself as outside the party. No matter your decision, I will remain a party member.

Expressing hope that the highest purge commission would overturn the decisions of the lower ones, he then departed. But the Central Purge Commission confirmed his exclusion from the party as a double-dealer and a degenerate, guilty of 'Menshevik vacillations'.⁴⁵

Many Old Bolsheviks were purged in 1933. Shliapnikov's comrade, Medvedev, made his bitterness clear towards those sitting in judgement of him. Excluding him as a 'bourgeois degenerate', purge-commission members absurdly charged that although he was a proletarian, he acted in a 'lordly' manner.⁴⁶ Upon learning of his friend's purge, Shliapnikov, who was on holiday in Kislovodsk, wrote him a message of condolence. He mocked charges in the press that Medvedev had undermined the work of the Commissariat of Heavy Industry, even while he was in the reserves and so not actively employed by it. Further, Shliapnikov pointed to the vanity of oblast-level officials, eager to make their careers by pillorying former oppositionists.⁴⁷

---

44   RGASPI, f. 589, op. 3, d. 9103, vol. 5, ll. 125–6; Iakovlev 1991, pp. 115–16. Ezhov was a CCC member at this time. In 1934 he became deputy chair of the Party Control Commission and its chair in 1935 (Getty and Naumov 2008). In 1936 he became NKVD chief. Ezhov may have had a personal connection with Shliapnikov through Shliapnikov's relatives in St. Petersburg and through mutual friends. In addition, Ezhov's secretary was a friend of Shliapnikov's wife.

45   RGASPI, f. 589, op. 3, d. 9103, vol. 5, ll. 122–3; l. 145, 31 October 1933. Knorin gave the report on Shliapnikov's case; also attending were Shliapnikov, Ivanov, Shillert, Mochalov (Gosplan RSFSR party cell bureau member), Sol'ts (Moscow oblast' purge commission member) and Karavaev. Iaroslavskii was secretary of the Central Purge Commission.

46   RGASPI, f. 589, op. 3, d. 9102, ll. 228–37, 22 November 1933; Sol'ts chaired; Karavaev and Filatov attended. Medvedev's troubles related partly to his history of oppositionism, but also to the reorganisation of VSNKh in 1929–30 and its replacement by the Commissariat of Heavy Industry in 1932 (Shearer 1996, pp. 81, 168–80).

47   TsA FSB, R33718, d. 499061, vol. 43, l. 164, 9 December 1934 letter from Shliapnikov in Kislovodsk to Medvedev in Moscow. Shliapnikov remarked in the letter that correspondence to him took about a week to arrive; he attributed the delay to perlustration.

As the purge was ending, Yaroslavsky and Knorin prepared new textbooks on party history. Both accounts erased Shlyapnikov's role in the party underground during World War I, with Knorin labelling him a conciliator on the war question and Yaroslavsky depicting him as 'primarily a trade-union organiser' before 1917. While Yaroslavsky presented Shlyapnikov as holding a Menshevist position during the February Revolution and taking a similar line in his memoirs of 1917, Knorin completely omitted his role in the February events, crediting Molotov with leadership of the CC Russian Bureau. Both overlooked the long development of the Workers' Opposition, casting it as an ephemeral movement that arose just on the eve of the Tenth Party Congress. Both echoed Lenin's condemnations of the Workers' Opposition's programme and referenced its members' continued struggle through the 1920s. While neither claimed outright that the Workers' Opposition merged with the United Opposition, the distinctions they drew between the two groups were so subtle that they may have escaped the attention of young, poorly educated party members.[48] These texts would influence NKVD investigators who would interrogate Shlyapnikov in 1935–7.

Conclusion

Shlyapnikov persistently struggled to refute outlandish accusations directed against his own past and towards his depiction of party history. During the purge, he preserved a spark of hope that he would not be excluded, because he had escaped similar attempts in the past. After all, some who sympathised with him had always been in a position to help. Perhaps he also thought that he could negotiate the terms of his exclusion and establish a basis for restoring his party membership. Although Shlyapnikov's purge surely was a foregone conclusion, purge-commission members seem to have negotiated among themselves the grounds on which he should be excluded. Nevertheless, at each level the charges became more serious and more encompassing. Interrogators at each level were expected to demonstrate their activism and commitment by adding new charges. Shlyapnikov could not bring himself to perform the humiliating ritual of self-abasement that was required. Rather than attempting to internalise Stalinist values and repudiate his past politics, he provided evidence of having defended the party's interests and of having criticised only within the framework allowed by the party. He employed the lightly ironic humour that had permeated party gatherings in the 1920s and earlier. More

---

48 Iaroslavskii 1933, ch. 2, pp. 6, 165–7, 252, 384; Knorin *et al.* 1935, pp. 136–9, 251, 295. Brandenberger 2011 has written about party history textbooks.

seriously, he offered himself to the party as a worker, as an organiser, who could contribute something of practical value. His stubborn self-defence in some ways resembled that of the Old Believers from whom he was descended, but the logic he employed offered hope to rescue the party's mission from the medieval path chosen by Stalin.

CHAPTER 12

Exile, Arrest and Prison

The party's so-called Congress of Victors (the Seventeenth Party Congress) in January–February 1934, which celebrated a large harvest and the completion of several large industrial projects, witnessed leading former oppositionists unite in praise of Stalin. Sergei Kirov, Leningrad party secretary, was a popular figure at the congress, but his assassination later that year led to a new, intensified campaign of repression against former oppositionists. Before 1991, many Western historians suspected that Kirov emerged at the congress as a moderate rival to Stalin, providing Stalin with a motive to kill Kirov later that year and unleash a final campaign against his old rivals, Zinoviev and Kamenev, as well as their supporters. Newly opened archives have not yielded information to prove the hypothesis that Kirov threatened to supplant Stalin, but instead have supported the contention that there were no radical and moderate factions in the Soviet leadership in the 1930s.[1]

Two exiles and two sets of arrests, interrogations and periods of imprisonment frame Shlyapnikov's personal and political life in this chapter, for which sources largely come from secret police archives. Not among those who attempted to redeem their political careers at the 1934 congress, Shlyapnikov, perhaps due to his intransigence, was subsequently ordered to depart Moscow for work in the far north. His experiences that year drove him to reflect, in his diary and personal correspondence, not only upon his personal fate, but also upon the changes that Stalinism had wrought on the working class and the party. He felt that Soviet socialism fell far short of the standard of his dreams, yet he maintained hope that socialism based on workers' initiative would eventually prevail in the USSR and other countries. The criticisms he privately expressed in 1934 served as evidence for the NKVD case against him in 1935–7, upon the conclusion of which he was executed. The Great Terror of 1936–8 spiralled outward to encompass not only communists like Shlyapnikov, but entire social and ethnic categories, resulting in two and a half million arrests and around six hundred and eighty-two thousand executions. Archives have yielded much data about the numbers of people involved, Stalin's role in guiding the terror, the NKVD's implementation of it, the responses of ordinary

---

1 Khlevniuk 1995 and 2008.

people and Gulag operations, yet there are still unilluminated aspects of this complex and confusing event.²

Memoirs published in the West before the collapse of the USSR and documents released subsequently provide diverse perspectives on the Great Terror. Evgenia Ginzburg survived arrest, interrogation and forced labour in the harsh Arctic north to write a two-part memoir, *Journey into the Whirlwind* and *In the Whirlwind*, describing the arbitrary, mad brutality of the Great Terror, but the archetype of the Old Bolshevik who perished in those years is the character Nicholas Rubashov, in Arthur Koestler's novel, *Darkness at Noon*. Interrogators employed the logic of party loyalty to persuade him to confess to outlandish crimes at a public trial. Koestler called Rubashov a 'synthesis' of the Old Bolsheviks who confessed in the 1936–8 show trials. These included Bukharin, Radek, Zinoviev, Kamenev and several dozen others.³ Koestler's compelling depiction of Rubashov's psychological transformation convinced many that it represented how all Old Bolsheviks felt towards their party.

Casting doubt on Koestler's depiction, Stephen F. Cohen contended that Bukharin employed 'double-talk' and 'veiled allusions' to subvert charges at his trial. Yet, historicising Koestler's literary approach, Igal Halfin argued, in his study of Leningrad University during the terror, that: 'A radical instrumentalization of their subjectivities rendered Party members selfless'. Without a sense of self, one could carry out any measures the party deemed necessary. Halfin relied for evidence on the published show-trial testimonies of the Old Bolsheviks and unpublished confessions by younger communists. Given the apparent solidity of his case and the rich store of documents released from archives, historians subsequently have shifted their attention towards the mass nature of the terror, although Wendy Goldman's recent book on the repression in Moscow factories returns focus to the individuals' motives to resist or facilitate escalating terror.⁴

This chapter introduces evidence that Old Bolshevik responses to terror were more complex than Halfin allows. Thousands of Old Bolsheviks who perished in the terror never came to public trial. Shlyapnikov and other key figures tried on the case of the Moscow Workers' Opposition did not confess because they did not regard self-slander as in the party's interest. Under interrogation, Shlyapnikov employed logic and denial to contest the 1935 charges of anti-Soviet agitation and counterrevolutionary organisation and the charge of

---

2 Goldman 2011 provides an excellent summary of the Terror and its historiography in her introduction and first chapter.
3 Ginzburg 1967 and 1981; Koestler 1986, dedication page; Zinoviev 1936.
4 Cohen 1980, p. 377; Halfin 2009, p. 2; Shearer 2009; Hagenloh 2009; Goldman 2007 and 2011.

terrorism added in 1936. Although at moments he wavered, he largely resisted implicating others in crimes against the Soviet state. Challenging Stalinist expectations for proper communist behaviour, he preserved his own sense of self as a Bolshevik.[5]

Exile to the North

By Politburo order, in 1930 construction began on the White Sea-Baltic Sea Canal (BBK), which was completed by summer 1933. Plagued by shortages of high-quality construction materials (especially metal), the canal never achieved the goals assigned to it. Too shallow for large vessels, it was not even of strategic value. Nevertheless, BBK served as the prototype for large-scale Soviet forced labour under secret-police direction. In 1934 construction continued on projects, including the Tuloma River hydroelectric power station. Aside from economic goals, BBK and similar projects had an ancillary goal: the 'reforging' [*perekovka*] of prisoners, who, by means of hard physical labour, would transform into the New Soviet Man. The term 'reforging' originates in metallurgy.[6] The human body and mind were to compensate in some ways for insufficient metals and other materials available for construction; spiritual regeneration would offset material backwardness.

Soviet leaders called upon Shlyapnikov, the Old Bolshevik metalworker, to participate in the BBK project soon after his purge from the party. His comrade, Sergei Medvedev, paved the way into exile, having been dispatched after his purge to BBK administrative headquarters in Medvezhegorsk, Karelia, where he worked as assistant chief of the mechanical shops. His ambiguous status there illuminates the arbitrariness of OGPU categories and procedures. Though he was listed as an 'administrative exile', the militia used his own passport to register him, which according to him was 'not done to even one administrative exile'. He had to check in monthly with the camp administration. Housed with freely hired personnel in a dormitory that reminded him of a tsarist transit prison, he was paid a salary (400 rubles/month), but the collective wage agreement did not apply to him and his term of work was indefinite. While he was in

---

5 Iakovlev 1991 published a summary of the case against the Moscow group of the Workers' Opposition (pp. 104–22). The former member of the Workers' Opposition, Mikhail Chëlyshev, a Soviet judge and former CCC member, died of a heart attack while under NKVD interrogation rather than confess to outlandish charges (Smirnov 2001, pp. 126–7).

6 Khlevniuk 2004, pp. 24, 35, 84, 335; Baron 2007, 129–49; Draskoczy 2012. The town was Medvezh'ia Gora prior to 1931, when it became BBK administrative centre (Baron 2007, 131–2).

exile, his sister cared for his daughters. Shlyapnikov and other comrades aided Medvedev's family.[7]

Despite Medvedev's turn of fate, Shlyapnikov seemed surprised when he, too, was administratively exiled to Russia's far north in spring 1934. Initially he embarked upon a quest to determine the legal basis of his exile and to negotiate its terms. He had been busy seeking work from Yezhov, who was then in charge of assigning party personnel. Even as a former party member, he could not get work without the party's permission.[8] Formerly a close comrade of several members of the Workers' Group, Yezhov had been personally acquainted with Shlyapnikov since at least 1922 and Shlyapnikov had rendered him assistance in the early 1920s. It therefore seems that Yezhov may have sympathised with Shlyapnikov, despite his harsh words at the older man's final purge hearing. Yezhov first assigned him to work for the People's Commissariat of Heavy Industry, but it rejected his candidacy. Other attempts similarly 'fell through'. When Yezhov offered work in Astrakhan, Shlyapnikov requested instead junior-level work in Moscow, so that he could continue to receive treatment for Ménière's illness. Yezhov finally explained that he wanted to remove him from Moscow, so that he would not tempt fate, perhaps meaning that Shlyapnikov's irreverent demeanour and banter antagonised some party leaders and so put him at risk. Still, Shlyapnikov hoped to be assigned work in Leningrad or Sevastopol, where he could receive medical treatment.[9]

But in early March, job negotiations took an ominous turn. After Yezhov missed an appointment with Shlyapnikov on 2 March because of illness, Shlyapnikov retreated to his dacha at Nikolina Gora (forty kilometres from Moscow), returning to Moscow only on 7 March. Upon his return, Yezhov's assistant, A.S. Rossov, unexpectedly instructed him that he should leave for Siberia within 48 hours. Astounded, Shlyapnikov interpreted this as a sentence of exile and set about appealing against it. First, he phoned his old comrades,

---

7   TsA FSB, R33718, d. 499061, vol. 13, ll. 68–70, Medvedev's letter to Shliapnikov handwritten on 4 July 1934 and delivered through his daughters; ll. 71–5 (typed version); vol. 14, l. 108 (packet of documents), 3 February 1934 postcard from Medvedev to Shliapnikov, sent through regular mail; vol. 43, l. 99, Medvedev's work booklet; unpaginated letter from M.P. Lushina to Medvedev, 8 January 1934.

8   Shliapnikova and Chernobaev (eds.) 2002, pp. 3–31, published version of Shliapnikov's handwritten diary, which I consulted in TsA FSB.

9   RGASPI, f. 82, op. 2, d. 178, ll. 28, 35, 21 September 1922 and [May] 1923 letters (copies) from Ezhov to Marta Berzina, referencing Shliapnikov, S.I. Maslennikov and V.P. Demidov; f. 671, op. 1, d. 22, l. 165, signed letter from Shliapnikov to the CC Secretariat, 17 January 1934; Shliapnikova and Chernobaev (eds.) 2002, pp. 3–4. I have rendered as 'tempt fate' Ezhov's more idiomatic '*ne draznit' moskovskikh guseĭ*'.

Politburo members Molotov (Sovnarkom chair) and Voroshilov (Military Commissar), and CC Special Section Chief, Alexander Poskrebyshev, who oversaw top secret documents. According to Shlyapnikov, Molotov did not offer help, but tried to reassure him that he probably was not being exiled. Poskrebyshev denied knowing anything about his work assignment, while the ex-metalworker, Voroshilov, was 'indignant' and promised to support him. Shlyapnikov submitted an appeal to Stalin, with copies to Molotov and Voroshilov. In it, he wrote of his 'elementary human right to medical treatment' (which the Soviet press often accused capitalist countries of denying to workers), objected that he could not receive treatment in Siberia and complained that without treatment he would lose his hearing and his ability to work.[10]

When Molotov informed him on 9 March that the Politburo had not yet discussed his appeal, Shlyapnikov became almost completely deaf due to nervous strain and left town for Nikolina Gora to seek quiet and recover his hearing. Late in the afternoon of 13 March, an OGPU employee came to the dacha. Shlyapnikov spoke with him outside, 'so as not to agitate the children'. The unexpected arrival of OGPU agents usually signified arrest, but this official had come to summon him to a meeting that evening with Anatoly Rutkovsky, assistant director of the first department of the OGPU Secret Political Section (SPO). The agent gave Shlyapnikov and Ekaterina a ride to their Moscow apartment in his official car, because the alternative, public transport, would have taken too long. Having prepared for a 'long journey', Shlyapnikov set off for Rutkovsky's office at the Lubyanka. Adopting a semi-humourous tone that belied his state of alarm, he inquired as to what 'case' he was being brought up on. Rutkovsky replied in a serious tone that the OGPU had nothing on him since Omsk and relayed to him orders to depart Moscow within three days for a work assignment at BBK.[11]

Determined to achieve an answer to his appeal, Shlyapnikov tried to reach Politburo members. Since he was too deaf to use the telephone, he enlisted his old comrade, Alexander Shotman, a high-ranking party member, to make phone calls for him, but without success. Kalinin expressed reluctance to talk openly because he was not alone, downplayed his concerns and said he had no time to intervene. Voroshilov could not be reached at all. At the end of the day, Shlyapnikov finally reached Molotov, who confirmed that the Politburo had still not discussed his protest. Their conversation ended abruptly; Shlyapnikov

---

10   Shliapnikova and Chernobaev (eds.) 2002, pp. 5–6; RGASPI, f. 74, op. 2, d. 49, l. 171, 7 March 1934 carbon copy, with Shliapnikov's original signature.
11   Shliapnikova and Chernobaev (eds.) 2002, pp. 5–6.

wrote that Molotov hung up on him. Much later, his wife told their children that Molotov only ended the call after Shlyapnikov denounced him as a 'swine'. Shlyapnikov thus finally understood that his 'former comrades' would not support his appeal, so he went to the OGPU early on 15 March to determine the conditions of his exile.[12]

Shlyapnikov found his status strange and confusing, since he had not been arrested, yet he had been placed under police authority. The OGPU had gradually expanded its duties beyond policing to include economic administration, but Shlyapnikov had no experience with its new powers, so he inquired about his legal status, the nature of his work, how his wife and children would obtain rations, how his travel would be funded and whether he could see his doctor before leaving for the north. Rutkovsky only knew that he was to do 'important' work on the Tuloma electrical station, but promised to find out the answers to his other questions within 24 hours. While waiting, Shlyapnikov packed for his trip, continued writing his Civil War memoirs and visited his former workplace, Gosplan RSFSR, to seek back pay. Formally he was still a member of the Gosplan RSFSR Presidium and was entitled to a salary, but he had been reluctant to visit there since he was purged from its party cell. Gosplan RSFSR chair, Rogov, had been trying to remove Shlyapnikov's name from the presidium, so that he would not taint it by association. Upon seeing him again, Rogov offered the unsolicited opinion that he could have avoided exile by appealing against his purge from the party.[13]

When Shlyapnikov returned to see Rutkovsky, he found that he was not deprived of civil rights, as he was considered neither an exile nor a prisoner. Yakov Rapoport, BBK director from 1933–5, would assign him administrative work on site. Rutkovsky issued him 500 rubles to cover his travel but could make no provision for his family, nor could he allow him time to see his doctor. Shlyapnikov immediately called Yezhov from Rutkovsky's phone and elicited a promise to arrange ration cards for his family. OGPU chief, Genrikh Yagoda, refused to give Shlyapnikov more time in Moscow but later, in a personal meeting, Shlyapnikov obtained Yezhov's promise to delay his departure for two days

---

12   Shliapnikova and Chernobaev (eds.) 2002, p. 7. Aleksandr Shotman (1880–1937) was a Finnish metalworker from St. Petersburg. He joined the RSDRP in 1899, was a member of the party's Petersburg Committee and a CC member in 1913. He organised Lenin's flight to Finland after the July 1917 uprising. After the revolution he worked in VSNKh and was a CCC member from 1924 to 1934. He was executed in 1937 (Protasov 2008; Bondarevskaia 1963).
13   Shliapnikova and Chernobaev (eds.) 2002, p. 8.

in order to see his doctor.¹⁴ This set of apparent incongruities accords with the picture, provided by Getty and Naumov in their biography of Yezhov, of Yezhov as a rising star and Yagoda as a declining authority. It is not clear whether Shlyapnikov was aware of their changing political fortunes, or if he was simply attempting all paths of appeal. Having exhausted all the avenues that occurred to him, he reconciled himself to the situation, probably realising that he could be arrested and exiled on less favourable terms.

Shlyapnikov returned to Nikolina Gora to spend time with his children and to repair the dacha. Rumours had already spread among adults there that the OGPU had arrested him. The distress of the nanny and the maid upset the children, so all were 'overjoyed' to see him return. Friends came to express sympathy and support. Since the OGPU was unable or unwilling to arrange his transport, Shlyapnikov had to reserve and pay for train tickets himself, placing him in the absurd situation of having to arrange his own travel into involuntary exile. Aware of the irony, he noted that his OGPU-issued travel document reminded him of one he had been issued in 1904 by the tsarist police. Having seen his doctor, he went to the train station accompanied by his wife and friends and departed just after midnight on 20 March. He had left money for Ekaterina to cover two months of the family's living expenses.¹⁵

The train only went to Leningrad, where Shlyapnikov stayed from 20–1 March, while he attempted to reserve a berth on a train to Medvezhegorsk. Travelling around Leningrad to see how it had changed since 1917, he reminisced about his earlier life there. In Vyborg he noted that new factories and dormitories had been built since the revolution. In Nevsky district he found some old factories had been dismantled, but the Obukhov factory to be much the same, with only some new buildings on the left side. He joked: 'The buildings and residences are new, but the dirt is old, as if it hadn't been removed for 33 years!' Nostalgia for his youth jarred with his impression that Leningrad's residents had changed greatly. Attentively comparing 'Leningradtsy' to 'Pitertsy', he found great differences between the intelligent-looking, well-dressed metalworkers of old and the tired and weak 1930s worker population composed of peasants in ragged clothing. No longer evident were the 'advanced workers of Old Peter', but instead 'the peasant prevails, primarily young ones hoping to start here a new or "different" life than in the countryside'. Malnourished women and children had in some cases been reduced to begging. On the first evening, he visited old acquaintances originally from Murom; conversation revolved around high prices and the greater availability of goods, which

---

14 Shliapnikova and Chernobaev (eds.) 2002, pp. 8–9.
15 Shliapnikova and Chernobaev (eds.) 2002, p. 9.

Shliapnikov referred to as a 'safety valve', implying that if shortages had continued, unrest could have ensued.[16]

On the second day in the Gavan neighbourhood, Shliapnikov found his nephew, Kostya, who in boyhood had assisted him in the revolutionary underground by watching out for the police. Kostya and his wife were factory workers; they had no tea or sugar, but served Shliapnikov hot water with lemon, bread, salted fish and candies. Their worry about low pay, poor rations and criminal charges for mistakes at work echoed the complaints of workers on the street. They reported that skilled workers were leaving factory work to take up higher-paid 'service' occupations, such as work in the fire service. The prevalence of peasant youth at the factories helped keep wages low and resulted in 'intensified exploitation and less money being spent on workers' safety and health'. To the peasants, this was better than starvation in the countryside. Shliapnikov saw this as a typical sociological process accompanying industrialisation, attributing it to the 'law of supply and demand'. Although he did not express explicit disappointment with Soviet industrialisation, he felt sympathy for the workers. Nor did he echo the newspapers' blaming of industrial spoilage on 'wreckers' or class enemies, instead attributing it to low wage rates and the newly arrived peasants' unfamiliarity with factory work.[17] He seems to have found that advances in Soviet industrialisation had caused class formation to start anew.

Having finally arranged passage on a train leaving late on the second night, Shliapnikov departed Leningrad. When his train made a regular stop in Petrozavodsk, he prevailed upon a disembarking fellow passenger to mail postcards to two old acquaintances, the Karelian party secretary, Kustaa Rovio (a founder of the Finnish Communist Party), and Karelian Sovnarkom chair, Edvard Gylling, alerting them to his presence in the region.[18] Perhaps he hoped that they might help him in some way. Very familiar with the Karelian land-

---

16   Shliapnikova and Chernobaev (eds.) 2002, pp. 10–11. Osokina 1993 discusses rationing policy. Davies 1997 writes about the Leningraders' expressed opinions.

17   Shliapnikova and Chernobaev (eds.) 2002, p. 12. Goldman 2007 confirms the picture of widespread worker flight from factories due to cuts in food rations (Goldman 2007, p. 22) and high rates of injury (Goldman 2007, p. 27). For vivid anecdotes about such occurrences, see Scott 1989.

18   A Finnish nationalist from a well-off middle-class family, Gylling (1881–1938) brought about the early 1930s return to Karelia of many Finns from the North American diaspora (Pogorelskin 1997, p. 262). Rovio (d. 1938) had expressed concern in 1930 that the large number of prisoners in Karelia constituted a security risk. Both men had sought local control over BBK and were disappointed when it came under the authority of the OGPU authority (Baron 2007, pp. 96, 135).

scape from his pre-revolutionary smuggling adventures, he derived pleasure from viewing 'its forested massifs and hills, hugged by little rivers and lakes, covered with ice and a snowy blanket'. Having arrived in Medvezhegorsk around 1 p.m. on 22 March, he set out for the BBK headquarters to learn his work assignment. Along his route, he met numerous acquaintances, many of whom he did not recognise because their camp sentences had changed them so dramatically.[19]

One old acquaintance was M.V. Petrosov, whom Shlyapnikov knew from party work in the North Caucasus during the Civil War. Alarmed, he was saddened to see that he was no longer the same 'unreserved, lively, curly-haired Southerner', but a:

> prisoner with a five-year sentence on a case without merit: some worthless fellow's denunciation, as if Petrosov knew that this guy had inside his skull 'criminal' Rightist ideas and besides that, counterrevolutionary intentions to organise the leader's assassination ... What could be more clumsy, more vile than such an accusation against Petrosov, for those who know him! But it is not we who know Petrosov who decide his fate now. We don't even decide our own fates!

'A dry rattling cough and thinning hair' spoke to him of Petrosov's ordeals, about which he did not ask for the sake of politeness. Expressing certainty of Petrosov's innocence, he faulted the southerner's old comrades, Mikoyan and Ordzhonikidze, for not speaking up on his behalf. Shlyapnikov's belief that individual agency could stem unfounded repression was reinforced by his success, a few years earlier, in getting an old non-party friend from Murom, Fyodor Kuritsyn, an engineer at Moscow waterworks, released from OGPU arrest.[20]

When Shlyapnikov arrived at BBK headquarters, he discovered that the chief, Rapoport, was in Moscow, and that his staff knew nothing of Shlyapnikov's mission. Moreover, his travel documents caused confusion, because they were not issued by the OGPU cadres department, but instead from the OGPU statistical department. After some consideration, Radetsky, one of Rapoport's assistants, graciously decided that Shlyapnikov would be considered a 'voluntary hire'. This meant that he would not be subjected to the indignities suffered by the exiles. Shlyapnikov pointed out honestly that this did not correspond to the way in which he had arrived. Radetsky allowed that in fact he was an exile,

---

19 Shliapnikova and Chernobaev (eds.) 2002, pp. 12–13.
20 Shliapnikova and Chernobaev (eds.) 2002, p. 14; Iurii Shliapnikov 2004. Kuritsyn died of natural causes in the 1950s.

but would work as if he were a voluntary hire; he was not, therefore, deprived of civil rights. Then Radetsky 'suggested' that Shlyapnikov should travel on to Kola to seek work from Sutyrin, chief of construction at the Tuloma hydrostation, the top priority project. Radetsky desired that he leave immediately, but the train that had brought him there had already left. Therefore, a staff person named Konovalov was assigned to arrange lodging and meals for him and to help him find a seat on the next train the following day. The administration covered his meals in the better-stocked cadres' cafeteria.[21]

Shlyapnikov was determined not to miss the opportunity to see and speak with Medvedev, but no one gave clear answers on how to find him. Having concluded that the OGPU did not want them to meet, he was still not deterred. When Konovalov finally left him alone, he went directly to the mechanical shop where Medvedev worked, but did not find him there or in his room. Disappointed, Shlyapnikov returned to his room to sleep on a straw mattress and pillow, under a regulation grey blanket for cadres. In the morning, Konovalov gave him a work voucher, but since the train was full, his journey was postponed for another day. Since 23 March was not a working day, he noted more people on the 'streets', some of whom he knew.[22]

One of these, Andrei Bachmanov, had worked as a businessman at the firm New Lessner and helped set up the Society of Factory Owners before 1917. After the February Revolution, Shlyapnikov wrote, Bachmanov had replaced Emmanuel Nobel as chair. He recalled that among others in the society's council were some who subsequently became Bolsheviks – the Krasin brothers, Leonid and German, and the engineer, Alexander Serebrovsky, who in the early 1930s was assistant People's Commissar of Heavy Industry. Shlyapnikov sympathised less with Bachmanov than with the Bolshevik Petrosov, but patiently heard his protests that he was innocent of the charge of being an 'English spy' and advised him to appeal against his conviction. Another acquaintance had been on the Narkomtrud board and was convicted in the Industrial Party case.[23] Despite many such accidental encounters, Shlyapnikov never did manage to see Medvedev; if the camp authorities prevented their meeting, it was likely due to fear of rebukes from OGPU higher-ups, so overwrought was concern about imagined conspiracies behind a simple reunion of old friends.

On 24 March, Konovalov finally obtained rail passage for Shlyapnikov, having had to trade a 'litre' (probably of vodka) for an upholstered seat. With

---

21 Shliapnikova and Chernobaev (eds.) 2002, pp. 14–15.
22 Shliapnikova and Chernobaev (eds.) 2002, p. 16.
23 Shliapnikova and Chernobaev (eds.) 2002, p. 17.

money from his travel funds, Shlyapnikov upgraded his ticket to a sleeping car, for the trip to Kola took 24 hours. Emotionally drained by his encounters in Medvezhegorsk, he appreciated the distraction offered by the changing landscape and by conversations with his travelling companions about nature. As they travelled, the environment changed from forests to boggy areas still in the grip of winter.[24]

Paradoxically, his 'express' train was often delayed by the mail train ahead of it. Attentive to signs of the forced-labour regime, Shlyapnikov noted that prisoners loaded and unloaded the train and that guards checked for escapees under train cars. Despite such vigilance, he found, when he arrived at Kola on the afternoon of 25 March, that no one met him and that administrators were surprised to see him appear at headquarters, because they had not been notified of his assignment. The chief administrator on site was Sutyrin, head of the seventh BBK territorial section, who Shlyapnikov described as an 'intellectual-type youth'. He recognised one of Sutyrin's assistants, Laptev, who had been secretary of the Foodworkers' Union when the oppositionist Ignatov had chaired it.[25]

While Sutyrin contemplated how to employ Shlyapnikov, Laptev arranged meals for him and housing in the administrators' barracks. As was typical, his room was poorly insulated, with an icy cold floor and cracks in the walls through which heat from the stoves escaped, and furnished only with a straw mattress, to which he requested that a table be added. At the post office, he found no mail waiting for him, but he sent a telegram, probably to his wife. On the next morning, after discussing goals and timetables, Shlyapnikov and Sutyrin decided that he was suited for 'operational planning'. Sutyrin's assistants gave him further orientation. He was told that there were eight and a half thousand prisoners in three camps. The Kola prison camp constructed railroads and roads, built administrative barracks and loaded and unloaded train cars. The second camp had begun work on the hydrostation, but also constructed prisoners' barracks, a dam on the Tuloma River and a spillway. They soon expected to have fifteen thousand prisoners in this camp. The third camp, sixty-five kilometres away on the Shovna River, felled timber.[26]

---

24   Shliapnikova and Chernobaev (eds.) 2002, pp. 17–18.
25   Shliapnikova and Chernobaev (eds.) 2002, p. 18. There were 15–20 territorial sections in BBK at any given time in the 1930s (Baron 2007 p. 136).
26   Shliapnikova and Chernobaev (eds.) 2002, pp. 19–20. The BBK prisoner population was 70,373 (not including forced settlers) on 1 January 1934 and 66,418 on 1 January 1935 (Baron 2007, p. 185).

Due to a shortage of space, Shlyapnikov shared an office with Sutyrin's assistants and so witnessed numerous interactions among the camp personnel. He wrote, perhaps ironically, that his location gave him the possibility 'to more quickly "assimilate" camp peculiarities, as well as the system of reforging spoiled human material into "new people"'. The first visitor was a young man with a peasant face, 'dressed according to military rules'. He was a member of the BBK third department, which was internal security. Joking that it was the 'OGPU within the OGPU', Shlyapnikov understood that the young man would check his correspondence.[27] Another visitor was an old comrade, former member of the central committee of the Metalworkers' Union, A.N. Kasperovich, who had served a sentence in Solovki for factionalism and had then become commandant of BBK camp no. 1.

Shlyapnikov noted that prisoners could work in 'secondary official roles', but only free hires or former prisoners could be top administrators. While free hires could address a superior as 'comrade', convict staff had to address a superior as 'citizen'. Superiors used the formal or informal pronoun 'you' depending on how well they knew or liked their subordinates. The personal requests of the rank-and-file prisoners included permission for a wife to visit, appeals to reduce a sentence or to grant amnesty. Shlyapnikov developed the impression that disenfranchised peasants (former kulaks) worked productively and reliably, but were 'less amenable to "reforging"'. Their sentences did not lessen their dislike of 'the regime, which had deprived them of their right of "free" existence, family and property'.[28] Shlyapnikov's placement of quotation marks may have signified not only that Stalinist terms like 'new people' and 'reforging' did not naturally belong to his own socialist vocabulary, but possibly also that he was sceptical about the extent to which a 'free' life was possible, even outside the camp system.

Most prisoners, Shlyapnikov found, were occupied with hard manual labour. Data indicated much overfulfilment of work norms at the hydrostation, which was rewarded by more and better food, including the privilege of purchasing goods for 'commercial prices'. High productivity and good behaviour could reduce sentences by half, but peasants convicted as kulaks got less of a reduction than did other prisoners ('three days reduced for two days of work'). Penalty rations, time in the isolator and going to work under guard were punishments. Rations for prisoners ranged from 300 to 1,300 grams of bread. The amount and type of food varied for prisoners who did engineering

---

27 The BBK third department took orders directly from the central Gulag administration (Baron 2007, p. 200).

28 Shliapnikova and Chernobaev (eds.) 2002, p. 20.

and technical work, for free hires, administrators and guards. Shlyapnikov concluded: 'Thus, everyone knows his place; egalitarianism has been completely liquidated'. His impressions coincide with the historians' accounts of Gulag operations.[29]

Shlyapnikov's prior experience in Rosmetizprom and Gosplan RSFSR had acquainted him with flaws of the Soviet economy that he also uncovered during his research into camp operations. Among these were incomplete and inaccurate data that were further distorted as they passed up the command chain, yielding an exaggeratedly optimistic perspective (a fundamental flaw in the Stalinist economy). He proposed to correct the picture by gathering more accurate and comprehensive data, which Sutyrin and BBK higher-ups approved. When choosing staff, however, he found it difficult to convince imprisoned accountants to take up planning work, as they received no reduction in sentences or improved food rations for office work. Instead, they faced the risk of longer sentences for mistakes. He nevertheless convinced four people to sign up and began work with them on 7 April. Yet on that very afternoon, Moscow authorities ordered him to return to the capital, for possible transfer to Kazan. The reasons for his return are not clear. Perhaps his old comrades had finally decided that he should have better access to medical care, or maybe they feared that he would try to escape across the border along the smuggling routes he had used before the revolution. Shlyapnikov's children tend to think that it was the latter reason, for their mother told them how she remembered that he had implied so in a telegram telling her to come to Karelia with the children, which she could not manage.[30] Nevertheless, it seems doubtful he would have considered such an attempt to be practical.

Before Shlyapnikov left BBK, he had to swear an oath to present himself at the OGPU SPO on the same day as his scheduled arrival in Moscow on 10 April. On the evening of 7 April, he departed by train. Alone in his sleeping compartment, he rested and enjoyed the passing landscape. Kem, one of the stations along the way, reminded him by its name of a Finnish town that had lain along his route for illegally smuggling revolutionary literature into Russia in 1915. His emotions spilled onto the pages of his diary, where he revealingly described

---

29   Shliapnikova and Chernobaev (eds.) 2002, p. 22. According to Khlevniuk 2004, p. 109, first-category prisoners in camps with extreme weather had sentences reduced by three days for two workdays and second-category prisoners by four days for three workdays. Shockworkers in both categories got further reductions. For more on the Gulag economy, see Gregory and Lazarev (eds.) 2003.

30   Shliapnikova and Chernobaev (eds.) 2002, pp. 22–3; Shliapnikova 1995 interview; Iurii Shliapnikov 2004.

himself as one: 'badgered and persecuted ... by people, who hijacked leadership of "Leninism" and of the party, strutting their achievements against the background of world reaction, but carefully hiding the true poverty of the working class and collective farmers'. After Kem, he shared his sleeping compartment with two local administrators who drank and smoked heavily. The fumes forced Shlyapnikov to seek clean air in the corridor. Despite his life-long revulsion against drinking and smoking, he compassionately attributed their excesses to work-related stress. When the train stopped for five minutes at Medvezhegorsk, he tried once more to find Medvedev, but again was disappointed. As the train approached Leningrad, he saw that local people rushed into the dining car to buy up 'everything that was edible, since they lived here in semi-starvation'.[31] When its agents confiscated the diary upon his arrest in 1935, the NKVD would find such observations to be anti-Soviet.

Interlude between Exile and Arrest

After Shlyapnikov returned to Moscow, he again appealed to the Politburo to allow him to remain in Moscow to be treated for his illness. Expressing dismay at his recent exile, he characterised it 'as an act of obvious administrative arbitrariness, as exile without a court'. Moreover, it had worsened the symptoms of his illness (deafness and vertigo). He maintained his innocence of anything that might have led to the decision to exile him. A month later he followed this up with a personal appeal to Yezhov, who replied that Shlyapnikov's request to be reinstated in the party was rejected, but that he would receive financial assistance and help finding work. Although he remained in Moscow until his arrest on 1 January 1935, he did not obtain new employment, but instead continued writing his memoirs. Attempts to receive a retirement pension dragged on and Shlyapnikov finally resolved to request permission to travel abroad for medical treatment.[32]

Shlyapnikov paid close attention to international events in 1934 and shared his views with Medvedev and perhaps other comrades by letter. From his reading of Soviet and foreign newspapers, he perceived the USSR as 'hungry and without marketable goods' and surrounded by capitalist enemies, who were eager to take advantage of its economic weakness in order to seize its raw

---

31 Shliapnikova and Chernobaev (eds.) 2002, pp. 24–5.
32 Shliapnikova and Chernobaev (eds.) 2002, p. 26, 16 April 1934 appeal; RGASPI, f. 671, op. 1, d. 22, ll. 166–7, 17 May and 26 October 1934 handwritten letters from Shlyapnikov to Ezhov, with Ezhov's handwritten comments.

materials. He thought that a war on a larger scale than World War I was imminent. He also regretted that the USSR did not do more to help Spanish leftist forces. Probably referring to the Catalonian general strike in October 1934 and its bloody suppression, he was astounded by the 'boundless heroism' of the Spanish workers and commanders, accompanied by their 'military-technical illiteracy'. Finding it foolhardy of them to hide in houses, where they were bombarded with artillery, he complained that socialist publishers issued much literature containing empty talk, but nothing practical about how workers might defend themselves.[33]

Medvedev's sad feelings about exile gave rise to a number of ironic asides about Soviet press reports on foreign affairs and domestic events, about which the NKVD would interrogate both him and Shlyapnikov in 1935. He expressed scepticism about reported *kolkhoz* achievements and scoffed at a rapid about-face in how the Soviet press depicted the League of Nations. Deriding the press for writing so little 'about the proletariat...as if it were a corpse', he complained that the press coverage of workers depicted a proletariat that had nothing else to do but parade in celebration of heroes and greet 'distinguished foreigners'. His only solace was in reading Marx and Engels, whose works gave him 'spiritual steadfastness and cheer'. He could not even celebrate the 17th anniversary of the October Revolution. Describing in detail the 'festive assemblies' with music and 'a river' of speeches by speakers shouting threats and waving their fists in the air, he wrote that they reminded him of characters from the plays of the nineteenth-century author, Nikolai Gogol, that satirised provincial officials in tsarist Russia.[34]

When Medvedev's daughters visited him in summer 1934, his gloom briefly lifted, but it returned when he realised that it was unlikely that he could travel to Moscow to see them, even though his service status gave him the right to take a holiday. In a forthright evaluation (made possible because his letter travelled through private channels), he analysed his and Shlyapnikov's political situation as the product of 'retribution' arising from 'a belated episode of political struggle' of the party leadership with those 'not accepting their ideology and interests'. He continued:

---

33   TsA FSB, R33718, d. 499061, vol. 14, l. 108 (packet of documents), June–December 1934 letters and postcards from Shliapnikov to Medvedev; all sent through regular mail.

34   TsA FSB, R33718, d. 499061, vol. 13, ll. 76–7, 3 August 1934 handwritten letter from Medvedev to Shliapnikov, ll. 78–81 (typed copy); vol. 14, l. 108 (packet), 9 November 1934 letter from Medvedev to Ivan Pivon'.

Our 'crime' is that we did not fit the Procrustean bed of the 'Stalinist epoch'. We cannot conceal this key fact by means of dodges. If we try to turn back the clock, we will have to subject ourselves to that vile self-abasement which all 'formers' have perpetrated upon themselves.

Such appeals as he and Shlyapnikov had written earlier, he pointed out, were as futile as 'the voice of one crying in the wilderness'. Admitting that many former oppositionists sincerely repented, he noted that this did not restore them to former positions of authority. Moreover, he did not care for returning to the party to serve its 1930s leadership. For him, repentance could never be sincere, but only a tactic to create 'an organising moment' for those who might sympathise with him and Shlyapnikov. Finally, he offered: 'I stake all my hopes for deliverance, as a prisoner of war of the existing regime, on the course of domestic and foreign events'.[35] He thus emphasised that his exile had not 'corrected' his political views, but only reinforced them.

Their old comrade, Maximov (of the Omsk case), died in spring 1934, apparently of natural causes. Mourning him, Medvedev reflected that it had taken a generation to forge such seasoned proletarians and active revolutionaries, and that another generation might pass before 'bright days will come for our country's workers and for the international proletariat'. By autumn 1934, he had begun to contemplate his own mortality, since he had been experiencing an 'irregular heartbeat', dizziness and the brief loss of control over his legs. Shlyapnikov did not engage with Medvedev's ironies and scepticism. The need to write via monitored mail services deprived him of the possibility to respond fully to his friend's troubled thoughts. Sensitive to Medvedev's dark mood, however, he tried to cheer him up and direct him towards positive goals, such as coming home to Moscow on leave. In his last letter to his comrade, Shlyapnikov tried to dispel his gloomy thoughts about mortality; he imagined for himself that he would live a long life.[36]

More optimistic than Medvedev, Shlyapnikov appealed to Kalinin, Yezhov and others, who all told him that only Stalin could decide his lot, so he wrote an appeal to Stalin in late November, sending it through Yezhov. Neither

---

35 TsA FSB, R33718, d. 499061, vol. 13, ll. 68–70, 4 July 1934 handwritten letter from Medvedev to Shliapnikov; ll. 71–5 (typed copy).

36 TsA FSB, R33718, d. 499061, vol. 14, l. 108 (packet), 17 June 1934 letter from Medvedev to Pivon'; 25 October 1934 letter from Medvedev to Shliapnikov (sent by registered mail, it travelled for almost a month) and an earlier draft written on 3 October; 11 December 1934 letter from Shliapnikov to Medvedev, sent through regular mail; vol. 43, l. 98, 16 August 1934 postcard from Shliapnikov to Medvedev.

lauding Stalin nor apologising, he focused on his rights and desire to work. Since his health had worsened during exile, he had in June applied to Sovnarkom for a pension, which he had not yet received. Insisting on his 'indisputable right' to a pension, which he asserted that Yezhov had confirmed, he also requested permission to travel to France for medical treatment. He thereby hoped to restore his ability to work on behalf of 'the revolutionary proletarian cause'. Finally, he requested that Stalin facilitate the publication of his manuscript on the Civil War in the North Caucasus, as publishers feared to conclude a contract with him. Among the sensitive subjects he addressed in his Civil War memoir was the sinking of the Black Sea Fleet to avoid its capture by enemy forces, which Stalin had delegated to him.[37]

Arrest and Interrogation

Stalin never responded to Shlyapnikov's November 1934 appeal, for a few days after it was sent, Leonid Nikolaev murdered Kirov. Stalin's role in ordering the assassination has been the subject of much investigation, but no smoking gun has ever been discovered, only an accumulation of circumstantial evidence.[38] Immediately after the murder, Stalin authored a Politburo decree accelerating the trials of those charged with terrorism (the 1 December 1934 Law); he followed this up with arrests of Zinoviev's associates in Leningrad, then of Zinoviev and Kamenev in mid-December. By February 1935 more than a thousand people had been arrested on the case of the Kirov murder.

Shlyapnikov and his close comrades were among the arrested. By the order of the NKVD chief, Yagoda, two of his officers arrested Shlyapnikov at the dacha in Nikolina Gora on the night of 1–2 January 1935. After searching the dacha and his Moscow apartment, they confiscated his diary, Civil War manuscript, correspondence, guns, bullets, a hunting knife, jewellery and over one thousand one hundred rubles in cash. He was detained at the NKVD's internal prison isolator of special assignment at the Lubyanka.[39] Immediately upon his arrival in prison, as arrestee no. 200, he demonstrated non-compliance by refusing

---

37 Shliapnikova and Chernobaev (eds.) 2002, pp. 27–8, 28 November 1934 letter from Shliapnikov to Stalin, with a brief accompanying letter to Ezhov.
38 Among the many books on this subject are Knight 1999; Conquest 1988; Getty and Naumov 1999, pp. 140–57 and Lenoe 2010 (the most comprehensive collection of documents translated into English on the Kirov murder).
39 TsA FSB, R33718, d. 499061, vol. 3, ll. 1–8. According to the NKVD list, Shliapnikov's weaponry included a Mauser 3008, Browning 102188, .375 rifle no. 234577 and more than

the prison supervisor's order to remove his boots when lying upon the bed. Mironov, the prison department's assistant director, investigated, stopping by his cell no. 95 as if on a routine visit. According to Mironov's report, Shlyapnikov became teary-eyed as he declared his innocence, but also asserted that by law his confiscated correspondence should be returned to him for examination in two days. Upon Mironov's inquiry, he replied that he wore his boots in bed because the cold temperature in the cell could aggravate his middle ear inflammation. Mironov noted in his report that the cell's temperature was 12 degrees Celsius and that he moved Shlyapnikov to a warmer cell.[40]

The NKVD interrogators of 1935–7 were around 30 years old, usually lacked higher education and knew only the party history that they intensively studied in distorted texts. They had no special training in interrogation, but were selected on the basis of apparent talent.[41] Shlyapnikov was first interrogated on the night of 2–3 January by Grigorev, the assistant chief of the Main Directorate of State Security (GUGB) First Secret Political Section (SPO).[42] Unaware of how long his detention would last and hopeful of quick release, he acknowledged that he had had 'differences with the policy of the CC VKP(b)' in the past, but he struck out the word 'anti-party' that was inserted into his own description of his positions in the interrogation protocol. Grigorev's evidence at this stage consisted of Shlyapnikov's 1934 diary notes and Medvedev's 3 August 1934 letter to him. Grigorev read from the portion of the diary where Shlyapnikov had described working-class women and children in Leningrad

---

300 bullets. Iurii Shliapnikov 2004 recalled that his father had more guns than these before a law was passed limiting firearm possession.

40 TsA FSB, R33718, d. 499061, vol. 3, ll. 11–12, handwritten letter from A.K. Bukol'd (NKVD isolator fourth corpus senior supervisor) to the isolator director, 2 January 1935, and report from Mironov, *Administrativno-Khoziaistvennoe Upravlenie* (AKhU) NKVD prison department assistant director to G.A. Molchanov, director of the *Sekretno-Politicheskii Otdel* (SPO) *Gosudarstvennoe Upravlenie Gosudarstvennoi Bezopasnosti* (GUGB) NKVD. The GUGB was the re-named OGPU, which was absorbed by the NKVD in July 1934 (Hagenloh 2009, p. 155).

41 Petrov 2012. Standard textbooks on party history were Iaroslavskii 1933 and Knorin 1934. Jeffrey Rossman has researched NKVD interrogators who worked in the provinces during the Great Terror. I know little about Shlyapnikov's interrogators beyond their last names.

42 TsA FSB, R33718, d. 499061, vol. 3, ll. 13–14 (handwritten), ll. 15–17 (typed). The files contain handwritten originals and typed copies of interrogation protocols, summarising interrogators' questions and Shliapnikov's answers. The protocols were dated but do not indicate the time of day or length of interrogations. Shliapnikov corrected protocols by hand and usually signed that he had read them and found them accurate. Kuromiya 2008 analysed many interrogation protocols from Ukraine.

as having 'gaunt faces, pale bloodless lips' and had written of 'low wage rates foisted on workers'. Shlyapnikov responded that he just wrote what he saw, but he acknowledged that this was not the entire picture. Grigorev found suspicious the indignation with which he wrote in his diary about Petrosov, the former comrade he encountered at BBK, but Shlyapnikov refused to elaborate. When Grigorev asked if he tried to bring Medvedev's August 1934 letter to the attention of the authorities, Shlyapnikov retorted that he supposed the letter had passed through censors and thus was 'known to those who were supposed to know about it'.[43]

In the face of Shlyapnikov's denials, the NKVD acquired testimony against him from others. By 5 January, Grigorev had taken statements from Georgy Safarov, accused as a Zinovievist, that Safarov and Shlyapnikov had discussed conducting 'joint counterrevolutionary work' in the previous three years. Shlyapnikov denied all of this. Grigorev claimed to have information that he had given counterrevolutionary directives to Mikhailov in December 1934, but he replied that Mikhailov had only asked for help finding work after losing his job as a factory director. The NKVD knew about a meeting at Shlyapnikov's apartment on 6 December 1934, the day of Kirov's burial. Shlyapnikov denied that it was a meeting of his 'organisation', but identified those who came 'for a cup of tea' as: Nikolai Sergievsky, Erazm Batenin, Mikhail Rozen, Genrikh Bruno, Alexander Pravdin, Lev Green (a U.S. citizen) and Mikhail Svechnikov. Allowing that they had discussed Kirov's murder among other topics, Shlyapnikov admitted that he had said that, no matter whether Nikolaev's motives were personal or political, the murder had 'a political character, since comrade Kirov was a Politburo and government member'.[44]

In the context of the time, it was enough to talk about controversial political topics to be suspected of possessing treacherous opinions and preparing to act upon them. At the third interrogation, on 6 January, Grigorev explored Shlyapnikov's allegedly counterrevolutionary organisation and activity, focusing on links to 'groups' in Omsk and Rostov. Shlyapnikov denied having given 'any counterrevolutionary directives about behaviour in case of war' or having had any organisational meetings. At the fourth interrogation, on 7 January, he continued to deny having expressed counterrevolutionary views in his conversations with Sergievsky and Mikhailov in November and December 1934. He had shared with Sergievsky criticisms of the Spanish republican forces' military tactics, but denied blaming the Comintern. When pressed as to how

---

43   TsA FSB, R33718, d. 499061, vol. 3, ll. 13–14 (handwritten), ll. 15–17 (typed).
44   TsA FSB, R33718, d. 499061, vol. 3, ll. 18–22 (handwritten), ll. 30–1 (typed). Safarov's and other Zinovievists' testimonies are in RGASPI, f. 671, op. 1, d. 121, ll. 84–94.

someone from Rostov found his address in December 1934, Shlyapnikov pointed out that this visitor could have looked it up in the telephone book (indeed, he was listed in the 1934 edition). He denied having characterised Kirov as an 'inconsistent Bolshevik' at the 6 December 1934 meeting, but recalled that he had said so to Sergievsky earlier that autumn. He thus conveyed his knowledge that Sergievsky had informed about the 6 December conversations. He denied having said anything about Stalin and other CC members being responsible for Kirov's murder. The interrogator accused him of having talked about the arrests of Zinoviev, Kamenev and Zalutsky on 18 December (they and others were arrested on 15–16 December) and of having said that Kirov's murder 'would be used by the CC for reprisals against the "oppositionists"'. Shlyapnikov denied all this, asserting that he learned about the arrests only on 24 December, from Chistyakov, a party member and teacher.[45]

Perhaps consciously challenging Stalin's entire concept of oppositionism and party relations, Shlyapnikov maintained his denials at the fifth interrogation, on 8 January, and at the sixth, on 9 January 1935, when Shtein and Grigorev tried to determine who was 'in the centre' of his alleged 'counterrevolutionary organisation', especially whether Medvedev was involved. Shlyapnikov repeatedly denied knowing anything about a centre, insisting: 'I do not construct my relations with comrades on the principle of their participation or non-participation in the former Workers' Opposition'. The 11 January 1935 interrogation was longer than any previous ones. Interrogators demanded repeatedly that he describe the structure and membership of the illegal organisation of the Workers' Opposition, but he continued to deny having engaged in 'anti-Soviet activity' or knowing anything about such a group. Interrogators claimed the existence of a Moscow centre with sub-groups headed by Mikhailov, Tarasov-Vichinsky and Bruno-Pravdin. Allegedly, Vladimir Tarasov and S.N. Barinov led another group in Omsk and Pivon led one in Rostov. The questions continued as if according to a template, despite Shlyapnikov's denials. He insisted that Safarov was lying about his having entered a bloc with Zinoviev. He also denied Illarion Vardin's testimony accusing Shlyapnikov of having developed

---

45   TsA FSB, R33718, d. 499061, vol. 3, ll. 26–9 (handwritten), ll. 30–1 (typed); ll. 32–7 (handwritten), ll. 38–41 (typed). Shtein, fourth SPO GUGB chief, joined Grigor'ev. The protocol does not indicate which interrogator was speaking. According to archival documents and Iakovlev 1991, Sergievskii was a 'secret NKVD informer' (Iakovlev 1991, p. 121), but Irina Shliapnikova 2012 attests that Shliapnikov knew from the beginning that Sergievskii had been asked to inform, because Sergievskii told him so (conversation). She accidentally saw operational files that were not available to me.

counterrevolutionary views based on the platform of the Workers' Opposition together with his comrades Rozen, Medvedev, Chelyshev et al.[46]

On 13 January Shlyapnikov requested permission to write a declaration.[47] In the next few days, he was allowed to receive parcels.[48] Perhaps NKVD officials thought that he was ready to confess. His statement, written in tiny script on the front and back of four sheets of paper, was addressed to Ivan Akulov, Procurator (Prosecutor) of the USSR and Yagoda, People's Commissar of Internal Affairs. Rather than confessing, he complained that the protocol recorded only truncated versions of his answers and that his request to write out his own answers had been rejected. Offended by the interrogator's characterisation of him as a 'person of undefined occupation', Shlyapnikov explained in detail his poor health, his attempts to seek a pension and the work on his memoirs.[49]

In discussing his memoirs, he elaborated upon remarks he had made about Kirov that were reported to the investigation. On the evening of 6 December, Shlyapnikov clarified, Svechnikov reported to the gathering of comrades that some time in the past, *Krasnaya zvezda* editors had asked him to provide reminiscences about Kirov's feats on the Southern front, but that he had declined, claiming that he did not recall Kirov (probably disingenuously, to avoid having to praise him). Shlyapnikov, either out of mischief or honesty, had reminded him that Kirov was among a North Caucasus delegation memorable for having crossed the Volga near Astrakhan in mid-February 1919, despite a ban.[50]

Refuting the accusation of having conducted counterrevolutionary work, he scoffed at the charge that he could have done so based on the 'old 1920–1

---

46   TsA FSB, R33718, d. 499061, vol. 3, ll. 42–3, 46–9 (handwritten), and ll. 44–45, 51–53 (typed), 8–9 January interrogations; ll. 59–66, 11 January 1935 session (typed); interrogated by Shtein and Grigor'ev. I did not see a handwritten version; Shliapnikov signed each page and at the end that he had read the protocol and it was correct.

47   TsA FSB, R33718, d. 499061, vol. 3, l. 71, note on a 3" × 5" sheet of paper in Shliapnikov's handwriting, addressed to Shtein. The NKVD isolator assistant director directed the note (marked urgent) to SPO chief Molchanov, with copies to interrogators Shtein, Grigor'ev and Braslina on 14 January.

48   TsA FSB, R33718, d. 499061, vol. 3, ll. 50, 72. The parcels contained 20 rubles, socks and underwear, two shirts, two collars [*vorotnichki*], sugar, lemons, glasses, medicinal powder, a handkerchief, butter, cookies, sausage and bread. The medicinal powder (probably for his ears) had to be examined by the prison doctor.

49   TsA FSB, R33718, d. 499061, vol. 3, ll. 73–6 (handwritten), ll. 77–92 (typed), 15–16 January 1935, from 'prisoner of cell no. 96 A.G. Shliapnikov'. Shliapnikov requested that it be attached to the 11 January 1935 interrogation protocol.

50   TsA FSB, R33718, d. 499061, vol. 3, ll. 79–80.

platform', since the Soviet economy had transformed greatly since that time. Moreover, he promoted comradely intra-party relations over rigidly hierarchical ones, insisting that it was ludicrous that he could be a 'centre' and 'leader' for Pravdin and Bruno, who were his old friends from before the revolution, not just collaborators in the Workers' Opposition. He pointed out that they were sufficiently senior party members 'to manage without my leadership'. Insisting on his legal rights, he asked to question Mikhailov personally. Regarding Pivon, he attested that they were not much acquainted, but he found it natural that Pivon would inquire after his health, especially as the press had reported the death of Shlyapnikov's cousin, Yakov, some months earlier. Yakov had belonged to the Society of Old Bolsheviks and some people had confused the two men. He also 'cleared' others, such as Tarasov of Omsk, of suspicion.[51]

Regarding Safarov's incriminations, Shlyapnikov asserted that Safarov's visit to him in 1932 'made a strange impression', since they were 'little acquainted'. He had formed an impression of Safarov as an 'adventurist', based on tales about Safarov's work in Central Asia. He declared that it would have been illogical for Zinoviev to have sent Safarov to propose a bloc to him, since he saw Zinoviev frequently enough for him to have posed the question himself. Besides that, Shlyapnikov knew other former Zinovievists far better than Safarov, yet none of them had proposed any illegal work. He found another logical fallacy in the notion that he would have joined the Zinovievist opposition in 1932, when it was already defeated, although he had not seen fit to join it in the mid-1920s, when it was most active. He had not joined then 'because of matters of principle'. Among these were the opposition's tendencies to 'allow into circulation insinuations', such as the phrase 'Thermidorian reaction'. He had advised Zinoviev and Kamenev that they should provide a straightforward factual analysis, rather than relying on hints and insinuations. Shlyapnikov then ridiculed the testimony of Illarion Vardin (Mgeladze), who he hardly knew, but met only occasionally at Rozen's apartment. Regarding Vardin's 'slanderous assertion [that] I became simply a bourgeois democrat I ... say to you just one thing: I have not arrived at such a state, in which I can spit in my own face'.[52]

---

51 TsA FSB, R33718, d. 499061, vol. 3, ll. 81–2. Aleksandr Pravdin (1879–1938) joined the party in 1899, participated in the 1905 revolution, was on the *Pravda* editorial board in 1912–14 and after the October 1917 Revolution worked in the NKVD. In 1924–5, he was Assistant RSFSR Commissar of Communications, in 1930–3 he worked in *Narkomtorg* and from 1933 in party and Soviet control bodies. See RKP(b) 1961, p. 843; Anderson et al. (eds.) 2007, vol. 1, p. 924; Heywood 2011, p. 150.

52 TsA FSB, R33718, d. 499061, vol. 3, ll. 83–7. He added, '*A te slushaiut, da chai kushaiut*', an idiomatic expression perhaps translated best as 'only fools listen'.

He had last seen Zinoviev in November 1933 in Kislovodsk in the sanatorium Turgenevka, but had not talked politics with him out of a tactful desire not 'to reopen his wounds' from the Ryutin case. In 1934 he had only met Kamenev 'in passing', as they were neighbours. Next, he explained his own perspective on oppositionism. Until 1929 he had viewed party politics as left (Zinoviev, Kamenev and Trotsky) versus right (Nikolai Uglanov and Rykov), with Stalin and Molotov in the centre. 'In the left was much that resonated with my moods, although their general position did not attract me'. But in 1929 his outlook changed due to the CC's commitment to industrialisation, which he supported. He had expressed his new perspective in his 1929 article and through work. Although he was sick with Ménière's syndrome, he worked in Rosmetizprom and in Gosplan RSFSR. Unable to comprehend why he was purged from the party in 1933 as a double-dealer, Shlyapnikov had interpreted his exile in 1934 as signifying how: 'I am guilty only in that I exist'. He nevertheless interpreted his return from exile as the recognition of a mistake. Since then he had written his memoirs, sold some possessions (including his metalworking tools) while awaiting a pension and sought medical treatment. Arrest was unexpected, but he:

> accepted it as a measure of verification, since I don't know about any crimes I have committed against the party. The materials of the investigation have revealed to me all secrets of my exclusion and my exile. And this one circumstance is valuable for me.

If he detailed these secrets, the protocol did not record it. Perhaps he thought his earlier woes were due to misinformation that agents had reported about him in 1932–4. He concluded with a long affirmation of his innocence.[53]

The NKVD nevertheless found sufficient grounds to accuse Shlyapnikov on 15 January, under article 58, paragraphs 10 and 11 of the RSFSR law code, of having been 'one of the leaders of the counterrevolutionary organisation of the so-called Workers' Opposition' who 'led illegal work, directed against Soviet power'. This required his continued detention.[54]

Zinoviev, Kamenev and seven others were tried in secret on 15–16 January; they were found guilty of organising a 'centre' and of 'moral complicity' in the Kirov murder. On 16 January, Shtein informed Shlyapnikov that Kamenev had implicated him in planning 'joint illegal work'. Shlyapnikov wholly denied

---

53   TsA FSB, R33718, d. 499061, vol. 3, ll. 88–92.
54   TsA FSB, R33718, d. 499061, vol. 3, l. 9.

this, but seemed to accept Zinoviev's admission of guilt.[55] On the next day, Shlyapnikov made a statement notable for its discordant style. It began: 'S.M. Kirov's villainous murder was a direct strike against the Leninist Central Committee by the Zinovievist counterrevolutionary underground organisation, revealing an ulcer many years old, parasitically adhering to the party's healthy organism'. But it continued rather differently: 'for a number of years (1925–8), although I did not join the United Opposition, I nevertheless supported and defended it and maintained acquaintances among those who have just unmasked themselves as repulsive counterrevolutionary monsters...'. Further in the statement, Shlyapnikov was induced to 'confess' that he 'insufficiently struggled orally and in writing with those moods, which the exile, S.P. Medvedev, revealed in his letters to me'. Nevertheless, he did not yet denounce Medvedev's views as 'counterrevolutionary' or 'anti-Soviet'. As required, he accepted his arrest as 'completely correct', but emphasised: 'I had nothing to do with the Zinovievist counterrevolutionary organisation and I knew nothing of its existence. As an opponent of factionalism, I did not create any centre, nor did I support any periphery'.[56] Under pressure, Shlyapnikov made some concessions to interrogators, but continued to maintain his own innocence and that of his close comrades.

Although Shlyapnikov was never permitted to question Mikhailov, he did have face-to-face confrontations with two other accusers: Vardin on 28 January 1935 and Safarov on 14 February. In a statement, he wrote that he found meaningful inconsistencies between the version of Vardin's testimony that he heard from Shtein during the 11 January interrogation and the version he heard directly from Vardin on 28 January. The earlier version portrayed him explicating his views to Vardin in the presence of Rozen, Medvedev and others, but the later version had him alone with Vardin. Shlyapnikov requested that Vardin's accusations be verified by Rozen and Medvedev. Surely he suspected that the change in Vardin's testimony was due to the lack of confirmation from Rozen and Medvedev. Furthermore, he pointed out a contradiction between Vardin's assertion that Shlyapnikov had argued that the Bolsheviks 'prematurely took power' and his other assertion that Shlyapnikov claimed to be loyal in 1932 to the 1921–2 platform, since it never referred to the premature seizure of power, which was a Menshevik position. He requested that the investigators confirm this by examining documents from 1921–2. Interrogators, of course, were under

---

55 TsA FSB, R33718, d. 499061, vol. 4, l. 93 (handwritten), l. 94 (typed).
56 TsA FSB, R33718, d. 499061, vol. 4, ll. 95–8. The statement was dated 17 January; Iagoda directed it to Stalin on 19 January. Only a typed copy was preserved in NKVD files, not a signed original.

strict instructions from above to produce confessions. They had no interest in conducting a genuine investigation, based on facts and evidence. Pressured to confess for the party's sake, Shlyapnikov asserted, unlike Rubashov: 'I am ready to do for the party all that is necessary... but I cannot accept Menshevik ideology'.[57]

When Shlyapnikov finally confronted Safarov on 14 February, Safarov repeated the testimony previously attributed to him, but Shlyapnikov retorted that it was all fabricated. He denied Safarov's allegation that he was linked to Vasily Kayurov, a leader of the Vyborg district party committee in 1917 and a former oppositionist, who Shlyapnikov said he had not seen in five years.[58] There was a month-long break in Shlyapnikov's interrogations from mid-February to mid-March, during which he was transferred to Butyrka prison. During this time his close comrade, Medvedev, was interrogated. Arrested in late January 1935 at his place of exile in Medvezhegorsk, he was quickly transferred to Moscow.[59] Characteristically, Medvedev was even less cooperative than Shlyapnikov and more hostile to interrogators.

Medvedev's chief interrogator was a Latvian woman, Lidiya Braslina.[60] Nikolai Sergievsky, the chief informer on the Moscow group of the Workers' Opposition in 1933–4, had reported to her, but had provided no evidence of an active underground organisation. Under pressure to produce results, Braslina summoned Sergievsky in early March and issued him an ultimatum to concoct false evidence of counterrevolutionary activity by Shlyapnikov and Medvedev, whereupon he appealed to the Committee on Party Control (KPK) for advice.[61] Braslina turned her attention to Shlyapnikov on 15–16 March, questioning him about Medvedev's 1922 trip to Germany. Shlyapnikov denied

---

57   TsA FSB, R33718, d. 499061, vol. 4, ll. 104–5 (handwritten by Shliapnikov and signed by him), 29 January 1935. He was still in the NKVD internal prison, but had been moved to cell no. 104.

58   TsA FSB, R33718, d. 499061, vol. 3, ll. 54–6, 67–9. This protocol has no original signatures. Interrogators were Shtein and Petrovskii, SPO GUGB first section chief.

59   TsA FSB, R33718, d. 499061, vol. 5. L.I. Braslina and N. Ivanov interrogated Medvedev on 31 January; 4, 5 and 15 February; and 11 and 14 March.

60   Protocols only provide Braslina's first two initials. Irina Shliapnikova 2000 and 2012, who had access to more NKVD files on her father's case than did I, told me that Braslina was a woman and provided her first name and nationality. Nikita Petrov of Memorial confirmed this in a 2012 email and telephone conversation, adding that at least several other women served as NKVD interrogators, one reaching the rank of colonel. Braslina was promoted to lieutenant in December 1935 (Petrov email 2012).

61   RGASPI, f. 671, op. 1, d. 87, l. 106, typed copy of a statement from Sergievskii to Shkiriatov (11 March 1935).

any conspiratorial purpose to the trip. She also quoted excerpts from correspondence between him, Medvedev and their comrades in the 1920s through to the 1930s. Shlyapnikov's answers include the word 'anti-party' to describe his own and Medvedev's 'evaluations', but he did not sign these answers. Perhaps Braslina inserted the word without his consent. In any case, he continued to deny the more serious charge of having given directives. Intriguingly, he added more information about his differences with the Leningrad Opposition in the 1920s: 'Leaders of this opposition wanted only one thing: return to intra-party democracy as it existed under Lenin. This degree of democracy did not satisfy us, the past for us was not an ideal; we demanded thorough worker democracy'. Conceding that Medvedev's 1934 views were 'deeply mistaken with a counter-revolutionary tendency', he argued that they arose from 'an exile's hopeless desperation'. He acknowledged guilt for not having surrendered Medvedev's 1934 letters to party authorities, but he adamantly refused to confess to having carried out anti-Soviet organisational work.[62] Behind the subtleties of the transcript's wording, there must have occurred a determined struggle between Shlyapnikov and Braslina over its composition.

Shlyapnikov tried to usurp control of the investigation from Braslina in a statement he wrote the next day. Referring to his interrogation of the previous night, he denied Sergievsky's testimony that Zinoviev and Kamenev tried to entice him into a bloc in 1933; he posited that Sergievsky confused 1933 with 1925–7. Moreover, he pointed out that a meeting between them was impossible then, since Zinoviev and Kamenev were in exile from mid-1932 to summer 1933. He concluded: 'It is time to end with this lie about a bloc: there was not one, there were not even suggestions of one'.[63]

Braslina was determined to extract some sort of confession. She first pressured him to confess that in December 1934 he had given Mikhailov directives to conduct underground work. When Shliapnikov rebuffed her, she tried another tack, arguing that he gave directives not to conduct underground work but instead to remain passive. He rejected all this, insisting: 'Neither my meetings nor discussions with former like-minded comrades were organised. My comrades and I criticised individual measures of the party and government,

---

62 TsA FSB, R33718, d. 499061, vol. 4, ll. 111–16 (handwritten), ll. 117–25 (typed). Here Shliapnikov did not sign each paragraph but only the bottom of each page; he wrote at the end 'Written correctly and read' and signed his name. In the typed version, this was changed to the usual 'Written correctly and read by me'. This leads me to wonder if Braslina only read the protocol to him and did not allow him to read it himself.

63 TsA FSB, R33718, d. 499061, vol. 4, ll. 126–7, 17 March 1935 (handwritten by Shliapnikov on a 3.5 × 6 inch sheet of paper), ll. 128–9 (typed).

but without malice or counterrevolutionary intentions'. He admitted that in 1930 he had doubted the methods of implementing collectivisation, considering that the initial instructions were unclear and led to excesses, that he had found the rate of collectivisation 'too high, not taking into account particularities of regions', but that in 1933–4 he had not disagreed with Soviet agricultural policy. Further, Shlyapnikov admitted that in 1931–2, based on conversations with Genrikh Bruno, who worked in the Urals then, he had 'doubted the feasibility of industrialisation tempos'. But through his work in Gosplan RSFSR in 1932–3, his doubts were dispelled. He said that he did not share Medvedev's criticisms of Soviet foreign policy (Soviet entry into the League of Nations), which 'S.P. Medvedev does not understand... and in his criticism slips onto an anti-Soviet path'. He also confessed to having had 'disagreements and doubts on discrete questions of party policy', which he voiced to his close comrades. But he maintained that he did not think that what he said 'could serve for any of my friends as a political orientation'. Finally, he 'confessed' for 'not bringing to the attention of party institutions my doubts and disagreements'.[64]

Despite having assured Shlyapnikov that the investigation was complete, Braslina interrogated him yet again, on 23 March 1935, asking him about friends and acquaintances. Regarding Bykhatsky from Kiev, Shlyapnikov barely remembered him as having passed through Moscow on the way to Chelyabinsk in 1933, but denied Bykhatsky's testimony about having belonged to the Workers' Opposition in 1933. Regarding Kolesnikov, who he knew from the Metalworkers' Union, Shlyapnikov gave a nuanced assessment of Kolesnikov's views in the 1920s, denied having given him 'tasks' or 'assignments' and refused to admit anything suspicious in their 1932–3 meetings, reporting that Kolesnikov asked only for advice on his 'troubles in the party or economic work'. Regarding Alexei Sidorchuk from Rostov, who had brought him letters from Pivon and Trifonova, Shlyapnikov denied knowing him. Required to elaborate further on his views on party economic policy, Shlyapnikov said that his views had changed in 1929 and that he had supported collectivisation and industrialisation. Moreover, he had understood that 'with the attraction into industry and construction sites of millions of workers, immigrants from the countryside, it was impossible to pose the question of intra-party and worker democracy as I had put it earlier'. Finally, Braslina introduced a new charge that in autumn 1933 Shlyapnikov and his comrades had an 'illegal meeting' at which they 'decided the question of

---

64   TsA FSB, R33718, d. 499061, vol. 4, ll. 130–2 (handwritten), ll. 133–6 (typed). Here again he signed each page, but not each paragraph. At the end he signed that he had read the protocol and that it was correct. He also signed that he had been informed that the investigation was over, as of 17 March 1935.

creation of a new party and about the transfer abroad of the leadership of the Workers' Opposition'. He denied all this.⁶⁵

On 26 March 1935, an NKVD SSSR 'special conference' heard Shlyapnikov's case (#705) and, 'for counterrevolutionary activity', sentenced him to five years in the Verkhne-Uralsk political isolator, where Zinoviev, Kamenev and other leading oppositionists were confined.⁶⁶ Yet one more interrogation was demanded of him. On 28 March 1935, N. Ivanov inquired into 'material aid' he rendered to Medvedev's daughters in 1934. Shlyapnikov verified that he had given 30–40 dollars in hard currency to Medvedev's sister Maria Lushina, to help the children, and had occasionally given them a few booklets to purchase items in hard-currency [*Torgsin*] stores. The interrogator attempted to render from this a 'common monetary fund', but Shlyapnikov drily replied that it was the first he had ever heard of it. Then he explained that some of the money remained from his trips abroad and some he had acquired in hopes of going abroad for medical treatment. He had borrowed some from his friend, Lev Green. Upon prompting, he admitted that some had also come from an NKVD diplomatic courier named Ryzhkov. He emphatically denied having a common fund with Medvedev. He acknowledged only giving money to Medvedev's family.⁶⁷

Prison, Exile in Astrakhan, Re-Arrest and Trial

There is still little information available on political isolators such as Verkhne-Uralsk, where Communist oppositionists were imprisoned together with Mensheviks and right-wing Ukrainian nationalists. A Zinovievist seeking release in August 1936, Boris Sakhov-Tsukerman, described squabbling among various political groups, attesting that the Trotskyists were more inclined than others towards protests, including hunger strikes. Although his agenda to seek an early release skews the perspective he offers, a few remarks about

---

65   TsA FSB, R33718, d. 499061, vol. 4, ll. 137–41 (handwritten, signed by Shliapnikov at the bottom of each page), ll. 142–9 (typed).
66   TsA FSB, R33718, d. 499061, vol. 4, l. 155, excerpt, verified on 18 May 1955 by Major Sychev, KGB archival registration section sixth division senior operational representative. The sentence was to be counted from 2 January 1935.
67   TsA FSB, R33718, d. 499061, vol. 4, ll. 150–1 (handwritten, signed by Shliapnikov at the bottom of each page), ll. 152–4 (typed). Shliapnikov was also asked about Fani Ezerskaia (a German communist), whom Shliapnikov admitted having known since 1912, having been aware that she was an NKVD (former OGPU) employee, and adding that the last time he saw her was in Berlin in 1928.

Shlyapnikov ring true. Singling him out as one of the few bold enough to state his views loudly and openly, Sakhov recalled that the former leader of the Workers' Opposition had taunted Kamenev, reproached Zinoviev for having slandered himself and others, and had asked sarcastically that if Zinoviev and Kamenev 'consider me an enemy, then why should I say that I am their friend?'[68]

While he was confined in prison, Shlyapnikov's deafness, vertigo and other symptoms of Ménière's syndrome grew worse. At times he suffered from a loss of vision and mobility. None of the doctors he saw at Verkhne-Uralsk prison, or in Magnitogorsk, dared advise the NKVD to release him for the sake of his health. Shlyapnikov contemplated declaring a hunger strike, but finally rejected this option, having realised that the Politburo would only react negatively to this as a hostile act. Having been returned to Butyrka prison in Moscow in autumn 1935, he wrote an appeal to the Politburo for his release, assuring its members that he could work for the party and international revolution. Fulsomely praising Stalin's international policy of a 'united proletarian front', he acknowledged that he had surrounded himself with 'unworthy people' and was guilty of having defended 'group interests', but denied charges of having participated in or advocated 'underground organisations, Siberian banditry or an uprising at the rear of the Red Army'. Offering to make a public confession of his guilt, he pleaded not to be tried as an 'enemy', not to 'allow the Communist Party's enemies to speculate on my name and behaviour'. He finally underscored his weak physical condition that would have prevented a public appearance until his recovery.[69]

Judging from the sentences underlined by Molotov in the text, party leaders may well have decided to release Shlyapnikov in order to restore his health prior to a potential show trial. Although Shlyapnikov had hoped to return to a free life with his family in Moscow, in December 1935 the NKVD converted his sentence to exile in Astrakhan.[70] In Astrakhan he found a community of fellow political exiles. He seems to have been on good terms with many; he rendered aid to one co-exile, Elizaveta Sandler (*née* Senatskaya), by selling the

---

68 RGASPI, f. 671, op. 1, d. 258, ll. 108–19, 23 August 1936, to Ezhov and Iagoda. Sakhov-Tsukerman (b. 1900) was Northern krai prosecutor before his arrest (l. 120). At a July 2012 conference in Memorial in Moscow, Russian historians noted that FSB archivists say that they cannot locate Verkhne-Ural'sk documents.

69 RGASPI, f. 82, op. 2, d. 198, ll. 133–8, copy of a letter from Shliapnikov to the Politburo, 20 October 1935, Butyrskaia prison, Moscow, verified by Braslina.

70 TsA FSB, R33718, d. 499061, vol. 3, l. 117, protocol no. 170 (excerpt) of the NKVD SSSR osoboe soveshchanie session, 10 December 1935.

motor that Kollontai had earlier obtained for him.[71] As soon as he arrived in Astrakhan, he appealed to Yezhov for 'medical aid' for his wife and children.[72] They suffered from isolation and material need while he was in prison. His wife not only suffered from illness, but had to support her husband for the first few weeks while he was in Astrakhan. She wrote to Yezhov for help in receiving medical treatment, material aid and work. In return, she promised she would strive to make her husband into a worthy candidate for party membership yet again. Perhaps moved by her appeal, Yezhov offered some aid.[73]

Shlyapnikov was allowed a brief visit with his oldest son. Having attended an elite boarding school ['*Lesnaya shkola*'] in 1933–5, Yuri had spent little time with his father during his last months of liberty. He long remembered how hurt he was that his parents thus deprived him of time with them in the period prior to his father's arrest. Yuri was permitted to visit his father in spring 1936 for about two weeks. He recalled that Shlyapnikov then worked as assistant director of the town transport section, which meant that he oversaw horses and a few vehicles. Yuri followed him on his rounds, which included a trip to a factory, where Shlyapnikov perhaps hoped his son would share his own fascination with mechanics. Yuri was most impressed with his father's skill in engineering a time-saving machine with rotating shelves for unloading bread from the horses. The time spent together reinforced his memories of his father as a man who was constantly busy, never able to sit in idleness.[74] Perhaps his son's visit inspired Shlyapnikov to request permission to visit Moscow for medical treatment and for transfer to Kazan, where he hoped to find a less inhospitable climate to recover from his illness than Astrakhan, where he found that the excessive heat worsened his symptoms.[75]

Forced to remain in Astrakhan, Shlyapnikov rose in responsibility; by summer 1936 he was working as a senior economist with the Lower Volga Steamboat Administration. Isolated from his family, he may have found comfort in an affair or intimate friendship with a female co-exile. His exile was disrupted by the onset of the Great Terror (1936–8). By early 1936, the chief of the NKVD, Yagoda, was viewed as insufficiently diligent in searching out enemies, so Yezhov, under Stalin's direction, re-opened the case against the Zinovievists and the Trotskyists for Kirov's murder and other political 'crimes'.

---

71 Iurii Shliapnikov 2004.
72 RGASPI, f. 589, op. 3, d. 9103, vol. 3, l. 114, telegram to Ezhov, 15 January 1936.
73 RGASPI, f. 671, op. 1, d. 22, ll. 169–71, letters from January–February 1936, with Ezhov's notation.
74 Iurii Shliapnikov 2007, interview, pp. 2, 7–8.
75 RGASPI, f. 671, op. 1, d. 22, l. 168, 26 May 1936 letter from Shliapnikov to the CC Secretariat.

New arrests of Trotskyists occurred in spring 1936. Unlike Shlyapnikov, Zinoviev and Kamenev had remained in prison since their initial arrests in December 1934. Under pressure, they confessed to planning the murder of party leaders, including Kirov and Stalin; they might have confessed to save their lives, or out of party loyalty, which was Bukharin's motivation, as laid out in a 10 December 1937 letter to Stalin. In August 1936 their confessions featured in the first public show trial of the Great Terror.[76]

Shlyapnikov's re-arrest followed on 2 September 1936.[77] New evidence included a testimony taken under interrogation from Kensorin Gidlevsky in March–April 1936 and Faivilovich in August 1936. Other evidence included an informer's July 1935 report that, in conversations with other prisoners in Verkhne-Uralsk isolator, Shlyapnikov had praised European democracy and had said that the unemployed in capitalist countries were better off than Soviet workers. Allegedly, he hoped that war would bring about revolution in the capitalist countries and change in the USSR. Gidlevsky reluctantly (probably under beatings and torture, as abrupt shifts in the protocol seem to indicate) confessed to having been in a Trotskyist organisation that formed a bloc with the 'Shlyapnikovists', including Bruno, Medvedev and Chelyshev. He nevertheless denied knowing of any counterrevolutionary acts perpetrated by the Shlyapnikovists. In a more smoothly flowing protocol, Faivilovich confessed that he, with others, planned the assassination of Stalin. He testified that another oppositionist had told him that 'Zinoviev was linked with Shlyapnikov' and that Shlyapnikov had advocated 'struggle with the party leadership ... with weapons in hand'.[78] The final piece of evidence was a letter Shlyapnikov sent to Ekaterina on 10 August 1936. In it, he shared with her that his readings of the correspondence of Marx and Engels confronted him with a marked contrast 'between the progressive character of the "future" which saturates the correspondence and that ubiquitous and overwhelming vulgarity one

---

76 TsA FSB, R27744, d. 3257, l. 14; Irina Shliapnikova 2000; Getty and Naumov 1999, pp. 247–60, 556–60; Getty and Naumov 2008, pp. 187–94.
77 A search of his residence at no. 30 Novikov street in Astrakhan yielded ordinary personal and household items, 376 rubles in cash, 35 brochures in French, five books in French, three books in German, three volumes of the works of Marx and Engels, 10 books in Russian, a folder of correspondence, two folders with copies of the correspondence of Lenin, Krupskaia and Zinoviev, three dictionaries (English-Russian, French-Russian, Russian-English) and periodicals including *Bol'shevik* and *L'Humanité* (TsA FSB, R27744, d. 3257, ll. 5–13).
78 TsA FSB, R27744, d. 3257, ll. 28–37 (typed), interrogated by Matusov, and ll. 38–42, interrogated by Lerner. This was probably Leonid Faivilovich, sentenced to execution in a case related to the August 1936 Zinoviev-Kamenev Trial (Lenoe 2010, p. 465).

encounters at every turn'. From any kind of rational perspective, none of this evidence directly implicated him in terrorist acts, but in the irrational context of the terror, thoughts led inexorably to deeds. The Astrakhan NKVD sent him by 'special convoy as an important state criminal' to Moscow.[79]

In Moscow he was first interrogated on 8 October 1936. The interrogator set the tone by declaring that Shlyapnikov did not give 'truthful testimony' in 1935, but he responded that he had 'nothing to add' to his 1935 testimony. He denied any knowledge of a Trotskyist-Zinovievist organisation, denied the existence of 'a counterrevolutionary organisation called the Workers' Opposition' and denied even negotiations about 'joint counterrevolutionary work'. Despite Zinoviev's testimony to the contrary, Shlyapnikov said their meetings had not been of a counterrevolutionary nature. When asked why he visited Zinoviev together with Medvedev, he responded: 'Medvedev was my closest comrade and we often dropped in on people together'. Shlyapnikov acknowledged having met Gidlevsky on occasion, but only in 'personal meetings of old comrades', where any criticisms voiced were not 'counterrevolutionary'. Somewhat intriguingly, he added that there were more people at the meeting with Gidlevsky than those listed by the interrogator (Medvedev, Bruno, Chelyshev and Gridasov), but oddly, the interrogator did not follow up on his implication. Usually they were eager to expand the circles of accused. The interrogator had repeatedly accused Shlyapnikov of lying, but his final answer was: 'I speak only the truth. The testimony of Vardin, Safarov, Zinoviev and Gidlevsky is false and therefore I deny it'.[80] Shlyapnikov's refusal to cooperate may have saved him from further prolonged interrogations and public trial.

Nevertheless, he could not be released. On 25 October 1936 the NKVD issued an order to accuse him on article 58, paragraphs 8, 10 and 11 and to keep him imprisoned.[81] No further testimony against him seems to have been collected. In April 1937 he was accused according to article 58-8 and 58-11 of the RSFSR law code of having led a counterrevolutionary group called the Workers'

---

79 TsA FSB, R27744, d. 3257, ll. 1–4, report prepared by SPO GUGB chief Molchanov; l. 7.
80 TsA FSB, R27744, d. 3257, ll. 16–23. Shliapnikov made minor corrections in the protocol, signed each page and at the end. He signed it as 'written from my words, read by me'. The interrogator's name appears to be Captain G.B. [illegible], SPO GUGB [1st or 7th] section assistant chief.
81 TsA FSB, R27744, d. 3257, l. 15, signed by junior lieutenant of state security, Fradkin. The only remaining interrogation of Shliapnikov was on 13 November; it seemed brief and inquired into his relationship with Konstantin Andreev, chair of the housing cooperative where Shliapnikov lived in 1923–9 (ll. 24–5 (handwritten), ll. 26–7 (typed), interrogated by Fradkin and signed by senior inspector Golanskii).

Opposition, of having linked up with the 'counterrevolutionary Trotskyist-Zinovievist terrorist bloc' and of having 'tried to conclude a bloc with Ruth Fischer for joint struggle against the policy and measures of the Comintern'. It alleged that he advocated 'individual terror' and that groups he directed in Omsk, Rostov-on-Don, Kiev, Odessa, Baku, Kharkov and Moscow had 'prepared and tried to realise the murder of comrade Stalin'. Acknowledging that Shlyapnikov did not confess his guilt, the accusation established it through the testimony of Zinoviev, Safarov, Vardin and others. It recommended that the Military Collegium of the USSR Supreme Court should try him and apply the 1 December 1934 law. Applying to cases of terrorist acts, this law ordered the immediate execution of capital-punishment sentences, with no appeals.[82]

The USSR Supreme Court Military Collegium met on 2 September 1937 in closed session to sentence Shlyapnikov, who appeared before the court in a two-hour long session. Refusing to admit his guilt, he also detailed his objections to others' testimony against him. Given the last word, Shlyapnikov declared that he was 'not hostile towards soviet power'. Perhaps as a last ironic remark, he confessed guilt only to 'a liberal attitude towards those around him'. Nevertheless, the court on the same day found him guilty under article 58, paragraphs 8 and 11, of having led 'an anti-Soviet terrorist organisation, the so-called "Workers' Opposition"', which carried out 'counterrevolutionary activity directed towards the toppling of soviet power'. He was convicted of having been in contact with 'leaders of Trotskyist-Zinovievist and Right-Bukharinist terrorist organisations' and of having ordered members of his 'anti-Soviet organisation' to carry out 'terrorist acts' against party and government leaders. Then the Military Collegium sentenced him to 'the highest measure of punishment – execution by shooting with confiscation of all personal property'. Below this was pencilled: 'the sentence was carried out on that day in Moscow'.[83] Despite 'eyewitness' tales that he survived for years longer, either abroad or under a false name in the Gulag (see the Epilogue below), documents attest to the fact that shortly after his 1937 execution, Alexander Shlyapnikov's body was cremated and buried in Donskoe cemetery in a common grave.[84]

---

82   TsA FSB, R27744, d. 3257, l. 98, 11 April 1937, signed by Braslina, lieutenant of state security; Serbinov, captain of state security; Kurskii, GUGB fourth section chief; and Rozovskii, senior assistant USSR Prosecutor; Medvedev 1973, p. 161.
83   TsA FSB, R27744, d. 3257, l. 102–4, signed by Ul'rikh (chair), Dmitriev and Kandybin. Kozlov was secretary.
84   Mil'chakov 1991, p. 4. Relatives are not certain whether his ashes were placed in common grave no. 1 or no. 2.

Conclusion

Exiled briefly in 1934, Shlyapnikov revealed in his diary pessimistic thoughts about Stalinist repression and the mistreatment of workers, but he did not give up hope, either in socialism's victory or in improving his own situation. Under interrogation in 1935–6, he did not interpret his web of relationships as a conspiracy, nor did he admit to having engaged in terrorism or to having ever been a co-conspirator with Zinoviev, Kamenev or others. In 1935 he did submit momentarily to pressure to denounce certain statements made by his closest comrade Medvedev. A health crisis induced by prison conditions also made him waver late in 1935, when he offered to make a public renunciation of his past, although not a wholesale one. Yet in 1936 he stood firm. There was no 'show trial' of the Workers' Opposition, either because it did not fit the narrative of oppositionism Stalin desired to construct or because Shlyapnikov and his closest comrades did not succumb to pressure to debase themselves and

FIGURE 35   *Alexander Shlyapnikov's ashes may have been buried in Donskoe cemetery, common grave no. 1 for victims of Stalinist repression, 1930–42 (photo by Barbara Allen, 2012).*

slander others in the service of the 'party'. For them, the party was not Stalin and his band, but a revolutionary political institution organised by workers in order to achieve a better life for the oppressed. This firm conviction helped them resist Stalin's rhetoric and narrative of the party's past and to imagine an alternative to his vision of socialism.

Epilogue: Retribution Upon the Family and Rehabilitation

Shlyapnikov's wife and children were allowed to remain in Moscow after his arrest and received some assistance through Yezhov's secretary, Sima Ryzhova, who was Ekaterina's old friend. Ekaterina wrote a letter to Yezhov pleading to stay in Moscow for medical treatment for Yuri, who she claimed was 'nervous'. Yuri, who later did not recall having been especially nervous, thought this was a subterfuge, suggested by Ryzhova, to play on Yezhov's sympathies. Ekaterina and the children seem to have visited Shlyapnikov in prison at some point, perhaps upon Braslina's arrangement. The children were told that he was sick and in hospital. Before 1936 Shlyapnikov's family continued to have normal social relations, but in 1936 they were shunned. Life became difficult, as Ekaterina's typewriter had been confiscated and work as a typist had been her main source of income. According to the children, Ryzhova warned Ekaterina to leave Moscow with the children immediately after Shlyapnikov's execution in order to avoid arrest, but she panicked and did not prepare in time.[1]

Ekaterina was arrested just days after her husband's execution. Yuri remembered the secret police rifling through the family's possessions and exulting when they found valuables [*zolotye rybki*].[2] While their mother was sentenced to eight years in prison, the children were first taken to a processing centre at the former Danilovsky monastery in Moscow, then to Gorky (formerly Nizhny Novgorod), where they were dispatched to separate orphanages. Irina remembered that she and Yuri spent several days at the monastery waiting for their younger brother, Alexander, to arrive. Although staff showed movies to distract the children, she remembered that she and her siblings just stood by the window and cried for their mother and caregiver. Irina's orphanage director (Dmitriev) in Kulebaki noted that she was withdrawn when she first arrived. When he asked her why, she explained that she did not like 'the collective', because she was accustomed to playing only with her younger brother. She insisted that her parents were on a trip to Astrakhan and would soon collect

---

1 Shliapnikova 2000; Iurii Shliapnikov 2004; RGASPI, f. 589, op. 3, d. 9103, vol. 5, l. 232, 14 March 1935, letter from E. Shliapnikova to Ezhov. According to Petrov 2012, it would not be surprising if the family were allowed to visit Shliapnikov in 1935; it would have been more unusual in 1937.
2 Iurii Shliapnikov 2004.

her.³ Her orphanage director reunited Alexander with her and facilitated the children's written correspondence with Yuri, who was able to visit them during World War II. Briefly after the war, they were re-united with their mother in Gorky, although they were not permitted to live together. All three children and their mother were arrested in 1948–51, when a new wave of terror broke. Irina's and Yuri's university educations were interrupted, while Alexander was snatched from his job at a Moscow construction site. Yuri served time in Komi and Alexander in Kolyma, but a sympathetic prosecutor changed Irina's prison-camp sentence to internal exile in Krasnoyarsk. Both young men were relatively fortunate to be assigned to engineering work that preserved their lives and health.⁴

Stalin died in 1953, after which his successors began slowly releasing prisoners from the Gulag. This became a flood after Khrushchev denounced Stalin's crimes in his 'Secret Speech' to the Twentieth Party Congress in 1956. After Ekaterina and the children were freed and returned to Gorky in the mid-1950s, they submitted the first of many petitions to clear Shlyapnikov of criminal and political charges. They were allowed to return to Moscow in the late 1950s, when Yuri earned a position as professor of chemistry at Moscow State University. The criminal case against Shlyapnikov was overturned in 1963 due to lack of evidence. Sergievsky recanted his testimony in 1956–7 and the authorities deemed Safarov's testimony 'untrustworthy'. The 1977 decision annulling Medvedev's case for lack of evidence emphasised that: 'None of those judged on the Workers' Opposition case confessed guilt'. Other evidence indicates that a few minor figures may have confessed.⁵ Shlyapnikov was only restored to party membership in 1988, as a result of the work of Alexander Yakovlev's commission on the rehabilitation of Stalin's victims. Irina Shliapnikova, a chemist and amateur historian, contributed much to her father's rehabilitation in the court of public opinion by writing and speaking about his life. Both she and her younger brother live in Moscow. Author of a textbook translated into English and used in university chemistry classes, Yuri began to travel abroad

---

3 Irina Shliapnikova 2012; Gusev 2006, p. 129.
4 Iurii Shliapnikov 2006–7, interviews.
5 Shliapnikova and Iurii Shliapnikov conversations and interviews; RGASPI, f. 589, op. 3, d. 9104, vol. 4 (E.S. Shliapnikova); TsA FSB, R27744, d. 3257, ll. 113–18; TsA FSB, R27744, d. 3257, ll. 127–9. Iakovlev 1991 asserts that some of those indicted on the case of the Moscow Workers' Opposition did confess guilt. Full access to FSB archives is needed to evaluate the testimony of all those prosecuted on the cases of the Workers' Opposition in Moscow and other cities.

to scientific conferences in the 1970s and, in the first decade of the twenty-first century, became a United States citizen. Residing in New Jersey with his daughter Marina, he remains in touch with his relatives in Moscow.[6]

Despite their father's rehabilitation of criminal charges and restoration to party membership, uncertainties about his fate still trouble his children, because survivors of the Stalin era have insisted that they met Shlyapnikov after his documented execution in 1937. One such account is Leopold Trepper's memoir of his time as a spy in World War II Europe. Trepper recounts that he met Shlyapnikov on an aeroplane above North Africa among a group of Russians being repatriated from France to the Soviet Union. Remembering the episode in great detail, even claiming that he and 'Chliapnikov' had mistakenly taken one another's suitcases at the airport in Moscow, he nevertheless relates 'facts' that could not have applied to Shlyapnikov, such as that Lenin arranged his resettlement in France immediately after the defeat of the Workers' Opposition and that he had worked there as a carpenter through the 1920s and 1930s, until 1945. In Trepper's tale, Shlyapnikov is a 'naïve' Old Bolshevik eager to return to the USSR to aid its recovery and continue working for the victory of communism, unaware of certain impending execution.[7] Another tale emerged in the late 1980s, as newspaper articles on former oppositionists prompted a Gulag survivor to write to Shlyapnikov's children, claiming that she had seen him in a prison camp after the war and that Stalin had called him to Moscow, after which, upon his return to the camp, he was beaten to death by common criminals. Still another account depicts him as having been on a secret mission in North Africa during the war. Because Irina has found a mathematical discrepancy in the records of the executions and burials in Donskoe cemetery on 2 September 1937, the family cannot discount such rumours, which taint their memories and leave them with uncertainty as to where they should mourn and for what time and the circumstances of death. I accept the version laid out in archival documents, but am inclined to think that alternative tales hold meaning for those who tell them, conveying Alexander Shlyapnikov's importance as a 'proletarian role model' and a symbolic carrier of the most idealistic hopes of the revolutionaries.

---

6 RGASPI, f. 589, op. 3, d. 9103, vol. 4, l. 43, Ekaterina Shliapnikova's 1956 autobiography; RGASPI, f. 589, op. 3, d. 9103, vol. 6, l. 296, Ekaterina Shliapnikova's undated autobiography; conversations with Iurii and Irina.

7 Trepper 1977, pp. 329–31, 336. If the tale is not entirely invented, Trepper might have met Gavriil Miasnikov and confused him with Shliapnikov in his memories.

Conclusion

As a worker in the Bolshevik leadership, with experience of having participated in Western-European socialist parties and trade unions, Shlyapnikov promoted meaningful participation from below in governing and economic management. His proposals had democratic potential, even though they were too narrowly class-based. He tolerated political differences among workers and demonstrated compassion towards workers' suffering, but he was too easily convinced, as a young man, that workers' rights could only be ensured by the political repression of the propertied classes. Among workers he was a natural leader. Many liked and admired him as a comrade committed to bettering their lives at the local level and on a grander scale, who had risen far in party and union ranks and who had proven himself professionally through developing his skills as a metalworker in the most demanding industrial jobs not only in Russia, but also in the most advanced factories of Western Europe. He sought to elevate talented proletarians to positions in the party, trade unions, economic administration and government. Moreover, he possessed sufficient self-confidence, reinforced by an ironic sense of humour, to speak and act autonomously in circles of the party intelligentsia. His charm, work ethic and intelligence won the friendship and respect of many European socialists – not only radicals but moderates as well. He became a high-ranking party official, trade-union leader and economic administrator, accumulating layers of identity throughout his life, yet the perspective he acquired early on as an industrial worker never completely left him.

Shlyapnikov's character and principles began to form in a youth of poverty; his mother raised him, since his father had died young, and the culture of the Old Belief shaped his early impressions of the Russian Orthodox Church and the tsarist authorities as capricious and oppressive. As a youth, Shlyapnikov was an eager and talented student, who continued to study after his formal schooling ended. His interests included the humanities as well as technical subjects. Lacking the opportunity to achieve a higher education, he regarded skilled factory work as a worthy career goal and his proletarian 'credentials' were unimpeachable. He began metals factory work at the age of 13, quickly became a skilled fitter, turner and draftsman and practised his craft for 17 years in Russian and Western-European metalworking factories. Shlyapnikov's experience as a factory worker shaped both his understanding of Bolshevism and his vision of the role of workers in the socialist state.

Having abandoned his childhood religious beliefs as he read more widely and entered the orbit of older workers who were atheists, he soon came under the sway of Social-Democratic political philosophy. Belief in the victory of the working class over capitalist oppression supplanted for him faith in God and redemption in the afterlife. In prison and in emigration he intently read the works of Marx and Engels, seeking a firm grounding in the philosophy to which he had devoted his life, in order to put it into practice. Although he was not a theorist, Shlyapnikov sought to understand Marxism and apply it practically. For him, deeds more than words proved who a person was and what he believed, and led to the creation of a better world. A tireless organiser for the Bolshevik Party and the unions of which he was a member, he also wrote valuable and respected memoir histories of the Russian revolutionary movement and of the 1917 revolutions, yet even his published memoirs had a practical orientation. They conveyed to workers an oblique call to action – for workers to emancipate themselves.

Turning points in Shlyapnikov's life coincided with pivotal events in twentieth-century Russian and Soviet history. From the Revolution of 1905, when he led demonstrations against tsarist rule in his native Murom and was imprisoned for his efforts, Shlyapnikov began developing into a dedicated, bold and experienced revolutionary. Forced to flee Russia in the reactionary year 1908 to avoid arrest, he resumed a life of factory work and political activities (legal and illegal) in Western Europe, from which he returned permanently to Russia only in late 1916. His work in Western-European factories and his involvement in the trade unions there acquainted him with more developed forms of worker organisation than he had seen in Russia, where unions were tightly restricted and for long periods banned outright. Moving in the circles of the Russian party intelligentsia, he grew closer to Vladimir Lenin and carried on an intimate relationship with the noblewoman and socialist feminist, Alexandra Kollontai. Kollontai's idealism and admiration of the working class resounded with Shlyapnikov; she encouraged him to develop his abilities as a worker-*intelligent* and as a politician. Under the tutelage of Kollontai, Lenin and Nadezhda Krupskaya, he wrote articles about working-class life and organisation.

Having worked in French, German and English factories and having participated in French and English trade unions, Shlyapnikov firmly believed that Russian workers could learn much from their Western-European counterparts. His investigations into wage rates, production practices, labour exchanges and other problems increased his understanding of the unions' practical role in workers' lives. Yet he saw the purpose of trade unions as not only to provide for workers in times of sickness or unemployment, but also to advance the cause of the 'workers' revolution'. He favoured new-style production unions, unifying workers of an entire industry, over trade unions that brought together workers of particular trades within industries. Through unions, he believed that workers would master production, manage the economy and cooperate in creating a new, more just, society, although he only began to flesh out the details of his vision in late 1917.

Despite his dedication to unions, Shlyapnikov was equally committed to the Bolshevik political party as a conduit for revolutionary struggle. The Bolsheviks drew him because they led the first socialist workers' organisations with which he formed ties and because he perceived them as more devoted to revolutionary action and more effective than other socialist groups in organising underground work. In his experience, the underground party organisation had proven most effective in pursuing revolutionary goals when legal options (such as those through unions) were not available. Other socialists saw him as a Bolshevik Party stalwart, with some reason. The fierceness with which Shlyapnikov had defended his Old Believer religion as a youth carried over into his devotion to the Bolsheviks. Nevertheless, he often collaborated with other socialists in practical work, as did many other radical left-wing revolutionaries before and during the October Revolution.

Shlyapnikov was closer politically to Lenin than to any other leading Bolshevik *intelligent*. Yet it is not entirely correct to regard him as a 'loyal Leninist', for he saw the party as an organisation of workers, rather than as an offering by the *intelligenty* to the workers. Indeed, the terms 'Leninism' and 'Leninist' only came into usage in the 1920s. He did not see himself as Lenin's subordinate in party matters, but as beholden to worker-Bolsheviks in Russia. He constantly reminded Lenin that conscious workers were the guiding force behind revolution and that organisational work should take precedence over partisan intra-party politics. Lenin often seemed to agree with Shlyapnikov on the need to rely upon 'conscious' workers to build the party's organisation, so Shlyapnikov in turn usually came around to support Lenin's stance on theoretical disputes. Shlyapnikov's preoccupation with revolutionary action, his respect for Lenin's erudition and his appreciation of Lenin's high level of activity in areas of practical use to the revolution led him often to ignore differences between Lenin and himself and the implications of these differences (as well as of Lenin's dominating personality) for worker empowerment.

Shlyapnikov's views on the role of workers vis-à-vis the *intelligenty* in the party grew out of his regard for ideas as tools for organising to create a more just world. He feared that *intelligent* influence could dilute that of the workers in the party and undermine its usefulness in empowering workers, but he respected those who were truly learned in Marxist philosophy. Until well after the revolution he saw theoretical differences as secondary in comparison to the great mass of unaccomplished practical work. When the Bolsheviks were confronted with the challenge of holding onto power after they had seized control of the state, differences in emphasis turned into strong disagreements over policies.

The exile, imprisonment or conscription of numerous revolutionaries during World War I allowed Shlyapnikov, as a man able to move quickly between, and function in, various European countries, to rise quickly in the Bolshevik Party leadership. When revolution erupted in Russia in February 1917, Shlyapnikov was one of the more prominent Bolshevik Party leaders on the scene in Petrograd. As a member of the Bolshevik Party CC Russian Bureau and of the Executive Committee of the Soviet of Workers' and Soldiers' Deputies, he opposed the Provisional Government, promoted a coalition government of revolutionary socialist parties and called for an end to the war. His decisions coincided with his views on the course that the revolution should take and on the role of workers' organisations. In a matter of weeks, more moderate Bolsheviks (especially Kamenev and Stalin), who were returning from exile, pushed him from the centre of political struggle; they downplayed calls for ending the war and did not actively oppose the Provisional Government. He was unable to obtain political victory, but he made a point of it to recall Kamenev's and Stalin's positions in his memoirs published in the 1920s.

Shunted aside from party leadership, Shlyapnikov transferred his attention by mid-1917 to work in the trade unions, particularly the Metalworkers' Union, where he was in his milieu. Leading first the Petrograd, and later the All-Russian, Metalworkers' Union, he became even more convinced of the unions' potential for realising his dream of worker emancipation. To him, the economic struggle of establishing tariff rates and unifying workers around industrial unions was as vital as that of achieving political victory. His ambitions were not limited to economic goals, however. As conservative leaders of industry placed obstacles in the way of tariff negotiations, he became more convinced in his belief that only another revolution could accomplish real change that would give unions a role in managing the economy and in regulating production. A notable result of his trade-union work in 1917, when he worked together with non-Bolshevik as well as Bolshevik metalworkers to accomplish change, was to deepen his appreciation of the contributions of non-Bolshevik workers (if not for non-Bolsheviks of other social classes) to improving workers' lives.

As Commissar of Labour after the Bolsheviks seized power in October 1917, Shlyapnikov relied on the trade unions to provide staff for government bodies, to provide input into government policy-making and to help implement government policy. He undertook important and difficult tasks such as extending wage-rate agreements (tariffs) to industry on a national scale, carrying out a programme to nationalise industry and elaborating a plan for workers' control, in which he promoted unions over factory committees as the preferable method to organise workers. His projects met with limited success. The tariff was published as a decree, but inflation rendered its rates useless. On the project of workers' control, Shlyapnikov's ambitions for the unions clashed with Lenin's political stake in the factory committees, which were far more pro-Bolshevik than were the unions in late 1917 and early 1918. Nationalisation of enterprises foundered at a time of economic crisis. Realising that the crisis threatened the survival of the working class (more and more workers were leaving industry), he requested enormous state subsidies to cover workers' cost of living, but was refused.

Increasingly disillusioned by the Soviet government's lack of support for his proposals to aid workers, Shlyapnikov welcomed assignments (to gather produce and to oversee military campaigns in the Russian Civil War) that removed him from Moscow (the new capital) and that provided the opportunity to achieve more immediate and visible results on behalf of the worker revolution. As the leader of an expedition to gather grain and other foodstuffs from the North Caucasus and later, as chair of the Caspian-Caucasian front, he recruited staff from the trade unions and went to great lengths to maintain good relations with local industrial workers. His military mission, however, was marred by the collapse, from disease and starvation, of one of the armies operating on his front. He was also entwined in political intrigues that he felt were detrimental to the military campaign. Poor health finally forced him to leave the front and return to Moscow.

When Shlyapnikov returned from the front to the Metalworkers' Union in 1919, he suddenly became aware that the attitude of party and soviet leaders towards workers had undergone ominous changes. He feared that the party and state were relying too greatly upon 'bourgeois' specialists, such as engineers and other professionals, in the management of industry and the state and he was horrified by the increasingly common tendency, in his opinion, in government circles to casually speak of and apply coercive measures towards workers to increase production. Moreover, he witnessed the deterioration of the working class – its leading members had been diverted to crucial work in the military, party and state and many other workers had been forced to leave industry by the economic crisis and to seek refuge in the countryside.

Shlyapnikov's response was activist – he spoke and published articles criticising the existing situation and demanded a concerted campaign to increase the influence of organised workers (in unions) over party and state policy. He called for the unions to replace state economic bodies as managers of the economy, for the reinforcement of workers' representation in higher party bodies and for the revival of the party's dedication to empowering workers.

The results of the Eighth Party Congress, where the Communist Party's economic programme was adopted, encouraged him in his campaign. The programme contained a clause that underlined the importance of the role of trade unions in the management of production, in combating bureaucracy in state economic bodies and in increasing worker participation in the management of industry. This clause became the linchpin of his theses on the role of the trade unions.

Although trade unionists largely lined up behind Tomsky's more moderate views, with a die-hard contingent following Trotsky, Shlyapnikov found support among fellow metalworkers and some other strong-willed union leaders. Together they formed the Workers' Opposition. As leader of the Workers' Opposition (1919–21), he presented a programme to realise his ideal of a worker-run state, advocating trade-union control of the economy and soviet control of politics, with an emphasis on workers' initiative. The Workers' Opposition gained strength and their proposals gained momentum during the winter of 1919–20, especially after Trotsky's call for the 'militarisation of labour' outraged many moderate trade unionists. In autumn 1920, the role of the trade unions became a hotly-debated topic, but intra-party democracy was another, which Shlyapnikov saw as connected to trade-union issues. Particularly concerned about ending the system of appointments whereby the party Orgburo and party committees appointed workers' leaders, Shlyapnikov called for the election of leaders by assemblies of workers, with confirmation from above. Moreover, he began to more explicitly attack the party leadership, calling for a wholesale 'workerisation' of the party CC at the next congress.

The trade-union debate was opened to the entire party membership in late December 1920, with proponents of various views airing their positions in the press and at assemblies of communists at all levels. Shlyapnikov's, Trotsky's and Lenin's supporters competed for delegates to the Tenth Party Congress. In the face of resistance from party and soviet leaders, non-proletarian members of the party and from many trade unionists who did not share its views, the Workers' Opposition was defeated at the Tenth Party Congress in March 1921. Furthermore, alarmed by the Kronstadt uprising and by Lenin's and Bukharin's frightening warnings of the ideological threat posed by the Workers' Opposition, congress delegates voted to ban it and any future opposition groups within the party.

Because Shlyapnikov and others from the Workers' Opposition were elected by the Congress to important posts, including CC membership, he imagined he would have the opportunity to realise some parts of the programme of the Workers' Opposition, one of which was to increase the proletarian composition of the party and to improve workers' living conditions. He also was optimistic that he and his comrades could wrest control of the trade-union movement from supporters of Tomsky and Trotsky. But the Politburo outmanoeuvred him, ousting him and his supporters even from their base in the Metalworkers' Union. Nevertheless, he struggled determinedly to regain control of the Metalworkers' Union, to halt reprisals against his supporters and to convince CC and Politburo members not to allow VSNKh to shape NEP.

A trial of Shlyapnikov in August 1921 for violating party discipline failed to dissuade him from his campaign, partly because it did not result in his conviction. In 1921–2 he and his supporters determined to make use of all possible legitimate means of appeal within the party and the international communist movement. Although their efforts were doomed to fail, given the control that the Politburo and other CC bodies exercised over the Comintern, the media and the assignment of party cadres, these efforts highlighted the deep contrast between the party leaders' words and their actions. Shlyapnikov and his comrades forced individuals to make decisions as to whether they would support or resist the suppression of dissent.

In 1923–6 Shlyapnikov and his comrades perceived the policy of Soviet leaders as increasingly favourable to the peasantry and they worried about its implications for the development of industry and of the working class in Russia. They saw this policy echoed in international affairs, as Bukharin and some other party leaders looked towards less industrialised Asian countries to spread revolution. Shlyapnikov and Medvedev fretted that party leaders were on a path that alienated more advanced workers from communist policies in European Russia. They shared their views with supporters, but only spoke publicly during periods of official debate in the party. Recognising that factional struggle would only back them into a corner, they sincerely disapproved of it, but they remained strong advocates of free intra-party discussion. Urging their supporters to remain within the party, they did not ally with Myasnikov's Workers' Group. Nor did they join the United Opposition. Stalin's supporters in the party and secret police kept changing the terms of political struggle and the definition of party discipline, so that in 1926 Shlyapnikov and Medvedev were found guilty of factionalism based on a private letter to a comrade in Baku.

Shlyapnikov served the Soviet Union well as chair of Metalloimport in 1926–9 by negotiating better terms for metals imports. Yet Stalin needed his own people in control of industry as the First Five-Year Plan jump-started intensive industrialisation. Shlyapnikov and his close comrades, despite their renunciation of factional struggle, were not Stalin loyalists. The most convenient way to be rid of them was through constructing a political or even criminal case against them. The Omsk case was a flimsy one, but it sufficed to exclude Shlyapnikov and Medvedev from economic work as the First Five-Year Plan got off the ground. A sign of the times, it also reflected far greater secret-police provocation and CCC manipulation of texts in order to broaden allegations against Shlyapnikov and Medvedev, who contested the allegations, as they had in the Baku affair. The context differed in that there was no open debate within the party in 1929–30. The Bukharinist or Rightist Opposition was defeated during the course of 1929. Trotskyists and Zinovievists were under attack, exiled and imprisoned. Trotsky was expelled from the USSR in 1929.

Determined to have his say on the revolution and earn a livelihood, Shlyapnikov finished the last volume of his 1917 memoirs in 1931, after which he took up work in Rosmetizprom. Again he contributed to the cause of industrialisation but he suffered from increased nervous strain over the contradictions inherent in implementing the plan, as well as from attacks on his published writings. Stalin could not tolerate any evasion of his agenda to reshape history to serve his own political goals, so he arranged harsh condemnations and bans on Shlyapnikov's books and those of many other party historians. Having written Shlyapnikov and those like him out of party history, Stalin purged him and many of his comrades from the party in 1933. In purge sessions, Shlyapnikov refused to distort his own past to make it serve Stalin's aims. He insisted that any mistakes he made were committed only in his strong desire to help workers. But his Bolshevism had to be written out of party history, for workers had to serve the interests of the state.

Stalin attempted to drive all possible wedges between the new industrial class (peasants being transformed into workers) and the older generation of worker revolutionaries, thus preventing the carry-over of Russian revolutionary labour traditions and moulding Soviet socialism in his image. With the removal of Rightist leader Tomsky and his supporters from the union movement in 1929, the unions no longer defended workers but instead came fully to serve the state's production goals.[1] Further, Stalin and his supporters unravelled the production unions Shlyapnikov and others had worked so hard to build, chopping up the Metalworkers' Union by the early 1930s into many specialised unions. Workers rose up against the harshest aspects of Stalinist industrialisation, but without adequate leadership they could not overcome state power.[2]

---

[1] Goldman 2007; Koenker 2005; Murphy 2005.
[2] Rossman 2005 vividly narrates details about worker strikes and demonstrations in the early 1930s.

CONCLUSION

In 1934 some former oppositionists repented and glorified Stalin, while others were in prison camps or abroad. Shlyapnikov, still respected and liked by many in the leadership but increasingly inconvenient in Moscow, was manoeuvred into a strange sort of exile in the far north for a short time. Upon his return to Moscow, he appealed for work, the right to publish and medical treatment abroad, but his appeals were not in the fawning, sycophantic terms required by Stalin. Like many other former oppositionists, he was arrested after the Kirov murder. Under interrogation, he waged a determined struggle, in the way he always had, against illogical charges not based on documented evidence. Willing to do all he could to help the party, he determined for himself what was necessary. He sometimes wavered, due to illness, exhaustion and despondency, but he could not accept that deceiving others and himself about his own past, about his comrades or about party history would be of any use to the party, to workers or to the revolution in which he continued to believe.

Bibliography*

Archival Sources

Gosudarstvennyi arkhiv Rossiiskoi Federatsii (GARF)
fond 102   Department of Police
fond 130   Council of People's Commissars (Sovnarkom)
fond 382   Commissariat of Labour (Narkomtrud)
fond 5451 All-Russian Central Council of Trade Unions Communist Fraction Bureau
fond 5469 All-Russian Metalworkers' Union Central Committee
fond 5667 Metalworkers' Union Central Committee Bureau of International Relations

Rossiiskii gosudarstvennyi arkhiv ekonomiki (RGAE)
fond 8346 Metalloimport

Tsentral'nyi arkhiv Federal'noi Sluzhby Bezopasnosti (TsA FSB)
R27744   USSR Supreme Court Military Collegium
         d. 3257, vol. 1, A.G. Shliapnikov
R33718   d. 499061, Workers' Opposition, Moscow Group (56 vols.)
         vols. 3–4, investigatory materials on A.G. Shliapnikov
         vol. 5, investigatory materials on S.P. Medvedev
         vol. 12, material evidence on A.G. Shliapnikov
         vol. 13, material evidence on S.P. Medvedev
         vol. 14, material evidence on I.I. Nikolaenko, Shliapnikov, Medvedev, and others
         vols. 36–43, materials confiscated from S.P. Medvedev

Rossiiskii gosudarstvennyi arkhiv sotsial'no-politicheskoi istorii (RGASPI)
fond 2   Lenin (Ul'ianov) Vladimir Il'ich, 1870–1924
fond 5   Secretariat of V.I. Lenin, 1917–24
fond 17   CPSU Central Committee, 1898, 1903–91
fond 19   Protocols of Sovnarkom, Little Sovnarkom, and STO RSFSR, 1917–22
fond 28   *Sotsial'-Demokrat* editorial board, 1908–17
fond 48   RKP(b) Eleventh Congress, 1922

---

* This bibliography provides a complete list of Shliapnikov's works. Not all of these are cited in the footnotes.

fond 70   Commission on the History of the October Revolution and of the RKP(b) [*Istpart*], 1920–8
fond 74   Voroshilov, Kliment Efremovich, 1881–1969
fond 76   Dzerzhinskii, Feliks Edmundovich, 1877–1926
fond 82   Molotov, Viacheslav Mikhailovich, 1890–1986
fond 95   VTsSPS Communist Fraction, 1918–24
fond 99   Metalworkers' Union Central Committee, Communist Fraction, 1918–25
fond 124   Society of Old Bolsheviks, 1922–35
fond 134   Kollontai, Aleksandra Mikhailovna, 1872–1952
fond 304   Shliapnikov, Aleksandr Gavrilovich, 1885–1937
fond 351   RSDRP foreign organisation, 1905–6, 1911–17
fond 589   Commission of Party Control, 1934–52;
             Committee of Party Control (KPK), 1952–91
             opis 3, delo 9102 Medvedev, Sergei Pavlovich
             opis 3, delo 9103 Shliapnikov, Aleksandr Gavrilovich
fond 671   Ezhov, Nikolai Ivanovich, 1895–1938

Tsentral'nyi arkhiv obshchestvennykh dvizhenii goroda Moskvy (TsAODgM)

fond 3   RSDRP(b) Moscow committee, 1917–29
fond 88   Frunzenskii raion committee of VKP(b) g. Moskvy
fond 267   Primary VKP(b) organisation, Moscow State Hydroelectric Station, Kirov raion
fond 390   Primary VKP(b) organisation of Gosplan RSFSR, Kuibyshev raion, 1928–40

Bakhmeteff Archive, Columbia University, New York City
Boris Sapir Papers

Library of Congress, Washington DC
Dmitry Volkogonov Papers

Published Books and Articles

Adibekov, G. et al. (eds.) 2001, *Politbiuro TsK RKP(b) – VKP(b) i Evropa: Resheniia 'Osoboi Papki', 1923–1939*, Moscow: ROSSPEN.

Albert, Gleb J. 2011, 'German October is Approaching: Internationalism, Activists, and the Soviet State in 1923', *Revolutionary Russia*, 24, 2: 111–42.

Aleksandrov, Kirill 2005, 'Bez zhalosti i sovesti: u istokov krasnogo terrora – 1917–1918 gody', *Novoe Vremia*, 34, 29: 36–9.

Alikina, N.A. 2006, *Don Kikhot Proletarskoi Revoliutsii: dokumental'naia povest' o tom, kak motovilikhinskii rabochii Gavriil Miasnikov borolsia s TsK RKP(b) za svobodu slova i pechati (1920–1922 gody)*, Perm: Pushka.

Allen, Barbara C. 2002, 'The Evolution of Communist Party Control over Trade Unions: Alexander Shliapnikov and the Trade Unions in May 1921', *Revolutionary Russia*, 15, 2: 72–105.

—— 2007, 'Friendship in Times of Factionalism and Terror: Aleksandr Shliapnikov and Sergei Medvedev', *Revolutionary Russia*, 20, 1: 75–93.

Anderson, Kirill *et al.* (eds.) 2007, *Stenogrammy zasedanii Politbiuro TsK RKP(b)–VKP(b): 1923–1928 gg.*, 3 volumes, Moscow: ROSSPEN.

Anikeev, V.V. 1974, *Deiatel'nost' TsK RSDRP(b)–RKP(b) v 1917–1918 godakh, khronika sobytii*, Moscow: Mysl'.

—— *et al.* (eds.) 1971, *Perepiska sekretariata TsK RKP(b) s mestnymi partiinymi organizatsiiami (ianvar'–mart 1919 g.): sbornik dokumentov*, Moscow: Politicheskaia literatura.

Anon 1916, 'Lektsii i sobraniia v N'iu-Iorke', *Novyi mir*. 736, p. 6, col. 1.

—— 1917a, 'Editorial', *Rabochaia gazeta*, 43.

—— 1917b, 'Iz zhizni soiuza', *Metallist*, 1–2: 19–23.

—— 1917c, 'Konflikty metallistov', *Metallist*, 1–2: 15.

—— 1922, *Materialy po voprosu o gruppe rabochei oppozitsii na XI s"ezde RKP(b), otchet komissii i rezoliutsii XI s"ezda RKP o nekotorykh chlenakh byvshei 'rabochei oppozitsii'*, Moscow: Izd-vo TsK RKP(b).

Anskii A. (ed.) 1928, *Professional'noe dvizenie v Petrograde v 1917 g.*, Leningrad: Len. Obl. Prof. Sov.

Antonov-Ovseenko, Anton 1981, *Time of Stalin: Portrait of a Tyranny*, NY: Harper & Rowe.

Artsybushev, Iurii K. 1918, *Diktatura proletariata v Rossii: politicheskie deiateli na zasedaniiakh sovetov rabochikh, soldatskikh i krest'ianskikh deputatov, Uchreditel'nogo sobraniia, krest'ianskikh s"ezdov i prochie v dekabre 1917 i v ianvare 1918 gg. Nabroski s natury Iu. K. Artsybusheva*, Moscow: PT-vo. I. Knebel'.

Ascher, Abraham 1988–94, *The Revolution of 1905*, two volumes, Stanford, CA: Stanford University Press.

Aves, Jonathan 1996, *Workers against Lenin: Labour Protest and the Bolshevik Dictatorship*, London: Tauris Academic Studies.

Avilov, V. 1917, 'Nashi zadachi', *Metallist*, 1–2: 3.

Avrich, Paul 1968, 'Russian Anarchists and the Civil War', *Russian Review*, 27, 3: 296–306.

—— 1970, *Kronstadt 1921*, Princeton: Princeton University Press.

—— 1984, 'Bolshevik Opposition to Lenin: G.T. Miasnikov and the Workers' Group', *Russian Review*, 43: 1–29.

Avvakum, Petrovich 1979, *Archpriest Avvakum: The Life Written by Himself*, translated by Kenneth N. Brostrom, Ann Arbor, MI: University of Michigan.
Bailes, Kendall E. 1977, 'Alexei Gastev and the Soviet Controversy over Taylorism, 1918–24', *Soviet Studies*, 29: 373–94.
―――― 1978, *Technology and Society under Lenin and Stalin: Origins of the Soviet Technical Intelligentsia, 1917–1941*, Princeton, NJ: Princeton University Press.
Barber, John 1976, 'Stalin's Letter to the Editors of *Proletarskaya Revolyutsiya*', *Soviet Studies*, 28, 1: 21–41.
Baron, Nick 2007, *Soviet Karelia: Politics, Planning, and Terror in Stalin's Russia, 1920–1939*, London: Routledge.
Beecher, Jonathan and Valerii N. Fomichev 2006, 'French Socialism in Lenin's and Stalin's Moscow: David Ryazanov and the French Archive of the Marx-Engels Institute', *Journal of Modern History*, 1: 119–43.
Berkman, Alexander 1989, *The Bolshevik Myth (Diary 1920–1922)*, London: Pluto.
Biggart, John 1976, 'The Astrakhan Rebellion: An Episode in the Career of Sergey Mironovich Kirov', *The Slavonic and East European Review*, 54, 2: 231–47.
Bondarevskaia, T.P. 1963, *A.V. Shotman*, Moscow: Gosizdat.
Bonnell, Victoria 1983, *Roots of Rebellion: Workers' Politics and Organisations in St. Petersburg and Moscow, 1900–1914*, Berkeley: University of California Press.
―――― (ed.) 1983, *The Russian Worker: Life and Labor under the Tsarist Regime*, Berkeley: University of California Press.
Bordiugov, G.A. et al. (eds.) 1995, *Neizvestnyi Bogdanov v 3-kh knigakh*, Moscow: AIRO.
Brandenberger, David 2011, *Propaganda State in Crisis: Soviet Ideology, Indoctrination and Terror under Stalin, 1928–1941*, New Haven, CT: Yale University Press.
Brokgauz, F.A. and I.A. Efron 1897, *Entsiklopedicheskii slovar'*, Sankt-Peterburg: Efron.
Brovkin, Vladimir 1990, 'Workers' Unrest and the Bolsheviks' Response in 1919', *Slavic Review*, 49, 3: 350–73.
―――― (ed.) 1991, *Dear Comrades: Menshevik Reports on the Bolshevik Revolution and Civil War*, Stanford: Hoover Institution Press.
Browder, Robert Paul and Aleksandr Fyodorovich Kerensky (eds.) 1961, *The Russian Provisional Government, 1917: Documents*, three volumes, Stanford, CA: Stanford University Press.
Bukharin, Nikolai 1998, *How It All Began: The Prison Novel*, translated by George Shriver and introduced by Stephen F. Cohen, NY: Columbia University Press.
―――― 2007, *The Prison Manuscripts: Socialism and its Culture*, translated by George Shriver and introduced by Stephen F. Cohen, Chicago: Seagull Books.
Bulkin, F. 1926, *Soiuz metallistov, 1906–1918 gg.: kratkii istoricheskii ocherk*, Moscow, 1926.
Bunyan, James 1967, *The Origin of Forced Labor in the Soviet State, 1917–1921: Documents and Materials*, Baltimore: Johns Hopkins Press.

Burdzhalov, Eduard N. 1956a, 'Eshche o taktike bol'shevikov v marte-aprele 1917 goda', *Voprosy istorii*, 8: 104–14.

—— 1956b, 'O taktike bol'shevikov v marte-aprele 1917 goda', *Voprosy istorii*, 4: 38–56.

—— 1987, *Russia's Second Revolution: The February 1917 Uprising in Petrograd*, translated and edited by Donald J. Raleigh, Bloomington, IN: Indiana University Press.

Bushnell, John 1985, *Mutiny amid Repression: Russian Soldiers in the Revolution of 1905–1906*, Bloomington: Indiana University Press.

Cameron, J. David 2005, 'To Transform the Revolution into an Evolution: Underlying Assumptions of German Foreign Policy toward Soviet Russia, 1919–1927', *Journal of Contemporary History*, 40, 1: 7–24.

Carr, Edward Hallett 1950–3, *The Bolshevik Revolution, 1917–1923*, 3 volumes, London: Macmillan.

—— and Robert William Davies 1976, *Foundations of a Planned Economy: 1926–1929*, NY: Macmillan.

Chase, William and J. Arch Getty 1986, *The Soviet Data Bank*, Version 1.0. [no longer available]

Chase, William J. and Vadim Staklo (eds.) 2001, *Enemies Within the Gates?: The Comintern and the Stalinist Repression, 1934–39*, New Haven, CT: Yale University Press.

Chernobaev, A.A. 1999, 'The Shliapnikov-Stalin Duel: From the History of the Intra-Party Struggle in the VKP(b) in the 1920s', *Revolutionary Russia*, 12, 1: 103–14.

—— (ed.) 2008, *Na prieme u Stalina: tetradi (zhurnaly) zapisei lits, priniatykh I.V. Stalinym (1924–1953 gg.)*, Moscow: Novyi khronograf.

Chernov, Viktor (ed.) 1922, *Cheka: materialy po deiatel'nosti chrezvychainykh komissii*, Berlin: TsK partii sotsialistov-revoliutsionerov.

Clements, Barbara Evans 1979, *Bolshevik Feminist: The Life of Alexandra Kollontai*, Bloomington: Indiana University Press.

—— 1997, *Bolshevik Women*, Cambridge: Cambridge University Press.

——, Rebecca Friedman and Dan Healey (eds.) 2002, *Russian Masculinities in History and Culture*, London: Palgrave.

Clowes, Edith W., Samuel D. Kassow, and James L. West (eds.) 1991, *Between Tsar and People: Educated Society and the Quest for Public Identity in Late Imperial Russia*, Princeton, NJ: Princeton University Press.

Cohen, Stephen F. 1980, *Bukharin and the Bolshevik Revolution: A Political Biography, 1888–1938*, Oxford: Oxford University Press.

Conquest, Robert 1988, *Stalin and the Kirov Murder*, Oxford: Oxford University Press.

Dahlke, Sandra 2008, 'Le soufflé lointain de la révolution et la terreur du quotidian: Le bolchevik Emel'jan Jaroslavskij dans les annees 1930', *Cahiers du monde russe*, 49, 4: 581–603.

Dan, Fëdor 1922, *Dva goda skitanii: vospominaniia lidera rossiiskogo men'shevizma 1919–1921*, Berlin: Sklad izd. Russische Bücherzentrale Obrazowanje.

Daniels, Robert 1988 [1960], *The Conscience of the Revolution: Communist Opposition in Soviet Russia*, Cambridge: Harvard University Press; revised edition, Boulder, CO: Westview Press.

David-Fox, Michael 1997, *Revolution of the Mind: Higher Learning among the Bolsheviks, 1918–1929*, Ithaca, NY: Cornell University Press.

―――, Peter Holquist and Marshall Poe (eds.) 2003, *The Resistance Debate in Russian and Soviet History*, Kritika Historical Studies, 1, Bloomington: Slavica Publishers.

Davies, Sarah 1997, *Popular Opinion in Stalin's Russia: Terror, Propaganda, and Dissent, 1934–1941*, Cambridge: Cambridge University Press.

Day, Richard 1973, *Leon Trotsky and the Politics of Economic Isolation*, Cambridge: Cambridge University Press.

Dazhina, I.M. (ed.) 2010, '"Pishu o tom, chto videla sama, o tekh liudiakh i vpechatleniiakh, kotorye vynesla lichno": A.M. Kollontai v gody grazhdanskoi voiny, 1919', *Istoricheskii arkhiv*, 3: 171–92.

Demidionova, L.N. and I.A. Shliapnikova (eds.) 1997, '"Gnusnyi paskvil' na partiiu": dokumenty TsK VKP(b) o vospominaniiakh A.G. Shliapnikova "Semnadtsatyi god"', *Istoricheskii arkhiv*, 2: 103–25.

Demidov, V.V. 1994, *Politicheskaia bor'ba i oppozitsiia v Sibiri: 1922–1929 gg.*, Novosibirsk: Izd. Sibirskogo kadrovogo tsentra.

Deutscher, Isaac 1959, *The Prophet Unarmed: Trotsky, 1921–1929*, London: Oxford University Press.

―――― 1966, *Stalin: A Political Biography*, second edition, New York: Oxford University Press.

Draskoczy, Julie 2012, 'The *Put'* of *Perekovka*: Transforming Lives at Stalin's White-Sea Baltic Canal', *Russian Review*, 71: 30–48.

Efimov, N.A. 2009, *S.M. Kirov: ot mifa k pravde*, Viatka: O-Kratkoe.

Eklof, Ben 1986, *Russian Peasant Schools: Officialdom, Village Culture, and Popular Pedagogy, 1861–1914*, Berkeley: University of California Press.

Elwood, Carter 1974, *Russian Social Democracy in the Underground: A Study of the RSDRP in the Ukraine, 1907–1914*, Assen: Van Gorcum.

―――― 2011, *The Non-Geometric Lenin: Essays on the Development of the Bolshevik Party, 1910–1914*, NY: Anthem Press.

Eremina, L.S. and A.B. Roginskii (eds.) 2000, *Rasstrel'nye spiski: Moskva 1937–1941*, Moscow: Memorial.

Evtuhov, Catherine 2011, *Portrait of a Russian Province: Economy, Society, and Civilization in Nineteenth-Century Nizhnii Novgorod*, Pittsburgh: University of Pittsburgh Press.

Farnsworth, Beatrice 1980, *Aleksandra Kollontai: Socialism, Feminism, and the Bolshevik Revolution*, Stanford, CA: Stanford University Press.

Fel'shtinskii, Iu. (ed.) 1990, *Kommunisticheskaia oppozitsiia v SSSR, 1923–1927*, 4 volumes, Moscow: Terra.

Figes, Orlando 1989, *Peasant Russia, Civil War: The Volga Countryside in Revolution, 1917–1921*, London: The Clarendon Press.

Filtzer, Donald, Wendy Goldman, Gijs Kessler and Simon Pirani (eds.) 2008, *A Dream Deferred: New Studies in Russian and Soviet Labor History*, Bern: Peter Lang.

Fischer, Ruth 1982, *Stalin and German Communism: A Study in the Origins of the State Party*, New Brunswick: Transaction Books.

Fitzpatrick, Sheila 1983, *The Russian Revolution*, London: Oxford University Press.

——— 1988, 'The Bolsheviks' Dilemma: Class, Culture, and Politics in the Early Soviet Years', *Slavic Review*, 47, 4: 599–613.

——— 1992, *The Cultural Front: Power and Culture in Revolutionary Russia*, Ithaca: Cornell University Press.

——— 1996, *Stalin's Peasants: Resistance and Survival in the Russian Village after Collectivisation*, London: Oxford University Press, 1996.

——— 2005, *Tear Off the Masks! Identity and Imposture in Twentieth-Century Russia*, Princeton: Princeton University Press.

Flenley, Paul 1991, 'Industrial Relations and the Economic Crisis of 1917', *Revolutionary Russia*, 4, 2: 184–209.

Fomichev, V.S. (ed.) 1984, *Vladimir Il'ich Lenin: biograficheskaia khronika, 1870–1924*, 12 volumes, Moscow: Politizdat.

Freeze, Gregory L. 1983, *Parish Clergy in 19th Century Russia*, Princeton, NJ: Princeton University Press.

Futrell, Michael 1963, *Northern Underground: Episodes of Russian Revolutionary Transport and Communications through Scandinavia and Finland, 1863–1917*, London: Faber & Faber.

Gambarov, Iu. et al. (eds.) 1989 [1927–9], *Deiateli SSSR i oktiabr'skoi revoliutsii: avtobiografii i biografii*, 3 parts, Moscow: Granat; reprinted Moscow: Kniga.

Gankin, Olga and Harold Fisher 1940,*The Bolsheviks and the World War: The Origin of the Third International*, Stanford, CA: Stanford University Press.

Gastev, A.K. 1917, 'Obrashchenie vsem rabochim-metallistam Rossii', *Metallist*, 1–2: 24.

——— 1927, 'K desiatiletiiu VSRM', *Metallist 1917–1927, iubileinyi nomer*, July: 67–8.

Georgievskii, R.P. 1919, *Ocherki po istorii krasnoi gvardii*, Moscow: Izd-vo Fakel'.

Getty, J. Arch 1985, *Origins of the Great Purges: The Soviet Communist Party Reconsidered, 1933–1938*, Cambridge: Cambridge University Press.

——— 1997, *Pragmatists and Puritans: The Rise and Fall of the Party Control Commission*, Carl Beck Papers in Russian and East European Studies, Pittsburgh: University of Pittsburgh/CREES.

——— 2013, *Practicing Stalinism: Bolsheviks, Boyars, and the Persistence of Tradition*, New Haven: Yale University Press.

—— and Oleg V. Naumov 1999, *The Road to Terror: Stalin and the Self-Destruction of the Bolsheviks, 1932–1939*, New Haven: Yale University Press.

—— 2008, *Yezhov: The Rise of Stalin's 'Iron Fist'*, New Haven: Yale University Press.

Getzler, Israel 1983, *Kronstadt 1917–1921: the Fate of a Soviet Democracy*, NY: Cambridge University Press.

Gill, Graeme 1990, *The Origins of the Stalinist Political System*, Cambridge: Cambridge University Press.

Gindlin, Ia. 1924, 'Tovarishch Lenin, kak stroitel' proletarskogo gosudarstva', *Molodaia gvardiia*, 5, *Leninskoe prilozhenie*: [26]–45.

Ginzburg, Evgenia 1967, *Journey into the Whirlwind*, translated by Paul Stevenson and Max Hayward, NY: Harcourt, Brace & World.

—— 1981, *Within the Whirlwind*, translated by Ian Boland, NY: Harcourt Brace Jovanovich.

Goldman, Wendy Z. 2007, *Terror and Democracy in the Age of Stalin: The Social Dynamics of Repression*, Cambridge: Cambridge University Press.

—— 2011, *Inventing the Enemy: Denunciation and Terror in Stalin's Russia*, Cambridge: Cambridge University Press.

Gol'tsman, A. 1918, 'Pervyi god', *Metallist*, 3–4: 3.

—— 1927, 'Kak byl sozdan vserossiiskii soiuz rabochikh-metallistov', *Metallist 1917–1927, iubileinyi nomer*: 64–6.

Gorelov, O.I. 1989, *M.P. Tomskii: stranitsy politicheskoi biografii, Novoe v zhizni, nauke, tekhnike: istoriia i politika KPSS*, no. 8, Moscow: Znanie.

Gorshkov, Boris 2009, *Russia's Factory Children: State, Society, and Law, 1800–1917*, Pittsburgh: University of Pittsburgh Press.

Graham, Loren 1993, *The Ghost of the Executed Engineer: Technology and the Fall of the Soviet Union*, Cambridge: Harvard University Press.

Graziosi, Andrea 1991, '"Building the First System of State Industry in History": Pyatakov's VSNKh and the Crisis of NEP, 1923–1926', *Cahiers du monde russe et soviétique*, 32: 539–81.

Gregory, Paul R. and Robert C. Stuart 1986, *Soviet Economic Structure and Performance*, third edition, NY: Harper and Rowe Publishers.

Gregory, Paul R. and Valery Lazarev (eds.) 2003, *The Economics of Forced Labor: the Soviet Gulag*, Stanford: Hoover Institution Press.

Gregory, Paul and Norman Naimark (eds.) 2008, *The Lost Politburo Transcripts: From Collective Rule to Stalin's Dictatorship*, New Haven: Yale University Press.

Gruber, Helmut (ed.) 1967, *International Communism in the Era of Lenin: A Documentary History*, Ithaca: Cornell University Press.

Gurevich, A. 1927, 'Desiat' let VSRM', *Metallist, 1917–1927, iubileinyi nomer*: 5.

Gusev, Aleksei 2008, 'The "Bolshevik Leninist" Opposition and the Working Class, 1928–1929', in Filtzer, Goldman, Kessler and Pirani (eds.) 2008.

Gusev, M. Iu. (ed.) 2006, 'Spasibo tovarishchu Stalinu za nashe schastlivoe detstvo!', in St. Pb. Gos. Univ. Fil. Fak. (ed.) 2006, vol. 10.

Hagen, Mark von 1993, 'The Archival Gold Rush and Historical Agendas in the Post-Soviet Era', *Slavic Review*, 52, 1: 96–100.

Hagenloh, Paul 2009, *Stalin's Police: Public Order and Mass Repression in the USSR, 1926–1941*, Washington: Woodrow Wilson Center Press.

Halfin, Igal 2000, *From Darkness to Light: Class, Consciousness and Salvation in Revolutionary Russia*, Pittsburgh: University of Pittsburgh Press.

―――― 2007, *Intimate Enemies: Demonizing the Bolshevik Opposition, 1918–1928*, Pittsburgh: University of Pittsburgh Press.

―――― 2009, *Stalinist Confessions: Messianism and Terror at the Leningrad Communist University*, Pittsburgh: University of Pittsburgh Press.

Hasegawa, Tsuyoshi 1981, *The February Revolution: Petrograd, 1917*, Seattle: University of Washington Press.

Haynes, John et al. 1998, *The Soviet World of American Communism*, New Haven, CT: Yale University Press.

Hellbeck, Jochen 2006, *Revolution on my Mind: Writing a Diary under Stalin*, Cambridge: Harvard University Press.

Heywood, Anthony 2011, *Engineer of Revolutionary Russia: Iurii V. Lomonosov (1876–1952) and the Railways*, Surrey/Burlington: Ashgate Publishing.

Hogan, Heather 1993, *Forging Revolution: Metalworkers, Managers, and the State in St. Petersburg, 1890–1914*, Bloomington: Indiana University Press.

Holmes, Larry E. 1979, 'Soviet Rewriting of 1917: The Case of A.G. Shliapnikov', *Slavic Review*, 2: 224–42.

―――― 1990, *For the Revolution Redeemed: The Workers' Opposition in the Bolshevik Party, 1919–1921*, The Carl Beck Papers in Russian and East European Studies, Pittsburgh: University of Pittsburgh/CREES.

Humbert-Droz, Jules 1967 [1922], *Die Taktik der Kommunistischen Internationale gegen die Offensive des Kapitals; Bericht über die Konferenz der Erweiterten Exekutive der Kommunistischen Internationale, Moskau, vom 24. Februar bis 4. März, 1922*, Milano: Feltrinelli.

Iakovlev, A.N. (ed.) 1991, *Reabilitatsiia: politicheskie protsessy 30–50-kh godov*, Moscow: Politizdat.

Iaroslavskii, Emel'ian 1933, *Istoriia VKP(b)*, Moscow: Partizdat.

Iarov, Sergei Viktorovich 1999, *Proletarii kak politik: politicheskaia psikhologiia rabochikh Petrograda v 1917–1923 gg.*, St. Petersburg: Dmitrii Bulavin.

International Labour Office 1920, *The International Congress of Metalworkers*, Geneva, Studies and Reports, Series A, no. 9, pamphlet.

Ioffe, G.Z. (ed.) 1990, *Fakel: istoriko-revoliutsionnyi al'manakh*, Moscow: Politizdat.

Iroshnikov, M.P. (ed.) 1988, *Utro strany sovetov*, Leningrad: Lenizdat.

Jansen, Marc and Nikita Petrov 2002, *Stalin's Loyal Executioner: People's Commissar Nikolai Ezhov, 1895–1940*, Stanford: Hoover Institution Press.

Kamenev, Lev Borisovich 1925, *Pis'ma V.I. Lenina A.G. Shliapnikovu i A.M. Kollontai, 1914–1917 gg.*, Moscow: Institut V.I. Lenina.

Kan, Aleksander 2007, 'Upolnomochennyi Ispolkoma Kominterna A.G. Shliapnikov v Skandinavii, mart-iiun' 1920', *Istoricheskii arkhiv*, 4: 162–71.

Kanatchikov, Semën 1986, *A Radical Worker in Tsarist Russia: The Autobiography of Semën Ivanovich Kanatchikov*, edited by Reginald Zelnik, Stanford, CA: Stanford University Press.

Kaptelov, B.I. et al. (eds.) 1992, *Delo provokatora Malinovskogo*, Moscow: Respublika.

Karamzin, Nikolai 1796, *Bednaia Liza*, Moscow.

Kashirskikh, O.N. 2006, 'Krizis v Sovetsko-Germanskikh ekonomicheskikh otnosheniiakh 1928 goda', *Voprosy istorii*, 9: 35–48.

Kelly, Catriona 1990, *Petrushka: The Russian Carnival Puppet Theatre*, Cambridge: Cambridge University Press.

―――― 2007, *Children's World: Growing Up in Russia, 1890–1991*, New Haven: Yale University Press.

Kenez, Peter 1977, *Civil War in South Russia, 1919–1920*, Berkeley: University of California Press.

Khlevniuk, O.V. 1995, *In Stalin's Shadow: the Career of 'Sergo' Ordzhonikidze*, edited by Donald J. Raleigh, translated by David J. Nordlander, Armonk: M.E. Sharpe.

―――― 2004, *The History of the Gulag: From Collectivization to the Great Terror*, New Haven: Yale University Press.

―――― 2008, *Master of the House: Stalin and His Inner Circle*, New Haven, CT: Yale University Press.

Kholopov, G.K. 1955, *Groznyi god: roman*, Moscow: Molodaia gvardiia.

Kii 1919, 'Ili diktatura, ili gibel', *Izvestiia VTsIK*, 65: 8.

Knight, Amy 1993, *Beria: Stalin's First Lieutenant*, Princeton: Princeton University Press.

―――― 1999, *Who Killed Kirov?: The Kremlin's Greatest Mystery*, NY: Hill and Wang.

Knorin, Vil'gel'm 1934, *Kratkaia istoriia VKP(b)*, Moscow: Partizdat.

―――― et al. (eds.) 1935, *Kratkaia istoriia VKP(b)*, second edition, Moscow: Partizdat.

Koenker, Diane P. 1985, 'Urbanization and Deurbanization in the Russian Revolution and Civil War', *Journal of Modern History*, 57: 424–50.

―――― Rosenberg and Suny (eds.) 1989, *Party, State, and Society in the Russian Civil War: Explorations in Social History*, Bloomington: Indiana University Press.

―――― 2005, *Republic of Labor: Russian Printers and Soviet Socialism, 1918–1930*, Ithaca, NY: Cornell University Press.

Koestler, Arthur 1986, *Darkness at Noon*, translated by Daphne Hardy, NY: Bantam Books.

Kolechenkova, V.N. (ed.) 1989, *A.M. Kollontai, 'Revoliutsiia – velikaia miatezhnitsa...': Izbrannye pis'ma, 1901–52*, Moscow: Sovetskaia Rossiia.

Kollontai, Alexandra M. 1921a, 'Pora proanalizirovat'', *Pravda*: 1.

—— 1921b, *Rabochaia oppozitsiia*, Moscow: 8-ia Gos. Tipografiia.

—— 1974 [1921], *Iz moei zhizni i raboty*, Odessa: Vseukrainskoe Gos. Izd.; rept. Moscow: Sovetskaia Rossia.

—— 1981, 'Thirty Two Pages', *A Great Love*, translated by Cathy Porter, NY/London: Ayer Co.

—— 2001, *Diplomaticheskie dnevniki, 1922–1940*, 2 volumes, Moscow: Academia.

—— 2004, *Letopis' moei zhizni*, Moscow: Academia.

Kondrashev, I.F. 1947, 'S. Kirov – organizator bol'shevistskogo podpol'ia v tylu u Denikina', *Voprosy istorii*, 7: 3–23.

Kommunisticheskii internatsional 1922, *Tret'ii vsemirnyi kongress Kommunisticheskogo Internatsionala: stenograficheskii otchet*, Petrograd: Gosizdat.

Kotkin, Stephen 1995, *Magnetic Mountain: Stalinism as a Civilization*, Berkeley: University of California Press.

Koval'chenko, I.D. (ed.) 1993, *Neizvestnaia Rossiia XX vek*, Moscow: Mosgorarkhiv.

Kowalski, Ronald 1991, *The Bolshevik Party in Conflict: The Left Communist Opposition of 1918*, Pittsburgh: University of Pittsburgh Press.

Kozlov, A.I. 1985, *Vo imia revoliutsii: potoplenie Chernomorskogo flota po prikazu V.I. Lenina v 1918 g.*, Rostov-on-Don: Izd. Rostovskogo universiteta.

KPSS SSSR 1954, *KPSS v resoliutsiiakh i resheniiakh: s"ezdov, konferentsii i plenumov TsK*, ch. 1 (1898–1924), seventh edition, Moscow.

Krasil'nikov, S.A. et al. (eds.) 2010–11, *Shakhtinskii protsess 1928 g.: podgotovka, provedenie, itogi*, 2 volumes, Moscow: ROSSPEN.

Krupskaia, Nadezhda Konstantinovna 1970, *Reminiscences of Lenin*, translated by Bernard Isaacs, New York: International Publishers.

Krylova, Anna 2000, 'The Tenacious Liberal Subject in Soviet Studies', *Kritika: Explorations in Russian and Eurasian History*, 1, 1: 1–28.

—— 2003, 'Beyond the Spontaneity-Consciousness Paradigm: "Class Instinct" as a Promising Category of Historical Analysis', *Slavic Review*, 62, 1: 1–23.

Kuromiya, Hiroaki 1998, *Stalin's Industrial Revolution: Politics and Workers, 1928–1931*, Cambridge: Cambridge University Press.

—— 2005, *Stalin: Profiles in Power*, Harlow, England: Pearson Education Limited.

—— 2008, *The Voices of the Dead: Stalin's Great Terror in the 1930s*, New Haven: Yale University Press.

Kvashonkin, A.V. et al. (eds.) 1996, *Bol'shevistskoe rukovodstvo: perepiska, 1912–1927*, Moscow: ROSSPEN.

Landauer, Carl 1983, *Corporate State Ideologies: Historical Roots and Philosophical Origins*, Berkeley: Institute of International Ideologies, University of California.

Landgren, Lars-Folke and Maunu Häyrynen (eds.) 1997, *The Dividing Line: Borders and National Peripheries*, Helsinki: Renvall Institute Publications.

Lane, A. Thomas (ed.) 1995, *Biographical Dictionary of European Labor Leaders*, 2 volumes, Westport, Conn.: Greenwood Press.

Lenin, Vladimir Il'ich 1914, 'Konets klevete', *Rabochii*, 4: 1.

——— 1915, 'Neskol'ko tezisov', *Sotsial'-Demokrat*, 47: 2.

——— 1926–37, *Sochineniia*, 30 volumes, Moscow: Gosizdat.

——— 1958–65, *Polnoe sobranie sochinenii*, 55 volumes, fifth edition, Moscow: Politizdat.

——— 1960–70, *Collected Works*, 45 volumes, edited by Iurii Sdobnikov, fourth English edition, Moscow: Foreign Languages Publishing House.

——— 1999, *V.I. Lenin: Neizvestnye dokumenty, 1891–1922*, compiled by Iu. N. Amiantov, Iu. A. Akhapkin, and V.N. Stepanov, Moscow: ROSSPEN.

Lenoe, Matthew 2010, *The Kirov Murder and Soviet History*, New Haven: Yale University Press.

Lepse, Ivan 1927, 'Petrogradskii soiuz rabochikh-metallistov v 1917 godu', *Metallist 1917–1927*, iubileinyi nomer: 69–72.

Lewin, Moshe 1968, *Lenin's Last Struggle*, NY: Pantheon Books.

——— 1975, *Russian Peasants and Soviet Power: A Study of Collectivisation*, NY: W.W. Norton & Co.

Lewis, Ben and Lars T. Lih (eds.) 2011, *Zinoviev and Martov: Head to Head in Halle*, London: November Publications.

Lih, Lars T. 2007, *Lenin Rediscovered: What is to be Done? In Context*, Historical Materialism Series, Leiden: Brill.

——— 2011a, *Lenin*, London: Reaktion Books.

——— 2011b, 'The Ironic Triumph of Old Bolshevism: The Debates of April 1917 in Context', *Russian History*, 38, 2: 199–242.

——— 2011c, 'Zinoviev: Populist Leninist', in Lewis and Lih (eds.) 2011.

———, et al. (eds.) 1995, *Stalin's Letters to Molotov*, New Haven: Yale University Press.

Lohr, Eric 2001, 'The Russian Army and the Jews: Mass Deportation, Hostages, and Violence during World War I', *Russian Review*, 60: 404–19.

Long, James W. 1992, 'The Volga Germans and the Famine of 1921', *Russian Review*, 51, 4: 510–25.

Longley, D.A. 1972, 'Divisions in the Bolshevik Party in March 1917', *Soviet Studies*, 2: 61–76.

Lorwin, Val R. 1954, *The French Labor Movement*, Cambridge, MA: Harvard University Press.

Lutz, Tom 1999, *Crying: The Natural and Cultural History of Tears*, NY: W.W. Norton & Co.

Malakhovskii, V.I. 1929, 'Kak sozdavalas' rabochaia krasnaia gvardiia', *Proletarskaia revoliutsiia*, 10: 27–79.

Malle, Silvana 1985, *The Economic Organization of War Communism, 1918–1921*, Cambridge: Cambridge University Press.

Maslenitsyn, S.I. 1971, *Murom*, Moscow: Iskusstvo.

Mawdsley, Evan 1978, *The Russian Revolution and the Baltic Fleet: War and Politics, February 1917–April 1918*, London: Macmillan.

—— 1987, *The Russian Civil War*, Boston: Allen & Unwin.

McCaffray, Susan and Michael Melancon (eds.) 2005, *Russia in the European Context: A Member of the Family, 1789–1914*, NY: Palgrave MacMillan.

McNeal, Robert 1974, *Resolutions and Decisions of the CPSU*, Toronto: University of Toronto Press.

Medvedev, Roy 1973, *Let History Judge: The Origins and Consequences of Stalinism*, NY: Random House.

Meijer, Jan M. (ed.) 1964, *The Trotsky Papers, 1917–1922*, The Hague: Mouton & Cie.

Melancon, Michael 1988, 'Who Wrote What and When? Proclamations of the February Revolution in Petrograd, 23 February–1 March 1917', *Soviet Studies*, 40, 3: 479–500.

—— 1990, *The Socialist Revolutionaries and the Russian Anti-War Movement, 1914–1917*, Columbus: Ohio State University Press.

—— 2006, *The Lena Goldfields Massacre and the Crisis of the Late Tsarist State*, College Station: Texas A&M University Press.

—— 2009, *From the Head of Zeus: The Petrograd Soviet's Rise and First Days, 27 February–2 March 1917*, The Carl Beck Papers in Russian and East European Studies, Pittsburgh: University of Pittsburgh/CREES.

—— and Donald J. Raleigh (eds.) 2012, *Russia's Century of Revolutions: Parties, People, Places*, Indiana: Slavica.

Miasnikov, G.I. 1995, *Filosofiia ubiistva, ili pochemu i kak ia ubil Mikhaila Romanova*, compiled by B.I. Belenkin and V.K. Vinogradov, *Minuvshee: istoricheskii al'manakh*, vyp. 18, Moscow: Atheneum; SPb: Feniks.

Michels, Georg Bernhard 1999, *At War with the Church: Religious Dissent in Seventeenth-Century Russia*, Stanford: Stanford University Press.

Mikoian, Anastas 1970, *Mysli i vospominaniia o Lenine*, Moscow: Politizdat.

Mil'chakov, A. 1991, 'Za inakomyslie k rasstrelu: naideno mesto zakhoroneniia pervykh dissidentov – Shliapnikova i Vuiovicha', *Vecherniaia Moskva*, 12 July, p. 4, cols. 1–7.

Molodtsygin, M.A. 1991, 'Chlen komiteta po voennym i morskim delam N.I. Podvoiskii', in Nenarokov (ed.) 1991.

Morgan, Kevin *et al.* (eds.) 2005, *Agents of the Revolution: New Biographical Approaches to the History of International Communism in the Age of Lenin and Stalin*, Oxford: Peter Lang Publishing Group.

Morris, Marcia A. 1993, *Saints and Revolutionaries: The Ascetic Hero in Russian Literature*, Albany: SUNY Press.

Murphy, Kevin 2005, *Revoluiion and Counterrevolution: Class Struggle in a Moscow Metal Factory*, NY: Berghahn Books.

Myllyntaus, Timo 1997, 'Electrical Imperialism or Multinational Cooperation? The Role of Big Business in Supplying Light and Power to St. Petersburg before 1917', *Business and Economic History*, 26, 2: 540–9.

Naumov, V.P. 1991, *Aleksandr Gavrilovich Shliapnikov: stranitsy politicheskoi biografii. Novoe v zhizni, nauke, tekhnike: seriia politicheskaia istoriia XX veka*, 8, Moscow: Znanie.

Nenarokov, A.P. (ed.) 1991, *Pervoe sovetskoe pravitel'stvo*, Moscow: Politizdat.

Nove, Alec 1984, *An Economic History of the USSR*, NY: Penguin Books.

Obolenskii, V.V. (N. Osinskii) 1918, 'Iz pervykh dnei VSNKh', *Narodnoe khoziaistvo*, 11: 11–14.

Olekh, G.L. 1994, '"Omskoe delo" 1922 g.: khronika i smysl' sobytii', *Iz proshlogo Sibiri*, vyp. 1, ch. 1, *Mezhvuzovskii sbornik nauchnykh trudov*, Novosibirsk: Novosibirskii gos. univ.

—— 1999, *Krovnye uzy: RKP(b) i ChK/GPU v pervoi polovine 1920-kh gg.*, Novosibirsk: Novosibirskaia gos. akademiia vodnogo transporta (NGAVT).

Oppenheim, Samuel A. 1973, 'The Supreme Economic Council, 1917–1921', *Soviet Studies*, 25, 1: 3–27.

Ordzhonikidze, G.K. 1956–7, *Stat'i i rechi*, 2 volumes, Moscow: Politizdat.

Osokina, Elena 1993, *Ierarkhiia potrebleniia: o zhizni liudei v usloviiakh stalinskogo snabzheniia, 1928–1935 gg.*, Moscow: MGOU.

Ostrovskii, A.V. 2002, *Kto stoial za spinoi Stalina?*, Sankt-Peterburg: Neva.

Papkov, Sergei Andreevich 1997, *Stalinskii terror v Sibiri, 1928–1941*, Novosibirsk: Izd. Sib. otd. RAN.

Pate, Alice K. 2002, 'Obshchestvennost' and St. Petersburg Workers, 1906–1914', *Revolutionary Russia*, December: 53–71.

—— 2005, 'The Implementation of Social Insurance Law of 1912', in McCaffray and Melancon (eds.) 2005.

Pavliuchenkov, S.A. 2008 *'Orden Mechenostsev': partiia i vlast' posle revoliutsii, 1917–1929 gg.*, Moscow: Sobranie.

Payne, Matthew J. 2001, *Stalin's Railroad: Turksib and the Building of Socialism*, Pittsburgh: University of Pittsburgh Press.

Perrie, Maureen 1972, 'The Social Composition and Structure of the Socialist-Revolutionary Party before 1917', *Soviet Studies*, 24, 2: 223–50.

Pipes, Richard 1994, *Russia under the Bolshevik Regime*, NY: Vintage Books.

Pirani, Simon 2008, *The Russian Revolution in Retreat, 1920–1924: Soviet Workers and the New Communist Elite*, London: Routledge.

Pogorelskin, Alexis E. 1997, 'Edvard Gylling and the Origins of Karelian Fever', in Landgren and Häyrynen (eds.) 1997.

Pospelov, P.N. et al. 1932, '1917 god v men'shevistskom osveshchenii', *Pravda*, 8.

Priestland, David 1997 'Bolshevik Ideology and the Debate over Party-State Relations, 1918–1921', *Revolutionary Russia*, 10, 2: 37–61.

Prokhorov, Aleksandr Mikhailovich (ed.) 1969–78, *Bol'shaia sovetskaia entsiklopediia*, 30 volumes, 3rd edition, Moscow: Sovetskaia Entsiklopediia.

Protasov, L.G. 2008, *Liudi uchreditel'nogo sobraniia: portret v inter'ere epokhi*, Moscow: ROSSPEN.

Rabinowitch, Alexander 1976, *The Bolsheviks Come to Power: The Revolution of 1917 in Petrograd*, NY: W.W. Norton.

——— 1991, *Prelude to Revolution: The Petrograd Bolsheviks and the July 1917 Uprising*, Bloomington: Indiana University Press.

——— 2007, *The Bolsheviks in Power: The First Year of Soviet Rule in Petrograd*, Bloomington: Indiana University Press.

Rachkovskii, V.A. 2011, 'Petrogradskii soviet rabochikh i soldatskikh deputatov v fevrale-marte 1917 g. v vospominaniiakh sotsialistov (chast' 1)', *Noveishaia istoriia Rossii*, 1, 2: 22–34.

Raleigh, Donald J. 2002, *Experiencing Russia's Civil War: Politics, Society, and Revolutionary Culture in Saratov, 1917–1922*, Princeton, NJ: Princeton University Press.

Raskol'nikov, Fëdor 1934, *Rasskazy Michmana Il'ina*, Moscow: Sovetskaia Literatura.

Razgon, I.M. 1941, *Ordzhonikidze i Kirov i bor'ba za vlast' sovetov na Severnom Kavkaze (1917–1920 gg.)*, Moscow: Gospolitizdat.

Ree, Erik Van 2010, 'The Stalinist Self: The Case of Ioseb Jughashvili (1898–1907)', *Kritika*, 11, 2: 257–82.

Rigby, Thomas Henry Richard 1990, *Political Elites in the USSR: Central Leaders and Local Cadres from Lenin to Gorbachev*, Aldershot, Hants: Edward Elgar.

Robson, Roy 1995, *Old Believers in Modern Russia*, Dekalb, Ill: Northern Illinois University Press.

Rosenberg, William G. (ed.) 1984, *Bolshevik Visions: First Phase of the Cultural Revolution in Soviet Russia*, Ann Arbor, MI: Ardis Publishers.

——— 1985, 'Russian Labor and Bolshevik Power after October', *Slavic Review*, 44: 213–39.

——— 1989, 'The Social Background to Tsektran', in Koenker, Rosenberg and Suny (eds.) 1989.

Rosmer, Alfred 1971, *Moscow under Lenin*, translated by Ian Birchall, NY: Monthly Review Press.

RKP(b) 1933, *Protokoly X s"ezda RKP(b)*, Moscow: Partizdat.

——— 1959, *Vos'moi s"ezd RKP(b), mart 1919 goda: protokoly*, Moscow: Gospolitizdat.

——— 1960, *Deviatyi s"ezd RKP(b), mart-aprel' 1920 goda: protokoly*, Moscow: Politizdat.

―――― 1961, *Odinnadtsatyi s"ezd RKP(b), mart-aprel' 1922 goda: stenograficheskii otchet*, Moscow: Politizdat.

―――― 1963, *Desiatyi s"ezd RKP(b), mart 1921 goda: stenograficheskii otchet*, Moscow: Politizdat.

―――― 1972, *Deviataia konferentsiia RKP(b), sentiabr' 1920 goda: protokoly*, Moscow: Politizdat.

Rossman, Jeffrey 2005, *Worker Resistance to Stalin: Class and Revolution on the Shop Floor*, Cambridge, MA: Harvard University Press.

Ruble, Blair 1981, *Soviet Trade Unions: Their Development in the 1970s*, Cambridge: Cambridge University Press.

―――― 1983, *The Applicability of Corporatist Models to the Study of Soviet Politics: the Case of the Trade Unions*, The Carl Beck Papers in Russian and East European Studies, no. 303, Pittsburgh, PA: University of Pittsburgh/REES.

Sablinsky, Walter 1976, *The Road to Bloody Sunday: Father Gapon and the St. Petersburg Massacre of 1905*, Princeton: Princeton University Press.

Sakharov, V.A. 2003, *'Politicheskoe zaveshchanie' Lenina: real'nost' istorii i mify politiki*, Moscow: Moscow Univ. Izd.

Schapiro, Leonard 1956, *The Origin of the Communist Autocracy: Political Opposition in the Soviet State, First Phase, 1917–1922*, Cambridge, MA: Harvard University Press.

Scott, John 1989, *Behind the Urals: an American Worker in Russia's City of Steel*, edited by Stephen Kotkin, Bloomington: Indiana University Press.

Serge, Victor 2002, *Memoirs of a Revolutionary*, translated by Peter Sedgwick, Iowa City: University of Iowa Press.

Service, Robert 1991, *Lenin: A Political Life*, 3 volumes, Bloomington: Indiana University Press.

Shanin, Teodor 1986, *Russia, 1905–07: Revolution as a Moment of Truth*, New Haven: Yale University Press.

Shcherbakov, A. *et al.* 1931, 'Men'shevistskaia fal'sifikatsiia istorii semnadtsatogo goda', *Bol'shevik*, 23, 4.

Shearer, David R. 1996, *Industry, State, and Society in Stalin's Russia, 1926–1934*, Ithaca, NY: Cornell University Press.

―――― 2009, *Policing Stalin's Socialism: Repression and Social Order in the Soviet Union, 1924–1953*, New Haven: Yale University Press.

Shkliarevsky, Gennady 1993, *Labor in the Russian Revolution: Factory Committees and Trade Unions, 1917–1918*, NY: St. Martin's Press.

Shklovskii, G.L. 1925, 'Bernskaia konferentsiia 1915 g.', *Proletarskaia revoliutsiia*, 5, 40: 134–93.

Shliapnikov, Aleksandr Gavrilovich 1912, 'Rabochii Parizh', *Prosveshchenie*, 5–7: 53–61.

―――― 1913a, 'Amerikanskie potogonnye systemy ("rabota na premiiu" and "khronometrazh")', *Metallist*, 10, 34: 3–5 and 11, 35: 6–8.

―――― 1913b, 'Bor'ba za "angliiskuiu nedeliu" vo Frantsii (pis'mo iz Frantsii)', *Prosveshchenie*, 5: 57–9.

―――― 1913c, 'Proekt ob"edineniia soiuzov po metallu v Senskom D-te', *Metallist*, 4, 28: 13–14.

―――― (Tokar' Belenin) 1914a, 'Na budnichnye temy (voprosy) naima', *Metallist*, 8, 45: 2–3.

―――― 1914b, 'O belgiiskikh metallistakh', *Prosveshchenie*, 4: 59–68.

―――― 1914c, 'O polozhenii inostrannykh rabochikh vo Frantsii', *Metallist*, 4, 41 (April 1): 10–12.

―――― [A.B.] 1914d, 'O rastsenkakh', *Metallist*, 8 (45) June 12: 6–7.

―――― (Tokar' Belenin) 1914e, 'Pis'mo rabochego', *Put' pravdy*, no. 89, 17 (30) (May): 2.

―――― 1914f, reports in *Sotsial'-Demokrat*, no. 33 (1 November) and no. 35 (December 12).

―――― 1914g, 'V lapakh kapitala: vnutrennii rasporiadok frantsuzskikh masterskikh', *Metallist*, 5 (12 April): 8–11.

―――― 1914h, 'Za granitsei: o polozhenii inostrannykh rabochikh vo Frantsii', *Metallist*, 4 (1 April): 10–12.

―――― 1915, 'Rabochii Peterburg i voina: nabliudeniia Peterburgskogo rabochego v nachale voiny', *Kommunist* (Geneva), 1–2: 161–7.

―――― 1917a, 'Beseda s G. Brantingom', *Pravda*, 18, 26 March: 7.

―――― 1917b, 'Bor'ba za minimum zarabatnoi platy v metallicheskoi promyshlennosti v Pitere', *Pravda*, 93: 9.

―――― 1917c, 'Eshche raz ob organizatsii soiuzov', *Metallist*, 5: 2.

―――― 1917d, 'Frantsuzskii ministr amunitsii Al'ber Toma v Ispolnitel'nom Komitete', *Pravda*, 46: 2–4.

―――― 1917e, 'Ko vsem rabochim', *Izvestiia*, 22 December, 258, p. 11, cols. 2–4.

―――― 1917f, 'Na fabriku', *Biblioteka proletariia, no. 8: sbornik*, Minsk: Zvezda.

―――― 1917g, 'Nash tarif', *Metallist*, 1–2: 3–6.

―――― 1917h, 'O konferentsii soiuza rabochikh-metallistov Moskovskoi oblasti', *Metallist*, 5: 11.

―――― (pseudonym A. Belenin) 1917i, 'O "krasnoi gvardii"', *Pravda*, 49: 5.

―――― 1917j, 'U nas dolzhen byt tol'ko odin soiuz rabochikh metallistov', *Metallist*, 1–2 (August 17): 13–14.

―――― 1917k, 'Zadachi rastsenochnykh komissii', *Metallist*, 3: 3.

―――― 1918, 'Novyi tarif rabochikh-metallistov', *Metallist*, 2: 14.

―――― 1919a, 'Aviatory', *Proletarskaia kul'tura*, 7–8: 59–62.

―――― 1919b, 'Moskva, 7 noiabria, 1919 god', *Metallist*, 12.

―――― 1919c, 'O spetsialistakh', *Pravda*, March 27: 1.

―――― 1919d, 'Voprosy proizvodstva i proizvoditel'nosti', *Pravda*, 27 April: 1–2.

―――― 1919e, 'Voprosy promyshlennoi proizvoditel'nosti', *Metallist*, 5: 2–3.

―――― (Schlapnikoff), 1920a, *Aus der Gewerkschaftsbewegung in Russland biz zur Eroberung der Macht*, Chemnitz: Chemnitzer Druck u. Verlagsanstalt, G.m.b.h.

―――― 1920b, 'Martovskie dni, 1917 goda', *Petrogradskaia Pravda*, 12 March: 1.

―――― (Schlapnikow), A.G. 1920c, *Die russischen gewerkschaften*, Leipzig: Kleine Bibliothek der Russischen Korrespondenz, 1.

―――― 1920d, 'Zadachi professional'nykh soiuzov', *Izvestiia TsK RKP(b)*: 21.

―――― 1921a, 'K chetvertomu s"ezdu VSRM', *Metallist*, 3–4: 1–2.

―――― 1921b, 'O nashikh vnutripartiinykh raznoglasiiakh', *Diskussionyi listok*, 1: 13.

―――― 1921c, 'Organizatsiia narodnogo khoziaistva i zadachi soiuzov: k diskussii o zadachakh profsoiuzov', *Luch* [*Organ Muromskogo i Melenkovskogo Uispolkoma i U"ezdkoma RKP*] 8, 194.

―――― 1921d, 'Politika Tsektrana i nash sindikalizm', *Biulleten' vtorogo vserossiiskogo s"ezda gornorabochikh*, 1: 4, and 2: 3.

―――― 1921e, *Les syndicates russes*, Paris: Bibliotheque du Travail.

―――― *et al.* 1921f, 'Tezisy rabochei oppozitsii: zadachi professional'nykh soiuzov', *Pravda* (January 25): 2–3.

―――― 1922a, 'K oktiabriu', *Proletarskaia revoliutsiia*, 10: 3–42.

―――― 1922b, *O zadachakh rabochikh soiuzov*, Samara: R.B.Ts.

―――― (ed.) 1923a, 'Fevral'skaia revoliutsiia v dokumentakh: listki, vozzvaniia, korrespondentsiia', *Proletarskaia revoliutsiia*, 1, 13: 259–351.

―――― 1923b, 'Fevral'skie dni v Peterburge', *Proletarskaia revoliutsiia*, 1, 13: 71–134.

―――― 1923c, 'Podpol'naia rabota v Muromskom raione (1902–1904 gody)', *Dvadtsat' let rabochei organizatsii v gorodakh: Murom, Kulebaki, Vyksa*, Moscow/St. Petersburg: Gosizdat.

―――― 1923d, '1905 god v Murome', *Dvadtsat' let rabochei organizatsii v gorodakh: Murom, Kulebaki, Vyksa*, Moscow/St. Petersburg: Gosizdat.

―――― 1923e, 'Sotsial'-demokratiia i voina (1914–1917)', *Proletarskaia revoliutsiia*, 3, 15: 178–95.

―――― 1924a, 'Nashi raznoglasiia', *Pravda*, January 18: 4–5.

―――― 1924b, 'Pamiati "uchredilki"', *Ogonek*, 5, 44: 9–10.

―――― 1924c, 'V.I. Lenin i Narkomtrud (po lichnym vospominaniiam)', *Voprosy truda*, 3: 3–5.

―――― 1924–31, *Semnadtsatyi god*, 4 volumes, Moscow: Gosizdat.

―――― 1925a, *Fevral'skie dni v Peterburge*, Moscow: Proletarii.

―――― 1925b, 'Oktiabr'skii perevorot i stavka', *Krasnyi arkhiv*, 8: 157–75.

―――― 1926a, *Les alliés contre la Russie avant, pendant et après la guerre mondiale (faits et documents)*, Paris: A. Delpeuch.

―――― 1926b, 'Iul'skie dni v Petrograde', *Proletarskaia revoliutsiia*, 4, 51: 46–89 and 52: 55–9.

―――― 1926c, 'Kerenshchina', *Proletarskaia revoliutsiia*, 7, 54: 9–56 and 8, 55: 5–53.

—— et al. (eds.) 1926d, *Kto dolzhnik?: sbornik dokumentirovannykh stat'ei po voprosu ob otnosheniiakh mezhdu Rossiei, Frantsiei i drugimi derzhavami Antanty do voiny 1914 g., vo vremia voiny i v period interventsii*, Moscow: Avioizdatel'stvo.

—— 1926e, 'O demonstrativnoi atake i pravoi opasnosti v partii', *Bol'shevik*, 17: 62–73.

—— 1926f, 'Pis'mo v redaktsiiu', *Bol'shevik*, 21–2: 135–8.

—— 1926g, *Po zavodam Frantsii i Germanii*. Leningrad: Rab. Izd. Priboi.

—— 1926h, *Zametki o Frantsii*, Leningrad.

—— [1926], 'Bor'ba Petrogradskikh metallistov za pervyi tarif', *Za dvadtsat' let*, 97–124.

—— 1927a, 'Otvet kritikam', *Bol'shevik*, 10: 82–91 and 11–12: 99–113.

—— 1927b, 'Pozitsiia "Rabochei Oppozitsii"', *Diskussiia o profsoiuzakh: materialy i dokumenty, 1920–1921 gg.*, edited by Jan Rudzutak, Moscow: Gosizdat.

—— 1929, 'Za industrializatsiiu—za sotsializm', *Pravda*, 16 December: 2.

—— 1982 [1923], *On the Eve of 1917*, translated by Richard Chappell, London/New York: Allison & Busby.

—— 1988, 'Oktiabr'', in Iroshnikov (ed.) 1988.

—— 1989 [1927–9], 'A.G. Shliapnikov (avtobiografiia)', in Gambarov et al. (eds.) 1989.

—— 1992 [1923–31], *Kanun semnadtsatogo goda; Semnadtsatyi god*, three volumes, commentary and preface by A.S. Smol'nikov and A.A. Chernobaev, Moscow: Politizdat.

—— 2002, 'Za khlebom i neft'iu', *Voprosy istorii*, 7–12 [continued].

—— 2003, 'Za khlebom i neft'iu', *Voprosy istorii*, 1–6 [continuation].

Shliapnikova, I.A. 1988, 'Pravda ob A.G. Shliapnikove,' *Voprosy istorii*, 3: 88–98.

—— and A.A. Chernobaev (eds) 2002, '"My ne reshaem nyne dazhe svoei sud'by": vospominaniia i pis'ma A.G. Shliapnikova, 1934 g.', *Istoricheskii arkhiv*, 1: 3–31.

Shukman, Harold (ed.) 1988, *The Blackwell Encyclopedia of the Russian Revolution*, Oxford: Blackwell.

Silin, P. 1922, 'Astrakhanskie rasstrely (mart 1919 g.)', in Chernov (ed.) 1922.

Slepkov, A. (ed.) 1926, *Put' 'Rabochei oppozitsii': sbornik statei*, Moscow: Izd. Pravda i Bednota.

Smirnov, N.G. 2001, *Repressirovannoe pravosudie*, Moscow: Gelios ARV.

Smith, Stephen Anthony 1983, *Red Petrograd: Revolution in the Factories, 1917–1918*, Cambridge: Cambridge University Press.

—— 2002, 'Masculinity in Transition: Peasant Migrants to Late-Imperial St. Petersburg', in Clements, Friedman and Healey (eds.) 2002.

Sokolov, A.K. 2012, *Ot voenproma k VPK: Sovetskaia voennaia promyshlennost', 1917–iiun' 1941 gg.*, Moscow: Novyi khronograf.

Solzhenitsyn, Aleksandr 1972, *August 1914*, translated by Michael Glenny, London: Bodley Head.

—— 1976, *Warning to the Western World*, London: BBC Books.

―――― 1983–91, *Krasnoe koleso: povestvovanie v otmerennykh srokakh*, 4 volumes, Paris: YMCA Press.

Sorenson, Jay 1969, *The Life and Death of Soviet Trade Unionism: 1917–1928*, NY: Atherton Press.

St. Pb. Gos. Univ. Fil. Fak. (ed.) 2006, *Russkoe proshloe: istoriko-dokumental'nyi al'manakh*, kn. 10, St. Petersburg.

Stalin, I.V. 1931, 'O nekotorykh voprosakh istorii bol'shevizma: pis'mo v redaktsiiu zhurnala Proletarskoi revoliutsii', *Proletarskaia revoliutsiia*, 6, 113: 12.

Startsev, V.I. 1965, *Ocherki po istorii Petrogradskoi krasnoi gvardii i rabochei militsii*, Moscow/Leningrad: Nauka.

Steinberg, Mark 2002, *Proletarian Imagination: Self, Modernity, and the Sacred in Russia, 1910–1925*, Ithaca, NY: Cornell University Press.

Sukhanov, Nikolai Nikolaevich 1922, *Zapiski o revoliutsii*, three volumes, Berlin: Z.I. Grizhebin.

―――― 1962, *The Russian Revolution, 1917*, two volumes, edited and translated by Joel Carmichael, NY: Harper.

Sunderland, Willard and Stephen M. Norris (eds.) 2012, *Russia's People of Empire: Life Stories from Eurasia, 1500 to the Present*, Bloomington, IN: Indiana University Press.

Svechnikov, M.S. 1926, *Bor'ba krasnoi armii na Severnom Kavkaze: sentiabr' 1918–aprel' 1919*, Moscow: Gosvoenizdat.

Sverdlov, Ia. M. 1976, *Izbrannye proizvedeniia: stat'i, rechi, pis'ma*, Moscow: Politizdat.

Swain, Geoffrey 2006, *Trotsky*, Harlow, England: Pearson Longman.

Thompson, John M. 1981, *Revolutionary Russia, 1917*, NY: Scribner.

Thorpe, Wayne 1989, *'The Workers Themselves': Revolutionary Syndicalism and International Labor, 1913–1923*, Dordrecht: Kluwer Academic.

Tivel, A. and M. Kheimo (eds.) 1967 [1929], *Desiat' let Kominterna v resheniiakh i tsifrakh*. Milan: Feltrinelli.

Tolz, Vera 2011, *Russia's Own Orient: The Politics of Identity and Oriental Studies in the Late Imperial and Early Soviet Periods*, Oxford: Oxford University Press.

Transchel, Kate 2006, *Under the Influence: Working-Class Drinking, Temperance and Cultural Revolution in Russia, 1895–1932*, Pittsburgh, PA: University of Pittsburgh Press.

Trepper, Leopold 1977, *The Great Game: Memoirs of the Spy Hitler Couldn't Silence*, NY: McGraw-Hill Book Company.

Trotsky, Leon Davidovich 1921, *O zadachakh profsoiuzov: doklad prochitannyi na sobranii 3 dekabria 1920 goda*, Moscow: Gosizdat.

Tsakunov, S.V. 1994, *V labirinte doktriny: iz opyta razrabotki ekonomicheskogo kursa strany v 1920-e gody*, Moscow: Rossiia Molodaia.

Tsereteli, Irakli 1963, *Vospominaniia o fevral'skoi revoliutsii*, two volumes, Paris: Mouton.

Tucker, Robert C. 1973, *Stalin as Revolutionary, 1879–1929: A Study in History and Personality*, NY: W.W. Norton & Co.

―――― 1990, *Stalin in Power: The Revolution from Above, 1928–1941*, NY: W.W. Norton & Co.

Turton, Katy 2007, *Forgotten Lives: The Role of Lenin's Sisters in the Russian Revolution, 1864–1937*, London: Palgrave Macmillan.

Ulam, Adam 1973, *Stalin: The Man and His Era*, NY: Viking.

Verigo, E. 1986, 'Slavnye stranitsy zhizni bol'shevika-lenintsa, k 100-letiiu so dnia rozhdeniia S.M. Kirova', *Kommunist*, 5: 111–21.

Vilenskii-Sibiriakov, V.D. et al. (eds.) 1974, *Deiateli revoliutsionnogo dvizheniia v Rossii: bio-bibliograficheskii slovar': ot predshestvennikov dekabristov do padeniia tsarizma*, Leipzig: Zentralantiquariat der DDR.

Vilkova, V.P. (ed.) 2004, *RKP(b): vnutripartiinaia bor'ba v dvadtsatye gody, dokumenty i materialy 1923*, Moscow: ROSSPEN.

Vinogradov, V. et al. (eds.) 2007, *Arkhiv VChK: sbornik dokumentov*, Moscow: Kuchkovo Pole.

Viola, Lynne 1996, *Peasant Rebels Under Stalin: Collectivisation and the Culture of Peasant Resistance*, London/NY: Oxford University Press.

―――― 2007, *The Unknown Gulag: The Lost World of Stalin's Special Settlements*, London/NY: Oxford University Press.

Voitikov, S.S. 2007, 'Razvitie vzgliadov vysshego rukovodstva Sovetskoi Rossii na voennoe stroitel'stvo v noiabre 1917–marte 1918 g.', *Voprosy istorii*, 10: 3–12.

Voline (Vsevolod Mikhailovich Eikhenbaum) 1974, *The Unknown Revolution, 1917–1921*, NY: Free Life Editions.

Volkogonov, Dmitri 1991, *Stalin: Triumph and Tragedy*, NY: Grove Weidenfeld.

―――― 1994, *Lenin: A New Biography*, NY: Free Press.

―――― 1996, *Trotsky: The Eternal Revolutionary*, NY: Free Press.

VTsSPS 1918, *Pervyi vserossiiskii s"ezd professional'nykh soiuzov, 7–14 ianvaria 1918; polnyi stenograficheskii otchet s predisloviem M. Tomskogo*, Moscow: Izd. VTsSPS.

Wade, Rex 1984, *Red Guards and Workers' Militias in the Russian Revolution*, Stanford: Stanford University Press.

―――― 2000, *The Russian Revolution, 1917*, Cambridge: Cambridge University Press.

Watson, Derek 2005, *Molotov: A Biography*, NY: Palgrave Macmillan.

Wcislo, Francis W. 2011, *Tales of Imperial Russia: The Life and Times of Sergei Witte, 1849–1915*, Oxford: Oxford University Press.

Weissman, Susan 2001, *Victor Serge: The Course is Set on Hope*, London/NY: Verso.

Werth, Nicolas 2007, *Cannibal Island: Death in a Siberian Gulag*, translated by Steven Rendall, Princeton, NJ: Princeton University Press.

White, James 1989, 'The February Revolution and the Bolshevik Vyborg District Committee (In Response to Michael Melancon)', *Soviet Studies*, 41, 4: 602–24.

Wildman, Allan 1967, *The Making of a Workers' Revolution: Russian Social Democracy, 1891–1903*, Chicago: University of Chicago Press.

Williams, Robert C. 1986, *The Other Bolsheviks: Lenin and His Critics, 1904–1914*, Bloomington: Indiana University Press.

Wolfe, Bertram D. 1960, *Three Who Made a Revolution: A Biographical History*, Boston: Beacon Press.

Wynn, Charters 1992, *Workers, Strikes, and Pogroms: The Donbass-Dnepr Bend in Late Imperial Russia, 1870–1905*, Princeton, NJ: Princeton University Press.

—— 2008, 'The "Right Opposition" and the "Smirnov-Eismont-Tolmachev Affair"', in Gregory and Naimark (eds.) 2008.

—— 2012, 'Young Tomsky: The Making of a Working-Class Bolshevik Leader', *Revolutionary Russia*, 25, 2: 119–40.

Zavadivker, Polly 2013, 'Blood and Ink: Russian and Soviet Jewish Chroniclers of Catastrophe from World War I to World War II' (Ph.D. dissertation, University of California Santa Cruz).

Zelnik, Reginald 1976, 'Russian Bebels: An Introduction to the Memoirs of the Russian Workers Semen Kanatchikov and Matvei Fisher', *Russian Review*, 35, 3: 249–89, and 35, 4: 417–47.

—— 1995, *Law and Disorder on the Narova River: The Kreenholm Strike of 1872*, Berkeley: University of California Press.

—— (ed.) 1999, *Workers and Intelligentsia in Late Imperial Russia: Realities, Representations, Reflections*, Berkeley: University of California.

Zen'kovich, Nikolai 2002, *Samye zakrytye liudi: Entsiklopediia biografii*, Moscow: Olma-Press.

Zenkovskii, Sergei 2006, *Russkoe staroobriadchestvo*, two volumes, Moscow: Institut DI-DIK.

Zhuravlev, Sergei 2000, *Malen'kie liudi i bol'shaia istoriia: inostrantsy Moskovskogo Elektrozavoda v sovetskom obshchestve 1920–1930-kh gg.*, Moscow: ROSSPEN.

Zinoviev, Grigorii 1921a, *O roli professional'nykh soiuzov v proizvodstve: doklady tt. Zinov'eva i Trotskogo, rech' t. Lenina, sodoklady tt. Bukharina, Nogina, Shliapnikova i Riazanova i zakliuchitel'nye slova tt. Trotskogo i Zinov'eva na soedinennom zasedanii delegatov 8-go s''ezda sovetov, VTsSPS i MGSPS, – chlenov RKP 30-go dekabria, 1920 g.*, Moscow: VTsSPS.

—— (ed.) 1921b, *Partiia i soiuzy (k diskussii o roli i zadachakh profsoiuzov): sbornik statei i materialov*, Petrograd: Gosizdat.

—— 1936, *The Case of the Trotskyite-Zinovievite Terrorist Center: Report of Court Proceedings*, Moscow: People's Commissariat of Justice.

Zlokazov, G.I. 1994, 'Ne vse u retsenzentov iskhodit ot nevezhestva', *Istoricheskii arkhiv*, 3: 196–211.

Zorkii, M.S. (ed.) 1926, *'Rabochaia oppozitsiia': materialy i dokumenty, 1920–1926 gg.*, preface by E.M. Iaroslavskii, Moscow: Gosizdat.

Websites

Ellis Island immigration database: http://www.libertyellisfoundation.org.

Unpublished Works

Allen, Barbara Carol 2001, 'Worker, trade unionist, revolutionary: a political biography of Alexander Shliapnikov, 1905–1922', Ph.D. dissertation, Indiana University Bloomington.
Glen, Billy Dale 1973, 'Alexander Shliapnikov and the Workers' Opposition', M.A. thesis, University of Virginia.
Kollontai, Aleksandra 1915, 'Letter to Aleksandr Shliapnikov, 10 February', Shliapnikov family collection, Moscow.
Kollontai, Vladimir 2006, interview by Barbara C. Allen, New York City, 25 March.
Kornilova, Elena Leonidovna 2008, 'A.G. Shliapnikov – revoliutsioner', istorik i memuarist', kand. diss., Ivanovskii gosudarstvennyi universitet.
Medvdeva, Irina 1995, conversation with the author, Moscow.
Peterson, Mark Richard 1987, 'The disillusionment of a revolutionary: a political biography of Aleksandr Shliapnikov', M.A. thesis, University of Washington.
Petrov, Nikita 2012, email to author, Moscow, 31 July.
⸻ 2012, telephone conversation with the author, Moscow, 1 August.
Rakov, Timofei N. 2012, 'Rabochaia oppozitsiia v RKP(b)', dipl. rabota, Iaroslavskii gosudarstvennyi universitet.
Sandu, Tat'iana Anatol'evna 2006, '"Rabochaia oppozitsiia" v RKP(b) (1919–1923)', kand. diss., Tiumen'skii gosudarstvennyi universitet.
Shliapnikov, Aleksandr 1908, letters and postcards to Khioniia Shliapnikova, Shliapnikov family collection, Moscow.
⸻ 1935, 'Otets – synu Iure', 23 July 1935, Shliapnikov family collection.
Shliapnikov, Iurii Aleksandrovich 2004, conversation with the author, Lawrenceville, New Jersey, 7 June.
⸻ 2004a, conversation with author, Lawrenceville, New Jersey, 25 June.
⸻ 2004b, conversation with author, Lawrenceville, New Jersey, 1 July.
⸻ 2006, interview by Barbara C. Allen, digital audio recording, Hopewell, New Jersey, 6 November (recordings and transcripts deposited at the Hoover Institution Library and Archives, Stanford University, Stanford, California).
⸻ 2007, interview by Barbara C. Allen, digital audio recording, Lawrenceville, New Jersey, 10 January (recordings and transcripts deposited at the Hoover Institution Library and Archives, Stanford University, Stanford, California).
Shliapnikova, Irina Aleksandrovna 1991, conversation with the author, Moscow.
⸻ 1995, conversations with the author, Moscow.

—— 1997, letter to the author, 13 July.
—— 2000, telephone conversation with the author, October.
—— 2012, conversations with the author, Moscow.
Spencer, Scott Sherwood 1981, 'A Political Biography of Alexandr Shlyapnikov', M. Litt. thesis, Oxford University.

Index

The index includes entries for people, institutions, places, and subjects discussed in the main text of the book. Because this book employs two systems for romanising Russian Cyrillic names and terms, both systems are reflected in the index. First is listed the name or term found in the body of the text, followed in brackets by the Library of Congress transliteration, if it differs. When an individual was known by a revolutionary alias, his or her birth name is added in brackets, if relevant. Parentheses are used for abbreviations and acronyms of institutions, information identifying individuals whose first names are not known, and designation of Alexander Shlyapnikov's family members. For organisations best known by their abbreviations or acronyms, the main entry is provided under the shorter term.

Achinsk   302
AFL-CIO (American Federation of Labor-Congress of Industrial Organizations)   3
Africa, North   368
Agranov, Yakov [Iakov]   293–5, 300 n. 44
agriculture, agrarian, farming   2, 25, 42, 61, 123, 141, 185, 191, 194–6, 229 n. 5, 253, 261, 265, 268, 297, 302, 304, 344, 357
Akulov, Ivan   351
alcohol, drinking, drunkenness   9–10, 13, 18, 21, 30, 128, 175–6, 271, 293–4, 301 n. 49, 302 n. 51, 316, 340, 344
see also sobriety
Alexander III   20, 228 n. 3
Alexandrovich, P. [Pëtr Aleksandrovich] [b. Viacheslav Dmitrievskii]   68
All-Russia Industrial and Art Exhibition   21–2
All-Russian Central Trade Union Council (VTsSPS)   86, 109–10, 113, 115, 119–21, 135, 137–48, 165, 167, 177–9, 197–203, 207, 209, 221–2, 224, 236, 238
    gubernia trade-union council(s)   197, 199, 223
All-Russian Constituent Assembly Committee (*Komuch*)   158
All-Russian Council of National Economy (VSNKh)   110, 112, 115, 120, 126, 132, 137, 141–4, 148 n. 63, 159, 165–6, 168, 179, 191–4, 196–7, 203, 208, 210 n. 45, 212, 216–17, 220, 222 n. 73, 223, 284–5, 288–91, 293, 305, 307, 328 n. 46, 336 n. 12, 375
    Electric Department   223

glavki   132, 137, 179
    Metals Department   137, 194, 222 n. 73, 223, 307
    sovnarkhoz(es)   137, 143, 170, 307
    VSNKh RSFSR   305, 307
All-Russian Executive Committee of Railwaymen (*Vikzhel*)   113
Amalgamated Society of Engineers (ASE)   59, 71
American Relief Administration (ARA)   225
Amsterdam International of Trade Unions   151, 155
anarchism, anarchists   47, 89, 132, 160, 162, 179, 183, 185 n. 74, 187, 189, 228, 232, 233 n. 17, 238, 252, 287
anarcho-syndicalism   47, 160, 162, 187, 189
    see also syndicalism
Andreev, Andrei   148, 165–8, 174, 176–7, 222, 235 n. 21
Andreev, Konstantin   362 n. 81
animal(s)   69, 124–5, 194, 265, 297, 313, 316, 360
Antonov (communist in Mongolia)   303
Antonov-Ovseenko, Vladimir   249–51, 271 n. 42
Anzhero-Sudzhensk   293
arbitrary, arbitrariness   19, 123, 192, 238, 284, 300, 314–16, 332–3, 344, 369
Armenia, Armenians   30, 257
artel(s)   13
artisan(s)   13, 30, 146, 160
    see also crafts
Artsybushev, Yuri [Iurii]   109

Artyom [Artëm] [Fëdor Sergeev]   148 n. 62, 165 n. 20–2, 176 n. 50, 198, 201–2, 208–9
Asia   32, 122, 266, 279, 301, 352, 375
  Central Asia   301, 352
  Far East   32, 122
Asnières   35, 42, 288
Astrakhan   123, 126–32, 317, 334, 351, 359–62, 366
Astrakhan Civil-War Fellowship   317
Astrakhan Council of Trade Unions   131
Astrakhan NKVD   362
Austria, Austrian   34, 89, 155 n. 69, 292
Avilov (Glebov), Nikolai   125
Avksentev, Nikolai [Avksent'ev]   96
Avvakum Petrovich, Archpriest   9, 42, 71
Azerbaijan   13, 123, 131 n. 26, 267–72, 275–7, 281–2, 284, 293, 363, 375–6

Babitsyn, A. (Metalworkers' Union investigator)   132
Bachmanov, Andrei   340
Badaev, Alexei [Aleksei]   50
Bakinskii rabochii   270–1
Baku   13, 123, 131 n. 26, 267–72, 275–7, 281–2, 284, 293, 363, 375–6
Baltic Fleet   182
banks, banking   103, 112, 192, 253, 286, 292, 307
  Ekonombank   292
  Prombank   307
Barchuk, Valeryan [Valerian]   267, 271
Barinov, S.N.   350
Bataille Socialiste, La   39
Batenin, Erazm   349
Battleship Potemkin   52
Bauman District   172–3, 216–18, 316–317, 324–5
Bauman group   158, 173, 218
BBK see White Sea-Baltic Sea Canal
Beethoven Hall   72
Begge, K.M.   287–9, 291
Belenin[1] (alias of Shlyapnikov, Alexander)   13, 72
Belenin, Alexei [Aleksei] (uncle)   12–13
Belenin, Nikolai (grandfather)   11
Belenina, Akulina (grandmother)   11

Belenina, Khioniya [Khioniia] (m. Gavril Shlyapnikov) (mother) see Shlyapnikova, Khioniya
Belorussia   221, 225
Berlin   42, 47 n. 19, 49, 244, 254 n. 2, 286–91, 358 n. 67
Black Hundred(s)   32, 174
blacklisting see labour
Black Sea Fleet   123, 125, 347
bloc   173, 268, 273, 276–7, 282, 350, 352, 356, 361, 363
Bloody Sunday   32–3, 77
Bogdanov, Alexander [Aleksandr]   39–41, 254
Bogdanov, Peter [Pëtr]   179 n. 58, 222 n. 73, 242 n. 41
Bologna   40
Bolshevik(s) see Russian Social Democratic Workers' Party
Bolshevik [Bol'shevik]   273–4
Bolshevik Military Organisation   89, 90 n. 36, 98–9
Bolshoi Theatre   270
Bosh, Evgenia [Evgeniia]   61, 66, 69, 70 n. 72, 127–8, 155
bourgeois, bourgeoisie   2, 8, 13, 16, 18, 49–51, 61–2, 72, 78–9, 81–2, 86, 88, 90–2, 106, 111, 114, 131, 153, 160, 171, 183, 187, 190–1, 194–7, 213, 216–17, 227, 232, 238, 259, 266, 268, 280, 306, 310, 328, 338, 340, 352, 373
  factory owners   18, 51, 61, 72, 86, 88, 90–2, 111, 114, 340
  merchant(s)   8 n. 2, 13, 131
  middle class   49, 78, 338
  petty bourgeois   51, 62, 160, 183, 194, 197, 213, 216–17, 266, 268, 280
  upper class   2
  see also capital
Branting, Karl Hjalmar   36 n. 2, 58
Braslina, Lidiya [Lidiia]   351 n. 47, 355–7, 359 n. 69, 363 n. 82, 366
Braude, L.I.   73 n. 78
Bronx   72
Bruno, Genrikh   206 n. 32, 232 n. 14, 242, 267, 349, 350, 352, 361–2
Bryansk [Briansk]   211

---

1   There is an alternate spelling of 'Belianin' for the family name 'Belenin'.

Bukharin, Nikolai 1, 5, 59, 66–73, 116, 134
  n. 32, 139, 142, 145, 147–8, 160, 162, 165–6,
  176–9, 184, 186, 188, 204–7, 213, 233 n. 15–16,
  238–9, 244, 253, 264–5, 267, 269–70, 272–4,
  279, 283, 291, 293, 297–8, 313, 332, 361, 363,
  374–6
bureaucracy, bureaucrats, bureaucratisation
  105, 115–16, 118–19, 132–4, 138, 141, 155–6,
  159, 166, 168, 175, 181, 184–5, 219, 232, 260–1,
  288–90, 310, 313, 374
  Bureaucrats' Union 115
Butyrka prison [Butyrskaia] 211
Bykhatsky [Bykhatskii] (Worker
  Oppositionist in Kiev) 357

capital, capitalism, capitalist(s) 1, 7, 24, 46,
  56, 62, 72, 84, 88, 92, 99, 111, 114, 137, 178,
  192–5, 213, 216, 223–4, 232, 236, 239, 243,
  265, 268–9, 272, 281, 286, 291, 293, 301, 322,
  324, 335, 344, 361, 370
  see also bourgeois, industry, and state
    capitalism
Carr, E.H. 110
Caspian Sea 126, 267
Catalonia 345
Catherine II (the Great) 16, 119
Caucasus 13, 30, 65, 118, 123, 125–31, 257,
  267–77, 281–2, 284, 293, 300–1, 313, 328,
  339, 347, 351, 353, 363, 373, 375–6
  see also North Caucasus and
    Transcaucasus
Central Board of Artillery Factories 179
Central Council of Factory Committees 86,
  148 n. 63
Central Council of Workers' Control 112
Central Union of Consumer Cooperatives
  (*Tsentrosoyuz*) [*Tsentrosoiuz*] 265
Chagin, Peter [Pëtr] 271
charity 10, 11, 20
Chechens 123, 125–6
Cheka (All-Russian Extraordinary
  Commission for Combatting
  Counterrevolution and Sabotage) 106,
  127–8, 131, 182, 201, 210, 214, 228, 239–42,
  255, 257–8, 268, 270, 295
Chelyabinsk [Cheliabinsk] 357
Chelysheva, Klavdiya [Klavdiia
  Chëlysheva] 278

Chelyshev, Mikhail [Chëlyshev] 185 n. 72,
  218 n. 63, 221 n. 70, 232 n. 14, 255, 267, 278,
  295, 333, 351, 361–2
Chernomazov, Miron 62–66
Chernov-Greshnev, Andrei 172, 206 n. 32
childhood 7–24, 26, 264, 292, 297, 303, 321,
  335–7, 343, 348, 358, 360, 366–7, 369
child labour 8, 10–11, 13–14, 16–18, 21–24, 26
children's games 10–11
Chistyakov [Chistiakov] (teacher and party
  member) 350
civil society [*obshchestvo*] 20, 35, 51
civil war 1, 56–7, 65–6, 106, 122–57, 162, 169,
  170, 179, 184, 189, 191, 194, 196, 201–2, 225–6,
  239, 252, 264, 290, 293, 295, 317–19, 322,
  336, 339, 347, 373
  Caspian-Caucasian front 126–32, 373
  civil war as a slogan 56–7, 65–6
  Eastern front 201
  Western front 139, 143
  see also Revolutionary Military Council
    (RVS)
clergy 8, 17, 19, 32, 131
  see also estate(s), social
coal 18, 21, 112, 223, 293
  see also fuel
Cohen, Stephen F. 332
collective farm(s) [*kolkhoz*] 261, 302, 304,
  344
collectivisation 261, 281, 283, 297, 300–2,
  304, 309, 312–13, 318, 344, 357
Commissariat of Agriculture 196, 229 n. 5
Commissariat of Enlightenment
  (*Narkompros*) 134, 267
Commissariat of Food Supply (or Produce)
  (*Narkomprod*) 98 n. 54, 126–7, 140
Commissariat of Foreign Affairs
  (*Narkomindel*) 59, 263, 286–91
Commissariat of Heavy Industry
  (*Narkomtiazhprom*) 328, 334
Commissariat of Internal Affairs see NKVD
Commissariat of Labour (*Narkomtrud*) 99,
  103–21, 175, 199 n. 16, 200, 237, 284, 340, 372
  Congress of Labour Commissars 112,
    113, 120
Commissariat (or Committee) of Military and
  Naval Affairs 105, 126–7, 140, 335
Commissariat of Post and Telegraph 125

Commissariat of Social Security (*Sobez*) 221
Commissariat of Trade (*Narkomtorg*) 285–91
Commissariat of Trade and Industry 116
Commission on Evacuation of Industry from Petrograd 103, 115–16
Commission on Improving Workers' Living Conditions 187, 219–21, 264, 325
Commission on the History of the October Revolution and of the RKP(b) (*Istpart*) 254
Committee of Soviet Youth (*Komsomol*) 260
Communist International, 'fourth' and Fourth 214, 241
Communist International, Second 56, 151
Communist International, Third (*Comintern*) 116, 139, 151, 153–4, 212–15, 217, 227, 231–52, 256, 268, 280, 349, 363, 375
Communist Party of China 279
Communist Party of France 263
Communist Party of Germany (KPD) 214 n. 53–4, 259
Communist Party (Russian or Soviet)
  Central Committee (CC) 119–20, 131, 134, 137 n. 37, 139–40, 142–8, 153–4, 156–7, 162–7, 169–70, 173, 175–6, 182–4, 186–9, 192, 196, 198, 200–10, 214, 216–20, 222, 227, 229–30, 233–5, 237, 239–43, 249–51, 254–9, 261, 264, 274, 277, 280–1, 285, 287, 290, 295 n. 27, 298–301, 312, 316, 318, 320, 327, 329, 335, 348, 350, 353–4, 374–5
  Central Control Commission (CCC) 4–5, 176, 192, 201, 206, 210, 214, 216, 218, 221, 241–3, 246–7, 255, 258–9, 267–82, 284, 293–303, 305 n. 55, 308, 311, 313–16, 318–21, 327–8, 333 n. 5, 336 n. 12, 376
  Central Purge Commission 187, 218, 221, 320 n. 26, 324, 327–8
  Committee on Party Control (CPC) 355
  communist fraction(s) 104, 135, 137, 142–3, 145–8, 166–70, 172, 175, 177–8, 198–209, 212, 216, 222–5, 234–7, 291 n. 17
  General Secretary 240, 258
  Orgburo 134, 137, 144, 148 n. 62, 164 n. 17, 189, 210, 221, 234–5, 240–1, 311, 374
  partiinost [*partiinost'*] 68, 308, 318, 321
  party cell(s) 135, 168 n. 29, 172, 211, 216–18, 228, 239, 248, 257, 259–60, 267, 270, 275, 292, 309, 316–25, 327–8, 336
  party committee(s) 4, 127, 134–5, 141, 147, 163–4, 166 n. 24, 170–3, 176–7, 189–90, 200, 211, 216–18, 234, 240, 258, 268 n. 35, 271, 275, 294, 301 n. 48, 317, 374
  Party Control Commission (PCC) 271, 328 n. 44
  party control commission(s) 176, 244, 247 n. 54, 266 n. 31, 269–71
  party court 65, 127, 167, 173, 175–6, 183, 215–16, 218, 231, 234, 237, 241–2, 325
  party discipline 50, 90, 135, 156, 167, 175 n. 47, 187, 189, 192, 201, 213–27, 233–5, 238, 240, 247–52, 268, 275, 281, 375
  party purge commission(s) 187, 218, 221, 242, 246 n. 51, 303 n. 53, 309, 320–9
  party secretary 128, 140, 163–4, 166, 204, 229, 240, 241 n. 39, 247 n. 54, 249 n. 58, 266, 268 n. 35, 271, 294, 298, 316–17, 319, 331, 338
  Politburo 2, 134, 137, 139, 142, 144, 151, 163–4, 193, 196–214, 218, 221–4, 226, 233–8, 240–3, 252, 257, 259, 262, 269–77, 282, 285, 295, 311, 313, 324, 333, 335, 344, 347, 349, 359, 375
  revolutionary self-discipline 70, 105, 129
  Secretariat 134, 144, 148 n. 62, 210
  Women's Department (*Zhenotdel*) 181, 243 n. 43
  see also RSDRP(b)
Communist Party (Russian or Soviet) Congresses and Conferences
  Eighth Party Congress 128, 133–4, 138, 147, 159, 168, 374
  Eleventh Party Congress 206, 211, 227–8, 230, 238, 243–54, 281, 323
  Fifteenth Party Congress 280
  Fourteenth Party Conference 264–6
  Fourteenth Party Congress 269–70
  Ninth Party Conference 162–4, 176
  Ninth Party Congress 143, 146–8, 163
  Seventeenth Party Congress 331
  Sixteenth Party Congress 302
  Tenth Party Conference 193–7
  Tenth Party Congress 3, 148, 157, 168, 173–4, 176–7, 179–92, 205–6, 209–10,

213–14, 216–20, 226–7, 230, 241–3, 246–8, 322, 329, 374
Thirteenth Party Conference 262
Twelfth Party Congress 255, 258
Twentieth Party Congress 367
see also RSDRP(b)
Communist Party of Ukraine 144, 164 n. 17, 169 n. 32, 170, 229 n. 5, 247 n. 54, 266
Communist Workers' Party of Germany (KAPD) 214, 241
conservative(s) 79, 89, 91, 106, 193, 372
Consolidated State Political Administration (OGPU) 255–8, 269, 281, 284, 292–303, 306–8, 311, 333–48, 358 n. 67
Constituent Assembly 79–80, 101, 103, 106–7, 158
Constitutional Democrat Party (*Kadets*) 79, 89, 106
consumer(s), consumerism 191, 194, 196, 220, 265, 267–8, 283, 285, 303
Copenhagen 58–9, 154, 288
corporatism, corporatist 161–2
Cossacks 95, 123–5, 300
Council of Labour and Defence (aka Council of Worker-Peasant Defence) 223, 285, 287–8, 292
Council of People's Commissars (*Sovnarkom*) 97 n. 53, 99, 100, 105–19, 123–7, 201, 219–20, 335, 338, 347
Little Sovnarkom 201
Council of Worker-Peasant Defence (aka Council of Labour and Defence) (STO) 223, 285, 287–8, 292
Cracow 42
crafts 46–7, 84, 87, 92–4, 146, 191, 193 n. 2, 195, 265
Czech Legion 122
Czechoslovakia 155 n. 69, 233 n. 15–17, 291–2

dacha 334–5, 337, 347
Danilovsky monastery [Danilovskii] 366
Declaration of the 46 259
Declaration of the 83 (or 84) 279
degenerate [*pererozhdenets*] 326, 328
delovaya oppozitsiya [*delovaia oppozitsiia*] 199
Democratic Centralists 134–5, 138, 143, 157–8, 174, 178 n. 56, 184

Democratic State Conference 96
Denikin, Anton 123
Denmark 58–9, 154, 155 n. 69, 288, 291
Département de la Seine 39
Deutscher, Isaac 275, 283
disease *see* medicine
'Dizzy with Success' 297
Dmitriev (orphanage director) 366
Dnieper Dam and Hydroelectric Station [Dnepr] 285
Dolgolevsky, Moshe (alias of Nikolai Bukharin) 72
Donbas 21, 63, 77, 169, 203, 246, 273, 291, 312
Donskoe Cemetery 363–4
Doschatoe 11–13, 18, 65
double-dealing [*dvurushnichestvo*] 323–5, 327–8, 353
Duma 33, 56, 58, 76, 78–80, 245, 250 n. 59
Dybenko, Pavel 99 n. 57, 100, 108
Dzerzhinsky, Felix [Feliks Dzerzhinskii] 106, 148 n. 62, 165 n. 20–1, 166 n. 23, 176, 201, 246 n. 50, 255–8, 284

education, schools 1, 5, 7–9, 11, 16–20, 22–3, 25, 30–3, 35, 37, 40–1, 49, 51, 63, 65, 75, 77–9, 99 n. 57, 134, 142, 148 n. 63, 165, 175, 194, 210 n. 45, 221 n. 70, 239, 249, 254, 264, 289, 308, 318, 332, 348, 360, 367, 369
boarding school 360
evening school 134
gymnasium 32 n. 51, 264
Minister, Ministry of Education 23
party school(s) 40–1
primary school(s) 8, 11, 16–20, 22, 148 n. 63
seminary 19
student(s) 16–20, 22–3, 25, 31–3, 51, 65, 77–8, 175, 194, 210 n. 45, 249, 254, 264, 308, 369
Sunday school(s) 30
university, universities 23, 99 n. 57, 221 n. 70, 264, 332, 367
Egorov, Alexander [Aleksandr] 124
Eikhe, Robert 294
Eismont, N.B. 313
Eismont-Tolmachev-Smirnov group 313
Ekaterinburg 172, 228

Ekaterinodar (Krasnodar) 125–6, 169, 171, 172 n. 41
Ekaterinoslav 65, 158, 171, 211 n. 47
election(s) 61, 64, 79, 83, 86, 96, 106–7, 130, 137, 159, 168, 174, 182, 190, 199–200, 202, 205–7, 210, 212, 218, 222, 236–7, 248, 260, 262, 280–1, 374
electrician(s) 93
electric power 22, 33, 193, 216, 223, 285, 333, 336
Elizarova, Anna 65, 67
Ellis Island 71–3
émigré, emigration 3, 34, 36–7, 39, 50, 69, 72, 81, 250 n. 60, 370
emotion(s) 9–10, 12–13, 17–18, 20, 24, 30, 41, 45–6, 74, 78, 107, 116, 135, 142, 163, 168, 174, 182, 206–8, 220, 236, 241, 256, 263, 279, 303, 307, 326–8, 335, 337, 339, 341, 343, 345, 348, 366, 376
Engels, Friedrich 110, 160, 180 n. 61, 182, 345, 361, 370
England, English 34–6, 45, 59, 61, 71, 125, 131, 181 n. 62, 249, 286, 289–91, 340, 361 n. 77, 367, 370
  see also Great Britain
Eremeev, Konstantin 83
Ershov (Bolshevik in Metalworkers' Union central committee) 111
estate(s), large land 80, 103
estate(s), social 2, 8, 10–11, 17, 19–20, 24–5, 29–30, 33, 41, 56, 61, 74, 76, 95–6, 99 n. 57, 131, 197, 210 n. 45, 264, 370
Estonia, Estonian(s) 30, 137
exile 51–2, 63, 76, 80, 98 n. 54, 110, 143, 176, 194 n. 6, 219, 245, 247, 256–7, 283, 295, 301, 305, 331, 333–47, 353–6, 359–61, 364, 367, 372, 376–7
Ezerskaya, Fanny [Fani Ezerskaia] 358 n. 67

faction(s), factionalism 6, 25, 30, 38, 41, 52, 56, 62, 69, 72, 77, 153, 157–8, 164–6, 173, 175–6, 178, 186–92, 199, 202, 205, 208–9, 212, 216–18, 228–30, 233, 238, 240–3, 246–82, 295–305, 312–13, 318 n. 19, 322–6, 331, 342
factory, factories 6, 8, 10–18, 21–4, 31, 33, 35–7, 40 n. 8, 42, 45–6, 49–51, 59, 61, 63–5, 72, 74, 78, 82–8, 90–3, 95–6, 98–100, 103, 107, 110–15, 130, 134, 137–41, 145, 148, 153, 156, 159–60, 167, 170 n. 35, 172, 179, 185, 193, 195, 200, 208 n. 40, 211, 216–17, 219, 222–3, 229, 241, 248, 249 n. 58, 257, 259–61, 263, 268, 283–5, 290, 299, 305–7, 332–3, 336–8, 340–1, 349, 360, 369–70, 373
Aivaz 63
automobile factory 35, 59
box 18
Electrical Station of 1886 33
Electrical Enterprise of 1886 193
Ericsson 50
factory committee(s) 84–7, 91–2, 107, 111–12, 148, 153, 156, 159, 179, 211, 219, 268, 373
Factory Law Code 45
factory legislation 17–18, 21, 45
factory owner(s) 18, 51, 61, 72, 86, 88, 90–2, 111, 114, 340
Factory Street 8
Fiat 59
foundry 11, 13, 18
Franco-Russian 65
Izhorsk 179
Jessop 290
Kondratov 22–3
match 8, 11
Metron 260
Moscow Hydroelectrical Station (MOGES) 193 n. 3, 216–17
Nadezhdinsky [Nadezhdinskii] 223
New Lessner 50, 340
Obukhov 33, 337
Putilov 78, 87, 100, 170 n. 35
Radio Morse 248
Saville 290
Semyannikov [Semiannikov] (aka Nevsky Shipbuilding and Machine Plant) 13–14, 23–4
spinning mill 17, 305
Torsk 24, 31
Tuloma hydroelectrical station 333, 336, 340–1
Valenkov Machine-Building 31
Vickers 290
Faivilovich, Leonid 361
famine 11, 20, 122, 130, 192, 194, 225, 253, 283, 312, 320
  1891 famine 11, 20
  1921 famine 194, 225
  1932–3 famine 312, 320

INDEX

feudalism 266
Filatov (Moscow purge commission member) 326, 328 n. 46
Finkel [Finkel'] (engineer, Soviet trade mission in Berlin) 287, 291
Finland, Finnish 41, 59, 62, 65, 73, 81, 90, 336 n. 12, 338, 343
Finnic 8
fire service 338
Fischer, Ruth 228 n. 54, 363
Fisher, Matvei 2
five-year plan(s) 305, 318, 375–6
Fontanka 90
food 10–11, 17–18, 21, 51, 76, 78, 80, 89, 98, 103, 118, 122–4, 130, 132, 134, 141, 157, 159, 162, 178–9, 182, 191–4, 196, 202–3, 219, 221, 225, 248, 253, 261, 280, 283, 301 n. 49, 303 n. 54, 305–6, 338, 340–3, 351 n. 48, 360, 373
food-requisitioning 118, 122–4, 130, 134, 157, 178–9, 182, 191–2, 221, 225, 373
Foodworkers' Union 341
'For Bread and Oil' 123, 311 n. 6, 336, 347
Ford, Henry 134
foreign(ers) 1, 5, 34–5, 50, 59, 65, 79, 81, 181–2, 191–3, 195, 213–14, 223–4, 227, 236, 243, 251, 257, 259–61, 263, 265, 269, 272–3, 279, 284, 286, 288, 291, 306, 344–6, 357
foundry 11, 13, 18
Fourth and 'fourth' Communist International 214, 241
France, French 3, 30–2, 34–42, 45–50, 52, 56, 71, 87, 94, 110, 126 n. 10, 153–5, 160–1, 233 n. 15–17, 245, 262–4, 290, 292, 303, 347, 361 n. 77, 368–70
Frolov, K. (MOGES party cell member) 216–17
Frunze, Mikhail 201–2
fuel 18, 21, 76, 89, 112, 123, 125–6, 134, 140, 162, 182, 219, 223, 267, 293
Futrell, Michael 56–7
Fyodorov, Grigory [Grigorii Fëdorov] 204, 208–9

Gagry 300–1
Galicia 89
Gapon, Father Georgy [Georgii] 32
garden(s) 8, 11
Gastev, Alexei [Aleksei] 40–1, 49, 85, 87, 114
Gavan 338

Gei, Konstantin 325
gender 7, 12–13, 20, 29–30, 174, 206, 213, 279
see also masculinity
Geneva 34
Genoa 34
Genoa Conference 243–4, 250
gentry *see* nobles
Georgia, Georgian 30, 258
Germany, German 3, 35–7, 39, 42, 45 n. 17, 47 n. 19, 49, 56–8, 61, 69, 72, 79, 81, 86 n. 27, 89, 91, 97, 99, 103, 115–16, 118, 122, 151–5, 175, 181 n. 62, 193–4, 210 n. 45, 213–14, 233 n. 15–16, 241, 243–4, 250, 254 n. 2, 256–7, 259, 263, 286–92, 303, 308, 355, 358 n. 67, 361 n. 77, 370
Getty, J. Arch 337
Gidlevsky, Kensorin [Gidlevskii] 361–2
Ginzburg, Evgenia 332
glavki see All-Russian Council of National Economy (VSNKh)
Glebov-Avilov, Nikolai 125
GOELRO *see* State Commission for Electrification of Russia
Gogol, Nikolai 345
gold 51, 261, 268, 281, 286
Goldman, Wendy 332
Goldstein (German communist and possible provocateur) 241 n. 38
Golikov (Gosplan RSFSR party cell chair) 316 n. 14, 317
Goltsman, Abram [Gol'tsman] 141, 166 n. 23, 177 n. 52
Gomel [Gomel'] 221, 225
Gomzy (State Association of Machine-Building Factories) 285
Gorbachev, Mikhail 4
Gorky (city) *see* Nizhny Novgorod
Gorky, Maxim [Maksim Gor'kii] 65, 70
Gosplan *see* State Committee for Planning
GPU (State Political Administration and Consolidated State Political Administration) 255 n. 4, 268 n. 35, 276, 281 n. 62
Great Britain, British 39, 59, 123, 155 n. 69, 194 n. 6, 233 n. 17, 279, 286–7
see also English
Great Reforms of the 1860s–70s 8, 16, 19
Great Terror *see* terror
Green, Lev [Grin] 349, 358

Gridasov (early 1930s social acquaintance of Shlyapnikov) 362
Grigorev [Grigor'ev] (NKVD interrogator) 348–51
Grozny 123, 125
Guerre Sociale, La 39
Guesdists 47
Gulag (Main Administration of Camps) 305, 332, 342 n. 27, 343, 363, 367–8, 377
Gylling, Edvard 338

Halfin, Igal 213, 332
Hamburg 259
Hansen, J.A. 154
Haywood, William 'Bill' 223
Hellbeck, Jochen 2
Höglund, Gunhild 60
Höglund, Zeth 57, 60
holiday(s) 10–13, 17–18, 23, 42, 50, 72, 78, 135, 221, 238, 272–4, 281, 298–301, 313, 328, 345
Holmenkollen 281
Holmes, Larry E. 4
Hoover, Herbert 225
hospital union 139
Hotel National 188
housing 8, 12, 21, 41–2, 63, 113, 159, 219, 255 n. 3, 257, 264, 275, 305, 314–16, 333, 335, 337, 341, 347, 349, 352, 361 n. 77, 362 n. 81
Humanité, L' 48, 361 n. 77
humour 3, 13, 45, 49, 96, 161, 188, 203, 206, 209, 214, 217, 245, 247–8, 268, 275, 277, 295–7, 299, 303, 308–9, 316, 319–20, 322, 327–9, 335, 337, 342, 359, 369
hunger strike(s) 358–9

Ignatov, Efim 158, 173, 180 n. 60, 184, 186 n. 75, 256, 341
Ilya Muromets 8
imperialism 8, 56–7, 96, 103, 122, 127 n. 15, 137, 266
Independent Social Democratic Party (USPD) 153
Industrial Party Case 306–7, 340
industry 6–7, 13, 20–2, 36, 45, 47, 84, 87, 91–2, 97, 103, 107, 110–16, 118, 124, 128–47, 153, 157–9, 162–8, 176, 179, 189–99, 212, 217, 223–5, 238, 242, 244, 253–5, 258–62, 265–9, 272, 280–319, 328, 334, 338, 340, 353, 357, 370, 372–6

concession(s), leasing 192–3, 195–6, 216, 223–4, 236, 269
evacuation of industry 103, 115–16, 118
industrialisation 13, 20–2, 193–7, 225, 253, 258, 261, 265–9, 283–319, 338, 353, 357, 375–6
nationalisation of industry 97, 103, 111–12, 132, 191–3, 195, 217, 225, 372–3
one-man vs. collegial management 113, 141–8
Ingush 123
Institute of Red Professors 310–11, 321 n. 29
insurance committees, groups, organisers 51–2, 65, 115
intelligentshchina 132
intelligenty, intellectuals 1, 4, 25, 29, 30–1, 36–7, 39–41, 45–6, 49, 51–2, 63–4, 66, 70–1, 73–4, 81, 94, 132, 141–2, 146, 157–8, 161, 170–1, 174–5, 181, 238, 245, 249, 254, 261, 291, 341
International Congress of Metalworkers' Unions, Eighth 151–5
International Council of Trade Unions (*Mezhsovprof*) 154
International Federation of Metalworkers 151–5
internationalism, internationalist 57, 66–70, 94, 224, 229 n. 5
International, Second 56, 151
International Socialist Bureau 52
International Women's Day *see* women
Internationale 40
interrogation 5–6, 19, 31–2, 242–3, 255 n. 7, 257, 268 n. 34, 270, 272, 275–7, 279 n. 58, 293–7, 325, 329, 331–3, 345, 347–64, 377
Iskra 24, 34
Istorik-marksist 310
Istpart *see* Commission on the History of the October Revolution and of the RKP(b)
Italy, Italian 40, 155 n. 69, 233 n. 15–16
Ivan IV (the Terrible) 8
Ivanov (Gosplan RSFSR purge commission chair) 321–3, 326–8
Ivanov, N. (NKVD interrogator) 355, 358
Ivanovo-Voznesensk 33, 52 n. 30, 171, 312
IWW (International Workers of the World) 287
Izhevsk 130, 172 n. 41
Izvestiya [*Izvestiia*] 266

INDEX 411

Japan 32
Jews, Jewish 30, 32, 70, 72–3, 119, 174–5
 anti-Semitism 174–5, 322

Kaganovich, Lazar 246 n. 50, 266, 295, 297, 312, 324
Kalinin, Fyodor [Fëdor] 40, 49
Kalinin, Mikhail 134 n. 32, 148 n. 62, 165 n. 20, 22, 176 n. 50, 262, 335, 346
Kamenev, Lev 50, 56, 76, 80–2, 97, 104, 106, 116, 121, 134 n. 32, 143, 145, 148, 165 n. 20–2, 167 n. 27, 176 n. 50, 178 n. 55, 246, 253, 255, 258–9, 267, 269–70, 272, 274, 277, 310, 323, 331–2, 347, 350, 352–3, 356, 358–9, 361, 364, 372
Kanatchikov, Semyon [Semën] 2, 8–10, 16, 22, 35, 37
Karamzin, Nikolai 20
Karavaev, P.N. 325–6, 328 n. 45–6
Karelia 333–4, 338–44
Karpych (Murom foundryman) 13
Kasperovich, A.N. 342
Kayurov, Vasily [Vasilii Kaiurov] 355
Kazakh(s) 283
Kazan 8, 343, 360
Kelly, Catriona 16
Kem 343–4
Kerensky, Alexander [Aleksandr Kerenskii] 79, 95, 99
Kharkov 65, 158, 169–70, 204, 211 n. 47, 363
Khlevnyuk, Oleg [Khlevniuk] 313
Khodynka field 20–1
Khrushchev, Nikita 3, 76 n. 1, 367
Kiev 77, 266, 357, 363
Kin, P.A. 251
Kirov, Sergei 128–31, 155, 246 n. 50, 271, 320 n. 26, 331, 347, 349–51, 353–4, 360–1, 377
Kiselev, Alexei [Aleksei Kiselëv] 52, 61, 144–5, 178, 180 n. 60, 185–7, 201, 215 n. 56, 235
Kislovodsk 273–4, 300–1, 313, 328, 353
Kizlyar [Kizliar] 125
Knorin, Vilgelm [Vil'gel'm] 321 n. 29, 326–9, 348 n. 41
Koestler, Arthur 332
Kola 340–1
Kolchuginsk [Kol'chuginsk] 293
Kolesnikov (metalworker, Worker Oppositionist) 357

kolkhoz (see collectivisation)
Kollontai, Alexandra [Aleksandra] 1, 3, 5, 36–7, 39, 41–3, 45, 49, 58–60, 62, 70–1, 74, 80, 105, 108, 116, 118, 130 n. 23, 132, 141–4, 158, 164, 178 n. 53, 180–4, 186, 188, 212–14, 217, 231–3, 239, 242, 245–7, 249–52, 256–7, 267, 269–70, 281, 288–9, 303, 312, 360, 370
Kollontai, Mikhail 37
Kollontai, Vladimir 303
Kolyma 367
Komi 367
Kommunist 66–70, 74
Konovalov (BBK staff member in Medvezhegorsk) 340
Kopylov, N.V. 140
Kornilov, Lavr (General) 82, 95
Kotkin, Stephen 2
Kovalenko, Iosif (brother-in-law) 54–5, 119
Krasin, German 340
Krasin, Leonid 263, 340
Krasnaya Zvezda [*Krasnaia Zvezda*] 351
Krasnodar 125–6, 169, 171–2
Krasnoyarsk [Krasnoiarsk] 367
Krestinsky, Nikolai [Krestinskii] 134 n. 32, 140, 143, 145, 148 n. 62, 165–6, 176 n. 50, 189, 287–91, 307
Kristianiafjord 71, 73
Krivov, Timofei 241–3, 295, 297, 300–1
Kronstadt 125, 127, 157, 174, 182–6, 189, 374
Kronstadt mutiny 157, 174, 182–6, 189, 374
Krupskaya, Nadezhda [Krupskaia] 36, 41, 68, 174, 258–9, 361 n. 77, 370
Krylov, N.S. 293–4, 302 n. 51
Krzhizhanovsky, Gleb [Krzhizhanovskii] 216
Kshesinskaya, Matilda [Kshesinskaia] 91
Kubyak, Nikolai [Kubiak] 194 n. 5, 249–50
Kuibyshev, Valerian 256 n. 10, 266, 277, 285, 288
kulak(s) see peasant(s)
Kulebaki 366
Kulikov, Ivan 136
Kuritsyn, Fyodor [Fëdor] 339
Kursk 137
Kutuzov, Ivan 144–5, 164, 172, 186 n. 75, 188, 194 n. 5
Kuzbas 223–4
Kuznetsov, Nikolai 232 n. 14, 247, 249, 251, 256

labour   8, 10–14, 16–18, 20–4, 26, 30–4, 35–9, 42, 45–52, 59, 63–4, 72, 74, 77–8, 85–96, 100–1, 103–22, 130–5, 139–43, 145, 157, 159, 162–5, 167, 176, 182, 188–9, 193–5, 197, 202–3, 219, 223–4, 230, 236–9, 244–5, 250, 253, 256, 259, 265, 270, 283–4, 294, 296–7, 306, 312, 320, 332–3, 337–8, 341–2, 345, 360, 370, 372–4, 376
   blacklisting   24, 38
   child labour   8, 10–11, 13–14, 16–18, 21–24, 26
   forced labour   35, 122, 142, 297, 332–3, 341
   labour armies   139–40, 142–3, 162–5, 176, 374
   Labour Code (1922)   237–8
   labour exchange(s)   46, 85, 91 n. 38, 238, 370
   labour history   2, 76, 124, 166, 236–7, 249, 254, 293, 295, 301, 309–12, 321–2, 326, 336
   labour law   17–18, 21, 45
   labour unrest   10, 20–4, 32–4, 38–9, 47, 51, 63–4, 72, 77–8, 87–93, 96, 104–5, 130–2, 135, 157, 182, 188–9, 219, 230, 236–7, 239, 244–5, 253, 256, 270, 283–4, 294, 312, 320, 338, 345, 376
   piecework   114, 132, 134, 306
   productivity   30, 88, 111–14, 131, 133–4, 159, 162, 165, 193–4, 197, 202–3, 237, 259, 283, 342
   tariff(s) [*tarif*]   85–8, 90–5, 101, 105, 111, 114, 120, 145, 165, 174, 260, 265, 372–3
   wage(s), wage rate(s)   21–3, 51, 59, 84, 86–9, 91, 93, 109, 114, 134, 139, 159–60, 202, 253, 259, 265, 284, 333, 338, 349, 370, 372
   women's labour *see* women
   see also Commissariat of Labour, factories, trade unions, women, workers
Lafargue, Laura   41
Lafargue, Paul   41
lapta   10
Laptev (former Foodworkers' Union secretary; in BBK)   341
Latin   37
Latin Quarter   34
Latvia, Latvian(s)   30, 148 n. 63, 355
law(s)   18–19, 21, 23–5, 31–3, 35, 39, 45–6, 50–2, 56, 59, 64–5, 74, 95, 106, 118–19, 127–8, 133, 166–7, 173, 175–6, 182–3, 206, 215–16, 218, 227, 231–2, 234, 236–7, 241–2, 248, 252, 258, 264–5, 294–7, 307 n. 60, 315–6, 325–7, 334, 336, 338, 343–4, 347–8, 350, 352–3, 357, 362–3, 367, 370–1
   comrade or party court(s)   65, 127, 167, 173, 175–6, 183, 215–16, 218, 231, 234, 237, 241–2, 325
   court(s)   19, 32 n. 50, 65, 106, 127, 167, 173, 175–6, 183, 215–16, 218, 227, 231, 234, 236–7, 241–2, 248, 295, 316, 325, 327, 344, 363, 367
   illegal   23–5, 31–2, 35, 39, 50–2, 56, 59, 64, 74, 173, 175, 258, 294, 296–7, 316, 343, 350, 352–3, 357, 370
   labour law   18, 21, 45
   Law of 1 December 1934   347, 363
   lawyer(s)   25, 33, 166, 326
   legal   19, 23, 35, 51–2, 64, 128, 232, 265, 297, 316, 334, 336, 352, 370–1
   legality   119, 206, 252, 265, 315–16
   martial law   95, 182
   RSFSR Law Code, article 58   353, 362–3
   USSR Supreme Court Military Collegium   363
League of Nations   345, 357
Leather Workers' Union   109
Lefortovo   33
Left Communists   110, 116, 118
Left Opposition   258–62, 283
Lena Goldfields   51
Lenin [Vladimir Ulyanov] [Ul'ianov]   1, 3–5, 24–5, 29, 34–70, 75–112, 115–21, 124, 128, 133–5, 139–44, 147, 156–98, 201, 204, 207–17, 220–2, 226–8, 231, 234, 238, 244–6, 249, 252–3, 258–9, 262, 265, 269, 273–4, 293, 299, 310–11, 329, 336, 344, 354, 356, 361, 368–74
   April Theses   81
   Last Testament   258–9, 269, 274, 293
   Lenin levy   262
   Leninism, Leninist   156, 170 n. 36, 344, 354, 371
   national self-determination   66–70, 77, 96
Leningrad   269–71, 285, 331–2, 334, 337–8, 344, 347–8
   see also Petrograd, St. Petersburg
Leningrad Opposition   269–70, 356

INDEX 413

Leningrad University 332
Lepse, Ivan 87 n. 29, 148, 177 n. 52, 207–9, 234–7
Lermontov, Mikhail 20
Lesnaya shkola [*Lesnaia*] 360
liberal(s), liberalism 32–3, 76, 78–9, 82–3, 89, 91, 94–6, 106, 250, 311, 363
Libet (*Tekhnoimport* head in Berlin) 287–8, 291
Lih, Lars T. 29, 40, 51, 80, 231
Litvin-Sedoi, Zinovy [Zinovii] 243 n. 43, 245–6
Litvinov, Maxim [Maksim] 59
Lives of the Saints 17
Loggin, Archpriest 9
London 34, 45, 59, 249, 289–90
Longjumeau 40
Lower Volga Steamboat Administration 360
Lozovsky, Solomon [Lozovskii] [b. Dridzo] 154, 167–8
Lubyanka 335, 347
Lunacharsky, Anatoly [Anatolii Lunacharskii] 40, 100, 175
Lushina, Maria [Mariia] 358
Lutovinov, Yuri [Iurii] 63, 143–8, 163–4, 167–9, 178, 214 n. 54, 255–7
Luxemburg, Rosa 233
Lvov, Georgy (Prince) [Georgii L'vov] 79

Magnitogorsk 359
mail *see* postal service
Maisky, Ivan [Maiskii] 41
Makh, I. 175
Makhaevism 161 n. 9
Makhova, Arisha 14, 29
Malinovsky, Roman [Malinovskii] 50
Manikovsky, Alexei [Aleksei Manikovskii] 105
Mann, Tom 223
Manuilsky, Dmitry [Dmitrii Manuil'skii] 229, 249–51, 256 n. 9
Marble Palace 119
Martov, Yuli [Iulii] 24–5
Marushevsky, Vladimir [Marushevskii] 105
Marx, Karl 1, 41, 182, 345, 361, 370
Marxism, Marxist 1–2, 7, 12, 18, 20, 23–5, 30, 37, 40–1, 66, 74, 79, 133, 145, 156, 160, 175, 187, 194 n. 6, 199, 236, 245, 279, 302–3, 310, 319, 370–1

Marx-Engels Institute (after 1931 the Marx-Engels-Lenin Institute) 110, 180 n. 61
masculinity 7, 12–13, 20, 30, 206
Maslov, Peter [Pëtr] 42
Mawdsley, Evan 119
Maximov, Nikolai [Maksimov] 293–303, 346
May Day 23, 42, 50
medicine
    medical care 99, 139, 219, 334–5, 343–4, 347, 353, 358, 360, 366, 377
    medical leave 135, 143, 208, 307, 309
    medical supplies, medicine 303 n. 54
    hospital(isation) 82, 139, 366
    hospital union 139
    disease, illness, sickness 51, 122, 129, 135, 139, 181, 238, 250, 253, 258, 264, 267, 297, 301 n. 49, 303, 307, 309, 321, 323–4, 326–7, 334–5, 344, 353, 359–60, 373, 377
    see also Ménière's disease, profession(s), tuberculosis, and typhus
Medvedev, Alexander [Aleksandr] 211–12, 232 n. 14
Medvedev, Sergei 5, 33–4, 42, 52, 144–5, 164, 166, 170 n. 35, 177 n. 52, 180 n. 60, 183–7, 194 n. 5, 197–8, 206–7, 209, 214, 217, 228 n. 1, 230–2, 235–6, 241–3, 245, 247–52, 254–8, 262, 264, 266 n. 31, 267–79, 281, 284, 294–303, 313, 323, 328, 333–4, 340, 344–6, 348–51, 354–8, 361–2, 364, 367, 375–6
Medvedeva, Aida 264, 345, 358
Medvedeva, Irina 264, 345, 358
Medvedeva, Maria [Mariia] 264, 278, 303
Medvezhegorsk [Medvezh'egorsk, Medvezh'ia Gora] 333, 337, 339–41, 344, 355, 359
Mekhonoshin, Konstantin 129, 131
Ménière's disease 129, 267, 307, 309, 323–4, 334–5, 344, 353, 359
Mensheviks *see* Russian Social Democratic Workers' Party (RSDRP)
Merrheim, Alphonse 154–5
meshchanstvo (townsmen) 8, 10–11, 17, 197
    see also estate(s), social
Metallist (alias used by Alexander Shlyapnikov) 37
Metallist (journal) 45 n. 17, 50, 85, 87 n. 29, 90
Metalloimport 285–92, 307, 375

metals, metalworkers, metalworking, metallurgy   1–2, 7–8, 10, 12–14, 20, 22–3, 30, 33, 35–9, 42, 45–6, 50, 52, 59, 61, 63, 71, 76, 78, 84–8, 90–4, 96–102, 109, 112, 114–15, 131–2, 135, 137–40, 144, 148, 151–5, 158–60, 166, 168, 170–2, 174, 177–9, 188–9, 192, 197–8, 203–12, 217, 221–8, 234–7, 241–2, 247–8, 254–5, 263, 267, 280, 284–92, 295, 305–7, 333, 335–7, 353, 357, 369, 372–6

Metalworkers' Union
   All-Russian Metalworkers' Union   73, 85, 94, 96–102, 109, 114, 132, 135, 137–41, 144, 148, 153–5, 158, 168–9, 177, 179, 189, 192, 197–8, 203–9, 212, 217, 221–8, 235–7, 254, 284, 291, 307, 342, 357, 372–3, 376
   Astrakhan Metalworkers' Union   131
   bureau of the communist fraction of the central committee   168, 205
   central committee   85, 97–8, 138, 144, 168, 170, 177, 204–5, 207, 209, 221–5, 234–7, 342
   communist fraction of the central committee   168, 205–7, 209, 222–4, 234
   Ekaterinburg Metalworkers' Union   172
   Fifth Congress of the Metalworkers' Union   227–8, 234–7
   Fourth Congress of the Metalworkers' Union   203–9, 223
   Kharkov Metalworkers' Union   170, 204
   Moscow Metalworkers' Union   204, 217, 248
   Nizhny Novgorod Metalworkers' Union   204
   Orenburg-Turgaisk Metalworkers' Union   172
   Petrograd Metalworkers' Union   61, 76, 84–8, 90–4, 96–102, 109, 114, 204–6, 372
   presidium of the central committee   168, 208–9, 223–4
   secretariat of the presidium of the central committee   206–7, 209
   St. Petersburg Metalworkers' Union   50, 52, 170 n. 35
   Tula Metalworkers' Union   140, 204
   Ukrainian Metalworkers' Union   148 n. 63
   Uralsk [Ural'sk] Metalworkers' Union   172
   Urals Metalworkers' Union   204

Meteletskaya [Meteletskaia] (Mosgorkom member, 1933)   317–19
Mezhraiontsy (Interdistrictites)   78, 229 n. 5
Miasnikov, Gavriil *see* Myasnikov, Gavril
Mikhailov, Mikhail   255 n. 7, 267, 349–50, 352, 354, 356
Mikhailov, Vasily [Vasilii]   189
Mikoyan, Anastas [Mikoian]   285, 287–8, 291, 339
military   32, 70, 78, 89–90, 98–9, 103, 105, 115–16, 122–33, 138–40, 144, 155, 163–4, 184, 199, 202, 219 n. 65, 257, 290, 292, 318, 322, 335, 342, 345, 349, 363, 373
   conscription   33, 162, 208 n. 40, 372
   militarisation   1, 140–1, 159, 162–4, 176, 374
   militarism   122, 155, 303
   Military Opposition   128
Military Revolutionary Committee (MRC)   99
militia(s)   76, 82–4, 90 n. 36, 333
Milonov, Yuri [Iurii]   171, 180 n. 60
Milyukov, Pavel [Miliukov]   79, 81
Mineralnye Vody [Mineral'nye Vody]   124
mining, miner(s)   11, 21, 144, 148, 159, 173–4, 195, 198, 201, 203, 223, 243, 285
Miners' Union   144, 148, 173–4, 198, 201, 203
   Congress of the Miners' Union   173–4
Mironov (assistant director of NKVD internal prison)   348
Mitin, Flor   206 n. 32, 210–12, 232 n. 14, 243, 246–51
Mitrevich, Anton   170–1
Molotov, Vyacheslav [Viacheslav]   77, 148 n. 62, 189, 203–4, 207–9, 248, 255, 257, 272, 274, 298–9, 326, 329, 335–6, 353, 359
monarchist   32, 79, 228
money   10, 12, 20, 36, 73 n. 78, 99, 115, 124, 128–9, 286, 295, 333, 336–8, 341, 347, 351 n. 48, 358, 361 n. 77
   dollars   358
   gold ruble   286
   hard currency   358
   Reichsmark   286
   ruble   73 n. 78, 99, 115, 128, 286, 333, 336, 347, 351 n. 48, 361 n. 77
Mongolia   303
Moscow   7–8, 20, 22, 31, 33, 52, 65, 77, 85 n. 24, 95, 97–8, 110, 115–16, 118–19, 124–30,

132, 134, 137, 139, 143–6, 148 n. 63, 151, 158, 162, 169, 172–3, 176–8, 180 n. 60, 193 n. 3, 197, 204–5, 212, 215–16, 218, 221–2, 225, 228, 238–9, 248, 256, 260, 262–4, 266–8, 270, 272, 275, 285, 292–7, 299, 303, 307–8, 313–17, 321–2, 325–6, 328 n. 45, 331–2, 334–6, 339, 343–7, 350, 355, 357, 359–60, 362–3, 366–8, 373, 377
   capital moved to Moscow   115–16, 118
Moscow city trade union council   146
Moscow Commissariat of Labour   116, 118
Moscow Metalworkers' Union   204, 217, 248
Moscow nonparty metalworkers' conference   160, 178–9
Moscow Oblast Metalworkers' Union Conference   85 n. 24, 97
Moscow party organization (city, gubernia, oblast)   172–3, 176–7, 183, 216, 218, 273, 275, 317, 321 n. 29, 322, 325–6, 328 n. 45
Moscow State University   367
Moscow Textileworkers' Union   144
Moscow waterworks   339
Murom   8–22, 24, 31–3, 59, 136, 149–51, 305–6, 337, 339, 370
Muromets, Ilya   8
Murom Group of Workers   31
Murom organisation of the RSDRP   31
Murom Social Revolutionary Party   31
Myasnikov, Gavril [Gavriil Miasnikov]   214 n. 54, 228–30, 232 n. 14, 240, 247 n. 53, 254–7, 281–2, 323, 375

nationalisation of industry *see* industry
nationalism, nationalist(s)   32, 66–70, 73–4, 96, 174, 279, 338 n. 18, 358
Nationalist Party of China (*Kuomintang*)   279
nationalities policy   258
national minorities   8, 13, 66–7, 76, 96, 174, 355 n. 60
   see also Armenia, Azerbaijan, Belorussia, Chechen, Estonia, Finland, Georgia, Ingush, Jews, Kazakh, Latvia, Poland, Tatars
national self-determination (national question)   66–70, 76–7, 96, 174
nature, appreciation of   12, 338–9, 341, 343

Naumov, Oleg   337
Naumov, Vladimir   4
nepotism   118–20, 176
network(s)   32, 58, 66, 83–4, 116, 171, 196, 229, 253, 275 n. 52, 284
Nevsky district [Nevskii]   337
Nevsky Shipbuilding and Machine Plant *see factories*
New Economic Policy (NEP)   179, 191–293, 323, 375
   tax-in-kind   179, 191–2, 196–7
   see also Communist Party congresses and conferences, industry, Left Opposition, Right Opposition, Shakhty Trial, syndicates, trusts, United Opposition
New Jersey   368
New Soviet Man, new people   333, 342
New York (city)   70–2
New York Times, The   274
Nicholas II   20–2, 32–3, 76, 78–9, 91
Nikolaenko, Ivan   266–7, 295
Nikolaev (city)   229
Nikolaev, Leonid   347, 349
Nikolina Gora   334–5, 337, 347
Nizhny Novgorod [Nizhnii Novgorod]   8, 21–2, 24, 30–1, 65, 77, 140, 169, 172, 204, 305, 366
   Gorky [Gor'kii]   366
Nizhny Novgorod provincial trade-union council   172
NKVD (Commissariat of Internal Affairs)   2, 5–6, 161 n. 10, 250 n. 60, 255 n. 3, 268 n. 34, 295 n. 26, 300 n. 43, 304, 328 n. 44, 329, 331, 333 n. 5, 344–5, 347–63
   Astrakhan NKVD   362
   NKVD informant   349–50, 355–6, 367
   NKVD interrogator(s)   329, 333 n. 5, 345, 348–58, 362
Nobel, Emmanuel [Nobel']   340
nobility, noble(s), gentry   2, 8, 19–20, 24, 29, 33, 41, 74, 131, 210 n. 45, 264, 370
   see also estate(s), social
Noé, Jacob   49
Nogin, Viktor   97, 99 n. 57, 116, 118–21, 148 n. 62, 154, 165
Nonferrous Metals Syndicate   295
   see also syndicate(s)

North Caucasus 118, 123, 125–6, 128–9, 300–1, 339, 347, 351, 373
Norway, Norwegian 39, 59–60, 68, 71, 154–5, 281, 288
Novorossiysk [Novorossiisk] 125
Novyi mir 72
Nyström, Ruth 60

Obolensky, Valerian [Obolenskii] (N. Osinsky) [Osinskii] 110, 134, 196
obshchestvo 20, 35, 51
Odessa 169, 363
OGPU (Consolidated State Political Administration) 255–8, 269, 281, 284, 292–303, 308, 311, 333, 335–48, 358 n. 67
  see also Cheka, GPU, NKVD, police
oil 112, 123, 126, 267
  see also fuel
Oka River 8
Olaussen, Eugène 60
Old Belief, Old Believers 5, 9, 11–14, 16–17, 19–23, 29, 40, 42, 65, 321–2, 330, 369–71
  Pomortsy 9
Old Church Slavonic 17
Omsk 169, 240, 284, 293–305, 308, 335, 346, 349–50, 352, 363, 375
opposition(ist) *see* Democratic Centralist, Left Opposition, Military Opposition, Right Opposition, United Opposition, Workers' Group, Workers' Truth and Workers' Opposition
opportunism, opportunist 58, 323
Ordzhonikidze, Grigory 'Sergo' [Grigorii] 128–30, 139, 258, 277, 294–5, 298–9, 339
Orel 137
Orenburg-Turgaisk, Metalworkers' Union of 172
Orlov, Grigory [Grigorii] 119
Orlov, Kirill 52, 63, 90 n. 36, 255
Ostroumova, Valentina 149

Palchinsky, Peter [Pëtr Palchinskii] 306–7
Panyushkin, Vasily [Vasilii Paniushkin] 210–11
Paris 34–5, 37–42, 47–9, 63 n. 52, 94, 257, 263, 275 n. 52, 290, 292
  Latin Quarter 34
  Parisian Mechanics' Trade Union 38
partiinost [*partiinost'*] 68, 308, 318, 321, 327

passport 13, 49, 56, 62, 71–2, 264, 290, 333
patron-client relations 291–2, 318
Pavlovo 305
peasant(s) 8, 11, 20, 24–5, 29–30, 33, 56, 61, 76, 95–6, 99 n. 57, 103, 105, 141, 146, 157, 160, 171, 182, 184, 190–7, 210, 212–13, 217, 225, 228–30, 245, 247, 252–4, 258, 261, 264–5, 267–8, 274, 283, 293–4, 297, 300, 302, 309, 317–19, 324, 337–8, 342, 375–6
  bednyak [*bedniak*] 61, 261, 265, 281, 317–8
  dekulakisation 300, 342, 297
  kulak 274, 283, 297, 300, 302, 324, 342
  state peasant(s) 11
  see also agriculture, collectivisation, estate(s)
pension 296, 344, 347, 351, 353
People's Commissariats *see* Commissariats
Perepechko, Ivan 169–70, 180 n. 60, 186 n. 75, 210–11
perlustration *see* postal service
Perm 140, 228
Peter I (the Great) 16
Petersburg Committee *see* Russian Social Democratic Workers' Party
Petersburg Metalworkers' Union *see* Metalworkers' Union
Peters, Yakov [Iakov] 321 n. 29, 322, 325–6
Petrograd 36, 56–7, 61–7, 70–1, 73, 76–116, 118–19, 130, 137, 148 n. 63, 157–8, 170–1, 174, 176, 179, 182, 184, 185 n. 72, 188–9, 204–6, 208 n. 40, 211 n. 47, 251, 372
  Petrograd Council of Trade Unions *see* trade unions
  Petrograd garrison 83, 99
  Petrograd Metalworkers' Union *see* Metalworkers' Union
  Petrograd Military District 83
  Petrograd Public Library 73 n. 78
  Petrograd Soviet *see* Soviets
  see also Leningrad, St. Petersburg
Petrosov, M.V. (Tenth Party Congress delegate; in BBK) 339–40, 349
Petrovskii (SPO GUGB first section chief) 355
Petrovsky, Grigory [Grigorii Petrovskii] 50, 148 n. 62, 165 n. 22, 246 n. 50, 249–50
Petrozavodsk 338
Petrushka puppet show 10
petty bourgeois *see* bourgeois

INDEX

philistine [*meshchanin, obyvatel'*] 258, 318, 326
Piter, Pitertsy 58, 337
Pivon, Ivan [Pivon'] 266 n. 31, 350, 352, 357
plan, planning (economic) 103, 112, 192, 194, 197, 216, 258–9, 261, 283, 285, 293, 297, 305, 307, 309, 312, 316–24, 327, 336, 341, 343, 353, 357, 375–6
  see also five-year plan, State Committee for Planning
Platform of Labour Industrialism group 114
Plastinin, Nikolai (brother-in-law) 149
Plekhanov, Georgy [Georgii] 24
Podvoisky, Nikolai [Podvoiskii] 105
Poland, Poles, Polish 30, 66 n. 61, 69, 163
police 2, 7, 9, 19, 21, 23, 25, 31–4, 37, 50, 56, 62–6, 71–2, 74, 77–8, 82–3, 106, 131 n. 26, 154, 175, 214–15, 250, 253, 255 n. 4, 257–8, 268, 270, 281, 284, 302, 305 n. 55, 331, 333, 336–8, 366, 375–6
  Okhrana 37, 56, 63, 65, 257
  gendarme(s) 21, 250
  German police 175
  Norwegian police 154
  police-sponsored unions 32
  Soviet secret police 2, 7, 19, 106, 131 n. 26, 214, 253, 255 n. 4, 258, 268, 270, 281, 284, 302, 305 n. 55, 331, 333, 336, 366, 375–6
  see also Cheka, GPU, NKVD, OGPU
  Soviet transport police 293
  tsarist-era Russian police 9, 21, 23, 25, 31–4, 37, 50, 62–6, 71–2, 74, 77–8, 82–3, 215, 337–8
Politburo *see* Communist Party
Poor Liza 20
Populists, Russian 20, 31, 302
Poskrebyshev, Alexander [Aleksandr] 335
postal service, mail 31, 34–5, 45, 69, 81, 124–5, 127, 131, 138, 153–4, 239–40, 275, 297 n. 37, 299–300, 328 n. 47, 334 n. 7, 338, 341, 343, 345–6
  Commissariat of Post and Telegraph 125
  mail train 341
  perlustration 328 n. 47
  telegram 81, 124, 127, 240, 275, 341, 343
  telegraph 45, 125, 131, 138, 153–4
Prague Conference of 1912 61
Pravda 49 n. 23, 50, 56, 58, 61, 80–1, 89, 139, 170 n. 35, 177, 181, 238, 242, 260–2, 271–4,

277, 280–1, 297–8, 311, 321 n. 29, 324, 352 n. 51
Pravdin, Alexander [Aleksandr] 232 n. 14, 255, 267, 349–50, 352
Preobrazhensky, Evgeny [Evgenii Preobrazhenskii] 148 n. 62, 163–6, 176 n. 50, 189
prison(s), prison camp(s), prisoners, political isolator(s) 7, 17, 19–20, 22 n. 36, 25, 33, 35, 78, 80, 137, 155, 176, 219, 235, 257, 291, 295, 298–9, 301, 305, 310, 331, 333, 336, 338–9, 341–3, 346–59, 362–4, 366–7, 370, 372, 376–7
  Butyrka prison 355–9
  Kolyma prison camp 367
  Komi prison camp 367
  Lubyanka prison 347–55
  transit prison 333
  Verkhne-Uralsk [Ural'sk] political isolator 7, 19, 358–9
  Vladimir prison 25, 33
  White-Sea Baltic-Sea Canal (BBK) prison camp 339, 341–3
procurator *see* prosecutor
professional revolutionary 39–40, 105
profession(s), professional(s) 4, 17, 19–20, 25, 29–30, 32–3, 37, 46, 59, 63, 71, 79, 113, 128, 139, 166, 188, 213, 287, 289–91, 306–7, 309–11, 315–16, 321, 323, 326, 336–7, 339–40, 342, 350–1, 359–60, 367, 373
  chemist(s) 4, 367
  engineer(s) 37, 46, 59, 71, 113, 188, 213, 287, 289, 291, 306–7, 339–40, 342, 360, 367, 373
  journalist(s) 20, 25, 128, 166
  lawyer(s) 25, 33, 166, 326
  medical doctor(s), physicians 20, 139, 315–16, 321, 336–7, 351 n. 48, 359
  professor(s) 290, 310–11, 321, 367
  teacher(s) 17, 19–20, 25, 29, 63, 350
  see also professional revolutionary
Profintern (Red Trade Union International) 154
prokurora see prosecutor
proletarian, proletariat 30, 35, 42, 45, 51, 62, 64, 67, 71, 81, 97, 99, 107, 132–4, 138, 140–1, 146, 160, 164, 174, 182, 184, 187, 194–7, 199–200, 217, 219, 230, 232, 236, 238–42, 245, 252, 254, 261, 265–6, 268, 280, 287, 289, 291, 307, 310–11, 320, 322, 326, 328, 345–7, 359, 368–9, 374

Proletarskaya Revolutsiya [*Proletarskaia revoliutsiia*] 310
prosecutor, procurator [procurator, *prokurora*] 32, 307, 351, 359 n. 68, 363 n. 82, 367
prosecutorial 233
province(s), provincial 1, 4, 24, 31, 52, 65, 77, 85, 139, 145, 164, 171–2, 196, 210 n. 44, 225, 240, 262, 345, 348 n. 41
  see also gubernias and oblasts by name
Provisional Government 62, 76, 79–83, 88–91, 95–7, 100–1, 104–5, 107, 119, 128, 372
  Ministry of Justice 79
  Ministry of Labour 88, 91, 100, 105, 107, 119
  Ministry of War 79, 105
Pskov 99
purge(s) 5–6, 19, 42, 56, 105, 161 n. 10, 175 n. 47, 176, 184, 187–8, 190, 209, 218, 221, 242, 246, 267, 298 n. 38, 301–3, 309, 316–29, 333–4, 336, 353, 376
  see also Communist Party
Pushkin, Alexander [Aleksandr] 20
Put' Pravdy see Pravda
Pyatakov, Georgy [Georgii Piatakov] 289
Pyatakov, Yuri [Iurii Piatakov] 61, 66, 69–70

Rabochaya oppozitsiya [*Rabochaia oppozitsiia*] 180–4
Rabochii Put' 301
Radek, Karl 66 n. 61, 69, 142, 145, 148, 163, 165 n. 20, 174, 213, 233, 239 n. 31, 244 n. 47, 332
Radetsky [Radetskii] (Rapoport's assistant at BBK) 339–40
Radus-Zenkovich, Viktor [Radus'-Zen'kovich] 119–20
Rafail [R.B. Farbman] 174
Railway Workers' Union 113, 162
  All-Russian Executive Committee of Railwaymen (*Vikzhel*) 113
Rapoport, Yakov [Iakov] 336, 339
Raskolnikov, Fyodor [Fëdor Raskol'nikov] 125
Red Army 122–4, 126–31, 139, 143, 163, 182, 290, 317, 359
  Eleventh Army 123, 126, 129–31
  Red Army Academy 290
  Red Army House 317
  Sixteenth Army 139, 143
  Twelfth Army 126, 129–30

Red Fleet 125
Red Guard 76, 82–4, 90 n. 36, 95, 100
Red Wheel 3
reforging [*perekovka*] 333, 342
rehabilitation 4, 270, 367–8
Reichsmark 286
Reichstag 56
religion 5–14, 16–17, 19–23, 29, 32, 39–40, 42, 65, 131, 174, 225, 321–2, 330, 369–71
  atheism 12, 369–70
  Christmas 17
  church(es) 9, 12, 16–17, 19, 22, 225, 369
  god builders 39–40
  icon(s) 11–12, 16
  martyr(s), martyrdom, saint(s) 9, 17, 42
  missionary 11–12
  Russian Orthodox Church 9, 11–12, 16, 19, 369
  seminary 19
  see also Old Belief
Revolution of 1848 32
Revolution of 1905 7, 25, 32–3, 52, 64, 85 n. 22, 110, 229 n. 5, 352 n. 51, 370
Revolution of 1917 5, 7, 31, 39, 45, 76–102, 110, 114, 116, 122 n. 1, 155, 179 n. 58, 247, 254, 262, 284, 292, 301, 309–12, 317, 322–5, 329, 336 n. 12, 340, 345, 355, 370–2, 376
  February Revolution 76–83, 114, 309–12, 325, 329, 340, 372
  June Days 89
  July Days 89–91, 95, 102, 336 n. 12
  Kornilov Affair 82, 95
  October Revolution 39, 76, 85 n. 23, 93, 95, 97–100, 102, 116, 122 n. 1, 155, 179 n. 58, 247, 254, 317, 322–4, 345, 371–2
  Semnadtsatyi god (Shlyapnikov's memoir of 1917) 7, 45, 76, 81–3, 87 n. 29, 97 n. 52, 254, 262, 267, 284, 292, 301, 325, 329, 370, 372, 376
Revolutionary Military Council (*Revvoensovet* or RVS) 126–31, 139, 143, 298, 351, 373
  RVS of the Caspian-Caucasian front 126–31, 351, 373
  RVS of the Sixteenth Army 139, 143
  RVS of the Southern front 126, 351
Right Opposition 2, 273, 283, 291–2, 298 n. 38, 313, 320, 325, 339, 363, 376
Rogov, Mikhail 316, 324, 336
Romanov, Mikhail (Grand Duke) 228 n. 3
Rossov, A.S. 334

Rostov-on-Don [Rostov-na-Donu]   349–50, 357, 363
Rovio, Kustaa   338
Rozen, Mikhail   349–52, 354
Rozental, Yakov [Iakov Rozental']   177 n. 52, 209 n. 42, 222
Rubashov, Nicholas   332, 355
Rudzutak, Jan [Ian]   148, 165, 167–8, 176 n. 50, 320 n. 26
Russian Orthodox Church   8–9, 11–12, 16–17, 19, 32, 131, 369
  clergy   8, 17, 19, 32, 131
  deacon(s)   17, 19
  priest(s)   9, 12, 19, 32, 131
  seminary   19
  see also religion
Russian Social Democratic Workers' Party (RSDRP)   23–4, 31, 38, 41, 157 (and below)
  Bolshevik(s)   1–3, 5–9, 25, 29–30, 33–7, 40–1, 46, 49–50, 52, 56–9, 61–9, 72–81, 83, 85–6, 89–91, 94–9, 101–4, 106–7, 109–13, 115–16, 118, 120–3, 125, 128, 130–1, 133, 155–6, 158, 160–1, 170, 176, 178, 182, 185, 189, 193, 198, 208, 210, 213, 225, 228, 233, 236–7, 242, 245, 247, 250, 252, 256, 262, 271, 273–4, 277, 281, 286, 295, 300, 309–11, 322, 328, 332–3, 340, 350, 352, 354, 368–73
  Central Committee   36, 52, 56, 58–9, 61–2, 64, 66–8, 74, 77, 80, 89, 96–8, 101, 104, 106, 110, 115, 249, 329, 336 n. 12, 372
  election(s)   61, 64, 83, 86, 96, 106–7, 137, 168, 174, 190, 218, 237, 248, 260, 262, 280–1, 374
  Fifth Party Congress   34
  Fourth Party Congress   249
  Menshevik(s)   3, 25, 37, 41–2, 50, 52, 72, 79, 81, 85–6, 94, 97–9, 104, 106–7, 109–10, 112–13, 130, 160, 170, 196, 211 n. 47, 213, 236, 245, 247, 250, 258, 270, 274, 276, 289, 310–11, 326–8, 354–5, 358
  Old Bolshevik   2–3, 6, 29–30, 170, 176, 185 n. 72, 198 n. 14, 247 n. 53, 252, 256 n. 9, 262, 295, 300, 328, 332–3, 352, 368
  party cell(s)   1, 63–4, 77
  party committee(s)   24, 34, 50, 56–8, 61–6, 77, 79, 80–1, 97–8, 355
  Petersburg Committee   34, 36, 50, 56–8, 61–6, 77, 79, 81, 97–8, 148 n. 63, 170 n. 35, 336 n. 12

Prague Conference (1912)   61
RSDRP   24, 98 n. 54, 211 n. 47, 336 n. 12
RSDRP(b)   34, 58
Russian Bureau of the CC   52, 61–2, 64, 66–7, 74, 77, 80, 101, 329, 372
SDs   24–5, 30–1, 33–4
Second Party Congress   25
Seventh Party Conference   81–2
Third Party Congress   249
Russian Soviet Federated Socialist Republic (RSFSR)   138, 145, 160, 197, 242 n. 42, 250 n. 60, 305–9, 312, 316–24, 327–8, 336, 343, 353, 357, 362, 376
  Gosplan RSFSR   309, 312, 316–24, 327–8, 336, 343, 353, 357, 362
  RSFSR Metals-Industry Association (ROMP)   305
  RSFSR Metalware-Industry Association (Rosmetizprom)   305–9, 343, 353, 376
  VSNKh RSFSR   305, 307
Russian Telegraph Agency (Rosta)   153
Russo-Japanese War of 1904–5   32
Rutkovsky, Anatoly [Rutkovskii]   335–6
Ryazan [Riazan']   169, 171
Ryazanov, David [Riazanov]   110, 114, 133, 146, 178, 199–202, 238
Rykov, Alexei [Aleksei]   97, 99 n. 57, 100, 115, 148, 154, 165–8, 274 n. 51, 283, 291, 353
Rykunov, Mikhail   179
Ryutin, Martemyan [Martem'ian Riutin]   313, 316
Ryzhova, Sima   328 n. 44, 366

sabotage   46, 106, 272–3, 291
Safarov, Georgy [Georgii]   349–50, 352, 354–5, 362–3, 367
St. Petersburg (Piter)   2, 8, 12–14, 20–4, 32–4, 49–52, 54–6, 58, 61, 98 n. 54, 99 n. 57, 110, 170 n. 35, 171, 193 n. 3, 194 n. 6, 328 n. 44, 336 n. 12, 337
St. Petersburg Technological Institute   194 n. 6
  see also Leningrad, Petrograd
Sakhov-Tsukerman, Boris   358–9
Saltykov-Shchedrin, Mikhail   247
Salygin, aka 'Stolypin' (agent or guard)   298–9, 301 n. 49
Samara   140, 158, 169, 171, 250, 264
Sandler, Elizaveta Senatskaya [Senatskaia]   359–60

Sandu, Tatyana [Tat'iana]   4, 140, 210 n. 44
Sapronov, Timofei   134
Scandinavia   36, 56–61, 67, 69–73, 151, 154–5, 163, 289
    see also Denmark, Finland, Norway, and Sweden
school see education
SDS   24–5, 30–1, 33–4
    Swedish SDS   58
    see also Russian Social Democratic Workers' Party
Second Communist International   56, 151
secret police see Cheka, GPU, NKVD, OGPU, Okhrana
'Secret speech' (1956)   367
Seine, Département de la   39
Seine Mechanics, Union of   46
self   2–3, 6, 20–1, 25, 29–30, 40, 52, 68, 70, 72, 74, 96, 105, 125, 128–9, 144 n. 53, 156, 170 n. 36, 173, 181, 239, 255 n. 6, 267, 276–7, 300–1, 305, 309, 311, 316, 322–30, 332–3, 337, 343–4, 346, 359, 369, 371, 377
Semnadtsatyi god see Shlyapnikov, Alexander Gavrilovich
Serebrennikov, Alexander [Aleksandr]   32 n. 51
Serebrovsky, Alexander [Aleksandr Serebrovskii]   340
Serebryakov [Serebriakov], Leonid   131, 148 n. 62, 165 n. 20–1, 166 n. 23, 176 n. 50, 189
Sergievsky, Nikolai [Sergievskii]   349–50, 355–6, 367
Service, Robert   57
Serge, Victor   167–8, 233 n. 17, 266
Sevastopol   334
Shadurskaya, Zoya [Zoia Shadurskaia]   116–17, 232, 239–40
Shakhty Trial   291–2, 306
    see also show trials
Shatov, Vladimir 'Bill'   287
Shcherbakov (Shlyapnikov's assistant at Gosplan RSFSR)   327
Sheffield   290
Shotman, Alexander [Aleksandr]   335–6

show trial(s)   291, 306, 332, 359, 361, 364
    see also Shakhty Trial
Shlyapnikov, Alexander Alexandrovich [Aleksandr Aleksandrovich Shliapnikov][2] (son)   7, 312, 214–15, 336–7, 359, 366–8
Shlyapnikov, Alexander Gavrilovich [Aleksandr Gavrilovich Shliapnikov]
    administrative work   99–100, 104–16, 118–21, 284–92, 305–8, 316, 323–4, 343
    arrest, imprisonment, interrogation
        1904–5   31–3
        1935   7, 332–3, 347–59
        1936–7   332–3, 361–5
    CCC investigations
        1922   241–4
        1926   268–77, 281–2
        1929–30   293–303, 308
        1932–3   314–16
    childhood   7–26
    civil war leadership   122–32, 139, 143, 155
    diplomatic work   262–4
    education   16–20, 22–3
    emigration   34–49, 56–62, 66–75
    exile   333–44, 359–61
    factory work   17–18, 22–4, 30–1, 33–8, 42, 50, 59
    family life   7–23, 54–5, 59, 119, 149–51, 264, 275, 278, 292, 303, 335–8, 343, 360–2, 366–8
    party purge in 1933   309, 320–30
    party underground work   24–5, 29–35, 40, 49–52, 56–9, 61–8, 71–7
    position on 1923–4 industrialisation debate   259–62
    position on Constituent Assembly   106–7
    position on socialist coalition government   103–4
    relationship with Gavril Myasnikov and Workers' Group   228–30, 240, 254–8
    role in 1905 Revolution   33
    role in February 1917 Revolution   76–84
    role in October 1917 Revolution   96–102
    role in 1922 appeal to the Comintern   227–52

---

2   For this entry and the next, the individual's patronymic is provided to distinguish two individuals who have the same first and last names. The patronymic is derived from the name of the individual's father.

INDEX

romantic relationships   37, 41–5, 58–60, 70–1, 74, 116, 264, 360
Semnadtsatyi god (memoir of 1917)   7, 45, 76, 81–3, 87 n. 29, 97 n. 52, 254, 262, 267, 284, 292, 301, 325, 329, 370, 372, 376
tall tales, rumors   125, 352, 368
trial in August 1921   215–19
trial in September 1937   363
trade union organising and leadership   31, 37–9, 46–51, 59, 80, 84–8, 90–102, 130–48, 151–209, 222–6, 234–8
writing   36–7, 45–9, 51, 56, 123–4, 135, 254, 261–2, 264–6, 280, 292, 309–13, 336, 343–4, 347
see also   holiday(s), masculinity, medicine, Ménière's disease
Shlyapnikov, Gavril [Gavriil Shliapnikov] (father)   9–10, 12, 15
Shlyapnikova, Anna [Shliapnikova] (m. Tyutereva) [Tiutereva] (sister)   10, 20–2, 54
Shlyapnikova, Ekaterina [Shliapnikova] (b. Voshchinskaya) [Voshchinskaia] (wife)   7, 185 n. 72, 264, 275, 292, 303, 312, 314–15, 328 n. 44, 335–7, 343, 351 n. 48, 359–61, 366–7
Shlyapnikova, Irina [Shliapnikova] (daughter)   4, 7, 12, 161 n. 10, 185 n. 72, 303, 314–15, 336–7, 343, 350 n. 45, 355 n. 60, 359–60, 366–8
Shlyapnikova, Khioniya [Khioniia Shliapnikova] (b. Belenina) (mother)   10–11, 13–14, 16–22, 28–9, 34, 54, 35 n. 57, 59, 65
Shlyapnikova, Maria [Mariia Shliapnikova] (m. Kovalenko, Plastinin) (sister)   10, 20, 54–5, 149
Shlyapnikov, Peter [Pëtr Shliapnikov] (brother)   10–11, 13–14, 16, 23
Shlyapnikov, Yakov [Iakov Shliapnikov] (cousin)   33, 352
Shlyapnikov, Yuri [Iurii Shliapnikov] (son)   7, 10, 12, 19–20, 264, 275, 292, 303, 314–15, 336–7, 343, 348 n. 39, 359–60, 366–8
Shmidt, Vasily [Vasilii]   61, 98, 111, 120–1, 142, 205 n. 30, 206 n. 34
Shovna River   341

Shtein (NKVD interrogator)   350, 353–4
Siberia   12, 35, 51–2, 63, 76–7, 98 n. 54, 122, 169, 180 n. 60, 228 n. 3, 240, 245, 284–5, 293–305, 334–5, 346, 349–50, 352, 359, 363, 367, 375
Sidor (pipefitter from the Caucasus)   13
Sidorchuk, Alexei [Aleksei]   357
Skliznev, S.   168, 177 n. 52, 235
Slav(s)   8
Smirnov, Alexander [Aleksandr]   256 n. 9, 298, 313, 318
Smirnov, M.N.   317
Smith, Stephen A.   30
smychka (worker-peasant alliance)   195, 274, 293
sobriety   7, 9, 23
Social Democrats (SDs)   23, 35, 50, 64, 73, 77–8, 81, 182, 232, 259, 265–6, 268–9, 370
   German Social Democrats   42, 56, 58, 153, 259
   Swedish Social Democrats   58, 60
   see also Mezhraiontsy and Russian Social Democratic Workers' Party (RSDRP)
'socialism in one country'   264–5, 267, 269–70, 274, 294
Socialist Party of France   38
Socialist Revolutionary Party (SRs)   3, 24–5, 31, 68, 79, 89, 94, 96, 99, 104, 107, 109, 118, 121–3, 130, 160, 178–9, 182, 196, 210, 213, 215 n. 57, 236, 247 n. 54, 270, 289
   Left SRs   89, 99, 104, 109, 118, 121, 123
   Right SRs   99, 122
socialist coalition government   98, 101, 103–4, 106, 113, 115, 118, 121, 322, 372
Society of Factory Owners   88, 90–2, 101, 114, 340
Sokolniki [Sokol'niki]   173
soldier(s)   30 n. 43, 32–3, 76, 78, 80, 83, 89–91, 95, 98–9, 103, 118, 122, 124, 126–7, 129–30, 157, 162, 208 n. 40, 245, 254, 372
   see also civil war, military, Revolutionary Military Council, World War I
Solovki   342
Solts, Aaron [Aron Sol'ts]   218 n. 63, 243 n. 43, 272, 275–7, 296 n. 30, 321 n. 29, 323, 325–6
Solzhenitsyn, Alexander [Aleksandr Sol'zhenitsyn]   3
Sormovo   7, 13, 20–4, 98 n. 54, 130, 172

Sotsial'-Demokrat 47 n. 19, 57, 61
soviet(s)³   76, 79–80, 88–9, 94, 96–8, 100–2, 106, 111–12, 130, 135, 137–8, 142, 145–6, 156, 160–1, 163–4, 171, 173, 175–6, 180, 182, 187, 210, 227, 229–30, 240, 254, 268, 322, 373–4
  All-Russian Soviet of Workers' and Soldiers' Deputies   96–7, 104
  All-Union Soviet of Workers' and Soldiers' Deputies   262
  Central Executive Committee (VTsIK)   104, 112, 119, 127, 262
  Congress of Soviets (Eighth)   175
  Congress of Soviets (Second)   97, 99, 104
  district soviet(s)   79, 83–5
  Executive Committee of the Petrograd Soviet   78–9, 90, 372
  peasant soviets   96
  Petrograd Soviet   4, 71, 76, 78–80, 82–90, 95, 98–100, 372
Soviet Union *see* USSR
sovkhoz   196
Sovnarkom *see* Council of People's Commissars
Spain, Spanish   345, 349
Spasopeskovsky Lane [*Spasopeskovskii pereulok*]   314–16
specialist(s), technical and managerial   42, 128, 132–4, 145, 147, 175, 179, 196, 222 n. 73, 284, 306, 373
SRs *see* Socialist Revolutionary Party
Stalin, Iosif [Djugashvili, Iosif]   1–7, 13, 19, 63, 76, 80–1, 100, 106, 108, 134 n. 32, 148, 165 n. 22, 167 n. 27, 176 n. 50, 186–7, 193–4, 198 n. 14, 201–2, 240, 246, 253, 255, 258–9, 264–75, 277, 279, 281–4, 291, 293–4, 297–302, 308–13, 318–20, 324, 330–1, 335, 346–7, 350, 353–4, 359–61, 363–5, 367–8, 372, 375–7
  Kirov's murder   347, 350, 360–1
  Koba   13
  revolution from above   193–4, 283–4, 293
  role in 1917   76, 80–1, 100, 106, 108
  role in Russian Civil War   123–6, 128–30, 139

socialism in one country   264–5, 267, 269, 274, 294
Stalinism, Stalinist   2–6, 124–5, 155, 283, 302, 305–9, 317, 319, 329, 331, 333, 342–3, 346, 364
Stark, Leonid   62, 65
starosta   33
state capitalism   265
State Association of Machine-Building Factories (*Gomzy*)   285
State Commission for Electrification of Russia (GOELRO)   216
State Committee for Planning (*Gosplan*)   216, 246, 258, 285, 309, 312, 316–24, 327–8, 336, 343, 353, 357
  Gosplan RSFSR   246 n. 51, 309, 312, 316–24, 327–8, 336, 343, 353, 357
State Construction Committee (*Komgosor*)   219–20
State Control Committee (*Goskontrol*)   135
Steinberg, Mark   37
Stockholm   57, 66, 249
strike(s)   10, 20, 22–4, 32–4, 38–9, 47, 51, 63–4, 72, 77–8, 87–9, 91–3, 104–5, 130–1, 135, 182, 230, 236–7, 239, 253, 256, 294, 345
  see also hunger strike(s), labour unrest
Sukhanov, Nikolai   80
Sutyrin (BBK administrator)   340–3
Svechnikov, Mikhail   126, 129–31, 290, 308, 349, 351
Sverdlov, Yakov [Iakov]   127
Sweden, Swedish   39, 57–9, 66, 81, 153 n. 66, 154–5, 223–4, 249, 288–9, 303 n. 54, 312
Switzerland   34, 61, 79, 155
syndicalism, syndicalist(s)   39–40, 47, 110, 113, 133, 142–3, 160–2, 170, 173, 182, 185, 187, 189, 232, 233 n. 17
  see also anarcho-syndicalism
syndicate(s)   244, 284–5, 289, 292, 295, 307

Tarasov, G.F.   235, 350
Tarasov, Vladimir (Omsk)   350, 352
Tashkin, A.   208, 232 n. 14, 235
Tatars, Kazan   8
Tauride Palace   89–90

---

3 This entry refers specifically to soviets as councils, not to the Soviet state and society in the broader sense.

taxation, tax(es)   179, 191–2, 195–7, 220, 253, 268
Taylor, Frederick W.   46
Taylorism   46, 114
Tekhnoimport   287, 289, 291
telegram *see* postal service
telegraph *see* postal service
telephone   299, 335, 350
Ten, the   165–8, 170–80, 183, 185–6, 189
Tenth Party Congress *see* Communist Party congresses and conferences
terror   1–2, 20, 122–3, 126, 130–2, 291, 300, 320, 331–3, 347–8, 360–7
   Great Terror of 1936–8   1–2, 126, 291, 300, 320, 331–2, 348 n. 41, 360–7
   terrorism, terrorists   20, 332–3, 347, 362–3
textile(s)   8, 20, 78, 93, 109, 132, 144, 159, 216–17
Textile workers' strike of 1896   20
Textileworkers' Union   109, 144, 216–17
'Thermidorian reaction'   352
Third Communist International (see Communist International, Third)
Thorpe, Wayne   161
tobacco   9, 12, 266
Tolmachev, V.N.   313
Tolokontsev, Alexander [Aleksandr]   144 n. 53, 172 n. 41, 177 n. 52, 179, 206, 232 n. 14, 242, 255, 264, 285, 287, 290, 292
Tolstoy (Murom nobleman and *okrug* court judge)   19
Tomsk   302
Tomsky, Mikhail [Tomskii]   2, 8–10, 16, 18, 22, 34–7, 120–1, 135, 137, 142–3, 145–8, 162, 165, 167–8, 176 n. 50, 198–203, 224 n. 77, 235 n. 21, 236, 238, 251, 256, 274 n. 51, 283, 291, 326, 374–6
Torgsin   358
townsmen *see meshchanstvo*
trade unions
   Bureaucrats' Union   115
   craft-based unions   46–7, 84, 87, 92–4
   guilds   93, 185
   industrial unions   46–7, 86, 92–4, 139, 144, 153, 155, 372
   Petrograd Council of Trade Unions   98, 112, 114
   police-sponsored unions   32
   political role of trade unions   36, 47, 91, 94, 98, 107, 109–10, 119–21, 123, 135, 137–9, 141, 146, 161, 165, 180, 191, 226
   production unions   46–7, 93, 168, 197–9, 370, 376
   profession-based unions   199
   trade unions in England   35–6, 39, 279, 370
   trade unions in France   35–9, 46–7, 49, 87, 94, 154, 160, 263, 370
   trade unions in Germany   35–6, 39, 151, 153
   trade unions in Russia before 1917   33, 36, 45–6, 52, 56, 63
   trade unions in Scandinavia   39, 151, 154
   trade union commission   165 n. 20, 167–8, 189
   see also All-Russian Council of Trade Unions, Amsterdam International of Trade Unions, Astrakhan Council of Trade Unions, Commissariat of Labour, Commission on Improvement of Workers' Lives, factory, hospital union, industry, labour, Metalworkers' Union, Miners' Union, one-man management, Railway Workers' Union, Shlyapnikov, strikes, Textileworkers' Union, Tomsky, *Tsektran*, Water-Transport Workers' Union, Workers' Opposition
trade union congresses and conferences
   Fifth All-Russian Conference of Trade Unions   158, 166–7
   Fifth All-Russian Congress of Trade Unions   237
   First All-Russian Congress of Trade Unions   106–7, 110
   First International Congress of Red Trade Unions   154
   Fourth All-Russian Congress of Trade Unions   197–204, 209–10
   Third All-Russian Congress of Trade Unions   142, 148, 200–1
   see also Metalworkers' Union, Miners' Union
Transcaucasus   268 n. 35, 271
transportation   8, 10–13, 20–1, 31, 35, 45, 52, 59, 70–3, 81–2, 90, 95, 97, 103, 112–13, 122–6, 135, 138, 140, 159, 162, 166, 173, 191, 222 n. 73, 285, 293–4, 306, 335, 337–43, 360

transportation (*cont.*)
  automobile(s)   35, 59, 82, 90, 135, 173, 335, 360
  oceangoing ship(s)   13, 52, 70–3
  railroads, railway(s)   31, 45, 81, 95, 113, 123–6, 138, 162, 166, 222 n. 73, 285, 293–4, 337–43
  steamboat(s)   8, 10–12, 20–1, 360
Trans-Siberian Railway   122
Treaty of Brest-Litovsk   116
Trepper, Leopold   368
Trifonova, Maria [Mariia]   266 n. 31, 279, 357
Trotsky, Lev [Trotskii]   1, 5, 99–100, 105, 123, 128–31, 134 n. 32, 139–45, 148, 157, 162–72, 174 n. 44, 175–9, 189, 198–9, 201, 203, 213–14, 232–3, 253, 255, 258–62, 266–7, 270, 272–4, 276–7, 280–1, 283–4, 293–4, 296, 310, 313, 320, 323, 325, 353, 358, 360–3, 374–6
Trotskyism, Trotskyist   214 n. 53, 253, 260–1, 283–4, 293–4, 296, 320, 323, 325, 358, 360–3, 376
Trud publisher   90
Trust(s)   132, 195–6, 225, 243–4, 284–6, 289–92, 307
  Association of State Enterprises on Mining and Nonferrous Metalworking (*Gospromtsvetmet*)   285
  Leningrad Machine Trust (*Lenmashtrest*)   285
  Moscow Machine Trust (*Mosmashtrest*)   285
  Southern Metallurgical Trust (*Yugostal*) [*Iugostal'*]   285–6
  State Association of Machine-Building Factories (*Gomzy*)   285
  Ukrainian Tobacco Trust   266
  Urals Metal Trust (*Uralmet*)   285
Tsaritsyn (Stalingrad, Volgograd)   123–4, 126, 129–30
Tsektran   162–3, 166–7, 199, 202–3
Tsyperovich, Grigory [Grigorii]   154, 167 n. 27
tuberculosis   264, 303
typhus   129
Tula   77, 130, 140, 172 n. 41, 178, 204, 211 n. 47
Tuloma River hydroelectric power station   333, 336, 340–1
Turgenevka   353
Turkestan   201, 285, 287 n. 8

Turk(s)   123
Turkestan-Siberian Railway (*Turksib*)   285, 287 n. 8
Tyuterev, Ivan [Tiuterev] (brother-in-law)   21–2
Tyutereva, Antonina [Tiutereva] (niece)   119, 278
Tyuterev, Kostya [Tiuterev] (nephew)   338

Uglanov, Nikolai   205 n. 30, 206 n. 34, 353
Ukraine, Ukrainian   21, 63, 65–6, 77, 123, 140, 144, 158, 164 n. 17, 169–71, 203, 211 n. 47, 228–9, 246, 251, 266, 273, 291, 312, 348 n. 42, 357, 363
  Communist Party of Ukraine   144, 164 n. 17, 169–70, 229 n. 5, 247 n. 54, 266
  Ukrainian Metalworkers' Union   148 n. 63
  Ukrainian Tobacco Trust   266
Ulyanova, Maria [Mariia Ul'ianova]   65, 272, 275
Union of Seine Mechanics *see* Seine Mechanics, Union of
United Front   227–8, 232–3, 244, 279
United Opposition   267, 274, 276, 279–81, 296, 323, 329, 354, 375
Urals   7, 65, 77, 140, 148 n. 63, 158, 172, 180 n. 60, 204, 222 n. 73, 228, 241 n. 39, 285, 357–9, 361
Ural'skii rabochii   172
USA (United States of America)   3, 36, 46, 59, 70–3, 134, 155 n. 69, 194 n. 6, 223–5, 275 n. 52, 286, 287 n. 8, 338 n. 18, 368
USSR (Union of Soviet Socialist Republics)   7, 126 n. 11, 193, 243, 255 n. 4, 257–8, 265, 283–6, 287–8, 293, 301, 303, 312, 331–2, 344–5, 351, 361, 363, 368, 375–6
  Supreme Court Military Collegium   363

Vacha   22
Vandervelde, Emile   52
Vardin (Mgeladze), Illarion   350, 352, 354, 362–3
Vasilev, S.P. [Vasil'ev]   217–18
Verkhne-Uralsk [Ural'sk] political isolator   358–9, 361
Vichinsky, Mikhail [Vichinskii]   295–6, 350
Vikzhel (All-Russian Executive Committee of Railwaymen)   113

Vladikavkaz 123
Vladimir 24, 32 n. 50, 33, 50, 65, 77, 115, 305
Vladimirov, Mikhail 85 n. 23, 97, 98 n. 54, 148, 168–9, 177 n. 52, 206–9, 222, 234–5, 255
Vladimirov, Miron 98 n. 54
Volga River 123, 126, 128–9, 131, 351, 360
Volga region 65, 225
Volkov, I.G. 85, 97
Voronezh 77
Voroshilov, Kliment 63, 298, 335
Votkinsk 130
VSNKh *see* All-Russian Economic Council
VTsSPS *see* All-Russian Central Trade Union Council
Vyborg 78–80, 83, 87, 337, 355
Vychuga 312

War Communism 122, 142, 157, 179, 191, 253
see also civil war, food-requisitioning, nationalisation of industry
Water-Transport Workers' Union 162
see also Tsektran
weapon(s) 33–4, 83, 90 n. 36, 96–7, 99–100, 107, 122, 124–5, 131, 153, 173, 252, 270, 302–3, 347–8, 361
Wembley 59
West, Western 2–5, 9, 34–7, 46, 49, 65, 76, 87, 128, 143, 153, 161–2, 232, 265–6, 268–9, 281, 331–2, 369–70
Western Europe 2, 5, 34–7, 46, 49, 65, 76, 87, 143, 153, 161, 232, 265–6, 268–9, 281, 369–70
White armies, forces 122–3, 126, 131, 137–8, 157, 174, 290, 293, 295
White Sea-Baltic Sea Canal (BBK) 333, 335–6, 338 n. 18, 339–43, 349
Wijk, Karl 41
Winter Palace 32, 99
Witte, Sergei 7, 21
women 16, 21, 29–30, 32–3, 37, 41, 60, 74, 78, 149, 174, 181, 231, 241, 243, 264, 289, 299, 337, 348–9, 355, 370
International Women's Day 78
'woman question' 41, 174, 231
women revolutionaries 29–30
women workers 78, 174
Zhenotdel 181, 243 n. 43
see also Belenina, Bosh, Braslina, Catherine II, Chelysheva, Elizarova, Ezerskaya, Fischer, gender, Ginzburg, Goldstein, Kollontai, Krupskaya, Kshesinskaya, Lafargue, Luxemburg, Makhova, Medvedeva (Aida, Irina, Maria), Meteletskaya, profession(s), Ryzhova, Sandler, Shadurskaya, Shlyapnikova (Anna, Ekaterina, Irina, Khioniya, Maria), Trifonova, Tyutereva, Ulyanova, Yanchevskaya, Zemlyachka, Zetkin
worker-Bolshevik 7, 36, 40, 63, 156, 371
Woodturners' Union 93
worker-*intelligent* 25, 37, 41, 45, 254, 370
worker-peasant alliance (*smychka*) 195, 274, 293
Worker-Peasant Socialist Party 210
workers (selected subtopics)
American workers' movement 72, 223–4
domestic servants 337
electrician(s) 93
ironworker(s), foundry men 11, 13, 18
metalworker(s) 1–2, 7, 13, 20–3, 30, 33, 37–9, 46, 50, 52, 61, 73, 76, 78, 84–102, 109, 114–15, 131–2, 135, 137–41, 144, 148, 151–4, 158, 160, 166, 168–72, 174, 177–9, 188–9, 192, 197–8, 203–12, 217–18, 221–8, 234–7, 247–8, 254, 263, 267, 284, 291, 307, 333, 335–7, 342, 357, 369, 372–6
printer(s) 30, 183
railway workers 95, 113, 124, 162
Swedish transport workers 57
textile worker(s) 78, 93, 109, 144, 216–17
unskilled worker(s) 10, 30, 87–8, 91, 93, 140
water-transport workers 162
welder(s) 30, 93
white-collar worker(s) 113, 159, 160
see also profession(s)
women worker(s) 78, 337
see also women
woodturner(s) 93
worker aristocracy 265
workerisation 147, 184, 187, 262, 374
workers' control 86, 88, 95, 97–8, 103, 111–15, 142, 373
workers' militia 76, 82–3, 90 n. 36
workerist [*ouvriériste*] 158 n. 4, 161, 210–11, 255–6

workers (selected subtopics) (*cont.*)
see also artel(s), artisan(s), craft(s), factory, industry, labour, proletarian, Russian Social Democratic Workers' Party (RSDRP), Shlyapnikov, soviet(s), trade union(s), Workers' Group, Workers' Opposition

Workers' and Peasants' Inspectorate (*Rabkrin*)   258

Workers' Group of the Russian Communist Party   175 n. 46, 228 n. 3, 247 n. 53, 254–8, 334, 375
see also Myasnikov

Workers' Opposition [*Rabochaia oppozitsiia*] 1, 3–5, 36, 39, 47, 52, 63–4, 74, 92, 123, 132–4, 138, 144–5, 148, 157–90, 192, 195, 198–9, 201–2, 204–5, 209–14, 216, 218–20, 222, 224, 228–9, 233–4, 238, 241, 244, 246–50, 253–7, 259 n. 15, 260–2, 266–8, 270–4, 276–7, 279–80, 285, 288, 293–5, 299–303, 305 n. 55, 308, 313, 322, 325, 327, 329, 332–3, 350–64, 367–8, 374
platform or programme   157–62, 166, 168, 177–8, 185, 187, 288
Rabochaya oppozitsiya [*Rabochaia oppozitsiia*]   180–4
reprisals against   173, 191–2, 198, 209–12, 216, 220, 375
resolution on party unity   186–7, 241
resolution on the 'syndicalist and anarchist deviation in the party'   186–7
support for   158, 161, 169–74, 178–81, 183–5, 198

Workers' Truth   254–7

World War I   36, 40, 52, 56–116, 119, 128, 135, 161, 174, 247 n. 53, 329, 345, 372
civil war as a slogan   56–7, 65–6
defencism and defeatism   56–7, 66, 81
social chauvinism   62, 69

World War II   257, 367–8

wrecking *see* sabotage

Yagoda, Genrikh [Iagoda]   294 n. 25, 336–7, 351, 354 n. 56, 360

Yakovlev, Alexander [Aleksandr Iakovlev]   333 n. 5, 350 n. 45, 367

Yanchevskaya, Vera [Ianchevskaia]   30–1

Yanson, Nikolai   208 n. 40, 209 n. 42, 235–6, 271, 277

yarmarka [*iarmarka*]   10

Yaroslavl [Iaroslavl']   130

Yaroslavsky, Emelyan [Emel'ian Iaroslavskii] 148 n. 62, 174, 176, 189, 246 n. 50, 269–72, 266–7, 294–6, 298–303, 308, 313 n. 10, 316, 320 n. 26, 348 n. 41

Yerevan [Erevan]   257

Yezhov, Nikolai [Ezhov]   2, 8–10, 16, 35, 37, 320 n. 26, 327–8, 334, 336–7, 344, 346–7, 359 n. 68, 360, 366

Yurenev, Konstantin [Iurenev]   143

Zalutsky, Peter [Pëtr Zalutskii]   77, 148 n. 62, 256 n. 9, 279 n. 58, 350

Zamoskvoretsky [Zamoskvoretskii]   217

Zelnik, Reginald   2, 37

Zemlyachka, Rozaliya [Rozaliia Zemliachka]   217–18

zemlyak [*zemliak*]   52

Zemlyansky [Zemlianskii]   270

zemstvo(s)   16, 20, 79

Zetkin, Clara   215, 233

Zimmerwald Conference   61

Zimmerwald Left   61

Zinoviev, Grigory [Grigorii Zinov'ev]   61, 67–7, 97, 104, 116, 121, 134 n. 32, 137, 139, 143, 148 n. 62, 151, 153, 160–5, 167–70, 175–6, 185, 188, 204, 206, 212, 231–4, 246, 251, 253, 255, 258–9, 267, 269–70, 272–4, 276–7, 280–1, 297, 310, 323, 331–2, 347, 349–50, 352–4, 356, 358–64, 376

www.ingramcontent.com/pod-product-compliance
Lightning Source LLC
Chambersburg PA
CBHW071145070526
44584CB00019B/2659